Programming Recreational Services

Jay S. Shivers

Professor Emeritus
University of Connecticut
Storrs, Connecticut

JONES AND BARTLETT PUBLISHERS
Sudbury, Massachusetts
BOSTON   TORONTO   LONDON   SINGAPORE

World Headquarters

Jones and Bartlett Publishers
40 Tall Pine Drive
Sudbury, MA 01776
978-443-5000
info@jbpub.com
www.jbpub.com

Jones and Bartlett Publishers Canada
6339 Ormindale Way
Mississauga, Ontario L5V 1J2
Canada

Jones and Bartlett Publishers International
Barb House, Barb Mews
London W6 7PA
United Kingdom

Jones and Bartlett's books and products are available through most bookstores and online booksellers. To contact Jones and Bartlett Publishers directly, call 800-832-0034, fax 978-443-8000, or visit our website, www.jbpub.com.

Substantial discounts on bulk quantities of Jones and Bartlett's publications are available to corporations, professional associations, and other qualified organizations. For details and specific discount information, contact the special sales department at Jones and Bartlett via the above contact information or send an email to specialsales@jbpub.com.

Production Credits

Publisher, Higher Education: Cathleen Sether
Acquisitions Editor: Shoshanna Goldberg
Senior Associate Editor: Amy L. Bloom
Senior Editorial Assistant: Kyle Hoover
Production Manager: Julie Champagne Bolduc
Asociate Production Editor: Jessica Steele Newfell
Associate Marketing Manager: Jody Sullivan

V.P., Manufacturing and Inventory Control: Therese Connell
Composition: Toppan Best-set Premedia Limited
Cover Design: Scott Moden
Photo Research and Permissions Manager: Kimberly Potvin
Assistant Photo Researcher: Carolyn Arcabascio
Printing and Binding: Courier Stoughton
Cover Printing: Courier Stoughton

Cover Images: main front cover: © Galyna Andrushko/ShutterStock, Inc.; bottom front cover, left to right: © Ints Vikmanis/ShutterStock, Inc., © Randy Faris/Corbis/age fotostock, © Emily Sartoski/ShutterStock, Inc.; top back cover, left to right: © Morgan Lane Photography/ShutterStock, Inc., © Tatyana Chernyak/Dreamstime.com, © Kuznetsov Alexey/ShutterStock, Inc.; bottom back cover: © Allistair Scott/Dreamstime.com

Library of Congress Cataloging-in-Publication Data
Shivers, Jay Sanford, 1930–
　　Programming recreational services / Jay S. Shivers.
　　　p. cm.
　　Includes bibliographical references and index.
　　ISBN-13: 978-0-7637-5198-2 (pbk. : alk. paper)
　　ISBN-10: 0-7637-5198-7 (pbk. : alk. paper)
　　1. Recreation.　I. Title.
　　GV181.4.S535 2010
　　790.06'9—dc22
　　　　　　　　　　　　　2009042693

6048
Printed in the United States of America
14 13 12 11 10　10 9 8 7 6 5 4 3 2 1

Dedication

This book is dedicated to Ellen Joyce (Joy) Shivers, who has brought me joy. By her compatibility, affability, creativity, sense of humor, willingness to explore other places and cultures, and tolerance of my foibles, Joy has lifted many burdens from me and has contributed to the remarkable sense of well-being and happiness that I now possess. We have experienced a relationship and an experience that makes life worth living.

Brief Contents

Contents

Preface

Recreational activities, particularly those consisting of socialization, creativity, educational enrichment, and aesthetic pursuits, offer stimulating and emotionally satisfying activities beneficial to an individual's self-perception. The comprehensive recreational program includes group, individual, passive, active, cultural, physical, cognitive, social, and artistic engagement. The vast range of possible activities enables an individual to select one in which he or she is most capable. By working from known to unknown activities, an individual's interest horizons are broadened so that he or she can have a deeper and more significant experience.

Recreational activity is valuable for all who participate in any way, at any age. Such activity is not obligatory or a social necessity. The greatest satisfaction does not rely only upon the individual's interests, knowledge, and abilities, but on how he or she occupies his or her leisure. It offers the opportunity to choose whatever motivates or stimulates appreciation and satisfaction.

Enjoyment is a singular characteristic of recreational experience. The expectation of pleasure in participation motivates people to engage in recreational activity. However the individual wishes to use his or her free time, whether by intense involvement as a participant or as a spectator and appreciator, he or she expects a satisfying and enjoyable experience. This aspect of recreational activity, the emotional reward, is its essential motivation.

The material presented in *Programming Recreational Services* is the distillation of almost 60 years of active involvement in a variety of recreational activities, observation of both facilities and recreational experiences throughout the world, assessment of recreational participation, and an understanding of the organization, operation, and management of the vast enterprise called recreational service. It is an intensely practical and self-evident discussion of the costs, leadership, equipment, places, timeliness, and programmatic techniques necessary for the provision of recreational services to those who will become active participants in organized and self-directed recreational activities. This text is a handbook designed to enable recreationists (professional practitioners) and others to call upon the incredible treasury of recreational activities for the benefit of those who are engaged in the pursuit of happiness.

This user-friendly text has been organized into two distinct sections. The first is concerned with elemental concepts of what programming is, how and why constituency populations are to be analyzed for eventual reception of recreational services, and the places where recreational activities occur. The second section deals with the twelve categories of a comprehensive and balanced recreational program, including suggested activities, methods of promoting them, how to instruct them, and the leadership necessary to guide them.

Illustrations and photos are provided throughout the text to emphasize program ideas and basic steps in understanding and performing recreational activities. Additionally, a selected reference section offers greater exploration into the recreational activities typically programmed and the organizations that have a fundamental role in giving assistance to those interested.

The teaching resources that accompany this text include an online instructor's manual, which details chapter overviews, key words, learning objectives, essential review questions, summaries, and resources.

Recreational service consists of all those arranged activities, planned spaces and facilities, and spontaneous and scheduled incidents that are basic to providing a comprehensive series of varied recreational experiences attractive to potential clientele. To develop and elaborate any specific program requires an elemental grounding in the organization, operation, and management of the personnel, materials, and financial resources of which such service is comprised.

This text offers the foundation from, and on which, a program of recreational service can be delivered, and provides programming ideas that are easily assimilated by recreationists and laypeople alike. The purpose of *Programming Recreational Services* is to ensure that the diverse recreational needs of all people are met. The concepts generated by assembling a full range of recreational examples may stimulate innovation and responses on the part of practitioners and lead to more effective and satisfying recreational experiences.

Those who act as volunteers will also benefit from the material in this text. Volunteers provide critical services that extend and augment that which is performed by professional providers. Volunteers perform their essential function by offering their time, talent, and effort in a service category that is no less satisfying and enjoyable than any other recreational activity.

Special emphasis has been offered in terms of activity technique, cost factors, facilities needed, supplies, and equipment, as well as leadership involved in the promotion of a comprehensive, balanced, and organized recreational program. The practical information in this text will assist in making the task and professional obligation of the recreationist of higher quality. To this end, *Programming Recreational Services* clearly presents the methods and materials necessary for the planning, organization, and operation of recreational services to all.

Acknowledgments

The following people assisted me in putting material together making up this text: Larry S. Waseile, local artist of note, whose rendering of my Walther P-38 depicts a semi-automatic pistol used for recreational shooting. Thank you to Dean David Wood, the University of Connecticut, School of Fine Arts, for his aid in obtaining pictures of theatrical equipment and the Nafe Katter Thrust Stage, and thanks also to Rod Rock, Director of the Jorgensen Center for the Performing Arts, the University of Connecticut, for additional help. I am particularly indebted to Dr. Jan L. Jones, Assistant Professor, Department of Recreational Service Education, Southern Connecticut State University, for her contribution concerning computer use in programming and establishing a recreational department Web site. Dr. Josh Shuart, Assistant Professor of Sports Management, Sacred Heart University, provided diagrammatic materials at a crucial time. In addition, I owe much to Minyong Lee, graduate student in the Department of Kinesiology at the University of Connecticut for his technical expertise concerning computer use. My thanks to Mr. Mark

Gordon, Webmaster of Prince William County Park Authority, Virginia, for his timely assistance. I deeply appreciate the critical analysis and modifications of the following reviewers, many of whose suggestions are included in the text:

- Dr. J. Thayer Raines, ReD, Green Mountain College
- Steven N. Waller, Sr., PhD, University of Tennessee
- Jerel Cowan, MS, University of Central Oklahoma
- Keith G. Diem, PhD, Clemson University
- Jennifer Livengood, PhD, MSW, William F. Harrah College of Hotel Administration
- Jan Louise Jones, PhD, Southern Connecticut State University
- Lee J. deLisle, PhD, Western Michigan University

Otia sapienter uti laetitiam et acquanimitatem parit.

PART

I

The Nature of Programming

The Program and Its Components

The only reason for the establishment of any agency purporting to deliver recreational services is the program. Recreational activity is any positive, voluntary, free-time experience whose sole attraction is the expectation of fun. A recreational program is composed of diverse experiences of a recreational nature that an actual or potential participant perceives to have intrinsic value with highly individualized benefits. Either the person views the activity as offering satisfaction and enjoyment or not. If the former, then the individual attempts to or actually participates in the experience. If the latter, rejection follows.

Programming is really the culmination of scheduling appropriate activities. It is combined with highly qualified and effective instructional personnel, who may also serve as guides or advisers, together with the necessary supplies, materials, and equipment, at a time and place both feasible and attractive so that a potential user has the opportunity to profit from the coordination. Essentially, the program is more than the sum of activities; it is a synergistic outflow, the result of which is greater than its parts. This is valid because much more than activities are involved. One vital ingredient to the mix is the intangible factor of personality—that of the recreationist and that of the recreator. In either case, personalities help to create an environment that is conducive to setting the tone of either a pleasant or dissatisfying experience. The participant brings everything that he or she is to the moment of the activity, as does the recreationist. This meeting of personalities contributes to the overall effect, whether positive or negative, and creates additional influences over and above that which has been accounted for by the various activities and their supporting structures.

Every program requires planning; allocation of resources; determination of the interests, needs, skills, knowledge, or appreciation of potential participants; and a smooth interweaving of all elements in the scheduled event. This means that people must know about the times, places, possibilities, costs, and whatever personal investment they have to make before satisfaction is forthcoming.

Professional personnel (recreationists) and volunteers need to be assigned to the supervision or instruction of activities. Funds must be segregated, if they have not been previously apportioned, so that infrastructure and logistics can be implemented. Maintenance of the areas involved, necessary material, and other indispensable commodities or properties need to be in their proper place for maximum use. In the final analysis, the program provides the formal structure for people to engage in many different experiences on a routine, sporadic, or special basis. These activities offer opportunities to develop latent talents, hone existing skills, interact with others, and gain whatever values or benefits are personally perceived. The assumption is that the chance to become engaged in activities, which tend to be attractive and stimulating, should result in satisfaction and enjoyment.

To be sure, recreational activity is not a panacea for the ills of the human race. Neither is it the means whereby crime, poverty, affliction, or other loss will be overcome. There are certain aspects of recreational participation that can void some of life's vicissitudes and reduce the stress imposed by circumstance; however, recreational participation should not be viewed as the cure for the disintegrating forces to which society is now subjected. Although recreational activity has a social component, it cannot compensate for a poor home life, truancy, substance abuse, or other negative behaviors. Although social activity diminishes loneliness and may reduce feelings of depression, it cannot remedy psychological problems that are only amenable to medical intervention.

Recreational activities are significant to the individual who engages in them because they provide real opportunities for acquaintanceship and for an interdependence with others that generates a sense of belonging, self-confidence, and self-respect. When individuals become absorbed in experiences that motivate interest and provoke achievable objectives, they tend to feel better about themselves. Just the attempts may be worthwhile, but it is the actual achievement of some end that makes the difference.

Recreational activity offers such a plethora of values to the potential participant that its universal attractiveness and expected realization of fun is apparent. Wherever people have leisure and some tradition for performance or previously have undergone or undertaken such activities that translate into cultural or physical performance, then recreational activity will be a major force for human betterment.

Recreational participation is a manifestation of social progress. By contributing to the enhancement of human life, recreational service justifies its inclusion in the functions of government at all levels. Furthermore, because it is considered to be a good rather than something that is dreaded or to be avoided, it is likely to be incorporated in the realization of the good life by those who are actively engaged of their own free will and without dependence upon organized assistance.

Satisfying Needs

The primary motive of recreational activity is to provide enjoyment or fun to the participant. Usually the participant is seeking a gratifying experience based on previous satisfactory experiences. Since this is valid, it is important for the recreationist to recognize which activities will best offer stimulation and pleasure for participants. Among the various classifications of experiences that are looked upon as basic recreational activities, the following have been found to be of considerable value or most beneficial. These categories contain almost all the potential positive leisure experiences in which one can be involved. Under each type are innumerable variations containing most, if not all, of the recreational pursuits in which people can engage. Through these experiences individuals can free themselves from the routines of living and become invested in occupations that are personally fulfilling.

1. *Art:* Graphic (painting and drawing) and plastic (molding any matter) representations may be undertaken to communicate ideas,

symbolize beliefs, register emotions, or define some aspect in the life of the performer.

2. *Crafts:* Through handmade objects using different substances, crafts may offer an opportunity for invention, creation, or reproduction that is inherently pleasing to the maker.

3. *Dance:* Activities performed in this medium offer highly personalized interpretations of moods, feelings, or emotions as well as stylized steps or formal accommodations. These are intensely satisfying because of the rhythmic movements or necessary postural shifts that occur for the performance.

4. *Drama:* This performing art may convey ideas, emotions, and interpretations of history or current social practices. It is a form of expression that uses facial expressions, gestures, speech, symbols, or silence to transmit meanings for the entertainment of an audience or the satisfaction of the performer.

5. *Education:* Without doubt, all recreational activities have some element of learning to them. Whether the effort is concerned with opportunities to learn new skills via instruction, demonstration, or emulation, there is some aspect of education. In fact, any subject found in the school curriculum could be the basis for a recreational experience.

6. *Hobbies:* Extremely personalized or stamped with the mark of the individual, hobbies are concerned with collecting, appreciating, or understanding some thing, object, or subject.

7. *Motor skills:* Sports, games, exercises, and other physical movements are part of this class of activities. Competitive or noncompetitive, single, dual, team, or group-oriented motor skills can provide both health and enjoyment benefits to those who take part.

8. *Music:* This art form can be performed in solitude or in front of an audience evoking pleasure and entertainment for those listening, performing vocally or instrumentally, or who have composed work.

9. *Nature-oriented activities:* Any experience that occurs in the outdoors and focuses on the environment or the natural habitat of animals, or is ecologically concerned comes within the scope of this classification.

10. *Service or volunteer activities:* Any activity that involves time or energy commitment in an effort to assist the performance of an organization or individual may be recognized as a service. Millions of people contribute their support to agencies and individuals that might otherwise not be able to succeed on their own, and gain tremendous satisfaction and enjoyment by providing help. This is truly a practical manifestation of the biblical injunction to "Cast your bread upon the waters . . .". It may very well be the most recreational of all categories.

11. *Social activities:* This catchall class may be looked upon as overlapping in many categories (e.g., parties, games, conversation, etc.); however, there are purely social experiences specifically designed to capture the attention and attract individuals into interactional situations. Thus, interpersonal relationships with two or more persons may be established in formal or informal settings and may consist of conversation in highly structured groups.

12. *Special events:* These experiences are deliberately organized, out-of-the-ordinary occurrences that are useful in augmenting routine activities or providing a spectacular and complex occasion to emphasize or focus attention on some program aspect.

Establishing the Program

Programming starts with an analysis of the population residing in the jurisdiction of the department in question. It incorporates all of the organized, sponsored, and administered recreational experiences operated by the department. However, the program is not an arbitrary series of scheduled activities imposed upon potential patrons; rather, it is a cooperative effort in which all parties, recreationists, and future participants and/or spectators provide pertinent information so that the largest number of people can be afforded the greatest opportunities. This is an integral part of the agency's function.

Certainly parts of the program will be routine and implemented using standard operating procedures. There may be specific activities that, because of past experience and comparison, have proved to be most satisfying to all concerned, and are therefore included.

Recreationists must determine the interests and needs of those whom they will service. Once this information is gathered, the programmer will be in a more strategic position to organize and conduct a program in concert with potential patrons. These future participants should be called upon to assist in the planning of their own activities. Their ideas, interests, skills, and knowledge will serve as a foundation for developing the program. Additionally, the recreationist must know where available resources, either material or personal, can be found so they may be brought to the planning process. In this manner, interested persons are given the chance for self-expression during the planning stage of activity development.

Participant Planning

The participant planning method is a process whereby interested individuals are included at the functional or programming level of recreational service. Such input is tremendously effective in composing immediate and future activities. The participants' assistance is emphasized in planning activities, although the recreationist is always available to function as a resource.

The ideas that are formulated in participant planning sessions are important to the development of an attractive program. Participant planning is necessary for the continued effectiveness and success of a program. Participant input is significant and may be vital insofar as program outcomes are concerned. Nevertheless, the recreationist should always be prepared to make additional or alternative suggestions whenever there is a paucity of proposals generated. Unless proper planning occurs, there can only be spontaneous activities offered without any thought as to whether they are appropriate, efficacious, or necessary, or actually satisfy the needs of the population for which they are intended. Another adverse possibility is that the program may coalesce around the skills and interests of the recreationist only. It is hardly likely that one person's range of interests would be so broad that everybody would be attracted to them. In this instance, there is no such notion as too many cooks spoiling the broth.

Programming is essential if progressively attractive activities are to be presented as an agency function. Programming avoids duplication and concentrates attention where it is needed. A basic objective of recreational service systems, whether in the public or private domain, is to foster socially acceptable mental and physical health patterns that will enhance the participants' quality of life. Therefore, the policy of the agency must not only be concerned with the numbers involved, but also include among its goals and ideals the concept of teaching socially acceptable behavior, respect for individual rights, good fellowship, and mutual appreciation.

Programming Practices

By profiting from the identified needs of community residents and capitalizing on the existing resources within the community to satisfy them, the recreational agency adheres to fundamental principles and practices that have been the mainstay of the profession. Programming owes a tremendous amount to the efforts of the many professionals who have promoted the cause of the recreational service field through the years. The following practices have become criteria by which superior performance can be evaluated. These standards of excellence are the floor of service below which no creditable recreational service department can afford to go.

1. Programming requires the personal participation of potential clients or patrons in a democratic context so that each individual has the opportunity to present ideas and is given a respectful hearing.
2. The recreationist is professionally obliged to offer diverse recreational activities by incorporating categories that cover all possible phases of recreational experiences.
3. Recreational service agencies must provide appropriate and adequate facilities in order to safeguard the health and welfare of participants.
4. Public recreational service agencies must cooperate with and coordinate their offerings with other public, quasi-public, and private agencies.
5. The recreational agency should utilize any material or individual resources available to better ensure maximum satisfaction and service to those who make up the constituency.
6. The recreational agency must design programs that do not discriminate against any person because of their ethnicity, gender, race, religion, or socioeconomic level.
7. All recreational activities need to be realistic and contribute to the obvious values that are attributed to recreational experiences.
8. A comprehensive recreational program must include activities that are active and passive in nature.
9. Continuity of activities should be conducted through the scheduling of activities at predetermined levels of skill. This ensures the likelihood of progress in skill development as well as greater enjoyment of the participant.

10. It is desirable to offer activities that can, by themselves, stimulate individual engagement.
11. The program should be as challenging as possible while remaining within the capacities of the participants.
12. Activities and facilities may have to be adapted to meet whatever physical or mental limitations are imposed on individuals by congenital deficits, accidental injuries, or disease.
13. Recreational activities need to be scheduled at times and places most suitable to satisfying the demands of potential participants.
14. Recreational agencies should disburse whatever financial resources are available to them in ways that will enhance the program, provide adequate facilities, employ professionally qualified workers, and acquire such space as will contribute to the most effective operation of recreational services beneficial to the residents of the community.
15. Recreational service agencies are responsible for maintaining good public relations within the community.
16. Recreational service agencies must be responsive to the needs of their constituencies. Therefore, they should continue to develop and evaluate their program, leadership, facilities, and other performance on the basis of the makeup of the population being served.
17. Activities must be integrated if the program is to have optimum benefit for participants.
18. Activities will depend upon the available personnel and physical resources of the department carrying them out.
19. It is the responsibility of the recreational agency to make sure that the constituency has opportunities to broaden their perspective by participating in cultural, social, esthetic, intellectual, and physical activities.
20. All recreational agencies should be receptive to and offer opportunities for potential participants to assist in the planning of activities.

Program Development

Every component involved with the initiation of activities designed to offer learning and enjoyment opportunities to those who participate is part of program advancement. The process concerns associating and interweaving a variety of elements into circumstances favorable for people to obtain personal satisfaction.

Planning for Skilled Persons

Of particular importance is the level of skill, knowledge, or appreciation that potential participants have in programmed activities. This is a primary consideration when building a program. Every community will always contain a certain percentage of the population who will be extremely competent or highly skilled in one or more recreational activities. These individuals may want to gain greater skill, deepen their knowledge, and derive greater satisfaction and enjoyment from continued participation. Such people may require nothing but space in which to perform. Others may need some instruction or have access to the recreationist as the resource person. Ordinarily, there will be those who want to participate in the program simply because previous exposure to the same or similar activities has given them pleasure.

Planning for Unskilled Persons

Another segment of the population that might want to participate may have had little or no previous experience with organized recreational service, either through lack of opportunity or because an earlier exposure was unsatisfying. This is the hard-to-reach group. The recreationist must use ingenuity to stimulate and encourage novices to give the activities a try. Perhaps a cafeteria of activities, which allows a judicious sampling of the offerings, could induce awakened interest and participation. The agency must make contact with this group if it is to serve the constituency. Repeated invitations through all of the public relations instruments, including personal visits by volunteers and by employees of the agency, may help arouse further curiosity and eventual engagement. Every attempt should be made to bring those reluctant to engage or uninformed individuals into the community recreational mainstream.

Planning for the Majority

Most people have some skills and a few have a great many or are expert in one or more activities. There are those who, for any number of reasons, have not been involved with any recreational activity except for passive entertainment. Among this group will be several whose passion for new ideas, skills, and things to do or places to go has never been thoroughly stimulated or partially satisfied. These persons will prove to be remarkably capable of being engaged, if prompted. On the other hand, there will also be many whose understanding of recreational activity is limited to sitting and rocking. This population will include those with long dormant skills who will require some selling in order to overcome their inertia. For this major potential clientele the agency must actively campaign to gain their attention, activate their attendance, and encourage the tentative. These individuals must be approached optimistically, offered attractive possibilities, actively persuaded, and introduced to their own capacities and potentials for the kinds of experiences that will draw them in.

For the most part, people tend to be apathetic about doing anything that requires leaving their home. Of course, this does not apply to almost all children. Most children happily take any opportunity for recreational activity that is offered. Adults, unfortunately, have to be shown and taught that there are countless recreational experiences that cannot be performed unless they are in specialized places and other people are around. The most productive of these recreational areas will be at the community recreational center or an analogous space, depending upon the agency making the provision. People must attend these recreational facilities, which are especially designed to accommodate activities of diverse types, if they really want to participate. Getting them to forego the simple pleasure of television watching may require efforts that go above and beyond what the typically dedicated recreationist may have to expend. If the information is worded carefully enough to arouse curiosity to the point of avidity, and provides sufficient stimulation, it can bring the pleasure seekers to an activity and expose them to whatever mind-grabbing attraction may be offered.

Timing and Program Development

Proper timing is essential for planning and developing the recreational program and scheduling specific activities. A well-timed activity may actually induce an indifferent person to participate. Conversely, activities that are poorly timed can prevent an otherwise interested person from attending. Tie-ins, that is, the performance of activities that utilize a current event or one that is designed to take advantage of a particular or familiar occurrence, may do much to promote participation.

Time Frames

Timely themes based on commemorative or seasonal happenings, holidays, community drives, religious or ethnic observances, or anything with which people can identify can be used to create maximum interest. Taking advantage of the relevancy of certain occasions to those who may be potential participants can provide the necessary stimulation to convince them that activity engagement is worthwhile. For example, Halloween can be the basis for a masquerade ball or town-wide "trick or treat" activities under the sponsorship of the recreational department. Additionally, other events may coincide with decorating windows, putting up displays, or inaugurating various game, craft, or performing arts activities.

Time of Events

The scheduling of activities—day or evening and particular hours—should consider the participants' insecurity about traveling far at night, whether the hours might interfere with nonleisure activities and demands, and if most people will be receptive to participation during those hours. All of these factors depend on the potential participant's physical condition, ability to attend with or without assistance, desire to spend time away from home during the day or evening hours, availability to accompany a child at a given time, and other impinging influences. Planning recreational activities, whether at a centralized facility or at one that serves a specific neighborhood, will be based on variable time factors.

Duration of Activities

Individual needs must be taken into account when determining how long an activity should be. Because people's intellectual capabilities vary, there will always be those who require a longer or shorter time to learn a given skill, technique, or subject. Its frequency, the time of day it is conducted, timeliness, or relevancy will also influence the duration of the activity. Thus, shorter or longer sessions or class periods may have to be introduced and juggled in order to accommodate participants. In any event, the activity must be arranged so that it will attract and focus attention, arouse interest, initiate and induce continuing participation, and accommodate potential participants.

Scheduling

Scheduling recreational activities is the process of coordinating all the elements comprising opportunities, time, personnel, location, facility, materials needed, and participants. The schedule is the concrete form of planning, developing, public information, maintenance work, and deployment of personnel at a time and place most appropriate for the performance of the recreational activity. It reflects the combination of people, places, interest, and time with advanced publicity so that no inconvenience results. Schedules permit flexibility. Prior release of information concerning routine or special arrangements for expected activities can be made. If emergency conditions occur, such as flooding, heavy snow, loss of electricity, torrential rain, or any one of many other possible incidents where something goes amiss, alternate times and dates can be preset so that participants have something to look forward to—thereby sustaining their interest and future participation.

The time interval used in scheduling may be hourly or shorter, depending on the attention span of those involved, on a daily, weekly, monthly, seasonal, or annual basis, and depending on the nature of the activity. For example, a course in life saving, first aid, cooking, sewing, conversational foreign language, or various other curricula-like subjects might take up to 10 weeks. Classes could be scheduled to meet once or more often per week contingent upon the type of activity, capacity of performers, and even the desire of participants. Some activities might be programmed monthly, or seasonal events could occur at suitable times. The significant element in programming is to rely upon the aims of the individuals involved and the quality of the experiences provided. All these variables need to be kept in mind when the schedule is developed (**Figure 1.1**).

This volume will concentrate on detailing all of the above topics in terms of how, when, where, and for how much, in order to describe pertinent methods dealing with the implementation of a comprehensive recreational program. Additionally, consideration will be given to staffing and leadership, physical plant, safety and risk management, and the financial support necessary for the production of a well-rounded and balanced program capable of serving the recreational needs of people.

Figure 1.1   The Programming Sequence

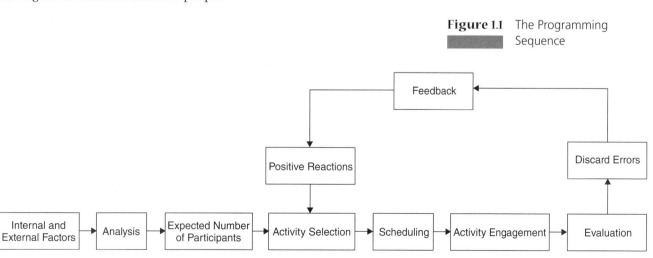

Summary

Programming is simple. It is merely the confluence of a participant, an activity, a place, supplies, and, if necessary, a recreationist. The difficult aspect is coordinating all of the disparate parts and bringing them together at a time that enables an enjoyable outcome. That is the ultimate function of the programmer. Of course, the preparation that is required to bring about this happy occurrence necessitates the collection of pertinent information about potential participants (population studies), their interests, previous recreational experiences, and current skills. Moreover, the scheduling of facilities, materials, assorted equipment, and personnel so that every component is present at the correct time needs scrupulous attention. Only a highly experienced recreationist/programmer can provide this effort.

Recreational service is the delivery of a comprehensive and balanced program of recreational activities that meets the needs and ambitions of any recreational agency's constituency. The twelve categories of recreational experience provide the patrons with a continuous series of routine, periodic, intermittent, and extraordinary events that are designed to satisfy the diverse interests, skills, and talents of all those who take advantage of the offering. This means that logistical support, physical plant, and administrative oversight must be focused on capturing and maintaining constituency participation and sustenance. Programming has to do with the public's education for leisure and its various positive uses. Finally, programming is concerned with the synchronization of personal and physical resources in establishing an attractive, stimulating, and all-inclusive program premised on the concept of ethical enjoyment. This is what the programmer's skill, knowledge, and background are concentrated upon. The outcome is a well-conceived and popular recreational program.

Selected Further References

Jurkowski, E. T. *Policy and Program Planning for Older Adults: Realities and Visions.* New York: Springer Publishing, 2007.

McLean, D., et al. *Recreation and Leisure in Modern Society.* 7th ed. Sudbury, MA: Jones and Bartlett Publishers, 2004.

Rossman, J. R., and B. E. Schlatter. *Recreation Programming: Designing Leisure Experiences.* 3rd ed. Champaign, IL: Sagamore Publishing, 2000.

Russell, R. V., and L. M. Jamieson. *Leisure Program Planning and Delivery.* Champaign, IL: Human Kinetics, 2008.

Shivers, J. S. *Recreational Services for Older Adults.* Teaneck, NJ: Fairleigh Dickinson University Press, 2002.

Vaughn-Williams, J. L., and P. Sander. *Recreational Activities for More Successful Programming.* Bossier City, LA: Professional Printing and Publishing, 2001.

CHAPTER 2

Demographics: The Population to Be Served

A droit and intelligent planning for recreational services must be based on the needs of the people to be served, whether they are citizens of a community or in the confines of a treatment center. To this end, the foundation of all recreational service, particularly that of the public sector, should be a mirror of diverse needs, abilities, and values, as well as similarly held areas of interest. Opportunities for participation should be available to all the people insofar as it is possible for any agency or consortium to serve the multifarious needs, interests, and demands of a heterogeneous population. In any case, there should be a routine program of recreational activities available to satisfy the chief recreational desires of those residing in the community, whatever its size or extent.

All programming is performed for whatever population the organization serves. Therefore, population factors are significant in planning for and developing a comprehensive recreational program. Poorly conceived programs arise because those whose responsibility it is to develop them rely upon their own experiences/biases or skills without regard for the people to be served. Programs are not created in a vacuum. They require information about the needs, interests, skills, knowledge, or appreciations that people have for leisure activity.

Well-planned programs, on the other hand, are not brought to fruition unless quantitative aspects of the constituent population are examined. The facts that are generated comprise the demographic features that portray people's differences and similarities.

Analysis of Demographics for Programming

The scope and participation in any community recreational program should reflect the variety and flexibility of human experiences involved. Stress should be laid on similarities and differences of age, gender, skill, previous experience, interests, traditions, mental or physical limitations, and the degree to which the recreationist can elicit participation through instructional or other public relations devices.

A comprehensive recreational program operated by professionals always recognizes several important points: (1) any community is composed of diverse groups whose special needs and interests must be incorporated into the would-be program; (2) program planning handles a variety of events and conditions that have application to the different groups and individuals who become the potential participants. Both of these operating facts are significant from the standpoint of program development.

Among the groups that make up the community are school-age youth, out-of-school youth, young adults, adults, and older adults. These, in turn, may be further classified by whatever affiliation they prefer; for example, interest groups, ethnic groups, racial groups, religious groups, fraternal or social groups, business and professional groups, service groups, the home bound, and/or people with disabilities. Although each of these groups may require specialized attention, it must not be forgotten that, taken together, they constitute the entire community. It may be necessary to have adapted activities to meet the distinct limitations of certain of these groups, but recreationists must recognize that these groups are not separated from community life and must, by their very nature, be considered an integral part of the total community constituency. As the needs of these groups and individuals are met through compassion and consideration, the fulfillment of a comprehensive program will occur. The delivery of these services is a responsibility that devolves upon both community authorities and those professionals representing other recreational-providing agencies, and consists of opportunities being made available to potential participants.

Age-Group Characteristics

The physical growth pattern of the individual through life is important if some understanding is to be gained insofar as the extent or limitations to which people may participate in recreational activities. We are interested not only in physiological development, but also psychological and social development. Interest in human growth and development provides the recreationist with guides that assist in any instructional aspect of the recreational program. Age-group characteristics help to indicate the individuality, apparent proclivities, and maturity of the person involved. Such characteristics suggest differences in the ability to manipulate tools, equipment, and concepts at various ages. By becoming aware of the most pronounced growth differences likely to occur at each age level, the recreationist becomes capable of determining whether, for example, a particular experience is appropriate for those exhibiting large- or fine-muscle dexterity. Specifically with children and youth, this knowledge can add to the value to be received by the potential participant. Recreationists should understand and recognize individual differences. On that basis they will best be able to recommend and/or guide activities for maximum advantage to the recipient of instruction.

Although age-group characteristics are offered on the following pages, they should in no way be thought to include all possibilities and permutations. Individuals are unique, if only for the differences in genetic construction, compounded by an overlay of environmental conditions. Thus, it must be understood that despite the attempt at specificity at particular age levels, each individual's development and growth vary greatly from anybody else's. Nevertheless, there are certain general tendencies referred to here.

Each person develops and matures at his or her own rate of speed. No startling changes will be observed within individuals as they pass from one age group to the next. Slight variations will be noticeable, but there will be no radical breaks with previous behavior or character. This pattern is usually observed in the same individual throughout the life process. Unless there is some cause, such as trauma, excessive pressure, or personal catastrophe, individuals maintain personality continuity throughout their lives.

In the use of age levels, an attempt has been made to show the probable general tendencies of a hypothetical average person. These factors, which condition and influence individual character, develop during the first 12 years of life—and are reinforced thereafter. Whatever salient marks are noted in the make-up of any person have occurred over many years; they simply do not arise overnight.

The 4-Year-Old

Typically, the child at age 4 is articulate and loves to use words whose sounds are enjoyable, rather than because he or she actually understands the meaning of the words. These children are active physically, verbally, and socially. Their large muscles are under control or almost so. These children enjoy a host of imaginative games, whether with playmates or by themselves. Generally, the child enjoys repetitive activity, is adventuresome, and is not restrained by fear of injury or the ridicule of peers. Heightened emotionality is common among 4-year-olds. Children of this age often feel that they can do more than their parents will permit them to do and rebel against rejections. Overestimating their own capacity to perform, they may become fatigued, irritable, and susceptible to emotional tensions. Contradictory behavior is also observed at this age. With equal ease the 4-year-old may be tractable and acquiescent or belligerent and obstinate.

The 4-year-old will engage in almost all physical activity that requires large-muscle effort. Large objects that can be manipulated are often favorites. Thus, blocks, clay work, finger painting, sand play, and construction activities are very popular. The make believe activities of children develop from life experiences. Construction experiences that demand the making of items or objects are essentially those seen in daily life. Running, jumping, climbing, sliding, swinging, and tag games are also part of the repertoire for participation.

The 5-Year-Old

On average, the 5-year-old appears to be calmer than the 4-year-old. The child of 5 miniaturizes the adult world. They prefer those things with which they are familiar and, therefore, comfortable. The children are attached to long-used toys, other possessions, and friends. They tend to resent the unknown, untried, or exploratory activities to which they are introduced. Their dramatic play focuses on the everyday world, rather than on the fantasy that intrigued the 4-year-old. They are at home with the familiar and rebel against intrusions that seem to attempt to change the known or substitute familiar situations. The 5-year-old has developed a social sense as well as the beginnings of a sense of humor. They have matured to a point where they appear to be at rest in preparation for a momentous developmental thrust.

At age 5, the child has relatively well-developed large-muscle control. The child's balance is better, and they show a marked inclination for rhythmics. They have greatly improved finger dexterity, and arm and leg coordination show up in such daily efforts as buttoning clothes, playing with small objects, and even sewing. The 5-year-old is at a developmental stage where craft activities can be more complex, insofar as manipulative experiences are concerned. The favorite crafts of 5-year-olds consist of plastic materials, housekeeping materials, action toys, beads, and clay. By age 5, the child is drawing with form and meaning. This child differentiates parts in drawings, which are clearly recognizable for what the child indicates they are.

Because the child at this age is stimulated by his or her ability to portray what is meaningful, any art activity will be able to offer opportunities for developing skill with the material used. The process of creating is more potent than the final outcome, so art material, for example, should be selected to meet the age group's needs for which it was planned. Consistent use of art materials will contribute to the child's ability to master the material sufficiently so as to be able to express personal feelings, reactions to his or her sensory processes, and personal perceptions of the environment.

In addition to play-acting, the young child spends much free time in making things. Given the opportunity, the 5-year-old is happy to play in mud, sand, water, and with blocks, beads, clay, crayons, and paints. Children enjoy drawing with crayons and they are not hesitant about using scissors, paper, or paste. All these materials enable children to construct items that abound in their everyday environment. These children are creatures of the moment and are invariably concerned with what is happening to and around them in the present.

The 6-Year-Old

By age 6, the child should be in complete control of all the activities required for clothing, feeding, and cleaning themselves. Rarely will they need assistance in performing these tasks, although there is a marked tendency to perform them in ways that leave much to be desired. The 6-year-old washes perfunctorily, puts on clothes without particular thought as to how they look or hang, and occasionally spills or dribbles food when at the table. Gradually, however, such routine activities become accepted and with steady practice are at last perfected. Now that they have entered the elementary grades, they will learn to write, form numbers, paint, draw, model, and manipulate tools for creative and constructive purposes.

Making things just for the pleasure of making them, with no thought as to the use of such constructs, is a popular form of recreational activity among 6-year-olds. Construction with wood and tools seems to be popular among young males, while females seek out such constructions as sewing, drawing, clay modeling, jewelry making, and painting. Arts, crafts, and materials associated with these activities are found to be satisfying to the child in whatever situation they find themselves. Thus, the schoolroom or the playground, camp, or other recreational setting may offer opportunities for this kind of participation.

Socially, the 6-year-old exhibits patterns of behavior that are extreme. They display emotions ranging from love to hate, joy to sorrow, and fear to daring almost simultaneously. They enjoy all opportunities to take part in games; they will not simply spectate for long. Friendships of lasting association are formed at this time. The child is building a foundation for adjusting to the social environment. Their emotional outcries are essentially experiments and explorations to determine what, if anything, can be accomplished. Social contact is a daily need and they seek out others for play. In most activities they throw caution to the wind and attempt the most appalling stunts. Nevertheless, they still also crave some solitude.

The 6-year-old demands action. They have developed physiologically to the point where large muscles are under control and fine-muscle coordination is beginning to assert itself. Most 6-year-olds have comparatively good manual dexterity and hand-and-foot coordination. The average 6-year-old is an old hand at using scissors and coloring within the lines of pictures; they enjoy manipulating plastic materials and building things. High energy output is characteristic of this age, and it is not unusual for the child to become exhausted unless stopped from doing so.

Good supervision is necessary for the child of 6. Limitations must be imposed to prevent undue frustration from participation in activities that are well beyond the capacity of the child to perform. This is an age where the child's ego can be bruised by criticism, and yet with competent guidance and counseling the child may be subtly led into areas more amenable to developing skills and talents.

The 7-Year-Old

Generally, the 7-year-old has reached the same plateau as did the 5-year-old. There appears to be a harvesting of strength for a similar growth spurt. Where the 6-year-old acted on impulse and never looked beyond the immediate results of actions, the 7-year-old calmly appraises each situation before acting. Other people are recognized as having certain rights and feelings. This child is now more concerned with rules and regulations than formerly, and leisure games are heavily laden with ritualistic activities that follow intricate procedures. Although children indulge in large motor activity, they have become better coordinated and have greater command of fine motor skills.

Activities at this time take on more or less popularity depending upon the child's ability to keep up with peers. In effect, the social awareness and sensitivity of the child to criticism from peers or adults may stifle participation in a variety of activities, particularly the creative ones. Poor performance in comparison with others leads to frustration or withdrawal. Only where the child shows precocity or unusual talent will creativity continue. Except when the child exhibits the gift of exceptionality or prodigality, the originality soon disappears. The child of 7 responds favorably to suggestions that do not carry overtones of rebuke or correction. Children are eager to learn and want to explore and be involved with many possibilities.

The 8-Year-Old

The child of 8 is growing rapidly both mentally and physically. This growth is shown in their socialization with peers and their attempts to accommodate themselves to the expectations of adults. Their motor capability is vastly superior to that of the 7-year-old. They have excellent control over large motor movements, and their coordination and fine-muscle command make for fluid and graceful actions. They enjoy almost any physical activity with which they are familiar, and exhibit the testing and exploratory ambitions that were first observed in the 6-year-old. Although children of this age like to show off, they are adept at team games and cooperate well with others.

Eight is the age where fine-muscle skills begin to show up. The ease and dexterity with which they use implements indicate the probability of future appreciation. The child of 8 has become more group- than ego-oriented, and sees him- or herself as part of a larger society in which they no longer are the center of the universe. They look beyond the here-and-now conceptions of the 7-year-old and attempt to plan and save for the future. Collecting becomes a very important activity at this time. Almost anything may be collected; however, a wide variety of objects within the special categories chosen make the collection all the more satisfying.

Because collections become important at about this age period, it is often consistent with school and recreational program objectives. Thus, for example, specimens may be collected and mounted as both an outdoor educational and a leisure experience.

More significantly, the 8-year-old requires leadership and competent supervision. They still cannot make accurate judgments about themselves, their capabilities, or things within their environmental sphere. Many accidents occur at this age because of the child's inability to take the precautions necessary for avoiding hazards. Professional instruction should be available and operating when children of any age are learning to work with tools, materials, or apparatus. Even more important to the health and welfare of the child is that good guidance be a part of the school or recreational situation because the mature judgment of the adult is substituted for the hit-and-miss patterns of the young child. With their increased span of attention and social awareness, they participate in a greater variety of social games and those activities where cooperation and group effort are manifested.

The 9-Year-Old

If anything characterizes the 9-year-old, it is the desire for increased social group activity. The early childhood stage has now been passed, and the individual begins to assume the social outlooks of future adulthood. This is a time for increased fine-muscle coordination and development. Activity is the hallmark, and there are no lengths to which the youngster will not go to test and explore his or her physical capacity to endure. Eye–hand coordination becomes more pronounced as skill and practice occupy a greater proportion of the child's free time. Most of their recreational activity is with members of their own sex, but under certain conditions socialization between the sexes will occur. In many respects they reflect a miniature image of the adult world. Ever active, they are sparkplugs bursting with energy and ready for anything.

Because of better coordination and almost complete command of finger movement, more intricate skills can be introduced to the child at this age. Both boys and girls are quite adept at manipulation of tools and small objects. It is not unusual at this time for children to be interested and active in drawing, painting, and clay modeling, with emphasis upon complicated details.

The Child from 10 to 12

Children between the ages of 10 and 12 have begun to turn to their peers for a wide variety of activities. This is the age of club or gang membership. This is still a time for secret societies, devotion until death, and the staking out of the group's domain. Of course, this is also a time for divided loyalties, hurt feelings, and the temporary withdrawal from the group, which is smoothed over and reconciled overnight.

Generally, children of this age cohort have achieved good neuromuscular development. Much of their physical activity calls for agility, strength, competitiveness, skill, and regulation. The rules are almost as important as the game, and a great deal of time is spent discussing whether or not a rule was broken during the course of the game. Almost any competitive activity requiring a high degree of skill in which rules are a constant source of reference will be of interest to this age group.

There will be "late bloomers" among this group, some children who have not yet attained the fine neuromuscular coordination that is normally evident for this age. However, most children will be able to compete favorably with their peers, and fierce rivalry results in interminable practice sessions to develop the degree of skill the child feels is necessary.

The attention span of children in this category has increased to the extent where they are content to watch without desiring to participate. They have developed an appreciation of the efforts of others and now remark knowledgeably about the skills involved in performance or silently observe performances as an entertaining medium. Span of attention also permits greater involvement in complicated activities requiring care and attention to detail. Group projects also develop, with each member contributing to the whole. Because they offer opportunities for the gradual development of social group interaction and mutual concern, craft activities have proved to be outstanding organizational forms for initiating close cooperation with others so that mutually beneficial outcomes are realized.

The Child from 4 to 12

As the child's social awareness broadens with entrance into school, new items of significance start to impinge upon his or her personal development. Their entire self-visualization must undergo frequent revision. Having seen themselves through the eyes of their parents during the first few years of life, it is understandable that they will view themselves with their prejudices. When they enter school they come under the scrutiny of those who are not automatically biased in their favor. They must now be concerned with attitudes and analyses of teachers, classmates, and other acquaintances. Parental attitudes will undergo modifications, and this will also serve to demolish the structure upon which an earlier self-concept was founded. As they grow older, the child's personality assumes a more settled pattern, exhibiting less flexibility than formerly. Whatever personality traits characterize the individual will not be changed, whether such traits contribute to peer and group acceptance or not.

As the child continues to spend more time with peers, there is increasing recognition of the fact that specific personality traits are admired and others are rejected by the peer group. Social opinion thus plays an important role in influencing the older child's personality. Children attempt to adapt their personality to suit the pattern that is admired in hopes of gaining the recognition and status desired. Children's ideas of personality traits change with age, and this is reflected in a hardening pattern of individuality. Whatever else they are or do to conform to the social pressures of their environments, children are individuals with certain needs, attitudes, and ambitions already crystallized by the first 12 years.

The 13- to 16-Year-Old

New interests develop throughout the adolescent years in consequence of the enormous changes made during the process of maturation. The onset of puberty with physical and hormonal modification and development of a heightened sense of status within social groups establishes emotional tensions. Adolescent interests may be looked upon as an attempt to throw off the previously held role of child and assume more adult activities. Personal interests are likely to center on their rapidly changing physique and accompanying bodily changes. There will be greater appreciation for the individual's appearance as there is increasing acceptance of social amenities between the sexes and between the adolescents and adults. At the same time, there is an increasing desire for autonomy as the independence that first appeared during the closing stages of childhood now manifests itself strongly.

Recreational interests also undergo changes during adolescence. Although a great deal of energy is still expended in competitive physical activities, there appears to be more selectivity toward activities. Males and females enjoy art activities, insofar as drawing and painting are concerned, but tend to be reticent about such productions.

Sexual interests are awakened during this postpubertal period. However, despite the need for recognition by the opposite sex, young adolescent boys and girls are rather timid when this desire is fulfilled. There still seems to be an attempt to reduce such shyness by group activities, but in the main most youngsters use the group situation to hide self-consciousness. It is only during the close of early adolescence that pairing off becomes characteristic.

The changes seen in personality patterns result, at least in part, from social pressures that are brought to bear on the individual. There are specific personality traits for both sexes, which receive acceptance or rejection. In their need to gain recognition by their social group, adolescents attempt to develop personality traits that will establish them within their group. Undoubtedly, most of the factors that influence personality development during the years of childhood will be the same for the adolescent. The significant difference, however, comes in terms of the stress placed upon particular behaviors. As the individual matures, childhood patterns that once were of dominant influence tend to diminish in adolescence, while formerly apparently unimportant factors assume important positions of influence.

The 17- to 20-Year-Old

The years between 17 and 20 are years of significant change. Adjustments must be made to an increasing adult role in society. The problems that seemed insurmountable to the early adolescent are now easily resolved. Perhaps the essential problem revolves around social adjustment. Physical growth that began with a spurt at the onset of puberty slows down dramatically during late adolescence. Whatever increases there are in height or weight become barely noticeable. Thus, integration of functions can be accomplished more swiftly, and with a coordination that finally rids the individual of the awkwardness displayed during early adolescence.

During late adolescence, selectivity of activities and acquaintances is even more pronounced than before. There will be fewer friends who may be termed intimate, while a broadened circle of social acquaintances is usual.

Individuals begin to assert themselves insofar as personal recognition is desired. Each sees him- or herself as having a distinct contribution to make in the group as a personality, and these efforts attempt to reveal the individual as distinctive from everybody else. Independence from adult authority is a particular issue, and every opportunity to rebel will be exploited.

Late adolescence is the age when the complete range of socially acceptable behavioral patterns for both sexes is imposed. There is a marked difference in behavior between the sexes. Males begin to take an interest in personal health, vocational choices, civic activities, learning, and recreational experiences. Females tend to reveal greater interest in personal attractiveness, social adjustment, lifestyle, and vocational choices. The desire for independence comes to a peak in late adolescence.

The recreational interests of the late adolescent appear to be even more restricted than previously. More time is spent on fewer activities. There is a gradual decline in participation in strenuous physical activity and greater inclination to be a passive spectator. Unless the individual excels in a particular sport or game form and there is peer pressure or other opportunity to participate, there is less likelihood of increased physical activity. Social activities, intellectual activities, and some hobby forms appeal to adolescents. Those who participate in hobbies tend to seek construction experiences. Reading also becomes an extremely pleasurable form of activity. A whole range of entertainments opens for late adolescents, as they have more money and greater discretion in the expenditure of money on activities they find enjoyable. Attendance at dances, concerts, movies, theater, and the like are popular.

What occurs to interests as the individual progresses through the varied opportunities provided by school and leisure to the stressful adjustments the adult assumes? The need to earn a living invariably forces a diminishing of recreational activity. There is a consequent narrowing of interests, although younger adults have a more varied series of recreational experiences than do older adults. Almost all participation in strenuous physical activity shows decline, while nonfiction reading and attendance at spectator performances appear to increase with age.

Up to a particular point, participation in hobbies seems to increase with age. Hobbies offer intense satisfaction, challenge, and enrichment lacking in other forms of recreational experience. Hobbies are thus likely to offer opportunities for satisfying basic needs when the other forms of involvement are no longer open or accessible. Of great meaning to the programmer is the increase in interest in craft activities, which occurs throughout the life span but is quite noticeable as spurts of interest after age 50 and again after age 65. Among the crafts most defined are those that are useful or serve a practical purpose. Automotive or mechanical repairing and tinkering, electric wiring, gardening, woodworking, sewing, cooking, book-binding, and furniture remodeling are among the craft forms frequently mentioned in studies that survey the recreational outlets of adults.

Interests are largely determined by social influences, cultural expectations, opportunities available, and the physical capacity and mental ability of individuals. Moreover, they mirror desire, needs, and drives representing fundamental outlets of satisfaction, either directly or vicariously. Striking differences exist among the interest patterns of individuals, each with their own special needs and unique model of personal-environmental relationships. The relative stability of interest patterns over the years is evident. Although change is rapid in the years from childhood to adolescence, certain general orientations may be noted as having been established by age 9 or earlier. By late adolescence interests have become crystallized to the extent that they are measurable for guidance purposes.

The fundamental relationship between broad and varied activities and good personal adjustment throughout the life span is well researched and substantiated. Recreational activities of all kinds offer enriched living potential and amply demonstrate the need to cultivate constructive and purposeful experiences of this nature. Children are a product of their nature and nurture. They must have wide parental guidance so that the development of satisfying interests will emerge with maturity and permit the individuals to invest their time creatively, pleasurably, and ethically.

Adulthood

The intelligent adult should attempt to develop a style of living offering depth, range, and intensity that will fulfill personal satisfactions and a sense of achievement despite the exigencies and ills of life. In this way, basic needs can be satisfied. The entire problem of good personal adjustment to life in relation to individual interests and capabilities has become of such significance that governmental agencies have properly been appointed to assist such adjustment and take responsibility for providing the opportunities for growth and learning. As leisure becomes increasingly prevalent, more people will be afforded ample opportunity to participate in recreational experiences of various kinds. Among these, there will be an appropriate avenue for finding individual achievement, enjoyment, acceptable social activity, constructive outlets, and the sources for satisfaction of a basic human need.

Program Planning Factors

Recreational program planning is only one aspect of comprehensive human ecological planning. It is a well-considered opinion that recreational activity is a basic human need, and as such, is an integral part of all social behavior. Recreational service planning develops directly from people's esthetic, educational, psychosocial, and biophysical capacities and desires. An essential concept for the logical conduct of program planning is that it cannot be performed without acknowledgement of and consideration for all elements composing the style of living of residents in whatever community the agency exists. In any given situation, recreational program planning needs to be based on all of the interdependent variables of the human community as well as the development of cohesiveness through the coordination of these factors. The entire range of human differences—age, gender, experience, social, political, economic, physical, ethnic, religious, racial, vocational—becomes the very foundation for a comprehensive recreational program. Only in this way will there be an assurance that individual differences, as well as commonalities, are taken into account so that opportunities for their satisfaction may be effectively offered.

Everything carried out in the field of recreational service is performed by people for other people. Moreover, the number of persons concerned, the way in which they are dispersed within the community, the rate at which they are increasing or decreasing in number, and the extent to which they are young or old, male or female, at work, in school, out of work, and other socially relevant characteristics are essential to the determination of the activities that make up any program.

Population study or demography has a well-defined content. Consideration of the divisions of this applied science for investigation is the surest means for ascertaining the nature of the constituency as well as the special needs or interests that can be ascribed to them. In undertaking population study, the recreationist must determine the facts and trends that will assist in the reasoned development of the recreational program. All of this requires the acquisition and utilization of appropriate space for facilities, arrangement of schedules, and deployment of personnel for the most effective and efficient service possible.

In brief, the following aspects of demography need to be considered to build a factual base for programming purposes.

Number and Area Distribution of Population

The number of people residing in the community is the single most important datum of any area. Primarily, an accurate determination must be made of the number of people living in the community. Almost as important as numbers is the currency of the information. Obviously, this material may be obtained from periodic census reports, but frequent post-census reporting may maintain accurately updated numbers. If the estimates are properly figured and separately given for smaller subdivisions, the foundation has been laid for serious study and analysis of the area distribution of the population.

Using the 10-year census carried out by the federal government as a base, population figures for particular local legal subdivisions should emerge. Clearly indicated will be the precise number of persons geographically distributed in the political subdivision within the community. Given such orderly arrangement, the recreationist should be able to extract facts and discern relationships from which program inferences can be made.

Population Features

A major division of demography concerns the make-up or traits of the population. These extremely significant characteristics, which distinguish one person from another, are used to classify populations into the most basic categories. For purposes of demographic analysis, age, sex, residence, race or color, and ethnicity are tabulated. These data are fundamental for population examination. Additionally, they serve as cross-reference material for all other characteristics.

Age is a prime characteristic for behavior determination. It represents a most significant classification that, employed in association with all other subclassifications of population information, determines to a great extent the value of census material. The recreationist *cum* demographer needs to study this feature scrupulously so the other relationships and differentials to be tested or demonstrated are not just reflections of differences or likeness in the age compositions of the populations being compared.

Gender is a vital characteristic because the ratio of males to females in a specific population is demographically significant. Appropriate classification of population data in consonance with the gender of the individuals concerned is one of the chief materials in the mosaic of scientific census taking.

The recreationist will make scant progress unless there is control through subsorting, or other techniques, to recognize the deviations in the gender makeup of the population being researched.

Residence is another characteristic of populations that promotes variance. Typically, residence is the distinguishing feature that separates classes of people. Usually, an urban–rural dichotomy is used to show vastly different values of style of living of those who live in the country as opposed to those living in cities. However, if the recreational service department is situated in an urban area, the factor of residence in terms of the section of the city in which people reside would displace the rural–urban continuum. In the same way, departments serving rural populations would also use local subdivisions to indicate differentials insofar as the other socially relevant characteristics are involved. In suburban communities, the analyst might find the rural–urban pattern more helpful and perhaps continue to break down the category into farm and nonfarm groups.

Race or color is an aspect of the picture that dominates population studies. Attempts to analyze and construe such demographic material reflect current societal prejudice toward these physical characteristics, and they continue to reveal fundamental divisions within the population. It does not matter that physical and social sciences indicate little to sustain the popular conception that race/color influences innate capacity, morality, or intelligence. Apparently, there is an ingrained belief by many people that it does, despite scientific findings to the contrary.

Ethnicity is another distinguishing feature of heterogeneous societies. The rise of hyphenated Americans during the past 25 years is a sign of the significance of ethnicity or national origin, to which individuals attach great importance. The classification of indigenous or foreign born, with additional subcategories for further distinction, provides considerable data on customs, language, cultural forms (dance, food, celebrations, holidays, music, religion, etc.), which the recreationist can use in the development of activities. Ethnically derived recreational activities tend to be extremely popular with those whose national origin serves as the reference for such programming.

The marital status of the population exerts considerable sociological influence. Census information invariably includes questions relating to this subject, and answers to such inquiries are incorporated into the tables of population characteristics.

Working and nonworking parts of the population could be included in demographic analyses by recreationists, because they may indicate a portion of the population's availability for recreational service at particular times. Thus, retired persons, preschool children, unemployed adolescents, homebound disabled persons, and others of similar circumstance might serve as the bases for developing outreach or facility-oriented activities.

The educational level of the population is a factor, which is quite evident from the enormous amount of data secured by the census. The literacy, educational status, or formal schooling of the population under study may heavily influence the kinds of activities, particularly those that have a heavy investment in intellectual pursuits that may be suitable for the population served by the department.

Increases or decreases in the population as determined by births, deaths, and migrations are the sole conditions that influence the size of a population or its geographic distribution. All three factors require analysis to determine whether or how much the population has changed, moved in particular directions, or dispersed according to need or desire.

Registration of births and deaths in any given year provides the basis for estimating the growth or decline in population. The migration of people either into or out of a specific area together with the natural increase or decrease indicates movement patterns as well as density in a community.

Population Distribution and Density

Material concerning the changing number and distribution of the population enables accurate projections of the movement of people. This, in turn, ensures that proper and timely planning of the acquisition and development of recreational places and spaces, as well as the scheduling of activities that depend upon such facilities, will be most effective. Trend lines indicating population flow and corroborating data depicting density are important for the current and future outcome of the program.

The number of persons residing in a given area has primary meaning for any policy adoption, planning stratagem, or administrative purpose relating to the provision of recreational services. Therefore, it is necessary to include every person residing in a given neighborhood, ward, precinct, or other local legal subdivision. All such census facts have reference to a particular time and are recorded separately for each individual. Any coverage needs to be of a meticulously defined area. If this kind of data collection is amassed, the product will be the number of people residing in a geographic location.

Place of Residence

Where a person lives tells the analyst something about the values of that individual. Communities can be divided up by tracts to indicate the number of persons residing in the area. This enables the recreationist to begin to collect information on the values, interests, educational level, ethnicity, race, religion, economic status, and other socially relevant characteristics that might assist in the planning and development of a comprehensive recreational program.

The continuum from rural to urban residence is neither sharply defined nor precisely calibrated. Indisputably, the rural end of the spectrum will undoubtedly contain a majority of persons who are in agriculture, but not everybody who is a rural dweller is a farmer. At the other end are undisguised urbanites—individuals who not only reside in the city, but also are influenced by social and cultural differentials only obtained by city living. A smaller community is more likely to suggest rurality. As the analyst looks at greater population density, local legal subdivisional components, building clusters, designated communities such as hamlet, village, town, city, or metropolitan center, not only will personal outlooks and opportunities change, but the areas that defy definition as rural or urban will also have to be taken into account. Variously defined as "edge-cities," fringe, exurbia, or some other designation, these represent varying degrees of urbanization or its opposite. The greatest number of communities are neither urban nor rural, but a combination of both. Any planning for the provision of recreational services must consider these attributes if intelligent and effective programming is the objective.

Community Growth

The rate of growth of a community must be considered in order to plan organized recreational services. The chief influences that work to increase population density and demand land annexation, on the one hand, and the chief forces that cause emigration and dispersal of the public population, on the other, must be examined. Social, political, and economic factors tend to act coincidentally and are reflected in the major population shifts within the community, into the community, or out of the community.

Technological innovations, for example, in one part of the country may have a profound effect upon the labor pool in a community somewhere else whose residents are made up of individuals who can take advantage of job vacancies created by the technology. Any number of cause and effect relationships may result in high-density shifts or scattered dispersions of the population. The forecasts that identify population gains or losses, and, most specifically, the trends within particular neighborhoods or districts of a given community, will necessarily dictate the placement and types of recreational spaces and structures as well as the program of activities conducted in or on them.

Economic Base

The foundation of the economy of the community is a vital factor in its viability. All of the economic activities that produce wealth within the community, and upon which the financial health of the locality is based, tend to greatly determine whether public recreational services will flourish or wither. Not only the physical plant, but also all aspects of recreational programming rest predominantly on the financial support and commitment of the community for the operation of recreational activities. Unless the community has the economic wherewithal and is willing to provide the financial assistance required for the expense of planning and development of a comprehensive program, little can be done that will have a salutary effect on the recreational enrichment of the lives of citizens. Financial considerations that include the tax base and rates, property value, outstanding bond issues, limitations on community indebtedness, community revenues, the ability of the locality to sustain capital expenditures over a generation for a system-wide physical recreational plan, and the means to support an operational program budget are also involved.

Race and Ethnicity

Of all the qualities that differentiate one population from another, or diverse parts of the same population from one another, the features recognized as race or color, ethnicity or place of national origin, and nativity are of greatest significance and most apparent. At most places and times during whatever constitutes the modern era, they have also been the characteristics people generally have considered to be of major importance.

Modern censuses classify populations by these features. Only the urban–rural polarization has priority over this primary subdivision. This is logical because the differences are enormous between the cultural backgrounds and economic levels of indigenous and foreign-born people. Also included here are the differentials in birth rates, mortality rates, and other social indices. The concept of race is formulated from that which is typically accepted by the general public. It does not scientifically mirror cognizance of biological origin.

Ethnic affiliations apply to populations distinguished on the basis of customs and characteristics. A person's ethnicity usually refers to the language spoken at home, the mother tongue, as well as identification of national connection or membership. All of these features are useful for analyzing the population of a community. The object, however, is not to cause or create conflicts within the diverse population elements. The main purpose of demographic examination is the development of recreational activities, using population origins and differences to better satisfy cultural expectations. By highlighting significant aspects of customs, cultural expressions of all types, and pride in the particular heritage, the recreational service department provides both thematic and the full range of experiences designed to enhance the enjoyment of potential and actual participants.

Residential Populations

The planning of any comprehensive recreational program, as well as the organization of the department providing such services, requires a fairly exhaustive compilation of relevant subject matter to become technical guides. In order to determine the facts necessary for making programmatic or policy decisions, an examination and analysis of the residential population has to be made. Neighborhoods need to be identified. The density of each neighborhood's population requires tabulation. The distribution of population by age, gender, or racial groups is necessary. Population distribution by occupational groupings (if feasible) could also be included. The distribution of population by ethnic, social, educational, and religious groupings needs to be considered. Investigation to determine opportunities for social interaction, civic service, community action programs, and/or social disintegration needs attention. Social agencies of the community in terms of organization, finance, relationships, program, possible duplication, and competition require scrutiny. Delinquency trends, problems, neighborhoods, kinds of offenses, and remedial measures could serve as the basis for recreational programming. Finally, public opinion and attitudes toward recreational services of all kinds must be gathered.

The following sources could be used for collecting data: the latest U.S. Census; school enrollment records; public utility corporate records; Chamber of Commerce records; and health, welfare, and various other public sector agency records. Reports and records of social agencies, law enforcement agencies, school attendance officers, and probation officers, personal interviews, analysis of newspaper notices and news items, court records, and juvenile or youth bureau records are available under the Freedom of Information Act, insofar as public agencies are concerned. Each of these investigations serves to clarify the picture of the public that is to be given recreational service. Thus, demography categorizes the disparate elements that constitute the total community. It reveals the special features and routine patterns whereby social, political, economic, and attitudinal factors can be more easily understood and classified for the provision of more effective and efficient recreational service.

Summary

Demographics, or the study of essential population characteristics, is needed to understand the diverse or similar features of the recreational agency's constituency. This, in turn, becomes the basis for determining the likely activities that could make up a program to satisfy whatever needs or interests such a population may have. Cultural background, previous experiences, or newly popularized ideas espoused by potential agency patrons serve as elements composing the program.

Age group characteristics constitute one of the detailed analyses that must be performed by recreationists if they are to deliver services of a recreational nature to those who reside in the community. Ethnic traditions, religious affiliation, gender, economic status, leisure available, and educational level attained all play a part in how people respond to the recreational offerings suggested by the agency in question. The recreationist/programmer must be cognizant of the similarities and differences manifested in the population to be served. In this way, a factual knowledge of probable recreational interests becomes the foundation for an attractive and satisfying comprehensive program.

Selected Further References

Bucher, R. D., et al. *Diversity Consciousness: Opening Our Minds to People, Cultures, and Opportunities.* Englewood Cliffs, NJ: Prentice-Hall PTR, 2009.

Davis, H. C. *Demographic Projection Techniques for Regions and Smaller Areas: A Primer.* Seattle: University of Washington Press, 1995.

Girosi, F., and G. King. *Demographic Forecasting.* Princeton, NJ: Princeton University Press, 2008.

Hobbs, F. B. *Demographic Trends in the 20th Century.* Washington, DC: U.S. Government Printing Office, 2002.

Martinez-Ebers, V., et al. *Perspectives on Race, Ethnicity and Religion: Identity Politics in America.* Oxford, UK: Oxford University Press, 2008.

Mitra, A., and S. Lankford. *Research Methods in Park, Recreation and Leisure Services.* Champaign, IL: Sagamore Publishing, 1998.

Riley, N., and J. McCarthy. *Demography in the Age of the Postmodern.* West Nyack, NY: Cambridge University Press, 2003.

Rowland, D. *Demographic Methods and Concepts.* New York: Oxford University Press, 2003.

Thomas, D. C. *Cross-Cultural Management: Essential Concepts.* Thousand Oaks, CA: Sage Publications, 2008.

Yaukey, D., and D. L. Anderton. *Demography: The Study of Human Population.* Prospect Heights, IL: Waveland Press, 2001.

Needs Assessment and Satisfaction

All people vary physically; in mental perception and acuity; emotionally; by gender, age, and race; and in opinion and attitude. Each individual possesses specific characteristics and attributes. Individuals have a physical structure of certain proportions; they may be counted upon to exhibit peculiar types of behavior; and, with maturation, they gain or should obtain particular skills that enable them to survive in the environment in which they find themselves. The individual is a product of his or her total milieu plus the biological inheritance. Thus, nature and nurture have had a hand in shaping both attitudes and aptitudes.

The fulfillment of physical needs cannot be made distinct from social needs or desires. From infancy to old age the individual is constantly concerned with the preservation of the self and the satisfaction of certain basic needs ranging from ego-centered and inner-directed to altruistic and other-directed behaviors. Such needs must be achieved in relation to the person's in-born and conditioned attitudes towards the individual's objectives that are felt to be self-fulfilling.

The various stimuli that produce, maintain, and direct human behavior have been classified as needs. The human organism has essential needs for survival, which can be divided into three component parts: physiological, psychological, and sociological. However, in all practicality, these fundamental needs neither are of separate aspect nor do they operate as distinct phases of behavior. Clinically or otherwise, it is literally impossible to separate the purely physical from the so-called mental or social needs of people. As a matter of fact, recent compelling scientific information leads one to believe that all behavior, whether of an emotional or social nature, stems from organic or physiological mechanisms situated in the central nervous system and modified by neurotransmitters.

Therefore, it is completely logical to say that these qualities are interdependent and interacting, not clearly seen as classifiable entities in and of themselves. The individual's needs or motivation for activity may operate overtly or covertly; they may be inherent or learned; they may be mental, physical, or social; but they never operate independently. Instead, they are dynamically interrelated instruments of the whole person in a total milieu. The intensity of the various desires or needs and goals is enumerated by the needs of the organism as a complete entity—in view of prior experiences and particular environmental situations.

When basic human needs are spoken about, there is usually referral to food, clothing, and shelter, as if these factors were all that is necessary for human beings to live well. Although it is valid to state that the human organism can survive when the needs for food, clothing, and shelter are being satisfied, that is all the individual will do—barely survive—because these elements merely cater to some physiological needs that can arise through pressures created by the type of environment in which the individual may be situated. It has been aptly stated that man (and woman) does not live by bread alone. Fundamental organic needs, arising from recurring stimuli that require organic adjustments, give birth to patterns of reactions. These essential physiological needs are innate and include visceral, adient, avoident, spontaneous, sexual, and rest reactions. These are vital to life.

The psychosocial needs of the individual are complex and oblique. In many instances they may be overt and lucid, but they are, nevertheless, complicated. Among the many psychosocial needs are goal-seeking activities, (i.e., love; affection; social, physical, and economic security; recognition; prestige; peer status; mastery; or dominance) with attendant impulses towards successful attainment, realization, or expression. The individual, with interrelated needs, must conform to the social environment in which he or she resides. This may sometimes cause a conflict of interest between personal needs and social requirements, which can become a source of irritation and frustration. The outcome of such conflict manifests itself in poorly adjusted individuals and, in the extreme, more severe emotional problems and maladjusted patterns of behavior. In order to ensure appropriate adjustment insofar as physical, mental, and emotional states are concerned, each individual needs to be stimulated in terms of personal ability. What is needed is a variety of experiences affording opportunities for achievement, self-esteem, and other valuable outcomes within the responsive limitations of the person's nature.

The recreationist must confront the problem of understanding human personality patterns (to the extent that is possible), needs, and motivations. For this study to be worthwhile, the possible variances of human behavior must be thoroughly considered. The behavioral pattern of any individual at any time in any environment must be recognized as having been produced by many factors, influenced by whatever it is that underlies human motivation.

Individuals seek satisfaction by meeting and compensating for deficiencies within themselves or their environment or by finding and concentrating on certain values that appeal and make the gratification of personal desires the stimulus to behavior. Thus the person is motivated to devise new ways of behaving that enable him or her to extend the scope and intensify the quality of needs satisfaction and to make certain of the replicability of those satisfactions previously experienced. The model for individual needs satisfaction is perceived to be founded in early childhood via the people, places, and things that provide aid and comfort, or that produce stress and pain. Probably one of the most important of all needs is that of acceptance by significant others, which incorporates such meanings as personal recognition and to be liked, admired, and loved.

Meeting Human Needs

The problem of providing recreational experiences to satisfy felt needs is, perhaps, one of greatest significance to the recreationist. As the professional gains comprehension of the problems of human behavior and motivation, activities that will provide satisfaction and stimulation for participants must be found. The fundamental activities that the recreationist considers are those that have generally been determined to produce positive benefits from engagement. After comparing recreational experiences, those activities that appear to have the qualities that are worthwhile for those who utilize them are incorporated into the program.

The experiences that occur at public recreational facilities of various kinds are known as the public recreational program. What responsibility is accepted by public recreational service agencies in relation to this program? Is their responsibility limited to the provision of facilities and the exercise of essential control, to the protection of public property, and to the regulation of the patrons' behavior? Or is it their responsibility to assume full control of the recreational program and to permit only activities that they have organized and promoted in accordance with certain preconceived objectives? These are two extreme viewpoints, and many adherents to them can be discovered. Originally, the park movement in the United States was built on the former concept. The playground movement in its early stages was concerned primarily with the welfare of children and tended to conform to the latter view. Schools, which assume limited responsibility for public recreational service, usually start with the concept that the school program of recreational operation must be conducted by teachers or recreationists employed as teachers, and that the program must be of a curricular and extracurricular nature designed to accomplish certain educational values.

Current public recreational service systems generally take the middle course. The modern recreationist recognizes that some types of facilities should be available for "free play" or unscheduled individual activities and for self-organized and self-directed group activities. The recreationist is also aware of the need for a determined amount of promotion and organization to multiply the number of activities and participants in the program, which tends to make for greater efficiency and larger usefulness of the public facilities. There is an appreciation of the necessity for supervision of some activities and the provision of positive leadership by recreationists so the desired educational, social, and cultural outcomes may be realized.

The recreationist has a mandatory obligation to fulfill. The professional must serve the recreational needs of the community in which he or she works and stand ready to deal with either individuals or groups. The recreationist is able to perform such tasks because of a thorough knowledge of individual needs, abilities, and experiences. People are led at their own pace toward the twin goals of enjoyment and satisfaction, which may be achieved through physical exertion, mental effort, skilled performance, cultural activities, education, conversation, or any one of countless activities the human mind is capable of creating.

There are several activities that, from prior experience and evaluative knowledge, the recreationist knows have had a beneficial effect upon individuals participating in them. Comparisons may have been made in various situations, and these activities were found to have worked whenever and wherever they were tried. Generally, these recreational experiences have been typified by providing an outlet for fun and personal fulfillment in ways that are completely valuable. In such instances, the professional person has a duty to the people who are being served to afford them such opportunities for performance.

By comparing experiences that have worked well in similar settings, the recreationist is able to construct a value scale of activities ranging from those that have proved to be worthwhile and satisfying to those that have proved degrading or demoralizing to the individual. Seen in totality, the consequences of the recreational experiences suggested by the practitioner should have a wholly beneficial effect upon the individual. By no stretch of the imagination does this statement preclude inventiveness on the part of the recreationist, nor should this be construed to mean regimentation, manipulation, or conformity to established programs. Simply put, it means the provision of recreational opportunities for all; whether such activities are utilized or not, they are made available.

Patron Needs

When discussion of potential patron needs is made for recreational purposes, the underlying rationale for such determination is the development of an appropriate program of activities that will satisfy those needs. Concomitantly, the second reason for assessing needs is to demonstrate the agency's understanding of and responsiveness to implicit or explicit articulations as perceived by the constituency. Finally, needs assessment permits the agency's clientele to voice their respective opinions and choices concerning experiences that impact upon their style of living, which they epitomize. It gives them an opportunity to participate in a decision-making process that directly affects their lives and social institutions with which they are acquainted.

Naturally, any assessment of needs will invariably turn up more expectations than can be gratified by any single agency. Therefore, recreationists must be capable of selecting a representative sample of probable activities based on potential participant input as well as educating for and influencing the best possible options. It must be presumed that recreationists, as professionals, have an understanding of activities that demean and those that uplift the engaged individual. This is not to be misconstrued as a patronizing, condescending, or judgmental point of view; rather, it is an accurate appraisal of the leisure qualities that recreationists should possess. In effect, then, it is a position that attempts to enlighten potential patrons by educating them to their own needs while also obtaining an understanding of the public's attitudes toward leisure experience.

Instead of merely reflecting majority points of view as the foundation of the recreational program, the recreationists must weigh the relative values of what has been requested. In some instances, majority opinion may be contrary to good morals, ethical standards, or decency. Simply because a majority, or an articulate minority, want the provision of an activity that is clearly reprehensible or of borderline worth should not make it a recreational mandate. The consumption of alcoholic beverages or other proscribed substances at public recreational places may appeal to a great number of people whose value system condones such usage, but it is not to be permitted or acquiesced to by the agency. Following the majority's desires in such circumstances would be investing undesirable and unacceptable behavior with the cachet of the agency and, therefore, would be irresponsible. In assessing the needs and desires of the constituency, a sense of proportion and value must be the determining elements when choosing activities or designing the program.

A variety of assessment techniques can be applied to ascertain the recreational needs of potential patrons. The essential function of any assessment is to discover constituency attitudes and preferences so they can be effectively satisfied through the recreational service delivery system. Logical determination of recreational needs may best be conducted by using statistical tools and analyzing the results; however, it is quite likely that the recreationist involved may not have the requisite background, skill, time, or financial means to undertake this effort.

It is probable that needs assessments can be carried out simply by asking a representative sample of the population to be served what their interests or enthusiasms are insofar as recreational experiences are concerned. From this information, analyses can be performed to elicit pertinent findings that can become the basis for future programming. A discussion of probability sampling will be offered later in the section titled "Sampling."

Advisory Committees

Citizen advisory committees may be developed at all levels of the locality. There could be neighborhood, ward, precinct, district, community, or city-wide committees formed of interested citizens by appointment or, in some cases, election. These citizens might be able to articulate the recreational needs of those who reside in the immediate area they represent. In whatever way the municipality or local government is broken down, its components could serve as the basis for an advisory committee. Each committee could then elect or select one of its members for the next higher level until a city-wide committee was formed. Each committee would become the conduit through which recreational deficits could be made up and activities developed and programmed.

Organizations are not above trying to subvert the functions of advisory committees. Agencies may attempt to use the committees to rubber stamp some position or to turn it into a lobby to achieve some preconceived end. Even if the objective is laudable, it is unprofessional to manipulate the agenda or outcome to suggest support for positions that have already been determined. After all, there are legitimate and ethical means to obtain desired goals. Such tactics may not work or may be exposed to public gaze if committee members are independent or strong minded enough.

Conversely, citizen groups may have certain attitudes that tend to promote particular points of view to the detriment of the whole in favor of the few; for example, departmental resources might be siphoned off to supply highly discriminatory experiences. These special pleaders can be harmful adversaries instead of objective or even relatively friendly advisers. These possible negative situations need not be the norm. It is much more likely that citizens who want to serve on recreational advisory committees do so because they are genuinely committed to community service, are well informed concerning their representative status, and are deemed to be competent advisers, thereby providing timely and effective communications between citizens and the recreational service department.

Open Meetings

In the early days of the United States, it was the custom to legislate at the local level through direct citizen participation. Thus, towns were operated as a result of an open town meeting to determine the budget and other appropriate questions of citizen concern brought up for discussion. Today, the town meeting is a quaint anachronism; however, the idea and format of such meetings may still be employed to determine citizen interest, attitude, and preferences with regard to recreational needs.

The conduct of such open meetings offers voters the opportunity to express their ideas and expectations, and give necessary input to the agency for the development of future programs. Of course, the open meeting permits the exchange of ideas as well as the exploration of innovative activity proposals. Lines of communication are opened between the agency and its constituents. Typically, citizens attending an open hearing have very strong opinions or emotions about issues and have no hesitancy in expressing them.

Town meetings may be effective in small communities, but in large urban centers they are neither representative of any viewpoint except of the person who is speaking, nor can such a format be easily organized. However, town meeting formats could be devised for small segments of the community, which would prove to be much more widely representative and offer the information being sought by the agency without further trouble. In fact, it is likely that this type of procedure is of great appeal to the practitioner who may not have the statistical or research skills required to conduct other investigatory prospects. For those who do have the requisite knowledge and skills, the following possibilities present themselves.

Surveys

Surveys examine or consider a situation with some specific objective in view. Although surveys may be used for delineation, elucidation, and discovery purposes, they are principally employed in investigations that have individuals as the units of analysis. Surveys are data gathering devices for collecting original information describing a population too large for direct observation. Deliberate probability sampling enables a group of respondents, whose characteristics tend to mirror a larger population, to provide data through a well-designed standardized questionnaire. Surveys are superior instruments for measuring attitudes and interests in a large population. Most urban areas and metropolitan regions would benefit from the use of a survey to determine recreational needs.

Three chief means for conducting surveys of the sample of respondents are self-administered questionnaires, interviews, and telephone surveys.

Self-administration by mail is typical. Although groups can be given a questionnaire if individuals are in the same place simultaneously, and they cooperate, it is more usual to mail the questionnaire to the potential respondents for completion and return. There are many texts dealing with social research that can supply the details for conducting the mailings and even provide examples of sample questions that could be used. Therefore, it should suffice merely to mention the practice here.

Interviewing is an alternative to having respondents reading and answering questionnaires. Interviewers question respondents orally and record the replies. Interviews can be done in face-to-face meetings or performed by telephone.

Interviews generally achieve a higher completion rate than mailings. Moreover, the interview tends to minimize the non-answer ("I don't know" or some other denial). Interviewers can be instructed to elicit responses, explain any ambiguities or misunderstood questions, and make observations about the individual respondent and his or her reactions, residence, dress, language, and so on. Ethical issues surface with this method because of the contact between the respondent and the agency seeking information.

Sensitivity to respondents' trust and confidentiality are essential in surveys of this type. No questionnaire is ideal. However, an appropriately designed and executed interview would try to achieve a level of consistency so that items tend to have the same meanings for each respondent and every response means the same thing when different respondents answer.

Interviewers must be trained to present a neutral front so there is little or no likelihood of influence on the respondent. In addition, different interviewers should be able to obtain the same responses from a particular respondent. The training is intended to reduce interference with the respondent through any influence and thus prevent bias.

Telephone surveys are simply non-face-to-face interviews. They save money and time. They may also be irritating to the potential respondent who has had previous telephone calls from various solicitors trying to sell magazines, gold stock, siding, or telephone service. Nevertheless, they are advantageous for obtaining honest answers as well as more direction over data gathering if several interviewers are employed in collecting needed information. One drawback to telephone surveys, however, is that people can end the call by hanging up.

Computer-assisted telephone interviewing (CATI) is also increasingly being used for surveying. The development of computer technology will eventually permit the machines to generate questionnaires, interview, analyze the data obtained, and perform other necessary, but time-consuming, tasks currently handled by humans.

Surveys, when well planned, administered, and conducted, are valuable data collecting mechanisms in terms of representative sampling. Despite several advantages, in terms of economy and the amount of information that can be gathered and analyzed, surveys tend to be superficial and contrived. There is also the danger of questionnaire and/or interviewer bias. Finally, surveys rely on sampling techniques, and it is with this aspect of surveys that recreationists may be least proficient.

Sampling

This is not the kind of text that dwells on the minutiae of research and the tools with which such research can be carried out. No attempt to develop a sampling workbook is contemplated. This section merely contains an indication of the concerns involved in sampling. Basic definitions and concepts will assist the recreationist, who may then refer to the voluminous literature on the subject of social research methodology, where the details of sampling procedures are spelled out.

It is necessary to understand that a population is the total number of all of the cases that conform to a set of defined specifications. A single member of a population is a population element. In general, it is much more economical in terms of resources to obtain desired information for only some of the elements with the objective of discovering something about the population from which they are taken. This designated group of elements is a sample. The expectation is that the characteristics of the sample reflect or are true of the whole population. Whether or not the collected information is an accurate picture of the population greatly depends on the way the sample is chosen.

The fundamental distinction in current sampling theory is between probability and nonprobability sampling. The basic quality of probability sampling is that one can denote the likelihood that each element of the population will be included. What is vital is that for every element there must be some explicit probability that it will be included. In nonprobability sampling, there can be no estimation of the probability that each element will be included in the sample, and no confidence that every element has some chance of being included.

Probability sampling is the only approach that possesses the capacity to estimate the extent to which the outcomes based on the sample are likely to differ from what would have been discovered by analyzing the population. With probability sampling, the sample size may be defined to provide a given degree of certainty that the sample findings will not differ by more than a particular amount (percentage) from those that an investigation of the total population would reveal.

The primary advantages of nonprobability sampling are convenience and economy; however, it may be that the risks of such sampling outweigh the advantages. Therefore, it is to probability sampling that we now turn. Among the chief forms of probability samples are simple random, stratified random, and a variety of cluster samples.

Simple Random Sample

This form of sampling is the fundamental probability design. It is included in all the more complex sampling designs. A simple random sample is performed by a procedure that makes certain that every element in the population has an equal chance of being included in the sample and also makes the selection of every possible combination of the desired number of cases equally assured. Populations of any size can have random samples drawn by utilizing a table of random numbers, which can be found in any statistics text. These are sets of numbers that have indicated absolutely no evidence of systematic order. Once all of the elements in the population are numbered, the table is then entered at any random point. The cases whose numbers arise as one moves down the column of numbers are used in the sample until the desired number of cases is obtained. The selection of any given case does not restrict the selection of any other case. Therefore, it is equally possible to select randomly all of the possible combinations of cases that are available.

Stratified Random Sample

The population for this sample is initially divided into two or more strata. The strata may be characterized by one or more criteria. In stratified random sampling, a single random sample is drawn from each stratum and then they are combined to form the total sample. If it is reasonable to assume that stratifying in accordance with a specific criterion or set of criteria will produce internally homogeneous strata, then it is desirable to stratify.

Generally speaking, the greatest degree of precision will be obtained if the various strata are sampled proportionate to their relative variability with regard to the traits being studied instead of proportionate to their relative sizes in the population. In sampling to determine the proportion of cases having a particular quality, strata in which it can be expected that approximately 50 percent of the cases will have the quality while the other half does not must be sampled with a greater degree of thoroughness than strata with a more marked uneven distribution.

Cluster Sample

In cluster sampling, the final set of elements to be included in the sample is obtained by initially sampling larger groups or clusters. The clusters are selected by simple or stratified random sampling methods. If all of the elements in these clusters are not to be included in the sample, the last choice from within the clusters is also performed on a simple or stratified random sampling foundation.

All of these methods may be easily applied and carried through if the researcher has the experience and skill to do so. However, most recreational practitioners may not have the background to conduct sampling procedures. In all likelihood, they will resort to open meetings, interviews, or suggestion boxes. Actually, these latter techniques may be just as effective as sampling. In any event, the basic principle for satisfying the recreational needs of a given constituency is to promulgate the most comprehensive and exhaustive program possible within the parameters of available resources. Under these circumstances, a comprehensive program will incorporate all of the categories of recreational experiences with a variety of subcategories that have been used and enjoyed before. Including more subcategories enables individuals to seek out familiar or unfamiliar activities that they feel they want to pursue. Thus, a program answering the recreational needs of the constituency can be developed.

The Balanced Program

The activities that are permitted and conducted by the public recreational service agency are legion. However, they may be classified into large categories for easier understanding and practical grouping. The normal recreational life of children and adults includes selected activities from all of these groups. Each major collection contains a huge variety of subcategories, which can be profitably utilized to provide a continuing series of experiences that are interesting, challenging, and eternally new to the participants. These groups may be graded from simple elementary forms to complicated expert forms. The following recreational activities have usually served as the basis for a well-rounded recreational program.

Arts and Crafts

These processes of communication along with other creative activities enable individuals to express themselves freely. These self-determining acts translate ego-centered involvement outward in a healthy process of self-realization. In woodwork, leather work, ceramics, and graphic arts, for example, the individual is able to forget the normal restrictions of social custom and thereby answer a felt need for originality.

Dancing

Dance in its many forms is met with interest because it concerns the universal and basic need for movement. It is a process of symbolic communication, expressing many sentiments, always serving as a fulfillment of emotional and physical feeling. It satisfies ambivalent desires and may be one method by which humans satisfy hostility urges and behave in socially acceptable ways. Normally associated with this form of expression are social, interpretive, square, round, folk, modern, ballet, and other types of dance.

Drama

Drama in its essence is a form of communication through the human voice and body. It is a communication process that provides satisfaction by transmitting ideas and emotions, as well as permitting self-expression either vicariously or directly. The elements of catharsis and empathy are closely related to dramatic productions.

Education

All experiences are informative, whether or not a participant is conscious of learning. Some learning occurs in the formal setting of the school, whereas other learning is informal (i.e., through recreational activities). Although it is valid to say that nearly all recreational activity results in some learning, there are specific educational aspects of recreational experiences. A formally organized class in baton twirling, social dancing, or furniture refinishing closely approximates a classroom situation. Adult classes in any number of subjects offered by the community school or the recreational service department may be both educational and recreational. Even formal subject courses, taken during leisure, may be recreational. Included, to mention but a few examples, might be typing, art, crafts, dance, photography, Christmas-package wrapping, cake decoration, citizenship, geography, conversational foreign language, history, or arithmetic.

Hobbies

A hobby is any individual interest that is self-sustaining, often engrossing, and stimulating to the participant without connection to the vocational experience. Typically, hobbies are of the acquisitive or appreciative type. Hobbies are not performance oriented, except in terms of manipulating that which has been collected. Thus, one may collect violins as a hobby, but playing the violin falls under the category of music. In the same vein, making a model airplane is a craft, whereas collecting model planes would be a hobby. One can also acquire knowledge about any subject or object and therefore appreciate or understand it better. This would also constitute a hobby. Although hobbies are idiosyncratic, certain hobbies are common on a worldwide basis, such as stamp collecting. Therefore, hobbies fulfill a certain desire for gregariousness because hobbyists may be expected to come into contact with one another as they explore manifestations of their particular, or peculiar, interest.

Service

All experiences concerned with activities that are normally associated with altruistic or humanitarian purposes may be deemed service-oriented. The fact that they are carried out by and for others indicates their social nature.

Social service activities have long been utilized by recreationists to fill leisure positively and productively where other forms of activity may not satisfy the human nature to extend sympathy, feel empathy, or offer aid. The release that one obtains from whole-heartedly giving service to others—the exchange of too much self-concern for selflessness—results in a feeling of personal satisfaction that cannot be underestimated. No other experience provides this sense of personal extension and self-realization. Activities subsumed under this category include teaching, acting as a counselor or group leader, volunteering in a treatment center, reading to blind persons, helping to build a community center, taking children to a zoo, chaperoning a teenage dance, taking part in civic affairs, and serving on many types of community-based committees.

Social Activities

Social needs are satisfied when people have to mix, mingle, get along, and/or adjust to others. Social activities of all kinds have a place in any recreational program where appropriate conduct and good mental health are objectives. Relationships developed through social intercourse contribute to the maturity of individuals and the development of empathy, catharsis, personal esteem, and self-expression. Activities related to social objectives include interest clubs, parties, mixers, banquets, outings, all volunteer work, and community service experiences.

Motor Activities

The enhancement of physical fitness and cardiovascular and pulmonary efficiency, the improvement of physiological functioning, and the release of hostility or the sublimation of socially disapproved feelings through games, exercise, and sports can provide a great deal of satisfaction to a participant. Although many people take part in gross or fine motor activities for achievement and self-realization, significant positive behavior toward others is also developed. Ego strength, self-confidence, high morale, or social tolerance may develop as a consequence of routinely participating in vigorous physical activity. Individual activities might include swimming, archery, hunting, gymnastics, or fishing. Team games such as football, baseball, basketball, soccer, or volleyball would be possible. Calisthenics, aerobics, or weight lifting might be competitive or noncompetitive forms of activity.

Music

The value of music to the individual varies from person to person. The effect music has on the individual, either as a participant performer or spectator/listener, illustrates its unique attraction. Whether music is listened to for the pure sensual pleasure of sound, for the esthetic effect, for the rhythm produced, or for a combination of these, or whether the individual plays an instrument or sings, empathy and emotional release are apparently generated. Except for the tone deaf, if such exist, there are few who do not appreciate some form of music. Musical activities include singing solo or in choral groups; playing instruments in orchestras, bands, or other ensembles; performing in opera workshops, operettas, or recitals; and so forth.

Nature-Oriented Activities

Outdoor activities of many types belong in the well-balanced recreational program. Among the most requested and truly important activities is camping. Whether it is day or residential, camping combines a variety of skills and satisfactions in its performance. Wilderness camping, in particular, provides the participant with the exhilaration that stems from being close to unspoiled nature. There is a need for some aspect of camping in every recreational program. All people have a traditional attachment to nature and instinctively seek to refresh themselves after the artificial environment of urban or suburban life. Outdoor experiences include camping of all types, hostelling, conservation, nature study, Indian lore, astronomy, meteorology, horticulture, canoe tripping, back-packing, rock climbing, and other stimulating outdoor contacts.

Special Events

These are activities that give color and zip to any program. They are out-of-the-ordinary experiences that punctuate the organized routine program. Special events are designed to appeal to the widest possible audience and participants. The nature of the activity is such that it must be scheduled only at specific times during the year and may represent some theme or commemorate an occurrence. Special events take up much preparatory time, money, effort, and in some cases, material. Thus, a special even might be a float parade, a circus, a theater production, an Olympic-type athletic event, or a pyrotechnic display. All these activities require inordinate preparation but attract much attention and may be the only vehicle that engages the interest or participation of persons who are uninterested in anything else.

All of these categories with their myriad activities should be a part of any balanced and comprehensive recreational program, for each experience contributes to satisfying people's recreational needs. It is important to the recreational agency to offer the broadest possible range of recreational activities so that an appeal can be made to all persons without exception. In this way, the likelihood of need satisfaction should be probable and obtainable. The tendency to emphasize one classification (for example, athletics) to the exclusion of other categories is a frequent error that must be avoided.

Summary

Every human is unique, and despite similarities in environment or culture has various personal needs specific to them. These needs arise from both genetic and experiential circumstances. Individual reaction to perceived conflict or harmony becomes the basis for behavioral motivation. How people respond to stimuli insofar as satisfying their needs, whether to assuage deficiencies or augment satisfactions, must be recognized by recreationists in attempting to deliver appropriate recreational services.

The development of a recreational program that appeals to the participants' innate need for self-esteem, personal acceptance by others, and goal-striving for ego satisfaction is the foundation upon which a balanced and comprehensive program of recreational activities can be built. By answering felt needs, through the medium of experiences that are known to be enjoyable, the most satisfying program is achievable. The method of selection used to determine appeal and sustained participation on the part of the agency's constituency will accrue from sampling technique, surveys, town/community meetings, questionnaires, and other means whereby the needs of people can be ascertained. Such effort should result in the production of a well-rounded continuing series of recreational activities designed to meet the needs of the individuals for whom it is intended.

Selected Further References

Bruni, L., et al. *Capabilities and Happiness.* Oxford, UK: Oxford University Press, 2009.

Kumar, D. D., et al. *Needs Assessment: An Overview.* Thousand Oaks, CA: Sage Publications, 2009.

Neuber, K. A., et. al. *Needs Assessment: A Model for Community Planning,* Vol. 14. Thousand Oaks, CA: Sage Publications, 1981.

Percy-Smith, J., ed. *Needs Assessment in Public Policy.* Independence, KT: Open University Press, 1996.

Reviere, R., et al. *Needs Assessment: A Creative Guide for Social Scientists.* Independence, KT: Taylor and Francis, 1996.

Royse, D. D., et al. *Needs Assessment.* Oxford, UK: Oxford University Press, 2009.

CHAPTER

4

Adaptation

Adaptation, when done well, permits individuals with disabilities to participate in recreational activities to the fullest extent of which they are capable. Every community contains numerous persons of all ages who, for whatever reason, are forced by injury, disease, or birth defect into a limiting role insofar as recreational activities are concerned. These people obviously have special needs, yet they do not require therapeutic recreational services. How can these needs be met? The answer lies in the changing of the community recreational service or other agency program. This means the adjustment or modification of activities, method of performance, environment, equipment, or facilities utilized for the activity, or in the nature of the activity itself. Anything that can be done to enable the individual with a disability to participate successfully entails adaptation.

In the past, the provision of community recreational services depended upon a certain degree of self-sufficiency on the part of participants. Those who had the capability to perform, either within the organized public program or in activities of their own choice, could participate. Others, with disabilities, were invariably omitted from recreational opportunities. These were persons residing within the community who were affected in a way that limited their ability to engage in the typical offerings available. They represented every age group and almost every socioeconomic level.

Of even greater significance was the lack of faith of those who are supposed to be ethically dedicated to upholding the rights of all persons. Public sector programs failed to respond to the needs of these individuals. Instead, a steady stream of excuses was presented about why the public agency could not undertake to serve this unfortunate minority. Lack of specialized personnel, insufficient funds to carry out the primary mandate for which the public department was originally established, poorly designed and equipped recreational facilities for serving the special needs of individuals with disabilities, and the realization of incompetence on the part of practitioners, all were used to mitigate the fact that a significant segment of the community was not being served recreationally.

Recreational programs were not adapted to meet the limitations of the disabled even though, often, a slight modification of activities would permit participation without any slackening of competition or skill. Those who should have cared enough to provide for those who could not run fast or exercise great degrees of skill, flexibility, control, or stamina, did not. This is the legacy of a culture that refuses to contend with the problems of victims of genetic deficiencies, degenerative diseases, crippling accidents, and war.

It is incumbent upon recreationists in all circumstances, but particularly in community or public recreational agencies, to ignore the prejudice and ignorance of society as a whole and begin advancing valid reasons for offering opportunities and service to all. The primary principle upon which the field of recreational service is founded is that of provision of recreational services to all people, not just to all people who are sound in mind and body or who have the personal resources to get along without any special assistance whatsoever. This most basic of all principles means what it says—service to all, whatever their condition, wherever they may be found, at whatever level they are functioning, as long as they are residents of the community. If they reside within the community, then the community and the agencies that represent it must provide continuing services designed to enhance their lives. Today, this nonconsideration of disabled persons is no longer a possibility. Either public departments must accommodate the individual with a disability or they open themselves to litigation.

Over the years, society's concept of disability has changed from absolute bias and disregard to the recognition that an otherwise disabled person, despite the impairment, may contribute productively to the community and may lead a satisfying life through socialization with peers and participation in the community. After considerable federal and state influence and legislation, the public, in great part, has come to the intelligent conclusion that disabling conditions need not exclude the individual so afflicted from normal human relationships nor restrict personal worth and self-expression. From the onus of stigma and overtones of guilt for some imagined sin to the realization that there are scientifically verified causes that produce the disabling condition, society is moving to establish an environment within which the seriously impaired or mildly incapacitated can achieve whatever potential they have for living the "good life."

The public must continue to be educated about the special needs of disabled persons who reside within the community. Although total enlightenment and public support have not yet reached the stage where the needs of all persons are being met, tremendous improvement has been noted. The U.S. Congress legislated Public Law 101-336 (Americans with Disabilities Act of 1990). This law requires reasonable accommodations of disabled individuals in public park and recreational places. This may mean some short-term financial crunches as departments make arrangements both environmentally and in the program to serve disabled persons. However, not providing services to these members of the community can make the public agency vulnerable to charges of bias and poor public relations, and cost them hard-pressed dollars when it comes to litigation.

Rationale for Adapted Recreational Service in the Community

As has been reiterated, recreational activity is as important to the health and well-being of people as physiological sustenance and social equilibrium. The disabled individual requires recreational activity to the same extent as, if not more than, the able counterpart. Two facets of adapted recreational service apply in meeting the needs of individuals with disabilities in the community setting. First, the adaptation of recreational experiences permitting the exercise of such pursuits transforms diversion into a restorative or preventative function. The act of modifying recreational activities decreases limitations placed on the individual by disabling circumstances, thereby enabling that person to compensate for the disability while stimulating whatever capacity remains. Second, adaptation supports the individual psychologically and encourages pursuits that build confidence in one's ability to perform what was previously thought to be impossible. This by itself should improve morale and sustain personal self-confidence.

The ability to cope with health, physical, or social problems, despite restriction, is an indication of the individual's capacity to be free of the despair brought on by impairment or dysfunction. If activity is to have any meaning in the life of the individual, it must be something in which the person can participate. What has been lost through accident, pathology, or age cannot be restored by recreational activity alone; however, the individual can be greatly assisted. Where the damage is permanent and the function or movement is gone forever, the person may still engage in compensatory activities if opportunities are provided. Once the individual has been stimulated to perform, personal drives may properly be directed to seek and develop new or latent interests and talents as well as to reintroduce old skills. Meaningful activity is fundamental to the health of the individual throughout the life cycle. Leisure activity, adapted to meet this need satisfactorily, serves therapeutically in both restorative and preventive ways.

Traditionally, recreational activity has been considered as a restorative. It was undertaken to provide recuperation necessary after performing the work of the day. There seems little question but that recreational activity does much to alleviate the distress and tension produced during the daily confrontations that all people experience. This has been the accepted role for recreational activity. In order to benefit from this recuperative aspect, in the psychological sense, physical, mental, and social limitations have to be bypassed. This may be accomplished by manipulating the activity, the environment, or the rules of procedure so that any restriction upon the individual's performance is nullified. By definition, a recreational service for persons with disabilities is conceived as adapted activities directed toward reinforcing the positive behavior of recipients of the service. To the degree that disabled persons are sustained in experiences of daily living and enabled to live more satisfying lives through recreational participation (i.e., permitting them to recoup their strength, mental equilibrium, or personal identity), behavioral changes may be noted.

All people require experiences that offer opportunities for relaxation, self-expression, cultural expansion, physical activity, and personal fulfillment. Without the opportunity to participate in recreational activities of some kind, individuals begin to deteriorate. Even the most interesting and stimulating work requires some abatement. Whatever the individual does during leisure provides that change. It serves, not merely as a restorative, important as restoration is, but as a preventative. In other words, recreational experiences are an effective agent of therapy and prophylaxis. This suggests that the fundamental purpose of adapted recreational service is to offer the diverse possibilities that can make life meaningful and rewarding, to prevent debilitation, and to assist individuals to exercise the greatest use possible of their remaining capacities.

Adapted recreational activities that open up new avenues and broaden the horizons for disabled persons in the community can be a remarkable barrier to the onslaught of mental illness and physical deterioration. While offering opportunities that do much to stimulate active physical participation or aroused attention to some heretofore neglected artistic, education, or social contact, the preservation of emotional stability and increased fitness are encouraged. An efficient, joyful, and satisfied person possesses the self-sufficiency and patterns of behavior that liberate him or her from emotional stress, irrational conflicts, presumed and imaginary slights, and illogical positions. Such an individual looks forward to the change and sweep of living while developing an attitude that facilitates coping with the continually changing panorama of his or her environment.

By utilizing personal resources to their fullest degree, the individual who has suffered dysfunction will be able to overcome some deficiencies and learn to adjust, thereby preventing preoccupation with morbidity, self-pity, despondency, and lowered physical capacity to respond to the changing forces and stimuli of the surroundings. This is the real preventative that adapted recreational service can bring to the disabled individual. It permits heightened interests and enthusiasms in place of despair or dependency. Once again, the person may view the open vistas of possibility in consequence of a program that allows him or her to enter and fulfill those necessary patterns governing all human beings. It is even possible that the individual may be restored to life fuller and healthier than was true prior to the disabling situation. Even those whose physical or mental incapacity was brought about genetically or through the deterioration of age or disease may be habilitated and borne up through the application of a well-directed program of recreational service.

Community Responsibility for Adapted Recreational Service

The development and cultural implications and consequences of qualitative recreational experience influence most governments to take positive action so as to provide the public with recreational services. But governmental enterprises in this field need not, nor cannot, preempt private endeavor. On the contrary, public recreational services only exist where and when the individual, either alone or in voluntary association with others, is thwarted in securing the recreational experiences necessary for personal satisfaction and enjoyment as a human right. Thus, recreational service ranks with education, public health, and safety as a necessary concern of government.

Those who have the greatest need for such services are typically those who are most frustrated in receiving them. Here is the perfect situation for community-sponsored opportunities to be made available and accessible to individuals whose age or dysfunction prevents participation unless special efforts are made on their behalf. These are the clients for the public field to serve. If such persons are not enabled to take part in the greater scheme of community involvement, at least through recreational experience, then the fundamental principle on which the community service is established is negated.

Methodology

The need to remove artificially created barriers to an individual's participation in gaining access to recreational places and activities is a paramount consideration. This is performed by enabling disabled persons to use ramps, elevators, and hydraulic lifts; widening doorways; and placing sensory guides for the blind or other conveniences that permit them to enter recreational areas without hindrance. Additionally, drinking fountains and telephones need to be lowered to accommodate those in wheelchairs or those whose stature does not allow comfortable use of these necessities. Finally, toilets need to be constructed to accommodate a wheelchair or those using crutches or braces. In constructing gymnasia or swimming pools, showers must be installed with the necessary privacy, space, and hand rails designed to give the person with a disability easy access and use.

The need for ingenious adaptations covers the entire range of recreational activities and facilities in and on which disabled people are welcome. Thus, tools may be shaped to fit a hand that no longer has the appositional grip, or other devices may be invented so the disabled person can participate without great effort. The use of certain colors can be employed to overcome the effects of color blindness.

Insofar as the physical environment is concerned, soft surfaces may be hardened to permit the passage of wheelchairs or those using crutches or canes. Hard surfaces also can be softened to avoid unnecessary injury. The use of non-skid materials in showers or on pool decks is simply a common-sense precaution.

Where physical activities are involved, rules can be changed, as can the space to be used. A person who cannot run may have a substitute runner. The number of hits on a volleyball may be increased; tees can be used for baseball or softball; and larger and lighter balls can be introduced for those with catching or strength problems. Distances may be shortened; more players can be injected into the game than are usually allowed; lighter weight equipment can be used; and modified equipment can be constructed for attachment purposes for those who need stability.

Whether an individual is in a wheelchair, needs a gurney to be ambulatory, requires Canadian braces (aluminum crutches with upper arm attachments and handles set below for easy use) or crutches, or is in bed, the ability to participate in recreational activities must not be hampered. Adaptation in terms of activity rules and regulations, numbers participating, colors, space, time, distance, height, access, sound, light, and design may all be included in the process of enabling persons with disabilities to take part.

In the final analysis, attitudinal changes must become a part of the indoctrination of every recreationist in any sector of society. People with disabilities do not need pity. What they require is sound common sense to allow them to participate in whatever way they can without artificially contrived barriers that set them apart from their fellows. Recreationists, above all, must recognize that despite disabling conditions, all people need to receive that degree of recreational service which they require for a quality of life that is both satisfying and enjoyable.

Summary

Disability should not prevent any individual from participating in one or more recreational activities, particularly insofar as a public recreational service department is concerned. But this applies to private sector programs as well. It behooves recreationists to live up to their professional obligation of serving those who are the constituents of the agency, no matter what limitations beset them. There is no excuse for failure to accommodate those persons with disabilities. If adaptations can be made to rules of participation, equipment, accessibility of facilities, and other areas that enable those who are personally challenged to engage in their choice of recreational activity, these changes must be made.

The federal government has enacted legislation that requires any purported recreational agency to arrange for the reasonable accommodation of those with disabilities. Failure to provide such inclusive programming lays the agency open to legal retribution as well as negative publicity. Therefore, adherence to ethical standards makes adaptation a necessity in carrying out the mandate imposed by professionalism.

Recreationists need to use ingenuity and common sense in developing the modifications of physical activity, tools, equipment, and other alterations to the environment so that those who are impacted by disability are not excluded or segregated.

The reason for this is obvious. All people need to be involved in some recreational activity. To reduce stress, attain personal satisfaction and enjoyment, and improve the quality of life, the pursuit of happiness through recreational experiences must not be denied. No one should be excluded from this form of engagement when adaptation can overcome whatever disability is present.

Selected Further References

Glazirin, I. D., et al. *Adaption in Physical Education and Sport.* Opole, Poland: OWPO, 2006.

Rouse, P. *Adapted Games and Activities: From Tag to Team Building.* Champaign, IL: Human Kinetics, 2005.

Scott, N., et al. *Special Needs, Special Horses: A Guide to the Benefits of Therapeutic Riding.* Denton, TX: University of North Texas Press, 2005.

Sherrill, C. *Adapted Physical Activity, Recreation and Sport.* 6th ed. Blackledge, OH: McGraw-Hill Higher Education, 2003.

Winnick, J. P. *Adapted Physical Education and Sport.* 4th ed. Champaign, IL: Human Kinetics, 2005.

CHAPTER

5

Computer Applications in Programming

Today's computers process information quickly, precisely, and economically. This is exactly what personnel in the field require for the systematic development of scheduled recreational activities to meet the diverse needs of whatever constituency the recreational agency serves. The variety of information is so extensive that it requires electronic processing if the most comprehensive program is to be offered. The generation and dissemination of information about persons, places, potential activities, and resources have grown exponentially. It is this increasing output of information that compounds the difficulty of producing a recreational program that can satisfy varied interests, talents, knowledge, skills, and appreciations of those people the agency was established to serve.

The need for informational services from which direct instructional and varied recreational offerings can be programmed has grown more quickly than was ever anticipated. In order to contend with this flood of material, recreationists must turn to technology to coordinate the physical, personal, environmental, and experiential resources, and leisure available to its public so that people's needs can be satisfied through recreational services.

Acquisition and assessment of data are fundamental to the planned program of recreational activities necessary to meet the expressed and unarticulated demands of an increasingly sophisticated and knowledgeable clientele. It is almost unimaginable for a recreational service agency to be without computer facilities. Today, data processing technology permits the recreational service enterprise to rapidly solve complex and intersecting problems concerning recreational activities.

Used in many ways—for record-keeping, retrieval of information, the planning of material requirements for the delivery of recreational experiences within the agency, the controlling of materials or inventories on hand insofar as supplies and equipment are concerned, and the development of a database that can almost point the way toward satisfying individual recreational needs—the computer has become indispensable.

Computer programs are able to ingest and retain whatever type of information is supplied and perform whatever is required in terms of comparing, offering alternatives, selecting best choices, or maintaining an intricate schedule of activities at different places and times without conflict, based on the information necessary for problem-solving.

Computer speed (power) and software capacity can solve the complex problems developed by the flood of data confronting recreationists. This complexity can be controlled by using existing technology.

Various programs are available to accomplish rapid and accurate logical calculations that are beyond human endurance or capability. In many instances computers permit acuteness in making choices or accuracy of control that was previously unthinkable. Today it is routine to compare extensive possibilities in order to resolve a problem or find the most beneficial alternative. Through the utilization of aids such as linear and dynamic programming, critical path analysis, factor analysis, network analysis, and simulation, recreationists can make recreational program decisions with precision and rationality.

Applications

The following are just a few specific applications of computers and data processors to the area of recreational program possibilities. A listing can be created of all possible areas, facilities, or spaces where potentially planned or independently occurring recreational activities might take place. The creation of a database containing all possible recreational activities in which people may participate on an organized or spontaneous basis is well within the grasp of the recreational programmer. Recreational activities require indoor and outdoor facilities in which the varied possibilities that satisfy personal needs occur. Scheduling all available spaces in terms of activity demand would normally be so burdensome that it would take enormous time, personnel effort, and monetary resources to undertake such a task. Yet, this type of duty can be performed with the touch of a button.

Displaying information concerning the maximum size of instructional activities for the most effective performance and participation not only saves time and money, but also is most efficient in terms of placing appropriate personnel at the right place and time to serve agency clientele. The ability to match participants' skills, talents, or knowledge with available activities as well as the development of new or additional activities to satisfy the full range of specific recreational needs can only be performed through the machinations of computer programs that are sufficiently endowed for the purpose. Additionally, the agency can offer various alternative choices to participants in terms of available personal leisure, skills, and interests.

Of course, computers are no more infallible than the data fed into them by human programmers. However, once the electronic data processing is initiated, it performs a job in seconds no single or even many humans could possibly do. Automatically matching people to activities, places, free spaces, free time, personnel on the job at any given time, and an almost infinite variety of information variables makes the computer an invaluable device for providing recreational services. With computer applications, it is more highly probable that individuals are going to obtain greater satisfaction from the recreational program because each person's individual needs may be more completely met. With computers and appropriate programs it is possible to develop activities that are designed to suit individual needs and preferences.

Computerized Program Development

Every ingredient that is part of the inauguration of activities implemented to offer instruction and pleasure for those participating is part of program development. These diverse elements require the coordination that only computer-driven outcomes can supply if the various facets are to be combined into opportunities in which people may find recreational satisfaction. The factors that determine the location, the means, the participants, the costs, and the time of activity are intermeshed with the reasons that stimulate individuals to participate or not and how they are informed about the program. Computers can do much to cut through the complexity of putting all of these items together so that they result in a coordinated and efficacious provision of activities.

Leisure and Timing

Free time is the essence of all recreational experiences—the planning and development of the recreational program and the scheduling of individual, group, or mass activities. The exact timing of activities, whether of an instructional, organized, or self-directed nature at any specific facility, may encourage or restrict opportunities to participate. In some instances the timing of the activity may be so convenient that it stimulates participation. The converse is also true. When an activity is poorly scheduled it may actually inhibit an interested individual from taking part.

Timeliness is extremely significant because of associations that can be made with current events, world, national, or local. The passing seasons or specific dates may stimulate remembrances of things past or induce interest in topics that encourage activities of the here and now. Timely subjects based on commemorations, memorials, national holidays, religious celebrations, ethnic traditions, or social customs can be employed to create high interest as well as to take advantage of the pertinence of certain experiences to potential participants.

Time Factors

The programming of activities during the day or evening hours needs to consider the potential client's ability to get to the place where the activity is operating. Some activity times may be inconvenient because they might interfere with other obligations, depending upon the age of the individual, whether they are employed, going to school, otherwise engaged in household chores, and so on. The appropriateness of the time when the potential participant will be most receptive to engaging in a recreational experience is an absolute requirement. All of these factors depend on the individual person's physical capacity, mental acuity, ability to attend with or without assistance, and any desire to be included. The planning of recreational activities, whether at a centralized facility or one serving a given neighborhood, will be based on variable time factors. Under such circumstances, it is hardly likely that the recreationist will be able to account for all of these multiple inputs and be able to mesh them seamlessly so as to best serve the conflicting needs and interests of the agency's clientele. The only hope for effective coordination with such a scattering of information is to feed the data into a software program with the expectation that the varied elements will be sorted out and made compatible. The recreationist then will be in a position to assess the variables in question and be better able to plan activities capable of satisfying the agency's clientele.

Individual Needs

The extent to which the conduct of activities is based on individual needs is increasingly important. Many independent and interdependent variables will have an effect on the duration of activities. Some people may require longer or shorter class periods if they are learning some skill or technique, or acquiring an understanding of some subject. Sometimes a person's attention span may not be long enough for an entire session. Other important considerations include the frequency of activities, length of activities, when the activities are offered, and the relevance of activities to the person's everyday life. Whether the activity is scheduled for a particular time depends on the person for whom it is intended. Therefore the activity must be arranged to stimulate and focus attention, arouse interest, and spur continued participation. The development of a database containing the constituents' profiles may be possible through the collection of information that potential clientele can provide, if the reasons for doing so are compelling enough. Such information will be forthcoming only by convincing people of the benefits of sharing actual or potential recreational interests, aptitudes, skills, or desires.

No recreational agency ever wants to gain a reputation of being paternalistic or having a "big brother" approach to people. Quite the reverse—the recreational agency needs to convince its constituency that it has no ulterior motives other than to serve the recreational needs of those who make up its catchment area.

Computerized Scheduling

The utilization of computers to schedule recreational activities is necessary because it facilitates the coordination of all the elements comprising opportunities, time, personnel, locations, facilities, supplies, materials, equipment, and participants. The schedule, then, is the concrete version of planning, developing, public relations and education, maintenance work, and deployment of personnel at a time and place most appropriate for executing the recreational activity within the program. Computer use undoubtedly offers the smooth combination of people, places, interests, and time with advance notification so that no inconvenience results and interested parties can plan for the occasion. Schedules enable flexibility. When planned correctly, personnel, money allocation, and material can be arranged, so that the activities will occur as expected. If emergency situations arise, such as flooding, heavy snow, loss of electricity, or other contingency, alternative times and dates can be established so that those who are actually or potentially interested will be able to plan accordingly, have something to look forward to, and have their interests maintained.

Activity Length

The duration of an activity depends on the needs of those who participate and the type of activity in which they are involved. Thus, rigorous activities may be scheduled for a shorter period of time than more passive activities. Surely, the capacity of individuals will be of immediate concern regarding whether strenuous activity is appropriate. The span of attention of persons attending a specific recreational activity might also influence the length of any session. An aesthetic experience might engage the attention of an artist for extended periods, whereas swimming, running, dancing, lectures, or other activities might not.

The duration of sessions has to be based almost completely on the interest, skill, needs, and desires of the participant. Also significant will be the availability of the facility to accommodate participants, recreationists available, and any competing demands made upon the agency for equal time and space for other members of the constituency.

The recreational program is the single most important function with which the recreational service agency concerns itself. Every conceivable means and effort must be taken to ensure a well-balanced, comprehensive, and varied program. Programming represents all the directed energy the agency has at its disposal to affect the most viable, satisfying, and attractive program possible. Programming is influenced by many far-reaching factors, including community fabric and milieu; individual needs, interests, and capacity; social, economic, and educational levels; previous experiences; occupation; and many tangible and intangible aspects of the culture of which it is a part.

All recreational programs are justifiable under the principle of providing something for each person who is part of the agency's constituency. That success in recreational programming depends on logical planning, standards of activity selection and development, and implementation techniques.

Programming is a complicated process requiring professional leadership and ultimately technological support. Detailed planning based on certain knowledge of the community and its people, resources, and potential are of inestimable value in establishing a sound program in which all people are recreationally served and may attain satisfaction, enjoyment, and a feeling of personal well-being. The use of computer applications as a tool for the implementation and operation of the broadest possible range of recreational activities at appropriate times and places carries out the responsibility imposed on the recreational agency.

Summary

In order to cope with the seemingly never-ending flood of disparate data concerning potential patrons and the various recreational facilities, supplies, materials, and equipment that can be used to satisfy individual and group needs, computer technology must be applied. Organizing such information so that it is intelligible and useful in the production of recreational services is a necessity. Recreationists must become knowledgeable of and proficient in the use of computer technology to accomplish the task generated by the continuous flow of demographics, physical and cultural resources, and the personnel investment required to develop a comprehensive and balanced recreational program.

Scheduling activities by bringing the patrons, recreationists, facility, materials, and activity into confluence at the right time is one of the functions that computer programs can offer. Of course, a well-qualified programmer must collect and install the pertinent information so the machine can transform the data into usable output. Specialized software is available to assist the programmer. Whether it is organizing an inventory of supplies on hand, analyzing population characteristics, or applying budgetary factors to the supply and demand for recreational services, computer technology is effective and efficient in the development of a satisfying program.

Selected Further References

Crowder, P., et al. *Creating Web Sites Bible.* New York: John Wiley & Sons, 2008.

Park, Y. H., ed. *Computer Technology and Applications.* Fairfield, NJ: American Society of Mechanical Engineers, 2004.

Parson, J. J., et al. *Computer Concepts.* 5th ed. Boston, MA: Course Technology, 2004.

Seppelt, R. *Computer Based Environmental Management.* New York: John Wiley and Sons, 2003.

Spalter, A. M. *Computer in Visual Arts.* Boston, MA: Addison-Wesley Professional, 1998.

Wei, D., ed. *Computer and Information Technology.* Piscataway, NJ: IEEE Computer Society Press, 2004.

6 The Environment: Natural and Artificial Settings

The natural and artificial settings used for recreational purposes comprise the full range of indoor and outdoor areas that can be employed. Some communities are fortuitously placed and can take advantage of the natural environment including scenic wonders, waterways, mountains, nearby forests, and other spaces that are particularly attractive for active or passive recreational experiences. The communities so situated can have their public recreational service departments exploit these conditions. Others, not so advantageously placed, must either create and develop artificial areas to accommodate recreational use or do without. The same holds true for private sector recreational agencies.

Commercial organizations have famously engineered facilities where natural places were unavailable. Thus, wave-making machines sited inland, where there is no access to the sea, have turned shallow pools into surfing areas. Water parks containing flumes, slides, and other created water activities have overcome the absence of the natural place. (**Figure 6.1**) In some instances, public departments working with sponsors, who underwrite much of the expense, are able to construct similar facilities.

What is not opportune outdoors may sometimes be manufactured inside to accommodate experiences of a recreational nature. However, the need to indicate the kinds and types of areas and facilities necessary to offer recreational opportunities to people during their leisure is the theme of this chapter.

Public Land Use for Recreational Services

In almost every community, but particularly the large urban center, there are sections of land reserved for public and quasi-public utilization. These uses are chiefly concerned with the provision of services to the entire community or some part of it. Contained in this classification are lands reserved for streets, public utilities, buildings, buffer zones, schools, and all types of recreational facilities. The policies under which these various land uses operate cannot be segregated from the agency responsibilities to which they relate. Therefore, it is necessary to omit additional mention of these services of government and concentrate on the one function of primary interest—recreational service.

Land and spaces categorized as recreational cover a wide variety of uses including playgrounds, parks, reservations, play fields, community centers, beaches, campgrounds, swimming pools, outdoor theaters, golf courses, riding trails, bicycle paths, tennis courts, auditoriums, gymnasiums, band shells, arboretums, zoological and botanical gardens, museums, scenic vistas, historical sites, waterways, forests, and other open spaces of different types. Recreational areas and spaces include quasi-public and privately owned lands and facilities that can be utilized for recreational purposes.

The amount of space segregated for recreational purposes in any given community varies greatly with the local conception of providing for public recreational service. If the community feels that recreational experience is a vital governmental function designed to meet the changing needs of people, the likelihood exists that a greater proportion of the available land will be devoted to recreational uses. Where a community does not accord value to recreational experience, the amount of land made available for recreational purposes decreases. Recreational spaces differ significantly from community to community and within different neighborhoods of a single community. The space necessary for recreational uses depends a great deal on the physical situation of the community, and on the interests, age groups, occupational factors, and educational, social, and economic level that are characteristic of its people. At this time, there are only educated estimates as to the space requirements for recreational use in any community. Such rules of thumb may run anywhere from 5 to 10 percent of all the community land available to 1 acre per every 100 persons residing in the community. The basic error of such figures is that they do not consider population mobility, density, or need.

Site location and variety of utilization are probably of greater importance than the total allotment of space set aside for recreational uses. Recreational facilities must consider all of the people residing in the community as well as transient populations. The chief factor concerning the amount of space devoted to recreational objectives is its accessibility to the population that most requires it. Facilities designed to meet the recreational needs of the local neighborhood have to be located within one quarter mile of almost every resident. The facilities must be easily accessible without hazard from vehicle traffic nor barred by any natural or man-made physical objects. On the other hand, regional parks and camping and picnic facilities need not be closely situated to the local population. They may be located on the outskirts of the community, or in distinct but accessible sections of the community without regard to distance. The utilization of such outlying or peripheral facilities is intended for a mobile population that will travel some distance to reach the site.

Figure 6.1   Aerial View of Splashdown Water Park

Figure 6.2 Hidden Pond

In the selection of sites for recreational purposes, every effort must be taken to make basic use of areas that for all other practical intents and purposes would prove to be uneconomical, unfeasible, or otherwise undesirable. Such areas are prime spots for scenic viewing, hiking trails, and nature trails, and have program value. Thus, steep hillsides may be converted to winter sled riding, skiing, or tobogganing areas. In the summer, the hillside might serve as an observatory, a beginner's hill for novice mountain climbers, as part of a cross-country or steeplechase run, and so on. Deep gorges, ravines, rocky promontories, so-called submarginal lands, swamps, bogs, and other equally unsuitable land for commercial or industrial development may very well be excellent for recreational purposes (**Figure 6.2**). These various areas may be easily incorporated into the program by making use of them as passive or active recreational spaces. Bird watching, hunting, geological explorations, collecting minerals, and studying the ecological processes of a given environment are all potentially worthwhile recreational experiences.

However, these lands should not be bought, leased, or accepted for recreational use unless they are situated in suitable locations. A deep ravine, for example, does not have to be accessible to the general public if it can be reached by an interested climber. In fact, accessibility may not be the only standard for selection. Availability for the purposes for which such areas are intended may make them desirable recreationally, if for no other reason. When the space is to be utilized for tot-lots or for a neighborhood playground, however, it must be of adequate size and situated within the neighborhood where it will be convenient to those whom it will serve.

Standardized Recreational Facilities and Their Placement

Every community should have a variety of basic recreational facilities in which all the people may find a balanced series of recreational experiences. Ideally, a small playground or tot-lot, with minimum equipment, should be situated at the center of every 100 children under 6 years of age. This area can be 10,000 square feet or less in size and situated in such a site that children could have access to it without crossing any street. The play lot can be fenced and contain a large sand pile and a few pieces of imaginatively constructed playscapes, gaily painted, and have benches set in on all sides. Parents would thus be the means of supervision in the sandbox and block play of early childhood could be satisfied.

The neighborhood playgrounds should be designed, although not exclusively, for children between the ages of 6 and 15 (**Figure 6.3**). The neighborhood playground may have from 2 to 10 acres, and multipurpose areas, a shelter, toilet facilities, quiet games area, core games area, and sufficient space to conduct a comprehensive and balanced program for the individuals who attend. In many instances the playground can be night-lighted and thereby serve an older age group. It is not uncommon to find tennis courts, volleyball courts, handball courts, bocce courts, and basketball layouts, as well as the aforementioned facilities in playgrounds.

The Neighborhood Park

The public space set apart for the habitual recreational use of residents in urban neighborhoods has generally been called the neighborhood park. Sometimes it is called the neighborhood playground, because being in a park-like environment it strongly attracts children, youth, and adults. It is one of the most numerous, if not the most important of all the components that are generally described as constituting the public park and recreational service systems of cities today.

To provide a comprehensive program of activities of a recreational nature, which all neighborhoods need, a full complement of facilities is required. To omit any renders the park inadequate by that degree. They should include the following (**Figure 6.4**):

1. Space for informal play, such as tag and circle games, folk and round dances, relay and other foot races, hopping and skipping games, stickball, bounce ball, and other adaptations of formal games of many kinds, modified because of limited space, all because they provide fun for the comparatively unskilled. Each space for informal games should be planted in durable turf; if not all of it, at least a portion. Too frequently the open play area for informal play is paved with asphalt, which contributes to many abrasions of knees and elbows and conditions adversely the kinds of activities that should be practiced on such an area.
2. Play courts marked out on pavement for games in which accurate bounce of balls and sure footing for the players are required. These courts include basketball, handball, volleyball, paddle tennis, and other less formally organized games. All of these games have official rules and dimensions that should be generally observed, not without some license in adaptation of them to players of junior age and moderate skill.

Figure 6.3 Neighborhood Playground

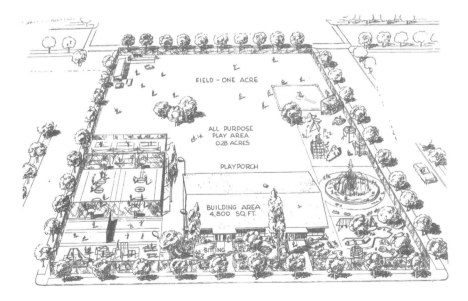

Figure 6.4 Neighborhood Park. This rendering shows all essential facilities accommodated on a minimal area of two acres.

3. Play apparatus arranged in groups for the play of preschool and elementary school children include swings, slides, climbers, tetherball, and sand areas, safely installed over well-drained subsurfaces. The surface beneath apparatus from which children frequently fall should be of sand, tanbark, or shavings. Where such materials are unavailable, synthetic or rubberized surfaces should be used, such as have been recently developed and are now widely used for pole vaulting pits and like facilities. Use of strap swing seats and the provision of two low rail fences make the swing as safe as any other piece of apparatus. Use of creative design features that virtually eliminate the possibility of accidents from side swinging and entanglements in the swing chains have proved beneficial in many instances. In the same vein, slides having wide sliding surfaces remove the impulse for children to push, because they accommodate a dozen or more children at one time, and have no ladder. The top of the sliding surface is reached by climbing up the sliding surface, an exercise in itself, with developmental function. In addition, slides have been developed that permit use of the contour of the play space for sliding. Artificially developed hillocks or banks have also been incorporated and serve equally useful objectives.

4. A spray pool, in lieu of a wading pool, for children to use on very hot days, and that may be used for in-line or roller skating and other pavement games in cool weather. Modern-designed spray equipment and attachments not only cool off users, but are versatile, being aesthetically pleasing, nearly vandal-proof, and portable.

5. Gymnasium apparatus, graduated in size for teenage youth, consisting basically of the types usually found in indoor gymnasiums, but adapted to the out-of-doors. These should include flying rings, horizontal and parallel bars, and the balance beam or variations of it.

6. Outdoor lighting for play under lights in the evening hours, especially for older teenagers, for whom the lighted outdoor gym may become a place of absorbing recreational activity when it is suitably equipped, and more so if the school teaches gymnastics. The outdoor gym should be adjacent to some of the court game areas and a field where field sports may be practiced informally. Altogether, they constitute an outdoor teenage recreational center.

7. Protective fencing, or other area separations, for safety and to confine balls to the playing areas. In playing games like paddle tennis, table tennis, and handball, there is great frustration when errant balls roll away from the playing area. Any fencing utilized should have as primary objectives the prevention of accidents to the players and the permitting of greater consistency in games. Fencing should not be used to prevent access to recreational places, particularly playgrounds or parks. There are places where fencing should be employed to serve this legitimate purpose, but denying entrance to non-fee or recreational places is not one of them.

8. Landscaping with trees, shrubs, grass, and other plantings.

9. Marginal areas, when the need is present, improved and set apart from areas used by children and containing outdoor facilities such

as horseshoe courts, shuffleboard courts, croquet and roque courts, benches and any tables, and shade structures if the preferred shade trees are lacking. Separate sanitary facilities should be provided.

10. A building, or portion of a building, providing, as a minimum, sanitary facilities, office, storage, kitchen, all-purpose recreational room, and club or craft room.

Design Plan of the Park

The area laid out and equipped for preschool children must be removed and protected from the hazards of the area where balls and other implements of play are used. Facilities used by older teenagers must be assembled in juxtaposition, encouraging use of apparatus and courts without crossing over areas used by other age groups. Parts of the park used most heavily by patrons should be closest to the center of supervision, which is at the building. The building, or part of a building, as in the case of the school, becomes the center of supervision.

All of the requirements of the neighborhood park, whether as part of a school or separate, could hardly be accommodated in an area of less than 2 acres. Since so many neighborhood schools have less than 2 acres not occupied by school buildings, compromises must be made. The same is true of neighborhood parks apart from schools.

Although every effort should be made to adhere to a minimal standard of 2 acres for a neighborhood park, there will be many neighborhoods in which smaller areas will have to suffice, owing largely to the high cost of acquisition of additional land. On smaller playgrounds, facilities for all age groups are not possible and programs must be adapted to the limited space. Derivatives of standard games and other activities must be substituted, as for example, stickball for baseball, and paddle tennis for tennis. Recreational professionals are skilled in devising substitutes.

Selection of Equipment and Apparatus

Important as the general layout and design of the park may be, the selection of implements, apparatus, and equipment—the outdoor furniture—is of equal importance. Selection of fixed equipment for a park calls for understanding of child, teenage, and adult psychology, as well as the changing patterns of behavior and recreational activity. It also requires knowledge of the use of equipment and its inherent attraction to users. Because educational and developmental objectives are always a concern, the inherent value of particular equipment in inducing activity, rather than mere amusement or entertainment, is important. The ability of individuals to perform and to derive value in use is also significant. Numbers who can be accommodated is still another criterion, related also to safety and economy.

Apart from recreational equipment for traditional athletic games, such as baseball, basketball, and handball, the apparatus selected should be designed to satisfy the urge of children and youth to climb, swing, slide, crawl, roll, lift, push, balance, and so on (**Figure 6.5**). These are ways of behaving that have, through the ages, provided the means of bodily development. The park designer would do well to recognize these natural urges, and select and design equipment that would induce developmental exercises,

Figure 6.5 Sculptured Climber

Figure 6.7 Yeehah

Figure 6.6 Chinning Cycle

Figure 6.8 Platform and Group Slide

preferably in unique and imaginative ways, to challenge achievement through repeated use (**Figure 6.6**).

There are infinite ways to do this. Some designers of recreational places for children have created innovative facilities and equipment (**Figure 6.7**). They strongly appeal to the child's ability to make believe, strive, and acquire physical efficiency and development.

The following is a summary of the neighborhood park area and the apparatus necessary:

1. Preschool children's area, ages 2–5
Baby swings, 8 feet high, strap seats
Platform or group slides (**Figure 6.8**), 4 and 6 feet high
Jungle gym, small
Pipe tunnel

Figure 6.9 Slide and Climber

Figure 6.10 Outdoor Gym

Sculptured climbing forms
Sand area
Benches and shade trees, table, and/or pergola
Spray pool (wading pool)
2. Elementary school–age children's area, ages 6–13
Swings, 12-foot frame, strap seats
Platform or group slide
Climber (**Figure 6.9**)
Traveling rings
Tetherball pole
Sculptured form
Spray pool, shared with younger group, available also for roller skating
Field for junior baseball, backstop
3. Youth area, ages 14–19
Outdoor gymnasium: flying rings, 12 to 14 feet high; horizontal bars; 5 and 6 feet high (**Figure 6.10**); parallel bars; balance beam; sand or shavings pit or synthetic or rubberized pad beneath apparatus
Handball courts, paddle tennis courts, alternately used for volleyball
Basketball courts (Figure 6.10), extra backboards
Lighting for all installations in this area
All courts with fences
4. Adult outdoor recreational area
Tables for table games
Benches
Bocce or horseshoe courts
Shuffleboard courts
Small shelter building, including sanitary facilities
Shade trees or pergola
5. All-purpose recreational area
Surface preferably of turf
Moderate reflected lighting from the corners, including junior baseball field; more concentrated lighting at infield

Figure 6.12   The Future District
Recreational Center

Figure 6.11   Multipurpose Room

6. Building area
All-purpose room, approximately 40 feet by 60 feet (**Figure 6.11**)
Craft and/or clubroom
Office, storage space, small platform stage
Recreational porch the length of the building, with table tennis and
other table games
Sitting areas at entrance, with moderate ornamental planting

The District Recreational Center or Community Park

The district recreational center is an indoor facility containing the space and equipment necessary for the ongoing year-round production of a highly effective and diversified program of recreational activities (**Figure 6.12**). It will serve all age groups and be open from morning until late at night to meet its primary obligations. It will be adjacent to or part of the community park of not less than 25, nor more than 40 acres, containing a variety of passive and active areas, including at least one fully equipped and staffed playground, walking paths, a variety of play fields, courts, appropriate plantings, and picnic spots. The district center should be able to serve the needs of people from an area within a radius of between one half and three quarters of a mile.

Facilities in Community Parks

- Outdoor swimming pool (**Figure 6.13**); if there is no pool in the nearby senior or middle school, an indoor pool is advisable).
- Tennis center (**Figure 6.14**). Not less than 4 courts and preferably 8 or 12.
- Archery range. Target points should permit at least 10 persons to participate in the activity simultaneously.
- Regulation baseball diamond or diamonds. (Outfields may overlap if space is not plentiful. The outfields should all be turfed.)

Figure 6.14   Bank of Tennis Courts

Figure 6.13   Outdoor Swimming
Pool

- Softball and/or junior baseball diamonds.
- Turfed field for soccer and other football play.
- Family picnic areas, with benches, tables, fireplaces, water supply, and so on.
- Picnic area for organization picnics, with conveniences as listed above plus outdoor stage or stand.
- Outdoor theater.
- Walking trails, bicycle paths, and emergency vehicular paths.
- Outdoor ice-skating rink, which may also be utilized as a roller-skating rink during the summer. This facility may also be converted to a dance floor when necessary.
- Roller-skating pad.
- Lighting installations for some play areas, including anti-nuisance lighting and the lighting of paths providing access to facilities.
- Spectator facilities at some locations.
- Sanitary conveniences where needed.
- Automobile parking area or areas.
- Maintenance yard and building.
- General and ornamental landscaping and conservation of natural features.

The community park may be an appropriate location for three very important facilities, but local circumstances may indicate preferred locations. The three are: (1) the comprehensive community recreational center (**Figure 6.15**), (2) the teenage recreational center, and (3) the senior citizens' recreational center. All of these are fast becoming essential facilities in communities in relation to population increments of 1 per 20,000 people. The three are separately described.

Community Recreational Center

A community recreational center, one of the elements designated above, is a term widely used to describe a multipurpose and multi-facility building serving the recreational needs of a total community consisting of several

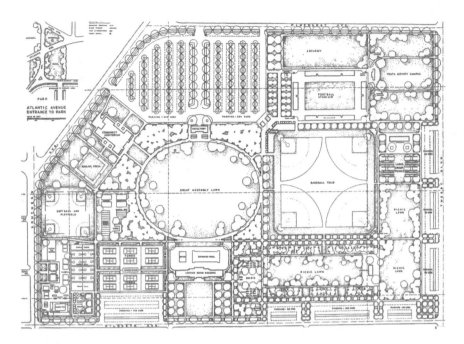

Figure 6.15 A Comprehensive Community Park

neighborhoods. It contains more indoor facilities than could reasonably be expected or planned for every neighborhood; it is essentially a community facility, in every sense of the word *community*. Although it is one of a number of facilities within a community park, because of its size it is more fully and separately described below.

Many cities with a population of 10,000 or more have established community centers. They have tended to become the focal point of the community's organized recreational and civic life. Very large cities, composed of several or numerous communities, have planned (and many have gone far to accomplish plans) to provide a community recreational center in each of the several communities making up the city.

A community recreational center usually includes the following minimal facilities in a planned arrangement, suitable to combinations of uses yet with compatibility of otherwise conflicting events when held simultaneously:

■ A large multipurpose room, minimum size 40 feet by 60 feet (2400 square feet), with additional platform stage and stage dressing rooms adding 20 feet to the length (800 square feet): total 3200 square feet.
■ Lobby, office, closets, laboratories, etc.: 1200 square feet.
■ Not less than four separate meeting rooms in variable sizes, average size 16 feet by 24 feet, with essential storage space, hallway, and utilities: 1536 square feet.
■ Gymnasium, minimum size 50 feet by 80 feet, 4000 square feet, plus dressing rooms, and ancillary facilities, 1400 square feet: total 5400 square feet. The multipurpose room or auditorium should not be designed to accommodate vigorous indoor sports. Where there are other indoor gymnasiums available in the community, as in high schools, the gymnasium should be eliminated.

The total minimal size of the community center described, less the gymnasium, would be approximately 6000 square feet. The community center should be planned for a central location within the community, preferably in a community park. It would not accommodate all the assembly needs of the people for which public provision should be made, but if it is complemented by a school auditorium, a community could be said to be well supplied with facilities of the type described.

The Teenage Recreational Center

The teenage center should preferably be a separate and distinct entity in itself. Indoor facilities should include an office with counter; an all-purpose assembly room big enough for parties and dances for about 50 couples; a snack bar; a game room; two or three club rooms; a craft workshop; a reading and study room; ample storage spaces; game equipment including billiards, pool, and table tennis; a television; and musical equipment.

The outdoor facilities should be immediately adjacent to the building, with free flow permitted either way. They should consist of such things as courts for table tennis, handball, and volleyball; gymnastic apparatus in sand, shavings, or foam rubber pit; basketball goals if not a small court; and, if possible, a softball diamond of restricted size. All of these should be well lighted for evening recreational performance. There should also be a drive-in, off-the-street parking lot. The teen center facilities should be in close order arrangement, without bleachers or the like, with due regard for safety in the use of units close to one another. The center must present multiple opportunities for varied activities, indoor and outdoor.

Older Adults' Recreational Center

In a community park, a senior citizens' center may range from those with minimal facilities, such as benches, roquet or croquet courts, horseshoe pitching courts, and the like, with a shelter from the sun and rain, and sanitary conveniences separate from those available to children, to a comprehensive center. A comprehensive senior citizens' recreational center would include indoor facilities for a whole range of experiences, encompassing such diverse forms as art, crafts, music, drama, forums, excursions, socials, and so forth. Whether a particular community park should be developed with the senior citizens' recreational center would depend on public demand, but no community park should be without the minimal features described.

The Athletic Field

Every community park should have an athletic field designed for highly organized competitive sports and for the convenience of audiences who attend athletic events. These include high school and college games and the athletic contests of teams and leagues that emerge from the less formal competition of the schools and the public playgrounds. Such contests require fields more adequately maintained than those used for informal contests at which admission is not charged. Building of conveniences for the comfort of spectators becomes as important as planning for the requirements of the competition. The facility, therefore, must be fenced, bleachers must be provided, and a lighting system of higher intensity installed, as is required for night use.

The athletic field should be incorporated into every community park. In very modified size and appointments, it is also a part of the neighborhood park. There are several kinds of fields, depending on the extent to which they are established for formal competition, as spectacles of interest to and attended by audiences of various sizes. Athletic competition organized by the recreational services is largely accommodated on fields in community and city-wide parks, sometimes also on high school athletic fields.

A running track for the quality of competition now current in high schools, colleges, and universities should have a six-lane straightaway to permit the standard 120-yard high hurdles race without using the curved portion of the track. To this must be added other lengths at the starting position and at the end, beyond the finish line, the total length then becomes 140 yards. The finish line should not be at the very end of the field so that those who occupy the seats in the center of the bleachers may observe the finish of races somewhat in front of their position.

Auxiliary Parks and Recreational Places

Every city of considerable size contains a miscellany of areas publicly owned or controlled that serve some park purpose and that may be called auxiliary parks. They are usually odd-shaped parcels of land that have been left over in the process of subdivision and that have fallen into the possession of the city. Included in this category are strips of land along important roads and streets, such as center dividers of major boulevards upon which landscape improvements may be made and sometimes benches provided for the convenience of pedestrians. These strips are often called parkstrips. Also included are triangles of land at street intersections that provide places for statuary, water fountains, benches, and bridges (**Figure 6.16**). In general there is little space for what can be termed active recreational experiences.

Incorporated in this category are small areas called vest-pocket parks and playgrounds (**Figure 6.17**). A vest-pocket park is a small parcel within a residential or commercial block that has a park-like appearance and is under control of the local public authority. The vest-pocket playground might yet find its place as a useful unit among the components of a comprehensive park and recreational service system.

Additionally, some recreational service departments set aside extreme activity areas for use by those who have the necessary skills and personal equipment to perform. These include banked and straightaway structures designed to accommodate trick bicycle riding, in-line skating, and skateboarding (**Figures 6.18** and **6.19**).

For those who have the developed skill to participate in such activities, facilities on which they may be accommodated may be set aside in enclosed areas where those involved may engage, where novices may be instructed, and from which the general public is excluded.

Depending on the geographic location of the community, other areas and facilities may include, but are not limited to, swimming pools, golf courses, beaches, marinas, stadiums, archery and rifle ranges, horseback riding trails, band shells, and other imaginative attractions.

Figure 6.16 Pass-Through Parklet

Figure 6.17 Vest-Pocket Playground

Figure 6.18   Skateboard Facility

Figure 6.19   Skateboard Facility: The Curve

The Regional Recreational Complex

The regional recreational complex is a tract of land not less than 100 acres and ranging up to 2000 acres. It contains a highly diversified series of terrain features, has facilities of many types, and may also be planned to house the community's zoological and/or botanical exhibit. It may be situated near a museum of natural history, art museum, or other educational center. There is every likelihood that the complex may have a field house constructed upon it for a variety of sports and game activities. It might have at least one outdoor theater and band shell, a relatively large lake, boating facilities in summer, and ice-skating facilities during the appropriate winter months. It may have an outdoor stadium as well as golf courses and one or two swimming pools or other aquatic areas (**Figure 6.20**).

Figure 6.20   Tower Slides at Splashdown Water Park

If the regional complex is located close to a major waterway (i.e., river, sound, bay, ocean, gulf, or great inland lake) it will probably have marine and beach facilities. Generally, there will be well-designed spaces for almost every recreational taste. Walks for strolling, bridle paths, bicycle paths, an observatory, a bird sanctuary, scenic vistas, fountain displays, reflecting pools, and picnic and camping areas may well be part of such a regional center. This may be considered to be the chief recreational plant of the community, and, depending upon the density of population, may very well be able to care for all of the people. Except in the largest urban metropolises, one such regional center is all that is necessary.

No community can be considered fully prepared to promote the most comprehensive coverage of recreational services unless it has within a short distance from its border a non-city-owned recreational reservation. Such a facility is usually operated by the county, state, or federal government and can be within a 2-hour drive by express highway from the city limits. The reservation may be part of the county park system, a state park or forest, a national park, a forest, or a monument. Any of these facilities will have natural or man-made special features that draw attendance.

Summary

The milieu for recreational activity occurs indoors and outdoors. The natural environment offers a myriad of settings for a variety of experiences that are either active or passive, depending upon the whim or need of the participant. Observation, engagement, or appreciation of various pursuits may require terrain features that are natural or manufactured.

Thus, parks, playgrounds, fields, and courts may have to be built or forests, gorges, rivers, lakes, oceanfront, or mountains can be put to recreational use.

Indoor activities that take place in gymnasiums, centers, pools, or schools become the focal point for year-round recreational activities that engage the interest, talent, and involvement of countless persons. Accessibility is a significant factor in determining use. Artificial barriers that prevent access of persons with disabilities must be eliminated. In the same way, dangerous crossings, traffic hazards, or other perilous sites must be avoided when placing recreational buildings or other facilities. No recreational service agency can afford to place its constituency in harm's way.

There are certain recognized standards for recreational sports and games. Zoning codes and local ordinances specify safety regulations. Precautions need to be taken insofar as playground and playing fields are concerned. Preventive maintenance can do much to offset the breakdown of equipment and surfaces.

A variety of recreational areas within and outside the immediate community can provide the space in which well-planned recreational activities can be conducted, all of which contribute to a balanced, comprehensive recreational program.

Selected Further References

Dahl, B., and D. J. Molnar. *Anatomy of a Park*. 3rd ed. Long Grove, IL: Waveland Press, 2005.

Douglas, R. W. *Forest Recreation*. 5th ed. Long Grove, IL: Waveland Press, 2005.

Gelb, A. *Playgrounds*. East Rutherford, NJ: Penguin Group, Inc., 1987.

Harper, C. A. *Environment and Society: Human Perspectives on Environmental Issues*. 3rd ed. Tappan, NJ: Prentice-Hall, Inc., 2003.

Jensen, C. R., and S. P. Guthrie. *Outdoor Recreation in America*. Champaign, IL: Human Kinetics, 2006.

Miller, G. T., Jr., and S. E. Spoolman. *Living in the Environment*. 16th ed. Belmont, CA: Brooks/Cole, 2009.

Morrison, G. *Nature in the Neighborhood*. Boston, MA: Houghton Mifflin Co., 2004.

Ravetz, J., et al. *Environment and the City*. Florence, KY: Routledge, 2005.

Seabrook, W., and C. W. Miles. *Recreational Land Management*. Florence, KY: Routledge, 1993.

Smith, D. L., and J. Hoffman. *Parks Directory of the United States*. Detroit, MI: Omnigraphics, Inc., 2004.

Stiles, D., and J. Stiles. *Playhouses You Can Build: Indoor and Backyard Design*. Westport, CT: Firefly Books, Ltd., 1999.

Williams, B. *Natural World: Biggest and Best*. Chicago, IL: Kelly, Miles Publishing, Ltd., 2004.

7

Program Development

The recreational program can never be an arbitrary measure imposed on people. It has to be planned, developed, and operated in response to constituency needs. In establishing a new program, it is desirable to offer a wide range of activities not only to serve the articulated interests of potential patrons, but also to discover where real participant interest lies.

All recreational agencies have finite resources upon which to draw. This means limitations on money, material, and manpower. Therefore, it is necessary for such organizations to be as efficient in their use of resources as they can be while satisfying the recreational needs that have been voiced by suggestion or action. By developing these specific activities for which a distinct call has been made, the agency does not run the risk of spreading itself too thinly. It also places the program on a firm foundation of interested participants. Although this will probably be ideal from a budgetary standpoint, it does present negative aspects as well. By addressing only those activities that are popular or for which a desire has been strongly expressed, the program may languish in the doldrums of special interests that really do not meet the recreational requirements of most citizens of the community. In short, the program may become unimaginative and stagnant. Simply because there are activities that meet the needs of some assertive individuals does not mean the agency is operating at its full potential.

There needs to be constant evaluation and appraisal of the program and its components. The agency must continuously build and actually create demand by stimulating the interest of the public in new and varied activities. It must offer its constituents opportunities to grow recreationally. It must provide the means and leadership to allow participants to find novel, creative, and innovative ways of obtaining wholesome methods of expression during leisure.

Motivation for Participation

The drives of human behavior also motivate recreational engagement. They are the human needs, wants, desires, and emotions. Some impelling desire or compelling force activates both children and adults. They are stimulated through a complex behavioral pattern by a conscious or innate striving until the objective is attained and the urge is satisfied. Some behavioral patterns are of short duration; others are prolonged and may be of a lifetime's duration. Creative activities stimulate behavior by engaging the senses.

Readiness to Learn

The readiness to learn is an important source of behavioral stimulation. When the need to know is such that it compels activity on the part of the learner, it may be said that such learning will not be frustrated until the need is satisfied. A specific point in development is reached. Energy outputs attain higher levels. Focus of attention is sharpened. Curiosity is released, and individuals pursue their desires with a single-minded purpose until success in mastering the idea, skill, or information is achieved. When learning is self-activated, individuals are interested in what they are doing and attempt, by whatever means are at their disposal, to undertake those experiences that will provide optimum enjoyment from achievement.

Attitudes

Attitudes and interests carry emotional baggage that apparently clouds knowledge and perceptions. Attitudes are developed and modified by home influences, and peer and social pressure groups. Favorable attitudes do much to motivate behavior. Appropriate incentives may activate behavioral patterns, which can develop healthy and desirable attitudes towards specific activities. Incentives are those extrapersonal elements that spur the individual on and arouse a latent or previously nonexistent desire to perform. Incentives that appeal to the ego are most often effective. The utilization of incentives should always be under the ethical control of the recreationist so that conduct is channeled to those behaviors that are socially acceptable and constructive for the individual or the community as a whole. Incentives may be personal or impersonal; however, with very few exceptions, impersonal incentives should never be used. They are invariably meaningless. Personal incentives, on the other hand, are those inner satisfactions received from doing something well, a sense of achievement, self-expression, approval, recognition, and a feeling of enjoyment or fulfillment when the goal is attained. The most appropriate incentives are those that serve to stimulate these feelings, which in turn tend to motivate reinforcing and consistent behavior.

Knowledge of Progress

Perhaps of singular importance to the person is knowledge of the progress he or she has made, which tends to encourage and extend the behavioral pattern. Personal knowledge of achievement may serve as motivation toward further goals. This technique is well within the command of recreationists to the extent that obvious indicators, such as skill, appreciation, and understanding, form a part of the verifiable elements involved. Subjectively, individuals know when they have made progress in terms of preset estimates or expectations. Individuals can see whether they are acting correctly by virtue of personal ability to perform. The individual undergoing some aspect of growth in development as a participant is aware of particular achievements as they occur. The satisfaction derived from knowing that one is capable of performance is sometimes more rewarding to the individual than any performance can be.

Tangible evidence of mastery comes about when the methods of work become smoother and well coordinated. Doing what is necessary to obtain anticipated results affords satisfaction. The well-planned program will permit opportunities for growth and exploration by offering the individual a chance to continue. The entire concept of gradation is formulated on the proposition that people will be motivated to participate in an activity if and when they are confident of their ability to achieve. They also know that they may remain in the same activity until they feel that their skill enables them to take on the next set of opportunities that promote mastery. Surely, the recreationist must recognize the means whereby people of differing abilities, backgrounds, and levels of skill may be stimulated to perform. One of the techniques that can be used positively to encourage participation and excite or renew interest is the concomitantly programmed graded level of activities that tend to supply individuals with the support or status they seek in such participation.

Personal Interests

Psychological studies have indicated that there are general tendencies toward which people of various ages, socioeconomic, educational, vocational, cultural, and other groupings veer insofar as personal interests are concerned. For this reason, program planning may be based on certain interests people are presumed to have. However, programming is never imposed on the group to be served. There is more to programming than the imposition of a recreationist's ideas upon those seen as potential participants. Essentially, the inventory of general interests that are assumed to be a part of every individual's make-up is utilized as a point of departure for the initiation of activities. To the extent that such interests are actually present and capable of attracting participation when established within a program, the recreationists can provide clear and present opportunities to arouse these interests.

Because of the special knowledge of age-group characteristics, growth, and developmental needs of individuals, the recreationist can assume that certain interests are present and that at a particular age level individuals have attained a physical, social, or intellectual ability to participate in specific activity forms. In some instances, individuals will express, without equivocation, their desire to perform or engage in activities. By trying out the suggestions of those who expressed interest, there is a great likelihood that the recreationist will better be able to serve participants. Where individuals expressed interest but perform in a perfunctory manner, exhibit boredom, or where attendance is sporadic, the recreationist can conclude that the expressed interest may have been feigned, something less, used to gain attention, or could have implied a desire for experiences of a similar type, but not necessarily the kind that were suggested.

As in many situations, the expression of interest in a given activity may merely cover the individual's real desire for social acceptance, broadened experiences within the community, the mastery of a skill and thereby gaining ego satisfaction, or to be innovative and independent. The recreationist who understands the clues people offer in their attempts to adjust to or cope with their respective environments may be better equipped to assist those who come to him or her in finding the means of satisfying felt needs through meaningful and valuable experiences.

Stimulating Interest

The recreationist can stimulate interest and encourage participation in a variety of ways. Depending on the nature of the activity in question, the recreationist could bring samples to the group or class in attendance. He or she may introduce potential participants to a highly skilled performer whose technique and knowledge may fascinate and attract their interest. By arranging for potential participants to see exhibits, demonstrations, or through visitation the group may be exposed to activities that could arouse curiosity and/or a desire to try. Members of the group may be the very reservoir of talent that the recreationist needs to stir excitement and create demands for activity. Some individuals are bound to have abilities that give them satisfaction and pleasure as they perform. These individuals may become the active agents who, by personal enthusiasm, can create attention and tempt others to try that particular interest.

Nothing stimulates a group as much as a hobbyist. Although individuals may not be prepared to adopt or even try to engage in the hobby immediately, they often can be introduced and exposed to the potential of the activity where before there was no basis for judgment. When people see others apparently having an enjoyable time doing some activity, their curiosity may be awakened as to why the activity should elicit such a response. The recreationist must recognize curiosity as a first step in stimulating motivation for participation.

Building Confidence

Some people are hesitant about joining a group or class because they feel less capable of performing well. Nobody wants to be made uncomfortable by having to participate in activities where knowledge or skill is the single distinguishing criterion. All people feel more comfortable in situations and activities that are familiar. Recreationists must assure novices that they will not have to compete to participate. Further, each participant should understand that all the others, with the exception of the instructor, are learners, too. To build confidence and help the individual who wants to participate but hesitates because of inability or lack of skill, the recreationist will schedule practice sessions for those who consider such assistance necessary. To prevent any individual embarrassment at having to attend tutorials, the recreationist may very well introduce a plan of practice so that everyone can improve.

Depending upon the maturity, education, previous experience, and other such factors participants display, the recreationist can adjust the presentation. If the group is composed of mature individuals who had previous experience with the activity, there is little reason why advanced experiences cannot be offered. When the group is composed of immature individuals or has had little or no experience, it is better for the recreationist to simplify the processes involved, take the group step-by-step through the methods of activity, and attempt to lead or guide participants by example. Activities should be analyzed so that their components may be treated separately. A very difficult activity can be effectively broken down into comparatively simple phases, enabling the participant to perform in a satisfying manner. Initially, exposure to any activity should be such that the participant can easily perform the movements or required techniques in a creditable way. As the individual's interest is continuously aroused, more complicated movements, knowledge, tactics, or techniques may be attempted. The desire to learn how to perform correctly or accurately will draw the participant repeatedly. In this way, participants are led to progressively more skilled levels of performance, better technical proficiency, and a deeper understanding and appreciation for the activities in which they are involved.

Continued Progress

As individuals begin to gain command of the activity and taste success in terms of strength, coordination, dexterity, range, or other aspects necessary for the experience, they may undergo a desire to broaden their newly found knowledge and skill. The program should be designed for just this purpose. People must be permitted to work intensively as well as inclusively. This allows for the development of latent talents, enhances self-expression, and gives range and scope to ideas that were formerly limited. The scheduling of learning or activity sessions should promote a feeling of progress and achievement within the performer.

The individual should have some objective in view, but the attainment of the objective must not be allowed to end interest in continuing on with the activity. By enabling the participant to progress from beginner to expert over a given period, the recreationists can add immeasurably to innate satisfactions and enjoyment received from an interest that will carry over for a lifetime. There is an enormous range of activities for people of every age group, skill level, level of appreciation, and mental capacity. Recreational activities are so varied that they can be used to focus attention and stimulate effort. The energy expended in such experiences is negligible in comparison with the self-fulfillment, confidence, and happiness obtained by those who desire this participation.

Experience, Talent, and Skill

Any recreational program, regardless of where it is situated or under whose auspice, must provide for the discovery of potential and the development of latent or obvious skills. Additionally, experiences for those with previous exposure to specific training must be offered. When such a program is formulated, it may then serve the greatest number of people by providing the widest possible series of choices for participation. In order for the comprehensive program to reach a maximum number of people and afford the broadest range of opportunities, provision should be made for every skill, talent, or background that people have. Accommodation should also be made for those without any previous experience or specific skill, or whose talent is negligible.

Relating Activities to Experience

Successful planning for recreational activities concerns the selection or modification of experiences to the level of skill held by those who desire to participate. Initiating an activity for a group of inexperienced persons using methods, materials, or equipment beyond their ability to appreciate or perform only leads to frustration. In like manner, an introduction of fundamentals to experienced persons can lead to boredom and disinclination to take part. Just as people are likely to become discouraged when they undertake activities that prove too difficult for them and in which there is little probability of success, the opposite situation among the highly skilled is conducive to ennui.

Activities must be offered that elicit varying degrees of skill so that everyone who is interested may find a level at which he or she can involve themselves successfully. As individuals develop greater skill, gradation permits them to seek out and join groups engaging in the activity at a more advanced stage. By no means should the recreationist attempt to plan activities to meet the needs of a single group to the exclusion of everybody else. This can in no way lead to the comprehensive program designed to account for all those who might possibly be interested in a given activity. Such exclusionary practice will definitely hinder the impact of an accommodating program within the community at large.

Development of Skills

Skill development is required if the individual is to attain command of materials, tools, equipment, or movements and the necessary control so that personal satisfaction is possible. For this reason, some instructional process must be offered or undertaken if the individual, whether child or adult, is to grow into a skilled performer. Instruction, then, is designed to foster the knowledge and develop the particular and special skills that can find outlet in activity performance.

The Nature of Talent

Recreational activities certainly furnish a desirable outlet for individual self-expression and self-realization for those who participate. They are a valuable means for those who have learned to appreciate their potential. For the novice, practice of an activity often leads not merely to personal satisfaction, but on occasion to skills beyond the dreams of those who first undertook it by chance or choice. Although little is known about what constitutes talent, there is a tendency on the part of recreationists (instructors) to indicate their ability to recognize talent. Sometimes what appears to be talent is nothing more or less than a superficial facility. This may cause a recreationist to spend an inordinate amount of time with the individual who shows such facility to the detriment of the rest of the group. Facility comes about because of exposure, practice, or maturity. It may be cultivated, as with any other skill, but it should not be confused with talent.

Talent is a natural ability or power that confers on the individual a special or superior ability to perform. In some instances of genius, it may spring full-blown upon a ready world, needing but a few refinements to reveal it in its glory. In other cases, talent implies a natural endowment for a particular pursuit, which must be developed by hard study and prolonged practice before the performer is ready to reveal it. Unlike a gift, talent must be cultivated in order to attain the full scope and range of ability. The gifted are already capable without having to resort to practice.

Talent may be latent or overt. Where it is revealed, as in actual performance or a product produced by the individual, the recreationist should encourage its development by every ethical means possible, for in this way the individual may be brought to a realization of self-expression that can be truly phenomenal. This is no less true of hidden talent. The individual who participates because of interest or stimulation and finds, to his or her delight, that he or she possesses an unexpected facility, should be judiciously guided along the paths of practice until, by repetition and constant exposure, a highly skilled performer develops. Between these two positions, the individual with latent talent may never perfect it unless there is some opportunity to have it exposed. The recreationist should enter the situation with the assumption that everybody has some talent, regardless of degree, and that it should be enhanced for the pleasure and self-realization it may bring to the possessor. Of course, the recreationist may be inaccurate in his or her assessment. Perhaps the individual has talent, but not in the specific activity in which he or she is participating. Something may still be taught to the individual without talent, if only an appreciation for the skill, process, product, or performance involved. However, when the recreationist can discover talent for any activity, he or she should do whatever can be done to stimulate and promote practice until the individual has the skill and confidence to continue without assistance.

For whatever reasons they have for engaging in the activity in question, there must be an organized structure through which experience, skill, or talent may receive optimum appreciation. Levels of performance attainment, simple intent or interest, a desire to learn something new—all require an environment that protects the inept while it promotes the advanced. Such structure may well be a graded series of activities based on the leadership available, financial support provided, community interest shown, and facility accessibility to accommodate the activities.

Each type of recreational facility has its unique problems in program organization and promotion. Some recreational places are established primarily for a single specialized recreational experience; golf courses, swimming pools, beaches, and cross-country ski trails are of this type. The program at such facilities, from the standpoint of the operating agency, tends to become a matter of mere routine. The patrons of these places desire only the freedom to pursue their interests and enthusiasms with a minimum of interference. Program administration, therefore, consists chiefly of arranging the physical environment for its efficient use, issuing permits for use (if necessary), establishing regulations for governing use of the facility by patrons, and promoting activities to ensure maximum participation. Programming administration on these recreational places may be in the organization of instructional activities, certain competitive events, staged shows, carnivals, or the like.

Program Planning and Development

Program planning necessitates the consideration of a number of factors that influence the selection and participation opportunities for potential participants. For example, some scheduled activities may require no special organization of participants in advance and may be engaged in at the whim of the player. These undirected activities or free play tend to become routine for certain regular attendees. Other activities, particularly group and team games, class meetings for instructional purposes, or group participation, must be planned a short time in advance and scheduled for a given time and place. Usually they occur again and again, but according to a schedule. Still other activities happen only once and require intensive preparation for days, weeks, or even months in advance and terminate in a performance, demonstration, or exhibition. They are the spectacular events that are eagerly antic-ipated and that sustain or create interest in the overall program.

Relative Value of Activities

The routine activities are of greatest value from the standpoint of development of the powers and skills of the individual because they are repeated day after day and their effects are cumulative. Their developmental value increases in proportion to the frequency of their repetition. The special events are valuable chiefly because of the preparation and instruction needed to make them possible, but also because they sustain or generate interest in a program that might otherwise tend to become commonplace and monotonous.

In planning the recreational program, care should be taken to observe a balance among routine, scheduled, and special projects. If only routine activities take place, the recreational program is dull, uninteresting, and lacking in novelty. If the program is dominated by scheduled events to the exclusion of free choice on the patrons' part, it will incline toward regimentation. Preparation for and the staging of frequent special events under high pressure often removes much of the joy and spontaneity that should always be manifest in recreational activity. Careful investigation of and attention to the physical environment and the interests and needs of potential users in a coordinated program can develop all kinds of activities to the benefit of those concerned.

Patrons' Involvement

Some people prefer only to "drop in" at recreational centers or other facilities and participate informally as interest moves them. These individuals may not want to take part in any scheduled contests or meetings. Others come only to attend special events, as either performers or spectators. Still others come only by appointment to meet in a regular session or class, or to play in a scheduled game. Some parents will permit their children to attend the recreational facility only when a scheduled event is to occur. At every center, playground, or other facility there is a regular clientele almost always present and ready to do anything that is suggested. The program should be planned so as to provide some attraction for all these potential patrons. These same preference factors also exist for private or commercial recreational programs.

Patron Assistance in Program Planning

Although not necessarily precluded because of its commercial orientation, the private recreational agency usually has a set menu of activities that patrons may either accept or reject. Only certain private organizations may involve participants in program planning. The participant-planning technique is a process whereby interested individuals help to plan activities. After all, the program does not develop in a vacuum, nor does it spring full-blown from the head of some recreationist-Zeus. Rather, it is the product of selected ideas, directed interests, and self-stimulating experiences. Participant planning is especially vital to the continuing success of the public recreational program. The ideas that may be generated from such groups are essential for the development of future activities.

The ideas of patrons are important to the health of the program and are probably significant to program outcomes. When potential participants have a hand in the development of activities within the program, they will feel, and rightly so, that these activities belong to them. Under these circumstances there is every reason to believe that individuals who took the trouble to express their ideas and interests in activity selection and/or planning will also develop a close feeling for and responsibility toward the success of the program. In consequence, they gain much greater value from their efforts, they find the activities more stimulating, and they bring to the situation new ideas and views to what might become mere professional routine. Recreationists should utilize participant planning assistance in attempting to satisfy the recreational needs of the public it serves.

Other types of recreational places—for example, playgrounds or public recreational centers—are established for participation in varied activities by patrons of all ages. Many of the activities desired are those that call for organized group participation. The playground and the recreational center are also distinguished from other specialized recreational places in that they have specific educational objectives, the achievement of which calls for program planning of a particular sort. Therefore, the problem of program administration presented by playgrounds and recreational centers is unique. In this section we are concerned chiefly with the types of centers that have more or less complete indoor and outdoor facilities for a varied program, which includes child and adult participation. The principles set forth, however, apply also to centers that are not so complete in their appointments.

Scheduled Activities

The activities schedule enumerates the activities that will be provided by any given recreational center or playground. Among the kinds of possible activities are those that are termed informal routine, recurrent, and special events. All the activities conducted or sponsored by the recreational service agency staff are scheduled so that prospective participants may know when those of particular interest to them are to be available. Even free play activities are listed so that children's parents are made aware that their services may be enlisted for supervisory purposes.

Informal Routine Activities

It should be the objective of every recreationist to encourage and initiate as many informal routine activities as possible. Ideally, the center should be so attractive and well equipped that it appeals to boys and girls and men and women at all hours of the day. For children, the customary equipment includes safe swings and slides, sandboxes, play houses, horizontal bars, flying and traveling rings, climbing apparatus, and sculpture equipment; areas and supplies for individual, dual, and team athletics; a natural area for camping, hiking, and picnicking; and a recreational building with materials and tools for indoor activities such as handicrafts, hobbies, table games, and various social experiences.

It must be remembered that routine activities are not all spontaneous; the recreationists in charge must plan many of them. But the planning cannot be obvious. The most common criticism of recreational programs is that they are repetitious and monotonous. Interesting ways to use the equipment must be constantly invented and taught, although most children's imaginations usually seethe with ingenious ways to use facilities and perform activities. Sometimes these uses are dangerous, but in many instances they are relatively safe and fun. New non-equipment games and events need to be introduced; old games and events should be revived. The director must constantly think of new stunts, new emphases, and new variations to suggest and introduce so the center comes to be thought of as a place where something exciting and different is going on all the time. The recreational center is a place at which to spend free time. Once there, however, patrons should be able to find many incentives and invitations to do interesting things and experience new thrills in learning new skills.

Recurrent Activities

Recurrent activities, as the topic suggests, are those experiences usually engaged in upon appointment and are typically group activities such as clubs, classes, and competitions in which so many members take part that a given time and place must be arranged for them. These activities are repeated on a daily, weekly, or monthly cycle until the schedule is completed, the season is concluded, or the program is finished.

Many of the scheduled events are self-managed. When the courts, fields, gymnasiums, and meeting rooms are not required for staff-directed activities, they are usually made available to self-managing groups. It should be the aim of public recreational facility directors to organize as many groups of this kind as possible without entirely relinquishing such staff control as may be necessary. The development of an extensive program of adult recreational activities in the public domain requires this technique to be used; otherwise, the number of groups will be limited by the size of the employed staff. Also, the educational value of the activity is greatly enhanced when the group manages itself and participates in the selection of its own leadership. In the private domain, comprehensively based facilities may utilize the same techniques, although management almost always operates on a first come, first served basis with competitive events such as leagues, flights, or other tournament formats being supervised in terms of rules or regulations governing participation.

Special Events

The special events at every recreational facility are the occasions that provide "spice" to the program. They attract new patrons, discover new talent, offer an incentive to practice, provide an ever-changing flavor or emphasis to the experiences, and create opportunity to secure some educational outcomes not otherwise possible. Their variety is literally infinite, limited only by the imagination of the recreationist in charge and the participants who may assist in the development and planning of the events. In general, they fall into nine divisions:

1. Demonstrations of skills learned, such as gymnastics, aquatics, group dancing, or instrumental music performance

2. Exhibits of objects made or collected, such as stamps; coins; books; historical objects; horticultural, zoological, scientific, or nature specimens; models; and hobby shows
3. Performances before an audience, such as holiday ceremonies, concerts, staged drama, and talent shows
4. Special contests, such as track and field meets, the final league game, dance, and forensic speech contests
5. Mass group participation in any activity practiced primarily in small groups, such as a seasonal play day or a folk dance festival
6. Social occasions, such as recognition ceremonies to reward civic service, parties, or a masquerade ball
7. Excursions to places of interest, which require detailed planning and usually indicate the need for logistical support
8. Spectacular displays, such as pyrotechnic shows, pageants, parades, carnivals, fairs, circuses, historical enactment (Pilgrims Progress, Civil War, or Revolutionary War battles), or *tableaux vivant*
9. Special instruction, such as visiting lecturers, sport "clinics," mass lessons in dance or music, open forums, debates, and public hearings

It is a very common error in planning and staging special events by recreational service agencies to emulate too closely the standards of professional entertainment and to expect comparable performances. The amateur theater, for example, cannot compete with professional theater or with other forms of commercial entertainment, despite the fact that some amateurs may be outstanding talents. Moreover, the objectives of professional entertainment are wholly different from those of the recreational program. The former caters to audience approval only, whereas the latter endeavors to provide satisfying experiences for the performers. In recreational events, the entertainment of the audience, although desirable, is secondary to the enjoyment of the participants who perform.

Special events should provide opportunities for as many as possible to participate. They should be truly representative of activities learned and/or undertaken in the recreational program and be the incentive for days, if not weeks, of anticipation and preparation. Such preparation, however, should not be arduous, but in the spirit of good recreational endeavor.

Scheduling

Every recreational facility should have a daily, weekly, monthly, seasonal, and yearly program. The facility director will find it helpful to chart the activities for the entire year, marking those events during the year, such as the opening and closing of the school term, holidays, historical commemorations, seasonal emphases, and thematic projects, that will influence the program. The activities for each month or season may be worked out in more detail as the year progresses.

The weekly schedule should be well publicized, posted in conspicuous places, and generally disseminated so that all may be aware of it and, perhaps, become interested in participating. Additionally, potential patrons might also suggest the provision of other stimulating experiences. The daily program is a recreationist's plan of work for the day. The director will plan each day's work in advance, always including something new or interesting and never depending wholly upon the inspiration of the moment. The professional practitioner may also use the good offices of a lay planning committee for whatever assistance they can give in formulating the program.

Playgrounds, for example, used to over-schedule activities. Each half-hour was devoted to some specific practice or class-type of activity and frequently to instruction. Such regimentation had its advantage and devotees in that it ensured emphasis upon varied activities and kept the playground patrons informed as to when each activity was to take place; however, it made insufficient allowance for novelty and for freedom of choice on the part of the participants. The playground took on a schoolroom atmosphere. Scheduling became the objective, rather than the means to a recreational end. Scheduled events should be the framework within which the program develops, but they should not preclude unscheduled activities nor the flexibility and spontaneity that often enhance recreational experience.

Agencies that operate more than one facility of the same type may want to prescribe a duplicated program for all the centers and playgrounds in the system. However, this is inadvisable. The program of each facility should be designed for and adapted to the needs, interests, traditions, and organizations of the neighborhood being served; the programs of other agencies in the community; the completeness of the facility itself; the available professional leadership required; and the skills, talents, and prior experiences of the people residing in the neighborhood. These factors vary greatly between neighborhoods and facilities. This should not signify that a coordinated series of events and some special activities cannot be observed throughout the system. These features are set forth in a master program for the entire year, announced in advance. The director of each facility should be given the freedom to establish the program for his or her center with no more control from the central administration of the department than seems necessary to ensure a well-balanced and varied program.

The program is merely a plan. Numerous unforeseen situations may arise that dictate the necessity for a change in the planned activities. Adhering blindly to prescribed or preconceived programs devitalizes the recreational facility and its activities. To arouse the new interests of people, to capture their transitory and changeable focus of attention, and to involve them in newly programmed events is a real test of the recreationist's discernment, leadership, and skill.

No recreationist can have at his or her fingertips at all times of the day all of the information necessary to conduct a successful program. The individual director will find it helpful to develop, for the facility and personal use, a library containing materials on all phases of activities that are organized and conducted. The director who refers again and again to such material generally has the most diversified program.

The physical equipment and the planned activities are not the only attractions at the recreational center. The opportunity to meet others under congenial circumstances is one of the most compelling incentives to attendance. The program should be arranged to provide happy social occasions. Similarly, the possibility of negative experiences should be minimized or, where possible, obliterated. For example, if the use of the equipment that is provided is attended by bickering, if timid persons are imposed upon by aggressive ones, or if orderly persons are intimidated by hostile ones, many prospective patrons will stay away. Definite supervision to prevent such obnoxious behavior is important for a successful program.

Gradation and Progress

Almost all recreational activities may be classified and graded by various methods. Every category, except hobbies, service, and special projects, will offer opportunities for instruction to be given and skills learned. A program that is free from the unpleasantness of stagnation and its attendant boredom must be progressive in scope. Progress is best maintained when individuals are enabled to develop proficiency in the activities that interest them. Gradation makes for easier program administration as well as comfort for the participants. To ensure a high degree of motivation and freedom from repetitive activities, which can become enervating, the process of gradation should take place in every recreational program.

Recreational activities, by their very nature, should be exciting to the individual, whether novice or expert. Yet, some recreational activities fail to elicit continued attention and interest after a specific level of skill or experience has been reached. The chief cause of loss of interest is a lack of progress beyond a particular level of achievement. Motivation is best sustained within the participant when each can develop a proficiency that is greater than that possessed when the activity was initially entered into. If the individual had no skill or knowledge to begin with, anything that is gained tends to stimulate continued interest and participation. If the person plateaus and shows no appreciable progress, he or she becomes discouraged and falters. It is usually on the basis of perceived progress that people make the effort to continue.

Gradation of recreational skills can be pertinent for almost any stage of the individual's development. It should not matter whether the participant has ever had any previous experience. Gradation offers opportunities to indicate something of value toward the patron's progress to the goal of enjoyment or satisfaction through skill achievement. Gradation also permits differentiation by age group, interest, motivation, and ability. Whatever the age or maturity level, skill, or interest, recreational activities suitable to meet both personal and group needs exist. As the participant becomes more adept at dealing with the various facets of activity, more possibilities and broader potentials are suggested. Although age, by itself, is not the single most important criterion for determining the likelihood of client intent, it does play a significant part in the overall development of the program.

Graded instructional activities can do much to sustain participant enthusiasm and to maintain the motivation necessary to accomplish the objectives the person anticipates. The use of the graded method encourages potential participants to explore new avenues of endeavor and attempts to satisfy the need for mental, physical, social, and developmental growth in surmounting previous experiential difficulties. Gradation should be a required process in the program for the very reason that the program exists—to assist the acquisition of skills, maintain interest, develop appreciation, and provide the support necessary for utilizing the individual's personal resources.

Gradation requires a tripling of program activities. This means that each skill taught at the recreational facility may be offered at the beginning level, intermediate level, or advanced level. Beyond this requirement is the division of classes into age groups. In crafts, for example, there are projects designed to familiarize the individual with tools, material, equipment, and finished product. At each age, there will be crafts appropriate to the needs of the group. With maturity and responsibility, more complicated and intricate crafts may be introduced. At the youngest age level, simplified and easily understood and completed projects are included. But even at the youngest ages there will be those who show such precocity or unusual advancements that to hold them back would be tantamount to retarding their ability to achieve. Such individuals should not be held back and deprived of more advanced techniques, for they will tend to drop out of the program if their interest cannot be maintained. Graded instructional courses prevent, in most instances, the withdrawal of participants because of boredom, possession of a high degree of skill, or association with individuals who are not capable of handling tools and materials. It is possible for this instructional sequence to maintain contact with programmed participants from earliest childhood through old age. The graded aspect of programming facilitates modification of activities to meet mental, physical, or maturational limitations. Gradation is necessary in the program because it allows people to acquire skills and interests that will have carry-over value for them.

The graded program can be broken down into five 10-week courses, thereby covering the year. Each 10-week session enrolls a number of participants in an activity session of anywhere from 30 to 60 minutes duration one or more times each week, always depending upon the interest of the participants and the availability of the instructor. Those who assimilate knowledge or skills more quickly than others may be transferred into the next level of instruction, if there is room. If not, such persons may have to be provided with more intense or individualized instruction to prevent their dropping out. In any event, the graded sessions, of three levels, may appropriately enroll all those who want to learn. It may be that the beginning level might have more than one session. Some of these participants will eventually find their way into the next level of skill. Some may have to repeat the activity in order to develop the necessary skill, and some may vault into a more advanced level because of innate talent or assimilative ability. However the sessions are scheduled, they should accommodate all those who desire to be active. The 10-week breakdown simply makes the administration of the program more manageable. A sample program is provided in **Figure 7.1** to illustrate time, level, session, and composition.

Program Implementation

Every function concerned with the implementation of activities designed for learning and enjoyment for those who participate is part of program development. The process involves combining and coordinating various elements so that opportunities are available in which people may find satisfaction.

Skilled People

The primary question to consider is the skill, level of achievement, or experience of potential participants. In every community a portion of the population will be highly skilled in one or more recreational activities. These individuals may want to deepen their knowledge, increase their skill, or

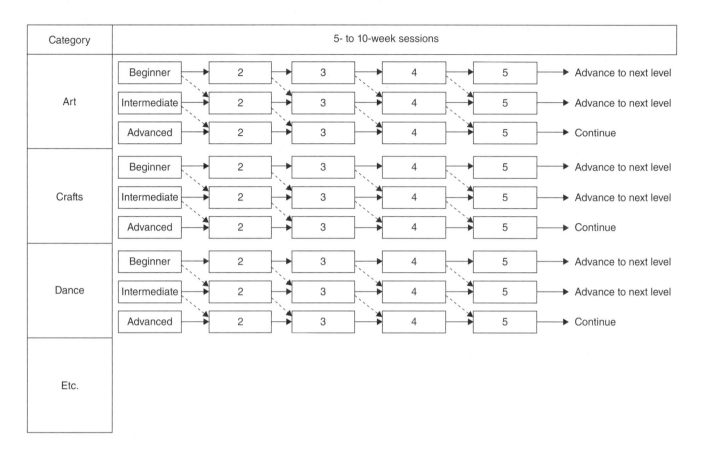

Category	5- to 10-week sessions					
Art	Beginner	2	3	4	5	Advance to next level
	Intermediate	2	3	4	5	Advance to next level
	Advanced	2	3	4	5	Continue
Crafts	Beginner	2	3	4	5	Advance to next level
	Intermediate	2	3	4	5	Advance to next level
	Advanced	2	3	4	5	Continue
Dance	Beginner	2	3	4	5	Advance to next level
	Intermediate	2	3	4	5	Advance to next level
	Advanced	2	3	4	5	Continue
Etc.						

Figure 7.1 The 50 Week Program: Gradation Sequence Per Year

merely practice and derive greater satisfaction from continued participation. Such individuals may not need anything but space in which to carry out the activity. Others may require some instruction or have recourse to the recreationist as a resource person. Finally, there are those who want to participate in the program simply to experience the enjoyment that previous exposure over the years has given them.

Unskilled People

Another portion of the population that may want to participate may have had no real prior experience with organized recreational activity, either because of lack of opportunity or because earlier exposure was unsatisfying. This is the hard-to-reach group. The recreationist-programmer must use ingenuity to stimulate and encourage novices to give the activities a try. Perhaps a smorgasbord of programmed activities that permits judicious sampling of the offerings may induce further participation. Contact with this group must be made if the agency is to serve the constituency. Repeated invitations through all of the public relations devices, including personal visits by volunteers and by professional employees of the agency, may help to arouse interest. Every attempt should be made to bring these reluctant individuals into the community mainstream. Routine outreach activities on the part of the department could be a vital factor in gaining attention and promoting at least a tentative attendance at some recreational function.

Most People

The majority of the population has skills and interests that run the gamut from very little to expert and highly developed. These are people who perhaps have not been involved with any recreational activity, except for passive entertainment. This group will have a few persons whose passion for new ideas, skills, and things to do or places to go has never been quenched. There also are many whose concept of recreational activity is sitting and rocking. Nothing is wrong with this form of activity, but there should be something beyond the front porch or living room that can attract individuals to take part in experiences that are exhilarating and fun. This latter group will include some individuals with long dormant skills who will require some selling in order to overcome inertia. The agency must actively campaign to obtain the recognition of this major potential clientele, activate the inert, and encourage the hesitant. These people must be approached confidently, offered attractive possibilities, actively persuaded, and introduced to their own capacities and potentials for the kinds of experiences that will involve them.

For the most part, people tend to be apathetic about doing anything that requires them to come out of their residences. Of course, this does not apply to most children. Happily, children seem to take any opportunity for recreational activity that is made available. Adults, on the other hand, have to be taught that there are countless recreational experiences that cannot be performed unless there are specialized places and other people around. The most productive of these recreational places will be at the community recreational center, or the facility that has been especially designed to accommodate recreational activities of particular or diverse types.

Depending on whether they want to use private facilities such as commercial operators provide or public places, people must, of necessity, come to these recreational centers if they really want to participate. To get them to forego the simple pleasure of television watching may require efforts that go beyond what the typical dedicated recreationist may have to expend. However, if the information is worded cleverly enough, arouses curiosity to the point of desire, and provides sufficient excitement, it can bring the pleasure seeker to the activity and expose that person to whatever mind-grabbing experience may be current.

Summary

Recreational program development must be founded upon the expressed interests of potential participants and the unarticulated, latent possibilities that can be incited by created demand. Routine activities can quickly become stagnant as programmers respond only to a vociferous minority. Recreationists need to be alert to the silent majority who will participate if an attractive stimulus is provided.

Recreationists have to be knowledgeable about behavioral motivation and use that information to develop experiences that will satisfy each individual's need to learn about new recreational forms, attitudes toward social engagement, self-confidence, and personal enjoyment.

Age-group characteristics may serve as a point of departure for recreational participation. Readiness to perform, arousal of interest, and attention-seeking may be the bases on which elements of a program can be built.

Among the techniques applied to gain potential participant awareness and interest are the use of patron planning, progress in skill development by gradation, the reliance on previous positive recreational experiences, and the stimulation derived by arousing curiosity and excitement about the program content.

A balanced and comprehensive recreational program should include regular or routine activities, discretionary or free-play activities, scheduled events, and special projects. All of these forms combined will contribute to overall patron enjoyment and satisfaction. This is a desired outcome if the community's people are to be well served.

Selected Further References

Edginton, C. R., et al. *Leisure Programming: A Service-Centered and Benefits Approach*. Blacklick, Ohio: McGraw-Hill Higher Education, 2003.

Jurkowski, E. T. *Policy and Program Planning for Older Adults: Realities and Visions*. New York: Springer Publishing, 2007.

Kujoth, J. S. *Recreational Program Guide: Organizing Activities for School, Camps, Park, Playground, or Children's Clubs*. Metuchen, New Jersey: Scarecrow Press, Inc., 1972.

McLean, D., et al. *Recreation and Leisure in Modern Society*, 7th ed. Sudbury, MA: Jones and Bartlett Publishers, 2004.

Mull, R. F., et al. *Recreational Sport Management*. Champaign, IL: Human Kinetics, 2005.

PART
II
The Recreational Program Categories

Art as Experience

Art is any personalized expression of a graphic or plastic nature representative of or symbolizing some concept. It is part of the process of communication. Fundamentally, it is a method of self-expression through visual factors arranged to satisfy the needs of the person who forms and creates them. It may be that only the artist can explain his or her work, but the explanation is neither important nor required. More importantly, art in any of its many forms provides a means of conveying ideas, moods, or personal feelings in a visual presentation. The art category may be divided into several easily distinguishable parts that readily lend themselves to incorporation in a recreational program. Among these parts are oil painting, watercolors, wash drawing, pen and ink drawing, collage, finger painting, charcoal sketching, pastel drawing, photography, dry point etching, silk screen printing, crayon drawing, stone sculpture, metal sculpture, clay sculpture, glass etching, ivory carving, wood carving, precious metal smithing, lapidary work, tapestry making, mosaic tile making, glass blowing, and mobiles.

All age groups may participate in art activities. Whether the child draws in crayon or the skilled artist creates in oil, each person is enabled to find expression (**Figure 8.1**). Art may be programmed on an instructional basis (i.e., graded classes can be organized to develop skill, technique, and ability to perform). There will always be those who are beginners. Primarily the youngest age groups will generally fall into this class; however, many older children, youth, and adults are also beginners. They need the stimulation and confidence building to be found among groups of people who come together to learn a new skill. As with all skills, other people have had some prior experience and they can be classified as intermediates. They are not highly skilled, but have basic knowledge of materials, media, and some technique. The third class is made up of highly skilled individuals who wish to continue in an instructional session, perhaps studying under a well-known artist. All of these skill levels must be considered in developing the category of art.

The noninstructional phase of art is for those persons who have the skill, talent, or knowledge to create, but lack a place in which to participate. The agency, through its schedule, can offer an art room in which people may perform without instruction, although commercial providers may attach fees for this service. One other facet of art comes in terms of appreciation. There are those individuals who cannot or will not want to draw, paint, or sculpt; however, they may have the desire to learn about art. Art appreciation classes organized to develop aesthetic interests in and an understanding of art may assuredly be incorporated into the art activity.

Art classes are scheduled according to the ability and capacity of the individuals so engaged. For younger children, short instructional sessions are programmed. For adults, longer sessions. Experience and exploration of community interests, needs, and requests will best assist in the establishment of the number of art classes, lessons required, equipment, spaces, and instructional leadership necessary.

Figure 8.1 The Young Artist in a Creative Mode

The following pages describe in detail a number of techniques important to a recreational program containing art as an activity. The presentation should prove beneficial to those individuals who are unskilled in the basic art processes of coloring, painting, sketching, and etching. Recreational instructors generally understand people in terms of growth and development. They understand the characteristics and behavior, but too often have a limited understanding of how children and others learn to work with paints, crayons, and other artistic media.

Any art activity should provide interested individuals with an opportunity to make a preliminary sketch, to make a deliberate and sensitive color choice, to develop contrasting patterns in detail, and most importantly to evaluate each stage of a technique. Too many programs are more concerned with the end product than with enriching the individual's knowledge and understanding of the properties and characteristics of materials. Limits should not be placed on the length of time participants have to create with crayons, paints, sketching materials, or other arts media. They should be provided with the time to experiment and think about the various techniques. These techniques should also expand and enrich the individual's concept of color and relationships.

Watercolor Painting

Watercolor painting is a very old art. Centuries ago the Chinese drew with a brush using light tints of color to brighten their designs and give them a sense of space and distance. Later, Michelangelo, like so many Italian fresco painters, used these thin pastel shades of color, called washes, to create preliminary drawings on paper of his great wall paintings, like those found in the Sistine Chapel in Rome. However, watercolors were not actually used to make finished paintings until the 18th century in England.

Fun with Watercolors

There are many techniques used in watercolors that, when used creatively, can assist the individual in painting an interesting and exciting picture. Experimenting with paintbrushes, paints, and paper can be fun. Playing with watercolor paints usually results in the discovery of new techniques that can be utilized in the painting process. The following suggests some of the techniques and materials needed for children, young adults, and adults to find satisfaction in watercolor painting. Try experimenting with these techniques. Can you think of other techniques and materials that can be used in painting with watercolors?

Materials

Very few materials are needed to begin a watercolor painting. A paintbrush, sponge, watercolor paints, paper, and plenty of water are the only materials that are required.

Watercolor paints are made from a pigment held together by a binder. The pigments for watercolor paints are obtained from rocks, soil, and plants ground into a very fine powder. The pigments are held together with a jellylike binder material called gum arabic. Watercolors can be mixed and thinned with water. Transparent watercolors are mixed with water and usually applied in washes or tints of color. The white paper shows through for highlights. There is also an opaque or nontransparent method for painting with watercolors called gouache. This method requires mixing transparent watercolors with white.

Look at a watercolor painting. Can you see its transparency and freshness of color? Once an object is painted in watercolors, it is usually allowed to remain that color. If the object is repainted or overworked, the watercolors usually lose their freshness and transparent qualities and become washed out, looking like old faded clothes.

Brushes

The first brush used for painting was probably a stick, mashed at one end into a clump of shredded fibers. Today's brushes are manufactured from animal hairs that have been carefully shaped so they come to a delicate point or broad flat edge. Different kinds of animal hairs are used to make brushes; some are very stiff, like pig bristles, and some are very soft, like sable and mink. The soft, easily managed sable brushes are usually used for watercolors. However, a stiffer bristle brush can be used to make some very intriguing stroke patterns.

Brushes are also manufactured in a variety of sizes and shapes. Pointed, flat, round, and dome-shaped brushes are used to obtain different effects when painting with watercolors. The dome-shaped brush is known as the wash brush. Because of its bushy shape, it holds a great deal of liquid and can be used to make long, sweeping strokes without having to be refilled with paint. The pointed and round-tipped brushes are used to make lines, while the flat-sided brushes are excellent for short, broad strokes. Brushes also come in sizes from very large with long, fat handles to very thin—at times having no more than three hairs at the tip. Brushes are numbered from size 1 to size 12. The big fat brushes, sizes 6 through 12, are the most fun to paint with. The tiny brushes are good for detail, but tend to make a painting look more like a drawing. These brushes sometimes limit the individual from really working with the wonderfully splashy liquid of watercolor. When painting, it is important to experiment with the different sizes and shapes of brushes and not stick to an old favorite. The finished painting will have a much freer, more enthusiastic look if different brushes are used.

"Puppy-Dog Tails"

Many other materials and things make superior lines and strokes that can give a painting a texture that no one else has created. By using one's imagination the individual can produce work that is unique. The would-be artist can use a stick mashed at one end. Matchsticks, cotton-tipped swabs, frayed rope, unwound string, and slivers of wood can be dabbled, dragged, and scribbled all over the surface to make spontaneous designs. Strips of cardboard, steel wool, and crumpled paper can also be used to paint a design with watercolors. It is important to remember that lines, shapes, and colors are the significant ingredients of the finished painting. It is interesting to see what happens when these techniques are combined on the surface of a piece of paper. The participant should ask as the painting takes shape: Is the line smooth and solid? Is it dry and broken? What happens if a small amount of paint is used? What happens if too much paint is used?

Paper for Watercoloring

Take a piece of white drawing paper and a piece of writing paper. Run both pieces of paper between your index finger and thumb. Notice the difference in the texture of the papers. The surface of the writing paper is smoother and almost shiny, whereas the drawing paper is rougher and harder to pull between the finger and thumb. Most recreational programs will probably use only drawing paper for painting activities because watercolor paper is so expensive. Individuals should be encouraged to experiment with different types of paper. Paints will react differently as they are applied to paper with a smooth or textured surface. Some watercolor papers are very bumpy, whereas others are as smooth as writing paper. The weight (thickness) of the paper also varies from very thin paper to the thickness of cardboard inserted into most new men's shirts.

The difference in texture and thickness is related to the watercolor technique used. Paint on some small pieces of paper using different amounts of water and pigment. Note how the paper curls and wrinkles. This curling and wrinkling occurs because water and pigments soak into the paper; they are not merely deposited on the surface. When the paint dries, the surface usually goes back to its original shape. A slight bumpiness may remain where the pigments are locked into and around fibers of the paper. If using a large quantity of water, a heavyweight paper should be used to prevent or minimize the wrinkling. For small amounts of water, a thinner paper can be used. The weight of the paper alone will not prevent wrinkling. Securing the paper to the working surface correctly can cut down on curling and wrinkling. One of the following three methods can be used for this purpose:

1. Brush a 1-inch strip of library paste around the outside edge of the paper. Turn the paper over and attach it to the working surface. After the painting dries, use a single-edged razor to cut around the border on the inside edge to free the painting. The glued piece of paper can be soaked off.
2. Sponge the working surface all over; then soak the paper thoroughly and while it is still dripping wet, lay it on the working surface. With a damp sponge, squeeze out the extra water from underneath the paper by firmly wiping the top surface of the paper. The sponge should be pushed from the center of the paper toward the edges. If the paper remains wet, it will not buckle.
3. Lay a piece of dry paper on the working surface. Tape around the four edges of the paper using 1-inch masking tape. The surface can be dampened by running a wet sponge across the top.

Preparing to Paint

Fill two large jars with water. One is to be used to mix the watercolors to make a wash. This water must be kept very clean in order to prevent dirty colors from getting onto the painting. The second jar of water is for rinsing the brushes. It is important to keep the brushes very clean and change the water often. A palette or dish should be used to mix the paints if the watercolors are not in a paint box. Some watercolors come in tubes. The little cakes of color in the paint box are the same as the paint in a tube except that they have been dried. When painting with colors from a paint box, the cover can be used to mix the watercolors.

Mixing Colors

It is important to understand a few basic color principles before working with watercolor paints. There are two ways of mixing colors with watercolor paint. One is to mix colors directly on the palette. A chart that describes the colors that can be mixed to make another color can be consulted, but the best way to find out what happens when colors are mixed is to experiment. By mixing different colors, one can see how many different colors can be created. An interesting record can be made by putting down on a piece of paper a little dab of each new color. Next to the new color, put the two or three colors used to mix it. This record can be used later as a guide for selecting colors. Remember, when mixing colors the amount of water used will determine the darkness of the color. The color will be dark when very little water is used, and it will be light when much water is used. The differences made to color by adding another color are called "tonal differences." The different tints of color are called "tones."

The second method of making new colors with transparent watercolors is by using washes. Washes are tints of color that are applied in a simple stroke. Once the wash has dried, a second colored wash can be brushed partially over the first. Because the watercolors are transparent, it is possible to see part of the first wash. To the eye, these colors seem to mix to form a third color. Participants should try this technique on a practice sheet.

If the second wash is applied before the first wash dries thoroughly, the method is called wet painting. When paint is put directly on top of a wet wash, one color blends into the other, creating a blurry line. This technique can be used to create a feeling of distance in a landscape painting, because distant objects do not have a definite line. The amount of blurring can be controlled by varying the amount of time that the first wash is allowed to dry before applying the second color.

If the first wash is allowed to dry completely before the second color is applied, the method is known as wet-on-dry painting. This technique is fine for building up shades of color with distinct lines.

In seascapes, colors can be blunted by using the following technique. Paint the surface using long sweeping strokes and very little water. Before the paint dries, rinse the brush in clear water, and without any paint on the brush at all, make a stroke right along the edge between the sky and water. The colors should blend together.

Finger Painting

Finger painting allows the individual to create beautiful and colorful paintings without knowing how to sketch or paint. It is a wonderful activity for children and adults and can be done anywhere. Finger painting is a good activity for releasing tension. Young children enjoy it because it provides them with an opportunity for large arm and finger movements.

It utilizes free, rhythmic motions of the closed fists, open hands, sides of the hands, lower arms, and knuckles. This technique lends itself to flowing designs rather than pictures. Pictures are usually rigid and do not bring out the characteristics of this medium. Good-quality finger paint can be purchased, but finger paints can also be made from a few common household ingredients.

Procedures for Making Finger Paints

- Mix dry starch with cold water until it is a smooth, thin paste. Place this mixture into the bottom of a large container and mix it with boiling water. Stir the mixture so that no lumps form. Do not mix the boiling water slowly because this will permit lumps to form. A small handful of soap powder or some liquid detergent will make it easier to wash the finger paints off anything. Powdered tempera paints can be added to the starch mixture to obtain the desired colors.
- Mix 4 tablespoons of cornstarch into ½ cup of cold water until smooth. Add this mixture to 3 cups of hot water. Place the mixture in a double boiler and stir over a low heat until the mixture thickens. Add food coloring or tempera to the mixture to obtain the desired colors.

The starch mixture can be useful for long periods of time before it gets tacky. If the mixture gets too tacky, a little water can be added to the surface and the paint should spread freely again.

Painting

Before starting to finger paint, cover the working surface with newspaper. Take a piece of shelf or butcher paper and wet it thoroughly in a pan of water. Drain the excess water by shaking or drawing the paper against the side of a pan or sink. The piece of wet paper is then placed onto the working surface with the coated side up. Press the surface of the paper with the side of the hand to remove all the air bubbles from under the paper. Once the surface is flat, put a teaspoon of paint in the center of the sheet and spread evenly with the palm of the hand over the entire surface. The surface is ready to paint (**Figure 8.2**).

The participant should work with different parts of the hands and fingers to learn the effects that can be obtained. Light forms and shadings can be created by using the elbows, knuckles, fingernails, wrist bone, palm, and heel of the palm. The effects can be changed by increasing or decreasing the amount of pressure used to form a shape. Add different colors to the design.

Figure 8.2 Finger Painting

Materials: shelf paper, scissors, spoon, sponge, finger paint.

1. Cut the shelf paper to the desired size.
2. Wet the paper with a sponge.
3. Smooth the surface of the paper with your hand.
4. With a spoon, drop some paint on the surface.
5. With your hand, spread the paint over the surface.
6. Using different parts of your hand, form a design.

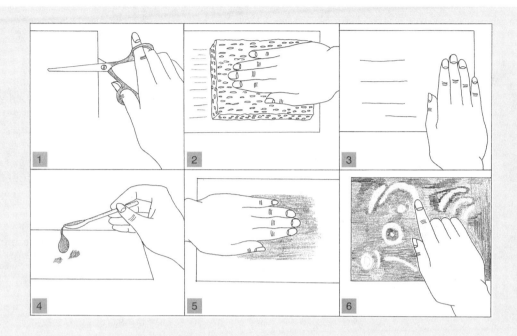

Tempera Painting

Young children love tempera paints because they lend themselves to bold designs. The various and complex possibilities of tempera painting can be explored by older children because of their ability to control the paint and brush. For example, they may explore with paint on moist, colored construction paper; utilize the dry-brush method to achieve texture; or try the mixed-media technique of tempera and crayon, tempera and India ink, or tempera and yarn. Children should be encouraged to use their imagination to create a painting that utilizes the properties and characteristics of tempera paints. They should be offered the opportunity to paint on materials such as burlap, corrugated cardboard, or papier-mâché. Older children should mix a variety of tints, shades, or neutralized hues rather than always painting with the available colors.

Construction paper in assorted sizes and colors makes an excellent surface or background for tempera paints because the color of the paper can be utilized as part of the design. The colored background will also help to unify the composition. Children should try painting on other background papers, for example, white drawing, cream manila, gray manila, bogus oatmeal, chip board, wallpaper samples, brown wrapping, or classified sections of newspapers.

Schedule sufficient time for children or participants to explore the various techniques that will enable them to develop a feeling for tempera paints. An individual cannot rush through a tempera paint project.

Acrylic Painting

Acrylic paints have many advantages over tempera and watercolors. They are water soluble and are versatile, ranging from watercolor to oil consistency. They also dry quickly. However, they are difficult to remove from the surface and are more expensive than watercolors or tempera paints. Special nylon brushes are manufactured for use with acrylic paints. These brushes have short stiff bristles and come in different widths.

Cover the working surface with newspaper and place all the material on it. Squeeze a little paint onto a palette (a piece of Masonite). When the participant decides on a picture or design to paint he or she may use one of the following techniques:

- *Transparent painting:* Acrylic paints, when diluted with enough water, can be used in the same manner as watercolors. Colors can be made lighter by diluting the paint with water and allowing the white paper to show through. If white paint is used to make a color brighter, the color becomes opaque.
- *Opaque painting:* Mix the paint with a small amount of water until it has a creamy consistency. Using a variety of colors, apply the paint in short strokes. Layers of paint should be gradually added until there is a three-dimensional quality to the painting.
- *Scrabble painting:* Mix the paint with water until it is creamy. With the paintbrush, quickly sketch the design or object in a scrabbling manner. The effects are quite interesting.
- *Flat two-dimensional painting:* Mix the paint with water until it is creamy. With a small brush or pencil, sketch a design or picture. Paint each form with one color. The participant will note how flat each shape looks.
- *Cartoon painting:* The participant should follow the instructions for flat two-dimensional painting but exaggerate the shapes. Black paint should be used to outline the shapes.

After the painting is finished, the participant must be sure to wash the brush and palette carefully. Once acrylic paint hardens on the brush, it is very difficult to remove. Acrylic paints can be used to paint many wooden or plastic objects such as toys, jewelry, picture frames, or screen posters.

Novelty Painting Techniques

Sponge Painting

This technique, like sponge printing, utilizes the textured surface of the sponge to obtain its effect. In sponge painting, a rectangular sponge is used to color shapes that are assembled to form a design or picture. The participant should draw a picture of a bottle, vase, or dish on a piece of white drawing paper, dip a one-inch rectangular sponge into a pan of tempera paint, and squeeze out any excess paint. Holding the sponge between the thumb and first two fingers, dab it against the surface of the drawing paper. The sponge is used to obtain a textured surface. Repeat the dipping and dabbing procedure until the total shape is completely colored. After the paint dries, cut the

Figure 8.3   Straw Painting

Materials: drawing paper, straw, paintbrush, paints.

1. Place a drop of paint on the paper.
2. Hold the bottom of the straw ¼ of an inch from the drop of the paint and blow into the straw.
3. Blow the drop around the paper.
4. Place another drop of paint on the paper.
5. Blow the drop around the paper.
6. Finished design.

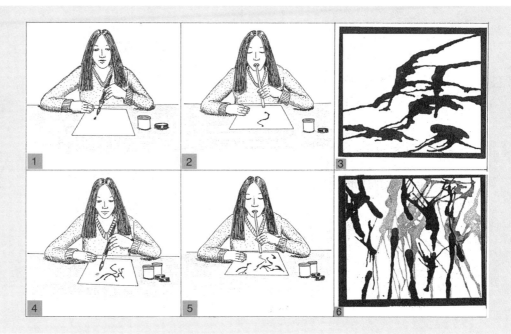

shape out with a pair of scissors. A second and third shape can be drawn and painted. These painted shapes are then mounted on a piece of colored construction paper. The shapes can be arranged to form an attractive still life.

Straw Painting

A soda straw can be used to blow a drop of paint into an interesting design or picture. This requires experimenting with the amount of water added to the paint to form the drop. Too little paint produces a drop that will not spread or run when air is blown on it (**Figure 8.3**).

With a paintbrush, place a drop of watercolor paint onto a piece of drawing paper. Hold a straw ¼ inch away from the drop of paint and blow through the straw. The paint should start to run; keep blowing the paint around the paper until it disappears. Place another drop of paint on the surface. This time hold the straw directly over the drop and blow through the straw. The drop of paint should spread in several directions. The participant should try adding different colors to the design or picture.

Start over again on a clean piece of paper and make a complete composition. Children, especially, usually have fun giving their compositions names.

Squeeze Painting with a Flour Mixture

An empty plastic detergent bottle can be used to deposit a mixture of flour and water onto a piece of cardboard to form a raised surface. With a pencil, sketch a design or picture on a piece of cardboard. Mix some flour and water into a thick paste in a detergent bottle. Turn the bottle upside down and squeeze the mixture onto a piece of cardboard through the small hole in the cap (**Figure 8.4**).

The mixture can fill whole areas or follow the outline of the design. A combination of both of these techniques can be used to make the picture or

Figure 8.4 Squeeze Painting

Materials: pencil, paintbrush, stirring stick, paint, flour, empty detergent bottle, drawing paper.

1. Sketch a design on a piece of drawing paper.
2. Pour ½ cup of flour and ⅓ cup water into the detergent bottle and stir until a thick paste is formed.
3. Squeeze the mixture onto the design.
4. Fill in whole areas and the outline of the mixture with the flour mixture.
5. Set aside to allow the flour mixture to dry.
6. Paint the raised areas.

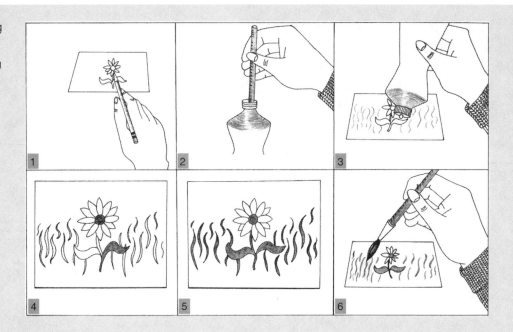

design more interesting. Set the design or picture aside and allow it to dry. After the mixture dries, paint the raised areas with either tempera or watercolors. The finished painting can be sprayed with a fixative to protect the surface.

Squeeze Painting with Tempera

In this activity, an empty plastic detergent bottle is used to squeeze tempera paint onto a piece of paper held on an easel. The paint is squeezed onto the top edge of the paper and allowed to run down the surface to form a series of lines. The lines will be straight, curved, or latticelike. Different colors will add to the design. Squeeze different colors on a surface and experiment with the thickness of tempera paint.

Sand Painting

Natural colored sands can be used to make beautiful sand paintings. If they are not available, white silica sand can be purchased from a sand and gravel dealer and tinted with different mortar colors. Sketch a design lightly on a piece of cardboard or wood. Cover those background areas that will not be covered by a sand coating with tempera, watercolors, or acrylic paints. Select one of the areas to cover with sand and coat it with a thin layer of shellac, varnish, or glue. A spoon or paper cone can be used to sprinkle the colored sand over the coated area. Allow the sand to sit for a few minutes and then pick up the cardboard or wood. Holding it in an upright position, tap lightly to remove the excess sand. Before using another color, gather up the excess

Figure 8.5   Sand Painting

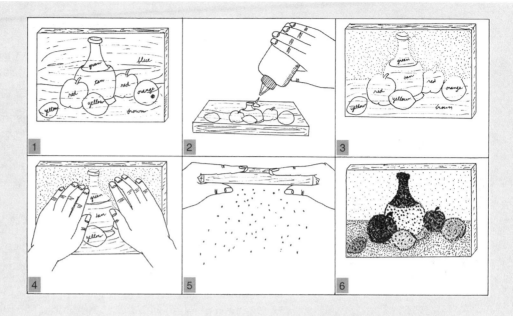

Materials: plywood, containers of colored sand, pencil, shellac, paint brush, glue.

1. Sketch a design on plywood and label the areas for various colors.
2. Apply glue to the areas to be one color.
3. Pour sand of this color onto these areas.
4. Press the sand down firmly.
5. Turn the board over and shake off the excess sand.
6. Repeat procedure for each color.
7. Shellac the finished design.

sand and put it back in the container. Repeat this process until all the desired areas are covered with sand (**Figure 8.5**).

A coarse black piece of emery cloth can be used as background material to obtain an interesting effect. The emery cloth is glued to a piece of stiff cardboard with contact cement. Care should be taken not to get any glue on the decorative surface. To dry, place the glued materials under a heavy weight for three or four hours. Draw a design on the mounted piece of emery cloth with chalk. White background areas can be painted with white acrylic paint to screen out the black background. The sand is applied to the surface in the same manner as for a cardboard or wooden base.

Drawing Techniques

Learning to draw requires an understanding of certain fundamental principles. Artistic talent cannot be taught; however, the techniques needed to express feelings and ideas can be learned. These fundamental principles usually represent the difference between good pencil, charcoal, crayon, or ink drawings and poor ones. But good drawing usually gives the feeling of being three-dimensional and utilizes the concept of perspective. The following eight fundamental principles are important to consider when sketching and drawing.

1. *Position:* Objects or parts of objects that are drawn near the bottom of the paper will appear to be closer.
2. *Size:* Objects or parts of objects that are nearer the observer will appear to be larger.
3. *Surface lines or texture:* Surface lines help give an object a three-dimensional appearance.

4. *Overlapping:* Overlapping is similar to position. The front object hides some of the lines of the rear object, thus creating an illusion of distance.
5. *Shading:* Shading gives an object a three-dimensional quality because it suggests thickness.
6. *Shadow:* A shadow shows the patch of darkness caused by an object blocking the light.
7. *Density:* Objects nearer the viewer should be drawn darker and with more detail than objects in the background.
8. *Foreshortening:* Horizontal lines are drawn closer together than they normally would be, thus distorting the shape slightly and creating an appearance of distance.

It is impossible to draw anything in perspective without using one or more of these fundamental principles. Therefore, it is safe to say that any individual who understands these fundamental principles can draw, provided he or she can draw the outline shape.

Success in drawing depends on more than knowing the various drawing techniques, however. The important thing is not how much is known, but what can be done with this information. Scientists may know all about aeronautics but not be able to fly a plane. The only way a person can learn to fly is to practice flying. The only way to learn how to draw is by practicing the various drawing techniques.

Drawing Cartoons

Cartoons are drawn by combining straight lines, curved lines, and circles into the basic shape of a man, woman, animal, insect, or some unusual creation. The first step in drawing cartoons is to practice making straight lines, curved lines, and circles, or combinations of these lines. These lines are then combined into a basic body shape. A head, arms, legs, and other characteristics are added to the body by modifying the basic lines (**Figures 8.6** and **8.7**).

Drawing Stick Figures

An endless variety of stick figures, both animal and human, can be drawn by connecting circles and straight lines. A head and spine are drawn first in whatever attitude the situation calls for. Arms and legs are added to the body in the necessary positions. The required characteristics or features are added to help the finished stick figure convey a message; for example, a skirt and long hair can help distinguish female from male. Size, clothing, and hairstyle help distinguish an adult from a child. Stick figures create easily recognized stereotypes.

Object Drawing

A rectangular prism, square, pyramid, triangle, cone, or sphere can be used to simplify the drawing of familiar objects (**Figure 8.8**). The first step in object drawing using the basic shapes is to analyze the model. Determine what basic shapes or modification of those shapes can be used to draw the object. For example, in drawing a house, the base may be a rectangular prism and the roof may be a triangular prism. These geometric relationships are common

Figure 8.6   Cartoon People

Materials: paper (newsprint or drawing), crayons or felt pen.

1. Draw a large circle for a head and a smaller one for a nose.
2. Draw two dots for the eyes and a curved line for the mouth.
3. Add hair to the head.
4. Draw a triangle for the body of a girl and a circle for the body of the boy.
5. Draw a neck to the connect the body to the head.
6. Add arms to the body.
7. Add legs and feet to the body.
8. Dress the cartoon character to look like a boy.
9. Dress the cartoon character to look like a girl.

Figure 8.7   Cartoon Animals

Materials: paper (newsprint or drawing), felt pen or crayon.

1. Practice making loops and curved lines.
2. Practice making basic body shapes.
3. Combine these loops, curved lines, and basic body shapes into cartoon animals.
4. Create a scene composed of cartoon animals.
5. Combine these loops, curved lines, and basic body shapes to create another cartoon animal.
6. Create another cartoon animal.

Figure 8.8   Object Drawing

Materials: paper (newsprint or drawing) and pencils (different shades: HB, 2B, 4B).

1. Use basic shapes to draw a picture.
2. Add texture and tone.

to innumerable objects. A candy box is a rectangular prism; a bowl, a hemisphere; a lamp shade, a truncated cone or pyramid. Even highly complex architectural structures can be resolved into comparatively simple geometric elements.

Contour Drawing

Contour drawing is not an outline of an object. An outline is a diagram or silhouette, flat and two-dimensional. It is the type of shape that is obtained by tracing one's own hand on a piece of paper. It is difficult to determine whether the drawing is of the front or back of the hand. Contour drawing, in contrast, has a three-dimensional quality because it shows thickness, length, and width of the form being drawn.

Set the object to be drawn in front of you and place a piece of drawing paper on the working surface. Focus your eyes on some point along the outer edge of the object to be drawn. Place the point of the pencil on the paper. In contour drawing, it is important to imagine that the pencil is touching the model instead of the paper. Concentrate on the model and without looking at the paper or pencil, start drawing the object. The eye moves slowly along the contour of the object as the pencil slowly moves along the paper. Imagine that the object is being traced. The key to success is developing coordination between the pencil and eye. It is important not to move the eye ahead of the pencil. Consider and concentrate on the point being drawn and not the total contour of the object. This requires practice and patience. When first starting to draw using this technique, the artist should not worry about proportions because they will become correct with practice (**Figure 8.9**).

Gesture Drawing

In gesture drawing, an endless line is drawn rapidly and continuously from top to bottom, around and around, without taking the pencil off the paper.

Figure 8.9   Gesture and
Contour
Drawing

Materials: paper (newsprint or
drawing) and pencils (different
shades: HB, 2B, 4B).

1. Contour drawing of a
   still life.
2. Gesture drawing of a
   still life.
3. Contour drawing of a
   baseball player.
4. Gesture drawing of a
   baseball player.

The end product may have the appearance of a scribble. Set the object to be
drawn in front of you and place a piece of drawing paper on the working
surface. Take a pencil and let it swing around the paper almost at will.
The form the lines take is determined by the action the individual sees in the
model. Let the pencil roam, capturing the gesture of the model.

The difference between contour drawing and gesture drawing is that the
purpose of the latter is to capture what the model appears to be doing and
not what it looks like or what it is. In contour drawing the essential thing is to
touch the edge of the form, whereas in gesture drawing, it is important to
capture the feeling of the object's movement. The finished drawing may be
meaningless to the observer once the model has been removed. There may
be nothing in the finished scribble to suggest the shape of the model. This is
not significant.

In gesture drawing, the edges of the form being drawn are not followed.
Instead, the pencil is allowed to meander, striking the edges of the form, but
more often it will travel through the center of the form being drawn. Many
times the pencil will travel outside of the figure and even off the paper to
create the desired gesture. Remember, it is only the action, the gesture, that
is being drawn and not a detailed illustration of the structure. Gesture drawing
should be dynamic, not static. The finished gesture drawing has no precise
edges, no exact shape, no jelled form, because the forms are changing.

Pencil Drawing

The first task in pencil drawing is to learn about the materials used in this
medium. All pencils are graded by degree of hardness on one end and should
be sharpened at the opposite end. The grades range from 6B (very soft and
black) to 9H (extremely hard). For preliminary sketches, the HB grade is the

Figure 8.10 Pencil Techniques

Materials: paper (newsprint or drawing) and pencils (different grades: HB, 2B, 4B).

1. Draw gray strokes first then add blacks. Outline with tone areas located. Add darker grays. Add the blacks.
2. Draw dark areas first and then add grays.
3. Apply lights and darks as needed.

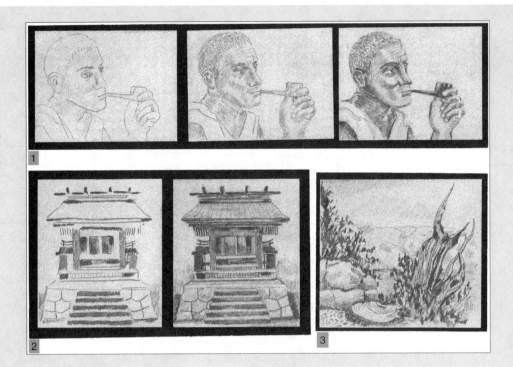

most commonly used, while the B and 2B are usually used for all-around purposes. The lead can be sharpened to a needle point or chisel point to obtain different effects.

Several types of paper can be used, and various effects may be achieved by using different grades of pencils. The surface of the paper is very important to pencil sketching, and it is important to learn the advantages and disadvantages of different surfaces before starting any sketch. A photographic effect can be obtained on a smooth surface, whereas the surface texture of rough paper will enhance the drawing of a stone wall. Apply even pressure or graded pressure as the strokes are drawn. Try cross-hatching, wavy or broken strokes, or accenting the ends of the lines to obtain different effects.

Any one of the following three methods can be used to make a pencil sketch (**Figure 8.10**). The first method is to draw the object and shade in the tone areas with light lines. With an HB pencil add the gray areas to the drawing, leaving the dark areas until last. These areas can be shaded with a 2B or softer pencil. The advantage of this method is that the picture gradually develops and is always under control. The disadvantage is that light pencil strokes sometimes spoil the tooth (texture lines) of the paper, making it difficult to add a dark shade to an area.

The second method reverses the previous order by adding tone to a drawing. The blacks are the first areas shaded, followed by the middle grays and finally the light grays. This approach presents two problems: first, once the dark areas are finished, it is difficult to keep from smudging the surface; second, this approach does not allow for any experimentation. The individual is forced to decide at the start of the drawing which areas will be dark and which will be light. This type of decision making is difficult for the beginner, who might prefer to build his or her value more gradually.

The third method does not use any rules for coming to or finishing the drawing with the desired light, gray, and dark tones. It is an experimental method in that once the basic sketch is made, the tones are randomly added to the various parts of the drawing to obtain the effect. Segments are shaded two or three times to obtain contrasts.

Black is important to the finished drawing, although many individuals are afraid of dark tones. Without dark tones, the finished sketch will appear wishy-washy and have little character.

Charcoal Drawing

As a medium of artistic expression, charcoal has been popular for many years. It is especially fine for quick effects. Charcoal's softness and generous size make it ideal for filling large areas of tone quickly. Errors can be easily corrected by dusting the paper clean. Charcoal also produces the most vivid blacks (**Figure 8.11**).

There are many kinds or grades of charcoal, and the price is usually a fair indication of quality. A few assorted sticks, soft and hard, are necessary to make a charcoal drawing. A number of imitation or synthetic charcoals in crayon or pencil form are available. These are more uniform and reliable than real charcoal, but are generally much more expensive.

Although charcoal can be used on many different types of paper, the best results are obtained by using paper made for this purpose. It comes in tints, as well as white. Charcoal paper is also good for drawings produced entirely in chalk or crayon. For the beginner, the inexpensive grades are satisfactory. A chamois skin is excellent for dusting the surface clean, and a rubber eraser is ideal for lifting tone and picking out highlights.

Because of the crumbly nature of charcoal, it is best to start drawing a large object. To lay out the subject, use a rather hard stick with a point. The piece of charcoal is sharpened by drawing a knife away from the point to prevent it from breaking. Sandpaper also can be used to sharpen the charcoal.

Figure 8.11   Charcoal Techniques

Materials: paper (newsprint, drawing, or charcoal), charcoal, eraser, chamois skin.

1. Tiny pits or depressions in the paper are allowed to show through the tone to give sparkle and vibration.
2. After applying charcoal, rub the surface with a finger and highlight with an eraser.

Block in the proportions freely, with an arm and wrist motion. Mistakes can be dusted off with a chamois and new materials added.

There are two common methods of adding tone to the drawing. In the first, each area is covered using a hard piece of pointed charcoal, and the tiny pits or depressions in the paper are allowed to show through the tone to give sparkle and vibration. If an area gets too dark, dust off the charcoal and start over or use the eraser to lighten the tone by gently rubbing the surface. Care should be taken to keep from smudging the charcoal surface.

In the second method, charcoal is applied in the same manner as in the first method and is then lightly rubbed with a finger and highlighted with an eraser. The eraser can be used to clean away some of the charcoal, allowing the white surface to show through. These white areas will represent highlights. The eraser should be cleaned by rubbing the edge on a piece of scrap paper after each highlight is made or the whole surface will be black, making it impossible to create the desired highlights.

These two methods can be combined in various ways. Areas can be smudged and then restored with a piece of pointed charcoal, producing a smooth, but vibrant texture. Another technique is to lightly rub the entire background and then erase the highlight areas. A sharp piece of charcoal can be used to touch up the surface. The success of charcoal drawing depends upon an understanding of the characteristics of charcoal and charcoal papers.

Colored Crayons

Crayons are an inexpensive art medium that can be used by very young children and adults for artistic expression. Crayons are usually misused because of incomplete understanding of their characteristics and properties. A crayon composition should have brilliant color, heavily applied to give character. A light crayon drawing is uninteresting, flat, and dull. Crayons are superb media for small, compact drawings utilizing a combination of strong dark and light contrast to bring out the details. Colored crayons are not an easel material, nor are they appropriate or effective when used to cover large surfaces.

How to Use Crayons

Many objects, such as fruit, are not just one color. An apple, for example, may have red, orange, green, brown, and even blue in it. Why, then, do we color the apple one shade of red? The answer is probably related to visual literacy and the lack of understanding of what techniques can be used with colored crayons.

The novice should try putting one color over another to make a different shade or to make a new color. As the colors are mixed, write the names of the colors used next to each sample.

The most effective method for learning how to crayon is by use. The following techniques can be employed to develop sensitivity to the properties and characteristics of colored crayons:

- The greater the pressure on the crayon, the darker the color will appear.
- Start with light tones and progress gradually to dark tones.

- The lightness and darkness of a single line used to outline an object can express depth.
- The appearance of distance can be obtained through light and dark tones.
- Cross-hatching tends to flatten an object.
- The direction of the strokes can be used to show depth.
- Rough crayon marks can be smoothed with a knife to give the surface a pastel appearance.
- Use colored crayons on different colored paper. The colored paper produces results similar to applying one color over another.

Flat Crayons

Short pieces of broken crayons can be flattened with a knife and used on their side to obtain some interesting effects (**Figure 8.12**). Place about 1 inch of newspaper under a sheet of paper. Hold the crayon on the flat side and, applying light pressure to one end, pull it across the paper. The line should be dark on one edge and fade to a light edge. This technique requires practice to obtain the desired line and effect.

Crayon-Eraser Stencil Designs

Oak tag, drawing paper, crayons, scissors, and an eraser can be used by children and others to make a stencil design. On a piece of oak tag, draw a variety of designs with a pencil. Then cut out each shape. Care should be taken not to damage either piece of material because both can be used to make the final

Figure 8.12 Flat Crayons

Materials: paper (newsprint or drawing), newspapers, crayons.

1. Place a piece of drawing paper on a ½-inch layer of newspaper.
2. Hold the crayon flat and push it across the surface of the drawing paper, applying light pressure to one end.
3. Practice drawing straight lines.
4. Practice drawing curved lines.
5. Draw a picture using a combination of these simple strokes.
6. Draw a second picture using different strokes.

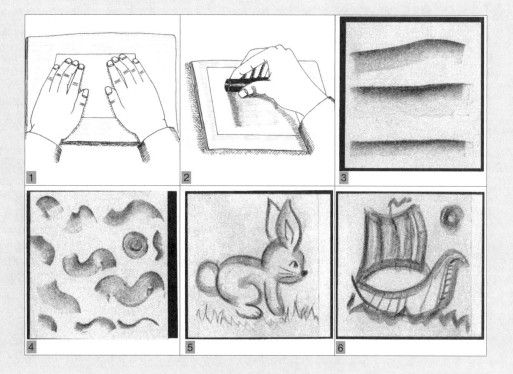

Figure 8.13 Crayon-Eraser Stencil Design

Materials: oak tag, scissors, pencil, crayons, eraser, drawing paper.

1. Draw a shape on a piece of oak tag.
2. Cut out the design.
3. Care should be taken not to damage the negative or positive parts of the design.
4. Color around the edge of the negative or positive shape with a crayon.
5. With an eraser, rub the crayon from the stencil onto a sheet of drawing paper.
6. Finished negative and positive design.

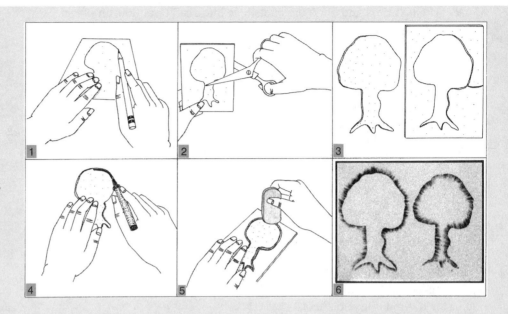

design. Color around the edge of the shape with a crayon. Place the shape on a piece of paper, crayon side up. Transfer the crayon to the drawing paper from the stencil by rubbing an eraser over the surface. The eraser strokes must be even and close together. Stencil designs can be used in a variety of combinations to obtain the desired effect (**Figure 8.13**).

Crayon Etching

Crayon etching can be used by any participant to obtain some interesting effects with color. The technique requires a minimum amount of supplies: crayons, paper (oak tag, coated paper, or shelf paper), and an etching tool (knife, nail, or toothpick). The working area should be covered and a piece of paper placed on the surface. Color the surface of the paper completely with bright colors, distributed randomly. Rub the crayon-colored surface with a facial tissue. Then coat the entire surface with black crayon. When the surface has been thoroughly blackened, rub it with a facial tissue. It is now ready for etching. The surface can be etched with a knife, nail, or other sharp object. The pointed tool is used to scratch through the blackened surface so that the bright colors underneath show. Simple lines can be scratched through the surface or large areas of black removed to modify the effect (**Figure 8.14**).

This technique intrigues participants because it removes some of the restrictions placed upon them when they use colored crayons alone. It also provides the individual with an unusual experience with color. If the participant edges a leaf shape, it may turn out to be red, green, and yellow, rather than just green.

Figure 8.14 Crayon Etching

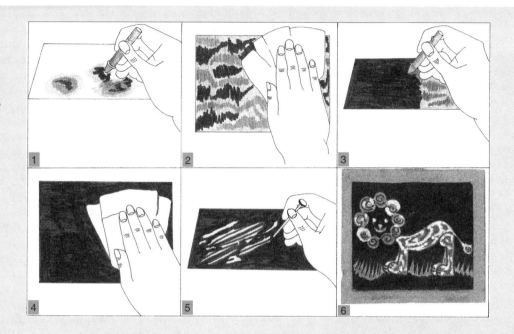

Materials: crayon, facial tissue, nail, paper (coated).

1. Cover the surface of the paper with small patches of different crayon colors.
2. Rub the crayon-colored surface with a facial tissue.
3. Cover the entire surface with black crayon.
4. Rub the blackened surface with facial tissue.
5. Scratch a design through the blackened surface with a nail.
6. Finished design.

Crayon-Tempera or -Ink Etching

The crayon-tempera or crayon-ink etching technique is similar to crayon etching in that the surface is covered with bright colors. The bright colored surface is then covered with black tempera or ink. If tempera is used, soap must be applied to the paintbrush before painting over the waxed crayon surface. When the paint or ink dries, a pointed object can be used to scratch a design through the blackened surface.

Crayon Shadow Pictures

Colored crayons rubbed across a piece of paper that has been placed on top of a cut out shape will result in a picture that has a shadow effect. Have the participants draw some shapes on a piece of thin cardboard or oak tag and cut them out with a pair of scissors. Arrange the shapes into a satisfying design or picture on a sheet of newspaper. Place a piece of construction paper, newsprint, or drawing paper over the shapes. Care should be taken not to move the shapes. Rub the side of a small piece of crayon across the surface of the paper. The edges of the shapes beneath the paper should appear darker, giving the finished picture or design a shadow appearance.

Crayon Resist

A waxed crayon drawing or design can be enriched by applying black tempera or watercolors over the entire surface. In fact, this technique can be used to change the characteristics of a picture or design. Many individuals are amazed and thrilled to see the difference that occurs when the black paint is brushed across the colored crayon surface. Areas covered with a heavy coating of waxed crayon will resist the water-based paint, while those not colored will retain the paint. Small amounts of black paint will be picked up between the strokes of crayons. The small patches of black add new dimensions.

The drawing or design can be planned so that large or small areas will be entirely free of crayon. Mix some black tempera paint with water or use watercolors to brush across the entire surface of the drawing.

Crayon Encaustics

This technique utilizes those small pieces of crayon that usually accumulate as participants draw and color. The small pieces of crayon are placed in an old muffin tin. The various colors are separated. The muffin tin is heated and the wax crayons melted. While the wax is in liquid form, it can be applied to a surface with a paintbrush. A stiff-bristle brush is better than a brush made of hair for applying the wax to the painting because of its consistency. The wax cools and solidifies quickly when the container is removed from the heat source; therefore, participants must work very quickly with these materials.

A crayon encaustic drawing and design will result in a picture with vivid colors. It can be painted on almost any surface—plywood, hardboard or Masonite, cardboard, posterboard, and wood. After the painting dries, one of the etching techniques can be used to obtain some surprising effects. Heat can be applied to the work for greater fusion of the colors.

An understanding of the properties and characteristics of material permits an individual to be more creative with the media. Understanding and sensitivity toward material can only be derived from use of the media.

Crayon Painting

Crayon painting uses heated crayons instead of brushes and paints. The crayons are only used on canvas, cloth, or Masonite. The surface to be painted can be held either horizontally or vertically. Have the participants plan a rough sketch of the design or picture that is to be painted. With a black crayon, lightly sketch the design or picture onto the canvas or Masonite surface. The sketch should be in outline form and not concerned with detail. Peel back the top edge of the paper on the crayons. As the crayons are used, the paper should be continuously peeled back. Place a candle into a holder of some type and light it. The tip of the crayon is placed over the heat for a few seconds. The crayon is then removed from the heat and dabbed onto the surface being painted. Simultaneously, it should be rubbed around, as when used to color a drawing. Because the crayon is soft, small lumps of colored wax will be deposited on the surface. The dabbing and rubbing process should be repeated until the entire painting is finished. A wide range of colors will make the painting more attractive. Colors can be mixed by putting different dabs on top of each other. As always, experimentation is of paramount importance.

Floating Designs

Floating designs can be used to decorate the surface of a piece of paper. Single-color and multicolored designs may be created by using this technique

Figure 8.15 Floating Designs

Materials: water, paper, turpentine, paint, large shallow pan, stirring stick, spoon.

1. Fill a wide shallow pan with water.
2. Add enough paint to a small quantity of turpentine to obtain desired color. Drop a small amount of the paint-turpentine mixture onto the surface of the water.
3. Add a second or third color to the surface of the water if desired.
4. Stir the water, causing the paint-turpentine mixture to form a series of swirl designs.

5. Place a piece of paper on top of the swirl designs.
6. Finished swirl designs.

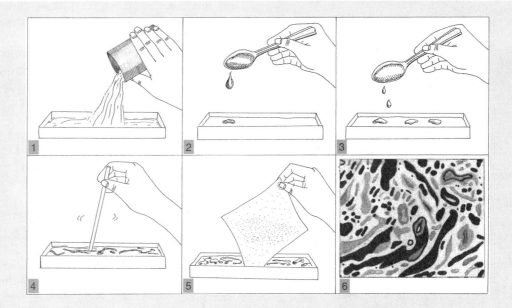

(**Figure 8.15**). Individuals enjoy interpreting the patterns that are formed as the paint-turpentine mixture is swirled. Fill a wide, shallow pan with water. Pour a small quantity of turpentine into a small jar and then add enough powder or oil paint to bring it to the required color strength. Pour a small amount of the paint-turpentine mixture onto the surface of the water. With a stick, stir the water, causing the paint-turpentine mixture to form a series of interesting swirl designs. Pick up a piece of drawing paper and place it on top of the water and swirl the design. Carefully lift the paper from the water and place it on a piece of newspaper to dry. The piece of paper can also be dragged across the surface of the water to pick up the design.

More than one color can be used at one time, creating a multicolored design. The second or third colors are created in the same way as the first paint-turpentine mixture and then added to the water. The designs may be controlled or they may be spontaneous, depending on the desired effect. If oil paints are used, the water and paints should not be washed down the sink. After emptying the container, wipe the surface clean with soap or detergent and cloth or paper towels.

Decoupage

Decoupage is the art of decorating a surface using cutout paper pictures. The picture is transferred to the new surface with a special medium that picks up the printed design but not the paper backing. Printed pictures can be transferred to wood, glass, china, plastic, and metal. The transfer medium can be purchased at most paint stores or craft shops.

Have the participants select a picture and cut it out. Brush four coats of transfer medium onto the front surface of the picture. Coats one and three are brushed on the surface vertically, while coats two and four are brushed horizontally. Fifteen minutes should be allowed between each coat or until the film covering the surface is clear. The brush should be cleaned between each application. Allow the final coat to dry for at least 2 hours.

Trim 1/16 inch from the edges of the picture with a razor blade or knife. Place the picture face down in soapy water and allow to soak for 1 hour. Remove from the soapy water and rinse the picture in clear water. After rinsing the picture, place it face down on a smooth, hard surface. Rub firmly over the surface with your fingers to peel the paper from the film. It may be necessary to add water or resoak the picture to remove all the paper. The picture will show through when all the paper is removed. Allow the surface to dry, and then apply a coat of transfer medium to the back of the picture. Also apply a coating of transfer medium to the surface on which the picture is going to be attached. The surface to which the picture is being transferred should be painted or stained before the picture is applied. Place the picture on the surface and use your fingers to press the picture flat. Care should be taken to remove air bubbles and excess transfer medium. Allow the picture to dry until completely transparent. Apply decoupage finish with a brush, brushing in one direction with long flowing strokes. Remove any brush hairs from the surface. The finish should be allowed to dry for 1 hour before a second coat is added. Repeat until the desired finish is obtained, and then clean the brush with thinner.

Summary

Many individuals ask, "What is the right way to use paints?" and "What is the right way to use crayons?" The answers are that any good art activity should provide individuals with an opportunity to express themselves in their own unique manner. The activity should provide an environment that encourages the participant to explore and create. Participants should also be afforded the chance to work with other materials that can be used to print, paint, or color a design or picture. Individuals will create their own techniques in using paints, crayons, and other art materials if provided with the opportunity to do so.

Art is in the eye of the beholder, and its meaning is in the mind of the artist. Although all art forms do not appeal to all people, there are particular genres that do. Therefore, art, or what is construed to be art, is popular almost everywhere. It is this popularity that underwrites its significance within the recreational program. The vast repertoire of art forms elicits appreciation, enjoyment, wonder, or creativity from those who observe its attraction or who participate in its creation.

Age is no barrier to art participation. The very young or old and those in between can express themselves in various ways. From scribbles to well-realized landscapes may be produced. Crayons, pen and pencil, watercolors, oil paints, acrylics, and many other media are available to use. It all depends upon taste and ability.

Those who have artistic talent may only require appropriate space in which to perform. Such activity needs to be scheduled at a time and place convenient for the artist and the agency. Others who want to learn may enroll in scheduled classes that are designed to accommodate every skill level from beginner to advanced. The timing of the sessions reflects the needs of the participants.

Of necessity, skilled instructors must be employed by the agency of record to teach basic or more complex skills to those who derive satisfaction and enjoyment from the experience. Either recreationists with the requisite talent can be used for this responsibility or other resource personnel must be sought out in the community and asked to volunteer their time or else must be hired to perform the teaching role.

Selected Further References

Bellamy, D. *Watercolor Landscapes Course*. New York: HarperCollins Publishers, Ltd., 2004.

Chandler, V. *Art in Action*. North Mankato, MN: Smart Apple Media, 2005.

Civardi, A. *Sculpture Secrets*. North Mankato, MN: Smart Apple Media, 2005.

Fletcher, A. *Watercolorist's A to Z of Trees and Foliage*. Cincinnati, OH: F&W Publications, Inc., 2003.

Gipson, R. *Crayon Activities Pack*. Manassas, VA: EDC Publishing, 2004.

Hector, V. *Art of Beadwork: Historic Inspiration, Contemporary Design*. New York: Watson-Guptill Publications, Inc., 2005.

Katter, E., and M. G. Stewart. *Art—A Community Connection*. Worcester, MA: Davis Publications, Inc., 2001.

Lindnerman, M. G. *Art in the Elementary School: Drawing, Painting, and Creating for the Classroom*. Blacklick, OH: McGraw-Hill Higher Education, 1996.

Packhurst, D. B. *Painter in Oil: A Complete Treatise on the Principles and Techniques Necessary to the Painting of Pictures in the Oil Colors*. Davenport, IA: Gustav's Library, 2004.

Payne, A. F. *Art Metalwork with Inexpensive Equipment*. Davenport, IA: Gustav's Library, 2004.

Robbins, C. *Art of Figure Drawing*. Cincinnati, OH: F&W Publications, Inc., 2003.

Russell, K. *Sculptured Foam Decorative Accents: 25 Fantastic and Fun Accent Pieces*. Iola, WI: Krause Publications, 2003.

Sanders, M. *Oil Painting Tips and Techniques: Painting with Oils*. Kansas City, KS: Search Press, Ltd., 2005.

Tappenden, C. *Watercolor Foundation Course*. New York: Cassell, 2003.

Winter, B. *Art Projects Middle Schoolers Can't Resist!* New York: Scholastic, Inc., 2003.

CHAPTER

9

Crafts

Crafts represent a particular mode of expression and are a vehicle for the inherently human desire to manipulate, fabricate, or experience the satisfaction of creativity. Indeed, the production of crafted objects may be likened to the process of communication where there is an attempt to transmit (or transform) ideas into concrete or synthesized entities.

Crafts are essentially represented by the utilization of a variety of materials for decorative, useful, or manipulative purposes. The creative process, of value to those who seek satisfaction and enjoyment from shaping, arranging, and changing materials, is enabled by craft activity.

Craftsmanship

The ability to utilize tools in the molding, treatment, or manipulation of substances and materials to fabricate something functional is craftsmanship. Among nature's evolutionary gifts to humankind was the appositional thumb. In consequence, people can manipulate objects, which in turn led to the use of things to work on other things. The clever hands of humans and a growing brain permitted an exquisite coordination to form. The capacity to grasp large and small objects and utilize them to create innovative designs by which materials are given form and substance is the essence of craftsmanship.

Another aspect of craftsmanship is the desire or ambition to complete a unit of work having the mark of one's own efforts forever stamped on the fabricated object. Perhaps craftsmanship should also be called pride of workmanship. It is the delight found in making the best effort possible by exerting an innately held talent or ability on the article crafted. It means the time taken for design, the energy expended in carrying out the design with quality, and the satisfaction derived only when form and function, together with such decorative design as is necessary, are brought to fruition.

Poor craftswork abounds everywhere. There seems little left of the pride of work that formerly marked the efforts of craftspersons in many trades. Perhaps the factor of machine-made goods precludes such individual ambition, but there are still many productive trades in which craftsmanship could manifest itself. The ideal of pride in the work being done has apparently been forsaken. Time, now, is looked upon as money. There is no intent to offer satisfaction or guarantee a job well done. Yet, there are those who do provide that last ounce of devoted work because they look upon their handiwork as a piece of themselves, carrying their reputation. Some people are concerned with reputation, and their work shows the unmistakable signs of pride.

Today, craftsmanship is more avocationally oriented than vocational. It is within the hobby activity, the recreational program, or the directed learning environment that individuals tend to exhibit craftsmanship. The real craftsperson, particularly, infuses a part of him- or herself into the craft activity. For these people, crafts have become a lifelong interest. They are not only learning by doing, but, perhaps, they have matured and attained excellence in the work of their own hands. Such individuals glory in whatever they make. They have freely chosen this form of self-expression and set to work with a willingness to spend whatever time, care, and attention to detail such activity requires. Crafts that become the focus of lifelong recreational activity involve meticulousness, classification, patience, and absolute absorption by the artisan. This almost fanatic and loving attention paid to performance and product has nearly passed out of existence. But those who spend the time and carry their devotion to full flower are repaid handsomely in terms of personal satisfaction and, sometimes, the mark of excellence.

Satisfying Individual Needs

Crafts permit the individual the occasion to experience fulfillment. Crafts offer the opportunity to personally identify oneself with an idea, carry it through every stage of development, and finally realize utter satisfaction as the finishing touches are added. The completeness of the project adds a dimension to the life of the craftsperson that seems to be disappearing from common life today—integrity and unity. A soundly developed program in crafts brings the individual in direct confrontation with a variety of problems, not the least of which is conflicting desires. Within the confines of the craft shop individuals can apply themselves, or, more importantly, their ideas to a medium. By using design, tools, and knowledge the person can subject any material to his or her will and create a new arrangement, new combinations, new proportions, and unique outcomes.

Handling tools and materials allows the inventiveness of the human mind to take a tangible form. Experimentation with possible avenues of productivity indicates individual potential and self-development. It is the total commitment creative experience demands that allows the individual to realize what can be done. What follows offers unending enjoyment, exploration of various materials, creation of designs, and upon completion, a sense of release and deep satisfaction. Fundamentally, satisfactions have origin in psychological and physiological needs that tend to motivate behavior.

Those who recognize the importance and character of needs can more intelligently select those courses of action that will lead to a fulfillment of needs. Such individuals can avoid experiences that do not coincide with the successful pursuit of satisfaction. This is not a hedonistic-oriented plan, but the opportunity to explore possible avenues that tend to offer a more harmonious style of living.

All individuals differ insofar as latent or overt skills, knowledge, talent, or desire is concerned. Each person, however, probably wants to achieve in some way. A vague feeling persists in us all that activates a drive to reduce tension. Participating in suitable behavior, which leads to actual accomplishment, alleviates tension produced by the urge to be active and achieve.

Unaccustomed experiences are worthwhile in satisfying the desire for achievement, but even more satisfying is the effective performance of some task. The human organism requires some purposeful activity in order to live a well-balanced life; some objective or work to complete satisfies the need to affect accomplishment. Crafts activities, providing an almost infinite variety of choices, new experiences, media, and purposes, can offer opportunities that end in genuine fulfillment.

The basis for program achievement in crafts lies in its ability to satisfy individual needs. Scrupulous attention must be paid to individual wants and needs. Accentuation of opportunities for individual participation should be held as a paramount goal. Because of individual differences, personal satisfaction may be derived in a number of ways. Group encounters will not always satisfy a person's desire for activity. There will always be people in every community who either cannot or do not want to participate in socializing experiences; they prefer solitary venues where they may express themselves alone. Some individuals especially seek out crafts as an outlet for solitary activity. Recreational programs should promote frequent opportunities for individual learning, skill development, and achievement. Being alone may very well be utilized as a means for self-development. In order to gain from an environment of people and experience, we must sometimes withdraw from it and find new experiences within ourselves.

Values of Group Experiences

Craft activities also provide the basis for group experiences, which people require for a balanced existence. A variety of classes for beginners, intermediately skilled persons, and advanced or expert artisans may be programmed to meet the diverse and special needs of those who desire the companionship of peers in attaining satisfying results of successfully completed projects. Recognition of individual achievement within the group may be an important means for stimulating participants to continue with their efforts, to try harder, or to progress to another level of ability. Although the best interests of the group are emphasized, the progress and promotion of individuals within the group are kept uppermost. As with all recreational situations, it is the individual for whom the total program is developed. The individual is the measure of the program's success. To the extent that all individuals within the group or aggregate are well served and satisfied by their respective endeavors, the entire group meets its goals.

Crafts provide program material through which individuals can obtain a rich experience in self-realization, secure confidence in decision making, become knowledgeable about materials, and perceive the significance of crafts in the lives of people. Participation can be initiated on an individual basis, because each person is involved with his or her own materials and works on something with his or her own hands. However, many craft activities are undertaken within a class or group setting, thereby offering an invitation for the timid to enter into group life. Although each participant is occupied with his or her own project, there is still opportunity to ask questions, compare styles, enjoy the companionship of others behaving in the same ways, receive inspiration from others' efforts, and maintain close contact without surrendering individuality. Members of any crafts group must share workspace, materials, tools, and the attention of the instructor. Cooperation is fostered and individuals are enabled to perform with peers. As skills develop, gradually there may also develop a concomitant feeling of integration with others. This is particularly helpful in extremely heterogeneous situations. Crafts offer opportunities for individual satisfaction and for combining into groups under conditions where intense feelings and tensions can be resolved. The individual can achieve status and recognition in consequence of performing in activities that are personally satisfying. At the same time there might also be a simultaneous build-up of contact and mutual confidence that goes into the development of group feeling.

Many persons, adults in particular, seek and find immensely satisfying avocational interests through their experiences in crafts. The craft instructor may have no motive beyond offering opportunities to create and enjoy through media, but there is recognition of talent and interest. In many instances the crafts instructor can serve as an important guidance or counseling resource in directing participants toward further employment of enhanced skills.

Factors in Planning Craft Activities

Whatever the agency involved, whether school, voluntary, commercial, or public recreational service department, the program is everything; that is, the total offering of services for which the agency was established. Participation has value for the individual, the agency, and the community at large. Program development in any recreational agency is never simple. Bringing interested potential participants together with competent leadership at a suitable and accessible time and place, for the greatest stimulation possible, with adequate materials and equipment, all smoothly organized to prevent friction and disaffection from arising, is an intricate process. To the extent that crafts instructors can coordinate all integral features, overcoming irritating irrelevancies, and matching participants to a group, class, or activity that will meet their particular recreational needs, the ultimate success of the program will be determined.

Aims of the Program

The program must contain the widest possible range of activities that have the capacity to attract interest, appreciation, and participation. To meet this aim requires knowledge of the community. This means an analysis of the people in terms of age, sex, ethnic, racial, religious, social, economic, political, educational, and interest categories. From such data the levels of skill, interest, need, previous experience, capacity to perform, and willingness to underwrite a diverse program will be ascertained.

Crafts can provide the variety of experiences necessary to meet the demands and needs of a diverse public. Crafts are so varied that in this category of recreational activity people may find a specific item, subject, or interest that will satisfy whatever need or desire they have.

Availability

Crafts activities are conducted at whatever outlets the community has and under widely differing circumstances. Simple crafts may be offered on playgrounds or at centers operated by the public recreational service department. The school system may offer every grade level, from elementary to postgraduate, in course work developed as an intrinsic part of the school curriculum. Voluntary agency offerings may include simple to complex crafts for artisans, avocationists, workers in specific trades, or others. These crafts activities will be located in YMCAs, Boys and Girls' Clubs, Boy and Girl Scout troop unit pavilions, church basements, or Grange halls. Wherever there are people who constitute the potential participants of the agency, crafts activities will be found. It is a most ubiquitous recreational and educational experience.

The fact that crafts serve equally well as a recreational activity for young children and older adults, for the healthy as well as the ill, for those who are institutionalized or not, indicates the surprising attraction that crafts have for most people. Crafts are both an intellectual and a manual enterprise permitting the most fanciful flights of imagination as well as the routine reproduction of ready-made objects or the simplified construction of models. Crafts accommodate the talented, the near talented, and those who want to participate, but have little or no talent.

Publicity

No crafts program can achieve full participation unless there is a well-thought-out public relations procedure that can inform potential participants about the times, places, costs (if any), materials, media, and so forth. People must know about an activity before they can participate. More importantly, the educational campaign must have an appeal that whets the appetite. The entire promotional preparation should be such that people are drawn to the activity as much out of curiosity as by previously satisfying experiences. Responsible leadership is required to see that every ethical advantage is taken of the diverse means for disseminating information about the program. Care must be taken to assure rapid and accurate information. The use of local mass media and displays in food markets, banks, movie theaters, and other popular places in the community should be used. Flyers, newsletters, posters, bulletin boards in strategic locations—all should be exploited if the widest dissemination of information in the most attractive way possible is to be developed.

Age-group classifications must be carefully fixed so that potential participants may make the best use of their leisure. Readily accessible and available facilities need to be provided so there is little in the way of extra travel to discourage some individuals from participation. In the promotion of a crafts program, the schedule should clearly reflect the needs, interest, skills, and attitudes of learners and craftspersons. Routine and special events should be mixed to maintain the activity's attractiveness. Innovative presentations, displays, and recognition of individuals for excellence should be encouraged. It is desirable that crafts activities become a staple in the overall community recreational program. In this way there will be continual growth and development of individual interests, and each activity will have reciprocal benefits for the other. Where the formal instructional aspect leaves off, the recreational endeavor may carry over.

Dependability of the program to do what it purports to do will be a significant factor in developing participation. When a crafts activity is scheduled to begin at a certain time and place, it must absolutely begin on time and in that location. Many parents may, in fact, send their children to a recreational activity when they feel that they can rely upon the routine operation of the activity to begin and end at specific times. This aspect may also eventuate in the parent becoming a student when crafts projects are made available to adults in the community.

Local Expectations

Conditions, that govern the attitudes of people may be a reflection of local history, custom, or mores. Shifts in employment may alter the make-up of a neighborhood or community so that previous plans have to be modified to accommodate an entirely new set of needs, interests, or circumstances. Political manipulation may freeze supporting funds with the consequent curtailment of planned craft activities. Economic, political, religious, ethnic, or any changing social situations may require strenuous efforts on the part of community agencies to change schedules, initiate new activities, omit certain productions, or operate in different locations under vastly speculative conditions. Employment, housing, and transportation may also force rapid development or accelerating abandonment of proposed craft activities.

Where there are great expectations for certain kinds of craft activities in the local community, such experience must be prepared. Starting from a familiar base permits craft instructors to proceed at a rate commensurate with the individual's ability and desire to learn. Working from the known to unknown quantities and qualities, the individual is introduced to new and unfamiliar items, media, and combinations that should do much to stimulate ideas and enthusiasm. Local expectations may only require that some craft activity is made available, but the adroit recreationist will build upon this conditioning factor in planning the craft activity.

Participant Planning

Perhaps one of the more significant facets of program planning is the role the layman takes in advising and assisting the development of the program. When citizens can be involved with the various considerations and problems that accrue as a program is being fleshed out, they are more appreciative and supportive of the end product. Even greater import should be given to the element of ego development, which results from participant planning. The individual who is intimately connected and concerned with the development of a program will also be concerned about its success. When an individual has taken the time and made the effort to contribute something of a positive nature and shared the exigencies of program planning, he or she is much more likely to work energetically for the ultimate success of the activity than if there had been no assumption of some personal responsibility for such representation.

Participant planning can be encouraged through the use of neighborhood recreational advisory councils; district committees; arts and crafts interest groups; state, county, and local arts councils; and other such legally established or purely advisory laymen's groups that can more completely represent the average citizen's interests and goals. Citizens may be enlisted to assist in community surveys, to determine the precise population composition of the community, to take population samples, and to serve on a variety of boards, commissions, councils, or committees all devised to permit a wider representation of the people to be served. The necessity of offering people a chance to participate in the intricacies of program development and administration cannot be minimized. Perhaps in no other way do the people come to accept responsibility and share the emotional involvement of doing something to help themselves and their peers. Through this method, the citizen is going to see that personal efforts are successful by encouraging participation, requiring cooperation, seeking coordination, and widely supplying information about the program.

Instructional Personnel and Leadership

There seems little doubt that the success of any recreational program is directly attributable to the quality, competency, and adequacy of personnel involved with leadership. No program can operate successfully without leadership. It is the key factor and determines, as no other single element can, the probability of program success.

Employment of a competent staff with well-grounded principles of recreational service education and practical skills assures a comprehensive program. The specialized education, abilities, and interests of recreationists make possible the widest possible offering of crafts. Competent workers soon discover the capabilities and skills of community participants and persuade them to volunteer, thereby additionally emphasizing the significance of leadership as a vital component in program planning.

Among the aspects of leisure that are crucial to the operation of a successful crafts program are those activities dealing with personal understanding and capability. Recognition of individual differences, insight into the needs of those who take part in the activity, and a philosophy that supports the ideal of service to all are essential for crafts program leadership.

Technical Competence

Of necessity, the craft instructor must possess specialized skill, knowledge, and a broad background of craft experiences. Special preparation is required because of the multiplicity of media, possibilities of design, and different technical skills encountered in crafts. The professional preparation of the craft instructor will probably be formalized as he or she receives exposure to aims, ideals, practices, and philosophies within a professional preparatory course in an institution of higher education. However, even before the craft instructor goes to college, there are the informal recreational experiences in crafts, which may assist enormously in the production of the skilled craftsperson. Self-directed activities may also prove of importance in the development of a competent craft instructor.

Understanding People

Although technical competence is one important factor in the make-up of the craft instructor, it is by no means the only attribute they must possess. The craft leader has to go far beyond craftsmanship. He or she must have the ability to communicate with the students. The instructor should be as capable of listening as of telling, of reception as of transmission. All this is confirmed in being able to teach others. The craft instructor starts teaching at the level of understanding the students have attained, and by slow and easy steps brings them to a more effective level of participation. This is performed by carefully noting the clues that each person offers. This means that the instructor is sensitive to both the articulated and unspoken needs of the students. The instructor's understanding of their behavior, attitudes, and expressions of satisfaction or deficiency enables the facilitation of their learning. The ability to empathize with the students often helps the instructor to resolve problems or provide an explanation that can clarify sometimes opaque situations. This sensitivity to people permits the instructor to discern benefits from the efforts of each of those being served, and by doing so the attention of the student can be directed toward recognition of desirable progress or outcomes. On those occasions when students do not detect improvement in their work, the instructor, who is more knowledgeable in the command of media and technique, may be able to pinpoint those areas of progress to further stimulate the students. It is the instructor's responsibility to provide instruction, guidance, and stimulation to students so they continue to make an effort that will eventuate in satisfaction and enjoyment.

The craft instructor should be concerned with differentiating between simple and complex crafts, with determining whether an individual is capable of handling particular activities, and with facilitating the efforts of students by anticipating design or construction problems before they become pronounced. Additionally, however, the instructor is aware of and has concern for the individual's need for recognition and achieving success. He or she should infuse the instructional groups with enthusiasm for the activity and realize that whatever accrues to students through craft endeavors will be valuable despite any imperfections noted in the completed crafts project. Surely the instructor will strive to teach those techniques that will enable the student to fashion crafts objects that are satisfying. More importantly, the process by which the individual may broaden personal horizons will be initiated, thus fostering creativity and arousing the desire for self-improvement. By assisting with the acquisition of skills and stimulating positive attitudes toward craft activities, the craft instructor increases the probability of satisfaction and enjoyment that derives from such participation.

Specialists

Adequacy of craft leadership within a community-operated program is a question of the number of competent personnel needed and available. The type of crafts program to be administered basically depends on how many specialists can be employed. If the community centralizes its crafts activities, it may require fewer specialist personnel to carry out the instructional and guidance function of the program. Of course, this will necessarily restrict the number of potential students (participants) because fewer persons will be able to be accommodated at any one time in a single facility.

In a decentralized program, where crafts activities are provided at neighborhood centers, playgrounds, and through mobile units bringing crafts activities to where the people are, rather than having people congregate to participate, many more craft instructors will be required. Any combination of the two plans is indicative of the philosophy of the operating department or system. If the primary objective is to provide the widest possible range of services, it follows that the combination approach will be used. The recruitment, selection, and the employment of professionals and specialists and the utilization of volunteers to supplement and complement such employed personnel will reflect the agency's understanding of its own function. To do the job there must be a sufficient number of craft instructors.

Leadership may be seen as a combination of special skills and a basic ability to work with and through people. It is concerned with learned abilities to function in instructional and inspirational ways. The professional person has the responsibility to help individuals to develop the skill to work out their own decisions and function as participants in the group rather than as isolets. In accord with this concept, the recreationist performs in ways that will lend support to individuals so they may gain confidence in their own strength and the respect of others while carrying out obligations that group dynamics thrusts upon them.

Volunteers and Part-Time Personnel

All voluntary leadership may be recruited from the general population of any community, but intensive and practical in-service education must be made available so that the purposes of the agency are promoted by those who assume some of the teaching responsibilities. This means setting aside time for the development of volunteer and staff personnel. It can require lectures, workshops, demonstrations, conferences, and other methods by which working personnel may be brought to the most effective and efficient state of readiness in serving people's needs.

Depending on the range and scope of the crafts program, recreationists who have specialized in crafts or commercial specialists may be employed for short term or seasonal work. Where local recreational centers and play-grounds are staffed with permanent personnel, it may be possible to program a complete craft experience ranging from elementary to advanced levels. These activities may be supplemented by traveling craft instructors who cir-culate through the system's program centers. By scheduling the traveling craft instructor one or more times each week at a given center or playground, specific crafts activities may be instructed and greater skill achieved by participants.

When the financial resources of the agency permit, mobile crafts units may be called upon to make the rounds of neighborhoods that are not served by any recreational structure. These mobile units are completely outfitted crafts shops and are capable of providing a facility where competent person-nel are available for guidance and instruction for all skill levels. Such units systematically make scheduled stops after public information has been dis-seminated. In conjunction with other municipal departments, the city block may be closed to traffic while the mobile crafts unit becomes the focus of neighborhood attention. Depending on the extent to which diverse crafts activities are carried to citizens in this manner, specialist personnel may have to be added.

Where the mobile unit operates out of a district or community recre-ational center or school, craft instructors already employed by the depart-ment may be utilized to attract and serve many more people who might otherwise never come to the structure or building. It is even possible to use the traveling craft instructors as the mobile unit force. By adroit scheduling on the part of the central administrative office, such traveling craft instructors may make the rounds of neighborhoods unserved by recreational structures during those hours when they are not otherwise engaged in instructing crafts at the centers.

However it is performed and maintained, the crafts program of any school system or municipality will only be as good as the quality of its leadership. Each crafts group that undertakes instruction in any aspect of crafts must have competent leadership personnel assigned to it. If sufficient numbers of professional personnel cannot be employed, skilled volunteers should be used to supplement the workforce. To the extent that some groups require little in the way of directed instruction, or are essentially self-directing adults, volunteers may be recruited to assist such groups. Craft instructors are basic to program survival, and they must be recompensed in a manner that will lead to the most satisfactory results for all concerned.

Financial Support

The amount of funds made available for the support of any municipal or school crafts program determines the scope or limitation of that program. Almost every aspect of program planning hinges on financial support. No program is possible unless funds are appropriated for all the elements required in operating the activities. Funding determines the quality and number of craft instructors. It permits or restricts the use of areas, facilities, and structures that can accommodate a wide-ranging and diverse program. The very pieces of equipment and supplies, without which no program gets very far, are dependent upon fiscal response. The budget will eventually determine whether all skill levels can be accommodated, how long the crafts sessions will be, whether they can be conducted in public places, whether custodial and maintenance functions can be assured, if there will be service for the homebound, and the type and variety of activities that can be programmed. The richness and variety of activities and when, where, and how such activities will be offered are all predicated on monetary support. A well-conceived budget affording generous support can do much to enhance and make vital any crafts program. Without adequate financial support, little will be done and very nearly total negation of program aims is likely.

Although it is true that there are many low-cost crafts activities, the funds necessary for leadership, facilities, and so forth should not be stinted. The community will benefit immeasurably from the fiscal support given to maintain and operate the crafts program in an effective manner. The benefits to people in terms of appreciation, skill development, and personal satisfaction far outweigh the monetary allotment required. Professional leaders may be able to cut down on the expenditures necessary for materials and equipment, they may be able to utilize make-shift spaces, and they will surely be able to recruit volunteers to assist in the program, but there is no substitute for high-quality personnel. This is where the major portion of the money must go.

Space and Facilities

Some crafts activities may occur on vacant lots, in parks, on playgrounds, at beaches, in camps, in vacant lofts, in offices, in church social halls, at libraries, in schools, and in other likely places. Where communities have realized the need and heeded the demand for the support of crafts activities, special facilities have been constructed. These craft centers are devoted to the operation of activities throughout the year. Such centers may maintain fully equipped rooms designed to offer a variety of crafts activities of particular types. Thus, there are rooms set aside for woodworking, ceramics, sculpturing, automotive, electrical, and leather crafts, as well as metalworking, furniture repair, or other craft forms. Those areas designed for one type of craft make possible the development of a highly specialized program concerned with individuals who may begin as novices and, in time, emerge as master craftspeople.

Such facilities feature the capability of maintaining a huge stock of supplies and equipment that can be utilized for every type and level of craft. Additionally, they serve as focal points for specialized interest and intent.

Centralized facilities enable the scheduling of crafts throughout the year and may be programmed to offer the widest possible range of crafts. Centers may be opened and accessible to the public from early morning until late at night every day throughout the year. The public's demand for such activity may more easily be met on this basis. Many skill levels, various crafts opportunities, and entire courses may be programmed simultaneously because there is no competition for space by any other recreational activity beyond crafts.

Typically, however, crafts activities must share space in a general recreational center with all other recreational activities that can be programmed indoors. More often than not, a crafts room or shop will be part of the center. Such a room can be well equipped for sophisticated craft experiences or, as is usually the case, be capable of accommodating very simple and basic craft activities. Where there is a general crafts room, many different crafts may be scheduled, but the probability of directed learning is limited when many different crafts are being performed at various skill levels. Of course, such activities may be more formally organized so that even when diverse crafts are programmed, those participants with the same skill levels may be arranged in groups or courses.

It is not unusual to find that no special crafts area is reserved and that crafts activities must compete for space in whatever nooks and crannies are available. When no special rooms are planned, little may be expected insofar as complex crafts or crafts that require machine tools or permanent equipment are concerned. Crafts that require nothing in the way of permanent equipment may do well, although there is a need for storage space. Leatherwork, sewing, knitting, model construction, and other handicrafts may be carried on in almost any space available. However, activities that need fixed or large tools, benches, and other nonportable equipment must be either neglected or handicapped for space.

The use of schools as public recreational centers has opened up excellent facilities for citizens. Usually centrally situated and serving local neighborhoods, districts, or communities, schools have special designated shops or laboratories that can be used. Any classroom may be opened and used for simple craft activities. The shops, when available, permit the schools to become crafts centers and also to perform as general recreational centers. When schools are employed within the public recreational service system, it may be feasible to hire the teachers who normally operate the shops, thereby reducing possible friction and disruption when crafts activities are conducted after school hours.

Craft Activities

Any number of crafts may be scheduled for a comprehensive program. Craft varieties are so numerous that thousands of books have been written about specific types. This section provides an introduction to the crafts that may be offered to those who wish to participate.

Fabric Dyeing

Elementary craft forms are useful for gaining the attention of children. One example of this is the use of dyeing techniques. Batiking, for example, utilizes wax to cover areas of a design that is not to be dyed during the dipping

Figure 9.1 Tie Dyeing

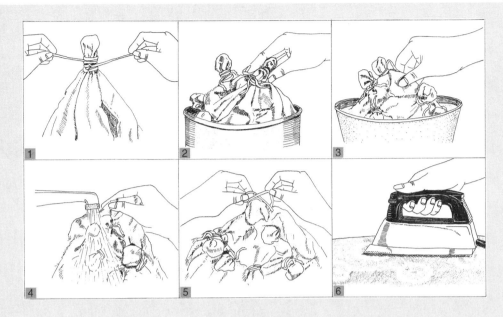

Materials: string, cloth, dye, large containers, water, stirring stick, iron.

1. Gather small bunches of material and tie them with string.
2. Place the tied fabric in a container of warm water. Remove fabric from the warm water and wring out the excess water.
3. Dip the tied fabric in the dye and stir for about three minutes.
4. Rinse the dyed fabric under cold water.
5. Remove the string and allow the fabric to drip dry until damp.
6. Iron the material with a warm iron.

operation. The wax can be removed and applied in different areas, forming a new design. The material is dipped again, adding another color to the design for an interesting effect.

Cover the working surface with newspaper. On a large piece of newsprint, use crayons to lay out the design for the batik. When the design is ready, tape a piece of muslin to a cardboard surface cut from an old container. Lay out the design on the piece of muslin. With a paintbrush, apply heated paraffin or beeswax to those areas of the design that are to remain free of the first dye color. When the desired areas are covered, the fabric is dipped into a bath of cold dye. If more than one color is used, lighter colors should be used first. Allow the material to sit in the dye bath for a sufficient length of time (see package directions). Remove the fabric from the dye. The wax is removed by scrubbing the fabric in a bath of warm water. Apply a second coat of wax, covering parts of the dyed areas to form a new design. The fabric is dipped in the dye bath of another color for the required length of time. Remove the wax and hang the fabric up to dry. The fabric will be covered with a multicolored pattern. Additional colors can be added to the design by repeating the process with different colored dyes. A crackling effect can be obtained by twisting the wax surface. Paraffin wax will crack, although beeswax will not. The wax will crack much more easily if it is cold.

Tie-dyeing is a craft that appeals to teenagers and others. In the tie-dyeing method, fabric is dipped in the dye bath after having sections twisted and tied tightly with string or cord (**Figure 9.1**). Tightly tying the material prevents the dye from penetrating sections of the fabric, resulting in areas that retain the original color of the cloth. When the fabric is untied a two-colored design will appear on the surface. The fabric can be retied and dyed with another color or different intensity of the same color. The fabric to be dyed should be free of all sizing. Sizing is removed by washing the fabric with soap and water.

The fabric can be tied in a number of different ways to obtain a wide variety of designs. If this is the first attempt at tie-dyeing, it is advisable to practice on a piece of scrap material. A circle design is obtained by picking up the fabric from the middle and folding the material as evenly as possible into a strip. Tie string tightly around the material at different intervals. After dyeing, these tied areas will appear as circles the same color as the original fabric. Varied shapes are obtained by tying marbles, pebbles, or different shapes of hardwood in the fabric. The material can be rolled into a tube and tied with string to create a series of strips.

When the fabric is tied, it is ready to be dipped in the dye bath. Mix the dye according to the directions that come with the package. Dip the tied fabric into a container of warm water before dyeing. Remove from the warm water and wring out the excess water. Dip the tied fabric in the dye mixture and stir constantly with a stick for about 3 minutes. Remove the fabric from the dye and rinse in cold water. Do not leave the fabric in the dye too long or the color will penetrate the tied areas, destroying the design.

A second color is added, if desired, by removing the string and tying the fabric in new locations. The fabric is dipped into the new dye solution and rinsed out in cold water. The fabric is allowed to drip dry until damp and then pressed with a hot iron, which helps set the color.

Print Making

Printing, silkscreen printing, and etching are all techniques to bring an added dimension to the creative process for those who are interested. Linoleum, cardboard, vegetable, stick, leaf, and sponge printing are common to most recreational crafts programs. However, silkscreen printing and etching are usually neglected in the planning of activities for these programs. Included here are detailed descriptions of these processes so that they may be incorporated in the development of the crafts program. They do not require any more equipment or skill than linoleum printing.

The important point to remember in any of the printmaking techniques is that they should be used to reproduce more than one copy from the original form. Too many crafts programs have children spend hours cutting the design to make a single print. Children should be encouraged to use a single design multiple times to create an overall design or to use a combination of designs to decorate a surface. Explore the different techniques presented here and see how they can be used to enrich any recreational crafts program.

Linoleum Block Printing

Linoleum block printing is the most difficult of the printing techniques. Therefore, it would be advisable for a beginner to try a simple method of printing (vegetable, stick) before attempting it. The beginner should first have experience with cutting the design into some material that is soft and easy to cut. A potato or carrot will be most suitable for the beginner to learn the "how's and why's" of block printing. A gum eraser, a discarded bottle cork, or a Styrofoam meat container also may be used to learn the techniques of block printing.

Linoleum-cutting tools are needed to carve the block print. These tools have replaceable blades, so that dull or broken blades can be easily and quickly replaced. The set of cutters consist of U-shaped and V-shaped gouges of different sizes, a flat chisel, and a cutting knife. The U-shaped gouges are used to scoop out large areas, while the V-shaped gouges are used to cut fine lines for detail. The chisel is used to smooth flat areas, and the knife is used to trim edges for clear, sharp lines. A few well-cared-for sets of linoleum-cutting tools will serve the needs of most recreational programs.

Selecting a design for the block print is the most important aspect of the printing technique. Block printing in most recreational programs too often means copying designs from Christmas or birthday cards. Participants in any crafts program should be encouraged to create a picture or design for their block print. The inspiration can come from a film, story, or experience. It may be the result of a discussion on nature, the future, or some other subject.

Draw the sketch or design on a piece of paper the size of the desired block. When the sketch is completed, it is ready for transferring to the block. Place a piece of carbon paper on top of the block with the carbon side down. Place the sketch on top of the carbon paper and tape to the block with masking tape. Use a pencil to trace the sketch on the linoleum surface. Darken the carbon impression with a pencil so that all the details and outlines are clear and easy to follow. Words or letters should be in the negative on the block if they are to print in the positive.

The cutting is done on a bench hook made of a flat board that has a strip of wood fastened across each end, with one strip on the top and the other on the bottom surface. The bench hook is held against the edge of the tabletop by the bottom strip, while the top strip provides an edge against which the block is held for cutting. This device protects the working surface and makes the cutting process easier and safer. The hand holding the block must be behind the cutting tool. This will reduce the chances of injury should the cutting tool slip.

Place the block on the bench hook. Select the most appropriate cutter for accomplishing the desired cut. Experimentation on a scrap piece of linoleum will enable the individual to determine the characteristics and advantages of each cutting tool. When using the cutters, always make a thin, shallow cut in the linoleum around the design. The small V-shaped tool works very well, and for this reason is usually referred to as the "liner." After the outline of the design has been cut, take the large V-shaped gouge and make a deeper cut directly over the fine cut made with the liner. Be careful not to cut into the inked area.

Remove those linoleum surfaces that are not part of the inked areas of the design (**Figure 9.2**). The cuts should be deep enough toward the burlap backing so that just the design stands out in relief. The U-shaped gouge is used to make long cuts from the edge of the design outward toward the edge of the piece of linoleum. These cuts should overlap so that no high areas or ridges remain. When cutting around the edge of the design, do not make the cuts perpendicular to the surface of the linoleum, but slope them gradually outward from the outline of the design. This sloped edge adds strength to the printing surface, and reduces the possibility of the edges breaking down during the printing operation.

After the block is completely carved, it is ready for inking. Cover the working surface with old newspapers and prepare an inking slab. The inking slab can be a piece of Masonite, Formica, metal, or plastic, or even a cookie sheet on which a small amount of printing ink can be squeezed. Water-based inks can be used for most activities; however, oil-based inks should be used for printing on textiles or any other surfaces that may be exposed to water.

Figure 9.2 Linoleum Block Printing

Materials: linoleum block, paper to be imprinted, printing ink, pencil, brayer, inking plate, linoleum cutter.

1. Draw the design onto the block.
2. Cut around the outline with a V-shaped cutter.
3. Cut away large areas with a U-shaped cutter.
4. Finish details with the V-shaped cutter.
5. Roll out ink on the inking plate.
6. Apply ink to the design.

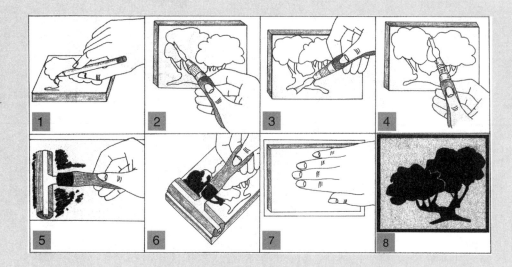

7. Press the inked design against the surface to be imprinted.
8. Set the printed design aside to dry.

Water-based inks can be cleaned with water, whereas oil-based inks require special solvents, such as paint thinner. Roll a brayer across the ink until it has a "tacky" sound and feel. Transfer the ink from the slab to the block with the brayer. Ink the block by rolling the brayer across it in both directions until the entire surface is evenly covered.

The inked block now is ready for printing. Place the material to be imprinted on top of a 1-inch padded surface of newspaper. The padded surface will compensate for the fact that the surfaces may not be flat and even. Pick up the block and carefully place it onto the surface to be imprinted with the inked side down. Press it gently but firmly against the surface. The back surface of the block can be rubbed with the hand. If the ink has been applied correctly and the padded surface used, the printing of the block design should require only finger pressure for a good-quality print. Care should be taken not to smudge the ink when removing the block from the printed surface.

The print should be checked to see if additional cutting is desirable. If additional cuts are required, wipe the block clean with a paper towel or cloth and return it to the bench hook for further cutting. If no additional cutting is needed, the printing operation can continue.

Colored inks can be used to make the block print more interesting and attractive. Another technique that adds to the quality of a print is the cutting procedure used. Instead of leaving large areas of solid or blank design, a textured technique can be used to break up solid areas. This technique makes the print more appealing. Students should be encouraged to explore with different types of printing. Emphasis should not be placed on the finished product but rather on understanding the characteristics and properties of the materials used in the process. Children have an intuitive feeling for design and need opportunities to foster this ability. They cannot succeed if forced to concentrate on finishing a block print without any provisions for experimentation with the materials and process.

Silkscreen Printing

Silkscreen printing is a process in which the stencil bearing the design to be reproduced is permanently affixed to a screen of silk, organdy, or some other meshed material. Colored paints, inks, or other printing mediums are forced through the screen with a squeegee and deposited on the printing surface, thus forming an impression of the original design. The technique is known as the silkscreen process because, originally, silk was exclusively used for the screen.

MATERIALS. *Silkscreen Frames.* Silkscreen frames vary in size and are constructed from wood or cardboard. Some frames are hinged to a piece of $^3/_4$-inch plywood to control movement during printing. For simple printing operations, the frame does not need to be hinged to a base. The hinged frame is effective for stencil designs utilizing more than one color.

The frame is covered with a coarse or fine meshed material, usually silk, nylon, nylon hosiery, or organdy. The mesh of the material used for a screen should not be too fine or it will clog during printing.

A simple frame can be constructed by cutting away the area from the bottom or top of a cardboard candy box. This open area is covered with a piece of meshed material pulled smooth and stapled to the sides. The edges around the opening are taped to the meshed material with masking tape to prevent the paint or ink from seeping under the frame, thereby spoiling the design. The cardboard frame has only limited use and is not as durable as a wooden frame. However, with young children and crayon-and-paper stencil designs, the cardboard frame is satisfactory.

A wooden frame can be constructed from 1×1 in. wooden strips mitered at the corners and fastened together with glue and nails. The frame size may vary with the design to be printed. The frame is covered with the meshed material stretched smooth and tightened over the frame and secured with staples. To secure the screen evenly, begin at the center of one side; staple, pull the material tight, and staple the center on the opposite side. Repeat this process on each end of the frame, then work the material from the center to the corners of the frame, stretching and stapling the material until the frame is covered.

Squeegee. The squeegee is pulled across the stencil design, forcing the ink through the screen onto the surface to be decorated. Squeegees can be constructed or purchased and should be as wide as the frame being used.

Inks and Paints. Both oil- and water-based inks can be used for silk screening. Oil-based inks and paints require special solvents for thinning and cleaning, while water-based inks and paints require only water. Colors are opaque when thick, and transparent when thinned. One color can be printed over another color when the first is dry. Dark colors are usually applied over light colors.

Fabrics. Any surface that will accept the paint or ink can be used for silk screening. Sized fabrics should be washed before they are imprinted; unwashed fabrics will not retain color when washed.

PROCEDURE. *How to Cut a Silkscreen Stencil.* Make an accurate drawing for the design on a piece of paper. With masking tape secure the four corners to a flat surface. Place a piece of lacquer film over the design with the lacquered side up and secure the corners with masking tape. The film should have a perimeter about 1 inch larger than the design. The design, clearly visible through the transparent lacquer film, is ready to be cut.

The design must be cut through the lacquer coating only. It should not be cut through the paper backing, which is a temporary carrier for the lacquer coating until it is transferred to the screen.

The stencil knife is used like a pen, and the operation is the same as tracing. A light even stroke is used. The stencil knife is held at an angle. A straightedge should be used as a guide for cutting straight lines while circles and arcs are cut with the aid of dividers. Irregular lines are cut freehand with a stencil knife, or a French curve can be used as a guide. Thin, straight, parallel lines are cut in one operation with a ruling pen. The points are set to the correct width and the lines are cut by pulling the pen alone the straightedge. Square or sharply intersecting lines are cut across corners.

When the complete outline of a part of the design has been cut, that area of the film is carefully stripped from the paper backing. To strip the film from the backing, insert the point of the stencil knife under one corner of the cut portion and carefully peel off the lacquer film which is in the traced area. Continue cutting and peeling the film until the design is completed. If a completely outlined area is cut through the paper backing, that area will fall out.

Attaching Lacquer Film to the Screen. To join the lacquer film to the screen, place the lacquer side up on a flat, smooth working surface. Then place the screen over the top of the film with the design in the desired position, so that the screen touches the film. Pour a small quantity of adhesive liquid (lacquer thinner) into a shallow tray or saucer. Moisten a cloth with the liquid and dampen a small portion of the screen. Immediately wipe this area dry with a second and larger cloth. If the adhesive liquid is allowed to settle, it will dissolve the lacquer film, thus ruining the design. Continue to moisten small areas of the screen and dry them immediately. Use a light rubbing motion to dry the screen and continue rubbing until the solution has evaporated. When the film has been attached to the screen, allow several minutes for drying.

Carefully place the stencil knife under one of the corners of the backing sheet and separate it from the film. Hold the paper backing with the fingers and slowly peel if off. Work slowly to prevent tearing. Should the film start to tear, stop and apply more adhesive liquid to that area. After the paper backing has been peeled off, check the design for any imperfections in the film. Imperfections are touched up by applying a lacquer filler to the area with a brush or pen.

Mask out the open spaces between the edges of the film in the frame with paper and masking tape. The inside edges should be taped so that the tape, which is first creased in half lengthwise, is half on the wood and half on the screen. This will seal the inside edges of the frame and prevent any paint from seeping under the frame.

Printing a Silkscreen Design. A smooth, level, and clean surface covered with a sheet of heavy paper should be used for printing. Before starting to print, mark the position of the two upper corners of the frame on the surface. These marks are not necessary if the frame is hinged. The position of the sheets to be printed must be marked for the proper placement of the design. This will ensure that the design is printed in the same position on all the sheets. Raised guides may be used where they do not interfere with the design.

Place enough ink or paint for several impressions in the upper margin of the screen. Use a rubber squeegee of sufficient length to reach across the design and push the ink over the open design, pressing the ink through to the sheet below. The squeegee is slanted slightly toward the operator as it is pulled with a side-to-side or wavy motion across the screen. This technique produces a more uniform impression.

After the sheet is printed, remove it by lifting the frame and inserting a new sheet in position against the guides. Each printed sheet should be set aside to dry. Sheets should not be piled one over another, because they will "offset"; that is, paint will be transferred from one sheet to the back of the sheet which is placed over the wet sheet.

Clean the Screen. The frame and squeegee should be thoroughly cleaned when the printing operation is completed. Oil-based colors are cleaned with a solvent. Remove the excess color from the screen with the squeegee or rubber spatula and return to the original container. Place the screen on old newspapers and press the solvent through the screen onto the newspaper with the squeegee or cloth. Continue until the screen is free of all color particles. Check the mash of the screen by holding it up to the light. Clear any clogged areas by rubbing the screen with a cloth soaked with a solvent. Soap and water can be used for the final cleaning.

To clean water-based colors, substitute cool water for the solvent and use the same procedures as for the oil-based colors. Remove stubborn spots by scrubbing the spotted areas with soap and water. Some screens cannot be cleaned, and others are not worth cleaning. These screens should be removed from the frame and discarded.

Dry Point Etching

The copy for an etching should be composed of fine lines made by utilizing a pen or pencil sketching technique. A line sketch lends itself to etching, whereas a design with solid areas lends itself to either block or silkscreen printing. Photographs, illustrations, and pictures containing solid areas must be converted into a pen or pencil line sketch or printed using another medium. The design to be imprinted must be etched in the negative, that is, in reverse, in order to produce a positive impression. Hence, the original copy from which the etching will be traced must be transferred into the negative before it is copied. To make a negative sketch, place a sheet of carbon paper face up under the copy or design and fasten the corners with masking tape. Then trace all the lines (**Figure 9.3**). The carbon impression on the back of the sheet will be in the negative. The design will face in the opposite direction when the sheet is turned over. If the design is on transparent paper, it will need only to be turned over to be in the negative.

Place a piece of clear plastic over the design and secure the four corners with masking tape. With a sharp scribing tool, an awl, or a compass point, scratch the lines of the design into the plastic. For artistic effect, a series of short lines should be used rather than a simple long line. The cuts are made by varying the pressure as the scriber is drawn over the plastic surface. Each line becomes a small trench with sidewalls to hold the ink.

The depth of the cut determines the intensity of the line printed. Deep cuts produce dark lines, whereas shallow ones result in light lines. Dark and shaded areas are obtained by carving and etching lines close together or cross-hatching an area. Cross-hatching consists of scribing a series of lines in one direction and then imposing a second series of lines in the opposite direction, crossing the first lines. Care should be taken not to remove the burrs formed as the lines are etched into the plastic. The burrs hold the ink in the etched lines. The progress and results of the etching may be observed by

Figure 9.3 Dry Point Etching

Materials: sheet of plastic, masking tape, carbon paper, scribing tool, ink, piece of cloth, water, paper (uncoated).

1. Transfer a design into the negative by using a piece of carbon paper.
2. Secure the design and clear plastic to working surface with masking tape.
3. Scratch the design into the plastic with a sharp scribing tool.
4. Press ink into the etched areas with a wadded cloth.
5. Wipe the surface clean, leaving only the etched areas filled with ink.
6. Wet a sheet of paper.

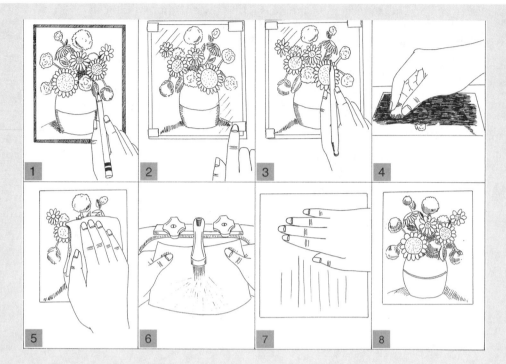

7. Place the paper over the inked surface and rub it to force the paper into the etched areas.
8. Finished print.

sliding a sheet of colored paper between the plate and the copy. After the scribing is completed, the plastic plate is ready to be printed.

The process of printing a dry point etching is called "gravure" or printing from any recessed surface. It is the opposite of linoleum block printing, which is performed using a raised surface. Ink the plate by pressing the ink into the etched areas with a wadded cloth. Apply the ink in a circular motion, making sure that all the etched lines are filled with ink.

After the plate is inked, the surface of the plate should be wiped clean of ink and ink smudges, leaving only the etched areas filled with ink. This will ensure the print has a clean background, with only the design actually printing.

Place the inked plate face up on a flat surface. Take a sheet of uncoated paper, which is first dampened with water to soften it, and place it over the plastic plate. The dampened surface makes it easier to pick up the ink from the etched surface, because the fibers are raised when wet. Place several sheets of blotting paper over the dampened paper and apply heavy pressure by rubbing the heel of the hand over the surface, forcing the paper into the scratches so that the sheet will pick up the ink. Separate the paper from the etched surface and check the print; additional lines may be added to the plate to obtain the desired effect. Two or three impressions may be made from one inking of the etched plate. The final print should be sharp and clear, free of any ink smudges. Set the print aside to dry before handling.

Clean the plate with a solvent. Cleaning will prevent the ink from hardening in the etched surface, which would make it impossible to make any additional prints of the design.

Papier-Mâché

Papier-mâché can be used to create interesting and beautiful objects. Many objects that are not well done with papier-mâché are the result of poor utilization of materials. This technique has been used for many centuries to create attractive jewelry boxes, trays, and other pieces. The ancient Chinese experimented with ways of tearing paper, mixing it with glue, and shaping and molding the papier-mâché into interesting forms. Today, Japan, Mexico, India, and Portugal produce large quantities of papier-mâché articles for export. Toys, vases, lamps, candleholders, and decorative furniture pieces are a few of the items made from papier-mâché and sold around the world.

Almost any type of paper can be used to construct an object from papier-mâché; newspaper, paper towels, tissue paper, or facial tissues are all suitable. Cloth or an old bed sheet can be used to add strength and texture to an object. Cardboard and egg cartons may be cut up, soaked, and turned into paper pulp.

A wide variety of other kinds of papers are used for adding decorative touches. Wallpaper, gift-wrapping paper, magazine pictures, colored tissue, and colored comics can all be used in a number of ways to add to the appearance of an object.

A number of different paste mixtures can be used as the holding agent when constructing any object with papier-mâché. The selection of the paste mixture usually depends upon available materials and personal preference. Strong holding agents, such as wheat paste and diluted white glue, should be used for large and complex objects.

Four basic techniques can be used to construct an object from papier-mâché. The most common is the layer-on-layer technique. Strips of paper are dipped into a liquid paste and then pressed and formed over a base. A second technique utilizes several layers of paper pasted together to make one strong flexible sheet. These laminated sheets of paper can be shaped or molded over a base, or they can be shaped and formed separately. They can also be torn and applied to a base. The third technique utilizes a pulpy, claylike substance that can be molded like clay. The fourth technique utilizes pieces of yarn or string pasted over a removable base to form a cagelike shape.

Mixing procedures to produce a holding agent may be performed in the following manner:

- *Flour mixture:* Mix 1 cup of flour with enough water to make a thin mixture. Heat over a low flame, stirring constantly, for a few minutes. When the mixture is cool, add a few drops of oil of wintergreen or formaldehyde as a preservative.
- *Wheat paste mixture:* Add 1 part of commercial wallpaper paste or wheat paste to 10 parts of water. Mix until the consistency of heavy cream.
- *Starch paste:* Mix 1 tablespoon of starch with 1 tablespoon of cold water. Add 1 cup of boiling water while rapidly stirring the mixture. The mixture should be the consistency of heavy cream.

Figure 9.4 Papier-Mâché Base

1. Crushed newspaper.
2. Cardboard box.
3. Rolled newspaper.
4. Chicken wire.
5. Laminated paper.
6. Wooden armature.

- *Liquid white glue paste:* Mix one part of liquid white glue with one part of water.
- *Liquid starch paste:* Mix 1 quart of liquid starch with 2 tablespoons of salt, sand, or plaster.

Selecting a Base

Papier-mâché can be used to cover a base made from almost any type of material. The importance of the base is directly related to how it minimizes the number of layers of pasted strips or paper pulp to obtain the desired finished shape. One of the following bases can be used to construct a papier-mâché object (**Figure 9.4**):

- *Removable base:* The base can be coated with a separator (petroleum jelly, waxed paper, or a sheet of wet paper) to keep it from sticking to the papier-mâché. If the base object is completely covered, it can be removed by cutting the papier-mâché in half and pasting the two halves together with masking tape or pasted paper strips.
- *Deflatable base:* An inflatable balloon or beach ball can be used as a base and then removed from the core by deflating. When covering the base with pasted paper strips, leave an opening around the intake valve. The surface must be coated with a separator.
- *Permanent base:* A base may become an important part of the finished object. For example, a plastic bottle can be used as a base, but it also provides a waterproof lining for holding water.
- *Chicken wire base:* Chicken wire is an excellent material to utilize as a base for papier-mâché objects because it can be bent and pressed

into shape. When the desired shape is obtained, strips of dry newspaper are woven into the chicken wire to provide a base for the pasted strips.

- *Rolled or crushed paper base:* Paper can be rolled or crushed into balls, cylinders, and ovals and then held together with string or masking tape. The shapes can be fastened together with string or masking tape to form the base for a great number of papier-mâché objects.
- *Armature base:* Wood, cardboard, hardboard, or wire can be utilized to make a stick figure resemblance of the desired object. Plastic bottles, tin cans, and wire can be used to build up the armature.
- *Cardboard base:* Cardboard boxes of varying sizes can be cut and folded and pieces taped together to form a wide variety of shapes.

Modifying the Base Shape

The base shape can be modified by using rolled, crushed, or cut paper. A balloon can be made to take on the appearance of an animal by using one or a combination of the following techniques to obtain the desired features:

- *Rolled paper:* Strips of paper can be rolled into a cylinder to form legs, horns, or other necessary shapes. Take three or four strips of newspaper the required width and roll them into a cylinder. The diameter of the cylinder can be changed by increasing or decreasing the number of paper strips.
- *Crushed paper:* Newspaper can be crushed into a ball to form a head, cheeks, jaw, or any other desired shape. Take a sheet of newspaper and crush it into a ball. The size of the paper sheet and number of sheets will determine how large the ball will be.
- *Cut paper:* Layers of newspaper or cardboard can be cut into a variety of shapes and used to add a new dimension to the base. Take three or four layers of newspaper or a piece of cardboard and cut out the desired shape.

Attaching the Shape

Hold the shape (leg, ear, jaw, etc.) with one hand while fixing it in place with a pasted strip of newspaper, string, or masking tape. Some shapes will require additional strips to hold them securely before the surface can be built up.

Once the rough shape is attached, additional strips can be applied to the surface to obtain the desired shape. The strips are added by running them from the base around the shape and back to the base in one direction and then in the opposite direction.

LAYER-ON-LAYER TECHNIQUE. Before starting to work with papier-mâché, cover the working surface with newspaper. A covered area protects the original surface and makes it easier to clean up after the project is finished.

Pick up a piece of newspaper and tear it into strips that are about 1 inch wide. Strips will tear evenly if the newspaper is torn with the grain. Torn strips are preferred to cut ones because the rough edges will mesh together, forming a smoother surface. Tear about 50 strips and store them in a cardboard box for easy handling.

Prepare the paste. If the paste was mixed earlier, stir again before using because the flour will settle on the bottom of the mixture after standing for about 20 minutes.

Hold a strip of newspaper between the thumb and index finger. Dip the strip into the pan of paste, making sure that it is completely covered with the mixture. Lift the strip from the pan and run it gently between the index finger and the middle finger to remove any excess paste.

Take the prepared base—crushed paper, actual object, plastic container, chicken wire, armature, or cardboard box—and cover the surface with pasted strips. With your fingers smooth out the edges of the pasted newspaper strips. After the entire base has been covered, a second layer should be placed on top of this wet layer. The strips for the second layer should run in the opposite direction.

Add three more layers of pasted strips to the surface and be sure to run each layer in a different direction. The last layer can be strips of paper towel, cloth, or wrapping paper to obtain a different surface. Remember that strips should be smooth.

PAPER PULP TECHNIQUE. Paper pulp is a claylike substance made from bits of paper that have been soaked in water and mixed with paste. The water–paste solution breaks down the paper and turns it into a pulpy, malleable substance. The paper pulp can be shaped or formed like clay and is very suitable for modeling small figurines and objects. It is also used to add texture to objects constructed by one of the other two techniques.

Tear newspaper, paper towels, facial tissues, egg cartons, or paper napkins into small bits and place them in water to soak overnight (**Figure 9.5**). The next day, pour off the water and squeeze the pulp until it is semi-moist. To

Figure 9.5 Paper Pulp

Materials: plastic container, paper toweling, facial tissues, wheat paste, water, paintbrush, paint.

1. Tear paper towel or facial tissue into small pieces.
2. Soak the small pieces of paper towel or tissue in a mixture of water and wheat paste.
3. Drain and squeeze out the excess water from the pulp.
4. Pinch the ball of pulp into a shape (*a* and *b*).
5. Paint the finished form.

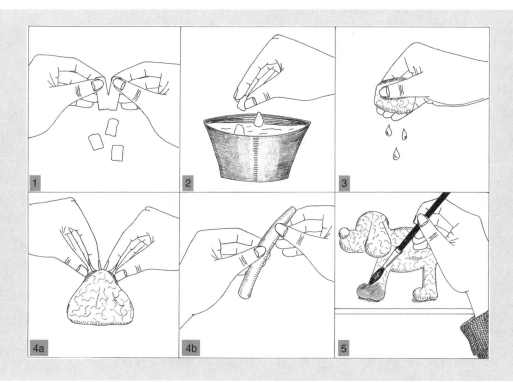

this pulpy substance, add enough paste to make a claylike mixture. Knead the mixture until the paste and paper fibers are thoroughly mixed. The paper pulp now is ready to be worked into the desired shape. It can be formed or shaped by using the pinch method.

The pinch method is used when forming simple shapes. The desired shape is actually pinched from the paper pulp. Each end is pinched, pulled, or pushed in various ways to obtain the desired shape.

Set the finished object to one side to dry. A piece of screening or wire over a box makes a good drying rack for paper pulp objects. The wire rack allows air to circulate around all surfaces, resulting in even drying.

Finishing Papier-Mâché

The possibilities of finishing papier-mâché objects are almost limitless. It is important to select materials and colors that complement the finished project. The surface can be covered with Suede Tex (a commercial product) where a durable suede finish is desired. A wide variety of other materials can be used to decorate a papier-mâché object—marbles for eyes, felt for ears, shirt stays for fangs, yarn for a lion's mane, or cotton for a rabbit's fur.

The dried surface should be sanded with fine sandpaper to smooth any rough edges before it is painted. Gesso is an opaque liquid that can be used as an undercoat to cover the paper surface. White latex paint can be used as a substitute for gesso. Gesso can be made by mixing 1 cup of evaporated milk with the powder from four sticks of chalk. Another mixture combines one part of white powdered tempera paint with one part of evaporated milk. Both mixtures are stirred until creamy.

Figure 9.6 Papier-Mâché Globe

Materials: balloon, string, newspaper, wheat paste, paintbrush, paint, plastic container.

1. Inflate a balloon and tie the stem.
2. Tear newspaper into 1-inch strips.
3. Dip the strips in wheat paste and remove excess by running the pasted strips between the fingers.
4. Apply the strips to the surface of the balloon.
5. Remove the balloon from the newspaper sphere.
6. Paint the continents on the sphere.

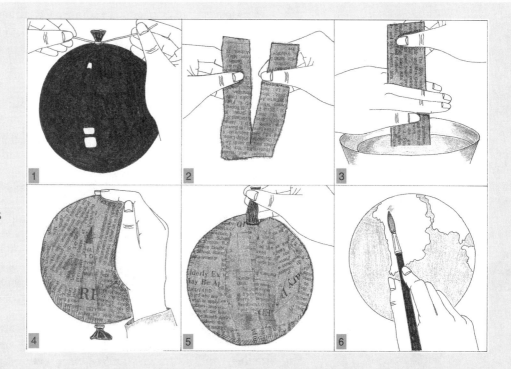

The paints most commonly used to decorate papier-mâché objects are tempera, poster paints, water colors, acrylics, oil paints, latex paints, and enamels. Each of these paints has its own characteristics and quality. For example, tempera paints have good covering qualities and are easy for children to work with. Enamels give the surface a glossy finish. Water-based paints are easy to apply and dry fast, and they are easy to clean up after use. Oil paints and enamels are extremely durable and make the surface water resistant. It is important to select paint for its particular effect, availability, or cost.

Sculpturing, Casting, and Mosaics

Sculpturing, casting, and mosaics are three areas important to any crafts program. Wax, Zonalite, plastic, soap, and Styrofoam are inexpensive materials that can be used for subtractive sculpturing, which is the process of cutting away those areas not essential to the finished form. It is one of the earliest forms of expression and dates back to the ability to fashion tools capable of carving wood and stone. Sculpturing need not be limited to solid forms; some interesting ones can be created from a piece of wire. Children and others enjoy manipulating wire, toothpicks, or wooden scraps into a wide variety of different forms. These materials enable participants to explore in an entirely new and different direction.

Casting provides participants with another process of reproducing a sculpture. A mold is made in sand or from rubber, and a liquid mixture is poured into the cavity. The mixture is allowed to harden, forming a reproduction of the original sculpture. Today many of the world's outstanding sculptures are cast from an original model carved from Styrofoam or another inexpensive material.

Mosaics can be used to decorate a flat surface. Although they are not used to construct a three-dimensional sculpture, they can be used to form some attractive two-dimensional decorations.

Sculpturing

Carving with soap can be fun. It requires only a limited number of tools and materials. This is an excellent introduction for children and other beginners. It is important to acquire a feel for the material before trying to carve an object or form that combines one or more of the basic shapes.

Take a bar of soap and prepare it for carving. Letters and raised designs should be scraped off to form a flat surface. All of the surfaces should be scraped to remove the powder coating. This outer coating is drier than the inner core, and its removal will prevent warping or bending during and after the carving of the object.

Place carbon paper, carbon side down, on top of the wide surface of the bar of soap. Put a piece of paper with the design on top of the piece of carbon paper. Check to see that the soap, carbon paper, and design are in correct order and that the edges are even. Secure the carbon paper and design sheet to the soap with masking tape.

With a pencil, trace the design, being careful not to tear the paper or smear the carbon. Remove the design sheet and carbon paper from the top of the soap. The design should appear on the surface of the soap. If the design is not clear or is smeared, a thin layer of soap can be scraped off the surface and the tracing procedure repeated.

When the design has been successfully transferred to the soap, it is ready to be carved. Right-handers should start carving in the upper right-hand corner; left-handers start in the upper left-hand corner. It is important to leave a one-quarter-inch border around the design when cutting out the general outline.

Start carving by gently cutting away soap around the outline of the design with a knife. Cut down through the soap from the top to bottom edge, being careful not to cut too close to the design. When the rough shape is obtained, the finished carving is ready to be started. Cut from the outer edge of the soap in toward the design. As the cuts get closer to the outline of the design, care should be taken not to cut into the finished shape.

Cuttings should be made on all sides of the shape so that the various parts of the object are gradually finished. Keep checking the design by rotating the object to be sure that it looks correct from all directions. When the carver feels the form or object has the desired shape, it is time to start finishing the small details. Surface details can be added by using either a knife or an orangewood stick (**Figure 9.7**).

This is also a good time to smooth out any rough surfaces with a knife. Rough edges also can be removed by placing the soap in slowly running water and rubbing the edges with the fingers. If water is used to smooth the rough edges, set the carving aside for about a half-hour to dry.

The finished object can be polished by rubbing the surface with a paper napkin, fingertips, or the palm of the hand. Polishing will give the finished object a shiny appearance. Color can be added by using tempera or acrylic paints. They can also be used to add detail to the finished object. Other materials such as Balsa wood and wax can also be used for carving purposes.

Figure 9.7   Soap Carving

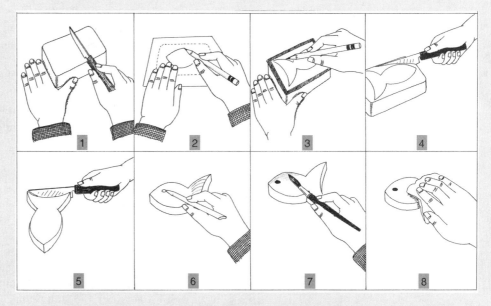

Materials: bar of soap, pencil, knife, paintbrush, paint, paper napkins, orangewood stick, paper, and carbon paper.

1. Take bar of soap and prepare it for carving. Letters and raised designs should be scraped off with a knife to form a flat surface.
2. Sketch a design on a piece of paper.
3. Place a piece of carbon paper on the bar of soap and trace over the design, pressing down lightly to prevent tearing the paper or smearing the carbon paper.
4. Start carving the bar of soap.
5. Gently carve the soap around the outline of the design.
6. Add small details with an orangewood stick.
7. Paint the surface.
8. Unpainted areas can be polished with a paper napkin.

Figure 9.8 Sculptures

1. Wire sculpture.
2. Scrap wood sculpture.
3. Toothpick sculpture.

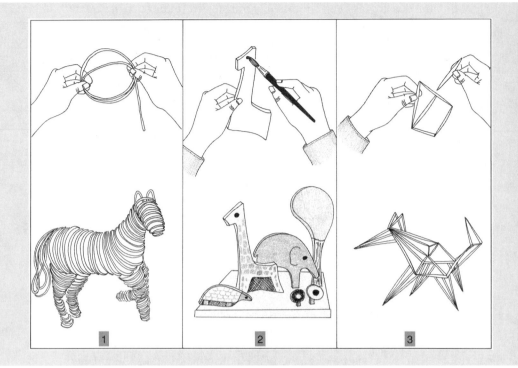

Wire sculpture can be created by using copper, aluminum, or bailing wire. Participants may experiment by bending and twisting the wire into various shapes (**Figure 9.8**). Some designs and figures may require the use of a coil. A wire coil can be made by wrapping the wire around a dowel, pencil, paper tube, or bottle. Be sure that the coil and base core can be separated.

Wire sculptures are usually conceived as one continuous length of wire, but they can be constructed from several lengths joined together. The pieces are hooked, twisted, or soldered together. The finished wire sculpture can be painted to improve its appearance. Wood, sponge, plastic, or paper can be combined with the wire to form an interesting sculpture.

Toothpicks can be held together with Duco cement to form various three-dimensional structures. Styrofoam, paper, plastic, and wood can be used to enhance the sculpture. A pencil sketch should be made to assist in the planning of a sculpture.

Scrap pieces of wood of various sizes, shapes, and colors can be placed together to create a sculpture. Collect a large variety of wooden shapes. Experiment with putting the various pieces of wood together to create an intriguing sculpture. When the desired arrangement is obtained, glue the pieces together. The sculpture should present an interesting view from all sides. Paint can be used to decorate the finished sculpture.

A mobile is a construction or sculpture of wire and a wide variety of shapes made from different materials that can be set in motion by air currents. They are created to produce movement with changing patterns. Constructing a mobile provides the individual with an experience in balance, design, sculpture, form, space, and color.

Decide on a theme for the mobile, the number of units, and the technique that will be utilized to construct the various objects. Wood, plastic, cloth, wire, paper, and numerous other materials can be used individually or in combination to construct parts of the mobile. There should be a relationship between the various objects that are used to make up the mobile.

Cut a piece of coat hanger wire or $\frac{1}{8}$-inch wooden dowel, the length depending upon the size of the objects used to make up the mobile. Tie a piece of nylon thread to one of the objects so that it will balance when suspended. (This single object suspended from the ceiling would represent the simplest form of mobile and is an appropriate activity for very young children.) Tie the other end of the thread to the end of the piece of wire. A second object is tied to the opposite end of the wire. The objects should hang so that they do not touch. A small drop of glue or cement applied to the thread and wire will keep the thread from slipping. The thread used to hold the objects should not be too long, and the lengths should vary.

Tie another piece of thread to the center of the wire or dowel supporting the two objects. Move the thread back and forth on the wire or dowel until the point of balance is located. Apply a drop of glue to secure the thread to the wire or dowel. This could be used as a simple mobile or additional pieces could be constructed and added to the mobile. Mobiles are constructed from the bottom up.

The thread holding the section can be attached to the end of the wire or dowel and secured with a drop of glue or cement. With a piece of thread, suspend another object from the other end of the wire or dowel. Attach a piece of thread to the center of the wire or dowel and balance both sections. Additional sections can be added as long as balance is maintained.

Casting

Sand sculpture is an inexpensive activity that children can use to create interesting wall plaques and other decorations. Plaster of Paris or Keene's cement are the materials typically used and are common shop room supplies. Paints, cardboard boxes, and sand are found around most recreational facilities.

Fill a small cardboard box with damp sand to within 1 inch of the top edge (**Figure 9.9**). With the edge of a piece of wood, level off the sand. Select

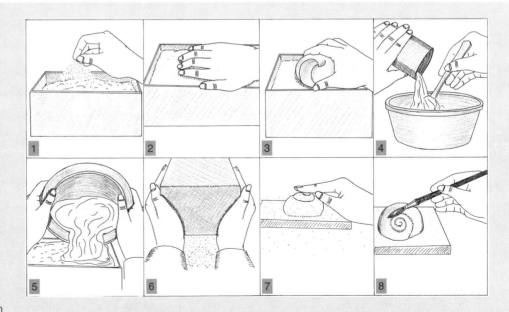

Figure 9.9   Sand Casting

Materials: cardboard box, bowl, measuring cup, paint, sand, paintbrush, plaster of Paris or Keene's cement.

1. Place sand in a cardboard box.
2. Level off the sand.
3. Press an object into the sand to create an impression.
4. Mix plaster of Paris or Keen's cement.
5. Pour the mixture into the sand mold and set aside to harden.
6. Remove the casting from the sand mold by inverting the box.
7. Brush the sand from the casting.
8. Paint the casting with tempera, watercolors, or acrylics.

an object that can be used to create an impression in the sand. It can be a seashell, plastic object, ceramic figurine, or wooden shape. Press the object into the sand. Lift the object from the sand; the sand impression should be clean and smooth. If it is not, level the sand and make another impression.

Mix enough plaster of Paris or Keene's cement to form a $^3/_4$-inch layer on top of the sand. Slowly pour the mixture over the sand. Make sure the surface of the mixture is smooth and level. A paper clip or bent piece of wire can be placed in the back of the plaque, while the mixture is wet. Allow the cement to dry overnight.

Spread a piece of newspaper over the working surface. With a knife, cut the sides of the box so they can be folded over and the plaque lifted from the sand mold. Place the plaque on the newspaper and brush all the loose sand from the finished piece. The plaque can be painted with tempera, water-colors, or acrylic paints. The painted surface can be sealed with a clear plastic spray.

Mosaics

Antique mosaics are surface decorations made of small pieces of colored glass, stone, or ceramic tile. Sketch several designs on a piece of paper, using crayon, paint, or cut paper to make a working model of the finished mosaic. If the design is one that utilizes tiles, the design can be planned by arranging the tiles. Transfer the design to a mounting surface. Hardboard can be used as a base for small mosaic projects, while plywood is used for larger activities. The thickness of the playwood depends upon the size of the finished mosaics (¼ inch—up to 2 ft. square; ½ inch—up to 4 ft. square; ¾ inch—larger).

Tiles are cut with nippers to fit the various areas of the design (**Figure 9.10**). Care should be taken when cutting tiles to shield the tile with a hand to prevent splinters from flying. Large tiles can be broken into smaller pieces by placing them in a burlap bag and smashing with a hammer.

Figure 9.10 Mosaics

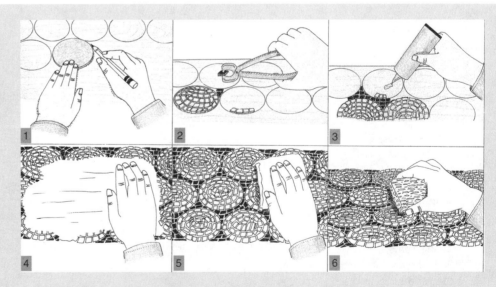

Materials: plywood, rag, tile, grout, tile cutters, cement, sponge, silicone or wax.

1. Outline the design on a plywood base.
2. Cut the tiles to fit the various areas of the design.
3. Cement the tiles to the surface, leaving a small space between each tile.
4. Rub grout into the spaces between the tiles and allow to set.
5. Remove the excess grout from the surface with a damp cloth.
6. Wash the surface clean with a sponge before sealing the surface with silicone or wax.

Tiles are glued with cement by spreading an even coating of glue over a small area. Care should be taken not to apply too much glue, because it will ooze up through the tiles, making it difficult to apply the grout. Press the tiles in place allowing a $1/16$- to $1/8$-inch space between the tiles for the grout. When the design is completed, it is set aside to dry. The spaces between the tiles are filled with grout. Grout and grout coloring (dry pigments) can be purchased at a hardware store or building supply house. The grout is mixed by adding the dry powder to a small amount of water. It is stirred until a consistency of heavy cream is obtained. It is spread over the surface, and rubbed with the fingers into the spaces between the tiles. A small stick is helpful in forcing the grout into the spaces between the tiles. The grout is allowed to set before the excessive grout is removed from the surface with a sponge, damp cloth, or paper towel. Before applying a sealer (silicone, marble polish, or wax) to protect the grout, clean the surface with a damp cloth or sponge.

Ceramics

Ceramics is a term applied to objects that are formed of clay and hardened by heat. Essentially, the freehand methods used today are the same as those that have been used since primitive times. They include molding a form from a lump of clay, pinching a shape from a ball of clay with the thumb and fingers, twisting coils into a form, joining slabs into the desired shape, and forming a piece of clay over an object. These methods require only limited materials, tools, and equipment. Slip, which is liquid clay, can be poured into a mold. The clay adheres to the walls and takes the shape of the mold. Another method is throwing on the wheel, a process of shaping the lump of moist clay while the wheel is turning.

There are various clays, each with its own unique properties and characteristics. These clays are used to create objects with completely different textures and appearances. Certain clays, because of their qualities, are much more suitable for particular kinds of work.

Any ceramic program for children or adults should provide a period for exploration and experimentation. An orientation is necessary to allow the individual to obtain an understanding of the properties and characteristics of different kinds of clay. Experimentation also enables the individual to feel his or her material, respect its limitations, and utilize it to build expressive forms.

Children enjoy patting, rolling, squeezing, thumping, pulling, and kneading clay. Doing so enables them to see and feel their ideas in three-dimensional form. Clay is malleable, flexible, and pliable, but it is also unpredictable, resisting, and often messy. However, it is economically feasible for use in any crafts program.

Clay is purchased in one of two forms: a dry powder referred to as "clay flour" or a prepared clay ready for use, which is called "moist clay." Dry clay is more economical; however, the moist clay is more efficient and the additional cost is negligible when compared with the convenience of having clay that is ready to use.

Mixing Clay

Mixing clay can provide children with another experience. The dry clay is mixed by sifting the flour into water and stirring until the mixture is thick. The mixture is allowed to sit at least 24 hours before working it. Excess water and air bubbles are eliminated by kneading and beating the clay on a hard surface.

The clay should be worked until it is easy to manipulate and no longer sticky. A good consistency is one that allows the clay to be manipulated without cracking and stiff enough so it does not stick to the hands.

An easy method of mixing clay is to put a pound of clay flour in a plastic bag and add a small amount of water. Press the air from the bag, secure the open end with a rubber band, and allow one of the participants to knead the mixture. If the clay is too dry, add more water; if too moist, add some dry clay. The mixture can be stored for an extended period of time in the plastic bag.

Clay should be workable, plastic, fine in texture, and possess good drying qualities. Clay of the proper consistency will not crumble and fall apart when being worked and will dry on the inner portions and outer surfaces in a reasonable length of time. If the correct consistency is not obtained and the clay is not workable or plastic, the next mixture can be improved by adding 40 percent talc and from 1 to 5 percent bentonite.

Fine texture can be determined by the satin smoothness of the clay flour or by rubbing moist clay between the fingers. If the clay is too coarse, the only alternative is to purchase a finer mesh clay.

Wedging

Clay should be wedged before it is formed into any shape. Wedging eliminates air pockets in the clay and gives it an even consistency. Both these characteristics are very important if quality work is to be obtained in the finished product. Clay is wedged by throwing it against a wedging board or other solid surface such as a table or workbench. After throwing the clay vigorously against a flat surface a number of times, cut it with a wire or knife to determine if all the air pockets have disappeared. Take the two pieces of clay and slap them together as hard as possible to prevent any new air pockets from forming. Care should be taken not to put two halves together in a way that allows air to be trapped in old air pockets. If air pockets appear on the split surfaces, continue to throw the clay ball against a flat surface until they have disappeared. This is determined by again cutting the ball of clay with a knife or wire.

Storing Clay

Clay should be stored so that it will retain its proper moisture level. Plastic bags, crocks, garbage cans, and other airtight containers are excellent for this purpose. A wet cloth can be used to cover the stored clay to retard the loss of moisture. Water can be added to moist clay if it starts to dry. Unused clay can be reclaimed by wrapping it in a damp cloth and setting it to one side for a few days. The clay can be returned to the main storage container when sufficiently wet again. Flour clay should be stored in a cool, dry place. Unfinished work should be kept moist by wrapping in a damp cloth until it is finished. An old refrigerator makes an excellent storage area for unfinished projects.

Modeling

Success with clay or substitute clay can be enhanced if participants understand the properties and characteristics of the material being modeled. Children should be urged to explore rather than create a finished product at first. They should learn that material can be returned to the clay container and reused to create a different form. Participants should be encouraged to pinch or pull their shapes from a ball, rather than just sticking shapes together. They should be provided an opportunity to see what happens when shapes are just put together. Those involved should experience how two pieces of clay can be worked together.

Making a Plan

Before modeling a dish, bowl, or sculpture, make some preliminary sketches of what the finished piece should look like. A sketch will assist the individual in planning the best method to construct the piece from clay. The template can be constructed from the sketches and used to check the inward or outward slopes of the walls of the piece under construction. Children will utilize the sketch to move from the play level to the craftsman level. The craftsman level requires controlling the clay to construct an object to certain specifications.

Pinch Method

The pinch method is the easiest method to use when forming simple sculptures or small bowls and dishes. The desired shape is actually pinched from a ball of clay. This method requires that a piece of clay be pinched, pulled, or pushed in a variety of ways to obtain the desired shape.

MAKING A BOWL OR LOW DISH. Form a ball of clay about the size of an apple and place it in the palm of the hand. Poke the thumb of the other hand into the top of the ball of clay (**Figure 9.11**). Continue to press the thumb into the center, while using the fingers to form the outer surface of the bowl. The wall of the bowl should be about $\frac{1}{4}$ inch or more thick. Care should be taken to keep the walls uniform in thickness. The top of the walls should not be thinner than the other parts.

Fingers can be used to smooth the inside and outside walls. Moisture can be added to clay by dipping fingers into water as the clay is being worked. This added moisture will help keep the clay in a workable condition. Too much water will make the clay difficult to model, however.

Figure 9.11 Pinch Pot

Materials: clay.

1. Roll the wedged clay into a ball.
2. Press thumb into the ball.
3. Pinch clay outward to form a pot.
4. Smooth the pot with the fingers.

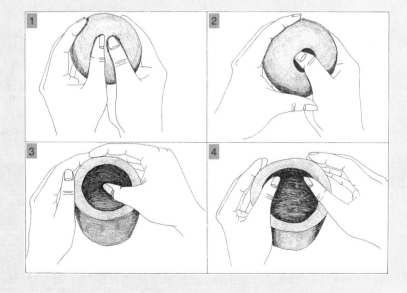

Figure 9.12 Coil Method

Materials: clay.

1. Roll a long coil for the base.
2. Wind the coil into the desired shape for the base.
3. Smooth the edges of the coil.
4. Place coils on the base to form the sides.
5. Continue winding the coils until the desired height is reached.
6. Weld the coils together.

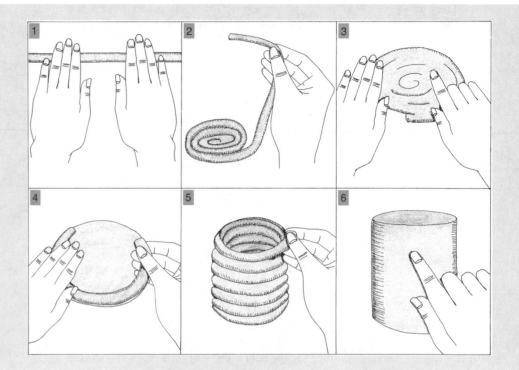

The finished shape can be round or a free form. If the finished object is not round, it should be free form enough to show that there was no intention to make it round.

Coil Method

This method utilizes coils of clay to model an object. This method is more difficult than the pinch method because it requires welding the coils into a uniform piece of material. Coils should be welded together so thoroughly that a seal is formed between them. The coil method can be utilized to create some sophisticated sculptures, bowls, plates, or pitchers.

FORMING THE BASE. The base can be oval or square; it does not have to be round. The base is formed by holding one end of the coil on a flat surface, while twisting the free end around the held end. Continue to twist in the same direction, being sure to push the coils close together. When the desired size of the base is obtained, press and smooth the coils together until the surface is flat (**Figure 9.12**). Turn the base over and flatten the opposite side. The base can also be constructed by rolling out a flat piece of clay to the desired thickness and cutting out the desired shape.

If cracks appear as the coils are being worked, it may be that the clay is poorly wedged or too dry. This problem usually can be corrected by rewedging or adding water. Some clays are not plastic and will not bend without cracking. These clays are not suitable for modeling objects using the coil method.

CONSTRUCTING THE WALLS. The walls of the object are also built up with coils. Coils should be firmly secured to the top edge of the base. Score the surface of the base at the spot that the coil will be connected to the base.

Figure 9.13   Coil Building
with a Template

Materials: clay, ¼-inch wooden dowel sharpened at one edge, cardboard template.

1. Form a base.
2. Score the base and moisten with slip.
3. Roll the clay into a coil.
4. Add the coil to the base.
5. Weld the outside.
6. Weld the inside.
7. Add another coil and check with a template.
8. Check the contour often with a template.
9. Completed project.

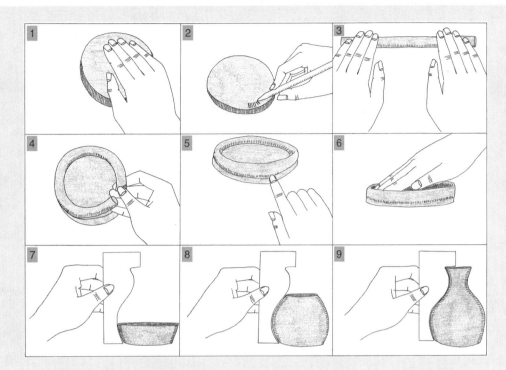

Apply slip to the scored area of the base before connecting the coil to it. Press the new coil very firmly to the base and cut off any extra material. The coil is welded to the base by working one hand on the inside of the wall, while using the other hand in the opposite position on the outside surface.

Before adding another coil, it should be decided if the walls are going to bulge outward or slope inward. An outward flair can be obtained by placing each additional coil toward the outer edge of the coil below. An inward curve can be obtained by putting each coil toward the inner edge of the coil below.

Score the top of the first coil and apply slip. A second coil is rolled and welded in place. Add another coil to the wall. Then, check the slope of the wall with a template (**Figure 9.13**). (A template is a pattern, usually of thin metal, wood, or plastic that is used for forming an accurate copy of an object. Depending on the project, the participant may be given a template or, if competent, may make one.) The clay should be worked so that it conforms to the contour of the template. Only three coils can be added at one time without causing the walls to sag. This is very important for large objects or those that have walls that flare outward. The unfinished object should be covered with a damp cloth and stored until the next time. The clay should dry to leather hardness before more coils are added.

Before continuing to build the wall, moisten the top edge of the last coil. Add the wanted number of coils to obtain the desired height. Remember that the coils should be welded together. Rough edges can be smoothed with slip and later the finished piece can be sanded, sponged, or smoothed with the fingers. When the piece is bone dry, the base can be rotated on a piece of sandpaper and the side walls sanded smooth. The piece is now ready to fire. If the piece is not going to be fired, it can be decorated with tempera paints.

Figure 9.14 Throughing on the Potter's Wheel

Materials: potter's wheel, clay, piece of wire, needlelike tool.

1. Slap a ball of wedged clay on the wheel.
2. Center the ball of clay.
3. Press both hands against the ball of clay to form a peak.
4. Flatten down the peak.
5. Make an opening in the ball of clay.
6. Widen the opening by pulling the clay inward.
7. Raise the clay wall.
8. Level the top of the piece with a needlelike tool.
9. Remove the sliced-off ring of clay.
10. Smooth the lip of the piece.

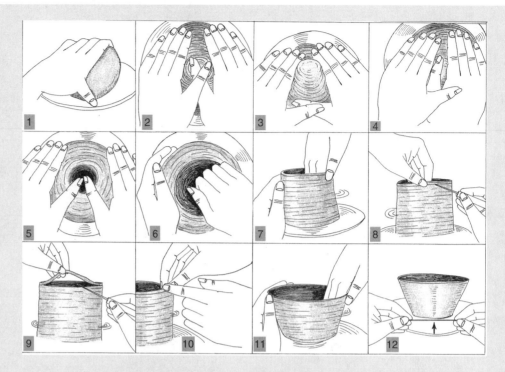

11. Continue the opening process until the desired shape is obtained.
12. Use a piece of wire to remove the piece from the wheel.

Throwing on the Potter's Wheel

Clay should be wedged thoroughly to remove all holes and air pockets before it can be thrown on a potter's wheel. Imperfections in the finished piece will result if these air pockets are not removed before working the clay. The clay can be thrown on a plastic bat or directly on the bare wheel. If a plastic bat is used, it is secured to the wheel with small pieces of clay placed at 120-degree intervals. Slip spread evenly over the bottom of the plastic bat can also be used to secure it to the wheel. The wedged clay is formed into a round ball and slapped onto the center of the wheel head. Place a container of water beside the wheel for wetting the clay as it is worked. Wet the clay. Center the clay by cupping it lightly in the hands as the wheel rapidly turns. When it stops thumping against the hands, it is centered.

Slow down the speed of the wheel and press both hands against the bowl of clay to form a peak (**Figure 9.14**). Support the sides of the clay with one hand and press firmly down with the palm of the other hand on the peak. Keep the fingers on the side of the clay while driving both thumbs into the center of the clay. Slowly separate the thumbs to form an opening in the center of the clay. Remember to maintain control over the outside contour with the fingers or the piece will be shapeless. The bottom thickness is determined now because it is too late after the sides of the piece have been drawn and the top is formed. If the base is too thick, shrinkage of the base and sides will not be equal, causing the sides to split. If the base is too thin, it will split.

Place one hand inside the hole and try to keep the forearm as perpendicular as possible to the wheel. The hand is pressed firmly against the inside of the piece as the other hand supports the outside wall. An elephant's ear sponge may be used on the outside to obtain a smooth texture. Create pressure on the sides between the two hands at the bottom of the piece and draw the clay upward to form the walls.

If the piece has a neck, it is formed by pressing inward with both hands in the desired position. Variations in the shape of the piece can be obtained by experimenting with different hand positions as the clay is worked. A needlelike tool is used to trim the top evenly. The piece is removed from the bat or directly off the wheel with a piece of wire. Stretch the wire taut and slide it underneath the piece. With careful handling, the piece can be removed from the wheel.

The piece should be set aside to dry. The neck of the vase should be covered to retard its drying, because the smaller diameter causes less shrinkage and creates cracks. When the piece is bone dry, it can be sanded, decorated, and fired.

Drying Finished Objects

An outstanding piece of modeling can be damaged if it is not properly dried. If thin edges and small parts dry faster than larger areas, they usually crack and fall off. This can be prevented by keeping these areas moistened during the drying process. A small brush can be used to apply water to these areas.

Objects with a flat base should not be placed on a table, but should be put on a surface that will allow air to circulate completely around all surfaces. This will result in a more even drying process.

Objects should not be placed directly over or near a heat source. The heat will cause the surface clay to dehydrate, while the core clay remains moist. The rapid shrinkage of the surface clay will result in cracks and small pieces falling off.

Sufficient time must be allowed for clay to dry properly. Some objects may need to be supported while drying. The heads and bodies of animals can be supported by wooden sticks or wire. The supports can be removed as soon as the clay is firm enough to hold its own weight.

Firing

Clay objects that are thoroughly dried are ready to be fired. These unfired pieces are called "green ware." Green ware can be stacked by putting the heavy pieces on the bottom and the lighter pieces on the top. Small pieces also can be placed inside larger objects. Clay pieces should be kept 1 inch or more from the side of the kiln.

Pyrometric cones (chemically prepared heat-measuring devices made to bend at certain temperatures) are inserted into small lumps of clay several days before firing to prevent them toppling over because the clay will shrink from the heat. Cones 08 and 07 are used for green ware. The cone should be located inside the kiln opposite the peephole.

Procedures for firing vary with the different types of kilns. No matter what type of kiln is used, the following procedures should be considered. Prefiring is an important process because it eliminates any moisture retained in the clay. Prefiring will usually prevent an explosion in the kiln caused by clay being improperly wedged or welded. Wet clay should never be fired.

During the prefiring period the kiln lid is propped open and the switch is turned onto the lowest temperature. The length of time for the prefiring depends on the size of the kiln. The prefiring time required in a large kiln may be overnight; for a small kiln, only 2 or 3 hours are needed. After the prefiring period, the door of the kiln is closed and the heat slowly increased. The length of firing can be gauged by the use of a mechanical heat thermometer, pyrometric cones, or a pyrometer. Firing temperatures vary with the type of clay. If using cones, watch them during the firing period. The number 08 cone should bend first. The other cones should be checked every 25 minutes because electric heat builds up rapidly toward the end of the firing period. The firing process for green ware is completed when all the cones are bent.

If the kiln has a pyrometer, the temperature should be checked to see if it coincides with the cone number. Any noted discrepancy should be corrected. A cone is a more reliable indicator of conditions inside the kiln than a pyrometer.

Fired ware should be allowed to cool in the kiln for as long as it took to heat the kiln. Care should be taken in removing pieces because some may still be hot. The fired ware is now called "bisque."

Glazes

Bisque ware can be decorated with an underglaze and covered with transparent glaze, or it may be covered with a single glaze and then refired. Appropriate glazes should be purchased for the clay that is to be used. The glaze is mixed with water to a creamlike consistency and applied to the bisque ware with a brush. More than one coat of glaze may be needed to obtain the thickness of the glaze coating. Glaze ware is stacked in the kiln on an individual stilt to prevent the glaze from fusing to the floor or shelf of the kiln. Pieces should be 1 inch apart to keep the glaze, which is a liquid glass, from fusing together. Cone numbers 08, 07, and 06 are usually used when firing glaze ware.

Some glazes can be used directly on green ware, requiring only one firing. These glazes should be painted on heavily when the pieces are going to be fired once. The kiln is stacked the same as for glazed bisque pieces.

Not all clay forms and objects should be fired. Clay figures and other objects for small-scale construction units, dioramas, and other such activities are usually not fired because they can be painted with tempera paints. Pottery, tiles, and figurines should be fired.

Techniques for Decorating Clay Objects

Some objects constructed from clay may require no decorations because of the shape, design, or material, whereas others can be made attractive by using a transparent or colored glaze. A number of techniques can be used to enrich a ceramic piece. It is important to consider how the design or decoration adds to the finished product. The decoration should be suitable for the size and shape of the object. One can experiment with the following techniques when the clay is damp (**Figure 9.15**):

- *Incising:* This technique utilizes a sharp-pointed object to cut a line design into a damp clay surface.
- *Carving:* This technique utilizes a sharp knife to cut out the design. Cuts should be made so that they slant from the outer edge to the center of the shape.

Figure 9.15 Decorating Techniques

1. Paint: Paint the design on the surface with slip.
2. Stencil: Use a stencil as a guide to paint the design.
3. Sgrafitto: Use a knife to scratch a design into the clay surface.
4. Wax resist: A. Paint the design with wax. B. Cover the surface with glaze.
5. Stamp: Stamp a design into the clay surface.
6. Incise: Use a sharp-pointed tool to cut a line design.
7. Carve: Use a knife to carve out a design.
8. Embossing or modeling-on: Add clay forms to create a design.

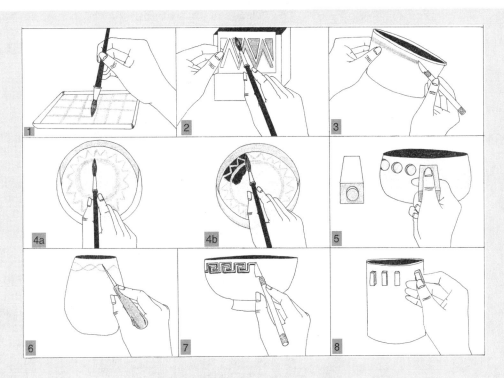

- *Embossing:* This technique utilizes thin clay forms or coils. The forms are cut from slabs of clay, and coils are formed from a ball of clay. They are arranged to form a design and are held in place with slip.
- *Stamping:* This technique utilizes a variety of objects to make imprints in the clay surface.
- *Slip painting:* This technique utilizes contrasting clay to make the mixture of slip. The slip is used to paint the design on a ceramic piece.

Substitute Clay

There are a number of excellent substitutes for clay and Plasticine. These substitute clays can be used to form and shape a wide variety of objects and figurines. Substitute clays are mixed by using common household items.

Children and other interested participants can cut, roll, and mold substitute clay into thousands of interesting objects like animals, flowers, boxes, and jewelry. The pinch, slab, or coil methods can be used to form or shape substitute clay.

Substitute clay objects should be placed on a screen or wire to allow the air to circulate around all surfaces. Finished objects should not be placed over heat or in bright sunlight because rapid drying may cause cracking. Substitute clay can be decorated with tempera, watercolors, or acrylic paints. After the paints dry, dip objects into clear shellac, spray with clear plastic, or brush on clear nail polish. Substitute clay can be stored in a plastic bag and used the next day. Among the substitutes are sawdust clay, salt–cornstarch clay, salt–flour clay, cornstarch–baking soda clay, and flour–salt–cornstarch clay.

Leather Crafts

Leather articles are durable and have a very pleasing appearance. Billfolds, key cases, purses, and belts are a few of the articles that can be made from leather. Calfskin, sheepskin, goatskin, cowhide, and pigskin are the most commonly used leathers. However, some articles can be enhanced through the use of deerskin, antelope, seal, lizard, or alligator.

Leather crafts include the process of cutting the leather, decorating the surface, and fastening the parts together with one of several techniques, such as lacing, stitching, or riveting. It is not always necessary to decorate the surface, because leather contains its own intrinsic beauty that can be enhanced with oil or wax. Carving, stamping, punching, tooling, and embossing are the techniques used to decorate the surface of a piece of leather. These techniques can be used individually or in different combinations to obtain the desired effect. Nail heads, fasteners, buckles, and clasps are also used to decorate the finished articles.

It is important for the beginner to practice cutting, stamping, tooling, and lacing leather before attempting to construct a complicated or large article. An understanding of how to use the various tools and materials is a requisite for the success of any leather craft activity. Small leather scraps are useful for practicing these operations.

Types of Craft Leathers

Many different types of leather are available for any crafts program. Each type of leather has its own unique properties and characteristics. These qualities should be utilized to enhance the beauty and durability of any project constructed from leather. Leather is available for purchase in many different weights and colors. The weight is designated in ounces, with 1 ounce equal to $1/_{64}$-inch thickness.

Planning the Project

Before designing any leather project, it is important to study leather articles in catalogs, magazines, newspapers, or stores. Such an investigation will provide the individual with an understanding of how leather is used, decorated, and finished. A series of preliminary sketches should be made of the proposed item. When an acceptable sketch is obtained, a model of the finished product can be constructed from heavy paper. The paper model should be accurate because it will be used to lay out the templates for cutting the various parts from the leather.

To obtain accurate patterns, be sure to make all necessary allowances for bends, overlaps, folds, and sewing and lacing seams. One thickness of leather should be added to the length or width for each bend and seam, while twice the thickness is required for each fold. These allowances should be included in the lines or widths of the paper patterns. Care should be taken assembling the paper patterns to utilize the same bends, folds, and seams as those that will be used in the construction of the finished leather article. For example, if the parts are laced, the paper model should be held together using a needle and thread in an over-and-over lacing method or buttonhole stitch to determine if the allowance is correct. The finished paper model should be checked for size to be sure the pattern pieces fit correctly.

Placing the Templates on the Skin

The templates should be moved around on the skin so that the leather is cut to advantage. The back is the best part of the skin and should be used for tooling, while the legs and belly sections are used for gussets and linings. Parts with straight edges should be placed together so one cut is sufficient for both pieces.

Cutting the Leather

Place the leather on an old board or heavy cardboard and cut it with a sharp knife along the edge of a steel square or metal straightedge (**Figure 9.16**). Cut along the line to within 1 inch of the end. Reverse the knife and cut from the opposite direction to prevent over-cutting and wasting leather.

Planning a Design

If the article is to be tooled, carved, or stamped, the design should be planned on scrap paper. Beginners should start with a simple design, with more difficult ones undertaken as skill and experience are gained.

The first step is to develop some preliminary sketches. The design should be selected and transferred to a piece of paper the same size and shape as the leather surface it will be used to decorate. Plan to leave an undecorated border of at least $1/2$ to 1 inch around the design, depending on the size of the article.

Figure 9.16   Cutting Leather

1. Using leather shears.
2. Cutting a large piece of leather with a head knife.
3. Cutting a small piece of leather with a head knife.
4. Cutting leather with a paper cutter.
5. Cutting a belt with a draw gauge.
6. Cutting leather with a knife.

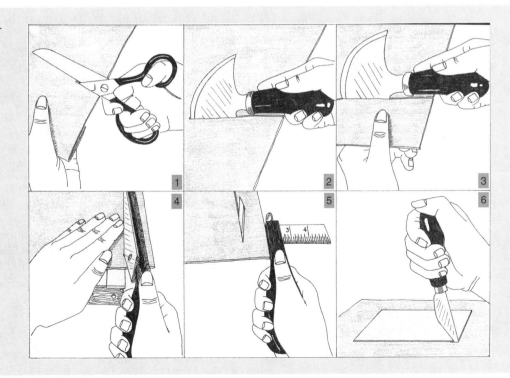

This allowance is needed for sewing, lacing, or just to offset the design. Lacing holes should be located $1\frac{1}{2}$ times the width of the lacing from the edge of the leather. All tooling, carving, or stamping must be done before the various parts of the article are assembled.

Tracing the Design on a Leather Surface

Make sure the design is complete and correct before transferring it to the leather surface. Once the design has been transferred to the leather, it is almost impossible to remove any lines. Carbon paper should never be used to transfer a design to leather.

The leather must be moistened before the design is transferred. Lightweight leather is moistened on the flesh side with a clean sponge and water until the finished surface darkens. The entire piece should be moistened so that any shrinkage or color change will be uniform. Set the leather grain side up on a flat surface and allow it to dry until it starts to resume its original color. The leather surface is now prepared to have the design traced on it.

Heavyweight leather is moistened by soaking the leather in water for a few minutes, removing, and wrapping in paper towels overnight. The soaking process will cause the fiber bundles to swell and makes the leather very pliable. Care should be taken in handling the leather once it has been moistened, because any undesirable impressions and marks will be impossible to remove. Set the leather grain side up on a flat surface and allow it to dry until the surface shows traces of the original color. The leather is now prepared to receive the design.

Place the tracing paper with the design on top of the grain side of the leather and secure it with masking tape. The design and leather should be placed on a smooth, firm surface such as a piece of marble, hardwood (maple), hardboard (tempered), or metal.

With a tracing tool, a pencil, the small end of a modeler, or a stylus, trace the design. Care should be taken not to move the design paper or tear it during the tracing operation. Apply firm, even pressure as the design is being traced, and use a straightedge as a guide for tracing straight lines. Raise one end of the design paper occasionally to check the impression. Make sure the impression lines are clear and that no lines have been skipped.

Tooling Leather

Tooling leather consists of decorating the surface of the material by stamping, carving, embossing, flat modeling, and stippling. By tooling, the leather surface is enhanced and becomes more attractive and personal.

OUTLINE TOOLING. Outline tooling is one of the simplest methods of decorating leather because it requires only the outline of the design being pressed down. Prepare the leather for tooling by moistening it as described above and then tracing the design on its surface. Place the piece of leather on a hard surface with the design side face up. Holding the modeler like a pencil and using the small end, trace around the outline of the design (**Figure 9.17**). Increase the pressure each time the outline is retraced until the desired depth is obtained. Care should be taken to keep the depth of the depressed lines uniform.

If water oozes up from the leather as it is being tooled, it is too damp and should be set aside to dry. The impression will not hold if the leather is too

Figure 9.17   Outline Tooling and Flat Modeling

1. Tool a straight line.
2. Use a template as a guide.
3. Draw irregular lines using the modeler.
4. Use a tool for outline tooling.
   FLAT MODELING
5. Bevel the background with a modeler.
6. Use the deerfoot modeler.
7. Push down the background with a tool.
8. Design with the background tooled.

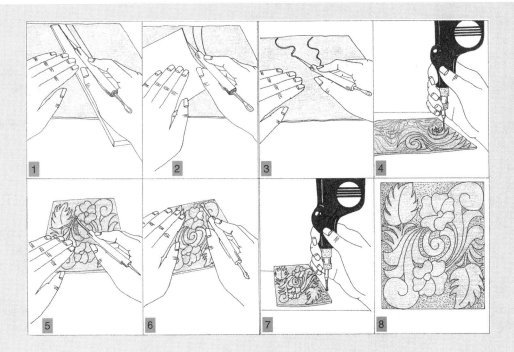

wet. If the modeler breaks through or scratches the surface, the leather is too dry and should be moistened. Dry leather will not tool correctly.

A straightedge should be used for all straight lines. On lightweight leather, straight lines should be tooled from the outer edge toward the center to prevent stretching the material.

FLAT MODELING. Flat modeling is the process of depressing or beveling the background away from the design, making the design stand out in bold relief. Prepare the leather for tooling. Place the leather design side up on a hard surface and trace around the design as in outline tooling. Using the broad end of the modeler, depress or bevel the background using a firm, even pressure. If the leather becomes too dry, a sponge can be used to moisten it slightly.

EMBOSSING. Embossing is the process of raising the design, or part of it, above the surface of the leather by working it from the flesh side. Prepare the leather for tooling. Place the leather on a hard surface and trace around the design as in outline tooling. This should produce a clear outline of the design on the flesh side of the leather.

Pick up the piece of leather and hold it with the grain side against the palm of the hand. Using a ball-end modeler, raise the design by working the tool over the flesh side of the leather, forcing it down between the fingers (**Figure 9.18**). An alternative method of raising the surface of leather is to place it on a piece of sponge rubber and force the design down into the rubber using the ball-end modeler.

When the desired proportions of the design have been raised, place the leather grain side up on a hard surface. With the broad end of the modeler smooth down the background around the raised parts of the design. If the design is not raised enough, it can be reworked until the desired effect is

Figure 9.18 Embossing and Stippling

EMBOSSING
1. Trace around the outline of the design.
2. Emboss the back of the design with the ball-end modeler.
3. Push down the background.
4. Back the embossed areas.

STIPPLING
5. Stipple with a modeler.
6. Stipple with a ball-end modeler.
7. Using a stippler.
8. Finished design with stippled areas.

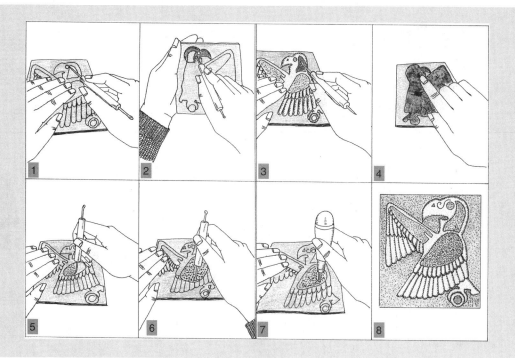

obtained. When the leather dries, fill the embossed areas with kapok, plastic wood, or cotton to prevent the raised surface from being pushed in. Cover the flesh side of the leather with a piece of lining leather.

STIPPLING. Stippling is the process of decorating the background with a series of small, dot-like impressions. A tracer, stylus, small end of the modeler, or stippler can be used to make different size impressions on the background. Prepare the leather for tooling. Hold the tool vertically and apply uniform pressure to the tool, being careful not to break through the surface of the leather.

An embossing wheel or carriage is used to create a decorative border or design. The leather should be in the same condition as for tooling. Lay out the lines to be embossed. Apply even pressure to the carriage, while pushing it along a straightedge. Sufficient pressure should be applied to ensure a clear, even impression the first time across the leather. It is impossible to go over the line a second time. Curved lines can be embossed by using a template for a guide or by using the carriage freehand.

STAMPING. Stamping is a technique that utilizes steel stamps to make simple patterns on a piece of leather. Craft catalogs list the different commercial stamps available for decorating a leather surface. The design produced depends upon the stamp shapes available and the ingenuity of the individual. Stamping is one of the simple methods of decorating leather and is suitable for use by young children and others. It is important to experiment with the different stamps on a piece of scrap leather before attempting the finished design.

Moisten the leather as for tooling and allow it to dry until the grain side of the leather has returned to its natural color. Leather that is too wet will not retain the impression.

Place the leather grain side up on a hard surface and select a stamp with the desired design. Hold the stamp vertically between the thumb and first and second fingers, while resting the other fingers on the leather. With a mallet strike the end of the stamp sharply, being careful not to cut through the leather. Arrange stamps in a pattern or in combination with other stamps to create an interesting design.

Carving Leather

Carving or incising is the process of cutting the design into the surface of a piece of leather, without actually removing or cutting away any material. The design is traced on the leather and the lines are cut with a swivel knife. Saddle stamps or a flat modeling tool are used to put down the background and decorate the design.

There is no definite procedure for carving leather. Each individual usually develops his or her own method and style of carving, but the fundamental process remains the same. Practice and experimentation are necessary if the individual is to become proficient in leather carving.

Prepare the leather for carving by moistening it and tracing the design on it. After the design has been transferred and before cutting, moisten the grain side of the leather with a sponge so that it is slightly wet.

Hold the swivel knife between the thumb and the middle and fourth fingers with the index finger resting on the yoke, while the little finger rests on the leather to help steady the hand (**Figure 9.19**). Practice making cuts on a piece of scrap leather. Cuts should be made with the corner of the blade and by pulling the knife.

Light pressure is applied to the knife at the start and end of the each cut, producing a shallow incision at both ends and a deep one in the center. The

Figure 9.19 Carving Leather

1. Using a swivel knife.
2. Hold the swivel knife at a right angle.
3. Using the swivel knife with a straightedge.
4. Using a Pro-gauge.
5. Using a camouflage tool.
6. Using a shader.
7. Using a veiner.
8. Making a dress cut with a swivel knife.
9. Finishing the dress cut.

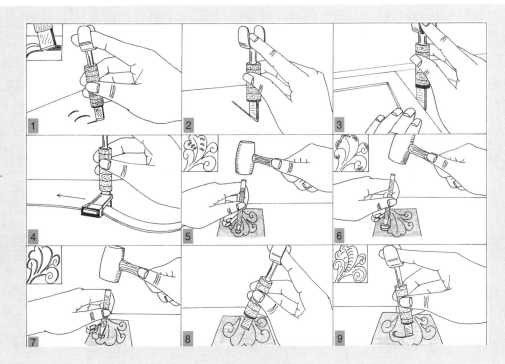

incision at the deepest point should not exceed half the thickness of the leather. Cuts should not be gone over a second time and should not cross one another. It is important to keep the knife in an upright position during the cutting operation. The design should be cut in the following order: border lines, flowers, stems, and leaves.

To obtain the desired effect, model those background areas that are to be depressed to make the design stand out in relief. This carved-out appearance is obtained by pressing the broad end of the modeling tool against the surface near the cut and working it back and forth.

Saddle stamps are also used to depress the background and decorate the design. If the impressions are stamped as close together as possible, a solid effect is produced. The raised areas contrast with the depressed ones to give a carved-out appearance. The following saddle stamps can be used: *Camouflage* stamps come in several sizes and shapes and are used to decorate flowers, leaves, and stones. *Pear* shaders come in several sizes and are used to produce a shaded effect on leaves and flower petals. The working surface of the tool may be smooth, checked, or ribbed. The *beveller* is available in several sizes and is used to make areas of the design stand out in bold relief. The working surface of the tool may be smooth, checked, or lined. *Veiner* and *shell* tools vary in size and shape and are used to decorate plain areas and leaves, stems, and flowers. *Seeders* vary in size and shape and are used for the centers of flowers or swirls. *Background* tools come in several sizes and shapes and are used to decorate the background of the design.

These are the basic stamps and their purposes. It is impossible to illustrate all the ways in which they can be used. With experience and practice an individual can develop skill in adapting various combinations of stamps to create an interesting design.

Edging Tools

Edging tools are used to round, level, and finish the edges of a piece of leather. They are available in different sizes for light and heavy leather, and in a variety of shapes (**Figure 9.20**).

Leather to be edged should be in the same condition as for tooling, because the edger will produce a smoother cut on damp leather. However, if the leather is not going to be tooled or stamped, there is no need to wet the leather just to bevel or round the edge.

EDGE BEVELLER. The edge beveller is used to bevel the edge on lightweight leather to prevent fraying, while the common edge tool is used to bevel or round edges on heavy leather. The tool is pushed along the edge, producing a uniform cut.

EDGE CREASERS. Edge creasers are used to crease lines along the edge of belts and open edges of pockets. A single or double metal edge creaser will produce the best results. The leather, in the same condition as for tooling, is held flat on a surface. Pressure is applied to the tool as it is pushed along the edge of the leather. Work the tool back and forth until the creased line is the desired depth.

SKIVING KNIFE. A skiving knife is used to reduce the thickness of leather, making it more pliable. Skiving may be used to thin edges that will be sewed or laced later, or where the leather is going to be folded or bent.

Figure 9.20 Using Edging Tools

1. Using the common edge tool.
2. Using an edge beveler.
3. Using a Bissonette edge tool.
4. Using a single edge creaser.

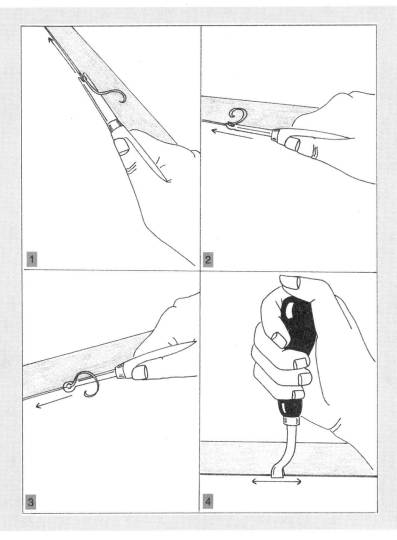

Place the leather grain side down on a hard surface and with a skiving knife remove a few pieces at a time. Care should be taken not to cut off too much material at one time, because there is danger of cutting a hole through the leather. The depth of the cut depends on the number of pieces to be assembled. The assembled edges should equal the original thickness of the leather. The cut should be $1/2$ inch in from the edge and down to half the thickness of the leather at the edge.

When used for skiving, the bevel-pointed knife, head knife, and bevel-end knife should be pushed away from the operator. The Skife, which is a patented skiving knife, is pulled toward the operator (**Figure 9.21**). It is an exceptional tool for cutting the edges of leather uniformly. Practice and experimentation are a must before skiving the pieces that are going to be used for the finished article.

Cementing Leather

Rubber cement can be used to hold linings, zippers, or edges in place for lacing or sewing. It can also be used to join two surfaces permanently. Apply

Figure 9.21 Skiving

1. Skiving with a bevel-end knife.
2. Skiving with a head knife.
3. Skiving with a bevel-pointed knife.
4. Skiving with a Skife.

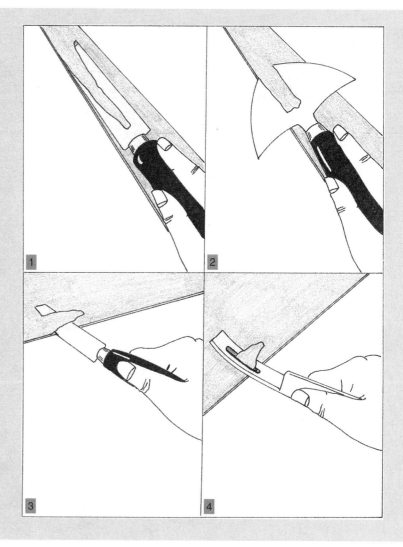

cement to both of the surfaces to be fastened together and allow it to dry until the shine disappears. If the surface is not to be folded, align the edges of the two pieces while holding the other end. Slowly work the surfaces together by pressing and smoothing out the material.

For surfaces that are to be folded, align the two pieces at the fold and press half of the material in place, working from the center out to the edge, while the material is held in a folded position. Keeping the leather in a folded position, reverse the material and press the other half in place. After the surfaces are cemented together, they can be trimmed, laced, or sewed. Excessive cement on any of the surfaces or edges can be rubbed off with a cloth.

Punches and Chisels

Round, oval, or oblong holes can be cut through a piece of leather using several different punches, which come in various sizes. Among these tools are revolving and round drive punches, thonging chisel, and oblong, tube belt, and strap end punches.

Lacing Techniques

The major purposes of lacing are to fasten two pieces of leather together as well as to provide decoration. Lacing leather is made of calf or goat and comes in an assortment of colors. It can be purchased by the yard or spool. The $^3/_{32}$-inch width is the most commonly used lacing, but a $^1/_8$-inch width is best for large projects. The length of lacing needed for any article depends on the size of the article and style of the stitch used. Because it is difficult to handle a piece of lacing longer than about a yard, it is advisable to add lace as it is needed. A new length of lacing can be spliced to the first one by skiving the top grain side about $^1/_2$ inch or more at the end and skiving the underside of the new strip. Apply cement to the skived areas and overlap the pieces of lacing together.

A special lacing needle can be used for lacing the leather through the small slits, or the end of the lacing can be cut at an angle and stiffened by applying cement to it. The end of the lacing is finished off by tucking $^1/_2$ inch or so of the end back under the last few stitches. Lay out and mark the guidelines for the lacing holes. One of the following stitches can be used to hold the edges together: running stitch, whipstitch, double whipstitch, cross-stitch, single buttonhole stitch, or double buttonhole stitch (**Figure 9.22**).

Hand Sewing

Hand sewing is considered superior to machine sewing because the stitches can be pulled tighter and will not loosen as easily as the machine lock stitch. For some articles, it is the only method that can be used to join leather together. Edges should be cemented before they are sewn together to prevent

Figure 9.22 Lacing

1. Running stitch.
2. Whipstitch.
3. Double whipstitch.
4. Cross-stitch.
5. Buttonhole stitch.
6. Double buttonhole stitch.

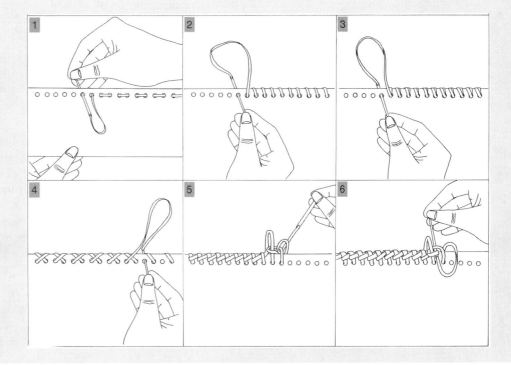

Figure 9.23 Sewing

1. Using a space marker with a straightedge.
2. Using a space marker with a template.
3. Using a stitching punch to make holes.
4. Using an awl to punch stitching holes.
5. Making a running stitch.
6. Sewing two pieces of materials together.

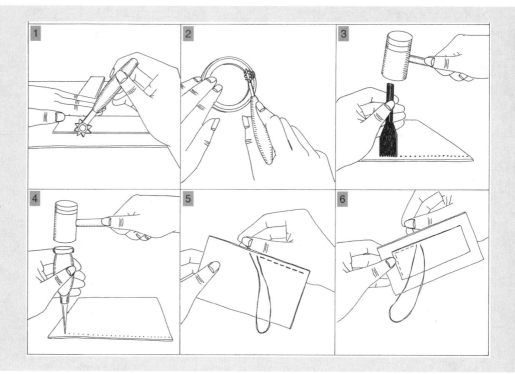

them from slipping. There are many kinds of needles (harness, sharps, or glover's) that can be used in sewing leather. These needles can be purchased in a wide variety of sizes at any notions counter. Waxed linen, nylon, or heavy cotton thread are all suitable for stitching leather.

Holes for sewing should be located $1/16$ inch from the edge for lightweight leather and $1/16$ to $1/4$ inch from the edge for heavyweight leather. The type of construction used will help to determine the precise location of the stitching line. The number of stitches per inch should be fixed; for lightweight leather there should be from 8 to 12 stitches per inch. A space marker can be used to locate the holes for stitching (**Figure 9.23**). Holes can be punched with an awl, or slits for sewing can be made with a thonging chisel. Holes in thick leather can be drilled.

RUNNING STITCH. A running stitch is preferred for use by beginners on lightweight leather. Start sewing in one direction by pushing the needle down and then up through the leather. Continue going up and down through the leather until the end is reached. Reverse the sewing procedure, filling in the alternate stitches. Pull each stitch tight, being careful not to cut the leather. When the sewing is completed, tie the ends of the thread and cut off any extra thread. A small amount of cement can be applied to the knot. If nylon thread is used, the ends can be burned to prevent the knot from untying.

SADDLERS STITCH. The saddlers stitch is used for heavy leather. Two threaded needles are used at one time, both going through the same hole from opposite sides of the leather. The positions of the needle are exchanged and returned through the next hole. This stitch fills in all spaces between the holes. Secure the end of the thread as for the running stitch.

Figure 9.24 Making a Key Case

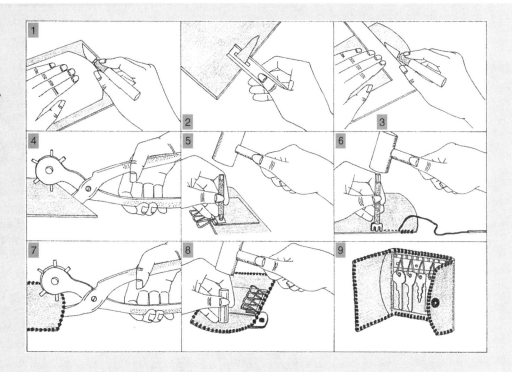

Materials: leather, template, key frame, rivets, thonging chisel, snaps, snap setter, lacing, revolving punch, drive punch, skiving knife, straight edge, rivet-setting device.

1. Carefully cut the leather, using a pattern as a guide.
2. Skive the edges of the leather.
3. Score the leather to facilitate folding.
4. Punch holes for the key frame.
5. Rivet the key frame in place.
6. Use the thonging chisel to punch holes for the lacing.
7. Punch the hole in the flap for the snap.
8. Set the snap.
9. Finished key case.

Snaps and Fasteners

Snaps are used to fasten together openings on purses, key cases (**Figure 9.24**), and other articles with an overlapping closure. Snaps consist of four parts, two of which go in an upper layer of leather and two of which go into the lower layer. These, in turn, snap into each other to hold the two layers of leather together.

There are two types of snap centers: the segma and birdcage. Care should be taken to use the correct part of the snap-setting device with the right part of the snap to prevent squeezing the wrong pieces. Other materials are eyelets, grommets, and rivets.

Dyeing and Finishing Leathers

Dye is used to color the surface of leather, while a leather finish is applied over both natural and dyed surfaces to soften, protect, and condition the leather.

All tooling should be completed before dye is applied to the leather. Clean the leather to remove all dirt and grease so that the surface may be dyed uniformly. Dissolve one teaspoonful of oxalic acid crystals in 1 pint of water to make a cleaning solution or purchase a commercial leather-cleaning solution. Apply the cleaning solution with a cellulose sponge and allow the leather to dry thoroughly.

Pour a small amount of dye into a shallow container and with sheep's wool or a cloth apply the dye in broad strokes and allow it to dry. If the surface dries streaky, a second coat of dye should be applied to the total surface. Small areas that are missed cannot be touched up. It is important to experiment on a scrap piece of leather before applying dye to the surfaces of the finished article. The scrap leather should be the same as that used in the finished article.

A small camel's hair brush can be used to apply dye to a carved background or small areas in a design. Care should be taken not to drip dye from the brush onto the leather surface, because it will cause spots.

FINISHING EDGES. Edges that are not going to be laced can be finished using one of the following techniques. A small brush can be used to apply dye to the edges of colored leather; care should be taken not to get dye on the finished surface. A solution of gum tragacanth is used on natural leather. A bone folder or the end of a modeler rubbed back and forth over a moistened surface will color the edge and set the fibers. Edges that will receive excessive wear should be covered with an edge or casing compound. Edge enamel or edged dye can also be used to coat edges that will receive excessive wear.

PROTECTIVE FINISHES. A special leather lacquer can be used to preserve and protect leather. Antique finishes that produce highlights and shadows are available in a number of colors. Waxes in liquid, paste, or cake form can be used as a finish or protective coat. Saddle soap is a mild cleaner and dressing for leather. Neat's-foot oil is a good preservative that will darken and waterproof natural leather.

Woodcrafts

This section is devoted to a simple description of some of the basic woodworking crafts. Of course, no crafts program can be called sufficient if there is no shop in which basic tools and supplies for the various woodcraft activities are stored. Whether there is a centralized facility or decentralized and mobile shops, they all need to contain measuring and layout tools; hand and machine saws of various types; planes and other smoothing equipment; and shaping tools such as chisels, gouges, carving tools, and knives. Additionally, files, rasps, and forming tools are also included. No woodworking shop can be complete without a bit brace, claw hammer, wood screws, nails, wood glue, sandpaper, and finishing products. Certainly, for advanced craftsmen, wood turning apparatus, power drills, and belt sanders are a necessity.

Each of these pieces of equipment and materials must have appropriate instruction for their use and safety. These tools and supplies are important to an individual planning a program that includes any aspect of the woodcraft area. Moreover, the information given will assist in considering the potential of woodcrafts and the dimension they can add to the crafts program. Familiarization with tool use is an imperative for beginners. Others will have had more or less experience with such equipment.

Common Joints and Their Uses

Joints are used in woodworking to provide for the connection of two pieces of wood so that they form a continuous surface. Various joints are used for different purposes and may be strengthened by gluing, nailing, dowels, or insertion of one piece into another.

Figure 9.25 Common Joints

1. End butt.
2. Edge butt joint.
3. Doweled edge joint.
4. Doweled end joint.
5. Doweled miter joint.
6. Splined edge joint.
7. Scarf joint.
8. Plain miter joint.
9. End lap joint.
10. Cross lap joint.
11. Miter spline joint.
12. Rabbet joint.
13. Dado joint.
14. Stop dovetail joint.
15. Mortise and tenon joint.

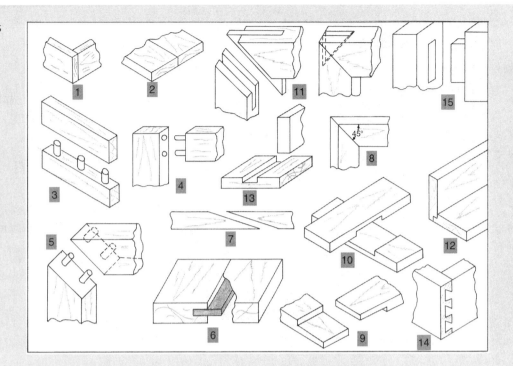

BUTT JOINT. The butt joint is used where great strength is required. It is constructed by planing the surfaces to be joined and then gluing them together. Dowels or splines can be used to give the joint added strength (**Figure 9.25**).

RABBET JOINT. The rabbet joint is used for simple drawer construction. The joint is constructed with a backsaw and then glued, nailed, or fastened with screws.

DADO JOINT. The dado joint is used in the construction of shelves, steps, drawers, and bookcases. It is constructed with a backsaw and trimmed with a chisel. The second part of the joint is fitted to the first and then glued. The dado joint is not noticeable from the front.

MITER JOINT. The miter joint is used in the construction of picture frames and the moldings around furniture. It is constructed by cutting the pieces with a miter box and then fitting the corners carefully. The pieces are fastened with glue, nails, or a spline.

LAP JOINT. The lap joint is used to fasten the legs of furniture, molding, and braces. It is constructed with a backsaw and trimmed with a chisel. The two parts are cut like dadoes and then glued together.

MORTISE AND TENON JOINT. The mortise and tenon joint is used for the construction of chairs and tables. The tenon is cut with a backsaw, and the mortise is drilled out and then trimmed with a chisel.

DOVETAIL JOINT. The dovetailed joint is used for drawer construction. It is cut on a jigsaw and then glued together.

Wood Turning

Wood turning introduces an experience that is entirely different from any offered in the other crafts areas. It increases the range of creative activities that can be produced in a crafts program. Bowls, plates, and trays can be turned on a lathe. The craftsperson will enjoy the particular satisfaction of seeing his or her material take shape, from a rough block to a graceful finished form, under the control of his or her hands. The satisfaction is similar to that of the potter throwing on the potter's wheel. The difference is that the potter uses a plastic medium, which can be shaped over and over with his or her hands, whereas the wood craftsperson works with chisels on a rigid material that cannot easily be altered once the shape is made.

A lathe is a special machine for holding and rotating a piece of wood while it is shaped with a chisel. There are eight chisels used for shaping the wood: large-gouge chisels, medium-gouge chisels, small-gouge chisels, half-round scraper, diamond-point scraper, parting tool, medium skew chisel, and large skew chisel. There are two main types of wood turning: spindle turning, in which the piece to be worked on is mounted and rotated between two centers, and faceplate turning, in which the work is mounted on a faceplate attached to the spindle of the head stock.

Faceplate Turning

In faceplate turning, the stock is mounted on a flat metal plate that fits onto the head stock of the lathe. As the faceplate revolves, the stock is shaped by the chisel scraping the surface. The round-nose chisel is used for concave cuts, the square-nose chisel for straight cuts, the diamond-point chisel for V cuts, and the parting chisel for depth.

Select a piece of wood that is free of knots and other defects. With a compass, draw a circle $1/8$ inch larger than the diameter of the finished turning. Cut the piece of wood with a handsaw. Select a faceplate smaller than the diameter of the work to be turned. Two methods may be used to attach the faceplate to the work. One is to screw the faceplate directly to the work, and the second is to glue a block of wood to the work and screw the faceplate to the wooden block. This method does not mark the base of the work with screw holes. The block of wood should be cut the same diameter as the faceplate. A heavy piece of paper should be glued between the wooden block and work to facilitate separating the surfaces when the turning is finished. Care should be taken on screwing the faceplate in position to make sure that the centers coincide. The live center is removed from the head spindle and the faceplate screwed in place. A piece of paper placed between the shoulder of the spindle and the faceplate will facilitate removal when the turning is finished. Before starting the lathe, adjust the belt to obtain the proper speed. Slow speeds of 600 rpm are usually used for large pieces, whereas a piece 3 inches in diameter or smaller may be turned at 1200 rpm.

The tool rest is moved into position to cut the edge of the work straight and smooth. The tool rest should be parallel with the edge of the work and $1/8$ inch away from the work. Before starting the lathe, turn the work one revolution by hand to make sure it clears the tool rest. To operate the lathe, take a position facing the lathe at an angle of approximately 45 degrees to the bed. Select a skew and hold the end of the handle with the right hand, while the left hand holds the blade to guide the tool along the rest. It is a good idea to get a feel for holding the tool and manipulating it before starting the lathe.

Figure 9.26 Faceplate Turning

1. Gluing the disk to a mounting block.
2. Cutting the edge of the disk straight with a round-nose chisel.
3. Smoothing the face of the disk with a skew chisel.
4. Shaping the edge of the disk with a round-nose chisel.
5. Testing the face of the disk for flatness with a square.
6. Marking circle with dividers set to the radius.
7. Cutting a hole with a round-nose chisel.
8. Shaping the inside of a bowl by scraping with the round-nose chisel.
9. Sanding a concave surface on a faceplate. Sanding is done below the center and on the down slope of the rotation of the stock.

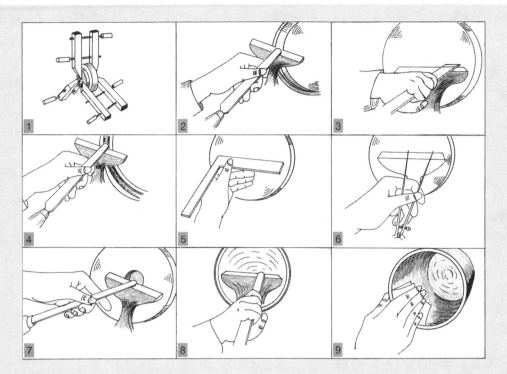

Turn on the lathe. The edge is straightened and turned by holding the tool perpendicular to the edge of the work on the tool rest (**Figure 9.26**). Keep the full width of the blade against the work while moving the tool across the thickness of the stock, taking small cuts until the shape is true.

When faceplate turning, the outside shape or form is usually turned before the inside. Concave cuts are made by holding the skew perpendicular to the work on the tool rest, while the handle is pivoted to form the desired arc. Concave cuts on the edge are made by using a round-nose tool. The tool is also held perpendicular to the work and pivoted to make a concave cut.

Convex cuts on the face surface are made by turning the tool rest so that it is parallel with the surface, $1/8$ inch below the center and $1/8$ inch away from the work. Place the skew chisel on the tool rest and pivot the cutting edge from the center out. Concave cuts on the face surface are made with the round-nose tool. Cuts are made by holding the tool perpendicular to the surface at the center of the work and moving toward the outer edge. It is important that the tool be held straight and level with the tool rest so that the end of the tool is doing the cutting. As the work takes form, the tool rest is advanced and adjusted to keep the proper working distance between the two surfaces.

The base and wall thickness of bowls and trays should be $3/16$ inch. The depth of an inside form can be measured by placing a straightedge across the opening and using a rule to measure the distance between the base of the object and the straightedge. The wall thickness can be measured with outside calipers.

Figure 9.27   Spindle or Between-Center Turning

1. Using the backsaw to cut diagonal lines $\frac{1}{8}$ inch deep for the spurs of the live center.
2. Using a wooden mallet to drive the live center into the wood so the spurs enter the kerf made by the saw.
3. Rough turning with a gouge using a scraping cut. Note the horizonal position of the tool.
4. Scraping with the skew chisel.
5. Using a parting tool to make a depth cut.
6. Using calipers to check the diameter of the turning.
7. Scraping a large bead with the diamond-point tool.

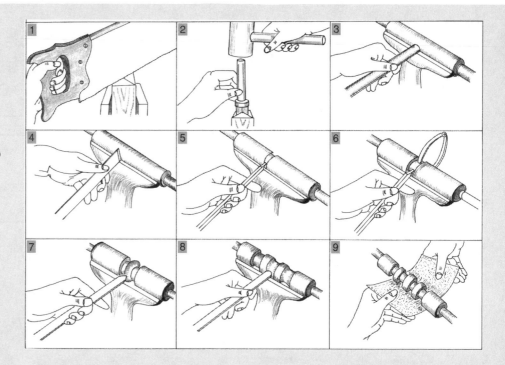

8. Scraping a concave surface with a round-nose tool. Hold the chisel flat on the tool rest and pivot the handle to form an arc.
9. Sanding in the lathe. Sanding is done by holding the paper either above or below the turning.

When the work is the desired shape, it should be sanded. Move the tool rest out of the way before starting to sand. Start sanding with $\frac{1}{2}$ garnet cabinet paper to remove chisel marks and then use $\frac{2}{0}$ garnet paper for the final sanding. When the surface is sanded free of all scratches and rough areas, the faceplate is removed from the lathe. If a wooden backing block was used, it is removed with a mallet and chisel. The chisel is placed at the glued joint between the wooden block and the finished turning and tapped lightly. Care should be taken not to damage the finished product. Apply the desired finish to the surface.

Spindle or Between-Center Turning

Select a piece of wood free of defects and cut to size, allowing 1 inch extra in the length and $\frac{1}{4}$ inch extra in the diameter for waste. Cut both ends of the stock square. Locate the centers of both ends by drawing diagonal lines across the corners. Place the stock in a vise and, using the diagonal lines, cut two saw kerfs $\frac{1}{8}$ inch deep with a backsaw (**Figure 9.27**). On the opposite end, punch a hole at the center. Remove the live center from the spindle by pushing a metal rod through the head stock. Place the stock in an upright position and, with a wooden mallet, drive the live center into the wood, making sure that the spurs enter the saw kerfs. Holding the live center in position, insert it into the spindle and slide the tail stock toward the head of the lathe until the point of the dead center enters the hole in the stock. Lock the tail stock in position and turn the spindle speed feed handle until the dead center is seated in the wood. Back off on the spindle feed handle to release the pressure slightly and apply a little wax, oil, or soap to the impression made by the dead center. Tighten the handle until the center is back in the original position. Adjust the tool rest by rotating the stock, making sure that the corners of the stock clear the edges of the rest by $^1/_8$ inch. The height of the tool rest should be $^1/_8$ inch below the center. The tool rest should be adjusted as the stock takes shape, and the gap between the two surfaces should not exceed $^3/_8$ inch. Stock larger than 2 inches square should have the corners removed before it is inserted in the lathe. Corners can be removed with a plane, spoke shave, or draw knife. Adjust the belt to obtain the correct speed; when the stock is square, the lathe should run at a slow speed of 600 rpm.

Select a large gouge and with the right hand grasp the handle toward the end. The left hand is used to hold the blade and guide the tool along the tool rest. A scraping cut is made by holding the gouge in a perpendicular position with the stock so that the tip end of the tool is doing the cutting. This method of turning will produce a rough cut. A shearing cut is made by lowering the right hand 10 degrees and turning the gouge slightly toward the direction of the cut. The gouge is moved along the tool rest, taking a fine cut. Scraping and shearing cuts are started in the center and the tool is worked toward the edge. Continue to turn with the gouge until the stock is cylindrical.

The higher the speed, the smoother the cut. The speed should be increased to 1600 or 1800 rpm. Speed is increased when the participant wants a smoother cut. This is determined individually and depends upon the user's skill. Use the large skew to smooth the surface. Hold the handle of the skew close to the end with the right hand, while the left hand is placed on the blade. The slope of the bevel should be pointing in the direction of the cut to be made and resting against the stock. Adjust the tool by moving the right hand until the blade is at an angle of about 120 degrees to the axis of the stock. Raise the tool until the blade starts to cut a shaving. Slide the tool along the rest, keeping the proper angle. Reverse and repeat until the stock is the correct diameter. The stock is ready to be shaped.

Making V Cuts

Mark the center line and the width of the V with a rule and pencil. Place a pencil against the surface and rotate the stock, making a mark around the cylinder for each measurement. Score the center line by placing the edge of the skew on the tool rest with the head down and the cutting edge on the center line of the V. Move the skew over about $^1/_8$ inch from the center line and turn it at a slight angle toward the center line. Cut into the center line. Repeat this operation on the other side of the center line. Continue this operation until the correct V is formed. A V shape may also be made by using a diamond-point chisel to scrape the surface into the desired width and depth. The tool is held horizontally and at a right angle to the stock, while being pushed against the surface.

Cutting Beads

Lay out the width of the beads with a pencil and rule. Rest the pencil point against the surface and rotate the stock, marking a guideline around the cylinder. For wide beads, a center line is helpful. The bead is shaped by placing the edge of the skew on the tool rest with the heel down. The cutting edge is rested against one of the lines that marks the width of the bead and pushed against the surface, scoring it. This operation is repeated on the other width line of the bead. Move the skew $1/8$ inch along the tool rest toward the center of the bead. With the heel of the skew doing the cutting, roll the tool toward the width line. Repeat this cut on the other side. Continue this process until the correct shape bead is formed. Calipers can be used to test the diameters of the crest and base of the beads.

Making Concave or Cove Cuts

Lay out the surface with a pencil and rule, marking the center and width measurements of the concave shape. With a pencil against one of the measurement marks, rotate the spindle, marking a guideline around the cylinder. This operation should be repeated for each mark. With a parting tool, cut a groove to within $1/16$ inch of the desired depth. Calipers are used to test the diameter of the cut. Both the round-nose tool and a gouge may also be used to form a concave shape.

Cutting a Long Taper

Lay out the points for the largest and smallest diameter with a pencil and rule. Make a full-size drawing on a piece of wrapping paper so that the diameter dimensions can be determined at several points. These points should be marked on the stock. With a parting tool, cut these depths on the side of the line with the smallest diameter. Calipers can be used to test the size of the diameter at these points. With a gouge, cut off the surplus stock. Adjust the tool rest so that it is parallel with the taper and, with a skew chisel, cut the stock to the finished dimensions, using either a scraping or shearing cut.

Sanding

Remove the tool rest for sanding. If the surface was scraped to the desired shape, use number 1, $1/2$, and $2/0$ garnet paper to sand the surface. For a shearing cut, $2/0$ garnet paper should be sufficient to obtain a smooth surface. Cylinders are sanded from above the work by holding a long piece of sandpaper between both hands and at a right angle to the stock. Apply even pressure as the paper is moved back and forth the length of the stock. Beads, V-grooves, and coves are sanded by forming the paper to fit small sections of the contour of the turning; sand from the bottom side so that the operation can be observed.

Metal Crafts

Copper, aluminum, and brass are metals that can be used to create a wide variety of decorative objects. Jewelry, trays, candleholders, dishes, and plaques are a few of the items that can be made utilizing the metal crafts techniques described in this section. Easy to work with, durable, and highly decorative, these metals are the most widely used in recreational crafts. Precious metals and their use are not discussed because of their expense.

Embossing is a simple activity that can be performed by very young children, but can also challenge the most accomplished craftsperson. Hammering represents another interesting technique. The forming of a flat sheet of metal into a three-dimensional form over a sandbag gives an individual a feeling of accomplishment. Etching and the decorating of a metal surface with a chemical process are most intriguing to participants. Enameling, a highly artistic endeavor, is another technique that offers the individual a great deal of satisfaction as the powdered glass used to coat the copper surface changes appearance as it is heated.

Tooling or Embossing

Tooling or embossing is a technique used to decorate the surface of a thin piece of metal with a design. Copper, brass, and aluminum foil are available in sheets or rolls 12 inches wide and with a thickness of 36 gauge (0.005 B&S). (Brown and Sharp [B&S] wire gauge is a standardized wire gauge system for indicating metal thickness used in wire and plates in the United States.) Tools needed are a liner or French molder, wide and narrow wooden spatulas, orangewood sticks of different sizes and shapes, a large felt pad $1/2$ to $3/4$ inch thick, a piece of Masonite, and steel wool numbered 000.

After selecting or drawing a suitable design, choose a piece of copper, brass, or aluminum foil. Place the tracing paper on top of the metal foil and secure it with masking tape (**Figure 9.28**). Put the metal foil on top of a felt pad and trace the design onto the foil using a hard number 6 pencil. Remove the tracing paper and masking tape from the foil and retrace the design on the foil with a liner or the pointed end of the wooden modeling tool.

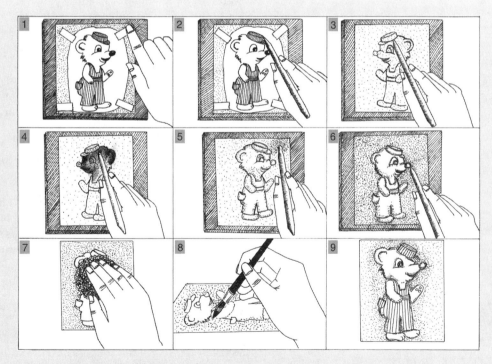

Figure 9.28 Tooling and Embossing Metal

Materials: masking tape, copper foil, modeling tool (wooden dowel), felt pack, number OOO steel wool, clear lacquer, paintbrush.

1. Place the design on the metal and secure it with masking tape.
2. Put the metal foil on top of a felt pad and outline the design with a sharp pointed instrument.
3. Turn the copper over and trace around the inside of the original line.
4. Start tooling by pressing out those areas to be emphasized.
5. Turn the design over and push down the background areas.
6. Decorate the background.
7. Clean the surface with number OOO steel wool.
8. Coat the surface with clear lacquer.
9. Finished tooled design.

Turn the foil over with the face side down against the padded surface, and with a tracing tool draw a line about $\frac{1}{32}$ inch on the inside of the traced design. This line should be slightly heavier than the first line. Should the tool accidentally slip and hit the line, turn the foil over and tool the line again from the right side.

Place the foil face down on a felt pad and press the design out with a wooden spatula or an orangewood stick, pushing out those areas that are going to be raised. Light, firm strokes should be used starting at the outline of the design and working toward the center.

Turn the piece of foil over and examine the tooled surface. If the surface is not raised to the desired height, turn the foil over and rework these areas. When the surface is raised to the correct height, place the foil face side up on a felt pad and retrace the design lines.

To tool the background, place the foil on a piece of Masonite and smooth the background around the design with a flat wooden tool. After depressing the area close to the design with a small flat tool, take the larger wooden tool and finish smoothing the background. The background should be flat without bulges or scratches. All the stretch should be taken out of the foil in one direction, either up and down or side to side, always starting close to the center of the design and working toward the edges. If the background is smoothed in both directions, the foil will buckle. Care should be taken not to overwork the metal because it will become brittle and hard.

If desired, a stippled background can be obtained. A shiny surface can be had by polishing the foil with number 000 steel wool. An antique finish is possible on copper by mixing a small piece of liver of sulfur in one half pint of water and applying to the surface. It will turn black and may then be polished to highlight desired areas.

Hammering

Forming by beating or hammering may be accomplished in two ways: beating over a stake and beating into a form. Forms of hardwood are used only when a limited number of articles are to be produced. Wooden forms can be purchased or are made by turning or carving into the wood a recess of the shape and depth desired. For beating down, a ball peen hammer or a mallet made of horn or wood should be used. To protect the metal surface, the peen faces are covered with a piece of leather or a rubber crutch tip.

BEATING INTO A FORM. Select or design a suitable form. Prepare a suitable form by turning or carving a recess of the shape and size desired from a 2-inch piece of wood. Lay out and cut a piece of 10- to 18-gauge copper or aluminum. When cutting the metal, every effort should be made to minimize the amount of material wasted. Cut the piece in rectangular form, allowing a little surplus for distortion when the metal is hammered into the form. The amount of surplus needed depends upon the depth the material is beaten down and the size of the object.

The piece of metal is centered over the form and fastened in place with brads driven through the corners into the wooden form (**Figure 9.29**). Locate the center, and with a compass draw the outline of the recess on the face of the metal. This line indicates the area that should be beaten down and the area that should not be hit.

Place the form on a solid surface. With a medium-size ball peen hammer or mallet start forming the metal by striking overlapping, light blows and

Figure 9.29 Beating into a Form

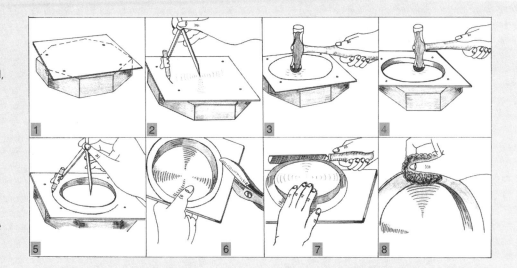

Materials: wooden form, steel wool, planishing hammer, tin snips, compass, file, sheet of copper or aluminum.

1. Fasten the metal to the wooden form.
2. Draw guidelines with a compass.
3. Hammer in center, working in circles to the outer edge.
4. Continue hammering the metal until it is the shape of the wooden form.
5. Lay out the guidelines for the finished form.
6. Cut around the guidelines with the snips.
7. File the edges smooth.
8. Polish with fine steel wool.

working in circles out toward the edges. Heavy blows are not needed; however, it is important to keep the handle of the hammer and the arm in a straight line, with the elbow close to the side. The handle is raised just enough to elevate the hammer head a few inches and on the down stroke exert little force. The hammer should hit the metal surface squarely.

Start again at the center and work in circles toward the outer edge. Be sure to use light, overlapping blows. Then move from the outer edge and work toward the center. Alternating the direction tends to equalize the internal strains that develop as the metal is stretched to form the required shape. Continue beating down the metal until it assumes the shape of the form. If the metal begins to work hard, it should be annealed. Annealing is the process of softening metal by heating. The copper or brass is heated evenly to a salmon red color and allowed to cool.

Raising a Shape over a Sandbag

A sandbag does not have the same limitations as a wooden mold. It allows for greater flexibility in the size and shape of the finished product. It can be used to form a great variety of shapes and sizes.

Make a sketch of how the finished product should look. Select, lay out, and cut a piece of 10- to 18-gauge copper or aluminum to the correct size. The size of the metal can be determined by bending a piece of wire to form a cross-section of the finished shape. A cardboard template should be made to check the shape as it is being formed.

Place the piece of metal on the sandbag with the guideline over the approximate center of the bag. Raise the rear of the metal about 2 or 3 inches, and with a horn or round-faced wooden mallet strike the metal with a light blow near the guideline (**Figure 9.30**). Rotate the metal slowly toward the

Figure 9.30 Raising a Shape over a Sandbag

Materials: sandbag, round-faced wooden mallet, tin snips, planishing hammer, compass, stake, sheet of copper or aluminum.

1. Draw guidelines with a compass.
2. Remove surplus stock with the snips.
3. Start hammering along the guidelines.
4. Increase the angle as forming progresses.
5. Continue to increase the angle until the correct form is obtained.
6. Planish the the surface over the stake.

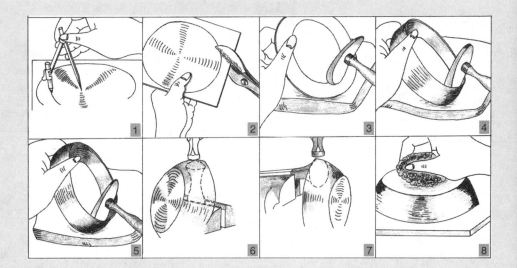

7. The stake should fit the contour of the bowl.
8. Finish the surface by rubbing it with steel wool.

right, striking another blow overlapping the previous one. Hold the metal at the same height and continue striking the surface with light blows until a complete circle has been made around the guideline. Move the metal back slightly on the sandbag so that another series of blows can be made that will slightly overlap the first ones. The height of the metal should be increased slightly.

Continue to move the metal back on the sandbag, while increasing the height. Care should be taken not to increase the height too rapidly because wrinkles will form. Wrinkles should be hammered out immediately. If the metal is formed gradually and carefully, wrinkles should not develop.

As the metal is being formed, the template should be used frequently to check the shape of the object. Continue to hammer and manipulate the metal on the sandbag until a suitable shape is obtained. If the metal is overworked, it will become hard and brittle and should be softened by annealing. When the correct shape is obtained, slight irregularities in the shape and indentations made during the forming should be removed by planishing. Planishing is the process of smoothing and stiffening metal by hammering the surface over a stake with a smooth-faced planishing hammer. If a planishing hammer is not available, a round-faced raising hammer or the ball end of a ball peen hammer can be used.

The top edge can be cut straight with a pair of tin snips and then smoothed with a mill file. A guideline may help and be necessary to obtain a straight edge. The finished product can be polished with fine steel wool or pumice.

Raising a Shape over a Recess

Select a block of hardwood 5 × 3 × 2 inches or a log of hardwood from a tree. Secure the piece in a vise and bore or gouge out a recess in the center, edge,

Figure 9.31 Raising a Shape
Over a Recess

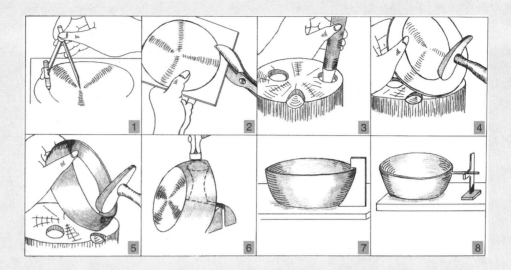

Materials: round-faced wooden
mallet, tin snips, planishing hammer,
compass, height gauge, file, stake,
sheet of copper or aluminum,
wooden log.

1. Draw guidelines with a
   compass.
2. Cut the shape out with
   the snips.
3. Gouge out a recess in
   the center, edge, or
   corner of the end of a
   hardwood log that fits
   the curvature of the
   form to be produced.
4. Place the piece of metal on
   the block of wood so that the
   guideline is over the center of
   the recess and at an angle of
   20 to 30 degrees. Strike along
   guideline with a round mallet.

5. Move the metal back and strike another series of hammer blows that slightly
   overlap those in the first row. The hammer blows should be just above the
   point where the metal and block touch.
6. Planish the surface over the stake.
7. Check the contour of the side with a template.
8. Mark the height of the finished bowl.

or corner to fit the curvature of the form to be produced (**Figure 9.31**). Select
a piece of metal and lay out the point where the curvature of the shape begins.
A cardboard template is helpful to check the finished shape.

Place the piece of metal on the block so that the guideline is over the
recess and at an angle of 20 to 30 degrees. While in this position, the metal is
formed by striking light overlapping blows with a round mallet, the peen of a
ball peen hammer, or a suitable raising hammer. Rotate the metal to the right
and continue to strike overlapping hammer blows along the guideline that
indicates the point where the curvature begins.

After a complete circle of hammer blows has been made along the guideline, move the metal back to allow another series of hammer blows that
slightly overlap those in the first row. The hammer blows should be just above
the point where the metal and block touch.

The metal should be manipulated on the block and over the recess to
obtain the desired shape. The shape of the recess may require some adjustments to obtain the desired curvature for the finished form.

With a template, check the shape during the forming operation. Wrinkles
should be hammered out when they form. However, if the piece is formed
gradually and carefully, wrinkles will not develop.

The metal should be manipulated and worked until the appropriate
shape is formed. On shallow shapes only a few complete circuits of hammer
blows will be required to raise the side of an object to the desired height. Trim
the top edge and file smooth with a mill file. Polish the surface with fine steel
wool or rubbing compound.

Figure 9.32 Etching Copper, Bronze, or Brass

Materials: sheet of copper, bronze, or brass; pliers; steel wool; turpentine; resist (asphaltum); paintbrush; acid bath.

1. Clean and polish the surface.
2. Transfer the design to the metal surface.
3. Paint unetched areas of the design with resist.
4. Use pliers to place the metal into the acid bath.
5. Wash off the acid in a pan of water.
6. Clean the resist from the surface with turpentine.

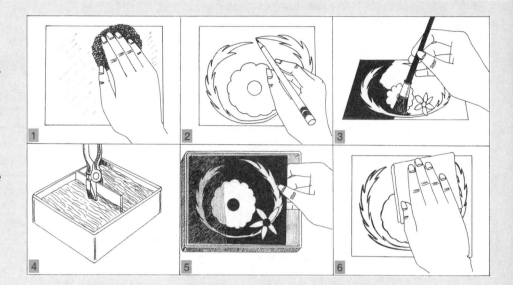

Other ornamenting techniques include *stamping*, which utilizes steel dies to make simple patterns on a piece of metal, and *chasing*, which utilizes blunt tools of various shapes to depress the metal on one side while raising it on the opposite side in the form of a design. No metal is removed in this process.

Etching Copper, Bronze, and Brass

Etching is a process that utilizes a chemical action to remove metal from the unprotected areas on the metal surface when placed in an acid bath. This technique is used to decorate bookends, paper knives, bowls, boxes, and jewelry.

Select or draw a design for the item to be etched. Cut and shape the piece to the preferred dimensions. It is a good practice to leave a little waste stock around the outline of the object, because the resist material has a tendency to crack and peel off along the edges allowing the acid to eat into the metal and produce uneven edges.

The metal surface should be cleaned with fine steel wool (**Figure 9.32**). With masking tape secure the design in position on the metal with a piece of carbon paper between the design and metal, carbon side down. Trace around the design with a pencil. When the design has been transferred to the metal surface, remove the design paper and carbon paper.

With a small brush, cover the areas from which no metal is to be removed with a resist material, usually black asphaltum, varnish, or stovepipe enamel. The areas from which the metal is to be removed are left unprotected. Allow the protective coating to dry for a few hours, and with a knife carefully remove any of the resist material that may have smeared onto the design.

Prepare the etching bath in a shallow glass or porcelain container. Mix one part nitric acid with two parts water. With a pair of tongs, slowly place the piece of metal into the nitric acid bath for from $^1/_2$ to 3 hours to obtain the desired depth, usually about 0.005 to 0.010 inch. Take the metal from the bath with tongs and wash under running water. Care should be taken not to handle the metal until the acid is washed off.

The resist material is removed by soaking the piece of metal in turpentine or naphtha for about 45 minutes and then wiping if clean with a cloth.

The piece of metal can be formed to the desired shape if this was not done before starting the etching process. Etched areas can be oxidized to make them stand out. A ball peen hammer can be used to decorate unetched areas.

Weaving, Sewing, and Hooking

No attempt can be made here to present all the intricate ramifications of weaving. It must suffice that elementary weaving forms, with some variations, are presented. The potential participant should be persuaded to seek a recreational outlet through this craft. If the urge to create can be aroused, if curiosity about advanced weaving techniques and designs is stimulated, then this presentation will have served its purpose. The interested person can read a variety of volumes that delve into the mysteries of the loom and its extensive modifications. Although the principles of weaving remain fairly constant, the technical aspects insofar as pattern and loom are concerned require thorough investigation. The general concept of weaving with fiber, cloth, paper, and reed materials is offered on the following pages. More significant, however, is the basic premise that weaving can be performed with or without a frame or loom.

Simple Looms

To rig a good, basic loom requires only a few pieces of wood, some small nails, and string. Weaving can be performed on any frame capable of withstanding the tension placed upon it by the warp. Take two strips of wood approximately $^1/_2 \times 1 \times 12$ inches, and two pieces about 20 inches long. Nail the two shorter strips to the longer ones to form a rectangle. This is the frame. Drive several nails into each corner to strengthen it. At $^1/_2$-inch intervals on the central line of the shorter wooden pieces, drive $^3/_4$-inch finishing nails halfway into the wood and slant them toward the outside of the frame. The loom is now ready to be strung by warp strands.

Tie the end of the warp to any corner nail. Putting tension on the warp, carry it to the opposite side of the frame and bend it around the back of two nails, carry it back to the starting side and bend it around the second two nails, then back to the opposite side in a continuous pattern until the entire loom has been warped. This will place the warp strands parallel to one another at $^1/_2$-inch intervals. The loom is easy to use, particularly for children. The process of weaving is simply to alternate the weft under and over the warp, packing each line tightly down, until the material is a size the weaver desires. When the weaving is completed, it may be removed from the loom, and the ends can be knotted and trimmed.

CARDBOARD LOOM. The cardboard loom consists of a piece of stiff cardboard cut to a size approximating the completed weaving. On the top and bottom edges of the cardboard a number of notches, spaced $^1/_2$ inch apart, should be cut (**Figure 9.33**). These will serve to hold the warp strands. Punch a hole in the upper left-hand corner of the loom and another at the lower

Figure 9.33 Cardboard Loom
and Weaving

Materials: cardboard, scissors, yarn,
Popsicle-stick shuttle.

1. Cut notches on edge of
cardboard.
2. Warp cardboard face.
3. Weave yarn through
warp.
4. Cut warp ends and tie
off.
5. Cut end knot and tie off.
6. Remove cardboard loom.

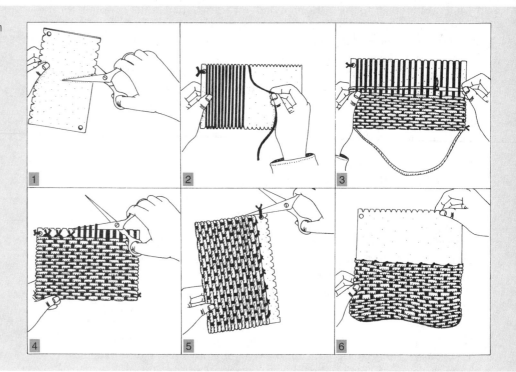

right-hand corner. The warp thread is knotted so that it cannot slide through the hole, passed through the top left-hand hole, and wound around the notches of the loom. The thread is pulled through the bottom right-hand hole and tied off. The entire card is now covered with vertical warp threads.

To weave, thread the weft thread through a large needle or shuttle and begin at the lower right of the cardboard loom by using a simple over and under pattern. Continue until the weft is across. Make sure that the weft is continually pushed down so the threads are tightly packed. This packing process may be done with a beater so that the work remains firm and even. When the line is completed in front, turn the loom over and weave again, until the starting point is reached. Continue this procedure until the weaving has reached within approximately $1/2$ inch of the top. The warp threads should then be cut and knotted two by two on each side. The warp knots may then be cut at the upper left and lower right. The weaving can then be taken from the loom intact.

CIRCLE LOOM. The circle loom, as its name implies, is used for weaving round objects. The loom can be suspended from any convenient branch, pole, or hook. Because it is lightweight, it may be comfortable for the weaver to hold the loom in one hand with the lower half resting in the lap. Almost any material may be used for the warp. Whatever is used for the warp, lighter material should be used for the weft. A barrel hoop is used as the basic frame for the loom. If a hoop cannot be found, a circle may be cut from a piece of $1/2$-inch plywood as a substitute. Notches are cut around the circumference of the circle frame. They should be 2 to 3 inches apart, directly opposite one another, and of an odd number so that continuous weaving may be accomplished.

Figure 9.34   Circle Loom
Weaving

Materials: cardboard, scissors, yarn, large needle or Popsicle-stick shuttle.

1. Notch edge of cardboard circle.
2. Warp strand from edge through center hole.
3. Continue warping circle.
4. Weave weft through spokes.
5. Cut weft and tie off.
6. Remove cardboard loom.

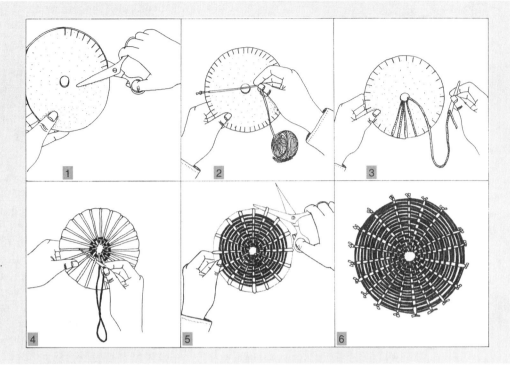

To thread the loom, pass the warp through a hole and knot the end. Carry the warp strand across the center and to a hole directly opposite; pass the thread through the circumference over the hole adjacent to it on the right, coming back through the circle from the outside to the hole on the opposite side of the circle to the left of the original warp strand. This process is repeated until the loom is strung or warped. The appearance of the circle loom completely strung is that of a wheel with radii or spokes (**Figure 9.34**). The last warp strand end should be fastened to the first.

To weave on the circle loom, simply knot the weft strands at the point where all the warp strands cross. Holding the frame securely, begin to interlace the weft. Initially, the warp should be divided into four segments where it cuts across the center. These parts will serve as the core and should be woven around three or four times until the midsection is even and tight. The warp should then be subdivided into eight sections, woven around three or four times, and subdivided again until the weft is being threaded under and over each alternate warp strand. The weaving should continue until the fabric reaches the desired size. On the final line, weave between the warp threads. Remove the material from the loom by cutting the outside threads. There should be several inches of warp remaining. Place the material on a flat surface and tie each warp end with a double knot. The ends may then be woven several inches into the material. The material is now ready for whatever purpose the weaver has in mind. If it is to be a mat, it may be lined with long-lasting and heavy fiber. The material should be steamed so that it will lie flat.

A Weaving Project

To produce a bag or other carryall from a woven piece, double it and sew the edges together. Line or finish it at the top with one of a variety of fasteners, such as a zipper, a cord and button, or a drawstring. The material could be folded in thirds, sewing two sides together and using the last section as a flap. A loop is braided, crocheted, or formed with a buttonhole stitch over strands of yarn and attached to the flap so that it can be secured over a button. Make a bag by weaving around a cardboard loom so that it is closed on the sides and bottom and open at the top. The cardboard is removed when the weaving is finished. Warp threads are retained in position and the crafts project is prepared as previously indicated in the section dealing with the cardboard loom.

Wrap Weaving

Almost any fiber may be used in wrap weaving. Typically, remnants or leftover threads are the basis for creating attractive hand-woven forms. A variation on the circle loom process of weaving is achieved by wrapping a number of threads around interesting pieces of wood or other small-diameter rigid materials. Tongue depressors, dowels, Popsicle sticks, and slightly longer pieces of wood may best be used for this weaving method.

The wrapping technique requires the thread to be passed from one spoke to another. To begin, place a solid circle of thick cardboard in the center of the crossed sticks. All the spokes are secured to the center of the hub. The thread is then wound over alternating spokes. Threads may be wound so that the lines will cover the top or the bottom of the frame. Combination weaving may also be performed, thereby giving the finished project a three-dimensional effect (**Figure 9.35**).

The fabric may be doubled by first wrapping the thread around alternating spokes and then turning the frame over to work on the spokes that were passed during the initial operation. Almost any pattern may be developed, depending only upon the ingenuity of the weaver.

Figure 9.35 Wrap Weaving

Materials: twine, yarn, thread, twigs, Popsicle sticks or thin dowels, acorns, buttons, wax (if desired), cardboard, scissors, glue.

1. Take a piece of cardboard and cut in a circular shape.
2. Take wooden sticks or thin dowels and cross them over the cardboard base.
3. Secure the sticks to the cardboard.
4. Make a simple knot at a point half the distance between the base and the tip of the spoke.
5. Weave over the alternating spokes.
6. A combined weaving effect may be achieved by turning the frame over and weaving around the spokes bypassed in the initial operation.

Other forms of weaving include spool weaving, paper weaving, bead weaving, inkle loom weaving, card weaving, and solid-core weaving. All of these techniques may be used in any comprehensive crafts activity depending upon the interest of participants.

Solid-Core Weaving

Among the variations on weaving is the utilization of the semi-braiding technique, worked on a solid base or core without a loom or frame. The warp strands, sometimes made out of plastic lace, are fastened to one end of an oblong piece of metal. The strands are permitted to overlap the edge and are then secured by some kind of tape (masking tape will do) or a paper clip. A flat metal blank may become a bracelet or, if a square, a brooch.

The warp strands are stretched from the point of attachment down to the opposite end, where they hang freely. The weaving or braiding design may be checkerboard weave, inverted V's, or other geometric shapes that please the designer. The weft strands are woven in the same under-and-over manner as in any weaving. They are drawn tightly across the surface of the metal blank and passed around the under part. Continued tension should be maintained upon the cross strands, and each successive strand must be positioned next to the strand that preceded it so that the two actually touch where the warp strands permit. Continue the procedure until the design and blank are finished. Tuck the end strands into the weft and clip for a neat finish (**Figure 9.36**). The single weft strand is tucked in under itself at the last line of the finished blank.

To make a bracelet, simply bend the metal oblong around some rounded object; a metal pipe will serve for this task. The metal blanks are flexible enough so that they may be bent around the human wrist to produce the kind of fit desired.

Figure 9.36 Solid-Core Weaving

Materials: oblong aluminum strip, gimp or pyrolace in various colors, masking or Scotch tape, scissors, paper clip.

1. Finished product.
2. Warp strands are taped to metal blank.
3. Weft strands are folded under metal blank.
4. Wrap weft strands to begin weaving.
5. Tuck end under warp.
6. Tuck end strand into the weft.
7. Clip ends for neat finish.
8. Twisting effect.

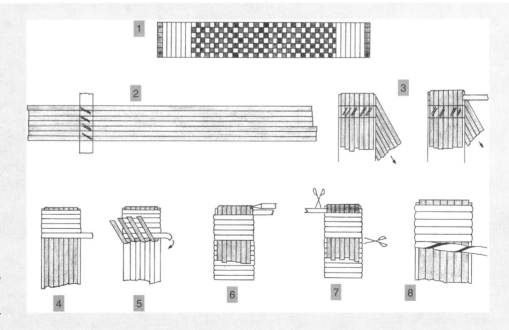

Where a complete circlet, without break, is worked, the following procedure may be employed. Cut three or more strips of flat plastic lacing long enough to go around the circumference of the band with approximately $1/2$ inch extra. Secure these for the base using a paper clip. The working strand or weft should be five or six times the length of the warp strands and is woven in the typical alternate pattern of weaving. Pass the weft through the ring, and continue weaving until the core is covered. Remove the paper clip, and carry the weaving directly over the loose ends it was retaining. When the pattern is finished, the working strand end is sliced to a sharp point and threaded through the first row of weaving taken. It is then tucked under a strand on the inside of the ring, drawn taut, and cut off.

Basketry as Weaving

Although natural plant reeds are available and can be gathered for use if one is close to a marsh area, most people turn to commercial reeds when basketry is considered for crafts. Commercial availability and convenience permit a wide range of reeds to be selected. Thus, flat and round strands of different widths and diameters are readily accessible. Commercial reeds frequently come in skeins and are typically dry and, therefore, brittle. However, soaking the reeds in water makes them pliable and easy to handle. Working strands of reed should be bundled into a loose coil before soaking. When being prepared for use as spokes or handles, reeds may be cut to short lengths before soaking. The reeds should be kept damp through the application of moist cloths.

Basketry is sufficiently different from flat weaving to have some terms with which the potential participant should become familiar. The "base" is the solid or woven core around and on which the basket will be developed. From the base there protrude "spokes." The spokes may be made by inserting several strands of reed through other strands when the base is woven. Spokes always lie flat and radiate from the center of the base. Reeds that are inserted into a solid base and stand vertically are called "stakes."

Using pliable reeds, select eight that will be used for the base. Slit four of the reeds slightly to the left and right of the center of each reed so the cuts are capable of accommodating transverse reeds. The other four reeds are then inserted into the lengthwise openings (see **Figure 9.37**). Align these four spokes so that they touch on the edges. When these eight reeds are arranged properly, they should form a symmetrical cross. The weaving process is initiated around these eight reeds.

To begin the weaving, take a thinner reed strand than was used for the spokes and loop it around one of the cross arms so that the ends of the strand are free. Push the strand close to the midsection of the cross. Weave the two free ends around the next cross arm so that one end goes over the spokes while the other goes under the same spokes. Cross the ends and weave them around the third cross arm. Continue this procedure until the working reed has run about four lines. Finish this core weave by tucking the working strands over or under the next arm. The base is enlarged by pairing the cross strands. Instead of having two cross pieces of four strands apiece, each bar will be divided into pairs so that eight spokes will emerge. This is accomplished in the same way that the core was created. Weave the reed ends over and under these pairs until the spokes are held securely in place.

Now, the paired spokes must be divided to provide single spokes. This is achieved by separating the double strands and weaving around the individual

Figure 9.37 Basket Weaving

Materials: reeds of appropriate length, wooden base (if necessary).

1. Slit four reeds slightly to the left and right of center and insert four transverse reeds.
2. Loop a weaving reed around one cross arm, pass one end over the next four, and pass the other end under the same four. Continue this procedure until all cross arms are secure. Tuck the working strands over or under the next arm.
3. Divde the four arms into eight pairs by looping a weaving reed around two strands and following step 2.
4. Divde the pairs again by looping a weaving reed around one strand and following step 2 to obtain 16 spokes.

5. Bend the spokes upward and weave a working reed over and under each spoke.
6. Continue the weaving process until the desired height is reached.

spokes until the base is of the size desired. It will be circular in shape and may be completed by finishing the edge. The edge can be finished by weaving each spoke around the other spokes or by bending each spoke and inserting the end into the base so that a series of closed curves are presented to view.

Oval and oblong bases may be made with any number of reeds, and solid bases may also be used with "waling." Waling requires three strands of reed. Position two strands on opposite sides of the stake; cross them and then bend them around the next stake. Repeat this procedure for one row. The third strand is then insinuated into the previous pattern by threading it over the top of the two crossed strands, then in front of the two next stakes, then under the next cross, and so on.

Sewing

Sewing is the attachment of one piece of material to another by means of inserting flexible fiber (thread) through the materials to be joined. The implement used for passing the thread through material is a needle. Needles are generally made of steel and have a pointed end for quick penetration and an eye at the opposite end so that the thread may be passed through and secured.

Almost any material can be sewn if it can be penetrated by the needle and the thread can maintain the attachment of closure. Sewing may be simple or complex, depending upon the need, the project contemplated, and the skill and artistic sense of the sewer. Sewing may be very practical, producing usable items, or it may have no utilitarian value, but great artistic or aesthetic value.

Stitches

A variety of stitches are used in sewing, and each one is useful for certain purposes. Among the more utilitarian stitches are:

- *Basting stitch:* A large straight-line stitch used to temporarily hold material in place until a finer and more permanent stitch may be used. Basting stitches are removed after the project is finished.
- *Running stitch:* A tiny straight-line stitch used for seams that are not put under any strain. The needle is passed through the material and back again, taking up a very small amount of material for each stitch.
- *Gathering or shirring stitch:* This stitch is performed as for running stitches. After the thread is knotted, fill the needle with stitches and draw them back on the thread. After all the material that is to be shirred is on the thread, pull the thread to the desired length and secure.
- *Overcasting stitch:* This stitch is used to secure a rough edge. If two pieces are to be attached, baste them in position and take stitches over the seam edge, holding the needle in a slanted position. All stitches must be of the same length.
- *Whipping or whip stitch:* A shallow overcasting stitch. Using the same kind of stitch as in overcasting, make smaller stitches closer together.

Without stitches there could be no needlecraft. Stitching is the technique by which thoughts, plans, and art may be transmitted to fabric. Stitches are selected because they suit the design. All stitches will attach one surface to another or permit the development of some idea with the insertion of thread through fabric, but a stitch becomes eminently appropriate for use when it expresses or reflects absolutely the subject to be worked. For this reason the craftsperson must have a good knowledge of the stitches available and the skill to use and select the right one for the subject matter at hand. There are literally hundreds of stitches that can be used for needlecraft. A few examples should serve to indicate the variety of techniques available. Among these are: satin stitch, Romanian stitch, chevron stitch, looped stitches, chain stitch, rosette chain stitch, knotted stitches, composite stitches, cross stitch, chain border stitch, and couching (**Figure 9.38**).

Quilting

Among the more pleasurable traditional social crafts activities in the United States and elsewhere is the quilting bee. For any patchwork quilt, select fabric scraps of the same type and weight. The pieces in each figure can be all different or show color variations. To design the quilt, cut two squares of cardboard and mark the desired figure on each one. Each square should be approximately 12 $\frac{1}{2}$ inches. Leave one whole to show the design and cut the

Figure 9.38 Different Stitches

1. Satin
2. Roumaniain
3. Chevron
4. Feather
5. Looped
6. Chain
7. Rosette chain
8. French knot
9. Pekinese
10. Cross
11. Chain border
12. Couching

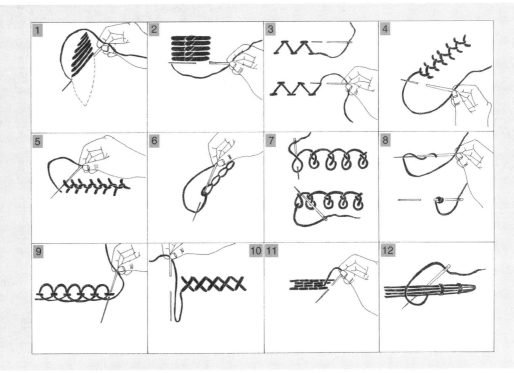

other up to use as a pattern. Cut out pieces of fabric around the cardboard patterns, allowing about $1/4$ inch on all edges. Sew the pieces into squares and press the seams open. Embroider over the seams on the right side with six-strand embroidery floss in a herringbone or other stitch. For cotton quilts, use two to three strands of floss. Join completed squares into strips with $1/4$-inch seams and embroider over the seams in the same decorative stitch. Connect strips of squares crosswise and embroider the seams. For the lining of a double size quilt, cut two pieces of fabric 40×104 inches; for the border, cut two pieces 4×80 inches. Join lining pieces with a $1/2$-inch seam and press. Sew border pieces to squares with $1/2$-inch seams, mitering the corners. Place the lining wrong side up on a flat surface and spread two layers of batting over it, trimming wherever necessary. Press the quilt top carefully and place over the batting, right side up. Turn under a $1/2$-inch seam on the lining, quilt the top edges, and fasten together. Baste to keep the batting in place. Whip stitch the lining and quilt edges. For decorative purposes, quilt along ornamental square edges, gathering in all thicknesses.

Appliqué

Appliqué is a technique that fastens pieces of a fabric to a background. Almost any material can be used. Fastening may be done by sewing, basting, or tacking. For the crafts instructor, there are unlimited opportunities to introduce appliqué work to youngsters as well as to the more mature individual. Children enjoy sewing if exposed to the process at an early age. In fact, both young girls and boys show a remarkable aptitude for it. All that is required are large quantities of scrap materials of various colors, sizes, and textures. Because appliqué is concerned with two-dimensional shapes, preliminary designs can be worked out with drawings, paintings, or colored paper before the actual cutting and sewing are undertaken.

Instruction should encourage spontaneity, surprise, and the ideas that come to mind as the work continues. Themes for appliqué may be derived from fantasy, history, everyday life, books that have been read, schoolwork, or any of the myriad ideas that contemporary life urges upon the individual. Environmental concerns and objects in their natural state may all serve as stimuli for this craft. When the design has been decided upon, pieces of fabric representative of the spaces in the design are chosen and cut to size. Initially, the pieces are tacked onto a ground and then sewed securely in place. Even at this stage, the instructor should encourage modifications of the basic scheme and changes in texture, color, and stitching if the participant is so inclined.

Hooking

Hooking employs a tool with a curved end to draw and press flexible material alternately in and out through some background material. It permits the combined use of weaving and stitchery and offers the participant an opportunity to experience the joy and satisfaction of creating a unique piece of work that is a delight to the eye as well as to the sense of touch. Arranging color, pattern, and texture in an appropriate design challenges the ingenuity and technical skill of the craftsperson. Hooking is simple enough to be performed by a child, yet its advanced forms require the greatest skill and talents of the artist. A variety of products from rugs to wall hangings of intricate design and great beauty may be produced in a range of textures from shag to sculptural effects.

Two fundamental techniques are utilized in hooking. One uses a backing of burlap or other such material and a hooked tool; the second employs a loop latch hook and a backing material of scrim. Generally, the former method is preferred. In the hook-and-burlap method, yarn or other material is held underneath the ground with one hand; the hooked tool is inserted through the ground and catches the yarn, which is then drawn up into a loop at the top. The process is repeated until 10 or 12 strands have been pulled up. The hooking must be done in such a manner that the loops are tightly bunched together to prevent their being pulled out. Of necessity, each loop should be at the same height. Different yarns or fibers may be used to create a mixture of colors, piles, and textures, which adds to the effect.

Among the tools used for hooking are the punch needle, shuttle hooker, and hand hook. A crocheting needle may also be used advantageously. When a rug is to be hooked, a design should be made. Burlap is stretched on a frame (which may be constructed or purchased commercially) and secured with tacking so it remains taut. The design should then be transferred to the burlap with charcoal, paint, dye, colored paper, or chalk.

To use the punch needle, pass the yarn through the eye of the tool and through the inside point. Pull approximately 12 inches of yarn through the needle, then draw the yarn back with sufficient tension so it will slowly slide into the tube and handle.

Set the loop gauge for the desired loop length. Slant the needle in the direction the hooking will incline. Press the needle through the backing until it meets the handle (**Figure 9.39**). Keep the hand holding the tool firmly on the backing. Draw the needle to the surface and smoothly move from loop to

Figure 9.39 Hooking

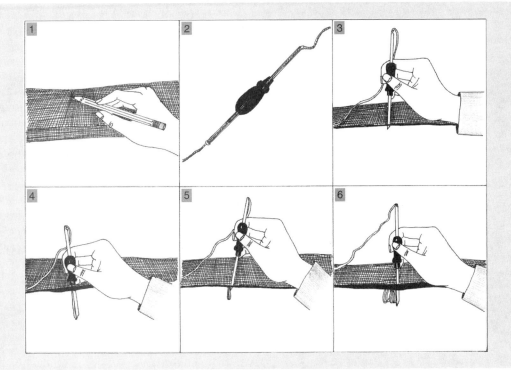

Materials: burlap, yarn, hooking tool, pencil, scissors.

1. Lay out design on ground.
2. Thread punch needle.
3. Insert needle into ground.
4. Push needle through ground.
5. Make pile loop beneath ground.
6. Repeat hooking process until completed.

loop. Continue the procedure as the clustering loops now secure one another in place. When all sections of the design have been completed, remove the material from the frame. Fold the edge back and apply appropriate stitching for an even and neat finish.

The second method of hooking employs a scrim background and the loop latch hook. Because scrim is a stiffened material, there is no need for a frame. The design should be transferred to the scrim before the hooking is started. The loop latch hook actually knots the yarn into the backing. The desired length of yarn for this technique is about 2 inches. Enough threads should be cut and piled so that at least one section of the design may be completed before more yarn must be cut to size. Join the two ends of the yarn so that a loose loop is formed, and hold it together between your fingers. Insert the loop latch through the loop and under one strand of scrim. Draw the two ends of the yarn up to the tip of the hook and position them between the hook and latch. Close the latch and draw the tool back through the scrim and through the first loop. Continue to hold the ends of the yarn so that a knot is formed. Repeat this procedure while making sure that the loops are close together.

Assorted Other Crafts

Among the possible crafts that can be incorporated into a comprehensive craft activity are nature crafts from natural materials including seashells, spores, fungi, hemlock cones, and various seeds that can be used for utensils, candleholders, necklaces, a variety of settings, and decorations. Natural baskets can be made from spruce and willow, or corn husks can be used to make sandals.

Candles can be made from bayberries, and other berries may be picked and crushed to make natural dyestuffs. Clay is a natural product that may be collected from lake or stream beds or from excavations. Clay may be found in almost any color. When the natural clay is cleaned it should be set aside to age or dry in the air for several days. When dry, clay must be broken into powder. The powdered clay is then placed into a pail or tub, covered with water, and allowed to soak until it is soft enough to be stirred. After stirring, the resulting thick liquid should be poured through a coarse and a fine filter to remove any foreign matter. Permit the mixture to stand until the clay settles to the bottom of the container. When all the clay has settled, pour off the water, spread the clay out to dry, and permit it to stand until almost all of the excess water has evaporated. The clay is now ready for use.

Whittling is an old custom that requires only a pocketknife and any piece of wood at hand. Sometimes whittling is done solely for relaxation, and the whittler makes little shavings out of sticks, blocks, or chunks of wood. However, a wide variety of objects can be carved with a small knife and a piece of wood.

Bird feeders, hanging flower baskets, log stools, knotting, lashing, and macramé are some of the forms that natural crafts may take. One should not forget to mention caning, mat weaving, fly-tying, netting, and braiding.

Theater crafts (which include puppet making, marionettes, dioramas, and stage and scene design), marine crafts, automotive crafts, electrical crafts, and junk or recycling crafts in all of their infinite shapes, sizes, textures, and projects are an intrinsic part of the total crafts program.

Summary

The manipulation of useful and sometimes decorative objects has a long tradition. Ever since proto-hominids, living in Africa's Olduvai Gorge, cracked pebbles and fashioned them into crude tools, handicrafts have been a uniquely human activity. Every type of material, whether animal, vegetable, or mineral, can be used for a craft. Moreover, categories of crafts including automotive, marine, nature, meteorological, culinary, and many others are available to the interested participant. Sewing, sawing, braiding, knotting, drilling, hammering, or weaving are only a few of the techniques that apply to crafts.

Crafts have been shown to offer a variety of experiences that can promote and produce satisfaction for the needs of a diverse clientele. From simple to complex forms occurring on the playgrounds of childhood to the sophisticated shops of advanced skilled adults, crafts attract those with no fabricating background as well as those who are technically adept.

The need for well-appointed craft shops at one or more locations within the community may be a significant factor in promoting this recreational activity. Of course, a good public relations campaign will also alert potential patrons to the possibilities. Simultaneously, basic craft activities at the lowest level may be implemented wherever some space can be found, indoors or outdoors, for this phase of the program.

Of vital importance is the employment of recreationists with appropriate craft skills, the recruitment of volunteers with the requisite skills for instruction, or the per diem hiring of craftpersons to teach specific craft forms and/or techniques.

Whether conducted at a centralized facility or distributed at numerous locations throughout the community, the craft experience should be scheduled to accommodate the greatest number of participants with the least inconvenience as to time and place. The crafts category is essential to a well-rounded recreational program.

Selected Further References

Allen, H. L. *Weaving Contemporary Rag Rugs: New Designs, Traditional Techniques.* New York: Sterling Publishing Co., Inc., 2001.

Anderson, E. *Art of Gold and Silver Metal Clay.* Iola, WI: Krause Publications, 2002.

Baker, M. *Wood for Woodturners.* New York: Guild of Master Craftsman Publications, Ltd., 2005.

Dean, J. *Craft of Natural Dying: Glowing Colors from the Plant World.* Kansas City, KS: Search Press, Ltd., 2004.

Eichorn, R. *Art of Fabric Collage: An Easy Introduction to Creative Sewing.* Newtown, CT: Tauton Press, Inc., 2003.

Gutner, Z. *Woodcarving: A Foundation Course.* Collingdale, PA: DIANE Publishing Co., 2004.

Held, S. E. *Weaving: A Handbook of the Fiber Arts.* Florence, KY: Wadsworth Publishing, 1998.

Irvin, C. M. *Craft Sticks Mania.* Danbury, CT: Scholastic Library Publishing, 2002.

Krupenia, D. *Art of Making Jewelry.* San Diego, CA: Advantage Publications Group, 2005.

McGuire, M. *Craft Workshop: How to Make Stunning Objects Using Natural Materials with 25 Step-by-Step Projects.* Blueridge Summit, PA: Anness Publishing, 2005.

———. *Leatherwork.* Blueridge Summit, PA: Anness Publishing, 2005.

Melville, S. *Crafts for All Abilities.* Kansas City, KS: Search Press, Ltd., 1997.

Peck, K. *Art of Handmade Tile: The Complete Instructions for Carving, Casting, and Glazing.* Iola, WI: Krause Publications, 2002.

Peterson, S. *Craft and Art of Clay.* 3rd ed. New York: The Overlook Press, Inc., 2000.

Research and Education Association Staff. *Leather/Craft and Weaving.* Piscataway, NJ: REA, 2003.

———. *Metal Shop and Metal Arts.* Piscataway, NJ: REA, 2003.

Schaefer, C. *Sew Any Fabric: 101 Fabrics from A to Z.* Iola, WI: Krause Publications, 2003.

Stohlman, A., and A. Stohlman. *Art of Embossing Leather.* South Fort Worth, TX: Tandy Leather Co., 1986.

Zieman, N. *Sew with Confidence: 100+ Tips, Techniques, and Projects Anyone Can Do.* Iola, WI: Krause Publications, 2004.

CHAPTER

10 Invitation to Dance

Any rhythmic movement, gross or fine, that is sustained by a regular tempo, beat, or music, may be termed *dance*. Dance has been conceived as a method of nonverbal communication, as kinetic movement to relieve tension, and as a means of social and individual self-expression. The dance category may, for ease of programming, be classified as: folk, social, choreographed, or rhythmic. Folk dancing includes square, round, line, and ethnic types. Social dancing includes waltzing, rumba, tango, fox trot, and any fad (e.g., twist, break dancing, hip-hop, and other current crazes). However, this material is specific to couples dancing. Choreographed dance includes all preplanned and sequenced movements to some score and includes ballet, modern, concert, and interpretive dancing. Rhythmics incorporates free exercise, some games, and synchronized movements to a selected tempo.

Dance, like all skills, must be learned. One of the most popular recreational activities, it has found almost universal expression in every culture. A dance may reflect traditions or a general contemporary feeling. Many dances are outgrowths of religious rites or of an ethnic variety depicting the celebrations and mores of different cultural patterns. Dancing is a graceful rhythmic motor skill whose performance can be enjoyed by spectators and participants alike. Dancing as an outlet of self-expression may also be of a solo type, dual, or performed in groups (**Figure 10.1**). Dancing fosters socialization and enables people to satisfy a basic urge to respond to a pleasing tempo.

Although social dancing still attracts the greatest number of people, square and folk dance have come to be extremely popular, and interest in this form of the activity is growing. The criteria for selecting specific types of dance forms are influenced by the age, gender, prior experience, degree of skill, and size of the group involved. Instructional phases of dance may be divided into the familiar beginner, intermediate, and advanced classifications.

Instruction in any type of dance requires the presence of qualified leadership. Recreationists qualified to teach dance are necessary to provide competent guidance for the inclusion of all who seek enjoyment through this medium. The various forms of dance enable almost everyone to achieve a sense of satisfaction. The techniques involved and the objectives to which people aspire vary greatly, thus offering opportunity for individuals to experience emotional outlets. Through instructional classes for the development of needed skills and in sharing the vicarious stimulation of watching the dance as a spectator, this activity proves of immense value as a socializing mechanism and contributes to the cohesion of any group so engaged. Dance is a compelling activity that permeates all cultures and provides opportunities for a sense of fulfillment in movement, enjoyment of the social occasion, and feelings of accomplishment as the individual exhibits the personal skills acquired through practice.

Figure 10.1 All Join Hands and Circle the Ring

Skills to Be Learned

In order to obtain the greatest satisfaction from any type of dancing, the participant must be competent in the fundamental skills and completely understand the activity. Among the basic skills are the following:

- Dance posture and body control
- Elegant dance movement
- Knowledge of appropriate couples dance positions
- Dancing techniques with a partner
- Sensitivity to rhythm, and the ability to move in time with a variety of dance meters
- Accordance with fundamental dance movements and a variety of step combinations in the most frequently performed social dance forms
- Ability to perform the most popular social dances in the appropriate style
- Etiquette for social dancing experiences

Posture and Body Control

Posture refers to how an individual carries him or herself, and is the basis for graceful and attractive dancing. Good posture is really natural, functional, and relaxed. It is typically upright without being stiff. In couples dancing, each dancer should be able to look at their partner directly.

The dancer's particular style of movement may change with the dance he or she is performing, but there are a number of common principles that should assist each individual to hold him or herself more gracefully and move in a more coordinated manner on the dance floor. One should stand with the body weight directly over the arch of the foot, with the knees slightly flexed. The upper body is inclined somewhat forward and the shoulders are open. The head is held high and is directly over the chest. The chin is parallel to the floor so the couple can look at one another without strain. The entire appearance is one of ease and standing tall. The feet are together and pointing straight ahead. The alignment of the body is evenly distributed or symmetrical. Slumping shoulders or a drooping chin or chest should be avoided. Good posture and a strong sense of balance are prerequisite whether standing or moving, and assure that the body will be under control for any dance movement.

Elegant Dance Movement

Walking is a fundamental movement in dance. The dance walk is a significant element in dancing that needs to be done with grace and appropriate style. If one can master this movement, dancing will be a success. The dance walk requires a forward or backward traveling step, in which the dancer usually takes two steps to a measure of music.

To start, the dancer begins with his or her feet close together, parallel, and pointing straight ahead. Usually the male begins by stepping forward with his left foot. In order to do this, he sways slightly forward with the upper body and, raising the heel of the right foot, swings the left foot forward keeping the leg straight. The left foot moves along close to the floor; when the left leg is completely extended, the weight is shifted to the ball of the left foot and then glides smoothly onto the entire foot. Continuing the dance walk, the male keeps moving at an even pace with the body weight held in a slightly forward manner; the next step is taken leading with the right foot. The dance walk must be made in an absolutely straight line, with the knees nearly brushing as they pass. Typically a single dance walk, from the heel of the leading foot to the toe of the supporting foot, is approximately the length of the dancer's foot.

The backward dance walk, performed by the female, is similar to the forward step, but done in reverse. The body weight is shifted slightly forward, and the dancer swings her right leg backward from the hip, with the knee straight, the leg and ankle extended, and the toe reaching straight back toward the floor. The weight is then transferred onto the toe, then the ball of the foot, and then the entire foot, although it remains primarily on the ball of the foot.

In doing the dance walk, the feet must be kept close together while traveling straight ahead or backward without swaying from side to side. The body must be held forward and moves just prior to the leading foot. The arms are held high and the body is erect. The traveling foot always moves along close to the floor. The weight is transferred smoothly without any sudden jolting. A graceful walk requires a small movement with the shoulders. When one steps forward with the left foot, the right shoulder should be brought slightly forward. The same movement occurs on the right foot.

Knowledge of Appropriate Couple Dance Positions

Knowledge of suitable couple dance positions is important because it enables the dancer's movements to be free, provides the opportunity to improvise steps or place them together in spontaneous sequences, offers the opportunity to lead and follow gracefully, and makes a good appearance. Essential, naturally, is good posture. The body must always be erect and appear graceful. A variety of dance positions may be used in social dancing; however, only four are vital. The others are adaptations.

The Closed Dance Position

The male stands facing the way he expects to move (i.e., counterclockwise). His partner faces him directly, looking clockwise. They should be quite close to one another, almost toe to toe, and usually with their upper bodies slightly touching. Therefore, when the male steps forward, he immediately gives his partner a lead, and she recognizes the cue to step backward. The pair's shoulders are held level and should parallel each other.

The male's right arm encircles his partner; his right hand is placed just below her left shoulder blade, palm in. The female's left hand rests lightly on her partner's right shoulder and somewhat below it, depending on their relative heights. The male's left hand with palm up holds the partner's right hand with her palm down. The arms are held away from the body with the elbows slightly curved and just below the shoulder level. The partners join hands at a level just above the elbows. Partners usually stand a little to their own left, so that they are looking over each other's right shoulder with their toes dovetailed.

The Promenade Position

The man stands facing away from the center of the dance floor. The female faces him and has her right shoulder toward the counterclockwise position. Taking the closed position, they subsequently turn their upper bodies and heads to the man's left and the female's right, facing counterclockwise. Whatever step is being done may require opening up more or less. Depending upon the step, the joined hands may be released, but the man's right arm remains around his partner's waist while her left hand remains on his right shoulder.

The Skating Position

Both partners face counterclockwise, shaking hands, while holding them in front. The male's right hand holds his partner's right hand over their joined left hands.

The Side Positions

Partners stand with their right sides adjacent to one another. The male faces counterclockwise, the female is reversed. Arms and hands are held as in the closed position. The male's left hand is held in front of his left shoulder and not out to the side. The left position is the reverse of the right position.

In each of these positions, particular hand holds can vary with relation to the type of dance being performed. In any case, all dancing positions should be natural and comfortable. Partners need to adjust to each other's height and build.

Leading and following are musts for graceful dancing. The lead must know exactly what he will do before attempting to lead. Timeliness is important. The lead must be given prior to the phase of music that signals to change position, direction, or step. The musical rhythm is extremely significant and, therefore, the individual needs to wait before starting or perform a simple maneuver that his partner can easily follow while compensating for the rhythm.

Dance Movement

All dance may be divided into four basic movements: swaying, pumping, gliding, and contracting. Swaying movements are characterized by rhythmic "to-and-fro" action. They have relaxed velocity and slowing, as with the movements of rocking in a chair. The recovery is not obtained until the momentum of the preceding effort has stopped. The effect is calming, which stimulates repetition.

The regular characteristics of the typical swaying movement are quickly changed to a forward-and-back pumping action if the moving part is pushed forward and retrieved before momentum is overcome. This "one-two" effect is rigorous, very physical, and fatiguing because of the effort required to stop momentum and alter direction.

Pumping movements are sudden and explosive; they are achieved in consequence of the rapid spasmodic free release of energy similar to pushing, punching, or throwing. Pumping occurs at the part of the movement that will offer the most strength and speed to the object being moved or contacted. Jumping, bouncing, running, and walking also have explosive release, but to a different degree in accordance with the activity. The preceding movement of these actions is swaying or gliding, or it may be a combination of both, and typically the movement finishes with a sweeping action.

Gliding movements are performed with a smooth, sustained energy release throughout the movement. Gliding movements differ from the temporary halting of the movement that, by using muscle tensions, occurs at the end of a rocking or sweeping movement.

Contracting movements are typified by the immediate release of energy throughout the entire body. Contraction may occur with some resistance at the start and then finish in a rapid sliding release, or there may be some resistance throughout the collapsing movement that would offer little in the way of contraction. Contraction occurs with or without resistance to the movement from upright to collapse. With resistance there is a gradual or controlled decline without reduction of posture, as in a split.

Dancing incorporates one, some, or all of these qualities. The actual bases for aesthetic experience in movement depend upon tension. The regulator of all movement in dance is rhythm. Rhythm may best be understood as the process by which action occurs over time. Rhythm is the length of time any movement takes; tempo is the rate at which movements follow each other sequentially.

Instruction

Successful dance experience may be achieved if the instruction enables the potential dancers to get along almost effortlessly. The instructor needs to be entirely familiar with the fundamental steps, music, and dance sequence before trying to transmit that knowledge. Additionally, the instructor must be skilled in demonstrating the steps and be ready at all times to take advantage of the attention of the learners so there is maximum use of class time. Any dance may be presented in a series of activities formulated for easy understanding. All dances should be analyzed for specific movements, and these should be taught in the clearest possible manner. There is a greater likelihood of success if the instructor does not use very technical terminology and focuses on the actual steps in coordination with the music.

To begin with, a small segment of the dance music should be played to familiarize the learners with its tempo, character, and rhythm. The participants should be arranged so that they can see and hear everything the instructor imparts. When the instructor has the attention of the group, fundamental step patterns of the dance should be taught. These movements should be mastered before any dancing is attempted. If the dance in question has steps that can be more appropriately learned from a line or circle formation, they should be taught in that way before the dance is practiced. If a specific step and pattern are included, the single step should be taught first and then the entire figure. The instructor should demonstrate the step while explaining to the class. After that, the entire group should be walked through the pattern together.

For dances with short sequences, the complete dance should be demonstrated and then the class should be taken through the sequence until it becomes quite familiar. When there are relatively long sequences, each separate part should be tried and then the parts should be coordinated. Initially, the steps should be walked through without musical accompaniment; the accompanying music should then be played. The important point is to get the group accustomed to new steps and patterns by demonstration, explanation, and slow movements and then to gradually increase the tempo as skill is gained.

A good instructor will always remember that there needs to be time for correction, review, and encouragement. Participants need to be given every opportunity to develop at their own rate, and reminded that the dancing is purely for recreational purposes and that enjoyment is more important than perfection.

Dance is enhanced by integrating many different recreational forms. Incorporating the effects of dramatic lighting and the kinds of music that are played to evoke mood and self-expression does much to stimulate interest, appreciation, and performance. Dancing is an excellent activity to maintain fitness and improve physical conditioning. Whether indoors or outdoors, dance stimulates concern about suitable appearance, proper etiquette, and personal hygiene.

The Values of Dance

Almost everybody seems to enjoy the stimulation of vigorous rhythmic movement, whether in company or alone. Dance offers the individual who has learned the skills a sense of personal power, mastery, and self-fulfillment that is derived from the exercise of both mind and body in graceful movements.

Dance is valuable for any participant because it enables the individual to be free of unnecessary inhibitions and breaks down some of the barriers that most people have devised for themselves as ego protection. Through dance, relaxation of excess nervous tension is possible. Dance is the most available of the various art forms because the medium through which expression is formed is one's own body. In dance, the body is the means and movement is the medium.

Dancing of all kinds—square, folk, round, social, modern, and classical forms—can be employed in a recreational program to correspond to any individual's needs, interests, experiences, and skills. Dance can offer the most strenuous of physical efforts or it may be performed in the most completely relaxed manner. Dance performance can be utilized in weight-loss activity, physical fitness and conditioning, and the development of poise, flexibility, and agility.

By far the greatest contribution that dancing can make to those who participate occurs in the social intercourse during an enjoyable session. Whether the individual is a beginner or expert, being with people in an atmosphere that permits pleasantries and small talk does much to encourage a positive attitude and an optimistic outlook. The ritualistic steps of folk, square, round, or social dance produce immediate gratification as the participant performs the beginning and then the more advanced steps and patterns making up these rhythmic movements. Under these circumstances, participants can focus their attention on their respective partners, instead of on the complicated steps, thereby promoting the process of social interaction.

Ethnicity can be an integral part of dance by incorporating a program of traditional folk dances. Whether newly immigrated or longtime assimilated, participants may derive genuine appreciation for the incorporation of ethnic folk dances in scheduled dance activities. Cultural heritage and the opportunity to demonstrate newly acquired or long-held skills offer participants a chance to obtain attention and ego satisfaction.

Among the dances that are popular will be a variety of folk and square dances, waltzes, fox trot, Latin American–based dance, and current fads. Dance can include the entire range of performance from novice to polished professional. It permits an individual to move at his or her own pace. There are dances with simple, easy-to-learn steps for the shy or reserved type as well as dances that employ more intricate movements and rhythms for the adept.

Dance may be divided into two categories, characterizing their primary objective. The *instructional* phase of dance includes all those functions and techniques designed to teach dance skills of any form. The *exhibition* phase deals with performance and demonstration of dance skills and complex movements. Both of these categories are recreational, and may be engaged in solely for enjoyment and satisfaction.

Summary

Dance has been likened to poetry in motion, and properly so because of its communicative character. Universally found, dance has ethnic, ritualistic, and interpretive meanings. People everywhere dance for the fun of it or to give expression to personal feelings. Dance elicits appreciation by observers, enjoyment for participants, and skill development with concomitant physical and mental health derivatives.

Everyone, at some time, has to learn how to dance if they are at all interested in the activity. No one is born with dance skills. This requires instruction, although some dances merely need to be observed and imitated. For a recreational program, instruction is key for those who wish to learn. Either a recreationist leader must be available or qualified volunteers must be sought and recruited. Private instruction is always accessible to those who can afford it.

The socializing effect of dance is one of the greatest contributions that this activity makes to any recreational program. Skilled dancers like to demonstrate their ability, while beginners are stimulated by the rhythmic tempo of the experience. In any case, the outcome is enjoyment and a feeling of accomplishment. Therefore, the timely scheduling of dance classes, formal or informal gatherings where dance is an integral part of the activity, or specific dance formats as part of the overall program must make up at least one twelfth of the activities offered by the agency.

Selected Further References

Aumack, S. *Art of Hula Dancing*. Philadelphia, PA: Running Press Book Publishers, 2005.

Cavalli, H. *Dance and Music: A Guide to Dance Accompaniment for Musicians and Dance Teachers*. Gainesville, FL: University Press of Florida, 2001.

Craig-Quijada, B. *Dance for Fun!* Minneapolis, MN: Compass Point Books, 2004.

Gray, J. A. *Dance Instruction: Science Applied to the Art of Movement*. Champaign, IL: Human Kinetics Publishers, 1995.

Pittman, A. M., et al. *Dance a While: Handbook for Folk, Square, Contra, and Social Dance*. 9th ed. Reading, MA: Benjamin-Cummings Publishing Co., 2004.

Pozo, C., et al. *Let's Dance*. Emeryville, CA: Hatherleigh Press, 2007.

Snoman, R. *Dance Music Manual: Tools, Toys, and Techniques*. New York: Elsevier Science and Technology Books, 2004.

Tortora, S., ed. *Dancing Dialogue: Using the Communicative Power of Movement with Young Children*. Baltimore, MD: Paul H. Brookes Publishing Co., 2005.

Votaw, M., and V. Rushmere. *Art of Belly Dancing*. Philadelphia, PA: Running Press Book Publishers, 2004.

CHAPTER

11

The Play's the Thing

Communication through aural and visual means, whereby an individual can emote and express him- or herself or reproduce the expression of others via interpretation, mimicry, symbolism, or spontaneous activity, may be defined as dramatics. Dramatics incorporates the element of performance, whether in front of an audience or not. The scope of dramatics is extremely broad and includes many activities, among which are those shown in **Table 11.1**.

The constructive utilization of a story, in either play form, pantomime, role playing, or spontaneous re-creation, enables participants to express themselves in terms of needs and interests. Dramatics and its various forms, using a medium of reality, fantasy, and wish fulfillment, make the individual aware of him- or herself and cause that person to empathize with others. Every age group enjoys some aspect of dramatics. Children love to tell stories and to hear them told, to play dramatic games, and to act out fairy tales. Adults enjoy a good story, as does the teller.

Dramatics also includes games, improvisation, plays, and other forms that convey ideas by means of speech, action, or both. Essentially the dramatic performance is the most highly personalized of all the categories. All attention is focused on the individual, and it is the individual who must interpret the idea or character about which the story is written. In creative dramatics there is no storyline; the role-taker must act out ideas spontaneously, as the mood or action dictates. Where there is a formal play, the actor has lines to memorize and must reproduce the character prescribed by the author.

As in all planned recreational activity, a prime requisite for a successful dramatics program is qualified leadership to serve in a directorial capacity, to act as a resource, or to supervise the entire presentation. Dramatics classes, appreciation of drama in its different forms, and actual performance upon the stage all require expert guidance. Dramatic presentation may be of the workshop variety where the participants learn by doing. On the other hand, when the play is performance oriented, many weeks must be taken for rehearsal, sets designed, lighting and other equipment accumulated, and all of the details of presentation planned. In many instances performers gain confidence through this participation and are able to overcome any emotional barriers that prevent them from taking part. Drama is valuable to the individual as a medium for self-expression, as well as representations of characters and roles that may be the creation of another person. Drama, in its essence, is a form of communication through the human voice and body. As a communicative process it provides satisfaction by transmitting ideas and emotions, and provides self-expression either vicariously or directly. The elements of catharsis and empathy are closely related to dramatic reproductions.

Dramatic arts include many activities that are virtual reality for both the audience and the actors and allow people to forget their anxieties for a short time by having their thoughts turned to new characters and events. In the theater, emotions are exercised or exorcised. Everyone needs to laugh or cry sometime, to feel independently about something other than personal cares or catastrophes, to have their sense of expectation sharpened, and to have affections aroused that have been dulled by routine and frustration.

Finally, dramatics offers intellectual stimulation through the interpretive comments on the human condition made by the author and performers. Sometimes this commentary is serious and is concerned about current events that impact on the lives of many people. Oftentimes the play is humorous, allegorical, satirical, or comedic. There are thoughtful plays that illuminate the foibles and strengths of people in situations that may or may not reflect real life, but contain aspects of truth in combining both the seriousness and humor met in daily life. The best of the theater assists a playgoer to gain a better understanding of him- or herself, other people, and the world at large. Whether they are classics or modern innovations, the stage compositions (and other dramatic forms) can clarify, stimulate, and inspire people with new ideas and objectives.

The fundamental components of dramatic performance are character, story, and interpretation, but the manner of presentation is an additional feature that tends to explain the fascination people have with performing and attending. The manner of presentation establishes dramatic effect. Patterns of movement and speech must be arranged for the theater because a certain amount of simplification and amplification is necessary to make the characters viable and poignant. Indeed, there is also a specific orientation to give the story a point of view, a sense of emphasis to make the playwright's ideas salient. If the players ignore the manner of their speech and acting, but instead stand around as people ordinarily do, the character, story, and commentary will be lost to the audience. Effective manner permits the plays to be projected into the vastness of the hall and to come alive.

Drama maintains a hold on people's lives that can be considered nearly universal. The observer sees this every day in the make-believe of little children, and the fascination with cartoons, movies, television, and stories that continually pull their attention. That this fascination is lifelong is apparent when one appreciates the great numbers of youngsters, teenagers, adults, and older adults who participate in plays, study dramatic technique, and attend or listen to performances via television, movies, radio, and theater.

Table 11.1   Types of Dramatic Activities

Manipulative Performance	Creative Drama	Forensic Performance	Theater
Marionettes	Pantomime	Monologues	Blackout plays
Puppetry	Improvisation	Dialogues	Demonstrations
Shadow plays	Games	Debate	Dramatizations
Juggling	Charades	Public speaking	Operas
Prestidigitation	Psychodrama	Story reading	Operettas
	Sociodrama	Storytelling	Tableaux
		Impersonation	Skits
		Choral speech	Stunts
		Radio plays	

Play Production

It is both impractical and facile to simply state that every community has talented and interested individuals who merely need to be summoned for community theater to occur. This is nonsensical. Dramatic production and the various elements that comprise this category require careful attention and consideration to details to be successful. Theater and all of its components is not acting by script, scene, dance, or music. It is, rather, a synergy of all the functions of which these things are composed. It consists of action, which is the soul of acting; words, which are the corpus of the play; color and line, which are the core of the scenes; rhythm, which is basic to dance; and tone, which is the essence of music. What is required is a producer, the individual who assists and directs the actor to interpret the role, who organizes the entire production, and who forecasts the potential audience's reaction to the performance—if there is one.

The producer may very well be a specialist employed by the recreational department to oversee all aspects of the drama category; however, it is probable that only large departments will employ such a recreationist. If a specialist is hired, that person will be able to exercise authority without being a dictator. On the other hand, it is much more likely that a department will not have the specialist personnel available and will therefore have to employ a competent individual from the commercial sector or seek out a person from the local school system. Elementary or high school teachers who are responsible for dramatic performances may be contacted for their suggestions or input. Failing that, a retired professional may providentially be discovered residing in the community who may have the requisite talent and a desire to lend it on a voluntary basis. Where the community contains or is situated close to an institution of higher education that has a school of fine arts, or at least a theater department, that department may be the locus of personnel who can provide the necessary expertise. Once a producer has been employed, the production of plays or other theatrical experiences may be programmed.

The producer's authority is like that of any leader who can guide and persuade other members of the ensemble to his or her point of view. The successful producer does not necessarily have to be a good actor, but must be aware of the difficulties that confront a performer so effective assistance can be provided as necessary. Possession of a sense of the play's meaning is as necessary as the correct pointing of the lines and relevant stage business in the make-up of the producer. He or she should have knowledge of the technical jargon used in the theater, scenic design, properties, lighting and sound effects, costuming, and furniture. Expertise in these specializations is unnecessary, although helpful. Among other things, the producer should have an appreciation of the performing arts, and the value of silence.

If the potential cast is made up of amateurs, the producer must be able to instruct the would-be performers in the execution of their roles. The help that is given is not merely dictating the moves without elaboration. By discussion, suggestion, improvisation, and paraphrase the skillful producer leads the actors by subtle cues toward the desired effect.

The main function of the producer, at the beginning of the production, is to read the script of the play that is to be presented. This means that the producer must read the play as though he or she was a member of the audience. There must be sensitivity to the written word that enables the specialist to visualize the characters on the stage, with its scenic flats, its artificial lighting, its own pace and sound. In this way the producer acclimatizes him- or herself to the rhythm and mood of the acted play as it seems to him or her for the first time. The producer is now ready to analyze the characterization, plot, and dialogue as well as look for clues as to the shape and layout of the scenery.

Setting the Stage

The producer will now have assimilated the primary themes of whatever play has been selected and is prepared to give directions to the scenic and costume designers. These individuals, again recruited from the community or employed by the department, have the background and experience to create the desired scenes and appropriate costumes. They will muster a cadre of paid or volunteer workers who can perform carpentry, scene painting, and sewing. Each of these significant prop departments should be overseen by an individual. However, because there is a dearth of necessary staff in these specialties, it may be necessary for one person to combine the functions of costume designer, tailor, and wardrobe master. This may also be true for the functions of carpenters, scene painters, electricians, and sound technicians. Handymen who can do all of these separate tasks are invaluable when there is a shortage of specialized personnel. Of course, it would be best if the functions could be filled by well-qualified individuals.

The sequential level of preparation necessitates the producer reading the script again, and focusing attention on the settings and any stage directions offered by the playwright. Going over the play one more time enables the producer to prepare a general ground plan together with other memoranda and sketches that might be assistive prior to a conference with the designer.

Planning for Effect

When developing a comprehensive plan for the proposed play, a sketch should be made of each scene indicating the layout of scenery and furniture. Drawn to scale, probably $\frac{1}{4}$ or $\frac{1}{2}$ inch to 1 foot, on appropriate graph paper, this sketch becomes the basis for further development of the producer's ideas in council with the other members of the design team. The plan displays the producer's conception in concrete terms. It also provides the designer with information concerning space availability for movement of the actors. Finally, the plan assists in determining the amount and dimensions of the furniture and other props that will be used. If an elaborate stage design is necessary, a model of the proposed set may be constructed. The plan, complemented by explanation and discussion of the plot, atmosphere, and characterization incorporated in the play, further enhances the consultation.

The fundamental plan relies on the method of staging. This depends on the kind of stage that is available or can be acquired by contract or short-term loan. The different types of stages are illustrated in **Figures 11.1** to **11.3**.

Stage Directions

In order to enable backstage operations of both the actors and the stage crew to be easily understood, common terms must be used. Having a common language prevents misunderstanding amid the typically complicated operation of play presentation. All directions, right and left, are presented from the stage facing the audience. Downstage is toward the footlights whereas upstage is away from the footlights. Off stage is away from the center toward left or right. All directions from the sides to the center are on stage. All space at the right or left of the stage unoccupied by the set is called the wings. The space above the stage is referred to as the fly or loft. The acting area on the stage

Figure 11.1 The Proscenium-Arch Stage. The performers are separated from the audience by means of a raised stage and archway at the front of the hall.

Figure 11.2 The Thrust Stage. This stage projects into the audience.

may be divided into upper left, left center, down left, up center, center, down center, up right, right center, and down right.

Stage Manager

The stage manager is essentially the assistant director backstage. The duties are numerous, and he or she may have one or two assistants. The stage manager checks to ensure that the cast is in the dressing rooms in a timely fashion for costume changes and make-up; indicates the time before the curtain rises; checks to see that scenery, props, and lighting are arranged correctly; calls places to the cast; gives curtain and light cues; gives all light and sound cues during the performance; and typically gives curtain cues at

Figure 11.3 The Aisle or Avenue Stage. The audience is seated on two sides of a hall, in the front of which is a platform.

the end of the acts. Assistant stage managers do the running because the stage manager needs to be available on stage at all times.

The Theater

It is probably good to assume that the local community theater has been developed by and for nonprofessionals. Simply stated, all theaters have two parts. The section in front of the curtain normally encompasses the seating area, lobbies, box offices, and lounges. This portion is for the convenience of the audience. The area behind the curtain comprises the stage, dressing room or dressing room facilities, and, perhaps, shops for building flats, painting scenery, making costumes, and storage space.

The Switchboard

Immediately inside the proscenium arch, on the right or the left side, is the switchboard, which controls stage lighting. See "Stage Lighting" later in this chapter for a detailed discussion of stage lighting.

The Pin Rail

On the same side of the stage as the switchboard is a pin rail, which is used for holding ropes used to raise or lower the suspended scenery. It is a 6 inch by 6 inch piece of timber, bolted to the wall approximately 3 feet from the floor and held about 6 to 8 inches away from the wall. A sufficiently large pipe may be used in place of wood. By drilling holes vertically through the wood or metal, pins of wood or metal may be inserted. A flange or collar halfway down the pin will prevent it from falling through the rail. When in position, the pin projects at least 6 inches above and below the rail. Obviously, several pins are used to line the rail.

The Fly Gallery

A fly gallery runs along the side wall of the stage from front to back, at least 16 feet above the stage floor. The pin rail may be situated on the fly gallery. This construction saves space for scenery and leaves available wall space against which scenery that is not being used can be stacked. Fly galleries have certain disadvantages, particularly if the stage crew is inexperienced. The different levels make it unlikely for the stage crew to double up their duties, and it is often necessary to have a crew both on the stage floor and in the fly gallery. However, even this disadvantage may be turned to advantage because the need for more participants in stage crew work permits the recruitment of more local people to join the theater company in a recreational experience.

The Grid

Just below the stage ceiling is a network of beams on which rests a special set of pulleys. Over these pulleys run the ropes that raise or lower scenery. No less than 3 feet and preferably more space between the grid and the ceiling is necessary to enable a person to work with some ease for the necessary alignment of those lines and rigging that reach to the stage floor and are tied to a piece of scenery. These lines extend from the scenery to the pin rail. Typically, these ropes and pulleys are arranged in sets of three or more lines. When there is no grid, pulleys may be attached to the ceiling. Community theaters are sometimes impromptu facilities where space is limited. Under these circumstances, the director will have to make adroit arrangements so that some system for raising and lowering scenery can be facilitated.

The Working Curtain

Most people in the audience take the theater curtain for granted. It is usual for theaters to have an opera drape. The opera drape is a two-piece curtain that opens in the center. On the back of the curtain, from both center corners diagonally up to the upper right and left corners, a sequence of rings are attached to each seam. Pulleys are fastened to each end of the batten to which the curtain is attached; a double pulley is used on the side from which the curtain is to be operated while a single pulley is placed on the other side. A rope is attached to the lower center ring on the single pulley side, threaded up through each of the rings to the single pulley, and across the top to the double pulley. The rope is then lowered and taken back up to the other half of the double pulley. The rope is finally threaded down through the other set of rings and attached to the lower center corner. The opera drape should be adequate in terms of height and width so that when it is opened it will not draw up at the outside.

The traveling curtain operates on one or two heavy smooth wires. The two halves of the curtain are hanging from the wire by rings or hooks that will easily slide along the wire. When two wires are used, they should be less than 6 inches apart. In this arrangement it is possible for the curtains to overlap as they close. This curtain is typically used in small community theaters.

Scenery

The typical scenic unit is the flat, consisting of a frame, almost always of wood, over which canvas is stretched. It can be of any height or width, varying insofar as the type of stage and the dimensions available in the theater. Flats can be joined together in a straight line or at an angle with hooks and guylines and kept firmly in place with braces of some kind.

The platform is another piece of scenery that offers a variety of movement and gives a satisfying composition through the use of elevation. Rectangular blocks, easily moved, can be used to change the shape of the stage on short notice. Steps provide easy access from one level to another.

Arches of different shapes are valuable for changing scenery quickly in a play that has many scenes. They can be filled with panels, curtains, or pictures. The space behind the arches can be changed while they are covered in this way. Arches used in this way become the permanent framework for a multipurpose set.

Door frames are solid units and have a special type of triangular support fixed to the main unit for greater rigidity when the door is slammed. Other elements that are usually seen in plays are windows, fireplaces, and curtains (**Figure 11.4**).

Changing Scenery

The producer needs to understand the technique of scene changing. Changing the set can be quite difficult. There are instances when the performance is ongoing in the fore-part of the stage in front of a traverse curtain while stage hands transform the scenery behind it. This enables the floor action to continue without interruption. Obviously, stage hands can remove set units to the sides of the stage. Scenery can be lifted into the flies, the area above the proscenium arch, by means of ropes and pulleys and left hanging there. If the theater has mechanical devices such as revolving stages, sliding panels, or lifts, these may be pressed into service for scene change. Finally, lighting can be used to effect scene change.

Figure 11.4 Scenery

$^{1}/_{8}"$ scale white model   *Artificial Jungle*   Set Design by Tim Saternow

Casting the Play

The person who serves as the producer/director uses the human material at his or her disposal. Whether a child, teenager, or adult, the individuals who want to perform must be given an opportunity to do so. It should always be kept uppermost that amateurs, even those with talent, are not going to offer Broadway-level performances. Even more significantly, the recreational drama activity is designed for the enjoyment of the performers, with the audience being a secondary consideration. Given this principle, it is still necessary for the play director to enable those who try out for parts to be selected for some role. Everybody cannot be a lead character. There will always have to be those in supporting roles as well as those who appear as extras in crowd or other scenes calling for people to be seen on stage, without having to say anything. They may have something to do, but they have no lines to speak.

Nevertheless, the director must, of necessity, have people audition for parts. Sometimes talent may be found in the most unexpected individuals. These persons should be nurtured and encouraged to perform. Often, talent is absent and the individual makes a mechanical presentation. Such people can still be a part of the theater and the play if they are willing to conform to the director's suggestions and the role that is offered.

Auditions are called quite some time before any play is to be staged. A talent pool must be collected. Actors need to read lines from the play and react to the directions given to adjust or strengthen the performance. If the director is satisfied that an individual can enter a role and project the character as the author has written and the director wants interpreted, then that person may be assigned to that role. Such auditions are continued until the entire cast of characters is completed. Not only does the director need his or her primary cast completed, it is also adroit to have a complete understudy cast available in the event that a principal or secondary actor is unable to perform. Those who audition have to understand that whatever performance they give is going to be supported. They will have every opportunity to be convincing in their stage persona. However, play limitations, competition for roles (if any), and an ability to assume the role will dictate the part they are to play.

The director understands that a community-based theater, organized by the local recreational agency, is primarily set up for the enjoyment of the actors. If and when a performance is scheduled, the actors will presumably do their respective best in their roles and trust that the audience will be receptive and appreciative. If this does not happen, no failure has been recorded as long as the performers are satisfied. It would be highly unusual if the hometown audience did not receive the efforts of the amateurs with enthusiasm.

What is the director looking for when casting a play? An actor who has stage presence, can project the character of the role in a creditable manner, and takes responsibility for fulfilling the obligation undertaken when the role is assigned. An ability to speak in a manner that can be heard in the farthest row of the audience is helpful. This does not mean shouting. It is voice projection and it can be learned with proper coaching. Diction is also important. A voice and diction coach may be extremely helpful to those potential actors who want a chance, but have speech impediments or other vocal drawbacks. These dysfunctions can be overcome with practice.

The director's primary function probably will be to lead his or her performers so they voluntarily cooperate with the demands of rehearsals and stage business without wasting time. It is the director's leadership that produces the willingness to subordinate oneself to the needs of the group and in so doing gains the greatest degree of personal satisfaction.

Stage Lighting

Common to any methods of lighting are general and specific illumination. The chief objective of general illumination is visibility, whereas specific illumination is for lighting particular stage areas. Light has particular qualities that are characteristic of the medium. One aspect of light is intensity. Thus, the lighting designer may use a range of illumination from the flickering of a candle to a sunlike glitter of brightness. Intensity enables flexibility for selecting the precise amount of light needed for any portion of the stage. The second attribute of light is color, which is at the behest of the designer. Every color of the visible spectrum can be used and contrasted artfully to increase or emphasize anything on the stage. Light distribution is a characteristic that can be used at the command of the designer to bathe the entire stage in light or to pinpoint one specific area. Finally, movement signifies the ability to change any of the other qualities of light abruptly or subtly.

Color mixing and color filtering are very important in stage lighting. Lighting fixtures give out rays of approximately white light, and the only real method to color these beams is to block them with a sheet of transparent colored material. In this way color filtering is obtained. Thus, two primary colors may be mixed to produce a third color. Typically, mixing and filtering are employed for more nuanced effects than would be possible simply by adding two primaries to produce a secondary. The lighting director or technician must comprehend the filtering and mixing processes that can be assimilated through the study of the primary and secondary colors. Technical competence will enable the lighting person to recognize that the same principles will apply to all colors, tints, and shades. Precision comes from experience.

Plastic, rather than gelatin, is the medium of choice. Although more expensive than gelatin, it has almost as many shades, is more reliable, and is longer-lasting. Glass filters may be used, but they are very expensive and probably will not be available in the budget of most public recreational agencies attempting to set up or operate community theater.

Color production and stage lighting are highly technical and require knowledge, skill, and experience of the person doing the lighting. Numerous published works on the topic are available (see the end of this chapter for some suggestions).

The most typical sources of general illumination are footlights, border lights, and floodlights. **Figure 11.5** shows a lighting setup using a variety of illumination sources.

General illumination is used to evenly distribute light over the entire stage. Although the color and intensity of light may be varied, there is very little control over the lighted area. In other words, everything is lighted equally. Of extreme importance is the fact that the audience must be able to see whatever the stage action is.

Specific illumination lights a particular area or series of areas on stage. This lighting is done with spotlights (**Figure 11.6**) because they are mounted

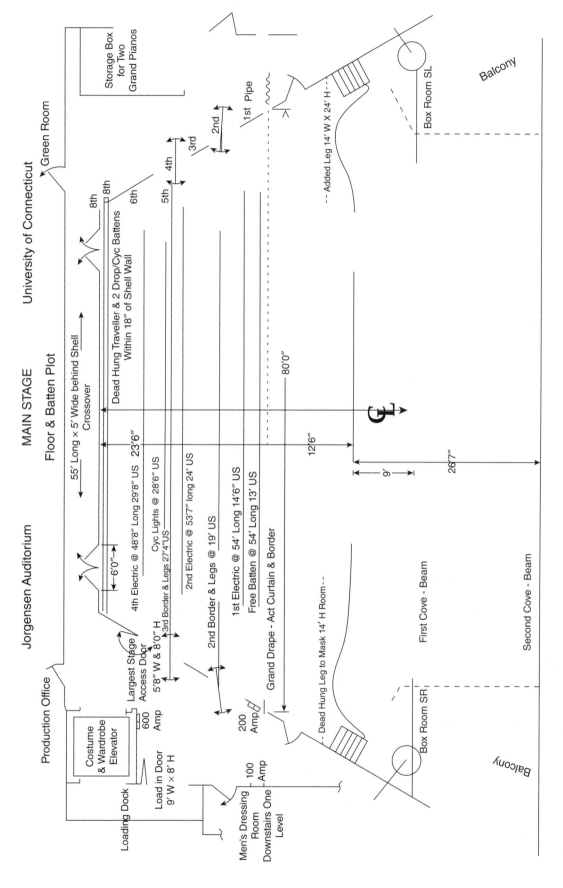

Figure 11.5 Stage Lighting Setup. Image courtesy of the University of Connecticut, The School of Fine Arts, Department of Dramatic Arts.

Figure 11.6 Spotlight

and constructed so that their beams can be directed to specific locations and the size and shape of the light can be controlled.

The spotlight focuses attention on some important area so that the rest of the set is seen as unimportant. This kind of lighting establishes a focus of interest and increases dramatic effect. Amateur productions, of the usual recreational variety, may sometimes overaccentuate action areas. When this occurs, it is likely that actors moving from one place to another may have to pass through unlighted areas. Footlights and border lights are very useful in preventing these dark spots; that is their function. By adroit use of footlights and border lights the accentuated pools created by spotlights may be blended to produce an even, yet vital, stage unity.

Successful lighting depends upon appropriate control of lighting instruments. These controls are used to turn lights on and off, dim lights, control the direction of lights in terms of mounting and hanging, control the size of the pool of light, control the shape of the spot of light, and control the color of light with filters or colored lamps.

All such control stems from the switchboard, which is situated on one side of the stage. Every electrical outlet terminates on the board. Every lighting instrument should have a separate switch and these, in turn, should be controlled by master switches so that any light may be turned on and off independently or in concert with any other light. Light intensity is controlled by dimmers. The switchboard can be simple or complex, but for the typical recreational theater production it will probably be one where a few dimmers would be used for footlights, borders, and floor pockets or spotlights.

Stage lighting provides the actor with an atmosphere in which the role being played may be interpreted. Simultaneously, stage lighting must help in bringing to the audience the full impact and psychology of the playwright's conceptualization.

As in all aspects of theater, leadership, in the sense of expertise, is essential if the technicalities of production are to be successfully brought off. Local recreational departments may have to avail themselves of volunteers who have the ability, through past experience, to operate the contrivances of lighting that give the production more meaning; otherwise they must seek out and employ paid specialists who are available in the community. In the latter case, this may mean electricians, carpenters, or other trades persons who can apply their skills to the needs of theater. Where the community is fortunate in having resident theater specialists, the enlistment of such persons is of inestimable value.

Summary

Community theater, little theater, creative dramatics, school plays—by whatever name it is called, all have a role in the dramatic performances engaged in by numerous persons in the community. Some organized group, such as an arts council, civic organization, lodge, or even a local drama club, may stage shows of various types. Sectarian agencies may put on religiously oriented works during holidays. Festivals, contests, ceremonial occasions, and tradition often have a role in spurring the production of dramatic moments.

The public recreational service agency has to be in the forefront of these efforts in providing the dramatic arts to, by, and for the constituent population. The department may be the instigator or the coordinator of community resources for stage presentations; it should include all of the performing arts in its program schedule.

Leadership is needed for direction, production, resource coordination, and facility if this activity is to be generally supported and participated in by community residents. All of the various forms dramatics takes may gain the interest and attention of would-be thespians.

Specialists are needed to carry out the functions that dramatics calls for. Thus, stage, lighting, and set designers may be called upon; make-up artists, producers, and their assistants need to be available. Voice coaches and song and dance instructors may be required, depending upon the type of production. Employed recreationists with the talent, skill, and experience to fill these roles are as important as volunteers to fill other positions.

Dramatics can be scheduled at every center, school, or other facility as the number of participants requires. This activity is carried on routinely through classes ending in some presentation. It is this culminating effort that brings the greatest satisfaction and enjoyment to the performers and the audience.

Variations of dramatics, in all their guises, afford a remarkable experience to the actor in building self-confidence, poise, and a sense of achievement that every person wants to have. Of even greater significance is that the activity is fun.

Selected Further References

Brockett, O. G., and R. J. Ball. *The Essential Theatre*. 9th ed. Boston: Thomson Wadsworth, 2008.

Corson, R. *Stage Makeup*. 9th ed. Tappan, NJ: Allyn and Bacon, Inc., 2000.

Doughton, M., and E. G. Stocks. *Stage 1 Design*. Independence, KY: Thomson Learning, 2000.

Doughton, M., et al. *Stage 2 Design*. Independence, KY: Thomson Learning, 2001.

Glerum, J. O. *Stage Rigging Handbook*. 2nd rev ed. Carbondale, IL: Southern Illinois University Press, 1997.

Lord, W. H. *Stagecraft 1: A Complete Guide to Backstage Work*. 3rd rev ed. Colorado Springs, CO: Meriwether Publishing, Ltd., 2000.

Miller, J. H. *Stage Lighting in the Boondocks*. 4th rev ed. Colorado Springs, CO: Meriwether Publishing, Ltd., 1995.

Patterson, J. *Stage Directing: The First Experiences*. Tappan, NJ: Allyn and Bacon, Inc., 2003.

Pura, T. *Stages: Creative Ideas for Teaching Drama*. Toronto, Ontario, Canada: J. Gordon Shillingford Publishing, 2004.

Sandstrom, U. *Stage Lighting Controls*. Colorado Springs, CO: Meriwether Publishing, Ltd., 1997.

Stein, T. S., and J. Bathhurst. *Performing Arts Management: A Handbook of Professional Practices*. New York: Allworth Press, 2008.

Stern, L. *Stage Management*. 8th ed. Tappan, NJ: Allyn and Bacon, Inc., 2005.

CHAPTER

12

Education

Education is a vital component in all recreational categories. Learning is fundamental for any activity that requires skill, knowledge, or appreciation. Thus, the principle of education belongs to all experiences where informational enhancement, growth of new knowledge, or the inculcation of a new idea or subject is paramount.

Any instructional activity may be undertaken for the pure joy of learning. Whether of the formal classroom variety or the informal learning that one assimilates in recreational participation, the personal satisfaction derived from knowledge acquisition meets all of the criteria that distinguish recreational experience from other forms of engagement.

An instructional activity where the primary reason for participation is the enhancement of knowledge or the learning of a new skill, idea, or subject may be termed education. Formal or classroom instruction of subject matter and informal learning experiences programmed specifically to teach a skill are part of this category. Although all recreational activity may be defined as educational, it is not the place of the recreational service department to teach subjects that might better be left to the school system. Certain educational objectives may be planned and noted in an organized program, but the atmosphere and the emphasis are quite different from those of the school classroom. The activities that typically form the educational category are:

Citizenship	Play writing
Civics	Poetry reading
First aid	Bible reading
Grammar	Letter writing
Mathematics	Foreign language for conversation
History	Debating (forensic speech)
Geography	Public speaking
Science	Choral recitation
Current events	Discussion groups
Industrial arts	Forums
Etiquette	Quizzes
Floral design	Storytelling
Horticultural arrangement	Story reading
Home gardening	Lectures
Accounting	Liturgical groups
Bookkeeping	Panel presentations
Typing	Seminars
Short story writing	Symposia
Book review	

Knowledge and Information

Nothing enhances enjoyment as much as having knowledge about a given subject and being able to bring that information to bear when a situation demands it. Knowledge opens many doors to quiet satisfaction. It extends awareness, recognition, and appreciation to any subject. The category of education lends itself most particularly to the recreational setting because learning can be absolutely enjoyable, especially when the information obtained is learned during one's leisure.

Subject matter that is typically taught in the formal setting of the school tends to place heavy emphasis upon the assimilation of facts, principles, or values while deliberately progressing toward some specified goal. So many units must be learned and examinations are employed to determine whether the expected information has indeed been assimilated. On the other hand, the recreational orientation of education stresses satisfaction on the learner's part without the need for examinations and the pressures that are integral when an individual is subject to achieving a particular grade. Instruction in recreational activities (regardless of subject) is designed to assist an individual to improve knowledge, increase skill, share social occasions, and develop physically, emotionally, and intellectually. It is the participant's sense of purpose, interest, and ability that dictate the speed of progress that will be made. Enjoyment is the motive that drives the desire to engage.

Educational Rationale

The whole purpose of the education category is not to displace formal schooling, but to complement it and extend the learning process into those informal settings where the pace of instruction offers the opportunity to obtain greater knowledge not otherwise easily experienced.

Almost any subject of the curriculum may become the basis for a recreational experience. Within schools, there are extracurricular clubs dedicated to the expansion of and appreciation for a particular subject that for some are pure torture or drudgery. Thus, for example, mathematics, chemistry, foreign language, history, or literature may be the attraction that draws devotees and enables the formation of an interest group or club. To those who do not have facility with these subjects, the very thought of belonging to such a group is anathema. They cannot conceive of anything more horrendous than participating in a program that contains school subjects they despise. Yet, for the aficionados these activities are not only pleasurable and satisfying, but also edifying. The same thing could be said for any recreational experience. For some, certain recreational activities are unthinkable, whereas for the competent these same activities are both attractive and completely enjoyable. As the adage says, "One man's meat is another man's poison." Nevertheless, any subject may be learned so that appreciation and skill replace ignorance, fear, and negative bias. This occurs when the activity is entered into voluntarily without the stress of having to learn in a specific period or where there is the intimidation of final examinations and grades.

Individuals who could never learn a foreign language in the formal setting of the classroom may, with proper stimulation, learn how to converse in that language. Perhaps they will, or have, traveled to the country where that language is spoken. They do not want to know the niceties of grammar or the rules of speech; they simply want to gain some fluency so they can better enjoy their travel experience. By setting up an informal learning experience, where the participant is immersed in the language of choice and merely trying to understand at a rate appropriate to them, facility could be gained. This may further encourage the individual to seek additional language experience in a formal setting or permit that person to practice the conversational art in a congenial environment.

Education during leisure has tended toward a variety of skills learning of curriculum subjects, such as typing, first aid, letter writing, short story writing, or civics. However, any subject might be offered. When literary, linguistic, or commercial courses are provided within the recreational program, they are there because a demand has been created and those who are interested desire them. Subjects are offered in the expectation that exposure to the information will prompt additional study and be the incentive for improvement.

Of course, it must be understood from the outset that all recreational activities must be acquired at some point. No one is born knowing recreational activities. These are assimilated during the growth and development phases of the young person's life; whoever has a penchant for a type of activity they have come to associate with enjoyment or is exposed to activity at an appropriate time may eventually develop the skill, knowledge, or appreciation that enables them to satisfy themselves through involvement. Other individuals are stimulated to learn new activities by observation, directed learning, or self-teaching. However it is done, education is the surest method for ingesting information or learning performance.

Timing the Education Program

Time is the basis on which the recreational program operates. During leisure people have the free time to participate in the recreational experiences of their choice. At almost any time during each day of any week there will be those in the community who have some free time. One of the elemental procedures necessary, if the agency is to serve its constituents well, is to determine who has leisure and when. On this foundation the program can be developed and maintained.

Activities for the youngest children must take into account the time when they are free to participate. Thus, preschool children may be involved during the mornings, and elementary school children may be involved in the afternoons after school closes, but before the evening meal. Other school-age youth must be scheduled when such activities do not interfere with schoolwork or homework. Out-of-school youth may be accommodated almost anytime they prefer to participate, particularly if they have the maturity, ability, and knowledge to engage in self-directed experiences. Where sufficient numbers of this group are collected, directed educational opportunities may be offered, if acceptable to those making up the group. For adults, the best times may come during the evening hours. For those who are employed in positions where odd-hour shifts occur, special accommodations may have to be arranged so that all those who are interested may participate freely. Older adults may have a great deal of leisure, especially those who are retired and find themselves with much time on their hands. To the extent that educational activities can engage all those who wish to participate without a feeling of crowding or formality, there is only the necessity to schedule various classes and groups.

Time becomes important in planning the program because it deals with all persons who live within the community. One requirement is that an analysis of potential educational participants is made to determine at what times various individuals and/or groups are free to participate. Planning the educational activities, whether at a centralized location or in various facilities situated throughout the community, will be based on time factors.

Length of Classes

Duration of activities is extremely important in terms of the participants' needs. The more mature and responsible the individual, the more probable it is that longer sessions will be necessary for work on time-consuming subjects. Children, on the other hand, have shorter attention spans and become restless even if they maintain an interest in the topic. Shorter activity sessions, more frequently given, may be the best response to the needs of young children. The time factor plays an important role for any age level insofar as frequency, length of period, time of day, timeliness or association, and other modifying factors are concerned. Whether the activity is prepared for morning, afternoon, or evening sessions, it must be well organized to sustain interest, stimulate repeated attendance, and be of a duration commensurate with the requirements of those who participate.

Punctuality

Punctuality is another time factor that must be considered. The clientele expects, and rightly so, that when activities are announced for a specific time, they will occur at that time, be completed on time, and not deviate from the schedule. It is poor public relations practice to frustrate people by making them wait. Not only is it discourteous, but it also may lead to outright disaffection with the activity and, perhaps, with the organization providing the opportunity. Certainly, no public department can afford to alienate its would-be supporters. Parents expect children who attend the activity sessions to be enrolled and participating in a group. They will not act favorably to a service that permits their children to wait around the door of the center or playground on the street because personnel have not yet arrived. Similarly, parents expect their children to appear promptly at the conclusion of the session. Schedules should be adhered to. Perhaps parents have made certain plans that include picking up their offspring at a specified time. If children are involved beyond a reasonable length of time, plans go awry. This does not lend itself to good feelings on the adults' part. Routines are important, and the starting and stopping times must be maintained. Whatever time must be taken for other considerations should be decided upon so that there are no last-minute problems that may cause an overlapping of periods, thereby stealing time from another group's activity. The same principle holds true for private agency programs of like nature and for similar reasons.

Scheduling

Scheduling is really concerned with coordinating time periods with participants, leadership, and space. The schedule is the visible result of planning, development, public relations, and personnel assignment along with suitable space and appropriate support of materials and equipment. It is dovetailing various elements into a harmonious pattern of the right place, people, time, and interests, coincidental with sufficient notice. Schedules also permit flexibility of arrangements so that emergencies may be handled with alternative plans. Should there be forced changes, substitute plans should be put into action to prevent loss of time or participant interest.

In scheduling educational activities, time may be considered in daily, weekly, monthly, or other increments, depending upon the nature of the subjects under consideration. There may be scheduled individual vocational sessions that occur at a given hour one or more times per week in which the content is progressive and is concerned with skill or knowledge building prior to entry into a sustained course. Such courses may be set up in terms of from 4 to 10 weeks, meeting once or more often each week. The course is designed to teach participants about some selected subject, to provide directed learning, or to offer the opportunity for continuous practice. In some instances the course may combine all of these attributes. Clearly, the goals of the course must be taken into consideration when planning the schedule.

The Instructor's Role

The function of any instructor is to enhance the development of the individual; this will necessarily include four aspects. The initial role is that of libertarian, where there is a democratic environment that encourages untrammeled inquiry. This atmosphere occurs when the instructor believes that each person has the unquestioned right to explore and seek the answers to whatever curiosity about subjects he or she has the urge to investigate. Thus, the classroom, playground, or other recreational area permits the learner to analyze ideas and evaluate them. The place, properly equipped with instructional tools and materials, is at least as important to learning as are ideas.

Instructional personnel also are resources for the learner. People should not be expected to initiate or create the concepts that will be employed by them in arranging, exploring, and interpreting their environment, although this is always possible. It is less important that each person originate the ideas used in the process of inquiry than it is for the instructor to be able to stimulate the learning experiences of every participant.

The process of coordinating plays a vital part in bringing together the diverse ideas, plans, and activities suggested and used by learners. The instructor must also encourage and stimulate the individuals in their respective efforts. As previously indicated, the instructor should not attempt to be the final authority. Participants can profit by making mistakes, specifically when the mistakes are recognized and corrected by the individual. It is unnecessary for the instructor to prevent any errors on the participant's part by anticipating them and supplying the right answer even before a request for assistance is made. There is no harm in permitting the learner to work a puzzle through to its conclusion, knowing that the attempted solution is wrong. If adequately guided, the individual will try to examine the given response and determine why it did not succeed. More learning may be gained by this approach than by dismissing the individual's wrong efforts, or by showing a correct method but refraining from going through a sequence of experiences that may illustrate how and why particular steps are important if a valid solution is to be reached. Naturally, no instructor will permit frustrations to develop if the participant becomes mired in a plan that has no answer. In this manner, the instructor ensures the smooth operation of the activity by supervisory expertise as well as the organization and coordination of materials and experiences.

Finally, the instructor assumes the role of evaluator. To do this, there must be effective plans that guide participant activities. The instructor has the responsibility for diagnosing learning problems, if any, and deciding on possible solutions. The instructor must determine what is to be taught, how the material should be presented, and how the learner can be evaluated. This really means that the structure of the learning environment cannot be completely spontaneous, haphazard, or unrestricted. The instructor must be able to arrange the space and materials, and extend the participant's curiosity into systematic knowledge. If learning is conceived as modified behavior in terms of directed learning sequences, the instructor has the responsibility for assessing the individual performer insofar as the behavior changes are contained in the aims of instruction.

Basic Learning Principles

Among the concepts that should be kept uppermost in guiding those who attempt to instruct are the following six:

1. Desirable behavior in terms of attainment of objectives should receive positive reinforcement. A conditioned pattern of response is thereby built up when appropriate learning or achievement of ends is effected. Verbal reward is the typical method used for reinforcing successful behavior. However, personal satisfaction, self-expression, and the pleasure of mastery of new skills, knowledge, or technical capability to perform probably contain a greater degree of sustenance for the individual because it is through personal effort that results are gained.

2. Signals that arouse the drive toward achievement of goals will certainly enhance the probability of attainment. The instructor must be prepared to emit those signals, which should elicit a positive response from the individual. However, not everybody is sensitive to, or capable of receiving, these suggestions for action. Anxiety can be applied to stimulate activity, and its reduction will serve to reinforce behavior. Too much anxiety can prohibit learning however. When the individual is placed in a position of jeopardy or such stress that anxiety about the situation replaces all other thoughts, learning is effectively blocked. Frustration leading to anxiety about performance restricts learning ability. An enriched atmosphere of learning combats excessive fears and promotes learning as the individual responds to the signals of instruction. This form of stimulation commends itself to the learning experience and may therefore be used effectively.

3. Transfer of training is a fundamental concept in all learning. Where activities require the same principles for solution, even though the problems are different, there is great likelihood that the principles will be applied. There is a great deal to commend the concept that

self-discovery offers greater opportunity for total involvement and real understanding of a given situation. When the individual has a chance to work out a problem for him- or herself, as opposed to being told what to do, there is every indication that the process becomes more deeply ingrained and permits a degree of insight that might otherwise not be a part of the learner's behavior. The opportunity of learning through almost any recreational experience will do much to inspire the involvement necessary for self-discovery to occur.

4. Activity consistent with the learner's current level of achievement will probably be assimilated. Intellectual comprehension, motor coordination, and span of attention are all significant factors in determining the capacity of the individual to learn. A variety of methods may be tried so the individual is enabled to achieve success with the least frustration and the maximum degree of satisfaction. This may be accomplished when the individual is facilitated by self-selection of activities and materials. This can be one of the innovative methods by which learning is supported and encouraged.

5. If an individual has been exposed to a variety of skills over a period of time, that person may be inclined to imitate such activities—especially when they appear to be interesting, pleasurable, stimulating, or exciting. Within a recreational context, there are countless opportunities for imitative learning to take place. Working with tools, manipulating materials, observing skilled performance, and copying movement to perfect skills are integral parts of any recreational program. The instructor should take every opportunity to promote this type of learning, and provision for practice should be optimized.

6. There is much to recommend the principle that individuals learn more effectively if they perform activities in response to problems posed. The individual who must work out a solution when confronted with a given situation is more likely to learn by such experiences than if he or she simply observes others making correct responses or attempting to solve problems. Vicarious experience certainly is a valuable method by which learning occurs; however, the most certain process is learning by doing. The carry-over value of this principle may have its most spectacular benefit in a novice learner's attempt to explore the environment, create a representation of what is observed, manipulate objects, use equipment, or subject him- or herself to the rigors of developing a new skill. Recreational activities of many kinds can be an outstanding avenue to employ in developing a well-rounded individual, in associating a series of apparently unrelated experiences to the learning process, and in assisting the individual to assimilate new skills by participation.

Individualized Instruction

The instructor has a mandatory responsibility to deal with each person as an individual. Every person, then, cannot receive the exact same educational exposure as every other participant. There is, therefore, a requirement for learning experiences that allow for the uniqueness of each individual. These learning situations should be organized with the objective of providing an educational program in which the participant's learning capability is enhanced by using whatever potential is evidenced.

A learning experience should be made available to accommodate the individual in terms of the method by which he or she best comprehends. In this way individuality may flourish and optimum learning will occur. Working with real objects and participating in specific projects or other activities that combine abstraction with visual and concrete materials may do much to facilitate learning, and incidentally be personally satisfying and enjoyable.

The program suggested here would provide optimized individual instruction by involving participants with activities that are enjoyable. Many people are bored in the formal, and sometimes stultifying, situation of the classroom. If much that constitutes the school curriculum could be offered in a manner that permitted the would-be learner unlimited freedom of inquiry, movement, pleasurable activity, and self-expression through many media, there might be greater likelihood of learning. Thus, many facets of the curriculum could be combined or singled out for attention in innovative ways that are stimulating and that tend to extend the individual's desire to know more and more about the subject.

Summary

Education is the broadest category in the recreational program because it encompasses all of the other activities as well as all curricular subjects. It has to do with directed learning through instruction. This is not say that the recreational service agency is attempting to undercut the school system. In fact, if anything, the recreational service program is a complement to the school curriculum. The informal aspect of education offered in no way infringes upon the requirement of school attendance or the subjects delivered by the school system.

Every possible concept that comes under the heading of education including the sciences, arts, mathematics, foreign languages, business, physical activity, vocational and industrial crafts, geography, and countless others may have recreational overtones for those who want more than a formal classroom experience. Clubs and interest groups are typical of the activities carried on by those who are absorbed by certain curricular subjects. Some individuals, for example, during their leisure, want to explore the intricacies of differential calculus, physics, biology, or history.

The educational category in a recreational program is informal, although classes may be scheduled so that some direct learning occurs. There are no tests or demands for conformity to rules and regulations, other than for common sense application and decent behavior. No required attendance is imposed. It is the participant and the interest generated by the activity that attracts and keeps him or her in the sequence. The sole objective is to have a good time; the concomitant role of learning is a bonus feature.

Selected Further References

Burriss, G. K., and B. F. Boyd (Eds.). *Outdoor Learning and Play, Ages 8–12*. Olney, MD: Association for Childhood Education International, 2005.

Campbell, K. J. *Art Across the Alphabet: Over 100 Art Experiences that Enrich Early Literacy*. Beltsville, MD: Gryshon House, Inc., 2003.

Gilbertson, K., et al. *Outdoor Education: Methods and Strategies*. Champaign, IL: Human Kinetics, Publishers, 2005.

Green, L., and R. Mitchell. *Art 7–11: Developing Primary Teaching Skills*. Florence, KY: Routledge, 1997.

Hickman, R. (Ed.). *Art Education*. 2nd ed. Harrisburg, PA: Continuum International Publishing Group, Inc., 2004.

Mundy, J. *Leisure Education: Theory and Practice*. Champaign, IL: Sagamore Publishing, 1997.

Sivan, A. A., and H. Ruskin. *Leisure Education Community Development and Populations with Special Needs*. New York: CABI Publishing Service, 2000.

Motor Skills

Motor skills of every kind are tremendously popular with children, youth, and adults who participate in recreational activities. This chapter expects to develop the purposes, professional practices, and program operation that can assist recreationists everywhere. Instructional methods have not been included in this material because there is a vast collection of published documents available for the interested practitioner. No detailed development of each and every motor skill has been attempted because the physical activitics can be grouped in such a manner that common procedures apply to any number of the experiences.

All activities requiring gross and/or fine muscle control that may be devised for physiological development, extension of capacity to endure, or competitive purposes are called motor skills. Sports, games, and conditioning experiences are one means of classifying and identifying motor performance. Sports are all those recreational pursuits that are not restricted by time, rules, or a distinct, specifically delimited, universally known area. Games, on the other hand, have special rules and codes to which all players must adhere. Games are conducted in carefully defined and distinguishable spaces, segregated from all other activities, and are usually relegated to a selected portion of time or by units in which the game must be completed. Sports, when so regulated, may be modified to become games. Games can never be sports. Conditioning experiences encompass repetitive movement of bending, stretching, pushing, or pulling. They may include isometric or isotonic activities designed to increase strength, flexibility, endurance, and/or speed.

Motor skills can be identified in several ways and contain the following activities:

Individual: archery, bicycling, bowling, diving, equitation, field events, fishing, fly-casting, golf, gymnastics, ice-skating, in-line skating, jogging, pistol shooting, rifle shooting, roller skating, sailing, skeet shooting, skiing, surfing, track, tumbling, walking, weightlifting, weight training

Dual: aerial darts, badminton, billiards, fencing, handball, horseshoe pitching, martial arts, paddleball, racquetball, shuffleboard, squash, synchronized swimming, table tennis, tennis, two-man sculling, wrestling

Team: baseball, basketball, cricket, crew, curling, field hockey, football, hurling, ice hockey, lacrosse, polo, rugby, soccer, softball, volleyball, water polo

Group: aerobics, apparatus play, ball games, bocce, calisthenics, circuit training, circle games, croquet, drills, goal-hi, hiding games, line games, relays, stunts, tag games, tug-o-war

It is unfortunate that too many recreational programs are so heavily larded with motor performance activities and little else. Sports and games are easily scheduled within any program and have almost universal acceptance; however, motor performance is no more important in a balanced recreational program than are any of the other categories. Nevertheless, sports and games have received an inordinate amount of emphasis. Motor performance can be very appealing to all age groups and to both genders. Cultural factors also may not affect its popularity. Motor performance is a part of living from the time a child expresses him- or herself in random kinetic movement until a mature individual takes a last evening constitutional. Every waking moment has some facet of motor skill or performance within it.

Traditionally, young males are attracted to and participate in a variety of motor skills. Young females also appreciate elementary games and rhythmical movement. As the individual matures, however, the females' interest in sports and physical games generally decreases. This is also true of active participation in team sports by adult males, although they may become golfers and fans or spectators who follow team sports and games. With the popularization of sports and game competition, a result in great part of the worldwide coverage of the last few Olympic Games by the mass media and, in part, of the increasing attention given to the physical fitness level of all Americans, participation has dramatically increased. Unfortunately, there is also a noticeable trend toward obesity in U.S. life, and this is most obvious in the curtailment of physical education classes in elementary through senior high school, as well as a falling off of active participation among adults. This apparent contradiction may be due to a reliance on television watching rather than rigorous physical involvement. Although public relations by establishments such as bowling centers have changed the image of the game and more women bowl now, and there is an upsurge in televised fitness activity commercials, there still remains a vast number of people who do not exercise at all.

Golf, swimming, gymnastics, and dance have been popularized by television. Where before women and girls might have considered sports and game participation unfeminine, they now realize the women participants in basketball, swimming, soccer, skiing, ice-skating, ballet, modern dance, tennis, golf, gymnastics, horseback riding, waterskiing, and track not only possess beautiful figures, but also are extremely feminine. No longer do women look with distaste upon motor performance. Despite this, there is a falling off of the number of participants. Therefore, much has to be done to foster a desire for physical activity participation, especially as a carryover recreational value long after the individual has left school.

The recreationist has the responsibility of programming all forms of motor skills throughout the year. He or she plans to meet the needs, skills, and experiences of all people in the community. The standard selection of motor activities for the program is based upon interest—not how many will be spectators, but rather, how many will take an active part.

The schedule of physical recreational experiences needs to include both highly organized, formal activities and self-directed, informal, and free play activities. Within this format there should be some motor performance that has an appeal for each individual according to his or her own skills, proficiency, experiences, and prior exposure. There must be instruction on each level of ability through clinics, workshops, and both individual and group practice. Competition is a real function in motor performance, but emphasis upon extrinsic awards and winning at any price must be avoided. The justification for participation should be the enjoyment and satisfaction derived from playing the game and taking part in the sport.

Whenever serious thought is given to competition, a program should be established for all those who wish to participate. A highly skilled performer certainly has a placc in the recreational games program, but so does the individual with little ability and no experience. The *intramural* program, with its intention of allowing every interested person to play the game, may be the best method available for meeting the needs of people. Intramurals should not be confused with the specialist team. They are designed to offer equal opportunity, where participation will be against those of average skill. The intramural program consists of competition among those persons who frequent one recreational facility. It may consist of double or single elimination tournaments, ladder or pyramid contests, or round robin tournaments. It may or may not be coeducational, although the latter might promote greater interest at one age and deter interest in another. In any case, the recreationist will be in the best position to organize such an activity.

Intermurals are those competitive activities organized between two or three neighborhood recreational facilities (e.g., centers or playgrounds), and are conducted on the same basis as intramurals. The difference here is that off-facility events in the schedule may stimulate an additional interest. *Extramurals* are those highly competitive events scheduled on an inter-district and city-wide basis, with great emphasis upon skills. They serve to focus attention upon the individual or single team and are useful in meeting the needs of those who have great ability, skill, and experience.

In whatever way the various forms of motor performance are programmed, they have a natural appeal. There are motor skills for the physically fit and unfit, for the strong, the weak, those who have endurance, and those who have little stamina. There are activities that demand poise, balance, flexibility, agility, speed, and grace. There are other activities that require hand–eye coordination. Sports have many values, not the least of which are the opportunity of belonging to a team, receiving personal satisfaction in attaining some objective, and simply enjoying the exhilarating effects of whatever game is being played.

Building Interest

The development of any organized motor skill activity necessitates the following of certain fundamental steps to ensure the success of the program. Among these will be the need to determine what interest there is in a given activity within the community. Of course, interested individuals may readily be found in terms of their coming forward and requesting that their particular activity be organized or developed. Sometimes, however, interest is latent or nonexistent. In this instance, it would probably be necessary to stimulate potential participation by exposing the constituency to films, demonstrations, exhibitions, and the like. This educational procedure might encourage those who have had little or no experience to step up for instruction and engagement. When interest is expressed and recruitment for the motor skills activities is ongoing, then individual, dual, and team competitions can be introduced.

Organizing and conducting physical recreational activities must, necessarily, vary depending upon local conditions and the organizations established to operate these activities. Public recreational service departments probably have to contend with laws governing the development and administration of the program. Extant and pertinent policies, money available, and facilities may enable some departments to have extensive physical activity while others languish or have greatly diminished athletic potential. This latter aspect also holds true for private agencies (e.g., youth organizations, sectarian organizations, or commercial enterprise). Local interest in traditions as well as geographic situation may also influence the type of motor skills program that can be operated. Some locations may advocate types of activities that are found in lumbering operations, agricultural enterprises, rock climbing in regions of hilly or mountainous terrain, and aquatic activities of various kinds depending upon the availability of or proximity to open or impounded waterways. Regional traditions may demand hunting, fishing, hiking, horseback riding, steeplechasing, and the like.

It is well known that people participate in motor skills of various types for the enjoyment they receive from engagement. The desire to have fun, achieve satisfaction, gain achievement, and engage in social interaction probably accounts for the millions of people who take part in these activities. Despite widespread reports of a decline in the number of people participating in vigorous physical activity, there is still a vast multitude of those who do. Due to the widespread interest and participation in such activities, uncounted thousands of individuals are exposed to the guidance and counseling of recreationists on a daily basis. Positive influence in the context of physical activity will assist the development of desirable qualities in those who take part. Particularly valuable will be the development of playing skills, companionship, ethical conduct, cooperative behavior, positive attitudes toward others, and fairness in dealing with questions of right and wrong.

The success of any program lies with its organization. Recreationists must recognize that the fundamental reason for the activity is that it meets the needs of all those who are interested. Activities must be arranged so that all age groups and genders have a choice insofar as their interest and needs are concerned. As with all other categories, provision must be made for the level of skill possessed by the participants, whether they are beginners, intermediates, or those with advanced skills. The schedule, enabling a variety of individuals to participate, should be arranged so that periods of play are appropriate in duration, time, and day for the varied population that is expected. Especially important is the need to provide facilities that are safe, well maintained, and attractive.

There should be a well-established public relations program that enables interested persons to express their opinions concerning the type of activities offered and their respective operation, and through this mechanism encourages participants to assist in the planning and management of the program. To the extent possible, those who are actively participating in any aspect of the motor skills conducted by the organization need to be stimulated to share responsibilities concerning leadership and cooperation. In keeping with the concept of good public relations, extensive coordination with other agencies operating in the community needs to be firmly established and maintained. Such an arrangement will effectively reduce any conflict of interest that might occur, be more capable of meeting the needs and interests of the population involved, and prevent competition among the various agencies for the same clientele.

Ongoing evaluation of the motor skills category needs to be conducted continuously. Activities presented, methods used, and participation may be some of the criteria utilized to determine whether this category is satisfying the purposes for which it was established. Weekly staff meetings to appraise the arrangements, activities, and extent of participation together with input from players and interested others should permit effective evaluation to discover if the values of the program are really being accomplished.

Organization and Conduct of Motor Performance

The single most important element in the general direction and administration of sports, games, and exercise is leadership. Although recreationists are supposed to be leaders, in the real sense of the term, there is also a need for volunteers as supplements and complements to the professional staff. Any person who is assigned to conduct competitive activities or any of the other motor performance experiences must be qualified to instruct to the extent necessary. Volunteers may be recruited from those who have an abiding interest and skill in the physical activity under consideration. Concerned parents may be helpful in working with children's groups, high school athletes may become involved with younger children's sports and games, and former professionals might be recruited to work with those who skills demand a knowledgeable proponent.

Organization of Motor Skills Activities

The success of any series of programmed motor skills depends upon organizational methods, competent guidance, and supervision. Recreationists with some general knowledge of sports and games, as well as those who have highly specialized skills, are invaluable to the production of a rationally planned and satisfying program. The recreationist detailed to motor performance activities must have the ability to lead whatever activities are assigned. He or she must have a genuine liking and enthusiasm for the motor skills to be instructed or supervised and for those who participate. Of course, physical education majors at the college level, if available, may be recruited as sport, game, and exercise specialists. These individuals, and their employed teaching counterparts, might be willing to serve as paid coaches or instructors, or become volunteer advocates for the promotion of motor skills. Beyond that, there will be a need for highly qualified game officials (i.e., umpires, referees, timers, etc). Such officials are necessary in any program where formal competition is a probable outcome of successful organization. Well-qualified officials can do much to instill the fundamental principle of fair and equitable governance of matches, games, tournaments, and other competitive events.

Among the factors to be considered when grouping participants for motor activities are age, gender, height, weight, maturity, interests, and current level of skill. Although there are variations within age groups, the following developmental characteristics influence participation in motor skill activities and should be recognized by recreationists to whom planning responsibilities are assigned.

Ages 4 to 6

The growth rate is much slower during this stage than at any other time between infancy and adolescence. Children may want to expend a great deal of energy, but they tire rapidly and must rest. During this stage, large muscle development is most pronounced. Children enjoy activities that require a great deal of running, jumping, hopping, skipping, and climbing. However, coupled with a tremendous energy output is a relatively short attention span. Children not only tire easily, but also are easily bored. Activities must therefore be fast, exciting, and quickly finished.

By the time the child is 5 years old he or she has some skill at ball handling and throwing. Individual differences in skills can range from poor to outstanding. Motor skills tend to show an increasing degree of sophistication by the age of 6. The child enjoys social activities, cooperates, and enjoys games that require chasing, dodging, tagging, and rhythmics.

There are a number of activities that children enjoy learning and performing during these years. Some are traditional, ethnic, or simply exploratory. The elements of suspense, rapid movement, simple roles, ease of understanding, and some competition characterize most of them. Line, square, and circle games can be used to maintain individual and group interest. Suggestions for typical games follow.

LITTLE BROWN BEAR. The children stand in line as though they are on the edge of a forest. A little brown bear lives in the forest. The children wish to go through the forest to the opposite side. They face a little brown bear crouching a short distance in front of them. In her wee voice she asks, "Are you afraid of a little brown bear?" The children answer no and run to the opposite side of the play space. The little brown bear stands up on her hind legs and chases them. She tags as many as she can. Those whom she touches become her helpers. The little brown bear then squats before the group, with her helpers in a line beside her. The little brown bear asks the question again. When the answer comes, all the helper bears chase the remaining children as they run across the play space, and the game continues until all the children become little brown bears. The last child tagged becomes the little brown bear for the next game.

TRAFFIC POLICE. The children stand in line as if on a curb ready to cross the street. One child is chosen to be the police officer. He or she stands on the opposite side of the play area. He or she calls "green light" and faces the opposite direction from the children, who move forward. The police officer suddenly calls "red light" and then turns toward them. The children must stop immediately. If the police officer sees any child move his or her feet, that child is sent back to the curb. The police officer continues to call, and the children move forward, or stop, according to the signal. The first child to touch the outstretched hand of the police officer is the new police officer.

SKYBALL. The players are divided into two teams. Facing one another, they stand on either side of a line marked on the playground. One player, throwing the ball high, tosses it to the other team. If a player on the opposite team catches the ball before it touches the ground, he or she scores a point for the team. The player who is able to place both hands on the ball first throws it up high to the other team. Each team is careful not to cross the dividing line. The game continues in this manner until five points are scored by one team.

Ages 7 to 9

The growth rate of boys and girls is slow and steady at this time. There is a decided integration of the sexes up to about 8 or 9 years of age, and boys and girls frequently play together without difficulty. After age 9, however, there is an equally strong preference for separation of the sexes. There is a need for group or peer acceptance, although individual achievement is a vital factor for motivation. Strong physical movements are noted; vigorous activity predominates. There is a desire for excellence, and the practice of various motor skills seems to come to the fore. One significant feature is participation in team or group activities in which cooperation is necessary. Youngsters at this age want to excel and seek approval from some authority figure—in this instance, the recreationist. Physical ability, lengthened attention span, and greater endurance enable participation in activities that have more complex rules and require more time. Games must still be relatively short, but the rest factor is no longer as restricting as before. Lead-up activities for far more highly organized team games should be scheduled.

Among the activities enjoyed by this age group are relays, jumping games, self-testing exercises, hiding and running games, and ball-handling games. The following are some examples.

CIRCLE CHASE. The players stand in a circle formation and number themselves around the circle from one to four. The leader then calls one of these numbers. If the leader calls "two," all players with this number run around the circle once, each player attempting to tag the number two runner in front of him or her. All players who are tagged step into the center of the circle. After each number has been called, the players in the center are counted. The group with the fewest players tagged is the winner. The game is played again with everyone participating.

GATHERING STICKS. Two base lines are marked at opposite ends of a playing space at least 100 feet long. This space is divided by a middle line. Six Indian clubs are placed on each base line. The players are divided into two equal teams and are scattered on each side of the center line. On a starting signal, the players attempt to run across the center line into the other team's area and pick up an Indian club without being tagged by an opponent. If a player successfully obtains an Indian club, he or she may walk back and place it on his or her base line. Any player who is tagged by an opponent in the opponent's play area becomes a prisoner and must stand on his or her opponent's base. His or her teammates rescue him or her by running to him or her if they can avoid being tagged by an opponent. After being rescued, the player may walk to his or her own side and continue playing. Whenever a prisoner is caught, his or her her teammates must rescue him or her before they can pick up any clubs. At the end of the playing time, the team with the most Indian clubs on their base line is the winner.

HOOK ON. Each player selects a partner. Players stand side by side, while the two hands that touch are inside hands. When the runner and chaser are chosen, the partners drop their hands in order to participate. Partners stand in a play area approximately 5 to 8 feet from the next couple. One player is chosen to be a runner and another to be a chaser. The chaser runs after the runner trying to tag him or her. The runner keeps from being tagged by hooking arms with another player's partner. The player who is left without a partner in this group of three becomes the runner, and the chaser continues after him or her. If a runner is tagged while running from the chaser, he or she becomes the chaser, and the chaser becomes the runner.

Ages 10 to 12

Most children between the ages of 10 and 12 continue to demand vigorous activity. Their muscular development, motor coordination, and stamina are quite good. They are therefore intensely interested in activities that permit them to exhibit skill, talent, and endurance. During these ages great stress is placed upon participation in competitive team activities. Boys particularly like experiences that require strength and agility for good performance, such as stunts, tumbling, and gymnastics. Girls, if athletically inclined, display similar characteristics. However, some girls show no interest in or desire for such participation. The early maturing girl is inclined to view such activities as unfeminine.

CORNER DODGE BALL. The game is played on a 40-foot square. In each corner and in the middle of the field, a 10-foot square is laid out. The groups are divided into several teams of seven to nine members each. Each team has a chief who stands in the center square facing the direction in which he or she intends to throw. Each chief has a rubber ball or volleyball. Each team stands in one of the corner squares. When the recreationist signals, all teams run counterclockwise to the next square. As they run, the chiefs attempt to hit players, below the waist, on the opposing teams with the ball. Players are safe when they are in a corner square. The players who are hit move to the outside of the square and return the balls that are thrown as the chiefs try to hit players. The game is concluded when the players have progressed around the square three times. Teams run only when the recreationist signals them to do so. The winning team is the largest number of individuals in a square at the end of the game.

SOCCER DODGE BALL. The game is played in a circle approximately 25 to 30 feet in diameter. The players are arranged in two teams. One team is inside the circle, and the other team stands on the circle. The team on the circle keeps the soccer ball in play by kicking it, attempting to eliminate the players on the inside of the circle by hitting them with the ball. When a player has been hit, he or she becomes a kicker. If any player inside the circle steps outside of it, he or she joins the kickers. The players on the outside must maintain their places. The players within the circle scatter to dodge the ball. The team eliminating the greatest number of players in a given time is the winner. No one is permitted to throw a ball. All balls must be kicked, and must hit the inner players below the waist.

Ages 13 to 17

The complex changes begun at the onset of puberty and adolescence directly relate to the kinds of physical activities in which this age group participates. Boys are more capable of balancing than are girls at this age, although there are girls who are extremely talented in balancing activities. Boys progress and improve their balancing skill, while most girls show negligible improvement. Girls seem to exhibit greater perceptual skills; they are more accurate than boys are during this period. Up to the age of 13, girls tend to be more agile than boys; boys easily surpass girls after that age. Boys always exhibit more strength than girls, but the degree of differentiation becomes even more pronounced with maturation. Nevertheless, there are always some females who exhibit great strength and stamina. The variations in primary motor skills must be considered by the recreationist responsible for the development of the athletic or sports program. Activities suitable to this age group include almost all the standard team, individual, and dual events.

Perceptual Activities

Perception is a process in which sensory information is evaluated concerning what is happening around us. All voluntary movement contains elements of perception, but perceptual activities are those that require intensive hand/eye coordination for skilled performance.

Archery

Archery is a perceptual activity that requires hand–eye coordination in the use of a propelling implement and a missile. Although bow hunting has become popular in the last several decades, most participants enjoy the activity by shooting at targets. There are many forms of target shooting. Field shooting requires targets of varying sizes situated at different distances; the object is to hit the target with the fewest possible number of shots. Field shooting, for which designated areas in parks are well-suited, necessitates a great deal of space for the targets as well as for safety. Target shooting, on the other hand, has fixed distances from which archers shoot (**Figure 13.1**); the object is to receive the highest possible score by hitting the scoring rings in the target.

Figure 13.1   At Full Draw

Archery golf, similar to golf, is played on a golf course or on a specific course designed for archers. The aim is to shoot an arrow from the tee to the green, where a 4-inch straw-ball target replaces the cup.

Clout shooting is long-range shooting at a 48-foot target laid out on the ground. This type of shooting is excellent for teaching the judgment of distances. A number of arrows, usually six ends or 36 arrows, are shot from 100 to 200 yards away from the target. The goal, or clout, is in the center of the target, which is 10 times larger than the standing 48-inch target. Scores are determined by totaling the points achieved for hitting the scoring rings.

Flight shooting is for distances only. Basically, the idea is to test the strength of the archer and the cast or ability of the bow to hurl the arrow. No accuracy is involved. In regular flight shooting, the archer stands and draws his or her bow to the maximum pull that can be attained and releases the string. In free-style shooting, the archer may assume any shooting position. Some archers lay down, place their feet on the belly of the bow, draw the string with two hands, and then let fly. Precautions must be taken against danger from stray arrows, because it is not unusual for an archer to shoot an arrow several hundred yards; therefore, a long space is required.

Rovers is a game of shooting at any inanimate object on the landscape. Any object—a clump of grass, trees, logs, bushes—constitutes a target. Each archer shoots one arrow at a selected target; the archer who either hits or comes closest to the target receives one point and may then select the next target. The archer with the most points at the end of a predetermined series of marks or period of time is declared the winner.

Standard rounds are commonly used for target shooting or in tournament archery competition. The rounds call for shooting a specific number of arrows at each of several fixed distances. Teams usually consist of four archers.

Target Shooting Rules

1. A regulation 48-inch target is used for all competitive and shooting purposes. The target is divided into a center, or goal, 9.6 inches in diameter and colored gold. Around the center are four concentric ratings, each 4.8 inches wide; they are colored from innermost to outermost, red, blue, black, and white. The color values, beginning with gold, are 9, 7, 5, 3, and 1.
2. An arrow cutting two colors is given the higher point value.
3. An arrow passing through the target face or bouncing off the target is given a score of 5 points regardless of where it hit the target.
4. Archers should stand astride the shooting line when shooting.
5. Archers should shoot one end, six arrows, and then all shooters go up to the targets at the same time to score hits.
6. An arrow leaving the bow for any reason is considered to have been shot, unless the archer can reach it without stepping across the shooting line.

Equipment

Archery equipment, or tackle, includes a bow, arrows, quiver, arm guard, and finger tab or shooting glove. The propelling implement, the bow, may be of the straight, reflex, or recurved type (**Figure 13.2**).

It may be made of wood, fiberglass, or laminate. The majority of fiberglass and laminated bows are recurved or reflex. The bow, particularly if recurved, should be shorter than the individual using it. The *draw weight* of the bow is the number of pounds of pull required to flex the bow to full draw. The average target bow should have a draw weight of between 25 and 40 pounds for males, depending upon age, height, weight, and strength. The average for females is from 20 to 35 pounds. Beginners should start with lighter bows; as proficiency increases, heavier bows can be used.

A bow is thickest at the grip or handle. The bow has an upper or lower limb. The part of the bow facing the archer is called the *belly*; that of the opposite side, the *back*. Two *nocks* are situated at the tips of the bow; these are grooves into which the looped ends of the bowstring are placed. Some bows have arrow rests and plates that permit the archer to align the arrow and also to protect the flesh between thumb and forefinger from being cut by the fletching as the arrow is released. If there is no arrow rest, the bow hand must support the arrow. Dacron bowstrings are widely used today and are relatively long-lasting. The bowstring has an additional protective covering

Figure 13.2 The Recurved Bow and Arrow

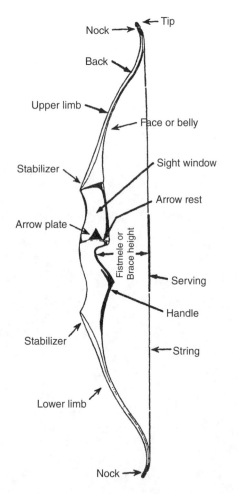

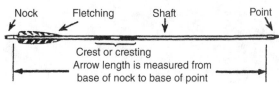

wrapped around the portion that receives the arrow nock; this is called the *serving*.

An arrow is a thin shaft of wood, fiberglass, or metal. It can be hollow or solid. The usual length of the arrow is from 24 to 30 inches, and it is 5/16 inch in diameter. Field, hunting, and fishing arrows are generally longer and heavier than target arrows. The tip, or pile, of the arrow is also differentiated depending upon the target. The main section of the arrow is called the *shaft*; the front, or pointed end, is called the *foreshaft*, or *footing*. The tip is called the *point*, or *pile*. The rear portion of the shaft is the *shaftment*. The feathered end, the *fletching*, is made up of three feathers. The feather set at a right angle to the nock is the cock feather; the other two are hen feathers. The color bands to the front of the fletching are designated the *crest*. The nock at the end of the arrow receives the bowstring. The correct length of the arrow is individually determined and depends upon the arm length of the archer.

All archers should wear some kind of finger and forearm protector in order to prevent blisters, contusions, or welts. A good archer will not hit his or her forearm with the bow string, but on occasion the bowstring may snap against the forearm, leaving a welt. If this continues, the skin may be bruised or even broken and lacerated. Leather or plastic guards are attached to the forearm by thongs, straps, or lacing on the back of the arm. Unless the three shooting fingers are well protected by finger tab or glove, they become sore with constant shooting. The tab or glove also permits a smoother release of the string.

Basic Archery Skills

When instructing fledgling archers, the recreationist must teach beginners the following skills.

STRINGING THE BOW. Place the bowstring loop in the bottom nock. Lay the lower curve of the bow over and across the left ankle. The lower limb of the bow is then taken over the right thigh. Grasp the upper limb of the bow with the right hand and bend the bow on the recurve. Slip the top loop of the bowstring on the upper nock and release the pressure gradually. Make sure that the bowstring is securely in place before drawing the bow. To unstring the bow, use the same method. Simply bend the bow until there is sufficient slack in the string to allow the loop to be freed from the nock.

STANCE. In addressing the target, have the archer stand comfortably, head erect, shoulders square, feet slightly separated and approximately 12 to 15 inches apart. The weight is evenly distributed on both feet. The archer's body should be at a right angle to the target. The archer should turn his or her head in order to look over the left shoulder directly at the target (**Figure 13.3**).

GRIPPING. The bow is held in the left hand by right-handed archers and in the right hand by left-handed archers. They should hold the bow so that the grip is

Figure 13.3   Basic Archery Skills

Stance

Gripping

Nocking 1

Nocking 2

against the base of the thumb and the handle is gripped by the thumb and forefinger. The other three fingers can be placed on the grip, but this is not necessary. The palm should be down. By rotating the elbow outward and keeping the palm of the hand facing down, the bow string can be released from full draw without having it slap against the forearm. The bow arm should be raised to shoulder height.

NOCKING. The bow should be grasped as just described. The archer should hold the bow directly in front of the hip and horizontal to the ground. With the right hand, an arrow should be placed in the rest with the arrow nock on the bowstring at the serving so that the cock feather is up or at a right angle to the bowstring. The arrow should be at a right angle to the string. Have the archer place the first three fingers of the drawing hand on the string at the first joint.

Rest the arrow nock between the first and third fingers. Rest the fourth finger on the serving. There is no need to pinch the arrow nock between the fingers. The arrow will stay on the bow string without any pressure if properly seated. A line drawn through the arrow would continue straight through the forearm. The elbow is neither raised nor lowered during this maneuver. The body posture should not change during the draw. Muscles in the back rather than the arms should be used to spread the bow.

Figure 13.4 Shooting Sequence

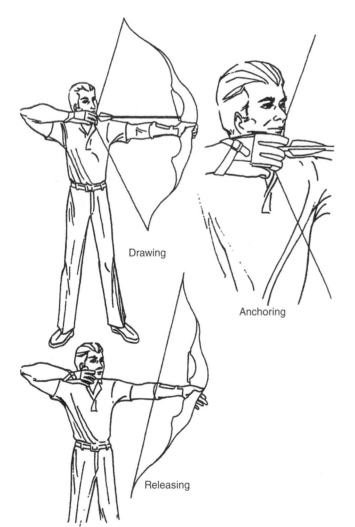

Drawing

Anchoring

Releasing

ANCHORING. Consistency is fundamental to good shooting. Therefore, the archer draws to the same spot each time. Individuals must find their own anchor point, but it is the spot to which the bowstring is drawn for each shot. It is a definite point on the face. Some archers prefer the tip of the nose; others the point of the chin; others the corner of the mouth or the corner of one eye (**Figure 13.4**). Wherever the anchor point is, it should remain the same. This prevents indiscriminate shooting or spattering the target with widely placed shots that cannot be corrected. One unvarying anchor point permits shot patterns and allows corrections to be made for height or wind variations.

AIMING. With recurve or reflex bows, which have a flatter trajectory than the standard straight bows, it is possible to aim directly at the target without having to compensate for an ascending or descending arc of flight. Recurved bows can be fired directly at the center of the target from distances of up to 40 yards, although the weight of the bow is a deciding factor in determining point-blank range. As with other bows, there is a tendency for the arrow to drop in flight over long distances, rather than flying on an even level. The aiming point must therefore be moved upward as the distance increases. The reverse is true of shorter distances. When at full draw and anchored, the archer should hold the arrow momentarily before releasing it. This action steadies the body as well as the bow and arrow and probably allows a more accurate cast.

RELEASING AND FOLLOWING THROUGH. The arrow should be released by permitting the string to roll off the tips of the fingers as they relax on the bowstring. The string should not be jerked. After the release, the body positioning is maintained, although there will be a slight reflex movement of the shooting hand as the string is released. The shooting hand tends to move backward about 1 inch as a result of the loss of tension.

CARE OF TACKLE. After shooting, the bow should be unstrung and hung on a rack in a cool, dry storage area. The bow should never be propped up against a wall. The bow should not be flexed nor the string released unless there is an arrow nocked and ready for flight.

To retrieve arrows that have been shot into the target, place the hand, palm up or down, against the target face with the shaft of the arrow extending between the first two fingers. Grasping the shaft with the other hand as close to the target face as possible, the shooter should withdraw the arrow with a twisting motion. Draw the arrow straight out in order to avoid bending it. If the arrow enters the ground or some other object, the process is the same. If the arrow penetrates the target to the fletching, draw the arrow through the target from the back. Arrows should be carried so that the feathers cannot be crushed, and stored so that the feathers do not touch; thus, the arrows must be placed in a standing position.

Safety Precautions

Archery ranges should be fairly isolated so that stray arrows do not damage persons or things. The shooting range should be banked at the area of the target butts. This prevents loss of arrows, and also eliminates the possibility of injury to a person inadvertently walking behind the targets. All archers must be cautioned about not stepping over the shooting line while others are shooting. To do so is not only a lapse of courtesy, but also dangerous. The shooting range official (recreationist) must make this absolutely clear.

Overdrawing can be dangerous because the arrow can be shot into the hand. This can be avoided by making sure that all arrows are of adequate length for the archer's draw.

An arrow placed in a 30-pound bow can be as dangerous as any rifle bullet. Archers must be warned to keep their arrows toward the target butts when shooting.

The commands of the range official must be obeyed instantly; there may be some emergency that the recreationist alone sees. All commands should be given loudly and clearly. If a cease-fire is given, all archers, whether at full draw or not, should immediately unnock the arrow. The wearing of protective gear is mandatory for all archers.

Bows, bowstrings, and arrows should be examined for signs of wear from friction or deterioration before any shooting takes place. Injuries from snapped bows can be avoided if tackle is properly inspected. Arrows with feathers that are not aligned or shafts that are warped are potentially dangerous and cause inaccuracies in shooting. Care of equipment, in most cases, prevents damage or injury and permits better shooting performance.

Riflery

Riflery, if the agency operates a shooting range, typically involves the sport of target shooting with a small-bore or 22-caliber rifle. Of course, indoor or

Figure 13.5 A Typical .22 Caliber Bolt-Action Rifle

REAR SIGHT (for aiming)
BOLT HANDLE
SMALL OF STOCK
COMB OF STOCK
BUTT OF STOCK
CHAMBER (holds cartridge ready for firing)
FRONT SIGHT (for aiming)
BREECH
BOLT
FORE-END OF STOCK
BARREL
UPPER SLING SWIVEL
MAGAZINE (feeds additional cartridges)
MUZZLE (front end of barrel)
TRIGGER GUARD
TRIGGER (releases cocked hammer or striker)
SLING (for carrying and steadying when firing)
LOWER SLING SWIVEL
HEEL OF STOCK
TOE OF STOCK
BUTTPLATE (place against shoulder when firing)

outdoor shooting ranges may enable rifles or pistols to be used. Usually, a public agency will permit a private association to operate the shooting facility and bear all of the expenses for such use. Commercial operations in the private sector allow any member to shoot with whatever weapon is chosen. Those few public recreational service agencies that operate shooting ranges may provide rifles and ammunition for rent, but almost always the individual must supply his or her own appropriate weapon and ammunition.

The object of shooting is to hit a target or series of targets from one or more fixed ranges. The rifle is a clip, tubular, or hand-fed shoulder weapon that is gas or hand-bolt operated (**Figure 13.5**). It has a grooved barrel in which spiral channels have been cut into the bore so that any bullet fired from the weapon rotates in flight. The rifling effect makes the shot more accurate and overcomes resistance from atmospheric friction.

The rifle has three basic sections: the stock, a barrel on the receiver, and the action. The *stock*, which is made of wood or other materials, is the part of the weapon that rests against the shoulder. The *barrel* is the metal part of the weapon through which the bullet is fired. The front of the barrel is the *muzzle*, while the rear is the *breech*. The *receiver* is the metal part of the piece in which the stock is attached. It contains the movable parts of the weapon and permits the bullet to be loaded, locked, and fired, and the rifle to be readied for another round. The action of the rifle contains those parts that perform the actual movements of loading, cocking, firing, and ejecting the cartridge.

The bolt is a sliding round metal plug that closes the breech in preparation for firing. The bolt contains (1) the firing pin, which strikes and fires the cartridge out of the barrel; (2) the main spring, which forces the firing pin forward; and (3) the extractor, which grasps the shell casing and pulls it out of the chamber after firing. The ejector is a small projection that flips the spent shell casing out of the chamber after extraction from the breech. The trigger housing contains the parts that release the firing pin in order for the rifle to fire; it includes the trigger, the trigger guard, and the safety, which prevents the trigger from being released accidentally.

The rifle sling is a leather strap arranged to fasten onto the rifle at the rear of the stock and at the fore-end of the stock by means of two metal swivels. The sling can be adjusted to fit the size and length of the arm. The purpose of the sling is not only to enable the rifle to be carried properly, but also to assist in steadying the rifle while aiming.

There are two sights on rifles: the front and the rear. These may be of three standard varieties: front blade sights, beads, and apertures. The blade is simply a thin piece of metal; it may be straight or curved toward the rear. The bead is similar except that there is a small bead of metal at the top of the blade. The aperture sight has a circle around the bead and a small opening through the bead; the whole is encased by a metal ring. The rear sights are attached to the top of the barrel toward the breech. They are either open notch or aperture. The open sight may have either a V-shaped or a square-shaped notch. The peep, or aperture sight, has a small hole set in a casing through which the shooter takes aim. The rear sight may also have screws attached by which adjustments for windage and elevation can be made.

The ammunition for small-bore rifle shooting must have a lead or alloy bullet seated in a rim-fire cartridge. The .22 long rifle cartridge is the one most frequently used, although the .22 short is available.

Firing points are spaces approximately 6 feet wide that are intended to accommodate the shooter and the coach. They are wide enough to permit both the shooter and the coach to assume a prone position. Any number of points can be used, depending upon the length of the firing line and the number of shooters on the range at any given time.

Shooting Techniques

The primary step in learning to shoot is mastering the technique of sighting and aiming. A training aid, called the sighting bar, can be easily and inexpensively made for such practice. It consists of a piece of wood approximately 2 feet in length. At one end of the slat there should be attached a thin, square piece of metal with a hole bored into it near its top. A 1-inch cut is made into the wood 1 foot from the eyepiece; into this is inserted another flat, square metal piece. This second piece of metal becomes the rear sight. An upright piece of metal is drilled into the wood 10 inches from the rear sight. This serves as the front-sight blade. Another slice is made 2 inches in front of this sight, and a target card can then be inserted. Using this device, the learner can be taught how to line up the front and rear sights with a target.

The front sight should be lined up with the rear sight so that the front blade or bead cuts the rear sight precisely in quarters. If a line were to be drawn vertically and horizontally from the front sight to the tip of the rear sight and from side to side, four equal quarters would be formed. When front and rear sights have been aligned, the bull's-eye of the target must be sighted so that it appears to rest exactly upon the top of the front-sight blade or so that the bead covers the bull's-eye.

Positions

PRONE POSITION. Among the four standard shooting positions, the prone position is steadiest and offers the greatest comfort and perhaps the greatest accuracy. The angle made by the body to the rifle is about 30 degrees. Spread the legs comfortably apart, with toes out and heels on the ground (see **Figure 13.6**). Grip the fore-end of the stock with the left hand; the left elbow should be directly beneath the forestock. Place the rifle butt firmly against the pad of the shoulder. Place the right hand on the small of the stock, with the right thumb along the stock and not around it. Press the right cheek against the upper portion of the stock, with the right eye as close to the rear sight as possible. The index finger of the right hand is in position to squeeze the trigger.

Figure 13.6 Riflery Positions: Prone, Sitting, Kneeling, Standing

LEGS WELL SPREAD
FEET FLAT
30 to 45 DEGREE ANGLE
LINE OF AIM

SITTING POSITION. Sit at an angle of about 45 degrees from the line of aim. Spread the feet comfortably. Bend the body forward at the hips without hunching the back. Rest the left elbow along the left shin or place it against the inner side of the left knee, supporting the rifle. Place the right elbow against the right knee. The heels of both feet should be solidly planted for a steady firing platform.

KNEELING POSITION. Kneel on the right knee so that the knee makes a right angle with the line of aim. Rest the left elbow below the left knee and well down on the shin. The left knee should be up toward the armpit for maximum support and steadiness. Place the right arm so that it forms a cushion for the rifle butt; place the right elbow comfortably out from the stock. Some shooters wish to hold the right elbow at a right angle to the stock or in an elevated position.

STANDING POSITION. The erect body should be at a right angle to the target butt. With the left hand, grasp the fore-end of the stock just behind the front sling swivel; the left elbow should be directly beneath the rifle. With the right hand, grasp the small of the stock; the right elbow should be held well up or out.

Trigger Squeeze

The trigger squeeze is one of the more important factors in accurate rifle shooting. Poor shooting usually results from spoiling the aim prior to firing the rifle. When a shooter flinches at the sound of the rifle being fired, he or she instinctively jerks the weapon. This throws off the point of aim, ruining the shot. Some learners anticipate the sound of the rifle being fired and flinch before the shot, thereby jerking the trigger. The trigger should be squeezed with increasing pressure so that the shooter is not surprised by the rifle's firing. The aim should be held while the trigger is being squeezed. Some shooters have the bad habit of jerking the trigger just as the sights and target become aligned; this invariably results in poor shooting. The shooter should hold his or her breath, aim, and deliberately squeeze the trigger. If the barrel of the rifle wavers too much, the shooter should relax and start again.

Safety Precautions

The shooting range should be carefully patrolled and designed so that no one can approach without seeing warning signs or without being seen by the range supervisor. When shooting is taking place, there should be a clearly designated signal that all must recognize. A red flag or some other such device can be used for this purpose.

Rifles should be inspected daily. They must be cleaned of carbon and dirt spots in the bore. Daily inspection is also necessary to make sure that chambers and bores are free of obstruction. Rifles should be placed standing in racks with bolts back and chambers open. They should never be rested on their sights or with the bolt underneath.

Rifle-range orders should be purposeful and clear. No learner should be allowed to load his or her rifle or to begin firing until all shooters are on the firing line and the range officer is prepared to supervise the firing. Rifles should always be pointed up- and down-range toward the target areas. Ammunition must be distributed only to those who are preparing to fire. At the completion of firing, all unused rounds should be collected and the rifles inspected for clearance before departing the range. Rifles should always be considered loaded. Strict rules should be applied to those who wish to receive shooting instructions.

Pistol Shooting

Another popular shooting activity is the use of a short barrel, handheld, aimed, and fired gun. Although there are many different types of pistols, the two kinds typically used today are the revolver and the semi-automatic (**Figures 13.7** and **13.8**). Most new shooters find that pistol shooting is extremely enjoyable, when performed safely.

A revolver is a pistol with a rotating cylinder constructed to contain cartridges. Pulling the trigger or cocking the hammer rotates the cylinder and permits the cartridge to be fired. The cylinder release latch permits the

Figure 13.7 The Revolver and Its Components

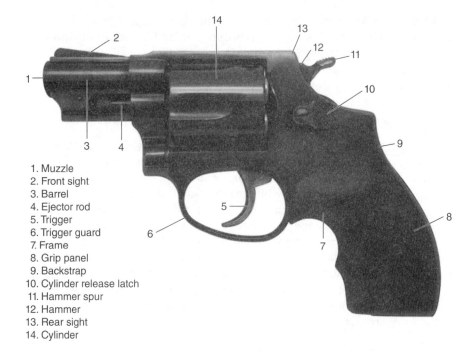

1. Muzzle
2. Front sight
3. Barrel
4. Ejector rod
5. Trigger
6. Trigger guard
7. Frame
8. Grip panel
9. Backstrap
10. Cylinder release latch
11. Hammer spur
12. Hammer
13. Rear sight
14. Cylinder

Figure 13.8 The Semi-Automatic Pistol and Its Components

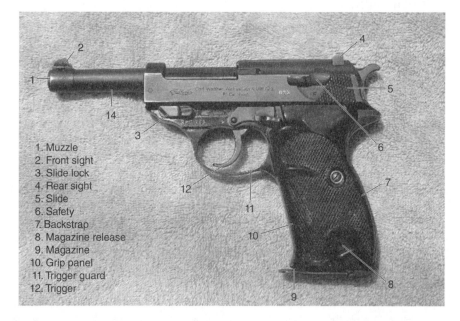

1. Muzzle
2. Front sight
3. Slide lock
4. Rear sight
5. Slide
6. Safety
7. Backstrap
8. Magazine release
9. Magazine
10. Grip panel
11. Trigger guard
12. Trigger

cylinder to swing out so that cartridges can be loaded and unloaded. Most revolvers have an extractor or ejector rod to remove cartridges from the cylinder. Revolvers are made up of a frame to which all other parts of the gun are attached. These attachments include the grip panels, backstrap, trigger guard, and rear sight, used for aiming purposes.

The barrel is the tube through which the bullet travels on its way to a target. The bore is contained in the barrel and has spiral grooves and lands cut into it so that it is rifled. Rifling puts a spin on the bullet, which permits greater accuracy and stability in flight. The distance between the lands indicates the caliber of the pistol. Common calibers include .22, .32, .38, .44, and .45. The front sight is situated on top of the barrel close to the muzzle.

The action is the moving parts used to load, fire, and unload the pistol. Obviously, the action is attached with a frame. The trigger sits underneath the frame. The hammer is attached to the rear of the frame. When the trigger is squeezed it causes the hammer to strike the firing pin and fire the cartridge.

Semi-automatics are pistols whose cartridges are loaded from a magazine inserted into the grip. When cartridges are fired the empty case is automatically extracted and ejected and a new cartridge is inserted into the chamber. All semi-automatics or autoloaders have the safety on the frame. The safety is a device installed to eliminate the possibility of accidental discharge of the pistol.

All semi-automatics have a slide. The slide either encloses the barrel or is located at the rear of the barrel. The first cartridge must always be manually cycled into the firing chamber by pulling back on the slide and then releasing it. As the slide moves forward, it takes a cartridge from the top of the magazine and inserts it into the chamber. The front and rear sights are normally located on the top of the slide. Some models have the sights situated on the top of the barrel or the frame.

When a semi-automatic pistol is fired, the slide moves to the rear, ejects the empty cartridge case, and cocks the pistol simultaneously. The cartridges in the magazine are forced upward by the magazine spring into the path of the slide. When the slide, under pressure, moves forward to a closed position it picks up and pushes the top cartridge into the chamber. After the first shot is fired, the movement of the slide will cock the hammer for the rest of the shots. The trigger will only be used to release the hammer.

Shooting Basics

For accurate shooting with a pistol, the beginner must learn proper body position, grip, breath control, sighting, trigger squeeze, and follow-through. These aspects need to be performed well every time a pistol is fired.

POSITION. The most common positions for pistol shooting are one-and two-handed standing. In all cases, the gun must be pointed in a safe direction with the finger off the trigger.

For one-hand standing, the body should be at an approximately 45-degree angle to the target with the right side of the body turned toward the target. The right arm is then extended and rotated in a small circular pattern. When the arm feels comfortable and is pointing at the center of the target, a point of aim has been established. The feet should be a shoulder's width apart and weight evenly distributed. The legs are straight, but not rigid. Both the body and the head are comfortably erect. The right arm is fully extended and the left hand is placed in the left trouser pocket. The gun is then brought to eye level ready for firing.

With the two-handed standing position, the gun is gripped in the right hand and the heel of the left hand is placed firmly against the heel of the right hand. The left thumb lies on top of the right thumb. The fingers of the left hand are then wrapped around the fingers of the right hand. The body faces the target squarely, with arms fully extended. The pistol is brought up to eye level ready for firing.

GRIP. In order to obtain a proper grip, the nonshooting hand is used to place the pistol in the grip of the shooting hand. Hold the backstrap portion of the frame as high as possible between the thumb and the index finger. The wrist and forearm are aligned with the backstrap. Hold the pistol firmly with the base of the thumb and lower three fingers of the shooting hand. The index finger should lie along the side of the frame or outside the trigger guard. The single most important aspect of the grip is that it should be the same whenever the pistol is held.

BREATH CONTROL. In order to be assured that the body remains relatively still, the breath must be held when shooting. Prior to each shot, inhale, let out enough air to be comfortable, and retain the rest when firing the shot.

SIGHTING. The sighting of the pistol is undertaken in much the same way as in rifle shooting. The eye must be lined up with the front and rear sights with the target appearing to sit on the front sight.

TRIGGER SQUEEZE. The smooth application of pressure to the trigger will surprise a shooter as to when the shot will occur. Of course, side alignment must be maintained during this sequence.

FOLLOW-THROUGH. This is a procedure for applying all of the shooting basics throughout the firing process. This prevents or reduces any unnecessary movement before the bullet leaves the barrel.

Gun Safety

Safety is a primary concern when handling or using a pistol or rifle. The essential gun safety rule to avoid accidents is to make sure the gun is always pointed in a safe direction (i.e., up- and down-range). The shooter must keep his or her finger off the trigger until ready to fire. Finally, the gun must remain unloaded until ready to use. If the gun has a detachable magazine it should be removed before the action is opened. If the magazine is not detachable, cartridges must be removed from it. When any gun is stored it should be unloaded.

Guns require regular maintenance to retain their operability. Cleaning and proper storage are part of preventive maintenance. Cleaning the pistol or rifle directly after the firing session is an obvious necessity to ensure proper operation. Cleaning rods, rod attachments, and patches can be obtained to fit the different calibers of pistols or rifles. It is vital to be certain that the gun is unloaded and the action open. There are some simple steps to follow to clean the pistol or rifle. Attach the bore brush to the cleaning rod and dip it in bore cleaner. Insert the brush into the bore a number of times. Cleaning from the rear of the barrel whenever possible prevents muzzle damage or wear. Attach a patch holder tip to the cleaning rod with a cloth patch at the tip. Dip the patch in bore cleaner and run it through the bore several times. Attach a clean, dry patch to the rod tip and run it through the bore. If, upon inspection, the patch is dirty, repeat the process. When the patch appears clean, run a lightly oiled patch through the bore. All surfaces of the pistol or rifle should be cleaned.

The novice shooter must learn how the gun operates, which includes how to open and close the action safely, and how to remove ammunition from chambers and/or magazines. Appropriate ammunition for the gun, specifically designed for the particular weapon, can be fired with safety.

This is merely a simplified version of gun handling and safety. It is extremely important that these potentially dangerous articles be used with extreme caution to prevent accidents from happening. By learning how to handle rifles and pistols, the novice shooter may have the most enjoyable experience in firing these weapons at appropriate targets.

Horseshoes

The object of pitching horseshoes is to encircle a metal stake with a horseshoe or, failing that, to pitch the shoes closer to the stake than does one's opponent. Each player pitches two shoes per round. The game can be played in singles (with two players) or in doubles (with four players). To start a match, players usually pitch one shoe to a stake. The shoe that rings or comes nearest to the stake permits that side to pitch first. In singles play, each player standing on the same side of the court throws two shoes in succession to the far stake. Both players then walk to the stake, tally the score, and throw the shoes to the first stake. The player who amasses 21 points is the winner. In doubles play, the opposing players stand at each side of the court and pitch in one direction only. Their scores are tallied and their partners on the far side pitch the shoes back. Again, 21 points are needed for a side to win.

The horseshoe court is 50 feet long and 10 feet wide. Two stakes, each 1 inch in diameter, are set into boxes 40 feet apart. The box is a wooden frame 6 feet square, projecting 1 inch above the ground. The box is filled with clay or some other material to a depth of 6 inches. Barnyard, or informal, horseshoe pitching does not require the regulation box. Stakes can be hammered into the ground for play.

The pitching type of horseshoe is an oval-shaped plate of iron or steel with one open end. It should weigh up to $2\frac{1}{2}$ pounds and can be no wider than $7\frac{1}{2}$ inches. The tips of the open ends of the shoe have projecting edges that may not extend more than $\frac{3}{4}$ inch. Shoes are tempered, and their resiliency depends upon their hardness.

Pitching Techniques

Horseshoe pitching requires much skill and practice; it is a perceptual skill that needs good hand–eye coordination. There are several methods of holding a shoe to hurl it with some degree of accuracy and control. The most common grip is holding the open end of the shoe away from the body and toward the aiming stake. The index finger is placed on the side of the shoe, but not hooked over the prong. The shank of the shoe rests on the other three fingers, with the third finger acting as primary support. The thumb is on the top of the shank. When the shoe is pitched, it should make one turn and the open end of the shoe should point toward the aiming stake.

A player may stand on either side of the stake, as long as he or she is within the outer edges of the box, which serve as foot-fault lines. He or she must be at least 18 inches from the stake. His or her feet should be close together, toes pointed at the opposite stake. The right-handed person takes an initial step toward the opposite box with the left foot; the right foot remains in place. The step is taken as the right arm nears the top of the back swing. A correct swing is essential to accurate pitching. The shoe can be held in any comfortable position, chest or chin high. Prior to the swing, the right arm is extended with the shoe pointing toward the opposite stake. The player may actually sight through the open end of the shoe to the top of the aiming stake. The player begins the back swing by bringing the right arm downward and backward in a straight line. As the arm swings past the hip the player turns the wrist so that the shoe is released with a turning motion. The release is made by turning the wrist out and to the right. This causes the shoe to spin and flatten in trajectory; it should thus reach the opposite stake with the open end forward. The player's eyes should be kept on the stake throughout the swing and delivery.

Bocce

In this game, two to eight players are divided into two teams. When eight people are competing, two players from each side are stationed at opposite ends of the court and play alternate frames. Each team, or side, bowls to determine who goes first. The team (side) closest to the cue ball gets to bowl first; therefore, they match to decide. A player from the side winning the toss initiates the game by throwing the cue, or small ball, from one end of the court to wherever it lands. The same player then attempts to roll or throw one of his or her game balls as close to the cue ball as possible. His or her side then retires and does not bowl again until the opposing side gets one of its balls closer to the cue. This procedure is followed until one side uses all of its balls. The other side is then entitled to bowl its remaining balls. Partners play alternately.

All balls must be delivered underhand, although they may be either rolled or tossed. A player must deliver his or her ball before overstepping the 4-foot mark that constitutes the foul line. The cue ball can be moved by hitting it. Opponents' balls can be knocked away from their position. Rebounds from the side walls are permitted. Any balls thrown out of court are considered out of play. If the cue ball is hit out of the court, it is returned to the midpoint of the far edge of the playing field. The side winning a point or points begins the next frame. Play is always in the opposite direction from the previous game.

One point is received for every ball that comes nearer to the cue ball than the closest ball of the opponents. Twelve points constitute a game. When the opposing side has 11 points, however, the game must continue until one or the other side has a clear 2-point advantage. A match is the best two out of three games.

Although there is no regulation length or width for bocce, a space 60 by 10 feet is generally used. This space is enclosed by wooden walls, between 10 and 12 inches high. Almost all bocce courts have shallow trenches no more than 6 inches deep at each end of the court to keep the balls from rebounding onto the playing area if they have been bowled too hard. Equipment consists of a cue ball, which is approximately 3 inches in diameter, and one 5-inch bocce ball per player. Some form of measuring device is necessary to obtain the distance of the bowled balls from the cue.

Lawn Bowling

Bowling on the green is essentially a combination of regulation bowling and horseshoe pitching. From two to eight persons can play. In order to start the game, a coin is tossed; the winner bowls first. Thereafter, the winner of each frame has the privilege of bowling first. A frame is completed when all bowlers and both teams have rolled their balls to one end. The player who bowls first is responsible for rolling the cue or jack ball and then his or her own two balls alternately with those of his or her opponent. When there are more than two players, the same procedure is used, with one team's player rolling his or her balls alternately with his or her opposite number.

The object of the game is to get as close to the jack as possible. The jack may be hit by a bowled ball, as may an opponent's ball. For each ball rolled closer to the jack than an opponent's ball, one point is scored. The basic game is 21 points, but any previously decided number of frames or period of time may also constitute a game.

Croquet

Croquet is played with a mallet that can be held in one or both hands. The object of croquet is to hit a ball with the mallet through a series of wickets in a specified sequence. Play begins by hitting a ball through two wickets on one side of the court, then through the right near wicket, the center wicket, the far right wicket, and a set of double wickets, to the far stake. The player then returns the ball down the court on the opposite side from the original course.

A player has one shot at the ball with the mallet to get through one or more wickets. A player may receive one additional turn for hitting a stake or going through a wicket. Two additional shots are received for hitting an opponent's ball. However, the player is permitted no more than two shots after a given shot. A player is permitted to shoot until the ball fails to pass through a wicket, misses a stake, or fails to hit an opponent's ball. As many as four players may compete in a match, either as opponents or in doubles combination.

A player may choose to knock his or her opponent's ball out of position. He or she must first hit the opponent's ball with his or her ball. He or she may then place his or her ball adjacent to the opponent's ball and use either a carom or croquet shot. In the former, the player simply hits the opponent's ball out of position while endeavoring to hit his or her own into an advantageous position. In the croquet shot, the player places his or her foot upon his or her own ball, to hold it securely, and strikes the ball with the mallet, thereby sending the opponent's ball in whatever direction he or she wishes, to a certain disadvantaged position. In doubles play, one partner may elect to move his or her partner's ball to a more advantageous position using the same technique.

A ball is considered to have passed through a wicket if a straightedge laid across the two wires on the side from which the ball came does not touched the ball. If a player plays a wrong ball, his or her turn is taken by the next player, and his or her own ball may be placed in any spot on the court. All misplayed balls must be returned to the places from which they were wrongly taken. Players must play in proper order. If any player goes out of turn, the strokes stand or must be played over at the discretion of the opponent.

The standard court for croquet is 60 by 30 feet. A 30-inch line from the boundary is inscribed all around the court; this is the playing line. Stakes are placed just outside of this line, equidistant from the sidelines. The stakes should be about 2 inches in diameter. The wickets are of wire, about $\frac{1}{4}$ inch thick, and should extend at least 10 inches from the ground. The arch formed by the wire should be no more than 5 inches wide. The nine wickets are placed so that two, one mallet's-head length apart, are situated directly before both stakes. Two additional wickets are placed approximately halfway between the center wicket and the paired wickets.

The equipment for croquet consists of wooden balls and wooden mallets. The balls are striped with various colors to permit easy identification. The mallet has a handle no less than 2 ½ feet in length, and a cylindrical head 12 inches long and 3 inches in diameter.

Equipment and Spaces

This section is not intended to discuss comprehensively the kinds of places, installations, or equipment that are necessary to supply adequately the facilities and materiel required for motor performance. Physically active recreational experiences necessitate appropriate spaces and equipment in amounts that guarantee quality and availability for those who wish to participate. When either adequate facilities or equipment are unavailable, due to budgetary constraints, the public department should attempt to raise sufficient funds through an intensive public relations program, or gain the needed places and supplies by seeking support from local businesses and professional organizations or civic service agencies. Certainly, association with other like-minded organizations may enable adequate facilities, supplies, and equipment to be made available.

Maintenance

Property and equipment maintenance is one of the major concerns of any recreational service agency, particularly for a public department. The type of program should dictate the kinds of facilities and equipment to be provided and, to some extent, the manner in which they are to be maintained. Routine maintenance consists of all indoor and outdoor janitorial and inspection duties. Indoor duties include the opening and closing of buildings and their rooms; sweeping, cleaning, scrubbing, and waxing; heating and ventilating; minor repairing and painting; and arranging furniture and equipment for indoor activities. For outdoor activity programs, watering and marking fields and courts; minor grading of grounds; repair of walls, pipelines, and water fixtures; irrigating, cultivating, mulching, fertilizing, and mowing; and inspection of recreational equipment for hazards to users are a must.

The objective of every recreational service agency is to create an environment conducive to recreational experiences or activities. To achieve this objective, the smallest details of maintenance must be attended to so that each step has a cumulative effect on the successful operation of the recreational activities that can be organized and conducted.

The department must supply the safest apparatus and equipment available, but such devices are not immune to damage or breakage, and require periodic inspection and, when necessary, servicing. Children's play areas should be serviced daily. The grounds should be level and free of objects that could result in injury. If immediate repairs cannot be made on a faulty apparatus, it should be moved or closed to use.

A number of places in every recreational service system receive constant use and require routine upkeep so that they may serve the public. Perhaps one of the most used places is the ball diamond. The intensity of use it gets justifies full attention to the fact that maintenance probably can sustain it in good playing condition. The rubber on both home plate and the pitcher's mound should be examined daily; spikes can cut the rubber, which might endanger sliding or pitching activities by causing cleats to hook into the rubber and injure the player. Home plate has a black margin that should be embedded below grade. All anchor points at the bases should be slightly below grade, and the strap buckles should be placed under the sacks. The areas around home plate and the pitcher's box should be hand-graded. The surface of the infield should be free of rocks, pebbles, or anything that may cause a ball to ricochet. All wire screening around the field should be free of holes and lose wire. The backstop should be kept in good repair so that there are no loose boards or splinters. All hose bibs and water boxes should be checked daily, and broken lids replaced as soon as they are discovered. The outfield should be kept free of holes. Benches must have no loose, weak, or splintered boards, nor protruding nails or bolts.

Cement surface courts should be kept clean by sweeping and washing down at least once a week. All of the nets should be checked daily. No shrubbery or vines should be permitted to grow inside the playing area. Surfaces that are prone to becoming slippery may need to be sand blasted or at least scrubbed to remove whatever might be causing the slippage.

Horseshoe courts should be serviced according to the amount of play they receive. The boxes must be kept graded and moist. Stakes with burrs should be lifted and sent for grinding. The backboard must be solid and free of splinters.

Sand that is thrown or kicked out of children's play areas, the playground, or the sand box should be shoveled back. When the sand is too dirty to clean by screening or raking, it should be removed and replaced with fresh sand. Dirty sand may be cleansed by sifting through a filtering material and washing.

Turfed areas are challenging because watering is the most important consideration. The frequency and amount depend on the type of grass, soil, weather, and other bionic factors. Perhaps the most difficult problem in keeping up fields is compactness of soil from heavy traffic. When a recreational center contains buildings and grounds, it is necessary to assign indoor and outdoor crews. Every maintenance person should be able to work any job on the grounds and provide assistance to fellow workers when needed.

Established standards are universally applicable and determine the size, shape, and quantity of equipment necessary for efficient operation. The safety of participants weighs heavily on the professional practice of those who operate motor skills activities. The safety of spectators is also a significant concern and must be recognized at all times.

Competition

Competitive activities play an important part in sports and games. From the individual, competing with him- or herself, to dual, team, and group efforts, competition may invoke a certain stimulation to try harder insofar as learning and using the skills involved. There is an equally important caveat that competition may spur the individual to an attitude of win at any cost. This must firmly be avoided. The primary consideration of participation in motor skills is for the fun or enjoyment derived. Competition provides an added stimulus to enjoyment, but it cannot be allowed to get out of hand. Therefore, every person with an interest should be enabled to participate regardless of skill.

Places in motor skill activities should be found for the unskilled, the highly skilled, and those of average skill.

To ensure this principle, instruction in skills should become a mainstay of the departmental program and this, in turn, can be the foundation for the development of competitions based upon age, gender, size, weight, and degree of skill. Thus, intramural, intermural, and extramural competition may be one part of the motor performance category. There will certainly be a role for highly skilled performers in the leagues and tournaments that are the natural outgrowth of these events.

Age Group Competition

There is almost no motor skill that is exempt from the current fixation on age group competition. Children as young as 5, presumably with talent, are being instructed in such efforts as golf, gymnastics, swimming, ball playing, soccer, ice-skating, and skiing, to name but a few. These competitions serve to open up opportunity for those with an inclination and desire to compete at highly skilled levels. Such activity continues until the individual either burns out, at a fairly young age, because competition is so stressful and eventual boredom sets in, or goes on to continue participation into maturity. In any case, recreational programs can and should offer these opportunities to those who want to participate.

Older Adult Activities

Participation in motor activities does much more than help older individuals maintain a reasonably higher level of motor ability and physical fitness. From the standpoint of mental health, sports and games offer excellent opportunities for necessary emotional release in a socially acceptable way. Many of the individuals in the older segment of the population have lost a spouse, relatives, or friends by death, which causes great emotional strain. For those whose relatives have been institutionalized in consequence of long-term debilitating diseases or disabilities, the strain is just as severe. Participation in motor performance activity has been found to ease stress during participation, and often beyond immediate engagement.

Opportunities to socialize with others who share the same interests in motor activity encourage new acquaintanceships. As older individuals become more proficient, there will be more opportunities to meet younger people, those of the same age, and some older than themselves. Participating with people of different age groups on a common ground in a shared interest often enhances an older person's self-esteem. While engaging in sports and games, an older person has the chance to regain some of the prestige and self-respect he or she may have lost when he or she retired, and a younger person replaced him or her in the job market, or on the social scene.

The motor activities that should be offered to clients of advanced years should range from mild and moderate to rigorous in the degree of physical exertion required. Whether an activity is mild, moderate, or vigorous will be determined by the participant's aerobic capacity, strength, and physical endurance. Older adults who are not in excellent physical condition and are not accustomed to vigorous activity should not participate in strenuous activity that raises the heart rate over 40 percent of the difference between the estimated heart rate and the resting heart rate. For a person 65 years of age with a resting heart rate of 80, the maximum pulse rate for participation would be 110. This rate indicates a workload in the higher level of moderate activity.

The guidelines indicating the degree of vigor of an activity enable the recreationist and the participant together to determine the level of exercise tolerance. If this level is not specified for the guidance of the individual, there is always the possibility that the person may overdo in the beginning because of failure to recognize that their capacity to perform strenuous work has decreased.

Participation may also be restricted in many instances by limits on movement capability. Some individuals may be unable to stand or may have poor sight or hearing or be afflicted by incapacitated joints. All such impairments affecting the person's movement potential require that adaptations be made in the way the skills of an activity are performed. This is also true concerning equipment used or how the facility is constructed. Generally, any modifications necessary to meet the special needs of individuals focus on the following factors:

- The development and increased use of other senses if one sense has been lost
- Support of the body in the correct position when it is incapable of self-support
- Change of the usual standing position for a sitting position
- Change of two-handed skills to one hand.
- Reducing the area through which a player must move on a court or field
- Revising the techniques of skill performance to protect a weak area
- Modification of rules of any sport or game that may aggravate a condition
- Permitting frequent rest periods as necessary

Body Control Sports

These activities are based on the difficulty and execution of bodily movements. In the sports, an individual recognizes how well he or she does because basal performance is measured against the criterion depicting "form." (See **Table 13.1**.)

Speed Sports

The elapsed time of an event is the concern of these activities (**Table 13.2**). Depending upon the event, achievement is measured by how much or how little time was used to complete the activity.

Target Sports

The focus of the activities shown in **Table 13.3** is to propel objects at a target with a high degree of accuracy. When the object hits the target, a point is awarded and the participant scores points according to the number of times the target is hit.

Table 13.1 Body Control Sports

Activity	Energy Expenditure	Suggested Modification
Diving	Moderate to vigorous	No modification necessary; lifeguard, buddy, or both should be present; swimming ability necessary
Ice-skating	Vigorous	Utilize music for rhythm development; skate with partner holding hands
Roller-skating	Vigorous	Utilize music for rhythm development; skate with partner holding hands
Skiing snow downhill cross-country	Vigorous	Rest frequently
Surfing	Vigorous	Wear life jacket; swimming ability necessary
Synchronized swimming	Vigorous	Little modification required; lifeguard and buddy strongly recommended
Water skiing	Vigorous	Wear life jacket; ski for short time; ski with two partners in boat
Water exercises	Mild, moderate, or vigorous	Water temperature of 87°F recommended; use shallow portion of pool; place benches, ropes to aid physically handicapped and poorly coordinated

Table 13.2 Speed Sports

Activity	Energy Expenditure	Suggested Modifications
Bicycling	Vigorous	Use three-wheeler for greater stability; begin with short distances and gradually increase distance
Rowing	Vigorous	No modification necessary; life jackets essential; swimming ability advised
Sailing	Moderate	Use life jacket; sail with partner
Track events	Vigorous	No modification necessary; follow planned work as scheduled by professional
Walking/jogging	Moderate to vigorous	Begin by walking at low intensity; increase distance and time and combine with jogging; watch for trembling, nausea, breathlessness, and palpitation of heart

Terminal Reciprocating Sports

These activities require an object to be put into play so that each participant alternately maneuvers, evades, or strikes the object (**Table 13.4**). Terminating the exchange in order to score is the primary goal.

Goal Sports and Games

The function of these activities requires objects to be propelled at a goal (**Table 13.5**). Success is determined by the accumulation of more goals than the opponent.

Unique Sport Forms and Games

These activities have a special primary intent and do not fit well into the previous categories (**Table 13.6**).

Table 13.3   Target Sports

Activity	Energy Expenditure	Suggested Modifications
Aerial darts	Mild	No modification necessary
Archery	Moderate	No modification necessary; a lighter-weight bow may be used by those with limited arm strength; reduce distance to target
Bait/fly casting	Mild	No modification necessary; use chairs for those unable to stand for long periods
Bocce	Mild to moderate	May be played without modification
Bowling	Moderate	Use lighter-weight ball
Bowling on the green	Mild to moderate	May be played without modification; emphasis on form not necessary
Croquet	Mild to moderate	Modify wickets by painting orange; use bigger wickets; reduce court size
Frisbee	Moderate	May be played without modification
Golf	Moderate to vigorous	Use electric golf carts; play nine holes; play level courses; utilize driving ranges and miniature golf courses
Horseshoe pitching	Moderate	Use rubber horseshoes if strength is poor
Quoits	Mild to moderate	No modification necessary
Shuffleboard	Mild to moderate	May be played without modification
Skish	Mild to moderate	No modification necessary; excellent game for those for whom fishing expeditions are too strenuous

Table 13.4   Terminal Reciprocating Sports

Activity	Energy Expenditure	Suggested Modifications
Badminton	Moderate to vigorous	May be played without modification; doubles recommended; reduce size of court
Deck tennis	Moderate	May be played without modification; doubles or team play recommended
Fencing	Vigorous	May be played without modification
Handball	Vigorous	May be played without modification; doubles recommended
Loop badminton	Mild to moderate	May be played without modification
Paddleball	Vigorous	May be played without modification; doubles recommended
Racquetball	Vigorous	May be played without modification; doubles recommended
Squash	Vigorous	May be played without modification; doubles recommended
Table tennis	Mild to moderate	May be played without modification; doubles recommended; lower table for wheelchair players
Tennis	Vigorous	May be played without modification; doubles recommended; reduce size of court

Safety

Before any activities are undertaken, potential participants need to undergo a thorough physical examination. The results, with any recommendations concerning specific limitations and restrictions upon physical activity, should be made known to the personnel in charge of the program. Then it will be

Table 13.5 Goal Sports

Activity	Energy Expenditure	Suggested Modifications
Curling	Vigorous	May be played without modification
Pocket billiards	Mild to moderate	May be played without modification
Polo	Vigorous	May be played without modification
Water polo	Vigorous	May be played without modification; reduce game area

Table 13.6 Unique Sports

Activity	Energy Expenditure	Suggested Modifications
Fishing	Mild, moderate, or vigorous	Fish from chairs on deck in substitution for stream fishing requiring walking
Sleighing	Mild	Group activity; wear appropriate cold-weather clothing; assist person in and out of sleigh
Softball	Moderate to vigorous	Use mush ball; provide base runners for those unable to run the bases
Swimming	Moderate to vigorous	Have participants remove dentures; maintain water and air temperature 85°F; have lifeguard and two instructors; provide rest area; limit class size; progress slowly; make flippers and swim boards available

necessary to discover the older person's tolerance for exercise. With this information, adequate precautions can be taken to protect clients from possible aggravation or injury to areas of the body weakened or damaged by illness or residual impairment. Necessarily, it also provides information about the need for rest periods during activity, for those who have low levels of endurance.

In addition to these physical concerns, the recreationist needs to attend to the social and emotional state of the older person. Usually attitude affects how safely a person participates. When all safety needs have been met, the older participant should concentrate on skill improvement and achieving good form. As always, in any recreational program, having a good time is more important than accuracy and form. Participants should be made to feel that acquisition of sufficient skill to enjoy the activity is adequate. Should they wish to become more highly skilled, they should be given the help they require to achieve the desired level of performance, if it is within their capacity.

The success of a program usually depends on the way in which it is introduced. As with other experiences, most people like to proceed from the known to the unknown, from the easy to the difficult. It is important, therefore, to begin a program of motor activities for older adults with games or sports with which they are already familiar or that they can learn easily. Shuffleboard, horseshoes, quoits, bocce, and other well-known games are examples that meet the suggested criterion. Whatever activity is selected to open the program, it must be one that many participants know and the others can learn rapidly. More importantly, it must be fun. With a successful base established, the recreationist can more easily move to other, somewhat more difficult and demanding experiences.

Actual instruction of elderly persons learning new motor skills essentially uses the same techniques as in teaching other age groups. However, older individuals often do not see or hear as well or respond as rapidly as younger people. Therefore, the speed of instruction must be slower and more repetitions of verbal directions and demonstrations of skills may be necessary.

Once the basics have been established the participants must be given opportunities to practice. It is only through practice that mastery can be achieved. It is a professional requirement that recreationists provide appropriate practice sessions in terms of need. Like the youngster, the older person requires practices close together for maximum benefit to be realized. Shorter time, intensity, and repetition are most efficient for learning. Once the participants become more skilled, they will be able to practice for longer periods, and the duration between practices may be increased without negative effects.

Intense Competition

It is not unusual for young children to be enrolled in private clubs or other organizations whose skilled instructors are there to provide intensive, individualized coaching designed to produce winners, champions, or future varsity team members. This is not the province of the recreational service agency, but comes under the auspices of those commercial organizations that are in business for such purposes.

Other activities can involve a larger percentage of the potential clientele who are not so driven. Under these circumstances, both public and private agencies should provide the appropriate instructional staff, sites, and organizational operation that can meet the needs of all those concerned. From early childhood, with its reliance on cooperation, achievement, and increasing skills, to the oldest able person interested in competing with peers or merely performing vigorous physical activity, the recreational service agency can supply opportunities for engagement.

Forms of Competition

For children attending different recreational centers including parks, playgrounds, or fields, typical activities include individual movement exploration, stunts, climbing, sliding, swinging, and other apparatus play. To this are added elementary games and simple ball games of the lead-up or introductory variety. Children tend to compete against themselves and obtain encouragement to do so, or they may be competing against other individuals. Because the child is at the recreational facility during his or her leisure, whatever activities are conducted or available can be formalized or be simply of the pickup variety. Intramurals, or competition within the facility, can occur when there are sufficient numbers to constitute a team. Whether it is a court game, baseball, softball, a soccer match, or activities involving track and field or gymnastics, the presiding rule is that there must be opportunity for all who want to participate to be able to do so.

Intermurals, or competition between teams from different facilities, occur when schedules are developed that enable participants to engage peers outside of the local playground or center. Extramurals are competitions that occur on a communitywide basis with representative teams taking part in a culminating tournament, exhibition, or playoff that includes all of the diverse recreational facilities.

Sports days may be scheduled when participants play on their own local facility teams, and more than one team from each facility competes. Depending upon the number of players interested and available, there may be as many as 5 or 10 teams from a recreational center. The teams may represent age levels or may be divided according to skill level. As always in such events, the emphasis must be on providing competition for many children. Field days tend to include essentially individual activities, such as

Table 13.7   Round Robin Tournament

1st Round	2nd Round	3rd Round	4th Round	5th Round
1–2	1–3	1–5	1–6	1–4
3–4	5–2	6–3	4–5	2–6
5–6	6–4	4–2	2–3	3–5

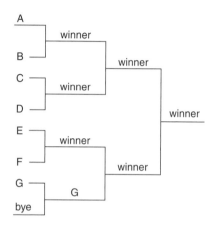

Figure 13.9   Single Elimination Tournament with a Bye

track and field events, gymnastics, and cross-country or novelty races (e.g., steeplechase).

Tournaments

Tournaments are used as a culminating event designed to display skill accomplishment, to be a unit of instruction, or to be recognition for previous participation in competitive activities. There are three fundamental types of tournaments: round robin, elimination, and ladder or pyramid tournaments. In order to determine the number of games that must be played in a given tournament, an automatic calculator may be devised. This technique enables tournament designers to formulate the type of competition most appropriate for a particular situation in terms of teams entered, time allotted, and facilities available.

Round Robin Tournament

The chief advantage of a round robin tournament is that every team or individual plays every other team and all teams play the same number of games without being eliminated. A more natural and realistic format applies when a percentage system of games won, lost, or tied may be worked out. The only disadvantage of the round robin is that it may take too long if many teams are involved. When there are many teams entered, the teams may be divided into several leagues, with winners of each league meeting for a play-off. Of primary consideration in round robin play, after the teams have been entered, is to specify the number of games necessary to complete all of the leagues, plus the play-offs. The formula $N(N - 1)$ will provide the number of games in a round robin. N refers to the number of teams entered.

A simple way to arrange the games is offered in **Table 13.7**.

Throughout the schedule, player or team number one retains the same position and the other teams rotate one place, counterclockwise. To determine the number of rounds required for the tournament, subtract one from the total number of players or teams. If there is an uneven number of players or teams, a bye, meaning that no game is played, is given to one player or team, and that unopposed player or team moves automatically to the second round.

Elimination Tournament

The obvious advantage of an elimination tournament is that it will enable a large number of teams to participate within a short span of time. The primary disadvantage is that some teams are eliminated after competing in only two games. In the single elimination tournament there will always be one fewer game than the number of teams (**Figure 13.9**).

To offset the immediate loss after one game, a double elimination procedure can be developed. To schedule this tournament, teams are placed in brackets, with two, four, or eight teams in each division. If the number of teams is not a power of two, it will be necessary to have byes. For example, if there are eight players or teams entered in a single elimination tournament, there will be a total of seven games. **Figure 13.10** shows four games, with eight teams participating. Teams one through eight play in the first round. The winner of each game in this championship flight moves to the right until a final winner is known. Each team that loses drops directly into the consolation flight. The winner of each of these games moves to the right until a final winner emerges from the consolation flight. The winners of both flights then play off.

In this tournament form the games are made more interesting if the teams are seeded or graded according to previously displayed strength or expectation of winning. In the eight-team bracket, the strongest team would be seeded as team one, the second strongest as team five. In seeding a third and fourth team, the third team would be team seven and the fourth would be team three. The advantage of seeding is that the best teams are more likely to compete in the final rounds.

Ladder and Pyramid Tournaments

These tournaments are continuous and are best used in individual and dual games and sports, such as racquetball, hand ball, squash, tennis, table tennis, paddleball, foul shooting, and so forth. Players tend to become placed by order of ability. No participant is eliminated. The chief disadvantage is that the tournament is never concluded unless a termination point is previously set. A ladder tournament may be followed by an elimination tournament where players are seeded based upon their performance in the ladder tournament.

In a ladder tournament, the participants choose for original places. A player may challenge any of the three players directly above him or her. For example, 6 may challenge 5, 4, or 3, but not 2 (**Figure 13.11**). If it is desirable, challenges may be limited to one or two places above. If 6 wins, his or her name card replaces that of the player who was defeated. If 6 loses, he or she cannot challenge the same player again until at least one other match has been concluded. Challenges must be accepted and played in the order they are received, and need to be posted to avoid any errors.

Pyramid tournaments are similar to ladder tournaments, with the proviso that the players may challenge only those in the row above them. For example, a player in row 1 may challenge all players; those in row 4 may challenge only

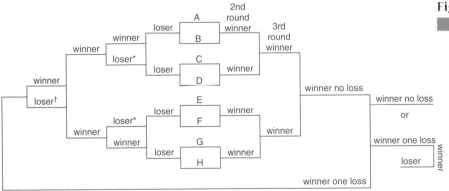

Figure 13.10 Double Elimination Tournament

*Losers of second round on right side.
†Loser of third round on right side.

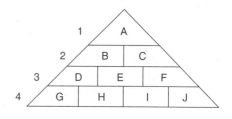

Figure 13.12 Pyramid Tournament

Figure 13.11 Ladder Tournament

players in row 3, and so on up to the apex (**Figure 13.12**). Only those in row 2 may challenge player 1. Names of the players may be placed on small round discs with metal rims and hung on a board.

Dual Competition

In every community there are people interested in any number of sport and athletic competitions of a dual nature in which only two players compete. Organized activities may be initiated by discovering what local interest there is in a particular dual sport or game. Organized activity may be performed by developing exhibitions of various types of activities that can be offered at a recreational facility. Investigating the probability of local athletes having the desired skills may provide a forum for display where others may be stimulated to try out for and participate in the activity. Activities may range from combat skills, such as wrestling, Kendo, the martial arts, and fencing to table tennis, horseshoe pitching, tennis, hand ball, badminton, paddleball, racquetball, or squash.

Generally, dual competition activities may be promoted by demonstrations and an effective public relations program augmented by the local media. It is highly likely that the local newspaper, television station, or radio station will encourage the activities as a public service. Of course, whatever interest there is in such activities must be based on having adequate space, supplies, materials, protective devices, and equipment. Particularly important is the concern for participant safety. No one engaged in the activity should be permitted to participate without being equipped with the required personal safety devices. This means the ownership or rental of plastic eye guards, masks, protective clothing or gear, helmets, and other similar items with specific reference to activity needs.

Diverse activities including fencing, rock climbing, aquatics, racquet games, or any other physical recreational experience assumes that those who have expressed an interest have been equipped with basic motor skills from the time they have been enrolled in elementary school. During their high school years they have learned many of the essential skills necessary for tennis, a variety of ball games, track and field exercises, and swimming. Surely, many of the same individuals have participated in playground and gymnasium activities where they have developed fundamental skills designed to enable them to participate in various games, sports, and exercises. Not everyone will have these experiences upon which to draw; these participants need additional instruction if they are to engage successfully. It is probable, therefore, that recreationists will be employed to teach many essential skills as well as to conduct a variety of sport, game, and exercise activities.

Summary

Motor skills offer a wide variety of potential activities designed to engage the physical, emotional, and social aspects of those who are interested. Physical activity offers something for everyone. From the rank amateur to the highly skilled performer and everybody in between, individuals may find a particular sport, game, or exercise worthy of their investment of time and energy. All such experiences are intended to promote enjoyment and satisfaction in those who participate. The pursuit of excellence during such experiences allows the individual to anticipate continued progress and eventual achievement for personal satisfaction. All such activities should be scheduled at a time and place that is accessible, safe, available, convenient, and congenial to the needs and desires of those to be served by motor skills.

Physical activity in all of its myriad forms has an important part in the development, implementation, and maintenance of a comprehensive recreational program. Sports and games play a significant role in the experiences of all people, at some period in their lives. This may be seen as appreciation of the skill exhibited by a well-coordinated gymnast or the talent displayed to an adoring fan of a basketball, football, baseball, soccer, or tennis star. Even more important is the participation of millions of people everywhere in rigorous physical activity. This runs the gamut from wrestling and the martial arts to squash, racquetball, handball, or table tennis. All require stamina, skill, and strength.

The well-balanced recreational program will provide for physical outlet in individual, dual, team, or group activities in competitive venues through leagues, tournaments, and contests. It will also enable those who do not care for competition to gain satisfaction and enjoyment through scheduled classes of exercise, skill development, or the use of appropriate equipment and facilities on a free play or discretionary basis.

All age groups may participate to the limit of their ability in physical activity of their liking. From toddlers to older adults, all may enter into the realm of motor skills for their own amusement, sense of well-being, feelings of confidence, or personal interest. Whatever the case, the recreational service program must provide the essential facilities, place, spaces, and equipment at the various times convenient for those who wish to participate or watch.

Selected Further References

Brown, J. *Tennis: Steps to Success.* 3rd ed. Champaign, IL: Human Kinetics, Publishers, 2004.

Crossingham, J., and B. Kalman. *Track Events in Action.* New York: Crabtree Publishing Co., 2004.

Engh, D. *Archery Fundamentals.* Champaign, IL: Human Kinetics, Publishers, 2004.

Gaiman, J. *Softball Skills and Drills.* Champaign, IL: Human Kinetics, Publishers, 2002.

Gallahue, D. L., and J. C. Ozmun. *Understanding Motor Development.* 6th ed. New York: McGraw-Hill Higher Education, 2006.

Gruber, B. *Gymnastics for Fun.* Minneapolis, MN: Compass Point Books, 2003.

Hobson, W., et al. *Swim, Bike, Run: Technique, Training, Racing.* 2nd ed. Champaign, IL: Human Kinetics, Publishers, 2001.

Jones, J. C., and P. Rose. *Physical Activity Instruction of Older Adults.* Champaign, IL: Human Kinetics, Publishers, 2004.

Martin, G., and D. Ingram. *Play Golf in the Zone: The Psychology of Golf Made Easy.* San Francisco, CA: Van der Plos Publications, 2004.

McGill, S. *Soccer Skills and Drills: Skill Developing Games and Activities for Girls Six and Up.* Terre Haute, IN: Wish Publishing, 2005.

Metzler, M. *Tennis: Mastering the Basics with the Personalized Sports Instruction System.* Reading, MA: Benjamin Cummings Publishing Co., 2000.

Motsuzaki, C. *Tennis Fundamentals.* Champaign, IL: Human Kinetics, Publishers, 2004.

National Association for Sport and Physical Education. *Physical Education for Lifelong Fitness: The Physical Best Teacher's Guide.* 2nd ed. Champaign, IL: Human Kinetics, Publishers, 2004.

National Soccer Coaches of America Staff. *Soccer Coaching Bible.* Champaign, IL: Human Kinetics, Publishers, 2004.

Remington Arms Company. *How to Start a Shooting Program.* Rev ed. Seattle, WA: Empire Publishing, Inc., 1977.

Schlegel, E., and C. R. Dunn. *Gymnastics Book: The Young Performer's Guide to Gymnastics.* Westport, CT: Firefly Books, Ltd., 2001.

Schmottlack, N., and J. McNamara. *Physical Education Activity Handbook.* 10th ed. Reading, MA: Benjamin Cummings Publishing Co., 2001.

Thompson, L. *Track and Field: Field Events.* Danbury, CT: Scholastic Library Publishing, 2001.

———. *Track and Field: Track Events.* Danbury, CT: Scholastic Library Publishing, 2001.

U.S. Marine Corps Staff. *Rifle Marksmanship.* Boulder, CO: Paladin Press, 2002.

Aquatic Activities

Aquatic activities can almost be said to be the most popular of all recreational activities. More than 160 million people in the United States enjoy some form of aquatics at some point during the year. Those recreational agencies that are fortunate to be situated on or near any water course, or have been foresighted enough to have had an adequate swimming pool constructed, have the potential for developing a comprehensive aquatic program. Although a swimming pool can accommodate only a few of the activities that constitute a balanced comprehensive aquatic program, it is at least a start in the right direction.

A well-sited recreational agency can establish a far-reaching aquatic program that reflects a range of activities: recreational and competitive swimming; plain and fancy diving; boating, rowing, and sailing; skin and scuba diving; lifesaving and water safety instruction; synchronized swimming; fishing; waterskiing; and surfing. The water pageant, another aspect of an aquatic program, is discussed in the chapter on special events (see Chapter 21).

The aquatic program offers the opportunity to learn an activity that will enhance the participants' satisfaction and give them a lifelong recreational skill. At the same time, the individual is learning a survival technique that will be useful in certain dangerous circumstances. Participation in aquatic activities contributes to the person's physiological growth and development because it promotes cardiovascular conditioning and fitness. Aquatics offer the individual a variety of experiences in which to learn and obtain advanced levels of motor skill. All people need to belong, to socialize, and to achieve mastery in whatever skills can be obtained through such activity. Participation is not restricted to any age group. Swimming can be taught to the youngest or oldest person.

Organization of the Aquatic Program

Recreational agencies have developed many schedules for the effective use of whatever waterfront they may have. The type of aquatic facility necessarily varies with the environment; depending on the resources available, the program may concentrate on instructional swimming, competition, water pageants, and shows; boating, rowing, sailing, surfing, and waterskiing; or any combination of these activities. The program director must determine the most suitable activities for the water resource available. The answers for the following questions will significantly influence the choice and scheduling of activities:

1. What is the agency's philosophy?
2. What is the water-resource capacity? Is the facility artificial, natural, a seacoast, a lake, a river?

3. How many participants are to be served at one time? How many can use the waterfront at the same time?
4. What effects will the weather have?
5. How far is the agency from the aquatic facility?
6. How many supervisory and instructional personnel are available at any given time?
7. How is the rest of the recreational program organized?

All these factors must be appraised because they have a definite bearing on the type of program that can be offered. The schedule for instructional swimming must make maximum use of qualified personnel at the times they are available. The aquatic program should be integrated with all other aspects of the recreational program so that no conflicts result. Positive relationships with all the parts of the program should be amplified; however, each phase of the program is valuable for its contribution to the participant. No one recreational category should be permitted to strip personnel or specialists from other activities.

Scheduling

The waterfront or other facility must be used efficiently, so activities must be scheduled. To the extent that all participants do not have the same water skills, an assessment must be made as to the level of skill the individual possesses. This can be performed when instructional classes are initiated. Those who cannot swim will be assigned to a basic or beginners class. Those who have a modicum of skill, if they wish to improve, can be assigned to an intermediate class. Advanced swimmers may desire instruction in water safety, synchronized swimming, or scuba diving. Instructional swimming may be arranged so that all who want to learn may be accommodated in a specific class at a convenient time for practice. Again, depending upon the facility available, classes may be scheduled to begin as early in the morning as is feasible and comfortable for both staff and participants. If night lighting is available, those who find evenings more congenial for their aquatic use can be accommodated at that time. It is not unusual for either public or private swimming facilities to be open at 9 a.m. and close at 11 p.m.

Swimming

The aquatic program cannot be limited to any one phase or approach. For this reason, every level of skill must be taken into account in each category of the program. The desirability of each participant attaining some degree of skill in swimming should not be underestimated. Successful achievement and learning all the water-related activities is also a main objective of the aquatic program. When the program concentrates on the instructional element of aquatics, it may fail to take advantage of the many facets of a well-rounded program. The recreational feature of free swimming without structured classes must have an important place in the schedule. But all aspects of the program depend upon the participants' ability to swim.

Figure 14.1 Beginner Learning the Flutter Kick

Swimming Instruction

Swimming instruction is given on three levels: beginner, intermediate, and advanced. Beginning swimming emphasizes introduction to the water. Basic patterns of water movement must be established and self-confidence in an unfamiliar element must be developed. Gradual immersion and games, including bobbing, blowing bubbles, bending over to pick up objects, learning to open the eyes under the water, and breath holding, are often initially employed to overcome a fear of the water.

When the beginner has mastered these experiences, flotation is introduced. This is taught in shallow water by having the person inflate his or her lungs, hold the breath, and attempt to sit on the bottom; because the individual is buoyant, the attempt naturally fails. With practice, this method becomes the basis for a tuck float, prone float, back or supine float, float with glide, and finally pushing off from the bottom or some stabilized side and performing the prone float and glide. Once this skill has been learned, almost 50 percent of the barriers to learning how to swim have been overcome. Other techniques for breathing, body position, arm and leg movements and coordination, and the elementary swimming strokes now can be taught (**Figure 14.1**).

Intermediate swimming emphasizes progressive skills. From elementary forms of swimming strokes, there now emerges the orthodox stroke pattern necessary for true propulsion through the water. The intermediate group is taught orthodox back, breast, side, and crawl strokes with emphasis on form, style, efficiency, and practice. Entry into the water from some type of diving position is also taught at this level; the participant learns how to jump and then dive into the water from any stable launching area.

Advanced swimming involves progress in mastering all stroke forms, with coordinated movements of arms, legs, breathing, body position, and alignment. Style and endurance are practiced in advanced classes. As the individual's competence grows, additional activities such as stunts, competitive swimming, fancy diving, and lifesaving techniques may be added.

Teaching Techniques

Instruction in any phase of swimming requires that the teacher build self-confidence in the learner. Those who have never been in or near the water fear that something bad will happen when they go in. For the fear of water to be overcome early and finally, patience and kindness are essential. A matter-of-fact voice and easily understood directions are necessary if successful learning is to take place. The individual must have everything explained before he or she even enters the water. The instructor must be prepared to take as much time as necessary to bring the participant along slowly but surely. Every step must reinforce those that have been performed and those that will come. The participant must be convinced that he or she cannot fail; he or she must be successful at each trial along the way. This can be accomplished by providing an easily obtainable objective during each practice session. At first these objectives may be blowing bubbles, opening the eyes under water, breath holding, or picking up objects from the bottom. As the individual progresses and begins to float, the goals become increasingly difficult, and success will continue to develop self-confidence. When strokes have finally been learned and actual locomotion is possible, the goals focus on distance covered, discipline of form, or other equally valuable standards in efficient swimming.

The dry-land drill is an excellent preliminary device for teaching swimmers correct body position and arm or leg motions. Each stroke can be learned without ever getting into the water by analyzing movements and then drilling. With this method, the participant has already made a habit of using the correct movement sequence when he or she finally does apply him- or herself to the water.

Backstroke

The backstroke is performed from a supine position. The legs perform a flutter kick, with the power being generated from the hips and thighs. The legs are flexed for a whip-like action. The ankles are relaxed and turned inward. The body is flat, and the head is erect with eyes staring upward. The arms are used alternately. If the swimmer starts with his or her left arm, it is brought up from the side in either a flexed or straight position. The arm sweeps the water in an arc that brings it to a 45-degree angle from the shoulder line. The palm of the hand is up. The arm is then pulled to the side and the same procedure is repeated with the other arm.

Sidestroke

The sidestroke is an extremely relaxing stroke, although it is most effective for rescue work. The swimmer, on one side, flexes the knees so that the topmost leg advances while the bottom leg moves back. The top knee moves toward the chin and the bottom knee moves toward the back of the head during the flexed aspect of the kick. To begin locomotion, the legs are moved in a slightly circular position. The top leg moves up, around, and then vigorously down. The bottom leg moves up, back, around, and then vigorously down. The two legs are thrust together, one atop the other, without actually touching; hence the term scissor kick.

The arm movements are quite simple. The starting position for the arm is an extended one. The foremost arm (either right or left, depending upon the side on which a swimmer is swimming) is extended straight ahead, but approximately 3 inches under water. The rear arm extends to the rear and lies parallel with the legs. The arms are recovered by flexing them and having the fingers of the hands meet almost under the chin. The stroke is taken by thrusting both arms in opposite directions so that the front arm is extended once again and the rear arm pushes through the water until it reaches a point of maximum extension. The procedure is then repeated. The swimmer begins the stroke in the glide position; that is, the arms are extended and the legs are held together. The legs are flexed and the arms are recovered simultaneously. The legs execute the scissor kick, the arms thrust away simultaneously, and the swimmer moves through the water in a series of smooth glides.

Breaststroke

The breaststroke is performed in a prone position. The arms and legs work simultaneously in the following sequence. From a glide position with arms and legs extended, the arms are pressed down against the water and pressure is exerted so that the stroke is made by separating the two arms down to a point just at the shoulder line. The head is lifted during the stroke to breathe. The arms are recovered by flexing them, and hands are brought together in a prayer attitude just beneath the chin. The legs are flexed in such a position that the soles of the feet may be brought together. The kick can be either a whip-like circular motion of the knees or a simple pressure by the soles of both feet against the water as the legs are thrust out, around, and then brought together. Arm recovery and leg flexion are performed simultaneously. The arms are thrust out together as the legs take the kick. The result of this movement is a prolonged glide. The only friction is caused by lifting the head for a breath at each arm stroke.

Crawl

The crawl is performed from a prone position. The legs execute a flutter kick while the arms alternately rotate. The head is turned slightly to either the right or the left, depending upon the swimmer's convenience; the mouth is cupped so that breath may be drawn in. The arm stroke occurs from an extended position. The body is held in a plane position, with the upper body slightly higher than the legs. There may be a very slight arch in the back. The right arm is dropped until it reaches a position to the rear and parallel to the thigh. It is recovered by lifting it almost straight up with the elbow leading. When the arm has cleared the water, it is again extended. The hand is low, the wrist is higher than the hand, and the elbow is higher than the wrist. The thumb should be lined up with the nose. The arm is relaxed so it can enter the water at an angle that permits the hand to catch approximately 6 inches below the surface. The first 6 inches of water from the surface down add nothing to the swimmer's forward locomotion, so it is wasted effort to press upon it. The hand should be placed into the water so that all effort is expended in an effective pull. As the right arm pulls and recovers, the left arm repeats the exact movement. The cyclical stroke continues alternately throughout the crawl.

The flutter kick is executed by driving the extended legs up and down against the water. Power is generated from the hips and thighs. The ankles are relaxed and turned inward. There are six to eight kicks for every complete arm cycle.

Dry-Land Drills

Flutter kicks can be taught by having the beginners sit on the edge of the pool or dock (if on a lake), or on the ground. The learners can lean back on their hands while they raise their legs. The drill consists of separating the legs vertically and kicking in an up-and-down pattern to get the feel of kicking with the entire leg from the thigh. Many beginners develop the negative habit of kicking with a flexed knee; they merely beat the water into foam, waste energy, and move slowly, if at all. Beginners must practice relaxing the ankle and letting it turn inward of its own weight.

The frog or whip kick for the breaststroke can be taught from the same position as the one just described. The beginners are instructed to bend their knees and place the soles of their feet together. On signal, they spread their legs horizontally and then bring both legs together. When this has been mastered, learners flex their legs and separate them outward by circling them slightly as they bring them together while keeping their feet turned out. In the whip kick, the knees are brought together and the legs are dropped to a vertical position and then circled vigorously together.

The scissor kick is practiced while resting on one hip, the forearm of one arm, and the hand of the other arm. If the beginner is on the right side, then the right forearm will be down and the left hand will be placed in front of the hips as an additional support. The legs are flexed so that the top leg moves up and forward. The bottom leg moves up and backward. During the kick sequence, the legs are simultaneously circled forward and backward and then brought together vigorously without actually touching.

Arm movements are plotted in precisely the same manner. For the crawl and backstroke, the arms are circled alternately in the appropriate manner. For the backstroke, the beginner stands erect. The two arms are held up over the head. The right arm begins by descending directly to the right side; the right wrist is turned so that the little finger of the hand is outward. As the right arm is moved up and back to its former position, the left arm descends to the side. The movements are repeated until the learner understands the pattern.

The crawl stroke is taught by having the beginners bend forward from the waist until their hands can rest on their knees. The head is raised. The two arms are extended to the front on either side of the head. The hands are relaxed so that the wrists are limp. The arms line up with the nose. The wrists are higher than the hands; the elbows are higher than the wrists. The right arm drops from its extended position to the thigh. As the arm is pulled slightly beyond the thigh, the head is turned to the right and the mouth is cupped to the right. The right arm is then recovered by lifting it straight up, with the elbow leading. As the right arm is extended, the head returns to its original position and air is expelled through the mouth and nose. As the right arm is extended, the left arm drops and the stroke is repeated.

The breaststroke is performed from a flexed position. The beginners bend at the waist, arms extended at the sides of the head. The stroke begins by separating the two hands and pulling out and down at an angle of approximately 45 degrees. The stroke stops when the arms reach a position in line with the shoulders. To recover the arms, the hands are circled and brought up beneath the chin and then thrust straight out to their original extended position.

The sidestroke is performed with learners standing erect. The right arm extends up and the left arm extends down. The arms are flexed and the hands are brought together under the chin. The right elbow is held up; the left elbow is down. The arms are simultaneously separated and thrust out to their original extended positions. The movement is repeated. The arms move simultaneously, but in opposite directions.

Water Drills

Kicking may best be practiced while holding onto a stationary object such as the side of the pool or dock. For the flutter kick, the left hand grasps whatever handhold presents itself while the right hand is placed down and flush along the side of the object. This elevates the body and permits it to assume the correct position for kicking. The kick is then initiated. Learners should be taught to kick with good vertical separation of the legs. Kickboards can also be used. Learners should be instructed to kick from between 12 and 15 inches beneath the surface of the water with their heels only. This produces the fountain effect from which the flutter derives its name.

The backstroke kick, or back flutter, is performed in exactly the same manner, except that the beginners are on their backs. They may rest their necks on whatever projection is available and grasp the side with both hands. The elbows are pointed straight up and will flank the head. The body is elevated to the correct kicking position. There is a slight arch in the back. The legs are moved from the hips and thighs, with a slight bend in the knees to produce a flexible action. The ankle is relaxed and is turned in by water pressure. Good vertical separation of the legs should produce an effective kick.

The breaststroke kick is performed first on the back. The body is brought into position in the manner just described for the backstroke. The knees are flexed and the soles of the feet are brought together. The legs are then thrust out vigorously, circled, and brought together with a snap. Assuming the prone position, as for the crawl flutter, the knees are brought together; the legs are dropped to a vertical position and then circled and brought together vigorously.

The scissor kick is performed in much the same way as it is during dry-land drills. If the learner is on the right side, the right arm is dropped and the hand placed flush against the side of the stationary object. The left arm is lifted out of the water with the elbow high, and the hand grasps whatever handhold is available. The head is turned so that the beginner looks back over the left shoulder. The knees are flexed with the top leg forward and the bottom leg backward. The kick is taken by stepping forward and around with the top leg and backward and around with the bottom leg. The two legs are brought on top of each other without touching. There must be a conclusive snap to the process of closing the legs in order to generate power for forward locomotion.

After these preliminary drills, the instructor may have the beginners practice kicking across the pool or crib area. The learner takes a deep breath, extends the arms, pushes off from side or bottom, and simply kicks until the required distance is attained. This drill should be continued until the kick is well executed and the action becomes smooth. The less effort put into the kick, the more energy is conserved and the greater the efficiency of the kick. When the beginner is proficient in the kick, arm strokes should be added. Combining arm and leg movements in short drills with some form of water game to maintain the person's interest will stimulate attention and hasten progress. It cannot be too greatly stressed that patience, simple directions, clear explanations, and kindness are absolutely necessary in all phases of instructional swimming.

Recreational or General Swimming

Free swims, where many individuals use the pool facility or other waterfront area for any reasonable type of aquatic play, are in the best tradition of recreational activity. During the instructional phase of the aquatics program, constant drilling, repetition, and correction are mandatory if skill development is to progress. In recreational swimming, however, the individual is free to move about the water with abandon. Naturally, good safety practices must be observed, but boisterous play, splashing, set games, racing back and forth—everything that gives enjoyment—is permissible (**Figure 14.2**).

Recreational swimming is enhanced by providing equipment that enhances fun. Slides can be installed (**Figure 14.3**), and odd-shaped rafts can be anchored in the swimming area to provide imaginative play for swimmers.

Diving and jumping contests to see who can make the highest jet of water can be part of this activity. Lap swimming, for those who are advanced enough to participate, should also be available through some separation of lanes so that swimmers will not be interfered with by other non-swimming activities. Recreational swimming can also include practice for pageants, stunts, games, races, water polo, water basketball, and many other water experiences.

Figure 14.2 Do Your Own Thing at the Lagoon

Figure 14.3   Kiddie Slide at Splashdown Water Park

Boating, Canoeing, and Sailing

Instruction in handling small craft can be an important asset to any recreational department. Many individuals have the opportunity to learn how to swim and dive, but few are given the chance to handle small craft. Although sailing is becoming extremely popular along seacoasts and inland regions where lake or river access permits it, only a small percentage of the total population has learned how to sail. This section discusses only equipment and methods, and the role of small craft in the aquatic program.

Boating

Rowing is the easiest form of boating that can be included in the recreational program. Rowboats are used on ponds, lakes, coastal waterways, and rivers. Rowboats provide a relatively safe means of transportation on waterways, even for unskilled swimmers. Rowing requires little demonstrable skill and is learned within a few minutes by the beginner. However, certain aspects of rowing demand a high degree of skill and therefore necessitate instructional assistance and a good deal of practice before the beginner becomes proficient in this method of water travel. Boating is useful for recreational experience, lifesaving, and competitive activities. For anyone who fishes, rowing is a requisite skill. Rowing is also used in water rescues. Skilled boat handling may prove invaluable in beating through high surf, if the facility abuts that type of water area.

Rowing is the propelling of a flat or round-bottomed boat along the surface of the water by means of oars. Oars are long, rigid, wooden blades made of spruce or ash (**Figure 14.4**). They are rested on or inserted into oarlocks or rowlocks, which become the fulcrum for maneuvering. The oarlock may be a U-shaped metal device that is fastened to the gunwale on both sides of the boat. The rower sits facing the rear of the boat on a seat, or on a thwart situated approximately in the middle of the craft. The rower moves the boat

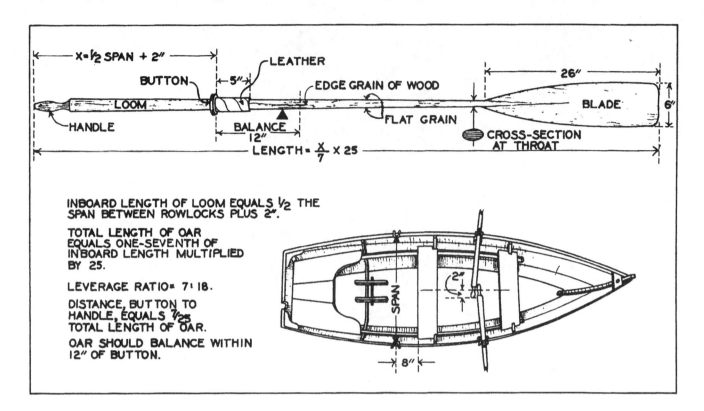

INBOARD LENGTH OF LOOM EQUALS ½ THE SPAN BETWEEN ROWLOCKS PLUS 2″.

TOTAL LENGTH OF OAR EQUALS ONE-SEVENTH OF INBOARD LENGTH MULTIPLIED BY 25.

LEVERAGE RATIO = 7:18.

DISTANCE, BUTTON TO HANDLE, EQUALS 7/25 TOTAL LENGTH OF OAR.

OAR SHOULD BALANCE WITHIN 12″ OF BUTTON.

Figure 14.4 Row Boat Nomenclature

by dipping the blades of the oars into the water at an angle so that the blades are toward the front of the boat. The rower pulls the handles of the oars to his or her chest so that the blades move toward the rear. The boat is thus propelled by means of leverage.

Techniques

The rower sits exactly in the middle of the thwart and places his or her legs on whatever rests are appropriate. The legs are kept straight and the feet braced against blocks. The back should not be bent while rowing and the shoulders should be square. Bending at the hips is permissible, but not at the waist. Each oar is grasped as close to the end of the handle as possible, with fingers on top and the thumb underneath. The blades of the oars are perpendicular to the water.

To perform the stroke, the body should bend forward with flexion at the hips. Hold the arms directly in front of the body. The oars should have a slightly forward angle to them so that the top of the blade is advanced. The arms are raised so that the oars are dipped into the water at about a 45-degree angle to the side of the boat. The blades are pulled through the water in a wide, shallow sweep toward the stern. The pulling is done with back and shoulder muscles, flexing at the hips until the rower regains an upright position. Elbows are kept close to the sides of the body.

The stroke should be a steady and even pressure. At the end of the stroke, there is a final dig that supplies the impetus for, and aids in, the recovery. At the end of the stroke, the body should regain its upright position. Feathering the oars helps them to lessen air resistance as they are returned toward the bow for another stroke. If a blade tops the water, it will hardly upset the rhythm of the stroke. To feather, raise the blades high enough so that they clear the water easily; however, they should not be so high that they splash into the water at the end of the recovery.

Backing up in water is accomplished by using the push stroke, which is the direct opposite of the pull stroke. Oars are slipped into the water toward the stern of the boat with the hands at the chest, elbows flexed. By pushing away from the chest and straightening the arms, the oars are forced through the water from rear to bow.

Alternate arm rowing can be used for either back or forward propulsion. In the forward movement, the arms are held in the flexed position; the body does not bend at the hips. The hand merely rotates over the wrist. The strokes are short and rapid. This form of rowing is useful when careful steering is required. The reverse motion is used for the push stroke. Instead of pulling toward the chest, push away, wrist over wrist.

Direction can be changed smoothly and quickly by shipping one oar—removing the oar from the water—and either pulling or pushing with the other. For very rapid turns and limited space, one oar can be pulled while the other is pushed. Thus, to turn to the right, pull on the left oar and push on the right, both strokes being completed together.

Landings alongside a dock or boat can be made by approaching the object at an angle. Approaches should be made into the wind or current whenever possible. When the bow of the boat is close to the object, the near oar should be shipped or pulled out of the water and into the boat. The outer oar is backed so that the boat swings up alongside the object.

Safety Precautions

The dangers of boating can be overcome by using common sense and maintaining control. All those who want to participate in boating should be qualified swimmers. At the very least, the person who uses a rowboat must be able to maintain him- or herself in the water. Rowboats should never be overloaded with passengers. The boat may be capable of accommodating two or more persons, but it is wiser to leave a space vacant than to risk the possibility of overloading. Horseplay on boats should be forbidden; it is dangerous and can result in capsizing or swamping the boat. Passengers should keep their respective seats. If changes must be made, the boat should be landed at the nearest shore. Seating arrangements can be changed, if it is absolutely necessary, by trimming the craft at each stage of the transfer. Individuals who change seats must crouch in order to maintain a low center of gravity. As the passenger moves, he or she grasps both gunwales and steps to the rower's seat. The rower shifts his or her weight to one side as the passenger slips to the other side of the thwart. The rower then vacates his or her seat and executes the same procedure to the vacant spot while the new rower shifts his or her weight to the middle. One other commonsense regulation should be observed: if a boat is swamped or overturned, it will stay afloat, although awash. Passengers should remain with the boat, which will maintain their weight.

Canoeing

Canoeing is a method of water transportation in an open, elongated, narrow, light-in-the-beam craft that is propelled by means of paddling (**Figures 14.5** and **14.6**). Good canoeing requires skilled handling of the craft and an ability

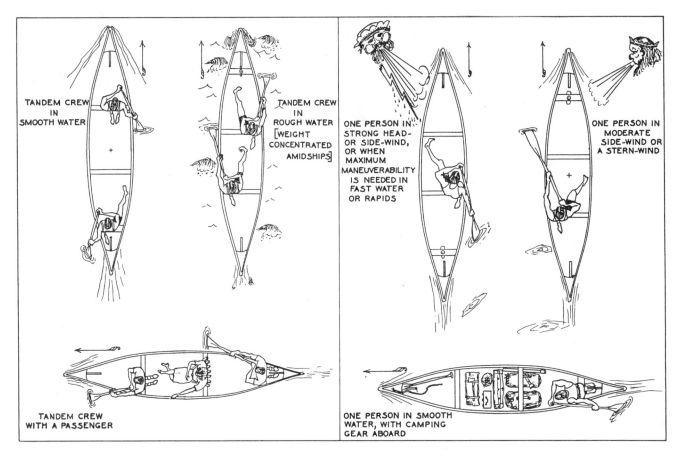

Figure 14.5 Proper Trim of the Canoe under Various Conditions

to use stroke techniques for rapid maneuvers as well as ease of paddling. Endurance, knowledge of the canoe's potential, manipulation of the craft under varying circumstances, safety precautions, personal conduct in the event of mishap, and care of equipment are all part of the knowledge necessary for the learner who wishes to use a canoe.

Techniques

Canoe strokes vary inasmuch as proponents of some stroking positions or methods profess to find particular paddling angles or movements more suitable than others; however, several strokes and techniques are known and held in common by nearly all canoeists. Agreement has also been reached on the most efficient positions to be taken by paddlers. Although most novices use the seats in the canoe for paddling, these high perches are not at all useful except for occasional rest, and then only when the water is calm. The ideal position for paddling is on one or both knees. The paddler kneels on the bottom of the canoe, resting a part of his or her weight against the seat thwart, but with more of the weight pitched forward onto the knees. This position is the safest to take in a canoe, because the canoe will afford a steadier ride when the center of gravity is lowered. Cushions or knee pads eliminate discomfort. The one-knee position requires that the leg away from the paddling side be thrust out and braced against the canoe bottom.

Whether the paddler strokes on the right or left side of the canoe makes little difference. The technique for the stroke remains the same. The upper

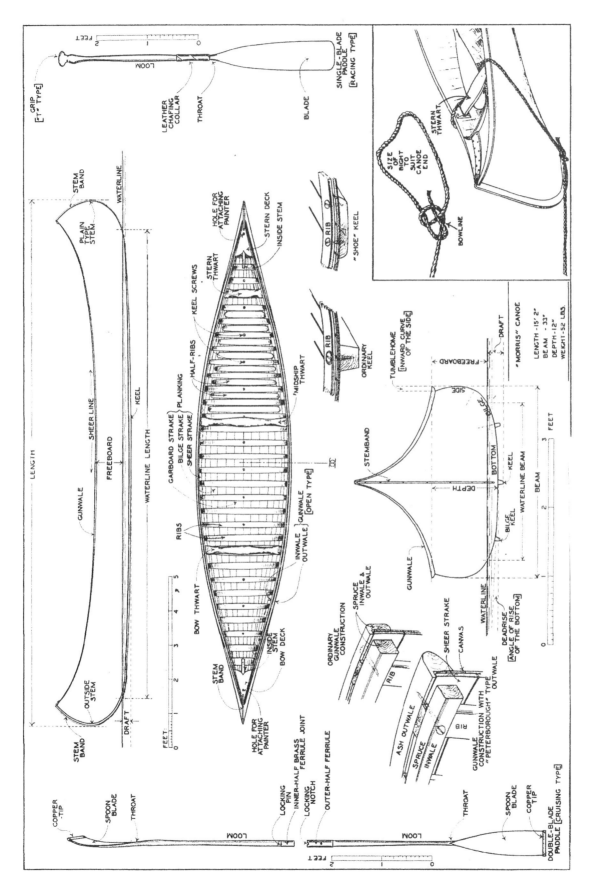

Figure 14.6 Canoe Nomenclature

hand is usually away from the side on which the paddle is placed in the water. The upper hand grasps the grip of the paddle, and the lower hand grasps the lower part of the shaft a few inches above the flair. The stroke should be taken in the most comfortable and natural manner possible. By using the paddle as a lever—that is, with the lower hand acting as a fulcrum and the upper hand pushing forward against the grip—a great deal of force is exerted and the canoe is sent skimming over the water. The paddle should be held as close as possible to the canoe side without scraping or dragging it against the canoe. The lower hand should be close to the water without actually dipping into it. At the completion of any stroke, it may be necessary to remove the paddle from the water to recover for the next stroke. The paddle should then be feathered; that is, the blade of the paddle should be turned so that its flat side is parallel to the water. This allows recovery and cuts air resistance. The more important strokes are described next.

THE J-STROKE. The J-stroke is always used by the paddler in the stern. It is effective in counteracting the bow's tendency to swing away from a straight course. Its name is derived from the course that the paddle takes as the blade is pulled through the water. The stroke is begun by reaching as far forward with the paddle as is comfortable, with the blade approximately 1 foot from the canoe's side. The paddle is levered from front to rear, and the blade is permitted to turn so that, at the end of the stroke, the back of the blade is turned away from the canoe. The blade travels in a tight arc away from the canoe and is jerked clear of the water for the recovery.

THE BOW STROKE. The bow stroke can be used from any position in the canoe. Insert the paddle into the water at a comfortable distance and then draw it to the stern with the blade at a right angle to the canoe side. Another stroke is started by feathering the paddle forward and replacing it in the water (see **Figure 14.7**).

THE FULL-SWEEP STROKE. This stroke is valuable when one person is paddling. The canoeist is usually kneeling at or near the center of the canoe. Place the paddle as far forward as can be reached, and sweep it around in a 180-degree turn from front to rear. The stroke is used to pivot the canoe away from the side on which the paddle is dipped. The recovery is made by feathering the paddle and returning it to the front with the lower end of the blade down.

THE BACKWATER STROKE. The backwater stroke is nearly the reverse of the bow stroke. When it is used, the canoe will be propelled backward, or its forward motion will be slowed and finally halted, or it will veer toward the side on which the stroke is being performed. The stroke is executed by cutting the blade into the water a comfortable distance to the rear of the hip. Then lever the paddle through the water from back to front as close to the side of the canoe as possible.

THE DRAW STROKE. The draw is accomplished by reaching out with the paddle at a comfortable distance from the side of the canoe, dipping the blade full-length into the water, and then pulling or drawing the canoe to the blade. Just before the blade reaches the canoe's side, turn the blade sideways and feather outward. Then begin the next draw.

THE UNDERWATER STROKE. The underwater stroke is used for stalking game. It is a silent stroke and does not give much speed. Begin the stroke by dipping the entire blade underwater and levering it through the water with

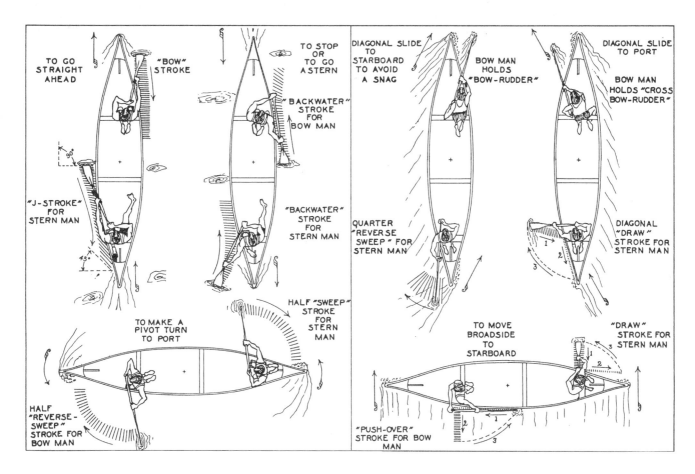

Figure 14.7 Canoe Paddling Strokes

the blade at an angle of less than 90 degrees. Rotate the grip of the paddle on every stroke to avoid riffling the water. The recovery is made by cutting the paddle through the water with one-third of the blade exposed.

SCULLING. Sculling is a useful stroke for pulling the canoe to one side quite rapidly. It is performed by manipulating the paddle so that it cuts a figure eight through the water. Hold the paddle sternward as if to make a draw stroke, with the blade parallel to the side of the canoe. The pressure comes from the draw phase of the stroke. This is an extremely short stroke; the lower arm does almost all the work, while the top hand and arm serve as guides.

THE PUSH STROKE. The push stroke is the opposite of the draw. It is used to move the canoe away from the side on which the paddling is being performed. Place the paddle into the water as close to the side of the canoe as possible in a vertical position; by extending both arms, the paddle is pushed away from the canoe. The upper hand pulls down and toward the canoe while the lower hand acts as a fulcrum.

Kayaking

The kayak has a covered deck or extension of the hull. The cockpit is covered by a water-tight spray deck and seats one paddler. The paddler uses a double-bladed paddle for efficient propulsion. The skirt or spray deck is used to seal the gap between the paddler and the deck. This makes for recovery from capsizing without flooding the interior with water.

Kayaks are usually made from a variety of materials including polyethylene, wood, composite (fiberglass and Kevlar), and skin. Today, skin boats are made with nylon or canvas deck, wood or aluminum frames, and a Hypalon rubber hull. There are inflatable kayaks for quick deflation for packing and transporting.

Kayaks are used on the open sea, for fishing, travel, racing, exercise, and stunts. They can be maneuvered so that the paddler may climb a series of stairs or opportunely placed rocks, slalom, or literally dive from cliffs into the water. In short, kayaks can be used in the same way as canoes. However, the kayaker must learn proficiency in using the kayak so that prevailing conditions do not unduly place the participant in harm's way.

Sailing

Sailing entails the propulsion of some form of flat-bottomed or keeled craft by means of wind power against spread canvas. A body of water that is at least 4 feet deep is required. There are many kinds of sailing craft, but recreational agencies usually use boats with one mast and one or two sails, such as the sailing dinghy and the sloop. The following discussion is based on the sloop, because it is most frequently used by recreational agencies. Of course, private individuals may use any form of sailing craft they wish.

The sloop has one mainmast with two sails (**Figure 14.8**). The mainsail is a triangular sheet attached to the mast on one side and to the boom or lower spar at the bottom. The second sail, or jib, a relatively small triangular canvas sheet, is forward of the mast. It is attached by lines rather than to wooden masts or spars. The sloop may come equipped with a retractable centerboard or keel. The keel can be used only where the water is deep enough. It provides additional stability to the sailing craft.

Fundamentally, all sailing is the same; the nautical terms that have been handed down for a thousand years remain constant. The only variation is in terms of the equipment, the size of the craft, and the number and dimensions of the sails.

Terminology is quite significant to the sailor, and it is necessary to learn the correct terms to designate parts of the boat.

The ability to give and obey orders when under sail makes the difference between a smooth, enjoyable ride and an uneven, and perhaps disastrous, one. Almost all sailboats require a two-person crew. The skipper steers the craft and handles the mainsheet, while the mate tends the centerboard and the jib sheet. All directions aboard a boat are indicated by port (left) and starboard (right), aft (back) and forward (front). The open space is called the *cockpit* and the remaining surface around the open section is called the *deck*. Forward of the cockpit is the *mast*, to which is attached a horizontal spar called the *boom*. There are generally three guide wires supporting the mast; these are called the port and starboard *sidestays* and the *forestay*.

Dry land practice may be used to learn tiller and sailing positions as the wind shifts direction (**Figure 14.9**). Models are sometimes used for this purpose.

Techniques

It is essential that the wind be brought to bear at the most efficient angle for use in propulsion. To obtain maximum forward momentum, a boat must

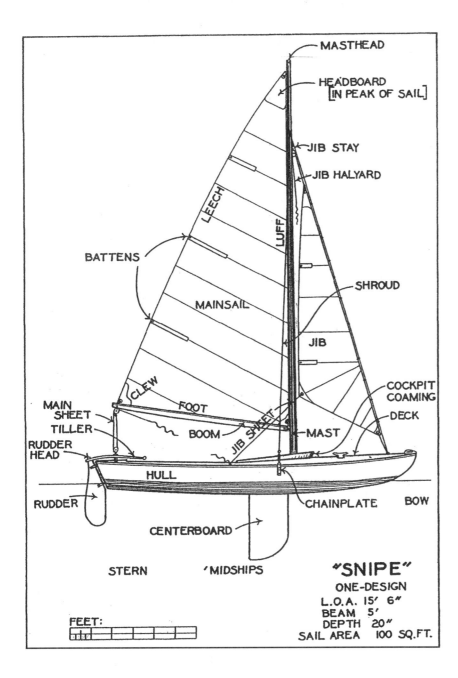

Figure 14.8   Sailboat Nomenclature

follow a zigzag course—that is, sail on alternate tacks at right angles to each other. As the wind fills the sail, part of the pressure is exerted against the sail to push the boat forward. The remaining pressure forces the boat sideways. As the sail fills, low pressure is created on the opposite side, forming a vacuum. The boat moves into this low pressure space and sails, as continued pressure is exerted against the sheets. It is impossible for a sailboat to sail into the wind. For this reason, the best course to follow when the wind is against the bow is at a 45-degree angle left or right of a course to windward.

The three basic positions are (1) *beating*, also called sailing to windward, tacking, pointing, sailing close-hauled, or sailing on the wind; (2) *reaching*, or sailing off the wind; and (3) *running*, also called sailing to leeward or running free.

Figure 14.9 The Points of Sailing

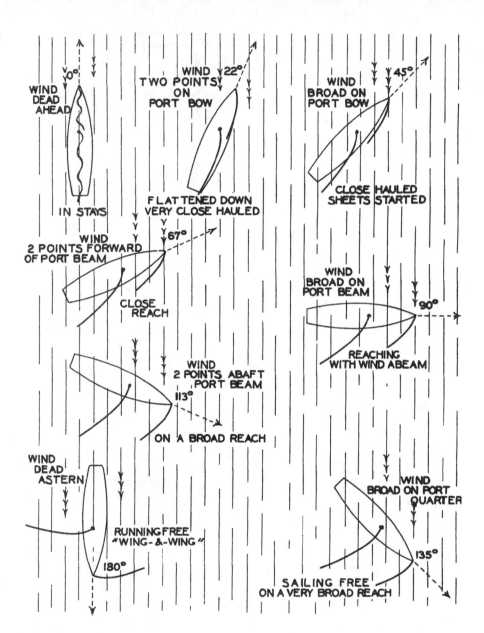

Beating

When the wind comes straight across the bow or to one side of the bow, a boat must be kept moving and the sails filled while the skipper keeps a course as close as possible to the direction from which the wind blows. The best angle for beating is 45 degrees to the wind. The centerboard will be down; the jib is trimmed in close, but not flat; the mainsail is trimmed close so that the end of the boom is directed in an angle toward the boat's stern, rather than straight back.

Reaching

This occurs when the wind comes directly to the side of the craft at a 90-degree angle to the boat. A close reach is any point of sailing between close-hauled and sailing at 90 degrees to windward. A broad reach is any point of sailing between 90 degrees to windward and running before the wind. Sails should always be trimmed in relation to the sailing position. Sails are best used when they do not luff or flap in the wind, and are slacked off.

Running

When a sailing craft moves in the same direction as the wind, it is running before the wind. With the wind blowing from directly astern, the mainsail is positioned at a right angle to the wind. If the water is fairly calm, the centerboard can be pulled clear of the water. This permits the boat to move through the water with the least amount of friction. When the boat is running, the skipper must be constantly attentive in order to prevent accidental jibbing. If the direction of the wind varies and the skipper has not been alert to the change, a jibe may occur; that is, the mainsail may shift from one side of the boat to the other. Such a condition puts excessive strain on the boat and is dangerous to all aboard. However, an intentional jibe can save precious seconds in a race, or can be performed as the wind changes direction from the stern. When this maneuver is adroitly performed, it is a swift and impressive procedure. To jibe a boat, the centerboard is lowered. The crew trims the mainsail in, while the skipper steers the boat off wind until the boom swings over to the other side. The main sheet is slacked off quickly and evenly, the course is resumed, and the centerboard is lowered. The jib will be reset on the opposite side. The skipper and crew normally shift their weight to the windward side in order to keep the trim.

Getting Away

Getting away from dock or mooring is not particularly difficult. There are some details that must be considered, however. First, the skipper should decide on his or her initial tack by noting the wind direction. The mainsail should be hoisted first, then the jib sheet. Depending on wind direction, the boat will sail to the wind. The bowline must be cast off and moved away from the dock so that the correct side of the boat is presented to the wind. The tiller is pulled over so that the boat clears the dock. The skipper trims the mainsail while the crew trims the jib.

Docking

It takes a high degree of skill to maneuver a boat to a dock. The general procedure is to come about directly into the wind so that the boat comes to a slow stop and gently touches the dock. Wind direction and speed must always be taken into account during docking. The boat may be running before the wind as it nears the dock. The centerboard should be lowered to permit easy maneuvering. The boat must be sailed parallel to the dock and at least two boat lengths away from it. The boat should be brought about so as to head into the wind while coming alongside the dock. The sails should be trimmed so as not to catch the dock. When the wind direction is across the dock, the approach to the dock should be on the side away from the wind and close-hauled. When the dock is fewer than three boat lengths away, the ship should be pointed into the wind while the main and jib sheets are let go.

Figure 14.10 Model Manipulation Helps One to Learn Tiller and Sailing Positions as the Wind Shifts

After Sailing

The ship must always be left in good condition. It should be clean and ready for other sailings. All sails should be lowered and battens removed. The sails should be stowed in bags. Damp sails should be laid out to dry. All traces of salt should be removed from the sails, if the voyage has been in salt water. All halyards should be fastened, leaving a little slack. Loose equipment must be secured, and the centerboard should be pulled up. The boat must be securely tied to the dock or mooring. The sailor must always consider the possibility of foul weather and secure the boat to ride it out.

Skin and Scuba Diving

Skin diving, or free underwater swimming, is performed without any attachments to the surface. The diver pursues some object of interest, or simply explores what others have never seen. The basic pieces of equipment for skin diving are a mask and faceplate, swim fins, and a breathing tube or snorkel. If the diver has an unusual capacity and can stay submerged for several minutes at a time, he or she may not even want the snorkel. The faceplate and snorkel permit the diver to swim slightly beneath the surface and observe the bottom. The fins enable the swimmer to attain relatively higher rates of speed and swim for long distances without too great an effort. When the skin diver reaches a point that seems worthy of exploration, a surface dive is performed and the swimmer submerges to investigate it or to collect specimens. The length of the dive is restricted by the diver's ability to withstand water pressure as well as to hold his or her breath. Some trained divers have attained a depth of more than 100 feet. Almost any body of water of sufficient depth and clarity offers a challenge to the skin diver.

If the diver carries a self-contained underwater breathing apparatus (scuba), he or she can remain under water and travel exceptionally long distances. Divers may operate under water on a tank of oxygen for periods up to 1 hour, at depths of 30 to 50 feet. The ability to remain under water for prolonged periods of time, coupled with a high degree of weightlessness and mobility, has attracted thousands of enthusiasts to this form of aquatics. With scuba gear, the diver can fish, photograph, explore, and collect specimens of underwater life and minerals.

Equipment

Several pieces of equipment are essential to any form of diving. The mask, or faceplate, is the most useful item. The mask is usually made of soft rubber and fitted with unbreakable glass plates. Good masks have a wide stainless-steel band holding the glass in place. The mask encloses the eyes and nose but leaves the mouth free for breathing. The mask can be molded to fit facial contours. The paramount function of the mask is to ensure a watertight seal. A strap holding the mask to the head should be attached to the front end; the mask is then more evenly pressed against the face and the insertion of a snorkel under the strap is permitted without breaking the seal.

Swim fins are also vital to the diver, because they increase forward speed considerably. Swim fins should be selected on the basis of the diver's

Figure 14.11 SCUBA in Use

swimming ability. Experienced divers and swimmers want a rigid fin that provides more power per kick; less-strong swimmers probably should select a flexible fin that reduces push but enables the diver to use less effort. Fins with adjustable or fixed rubber straps at the back of the heel tend to be less useful than those with enclosed heel guards that are designed for one person's exclusive use.

The snorkel, or breathing tube, is a device that allows divers to breathe while scanning the bottom from the surface. The head does not have to be lifted for air. The snorkel itself is a J- or U-shaped tube with a mouthpiece on one end that can be twisted to fit the mouth regardless of the tube's angle. The upper end of the tube should be flexible, so that it will not be torn out of the diver's mouth if it strikes some object.

For scuba diving, underwater breathing apparatus of the closed- or open-circuit variety is vital (**Figure 14.11**). The inherent dangers of the closed-circuit apparatus make it useful for experts only. The open-circuit apparatus, by far the most popular, is used by recreational agencies.

One or more tanks of compressed air are attached to the diver's back by means of a harness. The harness includes two shoulder straps and connecting straps across the chest, waist, and crotch. A demand regulator attached to the compressed air tank is used to supply on demand whatever volume of air the diver requires. The volume equalizes the air pressure within the diver and the surrounding pressure. In the single-stage system, only one operational phase is required. It reduces the high-pressure air, and, on demand, the air is supplied at the same pressure and volume as the surrounding pressure. In the two-stage system, the high pressure is reduced in one stage. The next stage is accomplished under a low pressure of approximately 100 pounds per square inch. In all two-stage systems, the diaphragm activates the low-pressure stage, which regulates the appropriate amount of air to be released to the diver for internal and external equalization.

A weighted belt is generally used to balance the diver. The lead weights counter the natural buoyancy of the body and the equipment. The belt has a quick-release that permits it to be dropped if necessary.

Protective suits are worn by divers if the water is cold, as it usually is when diving to depths of more than 50 feet, particularly in the sea or in unprotected waters where the sea has access. The dry suit is watertight; warm underclothing worn underneath it keeps the diver comfortable. The dry suit can be worn in very cold water, although any tear will reduce its effectiveness. If water gets into the suit, it seeps into the layer of insulating air around the underclothing. The wetsuit is usually made of foam rubber or neoprene. It fits closely, although a small amount of water is permitted to enter the suit to be warmed by the body. The suit insulates the body from outside cold water. The thickness of the suit determines the degree of insulation. Tears are easily repaired, and rips do not cause a loss of buoyancy or any loss of warmth in other parts of the suit.

Techniques

The diver should be well trained in swimming skills. Swimming with fins requires little instruction, but a good deal of conditioning is necessary for efficient use. Stamina should be gradually developed until the swimmer can propel him or herself over long distances without becoming fatigued. To use the mask properly, the diver must learn to adjust the pressure inside it by exhaling slightly through the nose. In order to get rid of any water that gets into the mask, the diver pushes in on the part of the mask closest to the surface and exhales through the nose. The air that is trapped in the mask pushes the water out at the bottom. This skill should be practiced in controlled situations by removing the mask under water and replacing it.

A skin diver breathes through the snorkel with his or her mouth. The diver must learn to inhale, pause, and then exhale. Breath holding when diving retains air in the breathing tube and prevents water from entering. It is important that sufficient air be retained to permit a forceful exhalation after returning to the surface, so that any water is expelled from the snorkel.

The air pressure in the ears should be equalized regularly during each dive to prevent discomfort. The diver must practice moving his or her jaw and swallowing during the dive. This may not be effective, however, and the diver must then compress the mask against the face and blow hard through the nose. A characteristic popping sound occurs as the pressure in the ears is equalized.

Scuba diving is much more complicated than skin diving because of the variety of physical and physiological problems that the diver must recognize before he or she is able to perform at any depth, particularly if the individual wishes to swim in open water. Knowledge of the physical laws as they apply to diving is necessary to prevent accidents. Perhaps the most important of these laws is Boyle's law, which states that the volume of a confined gas varies inversely with pressure at constant temperature. This means that when the diver, breathing compressed air or gas, is coming to the surface, he or she must continually exhale or else suffer the possibility of ruptured lungs.

The scuba diver must be able to clear both the mask and the regulator. With the two-stage regulator, a mouthpiece is removed and raised slightly higher than the regulator. This causes air to escape from the mouthpiece. The face is then turned toward the surface, and the bubbling mouthpiece is inserted into the mouth. The head is then turned in the direction of the hose to drain excess water to that side. A forceful exhalation pushes the remaining water out of the exhaust vent. The single-stage regulator requires a brief puff to clear the water from the mouthpiece.

Beginners must practice adjusting the equipment and using the regulator. Learners must be required to breathe with the apparatus on land before entering shallow water for continued practice. Clearing the mask is an essential skill that must be mastered. Buddy-breathing—that is, two divers breathing from one tank under water—must become a routine skill. Progressively prolonged periods of diving to greater depths should be practiced. Lifesaving skills, including treading and floating with the tank on, and the removal and replacement of equipment when underwater, must be stressed.

Safety Precautions

No diver should ever be permitted to dive alone, especially in a recreational agency–sponsored activity. The buddy system should always be used. All gear, including suit, fins, masks, and tanks, must be thoroughly checked for leaks, damage, or wear. Diving should be performed only when the individual is in good physical condition. Rough water, tides, and currents should be avoided wherever and whenever possible. A quick-release buckle should be a feature on all pieces of equipment. The diver should always exhale while ascending, never hold his or her breath while surfacing, and breathe normally while scuba diving. The tank should undergo a certified inspection and be filled at a recognized air station.

Beginners should not overexert themselves when under water. They must be aware of potential hazards before diving and remain calm. Slow, deliberate movements are more likely than rapid ones to release one from a dangerous situation. The individual should never swim in water that is colder than 70°F, unless an exposure suit is worn.

Lifesaving and Water-Safety Instruction

Material on new concepts and techniques of lifesaving and water-safety instruction can be obtained from agencies such as the American Red Cross and the YMCA, which are devoted to organizing and arranging the dissemination of this material. However, because lifesaving and water safety often play a key role in the modern recreational program, an indication of their function is required here.

Every individual should receive some instruction in water-safety procedures. This instruction should be offered at some time before the aquatic program is opened. A basic part of this activity will be information about the rules for use of any aquatic facility available for the program. Water safety includes using swimming and diving areas, keeping them in proper condition, using lifeguards, and buddy checks if the situation calls for it. Water safety practices are designed to eliminate hazards in the aquatic area.

Lifesaving classes can be offered in two categories to advanced swimmers: junior lifesaving for those less than 15 years of age, and senior lifesaving for those over the age of 15. Lifesaving courses are geared to the concept that a person is in trouble and might drown. The courses are therefore primarily concerned with the victim's immediate situation in relation to the nearest assistance. A rescuer does not have to swim to rescue a victim if other aids are available. The distance between the victim and the shore will guide the rescuer's efforts. If a victim is well off-shore and a lifeboat is within 100 yards

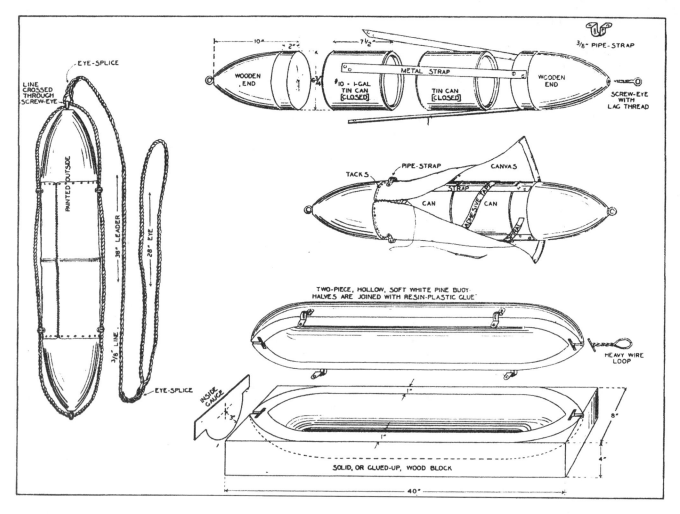

Figure 14.12   Homemade Rescue Buoy

of the rescuer, the best approach is to run to the boat and row to the rescue. Running would take no more than 12 seconds, and the boat could be launched immediately. Another 30 seconds would be needed to row the distance, and then the rescue could be made from the boat. If the rescuer were to swim out as fast as he or she could, he or she might reach the victim in less than 30 seconds, but then he or she would have to recover the victim and tow that person all the way back. It is therefore better to use some aid—reaching poles, ring buoys with lines attached (**Figure 14.12**), surfboards, and small craft—and to actually swim to the rescue only if these are unavailable.

Swimming rescues are classified as (1) entries into the water by jumping, running, or diving, followed by (2) front, rear, or underwater swimming approaches; (3) blocks and parries; (4) releases including front or rear strangle, and right, left, or both wrists; (5) carries, including cross-chest, head, hair, or tired-swimmer; and (6) shallow water carries, either camel-back or fireman's carry. Finally, there must be practice in the recovery of submerged victims and in resuscitation.

Lifesaving Techniques

The approaches and swimming rescues are from the front, rear, or underwater. The rescuer must be taught to keep his or her eye on the victim in making the approach, to reverse his or her position while maintaining correct distance, and to contact the victim in the proper manner and to level off for the tow to safety. In underwater approaches, the victim must be turned so that towing can be accomplished.

Once contact has been made with the victim, without conflict, the rescuer must then tow or carry the victim to safety by using a variety of carries. The cross-chest carry is useful to control the victim's panic-stricken thrashings. Arm and leg movements must be effective, and the victim must feel absolutely secure in the position. Generally, cross-chest carries are used for short distances only. The hair and head carries are properly used when the victim is unconscious and the distance to shore is quite far. The techniques for those carries require that certain arm and hand positions be maintained and the victim's face be held clear of the water. Leveling off from a vertical position requires a quick reverse by the rescuer and contact with the victim so that an initial movement to shore can be made while putting the victim into the proper position for a carry. The rescuer can correctly position the victim by engaging the victim's wrist with the rescuer's hand, palm and thumb down, and pulling the victim toward the shore while simultaneously turning that person. Leveling off is performed by cupping the hand under the victim's chin, thumb extended along the side of the head, and putting the elbow of the cupping arm into the small of the victim's back. This forces the victim into a supine floating position. A carry maneuver is then applied to tow the victim.

If, because of an error of judgment, the rescuer finds him or herself being attacked by the victim, a series of blocks, parries, or releases can be used. In executing the block, the rescuer keeps his or her arm outstretched and rigid, fingers spread against the upper part of the victim's chest. In some cases it might be necessary for the rescuer to spread his or her fingers against the base of the victim's throat to hold off any attempt to climb on the rescuer's head and shoulders. The parry is used to ward off a front strangle attempt in combination with contact so that the rescuer comes up behind the victim for a leveling-off procedure and carry. The block and turn is a combination that stops the victim and uses his or her own momentum to turn the person around so that leveling off and carrying can be applied.

In the event that the victim actually grabs the rescuer in a front head hold, the rescuer should turn his or her head aside, tuck in his or her chin, and push underwater. The victim will probably release any hold and try to fight back to the surface. In any event, the rescuer will place his or her hand between his or her own face and the victim's, hooking the thumb under the lower jaw. The rescuer will grasp the victim's elbow on top and just above the elbow joint and push the victim away with both hands while maintaining contact. The leveling off procedure is then carried out as the victim's arm is held by the rescuer's hand. The rescuer's arm becomes the fulcrum for leveling.

In the rear strangle, the rescuer turns his or her head to the side, tucks the chin in, and swims down by using his or her arms to submerge. Once underwater, the rescuer applies pressure to the victim's hand and elbow, bringing the victim to his or her front by leverage. The victim is then brought to the surface and leveled off at the same time. A carry can then be used. If the victim grasps one or both wrists, the rescuer should bring his or her hands close together and grasp the victim's wrist. The rescuer then takes a breath, forces the victim beneath the water, places his or her outer foot against the victim's outer shoulder (that is, on the side opposite the direction in which the victim will turn), and straightens the leg. The victim will lose his or her grip and be able to be turned and leveled off in one swift movement. A carry can then be used.

For shallow-water carries, either fireman's or camel-back, the following sequence proves adequate. In shallow water, the rescuer stands alongside the victim and places one hand over the near leg and under the far knee. The other hand should be under the victim's neck. The rescuer submerges to a squatting position and rolls the victim over his or her shoulders in a prone position. The victim's hips should be squarely above the rescuer's neck. The rescuer can then stand and, with the victim draped across his or her shoulders, move shoreward. The camel-back carry requires that the rescuer drape the victim's arm over his or her her neck and simultaneously reach over the victim's upper back to support his or her trunk out of the water. The rescuer than turns his or her back on the victim, brings that person against his or her own hips, and wades to shore in this position. With proper balance and applied leverage, almost any victim can be carried for relatively long distances without discomfort to the rescuer.

Synchronized Swimming

In synchronized swimming, strokes and patterns of movement are performed to some accompanying rhythm or music. Skill in standard swimming techniques and stunts, an ability to coordinate one's movements with those of others, and practice are all needed. Without a thorough knowledge of basic strokes, the endurance to go through the routines, and the skill to adapt easily to variations, a learner cannot contribute to the group's progress. For those who are just beginning to learn swimming in sets and simultaneous stroking, the group should move no faster than its slowest member. When advanced swimmers rehearse, however, any individual who cannot maintain the pace retards almost all activity. Teamwork, swimming style, and stamina are the three key factors for synchronized swimming.

Techniques

Standard swimming strokes form the foundation for all variations and stunts performed in synchronized swimming. The form of strokes should be consistent. Extensive practice is mandatory until all have acquired the degree of skill necessary to maneuver into various positions. Stroking should be rhythmic, powerful, and relaxed. The standard strokes are used to cover water space and for transitions. For synchronized swimming, some variations are noted. There is an absence of normal breathing techniques. The head is held above water so that performers can see each other and keep time. The body position in the water is lower than would normally be considered good practice, in order to avoid undue splashing. Combinations of strokes or variations on arm recoveries can be used to heighten the action or express emphasis. Body positions can be changed, directions can be changed, or the entry of the hand into the water can be modified.

The primary body positions are those of pike, tuck, and layout. In the layout position, the body is extended and aligned from head to toe. The prone or supine position can be used. Sculling can assist in maintaining a relatively stationary attitude. In the pike, the hips are flexed to a right angle. The knees are locked and the toes pointed straight up. The back pike requires that the hips be flexed at an acute angle, with the straight legs being brought closer to the chest. The toes are pointed and the ankles are at the surface of the water. In the tuck position, the knees and hips are flexed. The legs are drawn tightly to the chest, with the head held close to the knees. A flat scull is used to rotate the body. Tucks are executed near the surface of the water.

Sculling, used for support or locomotion, is merely pulling and pushing against the water alternately. The flat scull is performed by placing the hands, palms down, on the surface of the water and maneuvering them in a figure eight. The flat scull is used to maintain a stationary position. A standard scull performed at the waist will propel the body in the direction of the head. When it is used with arms extended above the head, the body moves toward the feet. With the reverse scull, the body moves in the opposite direction from that taken by the standard scull.

Stunts

All stunts are based on the standard positions, strokes, and sculling. Among the typical stunts are marlin, somersault, porpoise, kip, ballet leg, and dolphin. To move in one direction, the swimmer presses and swings the opposite arm under water toward the leg in the desired direction. The body should roll from back to stomach while the extended arm is swept under water. The roll is continued until the body position returns to a back layout at a right angle from the original position. The marlin is a transition movement and can be used to reorient an entire formation. Somersaults can be executed from either a tuck or pike position, front or back. In the tuck, the hands are used to complete the somersault. The porpoise is simply a pike surface-dive. The kip is begun from a back layout position to a tuck position. The body is rotated as it would be in a back somersault. The arms, with palms facing outward, press up toward the shoulders. The legs are held vertically, and the body is balanced in an upside-down position. The arms are then extended toward the bottom, and the body drops in the vertical position. The dolphin begins in a back layout. By sculling, the swimmer pulls him- or herself under the water in a complete circle until the body returns to a back layout and the surface. The ballet leg starts from a layout position. Either leg is flexed at the knee and hip, holding the other leg in extension. The flexed leg is then raised to a vertical position, while the trunk is extended on the surface and the head and shoulders are aligned. The vertical leg is then flexed and returned to its original position beside the extended leg. The other leg can then be raised in the same manner. An advanced stunt is the double dolphin, where both legs are raised simultaneously.

Synchronized swimming requires a good deal of practice on land as well as in the water. A series of drills should be designed, remembering that the movements are geared to be observed by an audience. Thus, if the audience is seated at water level, surface stunts and formations are effective. If the audience is situated above the water, then underwater sequences as well as surface formations will produce excellent results. The type of accompaniment is also important to the patterns that will be used. Analysis of rhythms will assist in choosing and developing the patterns and movements that can be used to best effect. All water movements must be appropriate to the setting, the accompaniment, the skills of the participants, and the safety of the performers.

Fishing

Fishing, although a part of the aquatic program, should be a part of the leisure of all those who are interested. It combines the excitement of competition with the peace and quiet that solitude brings. It offers opportunities for exploration, physical conditioning, and concurrent hobbies. From the sport of fishing for food and fun several competitive activities have developed that add to fishing skills. Among them are fly, bait, and spinning activities and casting games that require hand–eye coordination and much practice.

A location for the teaching of casting skills is easily selected. Selection of equipment, conservation laws, fish and game laws, dress, boat handling, and safety factors can be discussed almost anywhere. Any open space, whether on land or water, offers an adequate area for conducting classes and practice sessions. Members of the fishing and casting class fall into at least three categories: beginning, intermediate, and advanced. Beginners have never cast before and have probably never gone fishing. Intermediates may have done some bait casting, but their skills are limited and they still have difficulty with the equipment. Advanced individuals have had fishing experience and have some degree of skill; they no longer have difficulty with the equipment, but rather need practice to improve their skills.

Optimally, all three groups will receive instruction and demonstrations of casting techniques; however, it is neither necessary nor good practice to force the more highly skilled individuals to hold back for less-skilled ones. Once the groups are sorted out and the better casters have been identified, they can be assigned to some area where they may progress more rapidly. Inexperienced persons who obviously need more assistance should be grouped together. The station method of instruction can be quite useful here. As their skills increase, participants move to another section of the practice area where they receive additional instruction in more complicated movements. In this manner, learners can move as quickly as they are able through the various stages to advanced techniques. Another method, rotating participants to different stages of instruction at the end of definite time periods, can also be used.

Equipment

A sufficient number of satisfactory rods and reels may be made available by the recreational agency for participant use. Of course, many people own their own fishing tackle, but such tackle is usually of the bait-casting variety. The recreational agency can provide casting equipment of good quality so that each person can have individual equipment during the group practice. Eight or 10 outfits, including rod, reel, lure, line, and target, should meet equipment needs.

Bait-Casting Tackle

Bait-casting rods are generally made of fiberglass. They are durable and not damaged by moisture. They are strong and flexible, varying in length from 4 to 6 feet. Some rods come in several pieces for easy dismantling and carrying. The reel is a vital part of the equipment. The bait-casting reel has a revolving spool to pick up the line. The spool is geared to revolve four times for every turn of the handle. The narrow spool is recommended for beginners.

Preferable to silk lines are nylon lines, which are water-proof, require almost no care, and are extremely durable. All lines should be selected by weight and should be at least 75 yards long.

Fly-Casting Tackle

A fly rod of medium action that bends evenly is recommended for beginners. The best length for all-purpose use is approximately 8 feet. A good rod has at least seven and perhaps eight guides to the pole for the line. The windings that secure the guides must extend no less than $1/8$ inch beyond the foot of the guide. The grip should be of good-quality cork and at least 7 inches long. The single-action reel is preferred to the automatic by most experienced fly casters. The weight of the rod and reel together should be about $1^1/2$ times that of the rod alone.

The line is considered the single most important element in fly casting. The weight of the line is dependent upon the action of the rod. Flexible rods require a lighter line than do rigid rods. Most poles require a line of between 6 and 8 pounds. The weight of the line beyond the rod is the only weight that assists in the cast. Of the three types of lines—level, double taper, and torpedo—the level line is most commonly used.

Spin-Casting Tackle

The spinning rod is made specifically for spinning reels. The rods are usually between 6 and 7 feet long. The butt of the rod is either straight for open-faced reels or curved inward for the closed-faced type. The open-faced reel is mounted on the underside of the rod. The closed-faced type, recommended for the beginner, is mounted on top of the rod. A bail attached to the front of the reel wraps the line around the reel when the handle is turned. Nylon line is best for spin casting; it should be no more than 8 pounds test.

Skish

Skish bait casting employs regular tackle and serves to sharpen accuracy and improve technique when the participant cannot go fishing. In skish, the caster attempts to place a plug on a 10-inch target anywhere from 40 to 80 feet away (**Figure 14.13**). The caster has two chances at each target. Skish, which can be performed either inside or outside, is a perfect rainy-day activity for those who are learning how to cast.

Figure 14.13 Dry Practice by Flipping a Plug: (a) Ready Position, (b) Initiating the Back Swing, (c) Most Rearward Position, (d) Whipping Forward

Casting Techniques

For fly casting, the rod should be held firmly, but without tension, with the reel down. The fingers should be around the handle with the thumb along the side or the back of the grip. The line is held by the casting hand between the fingers and the rod handle. It is the line, rather than the lure, that is cast in fly casting.

The cast should be made with minimal arm movement, the forearm and wrist moving like a hinge. About 20 to 30 feet of line are stripped from the reel and laid out in front of the caster. The tip of the rod should be raised to take up slack. The line is loosely held in the left hand. The rod is lifted until the line is straight. The fly then lands on the surface of the water and the rod is held diagonally to the water. The rod is snapped to a vertical position and the line is permitted to follow around until it is behind the caster, with its weight bending the rod slightly. The forward cast is begun immediately; the rod is whipped forward until it reaches the original forward diagonal position. For greater distance, the line is released as soon as the fly starts to move forward. Just before the fly settles on target, the rod is raised to remove any slack and prevent the line from splashing into the water. The pickup must then be started slowly in order to remove the line from the water as quietly as possible.

In bait casting, the rod is held with the reel handle up and the thumb pressing lightly against the crossbar of the reel. The fingers are spread comfortably over the handle with the index finger around the fingerhook. In bait casting, unlike fly casting, the bait is thrown and the line follows it. The cast is overhead and the wrist does most of the work. The rod tip is lowered until the rod is nearly parallel to the surface and then snapped to a vertical position by the wrist and a negligible movement of the forearm. At the vertical position the rod is stopped, although the weight of the lure will bend the tip of the rod backward. The forward cast begins immediately, with the rod tip pointing at the target upon completion of the cast.

The spin cast is similar to bait casting. The chief difference is the control of the line during the cast. When using an open-faced reel, the grip of the rod is taken with the fingers holding the string close to the rod to prevent release on the back swing. The bail is open so that the line is free to run when the finger is straightened and the line is freed. With a closed-face reel, the line is freed by pressing the release button with the thumb.

Safety Precautions

There is almost no danger in practice casting, but there is a certain hazard when participants use hooks. Barbed hooks may be necessary for fishing, but it is inadvisable to use them in practice sessions. Before casting with a plug, the participant should always make sure that the area is clear so that no one will be hit accidentally. When fishing from a boat, the same rules apply as for water and boat safety.

Summary

Water-oriented activities are the most popular recreational pursuits in which people engage. Swimmers, sailors, boaters, surfers, fishermen, divers, and all those who take cruises, use water slides, or raft down rivers are also included as participants in aquatics.

When the community abuts or is in close proximity to any watercourse or body of water, it is perfectly natural for aquatic activities to abound. Even if nature has not been kind to a geographical area, artificially contrived water resources may be constructed. Indoor and outdoor swimming pools, water slides, wave making apparatus, and surfing slides are used to compensate for the natural deficit. Communities that are naturally endowed still have recourse to indoor and other man-made aquatic facilities.

The comprehensive and balanced recreational program can schedule all levels of swimming instruction, junior and senior lifesaving courses, scuba diving, small craft handling, and age-group competition. In addition, fishing tournaments, regattas of several types, and pools for aquatic exercises may be installed. Those who prefer to engage in lap swimming or just socializing in a pool can also be accommodated.

Obviously, both indoor and outdoor facilities can be built or nearby rivers, lakes, or oceanfront can be developed and roped off for similar aquatic experiences. Typically, those who are interested in water games and sports look to their respective communities for such areas as a convenience. When the community cannot or will not supply such recreational places, people will go elsewhere to satisfy themselves in water-related activities.

Selected Further References

Beard, H., and R. McKie. *Fishing: The Fine Art of Casting, Trolling, Jigging, or Spinning While Freezing, Sweating, or Swearing.* New York: Workman Publishing Co., Inc., 2002.

Ditchfield, C. *Kayaking, Canoeing, Rowing, and Yachting.* Danbury, CT: Scholastic Library Publishing, 2000.

Fawcett, P. *Aquatic Facility Management.* Champaign, IL: Human Kinetics, 2005.

Graver, D. K. *Aquatic Rescue and Safety: How to Recognize, Respond to and Prevent Water-Related Injuries.* Champaign, IL: Human Kinetics, 2004.

———. *Scuba Diving.* 3rd ed. Champaign, IL: Human Kinetics, 2003.

Jackson, J. *Scuba Diving.* Mechanicsburg, PA: Stackpole Books, 2004.

Kugach, G. *Fishing Tips for Freshwater Fishing.* Mechanicsburg, PA: Stackpole Books, 2004.

Malone, E. S., and T. Bottomley. *Boater's Handbook: The Essential Look-It-Up Book.* 3rd rev ed. Fairfield, NJ: Hearst Books, 2002.

Noble, J., and A. Gregeen. *Swimming Games and Activities.* 2nd ed. Kansas City, KS: A&E Black, 2004.

Scheck, A. *Fly Fish Better: Practical Advice on Tackle, Methods and Flies.* Mechanicsburg, PA: Stackpole Books, 2005.

Sova, R. *Aquatics Activities Handbook.* Sudbury, MA: Jones and Bartlett Publishers, Inc., 1992.

Thomas, D. *Swimming Steps to Success.* 3rd rev. ed. Champaign, IL: Human Kinetics, 2005.

CHAPTER

15

The Community Music Program

Music is universal. It has meaning for all people everywhere. It is produced by blowing in brass or on reeds; strumming, plucking, or bowing strings; striking keys, drums, or gongs; clashing cymbals; humming; whistling; or singing. Whether through the use of instruments or vocal renditions, the sound of music has the power to change the mood of the listener, evoke emotions, calm, arouse, and stimulate martial ardor, memories, piety, patriotism, sensuality, and pure enjoyment. "Music elicits emotions essential to life and vitality."[1] The same musical piece may move different people differently, but some music can affect different people in the same way. Of course, the sound must be produced in a manner that causes a response in the listener. Thus, by tempo, pitch, tone, loudness, softness, harmony, or discord, music creates a feeling or sensation in varying degrees within whoever hears it. There is music for every taste and ear.

The purveyor of music can be totally absorbed in the rendition with or without regard for those who hear it. Making music for oneself or others requires a desire to learn the rudiments of playing or vocalizing, and then by practice becoming capable of reproducing sound according to written notes or extemporizing material through skillful manipulation of the instrument or voice.

This brief chapter introduces one of the most important categories of any comprehensive recreational service program. All such programs must include some aspect of music to involve potential participants in whatever way they want to engage. It is a professional obligation on the recreationist's part to offer a musical dimension to accommodate people's need for this form of recreational experience.

Organizing the Locality for Music

The development of a music program at the local agency level requires a survey of interest and intent in the population as well as a cataloging of the resources available in the community. Questions that need resolution are:

- Where is music played or sung?
- Who performs?
- Does the school system have a music program?
- Are there any music teachers in town?
- Do sectarian organizations have choirs or choruses?
- Similar indications of musical performance, aptitude, or interest.

Leadership

Absolutely essential to the success of the community recreational music operation is the individual who has the competence and ability to develop, organize, and establish the program. This person's responsibility is to initiate a broadly based music activity that can appeal to anyone with the proclivity or intent to play or sing. If the department has such a person on staff, the organization and administration of the music segment of the program will go forward. On the other hand, the absence of such an individual on staff necessitates a search for someone who has the talent, preparation, and capacity to undertake the functions required. This means the employment (or appointment) of a music specialist whose competence includes being able to work with disparate groups and individuals in a recreational context.

The hiring of a music specialist exemplifies the idea that the executive of the department recognizes the music category as an integral part of the comprehensive recreational program and therefore needs both philosophical and material support. Without the assistance of a skilled specialist, the music aspect of the program will languish or never be developed to its maximum potential. Under these circumstances, the music specialist will not only have the responsibility of organizing and operating this program feature, but also be empowered with the necessary authority to discharge that responsibility.

The music specialist is charged with seeing to the implementation and execution of the total music program in all of its manifestations and ramifications. He or she not only administers and supervises the program, but also carries out a coordinating function with all organizations in the community that are, or want to be, involved in any aspect of performance. This specialist will be a musician in the fullest meaning of the word—that is, one who knows music as well as being able to make music. The specialist will act as a resource, assisting program-level employees (recreationists, part-time workers, and volunteers) in promoting more effective musical experiences for the participating population. This means that all age groups will be served in the various sections and sessions into which the total program is divided.

No community music program will succeed unless leadership is supplied by an individual who has the ability to influence others in achieving objectives that are of common concern and interest. If the recreationist is also a musician or well versed in musical knowledge, the groundwork will be readily laid for a far-reaching program that can serve the community desiring it.

The recreationist in charge, or music director, will need to gain the adherence of potential participants and contact organizations that have or can contribute to vocal and instrumental ensembles of various types. Although excellence in the production of music is one of the objectives of the program, far more significant is the feeling of self-worth, personal satisfaction, human development, and enjoyment evoked in those who sing or play within the recreational program. The entire outcome of the enterprise is predicated on the goal of enhancing and enriching human life through the enjoyment of music in all of its myriad forms.

Resources for Support

A community devoid of music seems improbable. People come into contact with this art form when listening to radio, CDs, tapes, or television; attending concerts, opera, ballet, or musical theater; and actually participating on an individual basis. In the unlikely event that a recreational staff person does not have the requisite ability, someone else must be employed to carry out the function of music specialist. The chief executive needs to know where to turn to find a satisfactory substitute. There are numerous sources from which to choose, not the least of which is the National Recreation and Park Association's personnel vacancy bulletin. This professional organization lists position vacancies in a twice-monthly periodical that is widely circulated to interested parties throughout the United States. Additionally, acquaintance with faculty at colleges and universities in the area or region may result in finding and employing a highly qualified recreationist.

The National Endowment for the Arts is a federal agency devoted to the encouragement of all forms of art. It was established for the development of art through grant proposals submitted by individuals and organizations. To receive funds for the implementation of a community music program, the recreational service department can apply for a grant by completing an appropriate application and writing a proposal in accordance with the established protocol. Based on the endowment's evaluation, the proposal may be accepted and sponsored with monetary support or rejected.

The department has many opportunities for obtaining financial assistance from state and federal granting agencies and should, therefore, employ a grant writer who can more than offset his or her salary by fulfilling the necessary specifications set forth and obtaining funds for the department's use.

The military services all have performing or exhibition bands made up of music specialists and virtuosi. These bands may be contacted for free performances through the Department of Defense, and arrangements can be made for a stimulating concert. The United States Army Field Band and Soldiers' Chorus is an example of this type of organization. Their concerts are eagerly anticipated by recipient audiences wherever they play. These concerts are eclectic enough to display band instruments in many different musical modes and can do much to whet the appetite of player hopefuls, as well as being entertaining.

The state arts council is another resource to which a local community may apply for advice concerning the employment of music specialists. It also may offer monetary support for the purchase of supplies, materials, and equipment. Information about locating personnel and organizing musical activities may also be available on a consultative basis.

Closer to home, the local school system will offer contact with the music director and/or music teachers who may want to supplement income by working on a part-time basis. In any event, these music educators have the necessary skill, talent, and experience to assist in the development of a community-based program that can complement what the schools have already developed. In fact, this may be considered to be a professional obligation in the process of the educator's goal of human development.

Sectarian organizations may be called upon for information or assistance in building the town's music program. Church or temple organists, and choir and chorus masters may be willing to lend a hand in the organization of an ecumenical vocal ensemble to perform on significant occasions. It is even probable that such individuals may be persuaded to lend their organizing and conducting abilities for the promotion of an age-specific recreational choir or glee club. These possibilities must be explored.

If there is an institution of higher education in the community, it may have a music department where students can learn both to appreciate music and to play or sing. Contact with this department may instigate a field work program where advanced music students go out into the community and instruct in their specialization or conduct a variety of ensembles for college credit. This would be valuable to both the student and the recipients of his or her skills, especially if the student intends to become a music teacher in some school system or a private instructor. The faculty of the institution might also be employed to organize a community orchestra, band, chorus, or vocal ensemble with the objective of eventually presenting prescheduled performances by those who are beginners, intermediates, or advanced learners in the program.

Community Contacts

Once a music director has been employed, the professional must seek out those in the locality who may be potential participants in the program or become resources upon which the department can call for assistance regarding materials, expertise, or information.

Music Teachers

Private instructors of instrumental music may, through association with the public department, identify clientele who are possible ensemble players. This contact is a *quid pro quo* arrangement because the cooperation offered by the teacher can lead to publicity and the attraction of additional students to the musician's clientele roster. Further, there may be learners in group sessions who are slower than their peers and, therefore, require additional help outside of the group session. This may also swell the number of students in the private teacher's classes. It is also possible that the teacher may either volunteer as a participant or receive a fee for performing with any orchestra or band that the department develops or sponsors.

Music Technical Services Personnel

Unless early contact and communication is established between the director of music and those who serve the musical profession, little can be expected or accomplished. The music publishers, sellers, instrumental tuners and repairers, and all others who supply the music field with goods and services require close personal association so that cooperative working arrangements can be solidified for the material benefit of the concerned individuals.

Retail Instrumental Outlets

The listing of any stores that sell musical instruments may prove helpful to both parties. The store will find it profitable to make sales presentations to an assembly of interested persons gathered by the department. Arousing interest in the purchase of musical instruments will directly benefit the retailers, the purchaser, music teachers, and the eventual ensembles that are produced through the music program. It also seems probable that the retailers may be too restricted to one instrument (e.g., keyboards). For that reason, wholesalers or manufacturers also need to be contacted.

Manufacturers' Representatives

Manufacturers of many instruments may be called upon to make their respective marketing promotions and provide instrumental exhibitions so potential buyers can inspect them and, perhaps, make a commitment to purchase, or at least discuss the possibilities of rentals with ultimate purchase in mind. These exhibits are also useful to introduce beginners to a variety of instruments from which they may select the one most suitable for them, with some guidance from the music director. In this manner, the seed may be sown that will later be harvested as bands, orchestras, or other groups of performers.

Public Library

Today, all public libraries have audio-visual materials on almost any subject, including compact discs, tapes, and computers with which to guide, advise, instruct, or offer music appreciation. All of these materials can be assistive in exposing the visitor to books about composers' lives, past and contemporary; informing about the development of musical ensembles; and other pertinent data retrieval that can be a part of stimulating interest and eventual participation. Books on the subject of music composition, organizing music groups, music manuscripts, and other writings are awaiting the interested reader. This kind of stimulation can do much to enthuse a community about the initiation of a music program.

Union Local

If the community is a major urban center or if the number of union members warrants it, a musician's local may exist. This is a resource that should not be overlooked insofar as obtaining volunteers and complementary amateur musicians for rounding out an orchestra or band, and invigorating the performance capacity of the program. The musician's local may also be a source of information concerning instrumental and equipment purchase or rental; copyright payments, where necessary, for the use of certain pieces of music or their arrangements; and personnel to lead or support the departmental effort.

Patrons

There will always be people in every community who are enamored of music and will do much to support and, perhaps, underwrite in part or participate in performing music or all of its production. Even more importantly, one or more of these individuals may be the catalyst who sparks an arts explosion in the community by approaching the local government and petitioning for a comprehensive music program. These inclined persons also become the cadres for a corps of volunteers to determine interest in, assist in the promotion of, and participate in performing music.

Once the idea of a music program has been planted, the public department must act to cultivate this receptive environment. Groups of interested individuals, young and old, male and female, need to be organized into the singing or playing ensembles of their choice. In this way the resources of the community are mobilized to effect a program in which music is a recreational outlet for the skill and talent of performers and the enjoyment of those who listen (**Figure 15.1**).

Participants

In the final analysis, a specific program will only be successful in terms of its ability to attract and hold participants. If the youth of a community can be induced to participate, through learning instrumental skills or developing

Figure 15.1   Local Residents Make the Band

innate vocal talents, then the parents of these children will probably become most supportive and demonstrative in favor of the program. It is not unheard of for both parents and offspring to participate in the same music group, thereby enjoying each other's company and bringing them closer together.

Open lines of communication must be easily available between the music director and other instructional personnel so that good public relations, as well as educational information, can be transmitted to all who are interested. The greater the involvement of parents in seeing to the musical development of their children, the more participation, popular support, and widespread music activities will accrue.

Ensemble Organization and Instruction

The basis for a music program in the community lies with beginners. Although the program will rely on the performances of advanced performers, the foundation will be laid with the identification and instruction of novices. Getting a number of people started in the right direction, insofar as instrument or vocal interest is concerned, is essential to the subsequent development of various performance ensembles.

A specific plan needs to be devised for the enrollment and instruction of beginners. The beginner sessions must be open to all of those interested. Whether singing or instrumental involvement, the music specialist will be able to offer a wide selection of opportunities for practice and eventual performance.

Class Method

It is likely that the class method of instruction will be employed. This means that all of the enrollees will learn to sing or play with the group. However, if someone experiences difficulties, so that the class is forced to slow its progress, private lessons may be the most practical answer until the necessary skill is attained.

Organized instrumental playing may begin as early as age 10, in some instances even earlier. It must always be remembered that this program is recreational in nature and that the participants' enjoyment is a primary objective. Certainly, skill and effective performance are also a goal, but recreational groups should be fun. Sometimes required practice and the effort that it takes is not enjoyable; however, as the player's skill and confidence grows the hedonic aspect will develop.

Recreational players and singers vary in innate talent and ability. Therefore, to ensure that all those who want to sing or play have the opportunity to do so, several sessions can be arranged in the schedule for both beginners who show clear aptitude and those who are not so gifted or mediocre, but still want to learn and perform. Either way, there is a place for all who have an interest.

Auditioning Talent

At some point, meetings will have to be called so interested persons can be placed in appropriate instructional and ensemble settings. Sooner or later performers will have to be organized if a comprehensive music program is to be accomplished. To do this, an initial meeting can be scheduled.

Instrument Demonstrations

It may be necessary for one or more capable persons to display and demonstrate the various instruments. In fact, the music director should be able to play all instruments and have the requisite skill necessary to demonstrate the range and capacity of every instrument. By exhibition, demonstration, and the first tentative experiments to play, interested individuals can be introduced to the instruments and subsequent instruction. As a precaution, the prospective player should be advised not to acquire an instrument until he or she has attempted to produce an appropriate tone in an easy manner. Once this has been accomplished, the beginner can either arrange for private instruction or become enrolled in group instruction with the department's classes. The community classes are never in competition with private teachers. Actually, both may equally benefit by cooperative action in that each supplements and complements the other insofar as participants are concerned.

After presenting the various musical instruments and explaining their place in a band, orchestra, or other ensemble, the session may be given over to the study of stringed instruments. Each novice should be offered the opportunity to hold the instrument, bow it, and find specific tones by fingering.

Another session may be focused on reed or woodwind instruments. Head-joints and mouthpieces, with reeds fitted, should be tested and available. Instruction on embouchure (mouthing) formation and mouthpiece position must be given. Then the students can try tones on the mouthpieces. When this practice becomes routine, a few tones may be played on the instrument of choice under careful supervision.

In further sessions, brass instrument instruction may be started with mouthpieces. Once the student is able to play a proper tone on the mouthpiece, instrument work may begin. In ensuing sessions the students should be enabled to attempt any instrument under supervision. Information needs to be disseminated about the study of the instrument of choice and the practice necessary to qualify for future ensemble playing in the types of groups being organized by the department.

Performing in a group is merely one outlet for the enjoyment of the individual. Skill must be acquired in playing an instrument, ability to read music is a necessity, and the person needs to be willing to practice. All such efforts may culminate in public or private performance, in an ensemble or as a soloist, or just for the sheer pleasure of the music maker.

Appropriately organized and guided, the first sessions of a music instructional program have the capacity for building and maintaining the beginner's interest. Additionally, they provide opportunities for determining whether an individual is suitable for the mental and physical demands to succeed in playing or vocalizing. Finally, the basis is developed for all with a talent or desire to accomplish the goal of making music.

Class Organization

A beginner will receive the same information and instruction in a group or class session as he or she would obtain from a private teacher. The difference is that in private the student receives the undivided attention of the teacher. This is not possible in a class of any appreciable size.

Once the introductory phase of orientation, instrument selection, and basic understanding has begun, the department groups all players into classes according to ability (or facility with the instrument), and organized instruction starts. The student must learn how to care for the instrument. The teacher will inspect each instrument to assure that it is easily playable. Properly holding the instrument for play or at rest and finger positioning are fundamental to tone and technique. Posture needs to be emphasized, as does deep breathing exercises for wind players. The sequence of learning now requires playing the first tones, bowing, embouchure formation, and other properties of a tone. The initial unit of playing devolves on quarter note technique within an octave range. Thereafter, incremental steps are taken to extend the range until the full instrumental range is achieved, along with new keys and rhythmic patterns.

Organizationally, the group sessions should be arranged for high efficiency. This means little time is lost in accomplishing the most work. All instruments should be brought together for ensemble training, but in the beginning, the most important focus will be on tonal purity, accuracy of intonation, and an appropriate level of technique. Therefore, sessions of the same instrument are likely to be most efficient in the initial phase.

Eventually, the various beginning groups will come together to work on common materials or problems. It is not especially difficult to instruct instrumental classes if they have been carefully selected and organized. Every student needs his or her own music and stand. There should be sufficient spacing from the other participants so that the individual can hear him- or herself distinctly when all are playing. Such spacing also minimizes any bother or interference that might develop while enabling the instructor to walk among the students for personal attention.

Group Instruction

The whole group should work together most of the time to accomplish whatever material there is. During each session every student should play alone. Every additional assignment needs careful attention, and new problems require thorough explanation so that incorrect habits will not gain a foothold. Students must be taught how to practice as well as play. Supervised practice may be an integral part of each class session, but students need to be impressed with the need for serious home practice.

The Advanced Ensemble

Progress, whether rapid or slow, comes to all those who practice assiduously. Group instruction should continue for the ongoing proficiency of each student, but with increasing skill, new assignments and greater ensemble playing will become the norm. Just as beginner sessions were organized, intermediate and advanced groups will be scheduled. As students progress to the point where specialized instruction is a necessity, private teachers may be called upon for individualized work. This should be encouraged as a form of collaboration between the community program and music teachers. There must never appear to be a conflict of interest or competition between public group sessions and private instruction. Of great importance is the cooperation that is fostered between these parties for the benefit of the entire community.

Instructional Need

All participants should be advised that continued instruction, in either the public or private sector, is required for performance in advanced ensembles. Progression will depend on the participants' ability to satisfy the demands imposed on performers by the music played in bands or orchestras. Of necessity, additional technical instruction may be provided during rehearsals for greater precision and ensemble flexibility. However, individuals should seek personal instruction from private sources to work out any problems encountered.

Ensemble Playing

As participants progress in technical proficiency and as musical ability improves, initial ensemble playing (duets, trios, quartets, or more members) will pave the way for elementary band and orchestra performance. With time, these participants should move into advanced organizations in accordance with their ability.

Advancement to a higher classification should be based on musical achievement. Together with performance in a band or orchestra, opportunities must be available to those whose virtuosity enables them to become soloists or work in small ensembles or chamber music groups. These latter groups require a higher degree of skill and musicianship than does playing in a band or orchestra.

All players do not exhibit the same capacity for skilled performance, and advancement among participants is usually uneven. Nevertheless, there should be an organization for all who want to play—from beginner to expert. Each person should be enabled to find his or her place in the community music program as long as they have the ambition and interest to learn and be a part of making music.

Space and Facilities

Every recreational center building has at least one large auditorium-type room that can be used for rehearsals and performances. Adequate space is a fundamental need for the music program, particularly for instructional purposes and rehearsals. The paucity of space or the use of only one area for all aspects of the program will do more to hinder than to help. Of course, the initial activity may have to make do with what is at hand, but eventually, sufficient space must be found or developed that will allow the music program to engage all who desire to sing or play. Space required for seating the players varies with the size of the ensemble. Adequate floor space permits the players, seats, and stands, together with the conductor's box or podium, to be accommodated.

Acoustics

The acoustical properties of the room must also receive attention. Sufficient air space or other medium is needed to soak up the volume of sound produced without excessive reverberation. Thus, any room used for ensemble playing must be capable of sustaining a tone exactly 1.1 to 1.8 seconds after its release by the performer, depending on room size. Available rooms can be made acoustically acceptable by lining walls and ceiling with easily acquired materials; even carpeting will have some effect. The greater the air space, the less the need for hangings. For best acoustical results, an expert should be consulted.

Floor Markings

The floor of both the rehearsal room and the stage should be unobtrusively marked for the location of chairs and stands. Seats and stands should also be marked in correspondence to the floor. This enables a reliable formation to occur at all rehearsals and stage performances. Typically, such formations are arranged in concentric semi-circles, with the conductor's stand situated at the focal point. Instrumental or vocal ensemble work needs rows that are sequentially higher or in ascending heights. Each row should be about 6 inches higher than the one in front. This permits performers to see and be seen.

Equipment

A straight, short-backed chair is preferred to a folding chair. Music stands of metal and adjustable for height and desk angle are required. The podium for the conductor is portable and must be at least 8 inches high. The conductor's stand should have a flat desk at waist height. When used in an orchestra pit, it should be independently lighted.

Storage Space

Storage space and equipment for department and privately owned instruments is almost as important to performance as are the rehearsal room and auditorium. Storage space for instruments can be included in the rehearsal room or in a separate room. Lockers and cabinets are preferred to open shelves, and if planned prior to construction should be recessed into the walls.

For tympani and other bulky or large and odd-shaped instruments, separate closets or floor-to-ceiling lockers should be available so as to offer easy access and protection. The precise size and kind of space required should be established prior to construction. If such planning is not considered, then roll-away racks need to be obtained for certain instruments. This lack of planning tends to be quite expensive in terms of costs and the possible damage that may accrue to improperly stored instruments.

The percussion cabinet is an ideal place for the storage and maintenance of percussion instruments and attendant equipment. A large cabinet on wheels, capable of being locked, is probably best. This cabinet will contain drawers to accommodate incidental equipment such as drumsticks, chime hammers, triangles, marimbas, clap blocks, and bird whistles. Shelves are also necessary for cymbals, tambourines, and similar instruments.

A music folder cabinet is the most efficient means for systematic storage of music folders for each extant music ensemble. The protected folders are given sufficient space so that separate instrumental or vocal parts, and the conductor's full scores, can be easily accessed. The cabinet is on wheels and can be locked.

At least one music sorting rack should be available for placing new music in rehearsal folders. After use, all music may then be returned to the music library for cataloging and easy access. The rack consists of several slanted shelves of appropriate size to accommodate the needs of any ensemble. Music sorting racks can be made in the recreational craft shop, if one exists, mounted on wheels for convenient movement, or purchased commercially.

The Music Library

The music library is the central repository for all music currently or potentially used for every organization that comprises the music program. Classified under four different sizes—folio, quarto, octavo, or march—these sheets are inserted in covers or envelopes suitable for the thickness of the set parts. If one envelope is insufficient as a container for all of the parts, an instrumental division may be developed so the complete set of parts is included. Parts are inserted in the envelope by instrument designation for easy access. The necessary filing information is inscribed on the exposed edge of the cover. All music is contained in standard-size metal filing cabinets as appropriate to the music classification. Today, computer files replace the old three-way card index that used to be employed to find any number by title, composer, or type. A volunteer staff can be recruited and well-trained to maintain the library and prepare the music for the various ensembles representing the program. New music must be filed, music must be distributed to the various folios, folios

Figure 15.2   The Concert Orchestra

must be issued and collected, and music taken from the folios must be refilled. This is a demanding job and requires the skill that a professionally prepared careerist would have or the dedication and enthusiasm that a loyal volunteer would bring to the task. Of course, a retired librarian volunteer might be the best of all possible worlds.

Performance

At some point, after skill is acquired and ensemble playing or singing becomes smooth and confident, it is reasonable to presume that a public performance should be given. Performance stimulates musical progress for all concerned. Performance, beyond that of the rehearsal hall, is the incentive that drives participants to show what they can do. Planned concerts and recitals for various ensembles and soloists bring attention to the program and offer entertainment to the public that attend (**Figure 15.2**). When musicianship is of high quality, performances will be appreciated and will be in demand. Under these circumstances, greater community support will be forthcoming and music achievement will rapidly develop.

Parents and others related to music participants tend to be avid boosters of the program. They are invaluable as a cadre of volunteers whose help in a variety of nonmusical activities can do much to lift the burden of necessary, but time-consuming, chores. Fund-raising by bake sales and teas or coffees can assist in supporting the different ensembles by off-setting costs that are generic to any such program. Additionally, boosterism spreads the word about the music offerings and does much to establish and maintain goodwill on the part of potential patrons, participants, and future audiences.

Fees and Charges

Costs to operate a music program will invariably include fees for the rental of equipment and instruments, and use of musical arrangements under copyright as well as scores. On principle, any recreational activity offered by the public department of recreational service should necessarily be included in the operating budget by which the department works. This is especially true if the activity is routinely provided as part of a balanced program. However, recent experience informs that this ideal situation is not always followed. Contingencies and other cost producers arise without warning and may not be covered by the budgeted funds. Municipal administrators also may not fully appreciate the need for a wholly funded department and require that the department either be self-supporting or make a profit for the community in which it is based. That this view is short-sighted and may defeat the purpose of the recreational service provision is glossed over; fees and charges will be imposed.

The most important expense to be met will be the salaries of key personnel—those who guide, advise, teach, and direct all of the phases of the music category. Where the community recreational service department has a talented individual on staff to oversee the development of the program as well as the instructors and conductors of various ensembles, the salary will be included in the human resources budget. If this talent is not available, then specialists must be hired to energize the program organization. Although music teachers may also be able to conduct a band, orchestra, or vocal group, it seems probable that securing these experts as volunteers is remote. Funds to employ such persons will have to be encumbered, or else the program will be in jeopardy.

Music is an integral part of a comprehensive recreational program, so sufficient sums need to be segregated and earmarked for this category of activity. Not to provide the monetary support required for developing and maintaining this experience tends to diminish, if not defeat, the entire concept of a community music program.

Fund-Raising

Some of the methods used to obtain funds include voluntary efforts, requesting audience members to make a specific monetary donation as they enter the performance hall, or seeking grants, gifts, or contributions from appropriate sources. The performers themselves also may be assessed dues or charges in order to become members of ensembles, thereby defraying costs that arise in the course of learning, rehearsing, or concertizing. In fact, a good analogy is to think of the performers as club members who are required to pay membership fees in order to belong and achieve the benefits that membership bestows.

Summary

Music has an important place in every culture everywhere. Ethnic tradition, religious plea, and secular outpourings all produce satisfaction and pleasure in performers or appreciation in those who attend and hear. By whatever instrument music is made, it has emotional power for the interested person. For this reason alone, it must be an essential feature of any balanced recreational program.

People everywhere respond to music because it appeals to their aesthetic sense, whatever that may be. The universality of music is well known and is a vital component of a comprehensive and well-balanced recreational program. In order to obtain the special benefits and unique contributions of music as an intrinsic recreational experience, public recreational service departments must hire recreationists with the talent, skill, and understanding of music and who recognize how it can affect people, or use substitutes. However it is done, music as an art form, in both performance and appreciation, must be included in any recreational program worthy of the name.

References

1. Scherer, B. L. "Practicing the Healing Art of Music." *The Wall Street Journal.* May 12, 2005: D1.

Selected Further References

Adey, C. *Orchestral Performance: A Guide for Conductors and Players.* Gordonsville, VA: Faber and Faber, Inc., 1998.

Burgess, R. *Art of Music Production.* New York: Omnibus Press, 2005.

Clendinning, J., and J. Philips. *Musicians Guide to Aural Skills.* Vol. 1. Scranton, PA: W.W. Norton and Company, Inc., 2003.

Coetzee, C. *Piano: An Easy Guide to Reading Music, Playing Your First Piece, Enjoying Your Piano.* London, England: New Holland Books, 2005.

Daniels, D. *Orchestral Music: A Handbook.* 3rd ed. Blue Ridge Summit, PA: Scarecrow Press, Inc., 1996.

Ganzl, C. *Musicals: The Complete Illustrated Story of the World's Most Popular Live Entertainment.* Riverside, NJ: Carlton Books, Ltd., 2004.

Gloag, K., and D. Beard. *Musicology: The Key Concepts.* Florence, KY: Routledge, 2005.

Gogerly, L. *Musical Instruments.* North Mankato, MN: Smart Apple Media, 2004.

Halston, K. R. *Marching Band Handbook.* 3rd rev ed. Jefferson, NC: McFarland & Company, Inc., 2004.

CHAPTER

16 Camping and Nature-Oriented Activities

All experiences based upon the physical and natural sciences and expressed by living in, collecting specimens of, acquiring knowledge about, and finding appreciation in the outdoor environment may be considered nature oriented. Broadly stated, nature-oriented experiences embrace all learning activities that deal with the wise utilization and maintenance of the natural environment. They consist of learning by actual performance in the laboratory of the outdoors.

Camping, one aspect of outdoor learning, has been part of the human experience since the existence of humans. By adapting to the outdoors and learning to obtain food, clothing, and shelter, early people used specific camping skills to sustain themselves. Among the methods employed were trailblazing, water source discovery, making fire, hunting and trapping animals, and constructing shelter for protection from inclement elements.

Outdoor education, the oldest form of education, has to do with contact with, esteem for, and knowledge about natural phenomena. It is concerned with the complete range of the environment, from ecology and biology to meteorology and zoology. Every science related to the outdoors is part of it. From our earliest ancestors who learned to make and control fire, to the camper who enjoys the camaraderie around the campfire, to anyone who has ever thrilled to the sight of the night sky filled with stars or of a stalactite- or stalagmite-filled cave—all have been caught up in outdoor education.

Historically, outdoor education consisted essentially of learning to survive in primitive environments. Over time, the elements of outdoor education transformed and developed into modern camping, which uses the natural environment for its setting. In fact, there is a resurgence of survival methodology in terms of bridging waterways, constructing shelters, fire building, food and water discovery, trail marking, finding one's way in the wilderness, and rope work.

Nature-oriented activity, particularly camping, offers excellent modalities and experiences for the development of participants who might otherwise be stifled in a less permissive atmosphere. For a little while, the individual is taken away from the normal routine of school, home, or business, and placed in a dynamic situation under the guidance of professionally prepared personnel. This type of organized activity may eventuate in the individual's own appreciation for and indulgence in outdoor educational activities on his or her own at a later time.

In an outdoor environment, individuals are able to express themselves most freely. There are no distractions, such as noisesome cities, densely populated neighborhoods, or the loneliness of isolation from one's peers, unless isolation is what the individual seeks. Here, the needs of the individual are satisfied. The child or adult has an opportunity to live in proximity to nature and see a clear moonrise, watch ribbons of light stream across the face of the earth at dawn, catch the first drops of a summer shower, stand in appreciation of a magnificent autumnal coloring, or gaze at the panoramic view after a long climb. Living close to nature teaches each person something of how best to appreciate the resources of the land. The therapeutic value of the outdoors comes from simply experiencing it, living at an unhurried and unharried pace, learning whatever new skills one is capable of performing, and experiencing an entirely new series of activities or relearning valuable skills that have been forgotten through disuse.

The quality of the leadership provided will determine the degree to which the aims of nature-oriented experiences are achieved. The leader of nature-oriented activities requires more than skill or technique in nature study, conservation, camping, or other specialties. Important as highly developed teaching skills are, they do not compensate for high-quality leadership. When soundly planned and administered, nature-oriented activities offer the best features of schooling, camping, recreational experiences, and skill development of the individual. Within the natural setting, each person has the opportunity of being him- or herself. This necessarily suggests, without temporizing, an optimal situation in terms of environment, facilities, program, and leadership. In order to obtain high-quality experience, the environment must be attractive, safe, stimulating, and developmental. It requires good leadership, programs, facilities, and resources that can provide those circumstances conducive to physical fitness (with all it implies) and promote good health habits, concern for others, and an appreciation of ecological factors.

The recreationist has an ethical obligation to help preserve and conserve natural resources. Every season of the year offers some aspect of outdoor education when nature-oriented activity can be incorporated into the general recreational program. Through the instillation of awareness of natural resources, participants may become a highly vocal and mobilized group to argue for the preservation of open space, wilderness areas, and other natural phenomena necessary for outdoor activities. By teaching people to appreciate the value and beauty of the outdoors, converts may be won. Those who are most vociferous for the maintenance of natural places in the face of entrenched opposition generally have had some chance to camp, climb, hike, or bird watch. The organization of nature interest clubs, gardening clubs, astronomy clubs, nature craft activities, wilderness tours, and other stimulating experiences of this kind are an essential aspect of the comprehensive and balanced recreational program. Recreational service agencies should take advantage of any open space, stream, waterway, forest, game refuge, or park in which to inculcate and dramatically present, to active and potential participants, the inherent value of recreational activities in the outdoor setting.

Camping

Modern camping was initiated when public-spirited and farsighted individuals recognized the value of outdoor living for participants. Although organized camping was originally viewed as a measure for getting young children out of sweltering cities and into a healthier environment or as a vacation for the young, today's camping is for all ages, serves those with special needs, and may be conducted throughout the year. Camping has become relatively institutionalized in the United States and elsewhere. It can satisfy the various recreational, social, educational, commercial, and conservation objectives of all campers.

Camping is the experience of living in or as close to nature as is possible. It offers a living situation in an environment untouched by urban culture, in a setting where the camper may have to fend for him- or herself. Camping does not have to be limited to one particular area, but may occur in solitude, without any permanent facility or boundary to prevent excursions into the wilderness. The camper may pack-in, live off the land, or use whatever method is available to transport an individual and supplies, and still retain the fun of camping.

The value of a personal camping experience does not depend on how one gets there or on encountering a variety of hazards—although this might make the experience more exciting to some people. Rather, the value derives from planning, anticipation of, and performance during the actual event.

Organized camping provides the individual, of any age, with the practical conditions for combining outdoor education, conservation education, and recreational experiences in a setting that encourages the development of self-expression and natural inclinations. Three elements are basic to the description and definition of organized camping. There is a permanent facility with appropriate space and suitable structures in which the camp experience occurs. Qualified counselors offer guidance and directed learning. Finally, all camping activities are oriented toward group needs in a democratic context. The distinctive feature of organized camping, in this sense, is that it is a version of social living in an outdoor environment. The individual learns to accept responsibility as a member of a group.

Countless organizations have become aware of the value in camping. They recognize that camping may serve to forward their aims and philosophies while serving the individual camper. Camps are therefore established to meet the specific objectives of whatever group or organization sponsors them. They may be classified as public or governmental, quasi-public or institutional, and commercial, private, or agency.

Camp Types

Camps may be classified according to the way they are organized. Typically, the sponsor chooses the type of camp that will best suit the needs of its members.

Resident Camps

A resident camp has a fixed site and permanent facilities. The campers live at the camp for varying periods and receive shelter and counseling as they participate in the planned program of nature-oriented activities. Structured groupings and occupancy periods characterize resident camps.

Duration of camp or occupancy also defines residential camping. It is not unusual for private and quasi-public camps to have two or more sessions operating simultaneously. If this is the case, the divisions are between campers who reside at the camp throughout the summer season and those who attend camp for 1 or 2 weeks only. Depending upon the capability of the facility to accommodate campers, permanent and temporary campers may be segregated in living quarters, have their own activities, associate infrequently, or be integrated. Whether of a temporary or permanent designation, the camper is a resident and participates to the fullest extent in every aspect of the program.

Day Camps

The day camp is typically established within easy commuting distance from the camper's normal place of residence. The child is transported or may walk to the camp in the morning and returns home before the evening meal. Generally, the only meal eaten at a day camp is lunch, which may be brought from home, supplemented with a beverage and dessert at camp, or be completely provided by the camp. The camping day lasts from 5 to 6 hours, usually at least 3 days per week. In most instances, the day camp has a 2-week session, although day campers may sign up for an entire summer season, if desirable. Fees are nominal; some agencies do not charge those who otherwise could not afford the experience.

Day camps may have no permanent structures, but rely upon tents or other quickly assembled temporary structures. Of course, there may be constructed facilities—sanitary facilities, swimming facilities, and a structure that can serve as a general recreational hall during inclement weather. Although it may seem contradictory, some day camps do offer at least one overnight stay each session so that campers will have the benefit of the continuity of a camping experience. The camper will sleep with his or her group at the camp. Some evening activities will be carried on around a campfire, and the evening and morning meals will be cooked out.

The day camp should stress outdoor living and camping-oriented activities such as nature study, crafts, cooking out, hiking, rock hounding, climbing, canoeing, or any other outdoor activity. Camper–counselor ratios (normally five to eight campers per counselor) should approximate those of the resident camp. The camper will be a part of a particular unit and be served by the same counselor each day.

Special Interest Camps

Specialized camps may be residential, day, or a combination of both. Characteristically, however, special interest camps always have one central objective. They are concerned with the development of a particular skill or talent, with assimilation of knowledge in one given subject or area, or with meeting unique or unusual personal limitations or needs. The distinguishing feature of the specialized camp is that it provides an enhanced background, a natural environment in which a specific interest or need may find fulfillment. Among special interest camps are those that cater to sports, particularly tennis, basketball, soccer, baseball, small craft handling, aquatics, or horseback riding. There are also camps that promote the performing arts. Others are for persons with disabilities. There are camps that specifically minister to older adults, terminally ill children, or those with tuberculosis, cardiac problems, blindness, cerebral palsy, muscular dystrophy, rheumatoid arthritis, developmental disability, or multiple sclerosis. In whatever way the special camp is concerned with individual problems or interests, it is first of all a camp with all of the values, leadership, facilities, and activities implied by that term.

Pioneer Camps

Pioneer or wilderness camps are never developed. The salient feature of this camp is that it is remote. This may be the only real camp in the most valid sense of the word. Pioneering or wilderness camp denotes outdoor living in its basic form. It is primitive; campers must forage for themselves. They learn to live off the land, accommodate themselves to the environment, and select sleeping sites with an eye toward possible flooding if it rains and warmth if the weather turns cold. All meals are cooked out. All activities are bent toward immediate survival. The sole concern is reaching daily objectives.

This by no means implies that pioneer camping is a life or death situation. It is one of the more fascinating aspects of organized camping. Pioneer or wilderness camps may be organized by resident camps or initiated by individuals and private groups. In some instances the pioneer camp is the investment of a single person. In general, however, pioneer camps are established for mature and highly skilled campers. It is a small operation with a skilled counselor-guide in nominal charge. The campers are transported to a jumping-off place and then either "pack-in" or secure suitable transportation by canoe, horseback, mule, or, if at all possible, wheels. Despite mountain bikes, there will come a point where the only transportation will be on foot. Then the campers must pack their supplies, shelter, sleeping equipment, and anything else deemed to be necessary, load them on their backs, and go. Very temporary quarters and continuous movement within a demarcated area characterize the pioneer camp. Typically, the pioneer camp operates for not less than 1 week; it may extend for an entire season. Naturally, the maturity and skill of the campers will play a significant role in the organization of such a camp.

On rare occasions, the pioneer camp may have a relatively permanent base. This means that the campers select the camping site, or erect tents or shelter halves that they have carried, and then forage from the base camp. The pioneer camps of permanency may be situated on lakes or mountain streams, or offer protection from the elements through rock formations. Such camps are designed to test the endurance, skill, and knowledge of the individuals who enjoy living under these conditions. The pioneer camp may be part of the program of activities organized by a home or resident camp; however, more often than not it is an organized entity significantly different from the better-known types of camping experiences.

Trip Camps

Camps without permanent structures or accommodations, and which are organized around continuous movement of the camper from place to place, are called trip camps. Designed to foster travel through a given geographic area or from one region to another in various modes, trip camps offer transportation by canoe, horse, foot, bicycle, automobile, train, bus, or sailing vessel. Trip camping is usually reserved for the mature and skilled older camper—one who can handle an axe, lash tent poles, feel at home where there are no trail markers, or climb a mountain.

Unlike the pioneer camp that has no destination and may be confined to a particular region, the trip camp may be cross-country, intrastate, or interstate, and has a predetermined destination.

Trip camps require scrupulous planning, specifically if the country one is traveling through is harsh. Some camps have limited time schedules. Whatever method the trip camp uses to undertake its responsibility to the camper, leaders will invariably need to determine destination, means of transportation, and duration.

Camp Administration

Camp management is concerned with providing outdoor and nature-oriented experiences through the employment and direction of specialists, supported by an optimum environment and appropriate facilities. Administration is fundamentally engaged in maximizing camping experiences without neglecting the health, safety, and public relations features that ensure the success of the camp.

The organization, initiation, performance, and maintenance of program, leadership, group effort, and supply operations are integral to administration. Camp management is immediately aware of the techniques and responsibilities necessary to execute its mission. Administration is accomplished by methods commonly used in every similar situation, including the following:

- Establishment, either by charter, incorporation, or contractual agreement, that the camp exists.
- The enactment of policies that provide a frame of reference to camp operations.
- Inauguration of fiscal management functions and revenue sources for the support of the camp.
- Policies and practices to recruit, educate, and retain the most highly qualified and competent staff possible; also, assignment of duties and responsibilities with commensurate authority to execute denoted obligations.
- Arrangement of the most comprehensive and varied series of nature-oriented opportunities so each camper may fulfill his or her capacity to participate; also, promotion of stimulating activities designed to meet the interests, needs, and range of abilities of the individual.
- Property acquisition, development, and maintenance.
- Public relations so that information about the camp and its value to campers is made known on a routine basis. A well-developed public relations program can do much to build staff morale, camper enthusiasm, parental support, and financial success.
- The establishment and maintenance of comprehensive records and reports dealing with every facet of camp life. Records and reports reveal every phase of camper background, camp program, personnel, property, and legally required accounts.

The amount of time and concentration administrators spend on these functions varies with the camp sponsorship, the physical resources controlled, the program's range, the number and quality of personnel involved, and the individual needs of campers.

Camp Organization

No one organizational plan works for all camps, but the diagrams in **Figures 16.1** and **16.2** may be helpful in understanding positions, functions, lines of

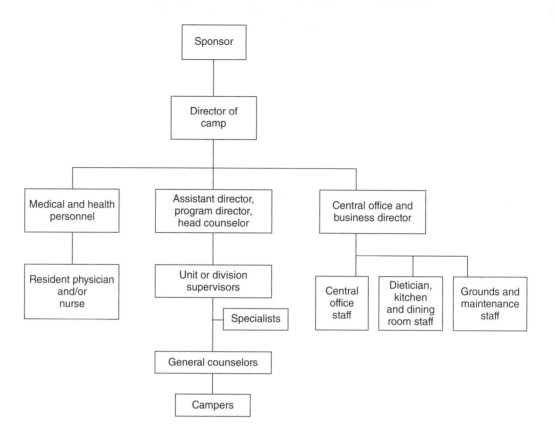

Figure 16.1 Typical Line and Staff Organizational Chart

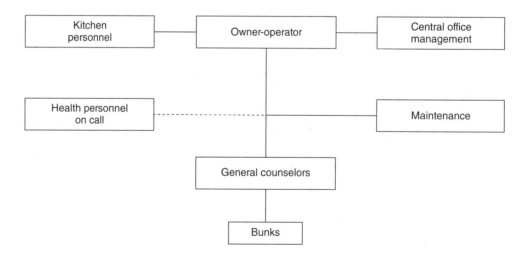

Figure 16.2 Camp Organization in a Small Private Camp

responsibility, and support personnel. The organizational levels include the executive or policy-making level, administrative or middle-management level, supervisory level, and functional level. Within these levels there may be a further division on a program or specialty basis.

To a greater or lesser extent, depending upon the size of the camp and the number of campers being accommodated, all camps are organized in terms of these functions and subdivisions. In large or elaborate camps, specialized facilities may call for managers, but few camps either have or require very specialized areas. In any event, specialists may be fitted into the organization at the supervisor level. Small camp operations may not require these line and staff combinations because the small camp expects personnel to double up in their functions. Thus, unit supervisors may also be specialized program counselors. In small operations, the camp director may combine the functions of business manager and program coordinator. Sometimes, although rarely, the camp nurse may assume dietitian responsibilities, but this is not recommended practice. In not a few situations, kitchen or dining rooms staff may also function as part of the maintenance and groundskeeping staff. The organizational development will reflect the size of the camp and the recognition on the part of the administrator of what efforts are necessary for the effective accomplishment of the camp's mission.

Division of Functions

The responsibility of the camp to the camper necessitates division of functions (**Figure 16.3**) or specialization, to ensure that its chief aim is carried out. The task to be accomplished requires a number of employees to be hired and assigned to various positions. Each of the employees then specializes in performing part of the responsibility, which leads to the success of the camp mission.

The division of work in any organization is rarely planned in advance. Normally, camp organization is thought of in single units, and expands by repeated subdivision whenever indicated. When a camp is established, the sponsoring agency appoints a camp director. If it is a private venture, the

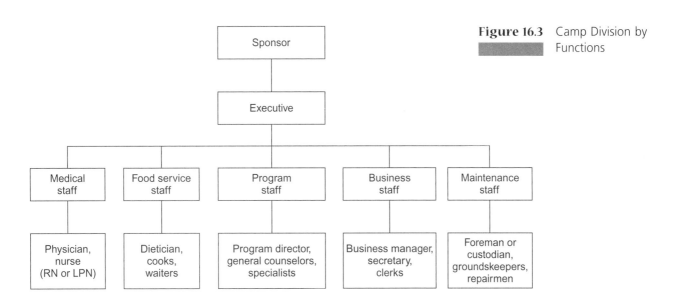

Figure 16.3 Camp Division by Functions

camp director may be the owner. In any case, the chief executive will soon find it necessary to consult others in order to determine the best methods of getting underway. As problems are identified, someone from the original consulting group or from the outside will be assigned to solve them. These people, in turn, may call on others for advice or technical services. In this way the original group is subdivided into secondary units that may further divide as the situation changes.

The arrangement of administrative, supervisory, and program personnel must be integrated if the experience is to be of value to the camper. To achieve this, each worker will need to know what others in the same division are doing so that all efforts may be coordinated. Traditionally, the supervisor is selected to coordinate efforts and to relate the activities of each person to those of others in the division. The supervisory process is, perhaps, most significant in affecting outcomes of value. The supervisor must recognize, for instance, that when the unit becomes so large that effective supervision is hindered, it is necessary to break it down into groups small enough to be coordinated by supervision.

Hierarchal Divisions

The executive or policy-making level consists of representatives of the sponsor of the camp and the camp director. The making of policy outlines the conduct of the camp. Policy is designed to carry out the wishes of the sponsor, but is also of primary importance in setting the operational standards of the camp.

Positions on the administrative level may carry either line or staff identifications, but are usually associated with the direction of a particular function and the staff assigned to it. Any employee who is directly responsible for carrying out the program function of the camp is a line employee. Any employee not directly involved in program work, but who, as a consequence of special skill or knowledge, provides technical aid and advice to line personnel in order to make those individuals more effective and efficient, is a staff employee.

Administrative personnel usually are concerned with the execution of policy and the manner in which daily assignments are handled. Consequently, middle management deals with subjects of a tangible nature directly related to personnel capacities for the production of output necessary to affect the camp program. With whatever title they are given, administrators perform identical functions at the same level within the camp. Some may be concerned with staff, such as personnel, fiscal, or office management; others may be responsible for giving direct personal assistance to line employees. Others may be called upon to act in the absence of the camp director.

There may be two or three departments, depending on the specialties needed. Normally, at least two departments assume responsibilities related to program and central office or business practices. Where the camp has the services of a physician, health becomes the third department. When the camp owns extensive properties, a fourth department may be created for plant and maintenance. This function, however, is almost always included within central office administration.

Administratively, certain functions are related to the overall operation of the camp, even though they are not directly involved with camping *per se*. These staff duties have to do with technical assistance in conducting the camp. Some of these services are situated in a central office where they are accessible to all for whom they are pertinent. Other central office operations are delegated through divisional status and have facilities outside of the central office from which they perform. The extent and specialization of the central office staff will, of course, be decided upon by the number of campers and all employed personnel. It administers a variety of business transactions, personnel classification, office management, fiscal accounting, and recording camp data.

In small camps the director-owner may also perform the duties of business manager. The inherent danger of such practice is that the details of office management; purchasing and dispersing supplies, equipment, food, and materials; keeping records; and maintenance of buildings, grounds, and equipment may prove too much of a burden. Where this occurs, the director may be forced to relinquish a primary function, that of directing camp activities, to the counselor staff. Large modern camps invest in a business manager.

Included within the range of responsibilities assumed by the business department will be divisions having to do with maintenance and kitchen and dining room personnel (if the camp requires waiters). Insofar as maintenance of the physical plant is a part of standard procedures, cleaning services (where appropriate), landscaping, and the repair of facilities and equipment are necessary for operation. Safe employment of all vehicles and tools, and enhancement of all structures, facilities, and areas is mandatory if the camper is to enjoy optimum satisfaction and benefit from camp participation.

The direction of good human resource practice has tremendous influence on the success of any camp. Human resource management in terms of records and reports must be updated so that the standards for staffing can be maintained.

Fiscal management is essential to the operation of all camps. Whether the camp sponsor is concerned about profit making, breaking even, or is unconcerned about money matters, there still remains the necessity of accounting for money as required by law. The custodianship of funds deposited by campers, records of purchases and disbursements, and receipts and voucher forms from the ordinary transactions of day-to-day affairs requires some form of control to assure correctness and honesty.

Office management and clerical work refer to the recording, filing, stenographic, supply, and inventory keeping that are part of all soundly arranged business offices. These functions are necessary even if done in the most perfunctory manner. Large camps dealing with hundreds of campers and many staff specialists would normally require an effective central office workforce. Smaller camps may assign one or two persons to perform these tasks.

The central office will also lend supervision to the kitchen and dining room staffs regarding the purchase of supplies, materials, and equipment. With the exception of waiters, specialists are employed to supervise and prepare food at camp. A dietitian may be hired to develop menus and ensure that proper safeguards are taken to prepare and serve nutritious, tasty, and attractive meals. Within this division there may be a head cook and other subordinates. Food preparation and service can be one of the most important functions of the resident camp; it contributes to the health and morale of campers and staff alike.

The single most important function, and a basic reason for the establishment of any camp, is carried out by the program department. This department may be administered by the camp director, an assistant director, or an individual variously identified as the head counselor or program director. It is the responsibility of this department, through its subdivisions and counselor staff, to promote the greatest variety and broadest possible range of nature-oriented and camp-based experiences to assure maximum satisfaction and enjoyment by each camper. The program department is directly involved with the health (exclusive of problems that are more properly cared for by competent medical specialists), safety, welfare, skill development, instruction, participation, and daily living experiences of all campers. It is through this department that the entire camping season is interpreted. So vital is this department to the success of the camp that camp directors leave nothing to chance in recruiting the most highly qualified and competent personnel to assume counselor positions. Clearly, the program department is supported by all other activities of administration. These other administrative functions would be meaningless if there were no program.

Counselors may play the most important role in any camp organization. They are the functional, face-to-face employees on whose shoulders ride the effectiveness of the camping experience. Nevertheless, all employees and owners who are part of the organization are of importance in making their unique contributions to the overall effectiveness of the camping situation.

The subdivision of the program department is the unit. Depending upon the number of campers and the extent to which the camp is centralized or decentralized, the breakdown into units and then bunks (camper groups) will determine the counselor–camper ratio and the supervisor–counselor ratio. An example of a good ratio would be to have about 40 general counselors for 300 campers. Each counselor would be responsible for one bunk of from five to eight campers. With 40 bunks, at least four unit supervisors would be needed, each responsible for 10 counselors. Added to this would be other supervisory specialists—waterfront or aquatic director, arts and crafts specialist, perhaps a nature science specialist. It is to be expected that where other skills are taught, general counselors are employed who possess the necessary techniques in various activities. They will be assigned to a bunk and can also be used for instructing in specific motor skills. Thus, a general counselor may teach or assist in teaching riflery, archery, tumbling, horseback riding, or tennis, as well as perform a bunk counselor's responsibilities.

Some large camps may employ specialists in a wide range of activities. These individuals are not given general counselor duties, nor are they assigned to a bunk. Specialists, in this instance, provide full-time instruction to campers in particular skills. It is not unusual for a camp to have an expert in dance, dramatics, music, crafts, nature, tennis, sailing, archery, rifle shooting, riding, or other activities who devotes all his or her time to the instruction of individuals and groups. In special camps, these highly qualified employees may be engaged to teach a more restricted area. In a general music camp, for example, instructors of all instruments are employed to teach whatever type of music the camp offers. In band camps, only band instrument instruction is offered. The same holds true for a general sport camp or for a camp solely devoted to basketball, baseball, or swimming. These special interest camps may utilize a camp setting as an attraction for the camper, but camping, as such, is not really practiced in these environments.

Where the camp has a medical department, the resident physician or nurse reports directly to the camp director. Health and medical forms originate from this department. Managerial functions relate strictly to the operation of the dispensary or the infirmary. Large camps may have both a resident physician and several nurses, either registered nurses or licensed practicing nurses. Smaller camps may have a resident nurse with clearance from a local physician or treatment center. All resident camps would be wise to make provision for any medical issue that may arise. Although camps are, or should be, conducted in the safest and most healthful way possible, there are always certain hazards that must be taken into account.

Camp Program Organization

Several factors must be considered in planning a program of activities. Among these are the owner's or sponsor's objectives for the camp, the campers' desires, parental requests, and the resources of the camp itself. These demands are neither so great nor so complicated as they might first appear. The camp generally has the resources to provide tremendously varied activities. The campers' quest for fun and excitement usually coincides with parental concern for skill development and learning, and with the camp's aim of outdoor education. In the best educational sense, the most logical camp program will not only use the campers as a point of departure, but also take their advice for initiating the program. Campers should participate in choosing what will be offered; this participation will evoke the most valid statements of campers' views. The campers will feel greater responsibility for the success of the activities and will take a more proprietary interest in the camp itself if they share in program planning. Self-expression, self-confidence, and independence will be fostered through camper involvement. From the campers' point of view, camp is for them. It is designed to please them. They should have a part in program development. Not all campers have the intelligence, skill, or experience to assist in this planning. Nevertheless, each bunk may have activities separate from those of larger units of the camp or the whole camp, so even less-helpful campers can be asked for suggestions or given several alternatives from which to choose.

Although it is important to plan for camper participation in many outdoor experiences, a too highly organized and routinized program denies spontaneity. It is desirable to have unplanned periods in the daily schedule so that there will be time to think, sit on a log, write a letter, read a book, hunt for frog eggs, gaze at clouds, or pursue special interests. Flexibility can be built into the program. As more campers are enrolled in a given camp, however, the necessity for detailed planning becomes essential. As mentioned, to reduce any rigidity that might ensue from early and systematic program development by the administration, counselors and campers must be given an opportunity to share in planning. Many successful programs are initially organized in skeletal form only and fleshed out later. The details of the daily schedule and some special events are introduced into the program after discussions in general sessions with counselors and mature campers. It is true that democratically derived programs are difficult to bring to fruition; but it is also true that such a program has a greater chance of fulfilling its aims. The adult staff should not attempt to hurry this process by manipulating the campers. Impatience at delay should not lead to a takeover by the staff of what must be thought of as the campers' choices.

The democratic concept being promoted in today's camps makes necessary the full participation of all those who receive value from camping activities. The interests and needs of campers are determined by means of questionnaires, personal interviews prior to camp, and discussions that occur in the bunks after camp has begun. These findings are used, or should be, as one basis for program arrangement. The production of a program is increasingly based upon sound educational, social, psychological, and recreational standards and principles. To be effective, camping must be guided by realistic objectives. In addition to the interests, needs, capabilities, and limitations of the campers involved, the environment and resources of the camp; the camp's philosophy; the duration of the camping period; the supplies, materials, and equipment at hand; and counselor and specialist competence to guide or instruct activities must also be considered.

Even the decentralized camp requires some all-camp or centralized activity. However, small group planning for decentralized living facilities and program structures identifies the bunk as the unit from which a daily schedule of activities originates. Unfortunately, the dynamics of daily interrelationships may also deprive the less articulate, aggressive, extroverted, bright camper from what he or she wants to do some of the time. The minority still has to be protected from the whims, overzealousness, and control of the majority. For this reason, a variety of program planning units may be initiated—the bunk or basic living unit, club or interest groups, instruction groups, and all-camp activities groups. These will offer each camper the opportunity to belong to many groups in which his or her own needs, talents, and skills may find satisfactory outlets.

Modern camps and associated agencies generally recognize that certain facilities, equipment, and supplies should be available for free play or unscheduled activities for individuals and self-organized and self-directed groups. There is also awareness of the need for a certain amount of promotion and organization that can multiply the number of activities and participants in the program, as well as a need for generating greater efficiency and usefulness of the available facilities. The necessity for supervision of activities and the provision of positive leadership by counselors must also be recognized so that educational, social, and cultural outcomes may be realized.

Summary

In order to effect the inclusion of the nature-based program and fulfill its responsibility for providing one of the 12 recreational categories to its constituency, camps are organized by recreational service departments. These camps, of whatever type, use nature-oriented activities as the basis for programming.

How the camp is organized, administered, and maintained is fundamental to satisfying the need for outdoor education, environmental protection, nature appreciation, and pleasure in the activities available to those who camp.

Camp structure is formulated on the different components that make up the division of labor. Administrative departments are required to carry out managerial functions for staffing, accounting/budgeting, maintenance, and programming. Larger camps require more subdivisional specialties than do small ones because of personnel needs and a greater camp population. Primarily, the camp exists to provide nature-oriented experiences to campers.

Too often, nature-oriented activities are either omitted or given short shrift by recreational agencies. Except for most organized camps, which can scarcely leave out such activity because of their location or orientation, the need for nature study, outdoor education, or natural science activity has been largely overlooked or relegated to a minor role.

However, this is being corrected because of the impact that knowledge of ecology, the environment, and the effects of man-made pollution has had on most thinking persons. Global warming and its consequences have created a condition of intense alarm. This, in turn, has stimulated a good deal of thought and activity concerning the natural world. One outcome is an increased awareness of and appreciation for involvement in nature-oriented activities.

To this end, therefore, recreational agencies must develop activities that reflect this new and continuing interest in the environment. Significantly and fortunately, such nature-oriented activity is absolutely enjoyable. It offers continuous opportunities to learn about and participate in the natural wonders that abound. As someone once said, "If spring were accompanied by trumpets and drums, everyone who takes the season for granted would stop and take new hope from the phenomenon." This is also true of every aspect of the natural world.

Therefore, it is the recreationist's professional obligation to program nature-oriented activities to increase the satisfaction, pleasure, and even amazement of current and potential participants. This requires leadership of the highest quality as well as a sense of responsibility to those who make up the agency's constituency.

Selected Further References

Conlin, J. "Camping? Yes. Roughing It? Not Quite." *The New York Times*. September 14, 2008: A4.

Freeman, S. C. "Camp Leads a Drumbeat for a Marching Band Style." *The New York Times*. July 23, 2008: A13.

Kelley, T. "Dear Parents: Please Relax, It's Just Camp." *The New York Times*. July 26, 2008: A1, A12.

CHAPTER

17 Practical Nature Science Activities

Although any recreational service agency can utilize the camp experience as the basis for its nature-oriented activities, there are many formats for such activities that are not camp based. All ages can interact with the outdoor environment (**Figure 17.1**). By observation, experimentation, collection, and appreciation, individuals who have the opportunity to be exposed to nature may experience personal satisfaction and enjoyment that is the essence of recreational activity. One does not have to be a naturalist or even a nature scientist to appreciate and enjoy the flight of a heron, the flash of a scarlet tanager, the thrill of finding what might be a gemstone, the feeling of apprehension and curiosity on approaching a huge wasps' nest built into the branches of a small tree, or observing bears, bison, fox, deer, or big horn sheep in their natural habitat.

Observing insects can fascinate an interested child for hours at a time. During the summer, especially if preceded by a wet spring, fields harbor a fantastic array of crawling, hopping, flying, and slithering insects. An uncut field will often be decorated by spider webs. Careful watching may be rewarded by a visit from a praying mantis or insects that camouflage themselves to look like twigs.

Rainy days do not have to be spent indoors. People can dress suitably for work in the woods, and look for mushrooms and bright colored fungi. The earth on which we live is 6 billion years old and contains an infinite variety of information to spellbind any audience. The very rocks can be collected, classified, and arranged by hardness or density.

Observing the variety of trees, ferns, and grasses; taking a look at a drop of water through a microscope; and living in harmony and with appreciation of wild things are all parts of nature lore and science. Individuals being introduced to nature sciences must learn that it is through conservation of natural resources that the greatest number of people can have the greatest enjoyment of these resources for the longest time.

Only the guidelines of a possible nature program will be presented in this chapter. The opportunities to learn, explore, and seek new wonders in the everyday world are infinite. If the recreational agency employs a nature specialist, as it should, that person can introduce an impressive array of things to do, places to go, and items to make and see. The natural sciences, with all their ramifications, are part of the nature program, not isolated classification subjects. The program should be presented so that the participant begins to realize the close relationship and intimate association among all things in nature. Instruction can help the individual to recognize a variety of plants, animals, and minerals, and encourage the collection of samples, in order to provide a greater understanding of ecology and the interdependence of natural phenomena. The program has an opportunity to stimulate the individual's curiosity and excite in him or her the desire to learn more about things he or she either has never seen or has simply taken for granted. For the participant, starting a collection of mineral samples can lead to a lifetime hobby, a life's work, or the study of other sciences.

The following sections present ideas for making the nature program informative and interesting. All projects are intended to foster conservation education.

Figure 17.1 Every Swampy Area Has Interesting Objects to See

Astronomy

One of the most impressive and beautiful sights is the black night sky filled with stars. On any clear night a luminous cloud appears to stretch across the heavens. The observer is actually looking edgewise through our own galaxy, which we know as the Milky Way. Our sun is only one of at least 100 billion stars that make up the Milky Way. It is situated on the outer edge of the galaxy in the center of our solar system. To arrive at some idea of how great the distances are that separate the stars in the galaxy, one must figure in terms of light-years. One light-year is the distance light travels in one year at the speed of about 186,000 miles per second. For example, the sun is 93 million miles from earth, or 8 minutes by light. Alpha Centauri, one of our closest star neighbors, is a mere 4-light-years away, or 26 trillion miles farther into space. The brightest star, Sirius, is 8.8-light-years off. The Milky Way is at least 100,000 light-years from one end to the other and measures 10,000 light-years through the center of the galaxy. The sun, with its system of planets, is approximately 30,000 light-years from the center of the galaxy.

Some interesting examples of distances in the universe illustrate the idea of the vastness of space. If the universe were to shrink to microscopic size, the sun would be the size of the period at the end of this sentence. The nearest star would be another period 10 miles away. Other stars even more distant would be reduced to the size of a penny, and would be hundreds and thousands of miles apart.

The Amateur Astronomer

During the summer, the night-by-night observation of the stars can be of great enjoyment to any viewer. Stargazing requires almost no equipment and very little preparation. Most important is that the participant be comfortable. Looking at stars high above the horizon can cause a stiff neck or an aching back. A blanket spread on the ground can be a comfortable observation point. It is important to dress appropriately, because the ground tends to cool off at night and the air may become chilly.

Figure 17.2 Introduction to the Stars

Little beyond one's eyes is really necessary to see the stars. Thousands can be observed on any clear night, particularly when there is no moon. With field glasses, however, enjoyment can be heightened because details of the planets and the moon can be seen. The higher the power of the optical instrument, the more details and stellar objects will be seen. Telescopes, bought or made, can contribute even more enjoyment because they allow for finer observations (**Figure 17.2**).

The enjoyment of stars requires merely a little practice in basic identification. For the beginner, the recognition of a dozen constellations and 10 of the brightest stars is usually sufficient. The systematic study of stars, the identification of lesser constellations, and the location and study of clusters and nebulae require more serious efforts. Even quite young persons, however, can learn to recognize nearly all constellations, bright stars, and visible planets.

Star Motion

The sun is about average size and brightness when compared to other stars. It moves at approximately 12 miles per second, along with the solar system, toward the great blue star Vega in the consolation Lyra. The sun, which is similar to all other stars, travels along its path as do all other stellar objects. Nothing remains motionless in the universe. Some stars travel hundreds of miles per second. Some are traveling in the same general direction as the sun; others are headed in precisely the opposite direction. Many stars are moving as parts of systems or clusters. Some stars consist of two or more components that revolve around a common core as they travel through space. The stars in a constellation are not necessarily related. They may be of completely different magnitudes, moving in diametrically opposed directions, and at varying speeds. Some are growing old; others are being born. Although the constellations present an unvarying picture to the observer, they are constantly changing shape. The stars that make up the outline of the constellations are steadily shifting their positions. In any constellation some stars may be farther away than others and unassociated with them. Because the stars are so far away, no one can possibly see them moving, except over a long period of time.

Those who observe the stars are looking into the past. Nothing in the night sky is actually there at the moment of observation. If, for example, one were to look at the stars in the constellation of Orion, the light from the brilliant stars that dot his right shoulder and left foot are so distant that it has taken 270 and 650 light-years, respectively, for eyes on earth to see them. A look at the great nebula in the constellation Andromeda brings to the observer something that occurred 750,000 earth years ago. It has taken the light shining from the great nebula that many years to travel to earth.

Constellations

The constellations have been extremely useful in assisting with the charting of the sky. Some constellations were identified several thousand years ago; others were identified by astronomers in the 17th century. The boundaries of constellations have been definitely established and recognized by astronomers everywhere by international convention.

Circumpolar constellations suggests that the viewer is somewhere between the equator and the North Pole. To an observer in the North Temperate Zone (between Florida and Maine) the stars seem to spread overhead as the earth turns on its axis every 24 hours. Stars near the pole remain in view as they turn around; stars closer to the equator rise and set. At the pole, all constellations are circumpolar. For stars located between the pole and the equator, latitude determines whether they are circumpolar. For example, the bowl of the Big Dipper does not set at latitude 40° north, but in Florida, at latitude 30°, it does set and is therefore no longer considered circumpolar. When the sun is north of the equator during the summer, it becomes circumpolar north of the Arctic Circle. Among circumpolar constellations of the Northern Zone are the Big Dipper, the Little Dipper, Cassiopeia, Cepheus, Draco, and Perseus. One of the thrilling moments for the amateur astronomer occurs when he or she first sees the Big Dipper and can then identify the other constellations nearby.

Circumpolar constellations with their key stars can be an effective guide in locating other constellations. Once the Big Dipper is recognized, the Pole star, Polaris, in the Little Dipper can be seen. Simply trace a line from the pointer (two outer) stars in the bowl of the Big Dipper, and Polaris, the last star in the handle of the Little Dipper, may be located. A line drawn through the base of the bowl of the Big Dipper to the east will lead to the star Castor in the constellation Gemini. A line through the handle to the bottom of the bowl will lead to Regulus in Leo Major. Following the curve in the handle of the Big Dipper will direct the viewer to Arcturus in the constellation Bootes.

Summer Constellations

Although the weather is generally favorable for stargazing in the summer, the sky is not as brilliant as in the early spring. There are, however, many constellations on view, and the Milky Way is rather impressive. The spring constellation Leo begins to sink into the west, but a number of constellations and bright stars rise in the east to replace it.

The constellation Bootes, although a late spring constellation, is visible for most of the summer. The major star in Bootes, Arcturus, is an excellent point from which to begin the examination of the summer sky. The observation of the night sky can open the way for many interesting and entertaining studies. Agency instructors can introduce the sciences of optics, light refraction, spectroscopy, meteorology, and hydrology through stargazing. Ancient Greek and Roman history, mythology, and literature can be touched on in discussing constellations.

Biology

Because biology deals with all living organisms, it includes many sciences. Biology may be divided into *botany*, which deals with plants, and *zoology*, which deals with animals. Botany, too, has several branches. One of these is bacteriology. Zoology includes entomology, the study of insects; icthyology, the study of fishes; ornithology, the study of birds; and anthropology, the study of man. Biology may also be classified in terms of form and structure. Morphology is the study of the form and structure of plants and animals. Physiology is the study of the functional organs and parts of organisms of plants and animals. Taxonomy is the study of the classification of plants and animals. Paleontology is the study of fossil plants and animals. Genetics, the study of heredity, is also a branch of biology, as are organic evolution and ecology. These latter two sciences deal with the succession of plant and animal types and the study of organisms in relation to their inanimate surroundings and to the other organisms that impinge upon and influence their lives. Morphology may be divided into anatomy, the study of the gross structures of organisms; histology, the study of tissues; and cytology, the study of cells. All of these studies are subdivisions of biology. The interdependence of living organisms illustrates the relationship that all sciences have to one another. Thus, the study of astronomy, while dealing with stellar objects and heavenly bodies, is concerned with the sun and the solar system. Without the influence of the sun and other necessary factors such as breathable air and good water, life as it currently exists on the earth would be impossible.

Living Organisms

It is relatively simple to distinguish a living plant or animal from an inanimate object. Nevertheless, attempts to formulate a definition of life in precise terms have been somewhat unsuccessful. Considering some of the distinguishing characteristics that separate living from nonliving things may be more valuable to nature program participants than teaching a disputed definition of life.

Organization for the performance of different but related functions is vital for life. The structure of organisms reveals that they are made up of viable units called cells. The cells are themselves highly organized. In multicellular organisms the cells are grouped to form tissues, and tissues are grouped to form organs. Inorganic matter has no such organization.

Movement of some type also is essential to nearly all living things; however, some kind of movement also occurs in the inorganic world. The difference is the responsiveness to stimuli. A *stimulus* may be defined as any physical or chemical change that activates modification in the behavior of an organism, but does not in itself provide energy for the response. There is nothing that corresponds to this phenomenon in inorganic matter. Growth by intussusception is probably the most unique characteristic of living matter. With the exception of crystal formation, which does not meet the specific criterion involved, there are no identical food intake processes like intussusception in the inorganic world. Living matter depends upon chemical balance and adjustment. The intricate chemical process of any living organism is due to molecules that are composed of atoms in an almost infinite variety of combinations. The organic substances—carbohydrates, fats, and proteins—occur only in organisms or their products.

Photosynthesis, with rare exception, is probably the ultimate source of energy for all living things. The chemical energy stored in foodstuffs is released when they are oxidized. It is true that photosynthesis can be promoted artificially without the presence of living organisms, but only on a very small scale;

for example, nearly everyone has had experience with the oxidation of materials in inorganic matter.

Water is the essence of life. Without water life ceases to flourish. The prototypes of all living organisms had their origins in water. These animals later moved onto the land. This is vividly illustrated by plants and animals alive today. Life is continuous, and continuity plays a vital role in evolution. It is unknown for living organisms to arise from nonliving matter. Every living organism is the end product of the continuous series of living organisms extending back to the initiation of life on earth. The chain will continue unbroken so long as nothing interferes with the environment in which the organisms abide. Unless some unforeseen natural disaster or artificially contrived holocaust develops, the continuity of life will remain in effect.

New living organisms arise from the process of reproduction. In asexual reproduction the entity develops as a result of cellular division. In sexual reproduction two cells termed *gametes* unite to form a zygote that is, fundamentally, a new living individual.

With this brief introduction to some of the concepts and categories of biology, the recreational specialist may be in a better position to answer questions that human beings have always wondered about. In fact, these are questions that can serve as the basis for recreational activities enlisting the sciences as a source of enjoyment. Why should life be so varied? Why are there so many different kinds of birds, fishes, trees, flowers, insects, and animals? The solution to these questions lies in the adaptation of each organism to the peculiar conditions of its environment. Organisms vary in size, shape, color, and internal structure because their environments require it. The converse is also valid. Organisms live in different environments because they differ in structure. Each species is adapted for the peculiar or unique conditions of its environment. In order to maintain life, plants or animals must be able to carry out functions under the conditions their environment presents.

Plants and animals are different not only in terms of the roles they play in the living world, but also in their essential features. Their functions may be complementary as well. Green plants produce organic food materials from inorganic matter in their environment. They are primarily concerned with building up a store of energy in chemical form. Animals are absolutely dependent upon green plants for their food. They are chiefly concerned with utilizing the energy that green plants have manufactured.

All plants do not contain chlorophyll, that remarkable substance that permits the utilization of light energy. Those plants that do not have chlorophyll must obtain food substances from other plants or animals, whether as parasites, while the host is alive, or as saprophytes, feeding on the excrement or the dead bodies of other organisms. Saprophytic plants are quite as important to the living world as are green plants. They cause decay and break down organic compounds that are returned to the inorganic world in a simple compound form. From these raw materials new life forms can be generated. One large group of plants, the fungi, are devoid of chlorophyll and live in parasitic or saprophytic form. Although the best-known of the bacteria are those that cause disease, the saprophytic group causes decay, without which life could not continue on earth.

Generally, animals obtain their food by eating other organisms, many of which eat green plants. Ultimately, therefore, all animals are dependent upon green plants for survival. They use the chemical energy that has been stored by the plants. The contrast between plants and animals is most marked by the features of food relations, energy relations, locomotion, cellular structure, organization, and evolution.

Observing Different Kinds of Living Things

The recreationist who is a specialist either in nature study or in one of the biological sciences must have a working knowledge of the natural resources that are available for use in a nature program.

Plants

An example of a nonvascular plant body displaying no clear distinction of roots, stem, or leaves is *algae*, or thallus plants with chlorophyll. Almost all of these plants live in fresh or salt water, the greatest number being found in the sea. Fresh water forms include minute blue-green algae that form the slime on top of water in ditches and dark films on moist ground. Pond scums and other threadlike algae are found floating in tangled masses near the surface of ponds and lakes. The branched candelabra plants that grow up in the bottom of ponds are also algae. Included in these forms are kelp, sea lettuce, and rockweed.

Fungi are thallus plants without chlorophyll. They include bacteria; various types of mold that attack bread, preserves, and fruits; mildews, which attack the leaves and other parts of seed plants; yeasts, which produce fermentation; and mushrooms and toadstools.

Mosses are small leafy plants found on moist ground, and also on trees, rocks, and fallen logs. Liverworts resemble mosses, but usually appear as a mass of small green leaves lying on the ground. Both of these plants reproduce sexually and asexually. The production of spores makes possible the wide distribution of this plant by wind.

Ferns are commonly found wherever the earth is moist. They have large, much-divided leaves or fronds that develop from an underground stem. By developing a more highly differentiated and independent sporophyte—a plant that reproduces by spores—the ferns have advanced their evolution a step beyond that of the mosses and liverworts towards the seed plants.

By far the greatest part of vegetation on earth consists of *seed plants*, which include all trees, shrubs, and herbs, and the most highly evolved of all plants. These plants reproduce on land through a seed that contains an embryo plant provided with resistant coverings to defend it while awaiting optimal conditions for germination.

The *conifers* are cone-bearing seed plants. Most of them are either trees or shrubs. The cone replaces the flower. The seeds formed on the scales of the cones are not enclosed as they are in flowering plants. Typical conifers are pine, hemlock, and ginkgo.

The true flowering plants have evolved to a point where their adaptation to dry land takes the form of pollination, protection, and dispersal of the seed. Insect pollination is involved in many species. Flowers' bright colors and scent attract insects that carry pollen from flower to flower. This has led to adaptation among specific species of flowers and most particularly to species of insects. Fruits, for example, are adapted to different methods of dispersion. Fleshy fruits provide food for many birds and animals. These, in turn, distribute the seeds. Other fruits, such as those of the dandelion, are adapted to wind distribution. These different adaptations to pollination and seed dispersal illustrate why there is such a variety of flowers and fruits.

Flowering plants are divided into two classes, the *dicots* and *monocots*. The dicot family seed has two seed-leaves, or cotyledons. The plants produced from these are recognized by their net-veined leaves and their flowers, which are never found in threes or multiples of three. Common dicot families are the buttercup, geranium, carnation, primrose, phlox, snapdragon, rose, cactus, maple, parsley, and aster. In monocot embryos the seed has only one leaf or cotyledon. The leaves of these plants are generally parallel-veined and their flowers are found in threes and multiples of three. Common families of the monocot group are the iris, lily, palm, fruit trees, and grasses.

Animals

A much greater differentiation exists in the animal kingdom than in plants. Except for those recreational places situated on or near salt water bodies, most of the animal life that can be observed easily is not found in water. However, any drop of water abounds with microscopic animals. For these reasons the following brief survey of the animal kingdom includes those forms as well as the higher types.

Unicellular animals consist of a single cell whose locomotion is by means of irregular streaming protoplasm, a small number of flagella, or many hair-like projections moving in unison. These animals exist in both fresh and salt water. They also may be observed as parasites in the bodies of other animals. The amoeba and paramecium are examples of this animal form.

There are 3000 species of sponges. These irregularly shaped creatures generally attach themselves to rocks or other objects in fresh or salt water. There are countless small openings on the surface of their bodies that allow water to pass through and be forced out again from one of the larger openings in the upper part of the animal. The common bath sponge is really the skeleton of one of these animals. Small fresh water sponges are found attached to sunken twigs in ponds.

Polyps and jellyfish most frequently occur in the sea. Polyps are cylindrically shaped animals that tend to attach themselves to some object in the water. The hydra is a fresh water variety of the polyp and is found in ponds, often attached to aquatic plants. Other recognizable examples are the sea anemones and corals. Jellyfish float in water and are bell-shaped.

Flatworms come in many varieties. Their bodies are elongated and flattened with one end differentiated into a head. There are four classes of flatworms. Planarians, whose locomotion is produced by undulating cilia, live in both fresh and salt water. Most of them are under 1 inch in length. Parasitic worms with suckers are commonly called flukes. Tapeworms are also parasitic and well known to human beings. They do not have a mouth or alimentary tract as do the flukes. The long-nosed free-living marine worm called the nemertine worm has an extremely flattened body. There are 8000 species of roundworms. They occur in water or on land and live as parasites in a variety of animals.

There are 6000 species of echinoderms. They are rather symmetrical animals with a skeleton composed of calcareous plates and spines. They move by means of sucking disks attached to tube feet. They live only in sea water. Sea urchins, sea cucumbers, starfish, and sea lilies belong to this family.

Mollusks have commonly been called shellfish. They are animals with soft inner bodies generally covered with a calcareous shell. Snails and slugs are examples of this group. They occur in salt and fresh water as well as on land. The cephalopods are marine mollusks with large eyes, a well-developed head, and long prehensile tentacles. The most well-known and common of these are the octopus and squid. Clams, oysters, mussels, and scallops are bivalves (two shells), while abalone is a monovalved creature residing in the ocean.

Segmented worms occur in the sea, in fresh water, and on the land. The most common and easily recognizable is the earthworm. Anglers and others will get to know these creatures after heavy rains or when seeking bait for fishing.

Arthropods account for nearly half of all species of living things. The term simply means joint-legged. The body is segmented like that of an earthworm, but the components are generally combined to form a head, thorax, and abdomen. Among the groupings that make up the arthropods are the crustaceans. These are animals that breathe by means of gills and spend their lives in fresh water or the sea. Examples of this type are barnacles, crabs, lobsters, and shrimp. Centipedes are also part of this group. They breathe by means of air tubes or tracheae and live on land. Millipedes are sometimes confused with centipedes, but are actually different by virtue of a cylindrical body whose segments each bear two pairs of legs. The centipede has a flattened body whose segments each bear one pair of legs.

Insects are arthropods that breathe air through tracheas. The body of the adult is divided into a head, thorax, and abdomen. The head bears one pair of antennae. The thorax bears three pairs of legs and usually two pairs of wings. The more highly developed insects metamorphose in their life cycle from larva or worm form to the winged segmented adult. For this change to occur the animal undergoes a quiescent stage when it forms a cocoon. The characteristics ordinarily used in distinguishing insects are the type of metamorphosis undergone, wings, and mouth parts. Some insects go through life without any metamorphosis. Other insects have a gradual or partial change whereby the young develop into adults without undergoing a quiescent period. Still other insects have a complete metamorphosis, the adult being so modified that its structure and lifestyle are unidentifiable with the larva stage.

Normally an insect has two pairs of wings. Sometimes, however, these are absent, as in the case of the worker ants. Flies have only one pair of wings. Wings may be membranous, parchment-like, form a protective covering, or be completely covered with scales. The mouth may be adapted for piercing, sucking, or chewing, or reduced to uselessness.

There are more species of insects than of any other animal. Grasshoppers, termites, dragonflies, lice, flies, fleas, bees, wasps, ants, moths, and butterflies are well-known insects.

The *arachnids*, or spiderlike animals, have a body that is usually divided into an anterior segment composed of head and thorax, to which legs are attached, and a posterior abdomen. Examples of these are spiders, scorpions, daddy-long-legs, mites, and ticks.

Animals that have a vertebral column and breathe by means of gills or lungs, with their nervous system on the upper or dorsal side of the body, and two pairs of appendages, are called *chordates*. Among the marine creatures of this type are sharks and rays. Although it will be a rare recreational center that is situated near enough to the sea for these creatures to be spotted, they are common enough so that their structure and class should be reported. The aquatic vertebrates that most people will come to know are termed *true fishes*. These creatures breathe by means of gills in a gill chamber, covered by a bony flap opening to the exterior on either side of the back of the head. Fish have two pairs of lateral fins. The true fishes are known for their great variety. Among them are trout, bass, perch, and sunfish.

Amphibians are species that begin life in water and, when fully adult, live in air. The young breathe by means of gills; adults use lungs. Adults have two pairs of five-toed limbs without claws. The body is without scales except in particular tropical forms. Frogs, toads, salamanders, and newts are typical of these creatures and occur in temperate zones. Almost everybody has been exposed to these animals when they hike across fields or investigate swamps, ponds, or bogs.

Reptiles are air breathers all their lives. Their scales are horny and formed from the outer layer of the skin. There are generally two pairs of appendages, snakes being a notorious exception. Examples of these creatures are all snakes, tortoises, and lizards. Except for those recreational places situated in the Deep South, it is not likely that participants will come upon other reptiles such as alligators.

Birds are feathered creatures whose forelimbs have been modified for flying. No birds have teeth, but all have horny beaks. Among the most common of all bird forms that can be observed throughout the year are swifts, hummingbirds, woodpeckers, geese, eagles (only in high country), hawks, and perching birds. The perching birds include more than half the known species of birds. They nearly always live in trees and bushes, and feed on fruits and insects. Examples are crows, jays, wrens, robins, sparrows, swallows, and thrushes.

Mammals nourish their young from breast glands or mammae. They are also characterized by having hair. There are several subclasses of mammals. The most primitive are egg layers. Pouched mammals are the second type. Their young are born in a very immature condition and are nourished and protected while being carried in a pouch on the underside of the mother's body. Typical of these animals is the opossum. Placental animals are the third class; these retain the young inside the mother's body until birth. Nourishment is transmitted by a special organ called the placenta. Among the more familiar placental animals are those that feed on insects, including the mole, shrew, and hedgehog. Other mammals may be classified by eating habits. Bats, another mammal, vary in their eating habits; some are fruit eaters, others are insect eaters, and some are bloodsuckers. Carnivorous animals are those that eat flesh. Among them are the skunk, wolf, dog, fox, bear, and cat. Other mammals that people will come into contact with are those that gnaw—squirrels, beavers, rabbits, mice, and rats.

Life is found in forests, marshes, streams, ponds, rivers, lakes, seas, and on the prairies. Almost everywhere on the surface of the earth and in its waters, plants and animals live out their lives and engage in the constant activity necessary for them to survive. The wide and varied distribution of living things has an order and logic that is quite consistent. Each species is adapted to the specific conditions of its particular environment. The various species of plants and animals inhabiting any environment are intimately associated and form communities. This plant–animal relationship is formed by the specific conditions of the environment, the abundance of organisms on which others feed, and correct amounts of heat, cold, moisture, and light, which allow survival. For example, the plants and animals inhabiting a fresh water pond are associated in a community. The kinds of plants and animals to be found depend on whether the pond will exist during the summer, how much or how little lime is contained in the water, the amount of decomposing matter available, and the amount of oxygen available. Depending upon these interrelated factors, certain species of plants and animals will be abundant. With them, those animals who are dependent upon the plant life will also be found. Just as the cells, tissues, and organs of a plant or animal are organized to form its structure and carry on those functions necessary for the maintenance of life, so the various species of plants and animals of a given environment are brought together to form a community in which each has a place and contributes to the conditions for life sustenance.

Entomology

Insects live everywhere—a few are even found in the seas. Where other forms of life are neither tolerated nor supported, insects can be found. This wide distribution is possible because insects can fly and are highly adaptable. They are tenacious, quick, strong, and aggressive. They can be carried by hosts, air, and water. Their habits and structures are so diverse that no unitary biological adaptation can be applied to them.

Insects are biologically the most successful of all the groups of arthropods. Although they are only one of 50 classes of animals, there are more species of insects than of all the others combined. It has been estimated that between 600,000 and 800,000 species of insects exist.

The influence of insects on other animals is significant. They are humans' primary competitor in the struggle for survival. They eat food that would normally serve people before it can be harvested, lay waste to forests and wood products, carry disease, infest the body, destroy clothing, and can make life unbearable. And yet insects have become so economically necessary and perform so many useful tasks that people would have many problems without them.

Insects that are beneficial to humans either produce valuable matter for use or protect human interests. An example of the first is the honeybee. Up to several thousand tons of honey and hundreds of tons of wax are produced annually by honeybees. As another example, silk manufactured by the silkworm and shellac produced from the wax of lac insects have been highly significant to the clothing and paint industries.

Some insects destroy others that are harmful to people. Ant lions, aphid lions, praying mantises, wasps, lady beetles, and tiger beetles are among the predacious insects that control destructive insects by parasitizing them, eating them, or breeding on them. Many insects perform valuable services through their eating habits—many beetles and flies live on both plant and animal leavings. Fecal matter, cadavers of animals, and other putrefying materials are quickly taken care of by the insects or their young. Many fish, herbs, and some mammals depend on insects for food. These, in turn, contribute food or other products to human beings.

More insects are destructive of people's interests than are helpful, however. Harmful insects include those that eat and destroy fruits and plants, those that annoy and harm domestic animals, those that transmit disease, and those that destroy wood and wood products, paper, cloth, and foods. Among these insects are grasshoppers, chinch bugs, boll weevils, corn borers, lice, mosquitoes, houseflies, fleas, moths, termites, and carpenter ants.

Insects are classified in at least 25 orders on the basis of their metamorphosis, type of mouth parts, and number and type of wings. In some instances other features are useful in classifying them.

The nature specialist in the recreational department should be responsible for providing participants with opportunities to observe and examine many different classifications of insects. The specialists can teach interested persons the basics of entomology. Little or no equipment is needed to collect various specimens for observation.[1] Active colonies may be collected with care and stored in a receptacle that permits interested individuals to watch the insects work, feed, and undertake their daily functions. When well grounded in entomology, the participant has the opportunity to spend fascinating hours studying this vast world that generally goes unseen by humans.

Figure 17.3   Collecting Specimens

Collecting Specimens

The type of equipment used for collecting specimens depends upon when and where explorations will be made. Necessary equipment for daytime terrestrial collecting includes a butterfly net, aspirator, umbrella, sifter and oilcloth, forceps, trowel, pocketknife, and killing jars (**Figure 17.3**).[2]

The Net

Although excellent hunting nets can be purchased, they are too costly and fragile, especially for the novice. A general duty net can easily be constructed. It will provide a sense of satisfaction as a personally made item, and also be less costly than a manufactured net.

The handle can be made from a broomstick that has been cut down to approximately 3 feet, saving the rounded end. On opposite sides of the stick, drill two ¼-inch holes. One hole should be 6½ inches below the sawed end. Grooves extending from the holes to the rough end will prevent the wire hoop from slipping. With a ½-inch diameter wire or a clothes hanger, make a circular shape with a diameter of 12 inches. There should be 6½ inches left at one end of the wire and 7 inches at the other. These loose ends will be used to secure the hoop to the handle. The tips are turned in ½ inch on the ends.

The depth of the net should be 1 foot longer than the diameter of the wire hoop. It should not be longer than the arm of the person who will use it. A fine mesh material such as bobbinet or voile can be used for the netting. Olive green or white are the best colors to use. The width of the net is measured by adding 2 inches to the circumference of the hoop. Lay a 10-inch strip of muslin across the top edge of the net and stitch it so as to present a cross-hatched appearance. Make a U-shaped slot at the outer edge of the net and

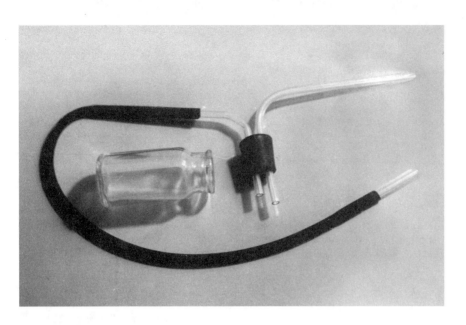

Figure 17.4 The Aspirator

through the two pieces of cloth. Fold the reinforced material in half, lengthwise, with the muslin on the outside. The rough edges must be stitched together. One inch of the unstitched material should be allowed to remain across the folded side so the wire hoop can be fed into the net in this space. The material is then slipped around the hoop. Turn the net inside out and sew the outside seam several times for reinforcement.

Place the hoop with its attached net on the pole. The two turned ends on the hoop should be placed into the two holes in the handle. Electrician's tape is then wrapped around the pole and the wire.

The Aspirator

The aspirator (**Figure 17.4**) uses suction to collect small insects. Tiny insects are easily damaged by the fingers; the aspirator reduces the amount of handling. It also permits the collector to be highly selective in capturing insects. The following materials are used to construct an aspirator:

- A vial 1½ inches in diameter and 5 inches long
- A two-hole rubber stopper that fits into the vial
- Sixteen inches of ¼-inch glass tubing about 6 millimeters in diameter, cut into three pieces, one 3 inches, one 5 inches, and one 8 inches long and curved; all ends should be fire polished
- Six inches of fire tubing

Place the 8-inch curved tube through one of the holes in the stopper so that it extends 1½ inches through the stopper. Place the 5-inch glass tube through the stopper so that three quarters of its length extends beyond the stopper. Attach the rubber tubing to the 3-inch glass tube that will serve as the mouthpiece.

Other Equipment

An old umbrella with a wooden handle is a useful collecting tool. Cut the handle and join the two rough edges by gluing a piece of leather between them. The piece of leather should be long enough to permit the umbrella to swing down when the handle is held horizontally. The umbrella may then be held directly beneath a shrub or branch in order to catch insects that drop off when the branch is vigorously shaken.

A sifter and an oilcloth are excellent pieces of equipment for finding insects in cut hay or leaves. It is a wooden frame with a screen attached to the bottom (**Figure 17.5**). The screen should have eight meshes to the inch. The white oilcloth is spread on the ground to catch insects that fall through the screen.

Forceps are essential in handling insects. Picking up specimens with the fingers may damage them because the legs and antennae, in particular, are very delicate.

Many insects hide under leaves or topsoil. A trowel is used to turn over topsoil. Insects also inhabit decayed trees or rotten logs. A knife is best for finding insects in dead wood.

Any wide-mouthed jar, approximately the size of a peanut butter jar, may be used as a killing instrument. About ½ inch of sawdust should be placed on the bottom of the jar. Cut ⅜ inch of ¼-inch glass tubing and place it upright on the sawdust against the side of the jar. Mix plaster of paris and pour a ¼-inch layer over the sawdust, allowing the glass tubing to protrude at the top. Any of the following may be used as killing agents in this type of jar: chloroform, benzidine, carbon tetrachloride, ethyl acetate. The killing agent is poured into the jar until the sawdust becomes saturated. Too much liquid will wet the plaster and damage any specimen. Excess liquid should be poured off. To recharge the killing jar, open it and place the jar in a warm, dry area. When all the moisture has evaporated put a new supply of killing agent in it.

Baiting is an easy way to attract different insects. A tin can or jar may be used. A large juice can (about 1 quart, 14 ounces) is the best size. Once the top lid has been removed, punch small holes into the bottom of the can to permit rain to run out. Place four stones around the can and a thin board on top of them so that the rain will be kept out. Set the can into a hole large enough for the top of the can to be slightly above ground level. Moss or other material is banked up to the top of the jar.

A baiting can is very good for wet or dry places, but a wide-mouthed glass jar is best for boggy or swampy areas. These traps may be checked every three or four hours. They are most productive during the day, but some specimens can be captured at night. Pieces of fish, meat, or sugar are the best bait, although almost anything can be used. Strong-odor baits attract more insects.

When collecting specimens in water during the day, rakes, seines, strainers, butterfly nets, and a shallow white pan can be used. An iron rake is useful to pull material from the edge of a stream or pond. The mud can then be put into a sifter. Seines are attached to poles that are about 3 feet long. The screen may be of the plastic window-screening type and at least 2 feet wide. The material should be wound around each pole and tacked securely in place. This seine works well in brooks and streams. One participant turns stones and churns up the stream bed. The person with the seine is stationed a short distance downstream. The bottom of the net should be pointed upstream with the handles directed slightly to the rear. In this way the loose debris rides up onto the seine. After enough material has been gathered on the seine, it should be shaken over a white oilcloth placed on shore.

A large kitchen strainer is a good instrument for stream and pond work, although it is helpful to add to the length of the handle. Such insects as water striders and boatmen can easily be caught with this simple tool. A butterfly net with heavy netting may also be useful for aquatic collecting. The shallow white enamel tray is fine for sorting out aquatic insects. Insects can be seen easily against the white background. Forceps are used to pick them up.

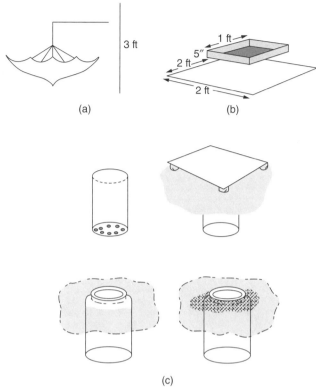

(a) Umbrella catcher, (b) sifter and oilcloth, (c) baiting cans or jars

Figure 17.5   Homemade Collecting Equipment

For collecting specimens at night, lights and sugaring are the best methods. A blue or white light should be suspended from a tree limb or tripod. A white sheet should be placed on the ground under the light. The insects will land or fall on the sheet and can be easily picked up with forceps. The best time to sugar is about one hour before sunset on a warm, cloudy night when there is a very slight breeze blowing. Brush the sugar solution on the tree trunks at chest height. Most of the insects can be collected by flicking them into a killing jar. Some insects will be very active and the net must then be used.

Geology

The study of geology is so broad that only a very brief description of some of its aspects can be presented here. Physical geology is concerned with the processes that deal with the rocks of the earth's crust, their composition and structure, and the forces that have contributed to the shaping of the landscapes visible on the surface of the earth. Among the sciences that contribute to the overall study of geology are mineralogy, the study of minerals; petrology, the study of rocks; geodesy, the study of the earth's size, shape, and other measurements; paleontology, the study of fossil plants and animals; and stratigraphy, the study of the order and sequence of rock layers making up the earth's crust.

The earth is undergoing constant transformation. We live amid the ruins of past worlds. Forces that modify the surface landscape are constantly at work. Some of these changes are extraordinary, sudden, and thrilling, but it is unlikely that most people will be able to witness them. Nevertheless, the recreationist can introduce the subject of these dramatic changes by talking about floods, earthquakes, or volcanic eruptions. He or she can illustrate the discussion by constructing a small pathway from a stream and showing what happens to the surrounding dirt when an artificially caused wave overflows the channel.

All earth movers are not rapid, however. The greatest modifiers take long periods of time. The development of mountain ranges, the creation of a desert, or the cutting of a valley or gorge by glaciers or rivers requires thousands and even millions of years. Recreationists should make participants aware that mountains are being worn down by frost, wind, running water, and gravity; that sea bottoms in some areas are rising; that in some regions the sea is inundating the land; and that the coastlines are being eroded by the constant pounding of the surf against the rocks or sandy beaches of the shore.

The earth on which we walk is really a crust or thin shell. Below this lies the earth's mantle, then an outer core, and finally a molten inner core. The crust is probably not more than 5 miles thick. The mantle, some 1800 miles thick, is a region of intensely heated matter and pressure. The mantle may very well be the reservoir that feeds volcanoes. The temperature at this level is approximately 5000°F. The rocks of the mantle are hard, to support the enormous pressure that weighs down on them. However, the pressure is so great that when there is a disturbance in the mantle the rocks bend, twist, and even flow. This is the region where the most severe earthquakes originate. Beneath the mantle is the outer core. This is composed of liquid iron and probably nickel. It is perhaps 1300 miles thick and the heat is even more intense than in the layers above it. The inner core or heart of the planet is composed of a shrunken bowl of nickel and iron under truly fantastic pressure. It is at the core of the earth that the geophysicists look for answers to questions concerning terrestrial magnetism.

There are three basic types of bedrock that make up the earth's crust—igneous rock, which was once molten; sedimentary rock, formed from crumbled rock materials, the fossils from living organisms, and minerals precipitated from water; and metamorphic rock, which is igneous or sedimentary rock that has been altered as a result of intense pressures, heat, liquids, or gases running through it. Examples of igneous rock are granite and the lava of volcanoes. Shale, sandstone, limestone, and salt are examples of sedimentary rock. Metamorphic rock is seen in marble and gneiss. Fundamentally the crust is composed of igneous rocks overlaid by sedimentary and metamorphic rock. The surfaces of the continents, for example, are mostly sedimentary formations.

The earth is thought of as a rigid, solid, hard object. It may be solid, but it is far from rigid. As gravitational force is exerted upon it by the sun and moon, and as the landscape of the earth changes because of erosive and developmental forces, there are changes in pressure. With these changes occur internal stresses, which are sometimes felt in terms of earth tremors, quakes, and volcanic eruptions.

The very forces that seem most destructive to the earth's surface are also those that assist in the birth and development of new matter. Erosive agents cause deterioration of rocks, and particles are broken off to be carried away and deposited in ever-growing layers. The debris builds up for millions of years and the pressure and heat on sedimentary rocks produce metamorphic rock. Continuous heat and pressure are applied to these rocks and a remelting occurs, which tends to produce igneous rocks. The cycle is never-ending. Sediments, the debris of earth erosion, are washed down into the valleys and sea bottoms. In some places they pile up until the sediments become rock. The process is extremely slow. Of all sedimentary rocks, conglomerate is the coarsest. It is composed of gravel and pebbles that have been stuck together by some mineral, thus becoming cemented. Such rocks are typically found in river beds, beaches, and at the foot of highlands.

Sedimentary rocks that form sandstone actually developed from grains of sand. Sandstones are usually made up of quartz particles. Water-made sandstone generally forms where rapidly flowing water begins to slow down. A few sandstones originated as sand in piles. These piles were buried beneath debris, turned to stone, and uncovered by erosion. Ripples in the rock, caused by wind blowing the sand before it hardened, may be seen clearly. Shales are usually composed of earth and plant matter. They are fine-grained and contain much clay rather than quartz minerals. Lake beds, deltas, and bays are the most likely places for this form of rock to be found.

Another type of sedimentary rock is limestone, which consists of small particles of calcite or calcium carbonate. It is white, gray, or bluish. The harder formations are quarried for building purposes. Some limestone, such as coral reefs, is made up of skeletons of creatures.

As sea bottoms rose to become dry land or mountain ranges, there were tremendous bending, squeezing, stretching, folding, and cracking movements. With the enormous pressures, heat, and other working forces influencing them, a vast array of minerals developed. From prehistoric swamps where giant ferns lived and died, deposits that produced peat, coal, and petroleum developed over millions of years. From sedimentary rocks a variety of beautiful minerals were created. Magnificently colored, shaped, and structured crystals are constantly being produced in consequence of the shifting nature of the earth's surface and inner strata.

Everywhere the recreationist looks he or she can find evidence of erosion and development. He or she should relate these phenomena to the participants in ways that will produce questions and further investigation. Each smooth pebble has a story to tell; the common quartz, often found, may begin a lifelong hobby.

Spelunking

The science of cave exploration, *speleology*, is intimately connected with geology and fascinates those whose interest is aroused by adventure in unique and unfamiliar places. The activity of cave exploration, or spelunking, requires little or no equipment, unless the group expects to remain in the cave for any length of time. In such cases, food and other supplies for warmth and sleeping are required. The adventure begins as soon as the individual enters the passage or opening that will take him or her into the cavern or underground excavation.

Caves exist in nearly every part of the United States, and particularly in those regions that have great limestone deposits. Evidence of subterranean waterways, such as surface sinkholes, are indications that underground caves exist. Thus, Indiana, Kentucky, Tennessee, Virginia, South Dakota, New York, Missouri, Illinois, Arkansas, New Mexico, and other states have small and large caves that have yet to be explored. Some of these areas are honeycombed with subterranean caverns. The Mammoth Cave of Kentucky, for example, is merely one of more than 200 miles of galleries that permit passage. The Howe Caverns of New York, the Luray Caverns of Virginia, and many others offer water-carved grottos, stalactites, and stalagmites of stupendous proportions. Some of these limestone drippings have been named after figures, faces, or scenes that they seem to depict or portray; their colors and formations are unique and wonderful.

The interior of some caves is gigantic. The domes of the largest rise almost 250 feet high and vary in width from 150 to 400 feet. In some of the caves that permit easy walking, a tour can take up to 9 hours. When uncharted caves are accessible, the possibility of weeks of exploration is not exceptional.

Formation of Caves

Caves are formed by groundwater that seeps into cracks and crevices in the limestone. Oxygen and carbon dioxide, accumulated in water from air and plants, help the water to dissolve the mineral calcium carbonate out of the limestone. When the water reaches an underlying rock structure that is not easily eroded, it begins to cut horizontally. Although the process is slow, it does admit water in considerable amounts. Carried by underground streams, material such as sand and gravel cut through the limestone and form the walls of the cave bed. Over a considerable period of time, great caverns are thus excavated. The vaults of caverns sometimes collapse because of the weight of the overhead rock. When the debris of the dome becomes pulverized and is washed away by natural processes, the result is a funnel-shaped cavity that, when it appears at the surface, is called a *sinkhole*. However, when the dome remains intact, a cave is formed.

The same chemical process that hollows out caverns also causes the same spaces to fill up. Above the water table, stalactites and stalagmites can form. *Stalactites* occur as the result of dripping water. The water, which is carrying carbonic acid that eroded the limestone to form the cave initially, continues to drip through crannies. As it falls, drop by drop, it deposits a ring of calcium carbonate around the point from which it drips. As additional mineral matter is deposited layer upon layer, the original ring becomes longer until a tube is formed through which the water maintains a steady flow. The tube hardens in consequence of crystallization and thereafter grows thicker and longer as more mineral is added. It may keep growing for hundreds or thousands of years as the flow of water passes along the tube and other deposits are added on the outside through evaporation.

Stalagmites are formed in almost a reverse process. The water that did not evaporate completely on the ceiling leaves the remains of its lime content at the places where it hits the floor of the cave. Here calcium carbonate builds upward in a series of accretions. In time a stalactite and a stalagmite might meet, forming a pillar. Where the seepage from above flows along some fissure, the dripstone will finally join along this line and make a solid partition. Thus the same chemical action that cut the cave literally reverses itself, and can seal up the excavation by the same process.

Spelunking Methods

Before attempting to explore a discovered cavern it is best to become familiar with the geography of the area. Topographic features should be learned, and streams and water courses should be noted for direction and depth. Most caves will have an entrance through a hillside. Some are located in the high mountains, such as those in the vicinity of Monterey, Mexico.

Recreational groups can take part in spelunking, but it is inadvisable for individuals to attempt cave explorations on their own. Only small groups should undertake a spelunking expedition. More than four people tend to make too much noise and the reverberations may actually cause some confusion. Under any cave exploration conditions, a recreationist should be in charge of the group. The recreationist should be adept at cave exploring and, if possible, be familiar with the particular caves to be explored.

Waterproof flashlights are the most important equipment for spelunking, and should be carried by each member of the party. The recreationist should also have three or four hard candles in his or her pack and a waterproof box of matches. The recreationist should carry a small lantern that can throw light in all directions as a supplement to flashlights that throw a beam in one direction only. All flashlights should have fresh batteries.

Clothing should be of comfortable, close-fitting wool or other warmth-producing materials. All participants and the recreationist should have jackets with many pockets for stowing food supplies, a canteen of water, and other paraphernalia. Headgear is optional, although it is a good idea to wear a hat that can absorb some of the force if an individual inadvertently strikes his or her head on a low edge or overhanging rock. Gloves may be worn to prevent the hands from getting gashed by sharp projections.

When entering a cave that has not previously been explored, it is wise to proceed carefully. Each participant and the recreationist should carry a large ball of white cord that will be unraveled as the exploration progresses. Each participant has a turn at the head of the group and plays out his or her line until it is unwound. The next person then takes his or her place and the procession continues. Either the party will be able to reach the end of the cave or will have to retrace its steps and pick up more cord. Some supply houses carry reels that permit playing out the cord so that it will not tangle. Whenever there is the least doubt of the return route, a cord should be utilized.

The collection of mineral specimens is a valuable part of spelunking. Pure alabaster, shales, parts of stalactites and stalagmites, as well as polished limestone and other minerals can be selected for acquisition. Obviously, collecting should not be marring or destructive of the observed formation or mineral. Any specimens taken should be detritus and not an integral part of a column, wall, or something chipped off. A variety of living things—blind fish, mice, and lizards—may also be collected for investigation later on.

Forestry

Forestry is an attempt to assist nature in making forests as productive as possible for present and future needs. Well-protected forests provide wood, game, furs, and minerals. They help maintain the supply of pure drinking water as well as cleaning the air. Much of our recreational activity depends on forests. Forestry involves a planned economy for the management and utilization of forest lands. Included within these lands are areas for mining, hydroelectric power development, irrigation dams, reservoirs for municipal water supplies, and land for the grazing of sheep and cattle. Propagation and maintenance of wildlife, the preservation of scenic and historic places and vistas, the prevention of erosion, the preservation of a regular and constant flow of water, and recreational development are all aspects of forestry.

Many recreational sites include forests. A variety of trees, each contributing to the splendor of the setting, will attract the interest of potential users. Some will want to study the different trees. Collecting leaf specimens and combining crafts and art by printing leaf designs or producing useful objects from twigs, branches, or other parts of the tree can be interesting aspects for study.

Fundamentally, a tree is a plant with a single woody trunk that does not branch for some space between the ground and the first bifurcation. It is composed of roots, trunk, branches, leaves, flowers, fruit, and seed. Tree roots are either surface or tap, depending upon their shape and penetration. Walnut, hickory, and oak trees are the most notable of the eastern region tap root species; longleaf and ponderosa pine are distinctive in the southern and western sections of the country. Spruce, birch, elm, lodgepole pine, and hemlock are known for surface-root systems. Other trees develop a combination system of surface and tap, depending upon the environment. Roots serve as an anchor for the tree and supply it with nourishment.

The stem of the tree is composed of inner and outer bark, heartwood, sapwood, and pith. The diameter of the tree is increased by the cambium layer; one layer accumulates each year. When the growth of the tree is stunted because of defoliation, drought, or disease, an additional ring may be added, but these rings are much fainter than those of normal growth and are easy to detect. The heartwood is located in the core of the trunk and is composed of inert matter whose primary function is to toughen and solidify the trunk. It is the sapwood that transmits nutrient solutions from the soil to the leaves. If the cambium layer or sapwood were cut into and the sap flow interrupted in any way, the tree would die almost immediately. Maple syrup collection is performed by superficially cutting the sapwood. The sap is then collected in pails and the wound is treated so as to heal the breach.

The leaves are the intricate chemical manufacturing agents of the tree. Thin liquid solutions are carried to the leaves and combined with carbon dioxide to form sugar and starches. The carbon dioxide is divided and combined with water. The extra oxygen and water are exuded, and the process of assimilation occurs in the presence of chlorophyll, which is the energy source for food storage.

A typical broadleaf forest is that in which maple, beech, and oak are most numerous, although hickory, chestnut, poplar, birch, and some conifers or soft woods such as pine and hemlock may also be prevalent. These trees will grow only where climate, soil, and other environmental conditions are suitable. There must be moderate rainfall, between 25 and 60 inches per year. The summer must be moderately warm with an average temperature of approximately 65°F. Trees of this type thrive when the winter temperature falls below freezing. The falling leaves in the deciduous (hardwood) forest are an adaptation of the trees to environmental differences between summer and winter. The broad leaves enable the trees to manufacture starch and carry on their life activities at a maximum rate throughout the summer when there are prolonged periods of sunlight, warm temperatures, and generally plentiful rainfall. During the shorter days of winter, when there is less sunlight and the air is dry and cold, leaves would be disadvantageous to the tree because of the evaporation of moisture through their broad surfaces. For these reasons, leaves are shed and the tree becomes dormant.

Trees, as the dominant plant in any forest, determine in great part what other life forms will survive in the forest community (**Figure 17.6**). Like all green plants, trees compete for sunlight. They are more successful than their competitors because they grow high and spread their branches and leaves to catch sunlight. During the summer they keep the forest in deep shade. Plants requiring much sunlight cannot survive. The leaves that reduce the intensity of sunlight entering the forest also maintain a moist atmosphere. Trees provide protection from wind and rain storms. Their dead leaves, shed bark, and fallen trunks are the source of much of the organic matter in the soil. Trees not only are the largest living organisms in the forest, but also are largely responsible for the existence of all living things in the community that they dominate.

Where the trees of a forest are spread out at greater distances and more sun is able to filter through the leaves, smaller trees and shrubs can grow. Sassafras, wild grape, wild cherry, and papaw, all of which produce food for game and birds, flourish. Trailing over the ground or climbing on nearby bushes may be

Figure 17.6   Trees Make Any Area More Interesting and Enjoyable

bittersweet, its bright scarlet berries aiding the coloring of autumn. Close to the ground may be many small herbaceous plants with soft stems and leaves. These plants grow rapidly during the spring before the trees get their leaves; they have stored up necessary nourishment underground during the winter in fleshy roots, stems, or leaves. These small plants produce most of the spring wildflowers of the forest, including hepatica, wild geranium, and Jack-in-the-pulpit. There are usually a few ferns scattered about, but they are not abundant in this type of forest. Mosses are abundant on fallen trees and stumps.

Beneath the green foliage the ground is carpeted with decaying twigs, leaves, bark, and grass, which gradually break up to form a mealy brownish matter called humus. The decay that leads to the formation of this material is produced by a variety of fungi as well as bacteria. Although the bacteria are invisible, many fungi emit reproductive bodies such as spores. These are the recognizable mushrooms, puffballs, and shelf fungi. These plants, which do not require light, thrive in relative darkness and moisture.

For many of the smaller animals the observer must look under dead leaves, in tree stumps, or under stones. Investigation of these places will reveal a miniature world. Centipedes run for cover, beetle larvae squirm, and millipedes curl up and play possum. If an ant nest is disturbed there is an anguished rush as workers scurry off carrying eggs and larvae. Insects are numerous in any forest. Each type of forest has its leaf-eating insect population. Many kinds of beetles, butterflies, moths, bees, wasps, flies, and mosquitoes are abundant. Where there are small flying insects, spiders construct their filmy webs. By digging under a fallen tree or stump a salamander may be found. These creatures are amphibious and require the moisture of the forest floor. They feed on insects.

As the order of life becomes more complex, there is an increasing dependence upon less highly organized creatures for survival. Trees initially produce the environment that permits other plants to grow. These, in turn, produce nutrients for small animals. Dead animals become part of the food chain of insects who, in their turn, supply food for larger predators and carnivores. Birds and mammals of every type are indebted to trees for their existence. By observing these phenomena, the nature program participant will understand the intimate and intricate connections between trees and all other forest life.

Hydrology

The study of water resources and the cyclical movement of water from sea to land and back to the sea is an interesting natural phenomenon of which nature lovers should become aware. Water directly and indirectly influences the daily life of all human beings in countless ways. In fact, most animated things are composed of large amounts of water. The sea was the origin of life. Humans carry this water inheritance in the saline character of the body's fluids. Human cells require constant bathing in what probably could be regarded as a sea water solution—blood.

Water is peculiar in its physical appearance. Although it is important in the gaseous state as part of the atmosphere, it is chiefly present on earth as a liquid. This is partially in consequence of the high temperature it requires for vaporization, which is uniquely higher than for most liquids with correspondingly simple molecules. Water's solid state, ice, is lighter than the liquid state.

For this reason, all water areas freeze from the top down. Almost no other substance has this characteristic. This property of water is indispensable to aquatic life. The part that water plays in the atmosphere and in bodies of water as a temperature control does not require further amplification here.

The water resources of the earth's surface can be divided into two categories—salt water, found in the oceans, and fresh water, a land resource. Even though human beings make greater use of the water found on the continents, salt and fresh water are not completely separable. All water will be salt water at one time or another. Through the action of solar energy and gravity, the water supply of the earth moves ceaselessly in a cycle from sea to land and back to the sea. Water is carried through the atmosphere, having been evaporated from the ocean's surface, over the land mass of the continents, where it is released by condensation and precipitation. Water loses the salt content in the process of evaporation and returns to a liquid from the gaseous state during condensation, so it is in its most desirable and utilitarian form insofar as human beings are concerned. This endless movement has neither beginning nor end; it is a complete cycle termed the *hydrologic cycle*. The water cycle plays an important part in terms of weather and annual rainfall in different regions of the world, and influences the type of food supply and living organisms that available fresh water maintains. An understanding of water resources and the water cycle is useful in studying the conservation problems and meteorological factors that affect all life.

Meteorology

Meteorology, the study of weather, can be a significant recreational activity. The best procedure for developing interest in meteorology is to encourage participants to study, observe, and perhaps even make predictions about the weather. As Mark Twain is supposed to have said, "Everybody talks about the weather, but nobody does anything about it." To a certain extent that is true today. We can record weather conditions, extrapolate from previous records and observations, and predict the weather relatively accurately for from 1 to 7 days in advance, but we still cannot change it or really do anything about it.

Human beings have been observing conditions that seemed to predict variations in the weather for centuries. Many old sayings about weather appear to have a reasonable basis in fact and survive to this day. Consider, for example, the saying, "Red sky at morning, farmer take warning; red sky at night, farmer's delight." In the morning, with the sun in the east, redness is seen in the west, and showers generally originate in the west. At dusk, when the sun is in the west, redness in the east means that any inclement weather has already passed. This is typical in middle latitudes where weather flows from west to east. Another saying tells us "Rain before seven, shine by eleven." In many instances where rain falls in the night and early morning hours, the weather usually clears before noon as the sun warms up the atmosphere, evaporating the clouds. "If you can see the painter's brush, the winds around you soon will rush." The painter's brush refers to the high thin cirrus clouds that usually mean foul weather is on the way.

Air Pressure

Human beings can be viewed as creatures that live at the bottom of a vast ocean of air. Held in place by gravitational pull, the atmosphere surrounds the earth to a height of between 300 and 700 miles. Without the atmosphere, there would be no life; there also would be no sound. The atmosphere is a protective envelope that shields the earth from the direct rays of the sun and keeps it from freezing when the sun sets.

The first and lowest layer of atmosphere is called the *troposphere*, where all of the earth's weather is initiated. This ocean of air is in constant motion. Many forces acting upon it cause prevailing winds, which blow steadily night and day, and tornadoes, which appear and disappear very quickly. The sun is one of the sources of energy that keeps the atmosphere in constant motion. The sun's rays heat the atmosphere and cause the gases in it to rise. When the gases have expanded enough they begin to cool and flow downward again. Because most of the circulatory flow happens at the equator, the motion is pushed north and south to the polar regions. Because the earth is also spinning at the rate of 16 miles per minute, the flow of air is not a straight circle between the equator and the poles. Instead, the earth deflects the flowing mass of air so that it flows at angles to the poles. To illustrate air pressure to youngsters, place a book on end on a flattened paper bag. Introducing air into the bag will upset the book.

The earth is slightly tilted on its axis. Because of this we have seasons. During the winter the sun's rays strike the earth obliquely because this part of the globe is tilted away from the sun. The northern hemisphere receives cold weather accompanied by snow. During the summer the sun's rays strike the same surface at a more nearly straight line, hence this region has warm or hot weather. One of the factors that determines how hot it gets in summer and how cold in winter is the distance one lives from the sea. The sea is always warmer or cooler than the land. This accounts for mild winter climate along the sea coast as compared to that of an inland region at the same latitude.

Cloud Formation

Riding on the moving air mass is water vapor. Because of the hydrologic cycle, water is constantly being transmitted through the air. Air temperature, water vapor, and billions of particles of dust form fog; air that is heavily laden with moisture is ideal for producing fog. As the air cools it is forced to emit some of its water vapor, which condenses on the countless dust particles suspended in the air. Around each speck of dust hangs a droplet of water. These droplets add up to form fog, and they remain in that state until the air warms sufficiently and the water is transformed to vapor. Clouds are simply high fog. In other cases, when the water vapor is cold enough, a cloud of ice crystals is formed. Clouds are formed in a variety of shapes and sizes. There is common agreement among meteorologists as to the names of particular clouds. Rainy, hot, or cold weather can be predicted with reasonable certainty when clouds are properly analyzed and interpreted in relation to other weather phenomena.

At least once during the summer, and probably more than once, there will be a thunderstorm. The most reliable warning of these storms is the majestic thunderhead cloud, or cumulonimbus. The afternoon may be clear and hot, but a storm is in the offing. The heat that has collected from the sun's rays causes the moist hot air to rise. When the air reaches cooling heights, water vapor in the air condenses and a cloud is formed. If the rising moist air currents are strong enough, the air will continue to push higher to cirrus levels, where the water vapor is transformed into ice crystals. As the cloud develops, water vapor condenses into rain and the storm begins. Lightning flashes and thunder booms. The sharp updrafts, downdrafts, and crosscurrents within a cloud cause the cloud's particles to rub against each other with such activity that electrical charges are set up. If a negatively charged cloud passes over positively charged ground, the cloud releases a bolt of electrons that strike as lightning. Lightning can strike from ground to cloud, from cloud to ground, and within a single cloud. Thunder comes directly after a lightning bolt and is created by rapidly heated air that expands at a great rate as lightning streaks through it. The distant rumbling is caused by the thunder's sound waves bouncing back and forth within clouds, or between mountains if they are in the vicinity.

Easy Meteorological Craft Activities

A small weather station can be constructed for the further interest of recreational participants. The weather station should consist of a wind vane, an anemometer for wind speed, a thermometer and shelter, an aneroid barometer, a mercurial barometer, wet- and dry-bulb thermometers or a hydrometer for humidity, and a rain gauge. The aneroid barometer and thermometer should be purchased because they are difficult to construct. All other instruments may be made by participants with the guidance of the recreationist.

Constructing instruments for meteorological observation is relatively easy. Few items are needed and most instruments can be built in the recreational crafts shop. To make a hydrometer, which determines the amount of relative humidity in the air, you will need two thermometers, a piece of gauze, and a saucer. Mount the thermometers side by side. Wrap the bulb of one in several layers of gauze extending below the thermometer. Fill the saucer with water at room temperature and suspend the wet-bulb thermometer over the saucer so that about 1 inch of gauze is in the water. The water should move up the gauze wick and keep the thermometer bulb moist. After several minutes, read the wet- and dry-bulb thermometers and determine the relative humidity. The amount of moisture in the air is compared with the maximum amount that the air could contain at the same temperature. The difference between the wet- and dry-bulb thermometers gives the relative humidity.

To make a simple barometer, use a test tube, a one-hole stopper, a curved length of glass tubing 10 to 14 inches long, and some water with iodine or methylate. Fill the test tube three quarters full of liquid and insert the stopper with the tube extending about 1 inch into the test tube. Invert and then mount the device. The level of the liquid in the glass tube will rise and fall as air pressure rises and falls (**Figure 17.7**).

If a discussion of lightning was initiated, an interesting and simple piece of construction to show electromagnetism may be devised by using a relatively long nail, a standard flashlight battery, a length of copper wire, and several paper clips. Take a 2-foot length of solid copper wire (not braided) and strip about half an inch of insulation off each end. Wind around a long nail until about 4 inches of wire is free at both ends. Tape one end of the wire to the end of an alkaline C battery marked with a minus sign (or negative). Touch the opposite end with the other end of the wire. A magnet has been made.

Figure 17.7 A Simple Barometer

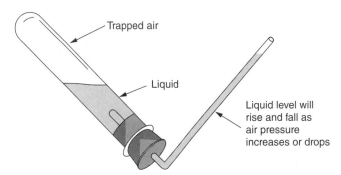

Test the magnet using metal paper clips. Take the wire off the battery. If the nail is made of iron, the paper clips will fall off. If the nail is made of steel it will be magnetized for a while.

Mineralogy

The study of minerals can be initiated at almost any recreational center. Wherever there is an excavation, cut, or eroded area, there will be ample opportunity to discover rocks of all types, sizes, shapes, hardness, and colors. *Minerals* are what rocks are made of; they are substances formed by natural processes out of basic elements such as iron, copper, sulphur, lead, and carbon. Some rock is composed almost entirely of one kind of mineral; sandstone, for example, consists mostly of quartz. Other rocks, such as gneiss, may contain minerals in varying proportions.

Minerals have several characteristics. They are found in every color of the spectrum. One mineral may appear in different places with different colors. Quartz is a good example. The various colors of quartz are derived from other elements in it. Thus, rose quartz gets its hue from the small percentage of iron oxide contained in it. Each mineral has a specific way of fracturing and splitting. Some split into flat sheets, as does mica. Calcite, on the other hand, divides into blocks. Flint breaks like glass, leaving a curved surface. Light reflection of minerals is another characteristic. Gemstones, for example, are known for their luster. Relative hardness is another feature. Heaviness indicates certain properties of the elements involved in the mineral.

The camp, park, or almost any outdoor setting is ideal for the identification and collection of mineral specimens. Walks and hikes can be even more stimulating than usual if participants can recognize rocks and minerals. Collecting samples and cutting and polishing them is an exhilarating experience. The most common rock forms—granite, basalt, and shale—are easy to recognize. Some minerals can be rapidly identified as well. Specimens can be looked for wherever bedrocks are exposed. Steep hillsides, excavations of any kind, stream beds, beaches, glacial moraines, and subterranean areas such as caves are likely places to find good samples. Some minerals will be very difficult to identify; even experts in laboratories may be hard pressed to recognize them without conducting some tests. But a pocket guidebook to rocks and minerals can assist anyone to learn the identity of many specimens.

Any collecting trip should involve particular objectives. The area to be visited should be studied in advance to learn how the land lies and what rocks and minerals might be found there. Sufficient time must be allowed for any fruitful effort to be made. Work should be systematically performed. Too much coverage or expended energy can be disappointing.

Equipment needs are few and simple. A knapsack for packing the collected samples, a few sheets of newspaper for wrapping specimens, and a notebook and pencil are all that are necessary when the material has already been broken. If the terrain features strata that have been sharply folded or invaded by magma, then other tools will be needed. The geologist's pick or mason's hammer is vital along with a cold chisel, a magnifying glass, heavy gloves, and a small knife. Each person should collect only what he or she can carry with reasonable comfort. There is always another day.

Specimens should be carefully selected. Very few should be kept from the many that are found. Although hand-sized samples are adequate, some collectors prefer small specimens that can be studied under a low-power microscope. Specimens should be wrapped in newspaper for safekeeping. To prevent scratching and chipping, the specimens should be laid on the newspaper and the sheet folded over. This process should be repeated until there are at least four thicknesses of paper covering the specimen.

Mineral specimen collecting can lead to other activities, including the collection of gemstones. Lapidary work with semiprecious stones can become a fascinating hobby. The cutting, polishing, and mounting of minerals can prove to be one of the more interesting aspects of specimen collecting.

Ornithology

So vast is the subject of zoology, the science dealing with all animals, that it is impossible to do justice to the field in a brief summary. The structures, functions, ecology, life habits, classifications, and all the laws and facts that pertain to animal life simply cannot be recounted here, nor should they be. Zoology leans heavily on other sciences. One of these is botany, since the relation between plant and animal life is so intricate. The physical sciences of physics, chemistry, and geology are vital if an understanding of zoology is to be gained. However, only ornithology will be touched upon at this point.

Birds represent one of the most interesting and widely recognized groups of all animals. They are distributed throughout the world. Both urban and rural dwellers come into contact with them. Most of these creatures are taken for granted, yet their identification and habits can prove to be endlessly interesting as a subject for observation and study. Countless bird watchers can attest to this fact.

Birds' unique method of movement, flying, which has caused humans to try to imitate them from early historical times, allows them worldwide distribution. There are more than 15,000 species of birds in the world, and their classification has been thoroughly worked out. Because birds appeal to amateur students, the study of birds can be a stimulating part of any recreational program. The habits, ecological relations, songs, and characteristics for bird identification make tireless enthusiasts of those who appreciate this animal form.

Although birds are gifted more than most animals in the ease and speed by which they can move from one habitat to another, many of them are restricted to particular areas. It is common for one species to be found in a special valley or on an island and nowhere else. Within climatic zones, many birds have adapted themselves to peculiar conditions and do not leave them.

Birds are among the most highly developed orders of the animal kingdom along with mammals. It is only in the development of the nervous system that mammals give evidence of a higher progress. In most body parts, birds have a decidedly greater specialization due to their adaptation for flight. They are an extremely active form, which corresponds to a higher metabolic rate and body temperature. The body is usually spindle-shaped with four divisions: head, neck, trunk, and tail. The neck is unusually long to afford balancing and other related activities. The limbs are paired, with the forelimbs adapted for flying. The other two limbs are variously adapted for perching, walking, or swimming. Fertilization is internal, producing eggs with the yolk surrounded by albumin enclosed within a hard calcareous shell. The incubation period is external, and the young are helpless and naked. Birds are the only animals with feathers, which provide insulation, support, protection, and body-heat regulation.

Perhaps no group of animals has more beautiful, striking, and varied coloration than do birds. Although tropical birds have plumage that is unique and magnificent, many temperate zone birds are equally famous for their brilliant colors. The colors are partially due to pigments and to interference colors produced by the reflection and refraction of light. Thus, under some conditions, bird colors will appear to vary.

Birds sing because air passes through the syrinx. This vocal organ has a membrane that vibrates to produce sound. In some species the range of sound is phenomenal. In others sound is rather restricted. Birds also produce characteristic calls when they are frightened, to attract mates, to call their young, or for other purposes. Some birds are voiceless, whereas others have a special talent for mimicry.

Birds are extremely active and require large amounts of food. Their metabolic and body temperatures are the highest of all animals. The food habits of birds vary among species. Some birds are strictly vegetarian; others are omnivorous. Some birds, such as the hummingbird, which lives on a diet of nectar from flowers, and the kingfisher, whose eating habits are restricted to fish, are totally dependent upon these items for food. The American crow, on the other hand, has an enormous range of diet.

Birds may be identified by their speeds of flight, territories in which they live, care of the young, mating habits, wings, feet, bills, migrations, behavior, and intelligence. There are about 27 bird orders with which they may be identified. Recreational participants interested in ornithology can use an illustrated pocket guidebook to help them identify the birds they see.

Summary

In order to take advantage of the present interest in the natural world, recreational agencies should program nature science activities. This requires leadership with specialization in the biological, botanical, zoological, meteorological, and other associated sciences. It is possible that some recreationists may have the prerequisite background for fulfilling this role, but if not, volunteers and/or paid instructors who can guide, counsel, and direct learners in appropriate directions must be recruited.

Participants can learn about the habitats of fauna and lower orders, about astronomy and the lore/mythology that tries to explain the constellations, the geology and geography of the continents and oceans, and other common knowledge of the world in which humans live.

Organized field trips for all age groups can be arranged and scheduled so that those whose interest is aroused by this activity can participate. Well-distributed recreational centers throughout the community can have natural science exhibits drawn from the collected specimens along with pictures of previous and present participants. Mobile units may traverse neighborhoods with biology, botany, geology, and other displays as well as a traveling telescope for astronomical observations. All of these experiences are designed to attract potential participants and awaken their personal wonder and enjoyment of natural science. In short, this is a recreational opportunity that cannot be overlooked.

References

1. Stokes, D. W. *A Guide to Observing Insect Lives.* Boston: Little, Brown, 1983.
2. Klots, A. B. *A Field Guild to the Butterflies.* Boston: Houghton Mifflin, 1951: 1–15.

Selected Further References

"Dethroning Coal." *The New Republic.* September 24, 2007: 2.

Espinoza, M. "Preserving Adirondack Land Where Emerson Camped." *New York Times.* September 19, 2008: B5.

Fairfield Minuteman. (August 16, 2007), In other Words, "Keeping the Beach Clean," Also in *New York Times.* August 26, 2007: 15.

Greenfield, B. "Land of the Giants." *New York Times.* September 19, 2008: F1, F8.

Hirshey, G. "Making Peace with the Woodpeckers." *New York Times.* August 17, 2008: 1–2.

New York Times. "Seeking Relief Where the Air Is Deemed Dirtiest." August 12, 2007: 17.

Nordhaus, T., and M. Shellenberger. "Second Life." *The New Republic.* September 24, 2007: 30–33.

Rosenthal, E. "In Italy, a Redesign of Nature to Clean It." *New York Times.* September 22, 2008: A5.

Slater, D. "Public Corporations Shall Take Us Seriously." *New York Times Magazine.* August 12, 2007: 24–27.

CHAPTER

18

Nature Exploration and Trips

The recreational program that is facility-bound serves only a limited purpose. Innumerable activities can be undertaken indoors, but the well-balanced and comprehensive program that will attract and maintain its hold on potential participants needs to provide more than in-house experiences. In order to offset the routine program typically found within the recreational center, recreationists must offer opportunities for new and exciting experiences outside of the facility or center.

Trips

The trip takes advantage of the skills and knowledge of more mature interested participants, gives them individual responsibility for maintaining themselves, and provides an experienced guide to assist with the day-to-day needs of food, clothing, and shelter. Any trip can be an ideal occasion for getting out of the facility and seeing what nature has to offer. Urban locations may have in-city parks, zoos, reservations, and heavily wooded areas. These may be the objectives for an initial trip before embarking on extended activities away from the center. Picnics or outings to the local park or a nearby beach or lake can introduce youngsters to the natural environment. Of course, recreational agencies that are fortunate to be situated in well-forested and appropriate outdoor settings may well look to the trip technique as a means by which the program and the outdoor environment may be vastly improved. In other words, the trip can give participants something new to anticipate, and with increased endurance and skill the possibility for getting out into remote wilderness regions, for observing the country first hand, and for the use of physical and mental skills.

Trip Planning

Trip planning requires the same diligence and coordination as all other scheduled recreational activities. Perhaps even more effective planning is necessary because participants will be away from the center and possibly exposed to hazards that could be more easily controlled indoors. Planning for trips begins as soon as the recreationist determines whether potential participants are interested in taking a trip. To generate interest requires exposing those to be involved to information concerning the nature of taking a trip, the likely activities that will be encountered, and the necessity for acquiring skills that will enhance the experience. Preparation can require participants to acquire fundamental skills in woodcrafts, camp crafts, swimming, canoeing, hiking, and, in some cases, horseback riding. The recreationist in charge of the trips program must take care that each trip is made with the safety of the participants as the highest priority, without reducing the potential risks inherent in the activity.

Although there are unlimited possibilities for taking trips to remote and primitive areas, most recreational agencies will prefer to plan their trips so that participants stop at established campgrounds on privately owned property or at state and national parks and forests. In such cases, a well-coordinated plan is mandatory. A great deal of detailed scheduling is necessary, including matters of food supply, method of travel (hiking, bicycling, horseback riding, canoeing, or by bus), protective gear (tents, foul weather clothing, sleeping bags), and utensils.

Conduct on Trips

The behavior of participants and any adults accompanying the group on any excursion is extremely important. Habits and attitudes towards the treatment of private and public property must conform to the highest possible standard. Those involved must be thoroughly indoctrinated with the idea that the proper respect for the rights and property of others is one of the most significant features of traveling. The good name of the recreational agency, as well as the reputation of the individuals participating, may necessitate absolute adherence to appropriate roles of conduct. All travelers should recognize the value of courtesy. When followed, outdoor manners will provide the greatest good to all participants without infringing upon their right to learn and without keeping them from enjoying their trip. The minimal rules and regulations that should be a part of the standard conduct of all travelers are:

1. Observe, collect, and learn about, but do not maliciously hurt, damage, or destroy wildlife or property.
2. Always observe the common rules of courtesy toward all persons met on the trail, in communities, or at campsites.
3. Always clean up the site in which the group bivouacked. Make sure that litter has been placed in proper containers.
4. Every precaution must be taken to eliminate waste and destruction of wildlife by fire. All fire making will be confined to proper areas. Safeguards will be taken to prevent fire damage by constructing fires only when needed, and making sure that they are extinguished.
5. Any and all trail signs and markers should be left intact.
6. In wilderness or primitive areas, do not strike out across unknown country. Do not become separated from the party.
7. Always have an emergency kit. This should include a compass, a waterproof box of matches, rations, and one sharp tool.
8. Never cut across a field or take any produce unless permission has been granted.
9. The directions of recreationists should be followed explicitly.

Safety Precautions

Recreationists with long experience programming out-of-facility trips realize that every safety precaution must be taken to prevent danger to participants.

Leadership is the most essential factor in reducing hazards, eliminating extraordinary risks, and providing the kind of guidance that most people require when they are taken out of a highly structured recreational program. The following safety policies apply to traveling and other out-of-center excursions:

1. Small groups are more appropriate than large ones for extended excursions, particularly orienteering, cross-country horseback riding, and canoe trips. If possible, the ratio (depending upon the maturity of the participants) should be no more than five individuals to each recreationist. On hikes, groups may be divided, but each group should be led by a recreationist.

2. Whenever groups or units leave the center on a scheduled hiking activity, one recreationist should head up the column while an assistant brings up the rear.

3. Those going on trips should be divided according to age, ability, endurance, and maturity. The individual's height may have nothing to do with his or her hiking capability, although it seems reasonable to group shorter individuals together and taller individuals together so that each group can keep its own pace. If such groupings cannot be devised, shorter individuals should be assigned to the front of the hiking group.

4. Rest stops for relaxation and recuperation should be as frequent as the participants require. No forced marches are necessary. The welfare of the individual is more important than covering any predetermined stretch of ground.

5. When walking along a highway, always walk in single file on the left side of the road facing traffic.

6. If any hiking is performed during the twilight hours, white clothing should be worn, and lights should be carried.

7. All participants should be accounted for at all times. It must be a rule that each person, when walking through brush on the trail, must be able to see the person ahead. Each hiker will hold any low overhead branches aside and not let them snap back into the face of the person following.

8. Never drink from any water source unless there is a sign indicating that it is a publicly approved water supply. Emergency kits and canteens of water should always be carried by each participant on any trip, route march, or overnight excursion.

9. In unfamiliar territory, make sure that the group arrives at its overnight site long before dark. The participants then will be able to complete whatever preparations are necessary for making their bivouac comfortable.

10. If the hike does not include an overnight stay, make sure that the return to the center begins early enough so that the hikers will reach the facility in good time.

11. Every person who participates in an out-of-center excursion must be capable of looking after him- or herself in an emergency. Even the youngest participants should be prepared to assume some responsibility for themselves. This can be assured if pre-trip instructions are given and proper training is offered.

Excursions

Excursions are travels undertaken to discover something new. The prospect of seeing new places for the first time, discovering phenomena one has heard about, and actually being a part of nature by living in it is a tremendously exciting one. The opportunity to combine the investigation of unfamiliar places with all of the preparation needed to be on one's own for a day or more is so compelling and attractive to most individuals that it becomes a project for developing the most ideal experiences possible. A variety of excursions, both within the facility's neighborhood and far beyond it, can be planned and carried out for the instruction and enjoyment of individuals of all ages. A variety of field trips can be taken to introduce the participant to natural areas in preparation for explorations and travel of increasingly longer duration. In some situations, where participants are older adolescents, a week to 2 months may be devoted to out-of-center travel to wilderness areas where primitive or pioneer camps are set up for living. The lure of the unusual maintains interest.

Some excursions can be accomplished by hiking or by bicycle, and not a few will require traveling by bus or train. In any event, most people have the desire to explore. It is extremely important that recreationists take advantage of this desire and adapt it to a directed learning situation. Active participants are quite interested in further investigation of the historical background, legends, and social meanings of specific land areas. If the recreational center is situated near an area of local, state, or national historical interest, or has such a place to which it can schedule visits, hikes and excursions can be made to these places for the pleasure and satisfaction derived from being in a location where history was made. Along the eastern seaboard, many Revolutionary War sites may be found. Additionally, the original 13 colonies may offer compelling attractions concerning the development of the United States. Every region and state in the United States has its own unique exploratory possibilities. Recreational agencies need to take advantage of them.

On such an exploratory trip, participants may learn research methods, discover new ideas, and develop a healthy and lifelong interest in subjects to which they may never before have been exposed. Exploratory trips may offer opportunities for the study of land use, biology, archeology, and many interrelated subjects enjoyable in their own right.

The recreational department should make good use of any unusual terrain or topological features, particularly if such areas have been examined by competent recreationists with an eye for offering the greatest degree of information and enjoyment. If the agency is situated in an area where there are nearby wetlands, a field trip can be organized to investigate them. Any exploratory trip to a swamp, bog, marsh, or other wetland is valuable for all concerned. Marshy ground invariably produces a phenomenon called a quaking bog. It is a unique experience to realize that one is walking out over water on a closely interwoven mat of sphagnum moss and swamp grasses. All of the plants observed in the vicinity are also living over the water. This can be shown by having the group jump up and down in unison. Trees, shrubs, and bushes will be seen to shake almost 20 yards away. Wildlife, plants, and a variety of specimens can be collected and classified, and the ecological significance of each, in terms of their relationship to the habitat, can be discussed endlessly. Such an experience can provide a full day of real and lasting value to the participants. It provides an appreciation of living things in relation to one another, and it introduces significant concepts of conservation practices so difficult to attain later in life.

Hiking

The necessity of knowing how to walk while on exploratory hikes through woods and fields or along trails seems to be taken for granted. And yet walking, like other motor skills, requires some adaptation to the terrain features through which the individual is moving. The hiker does not have smooth sidewalks to travel over. He or she must have his or her weight evenly distributed along the entire foot, rather than at the heel and then at the toe as does the city pedestrian. The hiker needs to keep his or her toes and therefore his or her foot pointed straight ahead or slightly inward. He or she does this to minimize the likelihood of tripping over small projections in the underbrush or on the trail. The hiker must learn to walk with a slight spring to his or her step. This means that his or her knees flex at each step. The hiker's stride is probably longer than that of an urban dweller, and there is a slight roll to his or her gait. Instead of a high knee-pumping action, the hiker must learn to swing his or her legs an inch or more to the stepping side. His or her feet are placed almost flat with each stride. Thus, the center of gravity is not on the front or back of the foot, but over the entire foot, meaning there is little chance of a twisted ankle or the loss of balance when walking uphill or downhill carrying a pack.

Foot Care

Nothing is more important to the hiker's comfort than having his or her feet in good condition to walk. Although it may not be necessary to toughen the feet, as do mile walkers or soldiers, the participant should be aware that any hiking requires that his or her feet be able to withstand the stress of a great deal of pressure. Good foot care begins with proper equipment. Heavy wool socks, preferably cashmere, should be worn for extensive hikes. Stout walking shoes with cut down tops are better than high laced boots. The socks will allow free circulation of air around the feet and will prevent saturation by perspiration. High laced boots do not permit ventilation of the feet.

Recreationists responsible for the hiking party should see that participants do whatever is necessary to prepare themselves for long walks. Before starting on the hike participants should rub talcum powder over their feet and dust some inside their shoes. Powder should be used freely over those parts of the body most likely to become chafed as a result of long walks. Feet should be kept clean and dry. Toenails should not be permitted to grow too long.

Blisters will usually form on any skin that is constantly rubbed. The heat developed as a result of friction between the outer layer of the skin and any material that it comes in contact with causes the rubbed spot to become raised with fluid, separating the outer skin or epidermis from the true skin or dermis. The dermis is quite sensitive and easily infected; therefore it should be kept covered by the blister until the fluid is absorbed, or at least as long as that can be managed. To maintain the blister, it should be covered with some kind of softening agent (such as petroleum jelly) and a gauze bandage. If the blister must be opened, it should be perforated with the idea of keeping the area as sterilized as possible. A lancet or needle must be sterilized. The point of the instrument should then be inserted at the margin of the blister and the fluid gently pressed out. Thereafter, it should be kept covered and dry. If the blister is broken before treatment is available, the edges should be trimmed with sterile scissors, and the area treated as a wound.

Building Endurance

Recreationists who regularly hike must remember that although they may be accustomed to a steady pace and experience no fatigue on a short walking trip, inexperienced walkers will find hiking difficult and quite tiring, even over relatively short distances. Walking is certainly not enjoyable if the consequences of it are fatigue, sore feet, muscle cramps, thirst, and frustration. Recreationists should accustom those who want to participate in the rigors of hiking by scheduling nature walks, field walks to nearby places of interest, moderately long walks to historic sites, and finally a full-fledged overnight hike to an area within a few miles of the recreational center. The gradually lengthened walks will build the needed stamina, skill, and degree of tolerance necessary for the participant to feel confident and comfortable on a hike. The recreationist should attempt to lighten the idea of physical effort by suggesting a variety of games, songs, and tactical stops for rest and relaxation. Although it is true that a hike can be organized to cover a particular distance in a given time, there is no reason why hikes cannot take advantage of the scenery and terrain being traversed, stopping for interesting features as they are found and taking time out for recuperation before continuing. The recreationist must know the limitations of his or her charges. He or she should be completely aware of their capacity to endure and sustain a steady pace and when they will require rest stops. Unless the idea of the hike is to develop endurance or is a part of a competitive exercise for speed and distance, there is no valid reason for pressing participants to do more than they are capable of doing. The fun of the hike comes not only in the walk, but in what is seen and done while walking.

Backpacking

Some hikes are planned for one or more nights to be spent outside of the recreational facility. These forays demand sound planning, adequate preparation, previous practice on the participant's part to develop endurance, the acquisition of certain skills, and a compact, fully equipped rig in which comfortable clothing, sleeping gear, foul weather protection, and basic tools are carried. Packs must be kept as light as possible and still provide whatever supplies are necessary for comfort and protection while living outside. Backpacking must be enjoyable. Participants should not be subjected to experiences that become frustrating because of poor equipment.

The best pack should be strong and long wearing, spacious enough to handle all required supplies and equipment, and easy to put on and take off. It should ride lightly on the lower portion of the back. Perhaps the best pack is made of waterproof canvas with a central pocket, small back pockets, and two smaller side pockets. Flaps are provided to close over objects placed inside; the flaps have buckles or snaps that may be closed for security. Loops are also provided for strapping or attaching other articles that cannot be accommodated in the pack pockets. A light metal frame is attached to the sack; leather shoulder straps are slung on the frame. A web of elasticized cloth is stretched across the bottom part of the sack and rests against the lower back or top of the hips.

The pack should be fixed to the participant's body so that it rests below his or her shoulder blades and on his or her hips. This will prevent a feeling of top heaviness by lowering the center of gravity. Instability will be lessened and the individual will be able to walk with greater ease and comfort. Because the harness actually flares out and away from the back, good air circulation is assured. This does away with overheating and chafing. The load comes directly down on top of the shoulders and does not pull the walker backward, thus preventing any back strain.

Overnight Hikes

The overnight hike is intended to offer the participant a chance to show his or her mettle. It involves the use of skills, knowledge of walking, and cooperation among peers, and requires that the participant, once he or she has begun a trip, follow through and complete the job. Each participant has to accept responsibility for a share of the work to be performed. Youngsters will probably not be taken on overnights because they do not have the necessary skills in camp crafts or the necessary stamina. But they can participate in a modified overnight hike if they indicate a desire and willingness to perform cooperatively with their companions. For a modified overnight hike, supplies can be trucked to the campsite (so youngsters do not have to carry them), or the youngsters themselves may be transported to and from the site to eliminate excessive walking.

The overnight hike can be planned for those individuals who have the necessary interest, skills, and capacity. The significance of an overnight hike as a method of promoting self-sufficiency cannot be overlooked. The participants, with the recreationist's assistance, arrange for their food, and plan for shelter, sleeping gear, and adequate clothing. Recreationists must be prepared for the work that such a hike entails. Being aware of the importance that the participant attaches to his or her first trip away from home or recreational center, the recreationist will extend him- or herself to make it a truly satisfying experience. There is little question that the recreationist's satisfaction is derived from realizing that his or her efforts have contributed a positive attitude and something of lasting value to the participant.

Path Finding

The ability to find one's way through unfamiliar territory or even over known ground under average conditions should be acquired very early by those who participate in outdoor living. Path finding is a learned skill that permits an individual to find his or her way without the use of a compass or map. There are times when, in the process of stalking, hunting, or observing, complete attention is absorbed in the activity and the individual may wander far afield. Under these circumstances it is relatively easy to lose one's bearings if either compass or map has been left behind. A basic rule for traveling in open or heavily wooded country is to carry a map, a compass, and a waterproof box of matches. The best advice, of course, is not to get lost. By taking reasonable and prudent measures, an individual can avoid having a search party organized for him or her, or finding him- or herself alone without knowing north from south.

Baseline

When a recreational group has camped out for several days in an unfamiliar place, it is best to explore the area immediately to the north and south of the site. Knowledge of the district above and below the camp, as well as familiarity with some terrain feature that clearly marks the section in which the bivouac is located, will be valuable when returning after a long hike. If the camp is established on a stream, lake, or river, the participant should remember to orient him- or herself in terms of flow. Thus, if the water flows north and south and the hikes are to the east or west, it is impossible to go beyond the baseline no matter how far one travels in a given day. If there is no water course along which the camp may be pitched, then other terrain features must be selected. A deep draw that runs the length of a valley, a range of hills against which the camp is nestled, or high ground that cannot be bypassed without instant recognition will do for a baseline. In any event, the participant should range above and below the camp for 1 or 2 miles in each direction and mark the baseline with blazes every half to quarter mile. The arrangement of blazes clearly indicates the direction from camp. (See the next section for more on blazes.)

Trail Marking

There is a well-known system of marking by which the hiker or hunter, in unfamiliar surroundings, can guide him- or herself. When following a poorly defined trail or establishing a new one through densely forested areas, blaze marks are made on trees at about chest height. One blaze indicates the direction away from camp; two blazes indicate the direction towards camp. The blazes are cut into the tree on opposite sides. This gives the hiker quick reference to his or her position so he or she may find his or her way back to camp.

Bush marks, on the other hand, do not require cuts into the plant. A bush mark is made by bending over the top of a bush in the direction being taken. The shrub may even be snapped or cut, but the attachment should be maintained so that the bush leans in the outward bound direction. Clumps of grass, tied together and folded in the direction of travel, a mound of stones erected in such a manner as to show direction, or sticks pushed into the ground in combination with stones or other convenient materials can tell the traveler in which direction he or she must move to reach his or her base camp.

Divides

In any region of the country there are bound to be rivers, streams, and watersheds. Divides are areas of land that run between streams and rivers as ridges. Instead of following a stream, which may necessitate several fords or even portages, where thick and tangled underbrush may grow to the water's edge, the hiking group would do well to keep to the ridgelines that divide water courses. The dividing ridge will generally have limited vegetation, thus making passage easier and allowing points of vantage to be reached where a long view may be obtained. The back of the ridge is the most dependable line of march to follow where there are no trails and where dense woods can hinder vision as well as progress. The ridge divides watersheds and permits access north and south or east and west, depending upon the direction of water flow.

Natural Guides

The Sky

During the day, when the sun shines, it is comparatively easy to find east and west. When the sun is hidden due to cloud cover, the hiker may still determined east-west direction by taking any thin, flat, reflecting surface, such as a knife blade, and holding it perpendicular to any glossy object—a thumbnail, a watch case, or a metal tool. Slowly rotate the blade. Unless the day is extremely dark, a faint shadow will be seen. The sun is in the opposite direction of the shadow.

At night, knowledge of the circumpolar stars will quickly indicate north. By scanning the skies for the Big Dipper (Ursa Major), spotting the two stars at the end of the bowl, and following them to Polaris, north may be approximately determined. Cassiopeia (the Queen) or Draco (the Dragon) can also be used to determine Polaris.

Moss Growth

Many people feel that the story of moss growing on the north sides of trees is a myth. Nevertheless there are indications that this natural sign indicates a northerly direction and may be detected by those who are sharply observant. First, moss grows more abundantly on both sides of trees where moisture is retained over the longest period of time. Moisture will evaporate last from the side that has a northerly exposure, so it stands to reason that more moss will be found on that side of the tree. The tree should be fairly straight, not leaning in any particular direction. The bark must be smooth; pay no attention to rough knots, forks, or dead fall. Trees having rather straight shafts offer the best evidence because an even distribution of moisture forms all around. Special attention should be paid to trees that have grown in isolated sections, free from competition to the point where they receive direct sunlight throughout most of the daylight period. Moss growth would almost invariably occur on the northern surface of these trees.

Conifer Tips

The topmost branch of any tall evergreen appears to incline toward the southeast. In almost five out of seven cases, conifer tips point slightly south of east. One must not look for such signs in deep, narrow valleys or on windswept ridges, however.

Bark

The bark of old trees appears to be thicker on the north and east sides of trees, with thickness also being present in a northeasterly direction. The predominant direction of bark growth is north.

Compass Use

One of the most important implements in a hiker's kit is the compass. The compass by itself cannot indicate to a lost person in which direction camp lies, but if precautions are taken before leaving camp by taking readings of prominent landmarks, compass reading will bring the individual back to camp. The compass does serve a major purpose by indicating an approximate northerly bearing. If the solitary hiker knows in which direction north lies, it is most probable that he or she will be able to reach his or her destination without undue apprehension.

The compass itself should be strong enough to withstand shocks, but sensitive enough to offer relatively accurate readings. It should have a non-metallic cover, preferably plastic, and a sight by which readings can be made. A compass should be large enough to read easily. The needle should be at least 2 inches long with an arrowhead so distinctive that north will be seen even when the logical thinking processes of a lost person are not functioning well. The compass also should have a release knob that permits the needle to swing freely when the user desires it.

Magnetism and the Compass

The compass works on the principle of magnetism. The earth has a magnetic field that runs from north to south, with one magnetic pole in northern Canada several degrees west of 90° and the other near Antarctica in the sea, so a magnetized compass needle tends to parallel the magnetic field and therefore appears to point in a north–south direction. Because the magnetic field does not lie due north and south, but wanders quite erratically, there will be variations in terms of a northerly direction depending upon the individual's location. Thus, if the hiker were in Maine, it is likely that a compass reading of north would actually point 20° west of true north. If the individual were hiking through Idaho the compass needle would point roughly 22° east of true north. The compass declination or variation from true north may be found from maps of local areas. Governmental charts show the difference between the compass needle and true north.

The places where the compass needle will point to the geographic north are those that follow a meandering line from north to south where there is no variation. This is called the agonic line. Generally it runs from the north magnetic pole in a southeasterly direction and is not static. It changes by moving westward at a very slow rate. Because of this, all locations to the east of the agonic line actually point west of north. All places west of the agonic line actually point east of north. No matter where the individual is located, as long as he or she understands compass declination, he or she can align him- or herself properly with a map and determine precisely where he or she is and how he or she must travel to reach a particular destination.

The difference in a specific region between true north and where the needle points may be learned from Polaris. To be accurate, the observation should be made when the tail star of the Big Dipper's handle is nearly in line with Polaris and the two pointer stars are lined up with the North Star. This phenomenon occurs when the handle of the Big Dipper is either directly above or below the Pole Star. It is at this time that Polaris is almost directly over the North Pole.

Inability to understand compass declination and to adjust for magnetic variation accounts for a great deal of difficulty in wilderness situations. The most common error is to assume that the needle always points toward true north, or that the error is slight. Thus a degree of declination error would permit a hiker to miss his or her target destination by almost a quarter mile if he or she had to walk 3 miles. In heavily wooded or remote places this inaccurate reckoning might be disastrous.

In compass reading, the degree-direction is called the azimuth. If the direction is to the northeast, the azimuth reading will be 45°. Theoretically, it should be relatively easy to retrace one's travels by simply reading the back-azimuth—the degree direction opposite of that which was originally taken on the outward trip. However, with the probability of changing direction, looping left or right, the back-azimuth might not bring one back to the original starting place.

Perhaps the easiest method for determining the location of the base camp is to first establish a compass reading of the camp in relation to two or more landmarks. The camp lies at the intersection of these readings. These headings should be indicated on whatever map or chart is available. No matter where one travels, the landmarks will be visible, within a reasonable distance. Simply line up the landmarks until they meet at the predetermined heading, and the camp should be at that point. If landmarks are sighted and the hiker is nowhere near camp, he or she should follow the preceding method and take readings of the landmarks, tracing the headings on his or her map. He or she will be at the place of intersection, and his or her camp, having already been indicated, will be determined in relation to where he or she is standing.

Another method to use is a single reading from a landmark. When in camp, take a reading of a distant mountain or other prominent place and draw a line on the map in terms of the degree heading. The line should run from the landmark through the campsite. After having traveled any distance from camp and desiring to return, spot the landmark and take a sight with the compass. Draw the degree heading on the map and compare it with the original reading. The relationship between the two will indicate where the individual is presently located. In order to return to the base camp, chart a course between the present position and the camp's position.

Timepiece Direction Finder

A wrist or pocket watch may serve in place of a compass, if it is keeping more or less accurate time. The watch should be turned so that the hour hand points to the sun. Take a relatively straight and rigid object, such as a nail or knife blade, and hold it vertically so that it casts its shadow across the face of the watch. Rotate the watch so that the hour hand is lined up with the shadow. Halfway between the hour hand and 12 o'clock will be the south point. Naturally, such reckoning is valid only in the northern hemisphere. It is precisely opposite below the equator.

Map Reading

Map reading is a rather simple task if the individual maintains the idea that a map is really a picture of the earth, drawn as if observed from a flying plane and including only the most prominent terrain features. The relationship between the size of a feature shown on the map and the corresponding actual feature on the ground is called the *scale*. Understanding scale is vital to reading a map. Scale may be explained in a variety of ways. The easiest is the verbal scale, which simply states that 1 inch equals so many miles.

The graphic scale is a graduated bar or line that indicates the distance on the ground of measured distances on the graph. This is usually expressed in some sort of ratio, such as 1 : 1,000,000. This means that one unit on the map corresponds to 1 million units on the ground. The significance of large-scale and small-scale maps comes in terms of the areas being portrayed. Thus, large-scale maps show a very small land area, whereas small scale maps show very large areas or the entire earth.

Signs and symbols attempt to convey pictorially the features they represent. Therefore, almost anything colored blue is water. A thin wiggly line can be a stream, a thicker blue line a river, and an irregular-shaped area in blue may be a pond, lake, or inland sea. All of these terrain features depend upon the size and area in question. Parallel lines indicate roads. Railroads are indicated with a single line and cross ties. Mines are symbolized by a crossed pickax and shovel. Contour lines that indicate vertical differences are drawn in black, vegetation is shown in green, buildings are sometimes indicated by crosses, or flags, or are outlined. Bridges, overpasses, underpasses, conduits, fences, and other features may all be indicated symbolically. A legend at the bottom of the map will usually explain any symbols used. Once the symbols are understood, the map is easily read.

Determining Location

Just as a compass can assist the individual to locate his or her position in relation to another known place, a map can help the hiker to determine his or her position. When traveling from one place to another, either by vehicle or by foot, it is necessary to find out where one is, both on the ground and on the map. Before one can decide on the best route to take in order to arrive at a particular place, it is necessary to orient oneself. Most outdoor enthusiasts will be on foot or on trips with canoes, horses, or bicycles, so it will be possible to climb the nearest high place and compare or orient the map with the terrain by turning the map until its signs and symbols match the visible terrain features. It will then be easy for the person to locate his or her position. It is the point where all lines between him- or herself and the features on the ground meet on the map.

Direction

When the map is oriented, it is usual to find that the top of the map is north, the right edge is east, the left is west, and the bottom south. During the day, the sun may be a guide to determine north and south. At night, the Pole Star will be of tremendous assistance in orienting the map.

Most maps use reference grids or intersecting lines as an aid in determining points on the map. Such index lines are really vertical and horizontal lines drawn over a map to form a pattern of squares or rectangles. These grids may then be divided into smaller boxes, say 10 vertical and 10 horizontal lines to each grid square. The map coordinates in terms of the major grid square and the lesser squares provide a fairly accurate method for locating any point.

Orienteering

Orienteering combines the use of map and compass. The activity may be performed as competition, with one or more persons pitted against other individuals or groups. The idea of orienteering is to traverse a given, unfamiliar area within a certain time limit. Variations of this activity include traveling over a specified distance and checking in at particular route points along the journey. The checkpoints must be reached at a given time. In route orienteering, the participants are given a predetermined route that is traveled by reaching various stations. These stations must be indicated on each hiker's map. The winner has the most station indications correctly designated on his or her personal map. In sequential orienteering, a given number of routes are designated, with each one needing to be reached in a particular order. The participant must decide which route to use in order to reach these points. The points may all be given initially when the competition is announced or the points may be revealed as each is reached in turn. Essentially, all map and compass work is orienteering. It can be made into a game, or have a decidedly serious, and sometimes a survival, purpose.

Hostelling

Hostelling is the term given to organized caravans or groups of people who set out either on foot, by bicycle, or by automobile and trailers and tour from place to place. Fundamentally, hostelling is very much like route orienteering, in that the participant or group travels from one preselected point to another by a route that is carefully established. Hostelling for older persons should be organized by a specialist responsible for such excursions. The distance between stops at predetermined points is based on the age and capability of the participants. Hostelling may even be designed to provide interested persons with traveling activities through a region with which they are unfamiliar or through areas with which they are vicariously familiar. Periodic stopovers may be established at homes, farms, or other domiciles by contact between those who own available property and a recreational department, or the participants can be expected to provide their own bivouacs as they journey.

Hostelling by bicycle can combine aspects of orienteering, survival activity, woodcraft experiences, and exposure to settings that would be denied to those confined to a recreational center in the city. The people who will participate in this type of activity must be mature, skilled in camp and woodcrafts, and have the stamina needed to pedal a bicycle for 20 to 40 miles each day. Naturally, there will be rest stops or stops to take advantage of a pleasing vista or some other interesting phenomenon. Side trips off the main line of travel may also be encouraged, although some sort of schedule must be honored. One or more recreationists will accompany any such group. The recreationists should have practical experiences in hostelling and be acquainted with the region of travel.

Hostelling participants must be equipped for the tour's duration. For a biking trip, for example, they should pack on their respective bicycles all the gear, except food, necessary to sustain them during their travels. It is more than likely that hostellers will be traveling along secondary or first-class highways. They will be able to purchase whatever food supplies they need along the way. However, they should be equipped with sleeping and cooking gear as well as foul weather clothing. Everything else in the way of supplies is superfluous.

Hostelling trips are designed to take participants to remote places; however, these natural areas may be approached by roads. Although it is true that participants may be out for weeks at a time, they can be scheduled to camp at state and national parks and forests on their way to and from a specific destination. It is unlikely that hostellers will cut across country and off roadways simply because bicycles will not travel well under such conditions. For these reasons, food purchases may be made daily, just before the meal is to be cooked, unless the group has reached the interior of a national park or forest. In this case, food will have been purchased prior to entrance to the park, the amount depending upon the length of stay, because prices are notoriously high in these enclaves.

The entire hostelling procedure can combine the best areas in outdoor expeditions. It is a tremendously social activity, being in company with others for one or more weeks at a time. The recreational department must secure recreationists who can function competently under hostelling conditions. The recreationist must have the respect and confidence of those who participate. He or she will serve as guide and confidant. Quite aside from knowing what to do and how to do it, the recreationist must have complete enthusiasm for the project. He or she will need physical stamina and mental alertness to carry participants through whatever difficulties arise. He or she must be able to stimulate additional effort from participants when necessary and gain cooperation when any disaffection threatens the harmony of the group. Close order living for extended periods can try the patience of almost any individual. The recreationist must be prepared to calm tensions that arise and ease the participants through what could become an unhappy situation. Hostelling is a great outdoor experience. It can be a highlight for those who are capable of participating.

Touring

Tours require intensive planning, expense, time, and energy if they are to be successful. Depending upon the age group concerned, excursions can be limited to natural wonders, places of historical interest, and tours for cultural maintenance and enhancement. For young and older adults who are interested, a radical change in scene can be tremendously benefiting. The entire concept of "getting away" has produced one of the most lucrative industries in the world today—travel and tourism.

Whether the recreational service department becomes the point of departure for tours or individuals decide to travel on their own, the world becomes a place of destinations, either next door or in another hemisphere. This is particularly true if a great deal of preplanning is required and the trip is to take a long time and cover a great distance.

Even if the trip is for a few hours by bus, train, or automobile, the preparations to accommodate older adults must be detailed and require great care. Rest stops will probably be necessary. Those who subsist on rigid dietary schedules and prescribed foods must be considered. Sometimes travel may be accomplished only through the use of specialized vehicles for non-ambulatory elders.

Journeys from the community, however, need to be treated with the care of vacation travel. The longer the trip and the greater the distance, the more it will cost. Careful planning must be devoted to all possibilities if interest, enjoyment, and personal satisfaction are to be achieved: Will transportation involve bus, train, automobile, airplane, or ship? Is there a need for combined travel accommodations? Will foreign countries be visited? What kind of residential accommodations are to be made and by whom? Where the excursion begins (the community center) and the trip's length, cost, and logistics are extremely important in determining whether travel is feasible. It is not expected that the recreational department will underwrite the costs of such ventures. However, the department may be able to get discounted rates for a group of a certain number on airlines, trains, buses, ships, at hotels, or on packaged tours. Of course, people may travel on their own whenever they are able to do so. Sometimes the recreational agency–sponsored excursion may stimulate further travel by individuals who never would have gone unless they had first experienced such exposure in an organized program.

Specialized Trips

All outings from the recreational center may be looked upon as special events, because they occur beyond the scope of the center's intramural activities. However, there are two very individual travel activities that require special skills, equipment, and experience beyond that normally needed for the less complex activities of hiking, cycling, or being transported by motor vehicle. These are canoe trips and horseback trips.

Canoe Trips

Canoe trips are especially favored by those mature and skilled enough to appreciate the experience. They may be of almost any duration because the canoe can be packed with gear and food supplies to last relatively long periods. Canoe travel requires an expertise in swimming, canoeing, camp crafts, and woodcrafts. The ability to travel great distances within a short time allows a canoe trip to be planned with the idea of covering vast stretches of territory. The participant who is involved in this outdoor experience should have developed stamina by taking short trips. He or she must pass whatever criteria are devised for those individuals interested in this type of trip. Standards of acceptance will be in terms of aquatics, boat handling, and the woodcraft skills that will be utilized each day. Because canoes can travel at speeds of up to 5 mph on smooth water and even faster when working with the current, it is probably wise to lay over every third day. The constant pounding of canoe traveling may begin to be tiresome after several days. It is best to spend time ashore enjoying the typical camping activities that one associates with wilderness travel.

Canoe trips are generally planned in regions where lakes, streams, or rivers abound and where there are connecting waterways or short portages from one lake to another. In some areas of the United States, such as the vast wilderness area of the upper Superior region or the Adirondacks of upper New York State, there are more than 2000 square miles of canoe-accessible waterways. The northeast is also well known for its hundreds of miles of rivers and lakes capable of being portaged.

Equipment

The traditional canoe is made of birch bark, but other wood products have also been applied. Modern canoes made of aluminum and fiberglass are available. Even though it is a rattletrap in rough water, the aluminum canoe is far superior to birch bark in construction and toughness. Styrofoam built into the canoe beneath the bow and stern decks keeps the canoe afloat when overturned. An additional safety feature of the aluminum canoe is its ability to right itself after being upset. If supplies are carefully packed and waterproofed, but particularly packed to float, complete recovery of all materials is possible regardless of water depth.

Canoes for wilderness and heavy travel should be approximately 17 feet long and 14 inches deep. The deeper draft allows for smoother sailing and greater stability in rough water or in troughs experienced on lakes during any weather where wind-lashed waves may threaten a shallow-draft canoe. Furthermore, deep-draft canoes are capable of carrying far greater loads than shallow-draft canoes.

The beam should be at least 36 inches, and the bottom should be relatively flat. Canoes with flat bottoms ride higher and are therefore easier to handle and maneuver in shallow water, riffles, and rapids. The canoe is made more completely stable and offers a better ride if the load is trimmed, that is, if it is equally balanced from side to side. It is more efficient to stow gear and supplies towards the rear of the canoe so that the bow rides slightly higher than the stern. The load should be distributed throughout the canoe, to the rear if feasible, but not packed into the ends. In a canoe with adequate depth, packs may be tied in place beneath the thwarts.

Portaging

When there is no connection between bodies of water, the canoe must be carried. The traverse is made around dangerous rapids, waterfalls, and where the watercourse ends. Usually, portaging is welcomed after incessant paddling. It offers a diversion in the sometimes monotonous regularity of sweeping the water. The easiest method for portaging canoes where there is only one paddler is to use the paddles as a yoke or shoulder rail. The paddles should be spaced so that the blades rest on the shoulders while the canoe is carried inverted over the head. Cushioning for the paddles may be made of any soft material. Wool or cotton shirts, jackets, or spare trousers may be rolled so that the weight of the canoe does not cause too much pressure on the back of the neck and shoulders.

Although one person may carry a canoe with comparative ease, it is likely that on any recreationally sponsored canoe trip there will be two persons assigned to each canoe. When there is any wind, it is best to have another pair of shoulders and hands to steady the load and help lift it. A comparatively easy two-person portage is to rest the bow seat on the back of the neck of one participant and the stern seat on the back of the neck of the other; however, this method is good only for short hauls. The idea of taking turns at packing the canoe may also be tested. Where a portage is a long one, it is better to carry a load part of the way and return for whatever is left. The empty-handed return allows for some recuperation. Constant portaging develops stamina, and in a short time the individual is capable of carrying loads without feeling tired or overburdened.

Tracking

When working into rough water or against a rapid current, it may sometimes be impossible to paddle the canoe. For this reason, it is a good idea to attach two ropes at least 50 feet long to the bow and stern of the canoe. Tracking consists of towing a loaded or unloaded canoe upstream or downstream. The canoe can be guided by manipulating the tracking lines at either bow or stern. Thus, the canoe may be turned away or towards the shore. By playing out the line or hauling it in the canoe may be maneuvered around any obstacle. There must, of course, be enough space along the bank of the waterway for an individual to walk. When two people are canoeing, both may take part in tracking or one may remain in the canoe and paddle while the other walks along the bank with the line.

Embarking

Getting into a canoe from either a landing, beach, or dock can cause damage to the canoe and an inadvertent wetting for the would-be canoeist if some care is not taken. The best technique for boarding a canoe from a sandy beach or sloping ground is as follows. Two individuals pick the craft up at its center of balance, the center thwart, and carry it stern first to the water's edge. The canoe is then slipped into the water stern first and by a hand-over-hand feeding along the gunwales. The bowman steadies the bow between his or her legs while the stern paddler walks down the center of the canoe to his or her stern position. He or she will hold on to the gunwales for support while getting to his or her place. The stern is heavier because of the added weight of the paddler, so the bow will rise slightly. The bow paddler may now enter the craft and push off from the shore.

Where there is a dock or landing, parallel embarkation is necessary. Where one person is using the canoe, he or she may tie the canoe to a mooring place and grasp the far gunwale at the center thwart. Holding the canoe fast to the dock, he or she enters the canoe from a crouched position and takes his or her place towards the stern. By releasing the trail line or painter he or she is free of the dock. When two individuals use the canoe, one may steady the canoe as indicated while the other climbs aboard. The embarked paddler steadies the canoe by holding it against the dock as the other participant enters. The occupants are then in a position to begin paddling. When landing the canoe, the reverse procedure from embarking is followed.

Safety Precautions

The canoe is thought to be a very unstable craft. This is a myth. In competent hands, the canoe is one of the safest and most seaworthy of all watercraft. Its extreme buoyancy makes it literally unsinkable. Nevertheless, some precautions must be taken in canoeing as in any other sport. Canoeing skills should be acquired before any individual is allowed to participate in any trip. Safety procedures should be deeply ingrained in every person who aspires to take a specialized trip. The ability to swim is of chief importance, but this skill alone does not guarantee safety. Several other conditions must be met.

- A mastery of all canoeing strokes is essential.
- Always paddle from a kneeling position except when the water is exceptionally calm or smooth.
- Never attempt to exchange paddling positions in a canoe. Land first and then shift positions.
- Carefully distribute the weight in the canoe. Keep the weight low and centered. Trim the craft by equally distributing the weight from bow to stern and side to side.
- When loading a canoe, load from the middle towards the ends. When unloading, the reverse procedure is the rule.
- Unless absolutely necessary, it is better not to take a canoe out in rough water or during high winds. In meeting high winds or waves,

either head the canoe directly to or away from the waves. When caught in high winds, it is best to shift the paddling position to the middle of the canoe if alone.

- If the canoe is overturned by broadside waves, do not leave the canoe. The canoe will support as many people as are paddling it.
- Attach tracking lines or painters to secure the canoe when mooring.
- Carry an extra paddle.
- Wear a flotation device.

Horseback Trips

Recreational center programs may sometimes schedule horseback trips if they are located in pack-horse country or if the facility has the financial resources (affluent interested individuals) to be able to provide participants with this unique experience. Although the acquisition of horses, stables, and gear is probably too expensive for most recreational departments, there is little doubt that the capital returns on the investment will be worthwhile to all concerned if the center is situated in a section of the country that favors this type of activity. Even where the recreational department has decided not to make the monetary investment in horses and equipment, horseback trips are still possible. The horses and equipment can be rented from a reliable outfitter, who will probably also send along a wrangler or horse handler. Horseback trips can be either the pack or riding variety.

On horseback trips, light gear is carried, similar to what individuals take for a hike. Instead of traveling on foot, however, a horse provides the transportation. Such trips can last one or more weeks depending upon the amount of feed carried and the terrain over which the trip is planned. The horse can easily carry a rider and 50 pounds of food and gear. The equipment will consist of bedding, tarpaulins for shelter, a few tools, changes of clothing, and perhaps a few more essential items that can be packed because of the extra load-carrying capacity of the horse. Insofar as the animals are concerned, they must be well fed, cared for, and given a certain amount of shelter from foul weather. The trip will have to be made where there are known water holes.

Pack-horse trips are somewhat different from horseback riding trips. If the recreational department has the pack horse and gear or tack, there will be at least one pack horse for every two potential participants. The trip will be much slower than the horseback riding trips because pack-horse trips normally cover rough terrain. Such outings may be away from the central facility for periods of up to 1 month at a time. For this reason, only mature individuals who have exceptional woodcraft and camping skills as well as the ability to ride and manage horses will be capable of taking advantage of this opportunity. The recreationist who supervises such trips must be expert with horses, and specifically one who has been or could be a horse wrangler.

Packing

In order to pack the horse most efficiently and effectively, it is best to place some stout padded material over a saddle blanket. The packsaddle may be of fairly rigid construction, but designed so as to fit only the padded back of the horse. It should have small edges or shelves on which the packs may be hitched or attached. Ordinary harness gear will hold the entire kit if the harness has rings for a breast or breaching strap. A waterproof pack cloth to protect the supplies during inclement weather is also necessary. All supplies may be strung across the packsaddle and tied down. Perhaps the safest and surest technique is to pack the supplies on the ground in two bundles of equal weight. With the horse tethered and harnessed, the two packs are simultaneously placed onto the packsaddle and lashed to it. This maintains balance and assures the comfort of the horse. The bundles should be made so that they can be tied high on the saddle. Part of the weight thus rests to the rear of the withers. The soft part of the bundle should be against the horse and the entire pack should be as flat as possible to prevent any back-and-forth movement.

Safety Precautions

As in all trips away from the recreational center, certain rules should be observed for the health and welfare of all the participants. Although the gait will probably be a walk, the speed of the group should never be more than the pace that the poorest rider can maintain. When riding hilly terrain, the rider should lean forward to free the horse's hindquarters, thereby giving him or her greater leverage and walking capability. Saddles should be designed to allow for the greatest ease in riding. For pack or horseback trips of any extended duration, the rider must learn to ride well up towards the withers. There should be a vertical line between the rider's eye, knee, and toe. Sitting in this position takes weight off the horse's loins and permits a much smoother pace. The rider should always move with the horse, not in an opposite direction. Kindness and gentleness are vital in handling horses. Relaxation is part of riding. Sit erect, guide the horse with neck reins, and enjoy the pleasant sensation of travel by horse.

Summary

Travel beyond the confines of the recreational center, playground, or park provides an enlarged experience for the participant. Trips to historical, cultural, and unique sites, in town as well as outside of the community, can do much to augment the knowledge and appreciation of the traveler and offer personal enjoyment.

All activities of this type require the knowledge and skill of a recreationist. This person's leadership qualities will enable proper planning for any off-site activity and the preparation of participants to engage in methods of travel. Skill development will determine, to a great extent, the opportunities, activities, and destinations of these outings.

As always, the safety of participants is of primary concern to agency personnel. No person should be placed in jeopardy because of an exploratory activity. Appropriate equipment, supplies, and material have to be distributed by the agency at pre-arranged times and places. Certainly, much equipment is personally owned, but it should meet whatever safety standards are set by the agency.

Excursions, trips, or touring may be conducted by automobile, bicycle, bus, canoe, train, horseback, or on foot depending on the ability to pay for travel and the accompanying expenses on the part of participants, or on the budget of the agency operating the activity. Travel should be available to all of the agency's constituents to the extent possible. Adroit planning and an interesting format may induce the participation of those who previously never would have considered such an experience. This aspect of the recreational program requires detailed attention, a high degree of knowledge and experience on the part of recreationists, and a place in the recreational program because of its value to those who become involved.

Selected Further Reference

Brooks, C. "The Preservationists' Trails." *New York Times*. September 28, 2008: 1, 8.

CHAPTER

19

Service Activities

All those activities voluntarily engaged in by people who wish to assist others in learning, appreciation, skill development, or making the community a better place in which to live as a result of their interest, talent, and sense of responsibility may be termed *service functions* or *volunteering*. It is the selfless giving of time, energy, and sometimes money, purely for the satisfaction derived from helping another person or an entire community. As Henry Home states ". . . there is a principle of benevolence in man which prompts him to an equal pursuit of the happiness of all."[1] Perhaps more than any other activity, service to others may be considered the most rewarding. It is just as enjoyable as any of the other activity categories, requires the same sense of personal expression, and may result in an even greater or more intense emotional response of well-being and warmth as the recipient of the service succeeds in the undertaking for which assistance was given.

Volunteering is concerned with all the activities normally associated with altruism, benevolence, or philanthropic programs. Service activities are a staple to fill leisure when other forms of activity cannot satisfy the human urge to extend sympathy, lend aid, or teach. The release gained from wholeheartedly giving service to others voluntarily, the expulsion of too much self-concern in exchange for self-giving, provides a sense of personal expansion and is a vital investment in the self with a magnificent return. Activities of this type might include voluntarily instructing a less skilled person in an activity, unpaid work in a hospital, reading to a blind person, helping to build a community center or playground, participating in community political or civic affairs, taking children to a zoo or beach, becoming a foster grandparent, or visiting a person who is homebound.

Watching an individual develop skill, knowledge, emotional maturity, or an appreciation of a variety of subjects as a direct consequence of one's own instruction, guidance, or support provides the donor with a feeling of achievement and a sense of self-esteem for being able to help another person. Service to others may be attained even when the volunteer does not work directly with other people.

By offering time, skill, or technical knowledge, a more valuable recreational experience can be provided. Service activity is as broad as the entire field of recreational service. However, for simplification, services may be organized around the classes shown in **Table 19.1**.

Every community has the potential personal resources of special skills and an infinite variety of talents waiting to be discovered. It is the responsibility of the recreationist to ensure a balanced program by investigating the possibility of incorporating the service phase of recreational experience into the program. To whatever extent an individual possesses some talent or ability, it may be useful to others and therefore a viable contribution to the community at large.

Lifelong skills acquired as a result of occupation, hobbies, education, or living within one community may be the basis on which one can provide voluntary services to others (**Figure 19.1**). Every phase of the program may be made more valuable to participants as the result of some volunteer's experiences and donation of time or effort.

Volunteers offer a variety of contributions that make possible a more comprehensive recreational program for participants. Bringing personal skills to the agency, volunteers enlarge the number of activities the agency can provide. Because their commitment is without remuneration, they may free up the budget for additional activities, equipment, or facilities. Moreover, they swell the ranks of participants simply by being present. Of essential importance is the fact that volunteers come from the local population and are therefore a direct line to the neighborhoods in which they reside and to the community at large. They serve as public relations carriers and are the most effective word-of-mouth informants to potential participants. Volunteers are probably very enthusiastic about what they do and how they do it, which makes them an ideal communication channel to the wider community. They bring new ideas, orientations, and broadened concepts of service to the agency insofar as satisfying community recreational needs.

Perhaps no other segment of the program provides as much good public relations and develops as much good will as does the service effort. The reasons for this are plain. Every volunteer becomes a disseminator of the positive outcomes of the activity in which he or she is interested. Volunteers not only aid the professional workers, but also are enthusiastic protagonists of the department. When volunteers receive the satisfaction typically derived from such participation, they almost always pass the word to friends and relatives. As people begin to find out about the activities available, more tend to participate in them.

Public relations are extremely important to the provision of recreational services, whether in the public, quasi-public, or private sector, and are significant in treatment centers as well. Allocations for expansion of the program,

Table 19.1   Service Classes

Committee Work	Direct Activity Leadership	Nonleadership Work
Membership on:	Art	Technician
Boards	Hobbies	Carpenter
Councils	Crafts	Cosmetician
Interest groups	Music	Clerical work
Resource groups	Dance	Receptionist
Committees	Nature	Fund raising
	Drama	Mechanic
	Motor performance	Transportation
	Education	Ushering
	Service activities	
	Social activities	
	Special events	

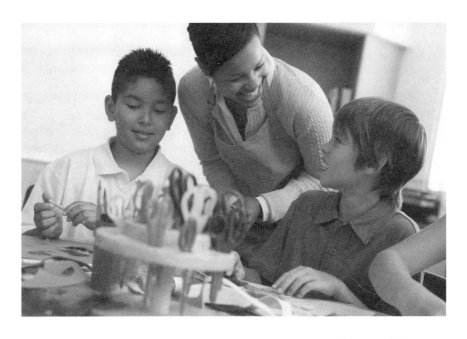

Figure 19.1   Building Confidence Is a Prime Example of Voluntary Leadership

personnel, and operation can be anticipated when there is a groundswell of support for the agency. High demand is usually a prelude to positive political consideration in the public arena. This is valid whether the department works within the public domain or within the institutional setting of a treatment center. To the extent that the department is meeting the needs of the constituency, there will be an increased demand for the continuation and augmentation of such services. Volunteers have tremendous impact on the community's population and therefore offer their personal testament to the good works the agency offers.

Recruitment

Of necessity, volunteers must be recruited. This is best done by a survey performed in the community by staff members of the recreational service department. Some volunteers simply walk into the agency and ask to be allowed to help in any way. However, for the most part volunteers must be sought. The department should maintain a list of possible volunteer positions needed in the conduct of the program, the operation of the agency, or assistance in enlisting support for the department. With these slots in mind, people may be recruited.

Many people would like to help, but feel they do not have special talent or do not realize they do not have to be skilled in order to be useful and make a valuable contribution. Unfortunately, too, some administrators do not recruit nor do they want volunteers assisting in the program because they feel that volunteers require more time than it is worthwhile to give them. Such an attitude on the administrator's part is not only bred of ignorance, but is completely out of keeping with the idea that volunteer service is an integral part of the recreational program.

Recruitment of volunteers may be facilitated if relevant sources are determined before any campaign is carried out. Retired individuals, high school–age youngsters, hobbyists, fraternal organization members, and labor union locals are prime targets as recruits. The same formula utilized in developing good public relations with the public should also merit consideration in developing a corps of volunteers for the department.

Another recruitment technique might be to involve individuals in short-term volunteer projects. They will obtain immediate satisfaction from their efforts, which may be just the stimulus needed to increase their willingness to attempt a long voluntary project. An individual who is not sure of being able to maintain a long period of service may be convinced of the effective use of his or her talents or knowledge, and thereby become more engaged and committed to volunteering for longer periods of time.

Once individuals have been recruited, a screening process must be instituted so they can be placed within the various voluntary classifications. Individuals with a high degree of program skills should be placed in a related sector, as should those who have administrative or clerical experience and those who may perform significant work for the department in other areas. An experienced interviewer for the department should be employed in the screening process, and written statements of potential volunteers should clarify their aims and primary sense of purpose in offering their time and energy.

After the initial action of recruitment and screening has occurred, there should be a basic orientation to the agency in terms of philosophy, functions, and goals. In this way the would-be volunteer can be made to recognize what the agency is attempting to do, why it performs in the way it does, and what contribution it makes to community betterment and welfare. Volunteers become the face of the agency. That means they represent the department to the public. It is therefore extremely important to make sure the volunteer understands his or her obligations and commitment to the organization. More significantly, the orientation should specify how the volunteer's particular service assignment is directly associated with the overall operation of the agency. Printed handouts or manuals should be prepared and distributed to all volunteers. This becomes a reference concerning the department's functions and the place of the volunteer in the overall setup.

After the orientation, there should be a period of in-service education to prepare the volunteers for service in any facet of agency operation. Those who will work with recreationists at a variety of facilities should receive scheduled observations and tours as well as a tutorial on skills and methods of instructing and supervision. For those who will be participating as administrative assistants, office management techniques should be thoroughly explained and demonstrated. There is room in the program's daily operation to include all who want to lend their time and energy.

There are certain drawbacks to the use of volunteers, but their positive benefits to the program far outweigh any undesirable characteristics. It is true that volunteers may not be as reliable as paid employees and that they will not owe first allegiance to the agency. However, the agency should do everything in its power to stimulate loyalty and dedication in the volunteer just as it does for the employed individual. Moreover, the dependable volunteer frees the professional worker to do a more extensive and inclusive job of programming than might be possible without additional help.

Despite any negative reasons listed as to why volunteers should not be assigned or utilized, there is one overriding fact in favor of their incorporation: service is a recreational activity and it must be considered if the recreational program is to be balanced with something for each person's taste and satisfaction. Recreationists have the mandatory obligation to serve people, and one way they can do this is by offering opportunities for providing service to others through volunteer efforts. The benefit volunteers contribute is so great that no program may be considered successful without them. The value received from a dedicated and skilled volunteer is incalculable to the agency. No program should be without as many as can be recruited.

Designated Volunteer Coordinator

If the agency's needs are extensive and decentralized, it might be valuable to employ an individual who has primary responsibility for the total volunteer program. This coordinator, when performing effectively, can tremendously enhance the program's efficiency. The coordinator is responsible for all aspects of the volunteer program from recruitment through evaluation. This is the individual whose primary function is to tap available persons from whatever sources are discovered. Under the coordinator's supervision, volunteers are prepared for work in areas of need.

When an agency believes that volunteers are important to its operation the management will allocate the necessary funds and provide the requisite material assistance to assure effectiveness. Whether the agency develops a new position (i.e., the volunteer coordinator) or simply assigns in-house personnel to be responsible for the service category, the individual so designated must assess agency needs and obtain the necessary volunteers.

Record Keeping

Records pertaining to all those who volunteer within the recreational program must be maintained to keep track of who does what with whom. Records need to show the number of hours spent by the volunteers performing the work for which they have been engaged. This also includes any in-service preparation, orientation, or external conferences that have been attended in order to provide more effective and efficient service. Not only is it important to make sure that the volunteer is engaged in the work he or she signed up to do, but records are significant signposts for the recognition of the volunteer's longevity and the exemplary effort the volunteer has given.

In this way, the agency has a systematic method for evaluating the performance of the volunteer, thereby enabling the recreationist to offer any assistance the volunteer might need in carrying out assigned duties and responsibilities. It is also an effective way of locating those individuals with special skills, knowledge, or talent when activities requiring their unique contributions are called for.

Recognition

Just as professional workers need acknowledgment of their dedication to the work of the agency, so too do volunteers, like any other person, need that stimulation of a pat on the back, "job well done," or more formal recognition of their loyalty, zeal, and devotion to the cause of recreational service. This recognition not only acknowledges the volunteer's commitment, but is a concrete example to the volunteer that the agency is concerned about his or her personal satisfaction and feelings of being needed.

Volunteers may be recognized in both intrinsic and extrinsic ways that can further stimulate the donor's desire to extend effort and be as effective as possible in the provision of service. As the occasion demands, informal recognition may include greetings, handshakes, compliments, and the like. Other awards may be pins, certificates, banquets, official ceremonies, letters of appreciation, or other means by which the volunteer is commemorated. Such recognition is offered not merely for time served, but for the continual progress in voluntary efforts.

Insurance

There is always an inherent risk in any recreational activity where people are involved. However, it is a good idea to avoid any volunteer assignment that carries with it high risk. Every volunteer needs to be informed during in-service education about the potential for injury to others and self. This means the volunteer must have appropriate orientation, training, and supervision. Even when a safety program is in effect, liability and accident insurance is required. Insurance coverage must be specific to the particular situation or condition in which the agency operates. Typically, volunteers can be covered under the same policy as professional employees. Understandably, this must be clearly spelled out in any contract that is undertaken.

Essentiality

Sometimes members of the professional staff who lack confidence or feel insecure view the recruitment of volunteers as undercutting their role or as potential replacements for them. Intra-agency communication and constant reiteration will assist in ending paid personnel anxieties. Actually, all recreationists should know that the service category is intrinsic to the offerings of a comprehensive program and therefore that volunteers are absolutely necessary if that category is to be effectually executed. A fundamental concept is that paid staff must be involved with the volunteer program. This means that paid staff needs to be engaged in the recruitment, preparation, and development of volunteers. In this way, staff member apprehensions will be assuaged by the understanding that volunteers are necessary to supplement and complement professional workers for an enriched and comprehensive recreational program. By coordinating the professionals' capabilities with the volunteers' skills, learning, and desire to assist, the interaction that develops between the staff and the volunteers should produce a sense of *esprit de corps*, or teamwork. Better understanding will ensue, confidence in oneself will be developed, and apprehensions should fade away.

Desirable Outcomes

If organized correctly, the service activity can be extremely valuable to the community and the individuals who participate in the program. The most obvious benefit of volunteer service is its contribution to the betterment of the community. There are many jobs that businesses and community organizations do not have the time or finances to undertake. Almost certainly volunteers can improve the efficiency of paid workers by doing jobs that do not require a great deal of expertise, but which are, nevertheless, essential. A volunteer will know from his or her experiences, as well as the reactions of those with whom he or she works, if the effort is appreciated. If it is not, the volunteer will experience no self-growth and will eventually leave. When the individual can be convinced that the volunteer experience is worthwhile there is often a sense of contribution and personal enhancement (**Figure 19.2**). As the individual continues to gain personal confidence and satisfaction from the participation, he or she will be encouraged, thereby stimulating the individual toward greater involvement. Essentially, volunteering is so rewarding that it sustains and, in fact, enlarges the service program.

Summary

Volunteers are the backbone of any recreational agency. The recruitment and retention of altruistic people enhance the delivery of recreational services to

Figure 19.2 Volunteer Instruction Can Be for Any Age Group

the community at large. Without the talent and input that benevolent people donate to the department, and other institutions, many of the varied activities that provide much pleasure to those who receive such services would be eliminated. Volunteers bring their own points of view to the agency's attention and by so doing enlarge the scope of the program.

Volunteers cannot replace recreationists because the professional is needed to organize, guide, and direct program implementation and those who participate in it. Volunteers are valuable, however, not merely because they offer their effort without remuneration, but because they augment and complement the work of recreationists. In the process they offer their time, experience, skill, and concern to the agency's repertoire, which results in a more comprehensive and enjoyable series of activities. Needless to say, the volunteer is compensated by receiving as much enjoyment in giving as any recipient does in getting the aid, counseling, or other service provided.

The utilization of volunteers to assist in carrying out the responsibilities of any recreational service program provides many benefits for those who participate. Those who receive services of a recreational nature will probably obtain greater exposure to the activities that a comprehensive program affords than they might otherwise if volunteers were not available. The probability of volunteers gaining increased skills or acquiring new ones is exponentially augmented when those who serve as volunteers lead or instruct. Both parties to the process are greatly helped in terms of services provided and services given.

There is no program of activity that cannot be made more efficient and effective with the participation of volunteers. Any responsible individual may assume the role and satisfy his or her altruistic tendencies and thereby offer greater interaction. Whoever becomes engaged in this vital category carries out a prime directive of the field of recreational service, which is the desire to better the condition of others through recreational participation. Both the givers and receivers of service are mutually benefited and obtain a sense of ego involvement, belonging, and personal feelings of enhancement.

References

1. Home, H. *Essays on the Principles of Moral and Natural Religion.* Edinburgh: Thoemmes 1751: 78.

Selected Further References

Buchanan, E. J. *Volunteer Training Office's Handbook.* Tulsa, OK: PennWell Corp., 2003.

Cloud, D. A., ed. *Volunteer Leader: Essays on the Role of Trustees of Nonprofit Facilities and Services for the Aging.* Washington, DC: American Association of Homes for the Aging, 1985.

Ellis, S. J. *Volunteer: A Recruitment Book.* Philadelphia, PA: Energize Books, 1996.

Grubbs, A., and E. Levine. *Voluntary Recognition Skit Kit.* Philadelphia, PA: Energize Books, 1992.

Hurke, N. R. *Volunteer Missions: Opportunities for Senior Adults.* Birmingham, AL: Woman's Mission Union, 1994.

Jackson, V. R., ed. *Volunteerism in Geriatric Settings.* Binghamton, NY: Haworth Press, 1996.

Kendall, J. *Voluntary Sector.* Florence, KY: Routledge, 2003.

King, R. R., and J. Fluke. *Volunteers: America's Hidden Resource.* Lantham, MD: University Press of America, 1990.

Kipps, H. C. *Volunteer America.* 4th rev ed. Rocky Mount, NC: Ferguson Pub. Co., 1997.

Kouri, M. *Volunteerism and the Older Adult.* Santa Barbara, CA: ABC-CLIO, 1990.

Lawson, D. M. *Volunteering: 101 Ways to Improve the World and Your Life.* Poway, CA: Alti Publishing, 1998.

McCurley, S., and R. Lynch. *Volunteer Management: Mobilizing all the Resources of the Community.* Madison, WI: The Society for Nonprofit Organizations, 1996.

Nair, M. D., and R. Brody. *Community Service: The Art of Volunteering and Service Learning.* 3rd ed. Wheaton, IL: Gregory Publishing Co., 2005.

Osborne, S. P. *Voluntary Organizations and Innovation in Public Services.* Florence, KY: Routledge, 1998.

Pearce, J. L. *Volunteers: The Organizational Behavior of Unpaid Workers.* Florence, KY: Routledge, 1993.

Pichler, T., and C. Broslavick. *Service Projects for Teens: 20 Plans That Work.* Dayton, OH: Pflaum Publishing Group, 2004.

Stebbins, R. A., ed. *Volunteering As Leisure/Leisure As Volunteering.* Cambridge, MA: CABI Publishing, 2004.

Williams, D. E., and K. O. Gangel. *Volunteers for Today's Church: How to Recruit and Retain Workers.* Eugene, OR: Wipf and Stork Publishers, 2004.

CHAPTER

20

Social Experiences

All experiences of a recreational nature where two or more people come into close contact and where there is some direct relationship so that communication exists are social. With the exception of solitary recreational activities, all situations of a recreational nature are intensely social. Communication, in this situation, does not have to be verbal. It is enough if people can satisfy their need to belong to a group by merely being present at an activity in which the group is involved. Close proximity, coincidental participation in the activity, and common interests often open avenues of receptivity and acceptance that are essential to sociability. Because social activities are generic to every category of recreational program, only a sampling of these experiences is listed. Social activities may be grouped as shown in **Table 20.1**.

Social interaction is assimilated when people exchange ideas or verbalize their thoughts concerning attitudes, feelings, and interests or simply relay whatever is interesting to someone else. Conversation, therefore, is the most essential and intensely social of all activities. It permits the exchange of points of view and is completely based on reciprocity. This means that mutual dependence or interdependence is involved. Conversation requires a speaker and a listener. It is of no matter whether the persons involved converse easily or it is a one-sided affair. It only matters that there is an occasional response—a nod, gesture, or verbal reply. To be sure, however, the best conversations are long and involved discourses that actually progress from one topic to another, totally absorbing the participants and offering an outlet for and reception of ideas.

Socialization as a Recreational Opportunity

Many of the most intense and influential relationships occur on a one-to-one basis. When an individual is free to interact with another, he or she is usually attracted by the physical presence, personality, intelligence, and availability of the other person. Commonly held values and beliefs tend to reinforce their correctness and promote self-confidence. It is easier to broach a new topic with another person if a similar attitude about the subject has already been expressed. Such unity facilitates interaction and encourages the process of communication.

Opportunity to socialize is an obvious outcome of proximity. The likelihood for greater or more frequent contact is promoted if attractive others reside nearby. If one person sees another daily, there is a good possibility that hesitant greetings will be exchanged as recognition is established. As familiarity grows, some interpersonal activity will be noted. This can take place in school, in a congregation, or at a food store, bank, mall, or other common meetingplace. The more frequent the contact, the more likely pleasant experiences will be shared. In fact, under such circumstances, unless the individual is misanthropic, behavior will be more amenable than usual. It is unpleasant to get along badly with those seen regularly; it is more typical to try to get along in an accommodating manner. The better one knows someone, the more expected and comprehensible are that person's behaviors and the greater the possibility that good interpersonal relations will develop.

Although proximity and regularity are significant in the development of interpersonal relations, another factor is compatibility. After all, familiarity sometimes does breed contempt, especially if the individual has undesirable personal characteristics or does not respond in a way that opens opportunities for an acquaintanceship to develop. Compatibility becomes important as people begin to assess the qualities of others and seek out those elements that may be involved in producing a lasting relationship.

People tend to prefer others because of perceived similarities to themselves. However, too much similarity, particularly in certain personality traits, rather than values or ideas, often produces hostility. Therefore, attraction will probably be based on some combination of similarity and correspondence. This means that when one individual has certain personality characteristics that complement the other's and has pleasing traits, attraction will occur. The other person has traits that not only are acceptable, but also fit in comfortably with the individual's own. It is the interaction between compatible people that enables social recreational experiences to occur. All of the occasions when familiarity, regularity, and agreement are operating produce conditions conducive to social intercourse. Recreational outcomes are an integral part of socialization.

Table 20.1 Grouping Social Activities

Formal Activities	Informal Activities
Parties	Games:
Banquets	Active
Ceremonials	Mental
Programmed dances	Musical
Concerts	Party
Dinners	Table
Balls	Community singing
Teas, coffees	Social dancing
Festivals	Conversation
Holiday celebrations	Coffee klatches
Commencements	Drop-ins
	Potluck suppers

Activities

The involvement of two or more people in some continuing and interactional experience comes about in nearly every kind of recreational activity that can be programmed or sponsored. However, socialization can be of a formal or informal type, spontaneous or planned. In some situations, coincidence plays a role in the social contact people make. In other cases, depending upon the nature of the individuals involved, a great deal of organization and effort is required.

Formal

Formal activities must be planned. Formality necessitates the organization of time, money, effort, and usually some theme around which the occasion is centered. Formal arrangements will be made for such various social activities as banquets, dances, weddings, wakes, teas, ceremonials, receptions, religious observances, dinners, and fashion shows, to name but a few. All these events are social to the extent that they involve two or more people who know each other. Moreover, the knowledge is typically of long standing with much in common between them.

The presumption is that individuals who participate in formal gatherings feel that they have an obligation to do so and are willing to make whatever effort is needed in order to attend. In such situations, communication between persons attending is absolutely clear, personal opinions are exchanged, and in most, if not all, of these occasions the event brings enjoyment and satisfaction to the participants. This is even true of some wakes, where the family and friends of the deceased share *joie de vivre*.

Planned

Not all planned activities are formal. In fact, many are decidedly informal. Informality, as used here, means that the individuals involved neither dress in a formal manner nor adhere to some protocol. No rigorous time schedule or precise format is anticipated, although in some informal activities the starting and stopping times are known well in advance. Informal activities permit strangers to meet initially for some activity and, because of proximity and the repetition of the activity, to become acquainted. Once they become acquainted, varying degrees of intimacy develop, permitting the free exchange of ideas, the production of affection or biases as the individuals come to know each other better, and the enhancement of personal enjoyment. There is always the possibility that such superficial exchanges may eventually ripen into friendships.

Some activities are planned to promote additional satisfaction and pleasure among old acquaintances and long-time friends. The reason for the activity is simply because people know one another and want to spend additional time together enjoying mutually satisfying and entertaining experiences.

Among planned activities that bring together people who may or may not have known one another previously are instructional classes, volunteer activities, meetings concerned with some particular issue that requires concerted action for successful resolution, or activities that are scheduled to meet the recreational needs of people. In the last instance, it is the activity that creates the social experience. Among these are parties, picnics, interest groups, games of all kinds, volunteering, meetings, classes, and recreational activities in general.

Informal

Activities of this type require little or no planning and are undertaken purely for the anticipated enjoyment. Participants usually have known each other for a relatively long period, fully recognize each other's foibles and strengths, and therefore get along well in each other's company.

For example, older adults may want to shop, drink, or travel with certain friends. This requires only an invitation and a little planning—unless the travel is expected to be of some duration, and even then, arrangements can be made easily if finances are not of concern. Children, on the other hand, may want to form "secret" clubs, meet at a certain playground for a variety of games, go fishing in season, or just come together for no specific reason. For some adults, shopping excursions require only the willingness to participate. Drinking is one of the most unequivocal of all social activities among those age groups who drink. It requires only the taste for the beverage and the desire for company either in the privacy of a residence or at a local tavern.

There are no restrictions in any of the informal activities in terms of time, dates, clothing, rules, or regulations. Participants must conform only to the standards of propriety and civilized behavior.

Spontaneous Experiences

Spontaneous activities occur on the spur of the moment without preplanning or expectation. These experiences are perhaps the most intensely social because they permit the greatest latitude in exploration at both the superficial and more profound levels of intimacy. Intimacy refers to the knowledge that one person has of another insofar as mutual acquaintanceship reveals the personal details of each other's lives. Intimacy is characterized by the nature of subjects discussed, reading styles, forms of address, and exchanges that presuppose knowledge of the reactions of others under vastly differing circumstances.

Among spontaneous activities are conversation, eating, visiting friends and relatives, walking, or visiting recreational places or commercial displays or exhibitions. Any of these activities occur as an individual casually goes about the business of daily living. Conversations may arise from a simple greeting and wander at will from that point. They can include chitchat about the weather with the discussion of family matters, health, or business affairs. Children, on the other hand, may talk about the latest video games, music, or any other subject that strikes their fancy.

Everyone must eat. Eating can be an excellent spontaneous social occasion if two or more people meet and decide to eat or have a snack together. It is an enjoyable activity and one that is enhanced for any individual by having others share the table and thoughts.

Walking requires only the capacity to walk. It enables an individual to get out and facilitates the chance of meeting others. Naturally, the walker may be accompanied by someone else from the start. Whether walking or riding a bike, an individual may decide to visit a zoo, beach, museum, art gallery, or concert hall. Proximity and capacity are involved in such decisions. Much the same is true of window shopping or viewing a commercial display. Nothing needs to be planned. As an individual finds him- or herself near a facility, only a quick decision is required to take advantage of the situation. The possibility for socializing with others who have the same idea at approximately the same time is obvious, although this too may be performed in company. The fact that one is thrown into proximity with others willy-nilly provides the opportunity for social interaction.

Interaction

Social experience means interaction. Social activities, however, can be learned, and there are definite techniques for their organization and implementation. There's no need to offer a complete catalog of activities or even to elaborate on instructional aspects. Nevertheless, recreationists should know how their constituents may be affiliated with their peers, how they can be introduced to strangers without the embarrassment that so often accompanies initial meetings, and what they need to feel they are welcome.

Someone needs to serve as a receptionist for any gathering or meeting as the official greeter. It is the responsibility of this person to provide whatever information a newcomer may need and to introduce him or her to others who seem to have similar interests, experiences, or knowledge. If the meeting is one at which each person is a "first-timer," a simple introduction to each other will reduce any tension and anxiety that first meetings usually entail. Once introductions have been made, depending upon the activity or location, the recreationist or other designated person must continually circulate throughout the gathering to make sure each person has someone to talk to, is participating, or is at least occupied with the group. No one should be left out or permitted to feel rejected. This does not mean that an individual cannot observe the group's activities. "People watching" is extremely enjoyable and may stimulate the desire to join in after any initial shyness or reserve has disappeared.

There are always risks in social activities, particularly when most, if not all, of the would-be participants are strangers to one another. Each person will be carefully feeling out others for support and will be quick to withdraw or feel rebuffed if he or she does not receive it. Food and drink are wonderful catalysts for providing activity that is not in the least threatening, enabling individuals to meet on a common ground and generally facilitating conversation.

Whatever the recreational activity, social programming requires the careful consideration typically given to other categories such as crafts, sports, or excursions. After all, each kind of recreational activity has social overtones. Whether the occasion is a party, picnic, bicycle trip, dance, or cookout, the recreationist must pay scrupulous attention to the timing, activities, and skills that will make it successful.

Whenever possible, patrons must be invited to assist in planning their own activities and given responsibilities commensurate with their abilities. Involvement with certain tasks tends to stimulate the individual's desire to have that aspect, at least, succeed. As the person becomes absorbed with the assignment, a much more satisfying experience will be created. If other participants have the same feeling, the socialization process will be rewarding and successful.

Social activities occur at any time. The interactions between people can make any activity pleasurable or horrendous. The difference between the two extremes requires advanced planning by the recreationist with the potential participants. Almost anything that can enhance social contact should be utilized, but proper planning, which avoids contingencies and unpleasant surprises, may be the single most effective technique. If each person has a role to play, knows what to expect, and then enjoys fulfilling the responsibility, the real value of social activity will have been achieved.

Courtesy

In order to obtain maximum benefits in social interaction, an individual must be true to him- or herself. Appreciation of motives, attitudes, and behavior is the greatest help in meeting and getting to know other people. The ability to appraise one's own personality or characteristics permits the same appraisal of others.

The chief way to establish good interpersonal behavior is common courtesy. There are no substitutes for good manners. A person who was unfailingly courteous, despite frustrations, will inevitably be wanted as a guest, acquaintance, or friend by many different people. Courteous people tend to be acknowledged as pleasant persons and therefore perceived as being far more attractive than discourteous individuals.

Personnel

Recreationists have a responsibility for a great variety of social activities. Because almost all recreational activities are social, no specialists will be required. However, it is important for recreationists to understand the nature of social activity, whether a dance, picnic, or other gathering, and be prepared to contribute to the organizational and operational aspects so as to assure success in the undertaking.

Paid personnel are not required in informal and spontaneous situations. Typically, people participate because they want to, at their own pace, and satisfy their own needs. In formal events a recreationist may have to assist in or plan the entire function to promote continuity and assure that needed supplies, materials, or equipment is available at the time and place desired. Space must be reserved, food and beverages ordered, and specific activities planned. The situation will determine the need for staff personnel.

Accessibility

Access to facilities always depends upon the capacity of the individuals involved. Almost any available space will be sufficient for social activities unless excessive mobility barriers preclude even the fittest individual from navigating entrances. Common sense plays an important role in terms of accessibility. If the space is appropriate it should be made accessible to those who want to participate. There is no rule of thumb for judging adequate facilities; however, the absence of mobility barriers may be one criterion.

Material Considerations

There is no standard for determining the kinds of equipment or material required for successful social activities. Some social activities need only people; others require a great deal of equipment and supplies, but these will be furnished by the program (e.g., sports, crafts, drama, etc.) in which the activity occurs. Because any activity involving two or more participants is social, creating a list of required recreational materials is impossible.

Costs

Costs, like materials, cannot be determined. Social activities often require no monetary expenditures, although some entail considerable expense. The cost depends entirely on the nature of the activity; the material, equipment, transportation, and rentals needed; and the personnel employed.

Public Relations

As with all forms of recreational activity, the general public relations program will provide the requisite information about social activities. Because of the type of experience, personal communication among friends, acquaintances, relatives, or even casual associates probably is the best means to inform others of the interests and needs that participation may satisfy.

Summary

A person's happiness depends not only upon satisfactory fulfillment of basic human survival needs, but also on affiliation, companionship, and the useful feeling of time well spent. For those who remain employed, the job may fulfill some of the requirements individuals have for social interaction and useful occupation. For young people, school becomes the socializing institution for as long as students remain in the mandated setting. However, as leisure becomes more prevalent, recreational activity may be the solution to satisfy any need for congenial companionship and other social stabilizers.

Recreationists may meet the social needs of their constituency by offering a wide variety of activities that are stimulating, interesting, and require cooperative involvement. To do this, the recreationist must make sure that whatever activities are planned or organized by and for actual participants are primarily enjoyable. Without the attraction of enjoyment, either immediate or remotely perceived, there is little likelihood that individuals will bother to participate. As has been stated previously, social experiences are intrinsic to all recreational activities except a few solitary ones. Whenever cooperation and coordination are needed for participation, social experience is involved.

With the exception of reclusive personalities and those who want to pursue solitary recreational activity, almost all recreational experiences have social overtones or direct social contact. Most people crave companionship of peers. Those whose interests, backgrounds, and likes are similar or identical to others will be more comfortable. Even strangers with different styles and experiences are acceptable acquaintances in certain recreational circumstances. Brought together by a common preference for some activity, social interaction is inevitably generated and continues to ripen. Eventually, empathy and stronger social bonds result. This is the power of sociability and is one of the essential characteristics of recreational experience.

Providing opportunities for social contact and allowing relationships to grow among participants is an integral function of the recreational program. This is one of the desired outcomes of recreational activity and is a required category of the comprehensive program. It is the professional mandate of recreationists to see to and supply the means by which this human enterprise can be accomplished.

Selected Further Reference

Kolata, G. "Keeping Up with the Pack." *New York Times*, September 23, 2007: 1, 8.

CHAPTER 21

Special Events

Activities that are out of the ordinary, conducted at intermittent intervals, normally require extra effort, and add variety and stimulation to the otherwise routine daily experiences of the program come under the heading of special events or projects. Such activities may involve participants who might not be attracted to the standard recreational program. Special events may be conducted throughout the year, but each special project is unique and is programmed only once in any given year. These feature presentations are complex and take strenuous effort at all stages, whether planning or actual operation, if they are to be successful. They must be colorful and exciting in order to draw active participants and spectators. Almost any idea or theme will serve as the vehicle for a special event; however, most projects are classified according to **Table 21.1**.

Special events spotlight, correlate, and include many if not all of the other program categories. The special event may be looked upon as a culminating activity for a season, a month, or a unique occasion. The special event must be coordinated with other phases of the program and maintain the balance between routine and the change of pace that such an activity provides. Special projects are those events calculated to stimulate the individual who participates in the daily activities offered by the department as well as the stay-away. A stay-away, as the term implies, is a person who rarely, if ever, attends or participates in a recreational program offering. It affords the once-in-a-while excitement necessary to attract new participants and sustain those who engage in the daily activities that are provided.

Key events that trigger the special project should be built around mid-year and year-end periods. The summer festival, Christmas carnival, or winter frolic requires, perhaps, 6 months to 1 year of planning and preparation for success. For this reason, the special project cannot be programmed on a routine basis. It would surely sap the energies and creative expression of those required to do the work. Special projects that take place too frequently lose their uniqueness and become commonplace. The recreationist must know when to inject the special project into the program. There is a natural progression of events that lead directly to a culminating activity inclusive of all the other recreational experiences that have proceeded. In the normal course of events, every 3-month segment of a program may terminate with a modified special event, and every 6-month segment with a major special project. Within these time periods special events may be programmed, but they cannot be of the magnitude of the semiannual projects.

Holidays make excellent themes around which a special event can take form, but there is no month within the year that does not contain a holiday or commemorative date of some note. Therefore, recreationists in charge of programming special projects would do well to limit the occasions for such activities. The less they are performed in any given year, the greater the anticipation and satisfaction at the occurrence. If, for example, pyrotechnic displays were offered every week, they would soon lose the typical reaction of spectators insofar as rapt attention and exhilaration are concerned.

Table 21.1 Types of Special Events

Exhibitions	Festivals	Musicals
Art show	Fair	Band day contest
Craft show	Circus	Parade
Animal show	Field day	Opera
Gymnastic exhibition	Carnival	Operetta
Horticultural show	Block party	Pageant
Tableau	Community picnic	Symphony concert
Nature exhibit	Holiday celebration	Talent show
Fireworks	Yacht regatta	Concert band

Special events can be programmed only once and are repeated annually, depending on the resources of the community or agency carrying out the operation. Some special events are magnifications of annual specials, such as a 10-year, 25-year, 50-year, or even a centennial celebration. Most special events, however, are annual. The fall harvest, Christmas, Washington's birthday, Halloween, or other similar occasions can be designed as special events. Naturally, special events may be utilized to terminate a specific series of activities, carry some theme to an obvious conclusion, or emphasize some aspect of the program.

When special events are thematic, then the program for a specified period is focused on one major theme and the special event is presented as a climax. If activities were scheduled that concentrated on developing skills of any kind, the special event may be held as a demonstration and exhibition of the skills learned. As the seasons change, special events may be employed to introduce another facet of the anticipated program. Thus the opening of a senior center, community center, or park may be the cue for a special event to stress the very activities and opportunities these recreational places can offer to prospective clients/patrons.

The special event must be coordinated with other phases of the comprehensive program in order to maintain the equilibrium between routine activities and the dynamic change the event provides. A great deal of planning is required for the successful operation of these events. The recreationist must know when to inject the exceptional into the program. There is a natural progression of experiences leading to one focusing activity that includes all the recreational activities that have preceded it. It is not hard to understand that every 3- or 4-month segment of the program may be underscored with a modified special event while major events are left for semiannual or annual exposure.

Benefits of Special Events

Special events offer an aspect of personal identification with some activity, group, or interest that may be lacking in other program experiences. Some individuals may be unable to participate in the standard offerings for one reason or another. Perhaps the routine activities do not interest them, or they simply do not have the time or inclination to join or even to observe. The special events may stimulate them to watch, if not actually to perform or to aid in the development of the event.

Special events can provide recognition of work performed and energy expended as well as an exhibition of skills, projects, or performance. Because of their rarity, the special events may attract potential participants. The sound, excitement, and bigness of a special event may motivate some to attend who might otherwise stay away.

Finally, integration of the many categories of activities within the special event heightens the sense of enjoyment and satisfaction of those who actually perform in, design, prepare, or implement the proceedings as well as those who observe them. To the extent that people do contribute their time, talent, energy, and interest in the production of a many-faceted project, they will receive the psychic rewards that accompany successful accomplishment of any activity in which there is ego identification.

Activities

The activities that can be considered special events are relatively few because of the extraordinary nature of the project. It is not merely that they are bigger than the standard activities of the typical recreational program; rather, they stand out in consequence of organizational structure, complexity, effort involved, time consumed in planning and execution, timeliness, integration of diverse parts, and rarity. Scale and dimension must be considered, but what really determines that an activity is a special event is the fact that it is a single annual event that affects everyone in some way, either as participants or as spectators.

Performance

Within the category of performance is the exhibition of skills, projects, or talents. Performances are not merely extensions of routine activities as, for example, the exhibition after completion of a course in crafts. These performances are displayed as a climax to an entire season or as part of a larger manifestation.

A *beaux-arts* ball might be designed for those who have been involved in the arts category of the program and utilize the skills of several other categories (e.g., art, crafts, music, dance, or drama). Such performances require weeks, if not months, of rehearsal. Uncounted hours of preparation are required to ensure that supplies, materials, and equipment are at the right place at the right time for maximum utility and to dovetail all parts and parties into this one grandiose spectacle. Of course, there will be elements of masquerade, social interaction, and exhibition of projects to enhance the theme of the ball, as well as the dancing, singing, and theatrical effects attached to this event. It is highly unlikely that the time and effort put into such a project could be expended more than once each year. Performances will depend, to a great extent, upon the capabilities of those who participate—their talents, skills, knowledge, and motivation to be involved. Furthermore, the expense occasioned in such an undertaking cannot be small. All such considerations must be taken into account in planning special activities of this kind.

Excursions

Excursions are considered a part of the special events category because of the intensive planning, expense, time, and energy involved. Whether community-based or from an institutional setting, participants can benefit tremendously from a radical change of scene. This is particularly true if a great deal of preplanning is required and if the trip is to take a long time and require a great distance. Even if the trip is for a few hours by bus, train, or automobile, the preparations to accommodate those who wish to attend must be detailed and require great care.

Excursions from the community need to be treated with the care of vacation travel. The longer the trip and the greater the distance, the more it will cost. Careful planning must be devoted to all possibilities if interest, enjoyment, and personal satisfaction are to be achieved: What transportation vehicles will be involved? Is there a need for combined travel accommodations? Depending upon the economic capability of those who wish to take advantage of local recreational department travel packages, out-of-state or foreign travel may be possible. These latter experiences will probably not be for the majority of citizens in the community; however, if a sufficient number of people wish to combine their resources and use the purchasing power of the local department as their travel agent, it is feasible that extended excursions and even foreign travel may be undertaken. What kind of residential accommodations are to be made and by whom? Whether the base of operations is the community center or treatment center, the length of the trip, cost, and logistics are extremely important in determining whether travel is likely.

Entertainment

Production of a stage presentation (e.g., play, musical, operetta, bazaar, carnival, commemoration) can involve as many participants as there are interested persons to fill roles, manage the production, act as technicians, and finally take part as spectators or participants in the various integral activities. A bazaar or carnival may consist of any number of skill activities, exhibitions, demonstrations, or social activities, including auctions, novelties, stunts, refreshments, speeches, rides, and other activities such as driving a nail or making ice cream. A great deal of coordination and participant support are required if each person is to gain a sense of accomplishment from the event.

The only real deterrents to the production of such projects are where individuals may be institutionalized for medical treatment, long-term care, or rehabilitation practices and the necessary adaptations of space, equipment, and activities are unavailable so that those with physical or mental disabilities cannot participate. Community-based special events of this type may also require some adaptations for persons with disabilities but they will be less formidable because community residents probably are not as severely restricted as are those confined to treatment centers.

Socials

Almost every special event can and does produce social interaction. However, within the format of the special event is the category of a social occasion that honors some person, recognizes distinguished service, commemorates a date, or offers thanksgiving by devotion or memorials. All of these occasions have intrinsic social attributes. The nature of the event demands preparation, personal effort, some economic resources, and certain supplies and equipment. Pageants, testimonials, tableaux, dancing, music, and other similar activities may be part of the proceedings. Nevertheless, the social aspect is fundamental to this event, and other categories are integrated to provide the attractiveness, gaiety, or, when necessary, the sober reflection that contributes to the significance of the program.

Other activities may be undertaken as special events, but they are characterized by intent. Thus, workshops, conferences, Chautauquas, and the like may fit the category by virtue of bigness, rarity, planning needed, and integration of other activities.

Instruction

Despite its major theme or purpose, a special event is made up of many diverse kinds of activities, so participants need few skills or knowledge to achieve pleasure or satisfaction from being part of the activity. There are no skills that cannot be taught for incorporation into the conglomerate that will produce a special event. Talents and skills in art, crafts, music, or drama are utilized in any stage production, and other skills used will depend on the theme of the special event. Instruction in whatever skills are necessary for participation, the honing of old skills by practicing new techniques, and the acquisition of new skills that capture the interest of the potential participant are all part of the learning environment.

The special event offers opportunities to demonstrate skill, knowledge, talent, enthusiasm, and the material results of directed learning. It includes color, spectacle, amusement, and celebrations that almost everybody considers significant. Ample consideration is given to those who need the special event merely to encourage them to attend something different. A special event is designed to attract those who might not ordinarily participate, those who want to gain recognition, and those who desire to be entertained. Thus, it is no different from any of the categories of recreational instruction.

Personnel

Requirements for recreationists in the development, organization, and operation of special events are somewhat different from those for the routine categories of the recreational program. Special events need recreationists who are ingenious and who will not be overwhelmed by the demands that are entailed in precise planning, detailed arrangements, and concern for the needs of both participants and spectators. The normal complement of staff employed by the community department or institution may be sufficient to administer this extraordinary project, but they can be greatly assisted by volunteers with the time, energy, and knowledge to create the necessary effects.

The development and successful accomplishment of special events requires detailed logistics: the number of individuals who will be expected to take part, the need for food and beverages, any vehicles that might be required, supplies, and equipment. In addition, interested persons must be included on various committees that will have the responsibility for advising on activities in the major event as well as for performing certain chores afterward.

Accessibility

Special events, whatever their nature, must be easily accessible to all those who will be participants. This means that organizational patterns must be established early so that personnel can be assigned appropriately. Furthermore, any mobility barriers must be removed, and suitable aids should be readily available in case they become necessary.

Material Considerations

It is impossible to say precisely what kinds of supplies, equipment, or other paraphernalia will be required to produce a successful special event. It is likely that material needed may range from little or none, to recycled scrap, to highly sophisticated substances. The amount of equipment and supplies required will depend upon the ingenuity of the recreationists and the participants, the type of extravaganza programmed, and the number of participants.

Costs

Costs for special events, like material, are variable. Some excursions, such as extensive travel, may cost individual participants hundreds or perhaps thousands of dollars, whereas a special topical or historical event held in the community may require only inexpensive costumes. Monetary outlays will depend on the organizers, but will probably be necessary for material, transportation, food and beverages, and equipment to produce special effects. The larger the celebration, the more activities will be integrated, and the more leadership and other accoutrements will be required.

Public Relations

It is generally easier to disseminate information to a specific public than to market a mass appeal to a vaguely determined potential clientele. If the messages sent out by the agency, whether directed from a community center or a treatment center, can persuade residents that it is to their benefit to attend or, more significantly, to take part personally, both the agency and the individual will have gained from the contact. Information should be factual and timely and include the place of activity, costs, recreationists available, alternate dates, transportation, and anything else that will serve to influence participation. It is also probable that public involvement will be guaranteed if the public relations program can utilize an idea that becomes a positively emotional issue for the target audience.

Perhaps no better public relations medium exists than word of mouth. An acquaintance, friend, or relative may do more than anyone else to cajole or persuade a somewhat reluctant individual to participate.

The recreational program serves as its own public relations device. If a program has attractive activities in settings in which many different recreational forms can be enjoyed without people getting in each other's way, and at a time that is convenient to those who want to participate, it is probable that people will be convinced that they should experiment just to learn what they can do. Convenience, attractiveness, ease of entry, helpful professionals, and a variety of activities all contribute to promoting attendance and active engagement.

A special event, because it focuses attention on one outstanding production, may activate newsgathering agencies to take notice and publicize the event in the mass media. Long before the event, the recreational agency should have sent copy to whatever print or electronic media exist in or are covering the community, but it is also helpful if newspapers and television and radio stations consider the occasion newsworthy enough to send someone to cover it. Such reporting will have little influence in promoting participation in the current year, but it may serve as a source for the next year. If the media can be advised that this kind of event is an annual affair, and that it generates news because of its bigness, the people it attracts, or its general interest and human interest appeal, they may assign coverage and even feature stories about the special event before it takes place. Thus, those who may have known nothing about the activity will be alerted to the possibility of involvement.

All of the methods for obtaining and maintaining sound public relations must be employed for any recreational program. Therefore, it is necessary that a barrage of appropriate information designed to educate all of the citizens to the offerings of the agency be constantly set before the target audience. This is no less valid for the institutionally based program. Although the number of residents/patients is smaller, there are just as many reasons for offering these people information about the program, particularly a special event. The methods used may be less mass-audience-oriented, but volunteers, posters, bulletin boards, flyers, and personal invitations can be effective in tempting institutionalized or home-bound disabled persons to the program. There will be those who cannot attend for physical or mental reasons. To the extent possible, some aspects of the program should be taken to them and modified in whatever way is necessary so that any physical or mental limitations will not automatically cause these people to be omitted or poorly served by recreational services.

Integration

Many special events are composed of activities that selectively use all other categories of the recreational program. Almost anything that can be programmed, depending upon the nature or theme of the special event, requires highlighting the many and varied recreational activities that display talent, skill, knowledge, performance, or an exhibition of things completed. The purpose of all the fanfare, spotlighting, and investment of time, money, and effort is to coordinate and integrate diverse aspects of the program so as to multiply the enjoyment, satisfaction, and ego involvement of those who seek outlets for personal expression in this manner.

Summary

All recreational programs need to attract resistive or non-participants. Some people are unable or unwilling to take part in the usual offerings of a recreational program. Special projects are specifically designed to overcome this apparent reluctance and stimulate interest for potential involvement.

Additionally, the special event injects a different offering from that of the routine or habitually entered recreational activities. It is attractive to nearly everybody due to the unusual focus of the production.

Because of the nature of the event, it requires much time for preparation. It also needs the assistance of many persons in the physical development aspect as well as those who will be the direct performers. Thus, there is a place to be found for those who prefer anonymity or those who wish to be seen and acknowledged. In any case, participation in any phase of the special event is rewarding to the participant by virtue of the satisfaction of achievement that it brings and the enjoyment that is discovered in the occurrence.

For some people, special events may be the single facet of a comprehensive program that will appeal to and have meaning for them. It can be the best means for introducing a reluctant individual to a potpourri of varied recreational experiences combined in one extravaganza, thereby exposing that person to the opportunities the program has to offer. In this way, people may be motivated to join in the presentation of more routine activities and so attain pleasure and the satisfaction of personal development and self-expression that might otherwise have been missed.

The special events in any recreational facility or institution are the occasions that add flavor to the recreational program. They have the potential to attract new clients or patrons, perhaps discover new talent or skill, provide an incentive to take part and practice, give an ever-changing format or emphasis to the program, and create opportunities to secure engagement that for whatever reasons have failed to be obtained previously. Their variety is endless and limited only by the imagination of the recreationist in charge and the participants who may assist in the planning and development of the event. In general, special events are categorized by:

- Demonstrations of skills learned
- Exhibitions of objects made or collected
- Performances before an audience
- Contests, tournaments, intramurals
- Mass group participation in any activity that has previously been practiced in small groups
- Social occasions, community picnics
- Excursions or prolonged trips
- Displays, tableaux, pageants
- Ceremonial occasions, memorials, historic re-enactments

Special events should provide opportunities for as many as possible to participate. They must be truly representative of activities occurring and learned within the recreational program of the community or institution. They should provide the incentive for days, if not weeks or months, of preparation. Such planning and preparation should not be arduous or overly fatiguing, unless the individual wants to indulge, and even then it must be in the spirit of good recreational endeavor.

Special events are a necessary component of a well-organized recreational program that confers benefits upon those who attend or actually participate. The project is a spectacular occasion and serves to arouse interest even in jaded appetites or encourages the hesitant to attempt some part of the experience. There is, in reality, something for everybody in the successful presentation of a compelling attraction.

Selected Further References

Barer, B. *Parade Day: Marching Through the Calendar Year*. New York: Holiday House, Inc., 2003.

Beck, R., and S. B. Metrick. *Art of Ritual: Creating and Performing Ceremonies for Growth and Change*. Berkeley, CA: Celestial Arts Publishing Co., 2004.

Davis, M. F. *Field Day*. Danbury, CT: Scholastic Library Publishing, 2003.

Eisenbichler, K., and W. Huskin. *Carnival and the Carnivalesque: Ludus, Medieval and Early Renaissance Theater and Drama*. New York: Rodopi, 1999.

Gardner, L., and S. Trepening. *Special Events Magazine Presents the Art of Event Design*. Malibu, CA: Milamar Communications, 1997.

Goldblatt, J. *Special Events: The Art of Science Celebration*. New York: John Wiley & Sons, Inc., 1990.

Huggins-Cooper, L. *Festivals*. North Mankato, MN: Smart Apple Media, 2004.

Jasso, G. *Special Events from A to Z: The Complete Educator's Handbook*. Thousand Oaks, CA: Sage Publications, 1996.

Lovegrove, K. *Pageant: The Beauty Contest*. New York: te Neues Publishing Co., 2004.

O'Rourke, B. *Pageant Master*. West Seneca, NY: F.A. Thorpe Publishers, 2003.

Twigg, N. J. *Celebrate Simply: Your Guide to Simpler More Meaningful Holidays and Special Occasions*. Knoxville, TN: Counting the Cost Publications, 2003.

Wexler, R. F. *Circus of the Grand Design*. Canton, OH: Prime, 2004.

CHAPTER
22 Program Evaluation

Evaluation is the continuous process of improving any enterprise by the application of information so that a deliberate selection of alternatives can be made. "Process" means a specific and consistent activity comprising a variety of techniques and concerning several procedures. Evaluation is an ongoing process and should not be perceived only as a finalized comparison between some objective and actual performance. The sole reason for evaluating anything is its improvement. Whatever information is generated is utilized with the immediate end of making the recreational service better. This betterment may come in terms of programming, facility planning, design, construction, operation, personnel performance, or any other condition, situation, or factor involving the development, organization, and provision of recreational service. Unless improvement is the net result of evaluation, evaluation has not been performed successfully.

Evaluation concerns the collection of actual information about any experience, concept, process, or thing. The information is then presented so that some judgment can be made. The judgment assumes that standards or criteria exist by which a factor may be measured. Thus, the value of one factor, such as an experience, may be determined on some known basis—for example, its promise of social contact or lack of interpersonal relationship. The value of each of several possible experiences may be assessed by comparison. In one instance, the intensity of relationship or social contact made is a sample, in contrast to another, of relative superficiality, denial, or rejection of interacting with the individual in question. How effective an experience is can be judged on the basis of information received about what the individual obtained from participation. The value of any experience may be determined by its impact upon the participant—that is, by the extent to which it, by itself or in comparison with other potential experiences, facilitates the specifically desired changes of those having the experience.

Recreational activity, although not a complex process insofar as the individual is concerned, is, as a social institution, among the more intricate procedures attempted within any sector of society. Recreational service is a complex process dealing with the selection of concepts, objectives, delivery systems, industry, and all of the functions that have come to be identified with the provision of recreational service. Choices have to be made in the design and implementation of a recreational service program, and the effectiveness of the program must be carefully scrutinized. The process of evaluation is a constant function to which all facets of the departmental system, organization, operation, and services must be submitted for study so that assessments can be made.

The application of intelligence is conceived not only in terms of intellectual command, but also as the gathering, analysis, and utilization of information designed to identify possible alternatives before any decisions can be reached. In this sense, intelligence is viewed as perspicacity as well as the means for diminishing ambiguity in making a correct choice from among the possibilities that present themselves. A deliberate choice must be made to monitor operations so their enhancement is forthcoming. Deliberate selection is based on differentiated alternatives that accrue in response to information collected about the action that might be taken concerning some enterprise.

Alternatives are two or more diverse measures that could be performed in reaction to some condition needing modification. Enterprise improvement takes place only when current behaviors, activities, or operations are changed. There are at least three situations that might require desirable altered action; if there is evidence that (1) some unsatisfied need exists, (2) a problem exists, or (3) a favorable condition exists that should be exploited. Where there are limited resources, as is so often true of public recreational service agencies, priorities must be assigned and decisions made on the basis of available means. The focus of evaluation is to come to some decision about a number of alternatives based on assessed values and benefits determined by careful analysis.

Determining Objectives

The process of evaluation is based on information that permits a comparison between any entity being scrutinized and its proximity to the objective or objectives that have been predetermined as achievable. The objectives of recreational service, regardless of their derivation and kind, have a number of sources. As an instrument for the benefit of society, recreational service is responsive to the needs or demands of the society from which it originates. Whether recreationists seek out these needs and initiate programs to satisfy constituent requests or actually propagandize the potential clientele, thereby creating demand where none existed previously, recreational service has responded both as a mirror of the culture and as an advocate for new and expanded horizons.

Societal Needs

The inexorable weight of society has required the establishment of the field of recreational service—at least in the public sector—to fulfill certain functions that otherwise would not or could not have been accomplished by other sector enterprises. Now that public sector agencies have demonstrated the feasibility of providing specific recreational activities for which there is a steady demand, private entrepreneurs have moved into the provision of services for commercial gain. There would have been little in the way of private racquet clubs, roller and hockey rinks, sports clubs, and other private sector delivery services unless the public sector departments had not first shown the popularity of specific recreational activities.

Individual Needs

The needs of individuals comprise a second source for objectives. The extent to which recreational service can supply experience, places, leadership, and instruction to meet the common needs of all people will constitute the potential participants of each agency, and must be recognized by each department sooner or later.

The law plays a significant role in the determination of objectives. The law, written as statute, code, or legislation, may define or specify the obligations and responsibilities that the recreational agency has toward its constituency. Although some legislation is broad and generally calls upon public agencies to perform in certain ways so that minimum services of a recreational nature are provided, other statutes or codes may itemize and specifically demand that public or other agencies offer particular recreational services to persons with disabilities, for example. The demands placed on social sector agencies by law offer an important source from which objectives may be selected.

Authoritative Statements

Another source of objectives is the scholarly statements issued by a number of recognized authorities, professional associations, conferences, institutes, or commissions. The objectives of the field, whether broadly or narrowly construed, may be developed by scholars in the discipline. These writings, almost by default, may become the authority from which objectives for the field are defined.

A number of objectives may be formulated from these sources, and these will serve as the goals determined to be achievable by the means available. Investigating needs and deciding which recreational services should be provided involve both systematic research and value judgments. Choices must be made by assessing the rationale and logic supporting the divergent alternatives. Study of the consequences of pertinent information and of their relevance to recreational service planning is a form of evaluation. Philosophical orientations, by their very nature, concern and compel consideration of values. If all of these factors are not involved in choosing objectives, the ones that have been omitted may nullify efforts at achieving the objectives. As with any objectives, there may be freedom of choice, but the accomplishment of goals will be determined by the ability to perform and the availability of resources to ensure success.

Establishing Objectives

The ongoing process of evaluation requires the establishment of well-defined objectives. Initially, consideration must be given to the items that allow the agency to be evaluated. Objectives should be chosen that set forth what the agency is attempting to accomplish and what its constituent personnel should achieve. Agency objectives will best be understood and accepted when there is cooperative effort on the part of all professional personnel at every level of the agency hierarchy. Neither the executive alone nor supervisors alone should set the objectives to be reached.

Objectives should be broadly stated; however, the wide latitude of objectives must still allow them to be accomplished by singular means. Other objectives will inevitably grow out of an appraisal of participant performance. Evaluation can never be looked upon as something apart from the provision of professional services to people. It is an integral factor of what the recreationist does to make his or her function more effective. Evaluation of performance is as significant as performance itself.

In establishing objectives, a distinct set of responsibilities is readily apparent. These factors can be grouped in general as programming, physical plant, public relations, participation, personnel and staffing needs, and financial support. Therefore, seven separate areas emerge as having need for evaluation. These may be stated as:

1. Programming recreational activities.
2. The development and maintenance of the physical plant including all structures and facilities.
3. Personnel standards, professional development, and management practices.
4. Adequate financial support from whatever the various sources available to the agency.
5. The development of an ongoing program of public relations.
6. The appraisal of the quality of participation in the number of users that the agency has.
7. Patron perceptions of recreational service.

Continual procedures designed to determine the value of the recreational service agency in the community are essential if the department is to realize its objectives in the provision of a comprehensive and balanced program of activities to meet the recreational needs of people. The idea of evaluating recreational agencies is not new. Everyone who has ever been to a recreational agency intuitively knows the good and bad aspects of the service received. Almost every layman fancies him- or herself an expert on the subject of recreational service. After all, "Isn't recreational activity a subjective and personal matter?" Because evaluation continues uninterrupted, it is absolutely necessary that its standards, devices, and techniques be understood. Methods must be developed for gathering facts so that judgments can be made as to how closely the recreational agency approximates its goals. Evaluation must be based on reliable information, and the sources of these facts need to be identified. Therefore, instruments or measuring devices that are accurate, consistently applicable to the areas undergoing evaluation, and easily administered by competent professionals are required.

Evaluation and Outcomes

Evaluation can be closely associated with every phase of planning and operational elements of any recreational service agency. Because of this fact, the process needs to become a cohesive force to assure that all activities fulfill and contribute to the goals of recreational service. Evaluation is both end-in-view and practice. As practice it includes studies and procedures designed to sustain or improve the quality of participation, methods of program presentation, professional personnel performance, and every other aspect of agency operation. It is a process that discloses evidence of inadequacy, evidence of progress, and evidence of proximity to any ideal that has been selected as the agency's goal.

To the extent that evaluation is also an end, it is improvement, which more nearly exemplifies its meaning. Evaluation includes both ends and means, for it permits a judgment to be reached concerning some person, place, or thing and may also be described as a process for reaching judgments.

How such judgments are reached and what end they may serve is a proper study for any recreationist who is concerned with evaluation procedures. It must be understood from the outset that evaluation is a process of determining information about the degree to which recreational service objectives are achieved by a provider. It should never be thought of as a mere collection of techniques, the total of which equals the process. Among the principles of evaluation that can effectively guide the evaluation process are those that deal with:

- Identification and understanding of what has to be evaluated. No method of evaluation can be chosen or initiated until the objectives of evaluation have been clearly determined. The effectiveness of the evaluation process relies as much on what is to be evaluated as it does on the validity, reliability, and technical stability of the instruments employed.

- Prior consideration should be given to the appropriateness of the evaluative technique chosen in terms of the aims to be served. Every evaluative technique has positive and negative factors with regard to gaining an understanding of what is being evaluated. Whichever technique is best fitted for the situation under examination should be utilized. It is not a question of which procedure to use, but which is most appropriate for a particular situation.

- An inclusive program of evaluation requires diverse techniques if it is to be effective and valuable. No one evaluation technique is adequate for determining all the significant products of recreational service. A variety of devices, including objective, subjective, and observational methods, is required to evaluate the host of possibilities included in the outcome of any recreational program. A variety of techniques may be fruitful, particularly when any single instrument is relatively limited in scope. Combining several procedures provides a greater likelihood that a more accurate and adequate judgment will be able to be made.

- Appropriate use of evaluation techniques requires a complete understanding of both the strategies and weaknesses of the procedure. The evaluation techniques can vary from quite precise instruments (e.g., quantitatively based statistics dealing with participant use of departmental facilities) to highly subjective narrative reports. Of course, there is always the possibility of incorrect analysis of evaluation results. Sometimes accuracy is imparted to instruments that are not precise enough. Evaluators should recognize that most techniques are limited and should not be credited with qualities they do not possess.

- Evaluation is a process that is justified only to the extent to which the results are put to appropriate use. If evaluation is considered an exercise rather than a means for delivering better services, it would be better left undone. When evaluation is seen as a process for obtaining information upon which substantive decisions can be based for improved services in every phase of departmental operation, then the process has served its purpose. Implied in this rule is the concept that objectives must be clearly defined prior to the initiation of the process; that the techniques utilized are appropriate for the purposes identified; that decisions will be guided by what the evaluation process elicited; and that the varied evaluative techniques employed are chosen on the basis of their value to improve departmental offerings, program operation, and supporting administration.

Factors for Evaluation

In developing an instrument to evaluate the recreational program of activities, it is necessary to include essential secondary elements in the process. These elements are vital to delivering the kinds of services required in a comprehensive and balanced recreational program. In fact, the organization and operation of delivered recreational services could not be accomplished without them. It is not merely that the recreational program is not operationally possible if these elements are not present, but that these functions underwrite every aspect of the program.

Among these functions are those of leadership or human resource factors, financial support, area and facility development, maintenance operations, and an adequate supply of materials including apparatus, equipment, tools, and other basic supplies necessary for carrying out activities. In the following topics, standards and recommendations are offered as an illustration of selected areas for examination that any recreational service agency might want to evaluate.

Topic 1: Financial Support

REQUIREMENT. An appropriation should be made equal to the amount needed for the full operation and administration of all recreational services. The amount depends on the interest of the community, the economic status of the community, and present or anticipated recreational resources, areas, or facilities of a personal or physical nature, but would be whatever is available and appropriate to supply the recreational needs of the people in the community.

RECOMMENDATION. An annual appropriation made from the general subdivisional fund will be earmarked for recreational service operations. This sum depends on the willingness and need of the citizens to pay for and receive recreational services. The same requirement is true for private or commercial agencies in terms of their budgetary capability. Presumably, fees collected by an agency for recreational use will be the basis for its fiscal policy.

DETAILED DEVELOPMENT OF THE RECOMMENDATION.
1. *General fund appropriations:* Money supplied from general taxes received from the community and appropriated to the recreational service department for current fiscal operations. This appears to be the most uncomplicated and direct means for providing financial support to the recreational agency, if the sum appropriated actually allows effective operation of the recreational service department.
2. *The recreational mill levy:* An amount of tax money stipulated by state law, which may be collected from the citizens of the community in order to operate a recreational service agency. A popular referendum must take place in order to pass a mill levy,

which generally does not exceed three mills. Upon the completion of the referendum, and if the motion for a millage levy is passed, the money collected will be utilized exclusively for the operation of the recreational agency. The mill levy may be for a stipulated number of years or longer and may also be rescinded by popular vote.

3. *The bond issue:* A legal instrument indebting the community for a specified sum within a particular period of time. It is utilized in the construction and development of large capital outlays for land acquisition, construction of buildings, and purchase of expensive equipment. It is only passed by popular referendum.

4. *Special assessments:* Those levies laid upon specific individuals for improvements within a particular area when such improvements affect only the residents of that area rather than the community at large.

5. *Fees and charges:* Utilized to supplement any financial support appropriated to the agency. Such fees and charges must never be utilized for profit making, nor should they be excessive, exorbitant, or of such nature as to prohibit individuals from entering into or participating in recreational activities sponsored by the recreational agency. The fee and the charge must be used sparingly, and may be justified only in terms of providing extraordinary services or activities not possible under the appropriated funds for the operation of the agency. Corollary: It is better to allow an individual to participate in a recreational activity than to omit that person from that activity because he or she does not have the monetary means for entrance.

Topic 2: Planning for Recreational Services

REQUIREMENT. A broad framework guiding future substantive actions and operations in the recreational agency. These principles are concerned with the development and accumulation of basic information, the analysis of that information for categorizing into classes for easy comprehension, the projection of alternate courses of action, and the appraisal of the consequences of such diversified courses.

RECOMMENDATION. Planning procedures and the guided development of a recreational agency must be implemented to enhance the functions of that agency, in order to avoid the waste of duplication, inefficiency, and deficient concepts.

DETAILED DEVELOPMENT OF THE RECOMMENDATION.
1. *Analysis and research:* The collection of basic material and information relating to current concepts of recreational programming; design, construction, and maintenance of structures and facilities; investigation of comparative agencies; study of professional literature pertinent to the field of recreational service for philosophy, principles, ethics, and practices; and examination of the collected data to determine whether the agency is keeping abreast of current professional concepts in each of the aforementioned areas (i.e., physical plant, program, and practices). Research may be carried out using statistical representation,

survey, or open forums. Research will attempt to determine whether the recreational services provided by the agency are adequate and effective in meeting the needs of the agency's clientele and the population of the wider community.

2. *The master plan:* A detailed construct concerning the socioeconomic, political, geographic, demographic, and educational investigation of the community in order to determine the most effective placement of physical recreational resources. It also allows for the employment of competent, professionally prepared individuals to operate the activities afforded by such physical resources to meet the potential population trends and recreational needs of present and future residents of the community. Such a plan must be coordinated with other institutional physical structures of the community including the school system and other municipal agency services (i.e., police, fire, health, public works, streets, parks, parkways and lighting developments). The master plan is usually undertaken as a 25-year directive. Among the factors to be considered are:
   a. The economic feasibility of such a master plan
   b. Whether the community is interested
   c. Demand upon the citizenry
   d. Increased and more interesting activities
   e. Whether the community is involved with the planning procedures
   f. The city's political institutions
   g. The agency under which the recreational department operates
   h. Population demographics

3. *The priority schedule:* A timetable for the implementation of physical recreational facilities in accordance with a master plan. The master plan is a policy statement, but the priority schedule is a timetable for the construction of the facilities laid out in the master plan. This takes into consideration what is most important, what is needed immediately for the greatest number of people, and what can be done with the amount of money available.

   The acquisition of suitable land for recreational purposes has first priority. When the land has been obtained it must be planned appropriately in terms of open spaces, various facility emplacements, structures, access areas, and so on, so that community recreational needs may be satisfied.

4. *The 5-year plan:* An immediate appraisal of the community, which includes past studies concerning traffic placements, water mains, sewer, and lighting systems within recent periods. The master plan is enacted in 5-year segments. This permits flexibility and allows adjustments to be made as population density fluctuates or movements are noted. It also allows for technological innovation and natural or man-made events that might occur, thereby changing the variables that influence the plan. This plan is conceived as carrying out the provisions indicated in the master plan and is related to those community-wide and regional installations that typically enlarge the kinds of comprehensive program services offered within the community.

5. *The 3-year plan:* Concerns the relationship of immediate population movement, and takes into consideration the necessity

of developing facilities in accordance with the latest population increase. It is only concerned with that 3-year period. It is, therefore, a plan of considerable limitation and restricted physical developments.

This plan is generally concerned with specific neighborhood developments rather than community developments. The content of the plan will therefore be oriented to several neighborhoods within the community that appear to be gaining in population and with the provision of facilities to accommodate that increase. The development of facilities will necessarily be concerned with building structures, individual playgrounds, individual parks, or other facilities rather than complex installations.

6. *The 1-year short-term plan:* Initiated for any population increase for one neighborhood within the community. Rather than concerning many aspects of the community, this plan will be related to meeting the needs of the fastest growing neighborhood of the community and the provision of recreational services and facilities in that neighborhood. Such a facility would usually be the neighborhood playground or the renovation of an existing building for increased use.

7. *The emergency plan:* Concerned with the provision of recreational services and development or renovation of facilities in densely populated sections of the community. It is intended to meet recreational deficits within heavily populated regions of the community rather than acquiring land or developing new facilities in outlying areas. The emergency plan, as its name implies, is concerned with meeting the urgent and immediate recreational needs caused by underdeveloped property or lack of adequate space and facilities. This plan must be undertaken because of lack of foresight on the part of the administrators or government authorities to see the necessity of recreational planning in relation to the growth of the community. Such a plan will never keep up with population growth, is inadequate to say the least, and is instigated as an expediency measure in response to demand. Such a plan indicates that no master plan has been developed or is available.

8. *Spot surveys:* Appraisals of the community taken at random that indicate whether the provision of recreational service programming is adequate and meeting the needs of the citizens of the community. The spot survey may be made using a questionnaire, personal interviews, or observation. Its most useful function is to indicate whether the program and the facilities are adequate, well attended, and well operated.

Topic 3: Human Resources Standards

REQUIREMENT. Incumbents in recreational positions must have an educational and experiential preparation that will enable them to perform the essential work of serving the public's recreational needs. Such personnel will be on a professional level combining qualities of competence, dedication, knowledge, and personal integrity to effectively function and carry on the duties and responsibilities of office.

RECOMMENDATION. Only personnel who can demonstrate their theoretical and practical knowledge and professional efficiency will be employed on a full-time professional basis. Minimum standards for entrance into the field of recreational service include graduation from an accredited college or university with major work in recreational service education, additional experience, and educational preparation necessary for the position level. The attendant salary becomes higher as duties and responsibilities become more complex. With progressively more responsibility, authority, and higher salary as tenure on the job lengthens, job pressures also mount. As the employee obtains more experience and is, consequently, given more authority and responsibility, the complexities at this level of the organizational hierarchy become more intense.

JOB ANALYSIS. Employees are required to report the duties performed hour by hour for a given period. Forms are prepared on which the standard tasks (general supervision, instruction, counseling, program organization, planning community context, preparing reports) are shown. Places are also provided for description of other non-standard duties, analyzed as to duties performed and time-consuming, and general tendencies as noted.

ANALYSIS OF EDUCATION AND EXPERIENCE OF WORKERS IN RELATION TO SPECIFIC SKILLS EMPLOYED ON-THE-JOB. They have proved of assistance in indicating the skills that should be sought in selecting employees and suggesting the nature of in-service instruction to be provided.

RATING SYSTEMS. Several systems for rating the work and value of employees have been devised. They are difficult to apply to employees whose work does not lend itself to objective measurement, but, within certain limits, they are helpful in systematizing the appraisal of employees and in emphasizing the relative value of qualities that contribute to success.

Topic 4: Recreational Spaces

REQUIREMENT. Any land, water, or physical structure, space, or area (i.e., physical property) that may be utilized for recreational purposes or that has historic, aesthetic, scientific, or scenic value should be acquired as part of the public's legacy in conserving the natural open, wooded, and water spaces for present and future utilization.

RECOMMENDATION. All land that has historic, aesthetic, scientific, or scenic value that can feasibly be acquired and held for public benefit should be so acquired and held. All current space holdings should be carefully investigated in order to discover present and potential recreational use insofar as population movement, subdivisional development, arterial construction, or other land-diminishing encroachments on the public domain are concerned.

DETAILED DEVELOPMENT OF THE RECOMMENDATION.
1. *Land acquisition:* Vital in acquiring sites for recreational purposes. These sites must be located in areas that are accessible for utilization and acquirable for the amount of money the community has to spend. The land itself must not need too much development before it can be utilized. Land acquisition is necessary if recreational services in the community are to keep pace with the growth of the community. It is unnecessary if the community

shows no growth over a period of time. As people realize the possibilities in recreational activities and recreationists educate them about the need for acquiring various spaces, the public will want to acquire these areas for their use. Much of this land will be inside the community, as well as in possible and/or annexed areas outside of the community, to take care of the newly educated public. These acquisitions are necessary to conserve potential recreational space in the face of encroachment of all kinds. Land should be acquired and dedicated in perpetuity before any of the many commercial and private organizations stake a claim.

2. *Nomenclature, size, site, and characteristics:* What the land is called—park, playground, reservation, refuge, conservation site, wilderness area, and so on. The size of the spaces should range from 5000 square feet to several hundred acres within the community for any one area. There should be at least 1 acre of land for every 100 people. Any site selected should be well located, be dry or able to be quickly drained, not need to be cut or filled extensively, be easily accessible, not be dangerous, and be placed so it can be utilized by people who need to use it. These characteristics are referred to as topographic and terrain features (i.e., the characteristics of the land).

3. *Land-use patterns:* Examination of zoning laws in the community or to determine land-use patterns. This involves determining where transportation, industry, and schools will be placed so that placement of recreational facilities, structures, and areas will be more feasible and appropriate. The land should be dedicated in perpetuity by the public for provision of recreational services. To fight encroachment, an aroused public is the best bet.

Topic 5: Recreational Structures

REQUIREMENT. Any physical structure designed and built in such a way as to serve primarily and directly as a center for recreational activity or that may have a secondary recreational potential (i.e., indirect value for recreational experience, although the principal purpose is oriented towards some other endeavor).

RECOMMENDATION. Physical structures will be designed and constructed to serve primarily as functional recreational centers, where feasible. When existing physical structures have been designed with some purpose other than recreational service as the main function, they should be utilized as supporting centers until such time as specialized structures may be erected.

DETAILED DEVELOPMENT OF THE RECOMMENDATION.

1. *Primary structures:* Buildings constructed for functional recreational activities and experiences (e.g., pools, parks, zoos, centers, botanical gardens, and so on). These facilities may have secondary purposes also, but they are primarily designed and used for recreational purposes.

2. *Supportive structures:* Structures utilized primarily for purposes other than recreational experiences, such as schools (activities for

directed learning), hospitals (facilities for the delivery of medical and health services), and churches (buildings for religious purposes). These structures should be used for recreational service, providing such use does not interfere with the purposes for which the structures were originally intended.

Topic 6: Recreational Facilities and Traffic Patterns

REQUIREMENT. All facilities that may be utilized for some recreational purpose should be considered in an inverse priority order (highest to lowest), in terms of their primary purpose. Facilities and equipment may be appraised only in view of population size, density, and actual usage involved, particularly expendable equipment.

RECOMMENDATION. Such facilities as are necessary to accommodate public usage within or around a specific community should be built, maintained, and operated in accordance with enumerated supervisory processes, design details, the relationship of the population to any single facility (i.e., density), and construction types in conformity with local zoning and inspection codes.

Topic 7: Public Relations and Recreational Service

REQUIREMENT. This is a procedure that serves as an information gatherer and distributor (i.e., reception and transmission of data). It functions as a sounding board and analytic machine in defining the public's interests and desires and how the policies, plans, and services of the recreational agency may be interpreted. This procedure utilizes many media—oral, visual, and physical—in reaching the public eye, ear, and taste. There are many instruments for gathering and analyzing public demands and interests.

RECOMMENDATION. The inauguration of a specific section within the recreational agency (if the organization is large enough) or the delegation of the public relations function to one employee of the organization (i.e., a public relations specialist) for the gathering, dissemination, and interpretation of information concerning agency policy and service to the public and the collection, analysis, and assessment of the recreational needs of the public.

DETAILED DEVELOPMENT OF THE RECOMMENDATION.
1. Transmission:
    a. Program
    b. Evaluation of the program
    c. Utilizing mass communication
    d. Listing of material via fliers, leaflets, brochures
    e. Advertising gimmicks
    f. Meetings, forums, discussions
2. Reception:
    a. Suggestion boxes
    b. Interviews
    c. Conferences
    d. Inventories
    e. Checklists

Topic 8: Patron Perceptions of Recreational Service

REQUIREMENT. Monitoring of provided recreational services must incorporate the views and understanding of those who actually participate in the activities offered by the public department as well as the opinions held by other citizens who do not participate.

RECOMMENDATION. To the extent possible, a variety of surveys, polls, interviews, or other feedback procedures should be implemented so the department is made aware of the criticisms, deficits, or inadequacies of the public recreational service as well as the successes and strengths of the system.

DETAILED DEVELOPMENT OF THE RECOMMENDATION.

1. Creation of instruments that can record and assist in assessing the adequacy, variety, and availability of recreational activities.
2. Development of recording instruments that can measure citizen use of facilities.
3. Utilization of instruments that will determine citizen perception of overall departmental effectiveness. Such an appraisal device should be concerned with participant and nonparticipant perceptions of personal security/safety at the various facilities operated by the department; the public's knowledge of available activities; whether the hours of operation are appropriate in meeting citizens needs; whether citizens find the facilities attractive, well maintained, and accessible; and any difficulties people have in obtaining information about the program, the facilities, or special services offered or supplied by the agency in question.
4. Determination of whether participants are given the assistance and/or information they appear to want from employees of the department. Additionally, attempts should be made to determine citizens' attitudes toward employees regarding helpfulness and concern for participants.
5. Determination of why citizens do not participate in the recreational activities offered by the department. What negative factors are involved that cause rejection of program offerings?
   a. Facilities too far for potential participant to travel
   b. Facilities overcrowded
   c. Fear or feelings of insecurity aroused by actual or supposed knowledge of danger associated with facility or activity
   d. Lack of knowledge of activities (i.e., poor public relations)
   e. Lack of personal skill required for participation
   f. Fees or charges for activities or facility use are excessive
   g. Variety of activities is insufficient to attract potential participant
   h. Hostility to other potential participants
   i. Hostility to agency
   j. Discourteous personnel; not helpful to citizen
   k. Unattractive, poorly equipped, or poorly maintained physical plant, or insufficient supplies, materials, or equipment for satisfactory participation
   l. Physical inability to participate due to age, disability, or illness

Topic 9: Program Standards

REQUIREMENT. The program of any recreational service agency consists of all those activities provided by the agency that meet the recreational needs of the constituent public. The program contains a balance of activities produced on a full-time, year-round basis in which all age, gender, racial, ethnic, religious, economic, disability, or social status groups and the individuals who make up these groups may participate according to their respective abilities and experiences. The program will consist of the following activities, which may be further subdivided:

1. Art
2. Crafts
3. Dance and rhythmic experiences
4. Dramatics
5. Education
6. Hobbies
7. Motor skills
   a. Individual, dual, group and team, competitive, and noncompetitive activities
   b. Games
   c. Aquatics
   d. Sports
8. Music
9. Outdoor education and camping
10. Service or volunteering
11. Social experiences
12. Special projects or events

RECOMMENDATION. The program will contain a balance of activities featuring recreational experiences that provide social, cultural, emotional, physical, and moral values for participating individuals.

DETAILED DEVELOPMENT OF THE RECOMMENDATION.
1. Possible activities and criteria for their selection. It is patently foolish to select activities on any basis other than considering the objectives of the activity as being measurable. Some concepts are already inherent within the activity. They are not valid as criteria. The recreationist has to develop other forms of criteria for the activity. Some criteria that can be measured are:
   a. Social acceptability. (Is it legal and ethical?)
   b. Enjoyment (by attitudinal survey). It is up to the recreationist to determine if the person engaged enjoys the activity. If enjoyment is not achieved, the recreationist has to find out why and do something about it. The recreationist serves a leadership function and is not there just to provide a presence. Some people go into an activity for reasons other than enjoyment, and the recreationist has to determine what those reasons are.
   c. Safety precautions. With precautions no activity is dangerous. Human uniqueness is the factor, not the inherent danger of an activity. The behavior of people involved in an activity is the

determining factor of safety. A person's attitude toward a specific activity may put him or her in harm's way. Poor judgment as to the action taken often leads to jeopardy.

d. Skill (by rate of return to the activity, perseverance in the activity, and achievement). Skill is measurable and indicates whether the recreationist is performing the instructional obligations.

e. Participation (by number who participate and the quality of it). Evaluation by number simply involves "how many" in terms of a count. The recreationist evaluates the activity in terms of the intensity or extent of the individual's participation.

Selection of activities should be determined by geographic region, climate, or tradition.

2. Evaluation.

3. A balance of the full range of activities offered. By utilizing the 12 categories of the well-balanced and well-rounded program, an adequate presentation of all these activities must be made.

4. Equal opportunity in terms of age, gender, race, ethnicity, social status, economic status, or disability.

Based on the standards and objectives identified and defined by the agency, a simplified score sheet may be drawn up to facilitate the comparison of the public department (and private or quasi-public agencies) to the suggested criteria. The score form can contain a listing of all pertinent items that should be evaluated, a standardized score may be devised pertaining to the significance of the item insofar as provision of recreational service is concerned, and then the department's operation may be carefully analyzed and scored. Where the department obtains maximum scores, it may generally be stated that the item is being successfully fulfilled. Where any deficiencies are noted, either no score will be given or a lesser score will be appropriate. It will then be necessary to make recommendations for future substantive action if the evaluation process is to serve any worthwhile purpose. Thus, inadequacies will eventually be alleviated. The score sheet in **Table 22.1** is one type of standardized form that may be utilized in the evaluation process.

Table 22.1   Evaluative Instrument

Financial Support (100)	Maximum Point Score	Department Score
1. From the general tax board appropriation	25	
2. Earmarked funds	20	
3. Bond issues for capital improvement	15	
4. Fees and charges appropriate to the situation	5	
5. Minimum operational budget $20 per capita	10	
a. Debit one point for each $1 under		
b. Credit two points for each $1 over		

6. Personnel appropriation: 82 percent 15

 a. Credit ½ point for every 1 percent over

 b. Debit 1 point for every 5 percent under

7. Facilities maintenance: 15 percent 5

 a. Debit 1 point for every 5 percent over

8. Expendable program items: 3 percent 5

9. Millage levy appropriation 10

10. Special taxes 10

11. Operational expenditures: 75 percent 5

 a. Debit 1 point for every 5 percent under

12. Capital expenditures: 25 percent (equipment) 2

 a. Debit 1 point for every 5 percent over

Personnel Standards (250)

1. Minimal educational qualifications 25

2. Position classification under either civil service or merit system 25

3. Listed personnel salary ranges and step increments 25

4. Written job analysis for each position 20

5. Experience required depending on job analysis 15

6. Written job description 10

7. Personnel practices 25

8. Recruitment programs 10

9. On-the-job educational practices 10

10. In-service educational program 15

11. Orientation of personnel 5

12. Retirement plans 5

13. Fringe benefits 5

14. Part-time functional workers as required 5

15. Line and staff organization 60

 a. Requirement for executive officer full time 15

 b. General supervisory positions on full-time basis 10

 c. Facilities director full time at year-round facility 10

 d. Full-time program leader; also serves as director of playground or director of facilities 10

 e. Specialists or instructors for activities 10

Planning (50)

1. Comprehensive study of the community 20

 a. Physiographic factors 3

 b. Economic factors 3

 c. Community features and characteristics 2

 d. Recreational resources of a personal nature 2

 e. Recreational resources of a physical nature 2

f. Current recreational services provided	3
g. Population factors	1
h. Population trends	1
i. Metropolitan movement	1
j. Housing data and subdivision growth	1
k. Recent municipal studies	1

2. Three- to five-year recreational projection

a. History and location of community	10
b. Local governmental structure	1
c. Economic factors	1
d. Current recreational services	1
e. Physical recreational resources	1
f. Recreational personnel duties and number	1
g. Activities making up the recreational program	1
h. Land acquisition	1
i. Commercialized recreational services	1
j. Community agencies performing any recreational services	1

3. Property schedule (10)

a. Land acquisition	2
b. Construction of facilities	2
c. Construction of permanent structures	2
d. Construction of special areas	2
e. Construction for present emergency needs	2

4. Recreational surveys (10)

a. Factual data on outdoor physical resources	1
b. Factual data on indoor physical resources	1
c. Factual data on current recreational services	1
d. Actual data on the operating recreational personnel	1
e. Density of population to be served	1
f. Characteristics of the population	1
g. Geographic boundaries	1
h. Agency that administers recreational program	1
i. Probable resources available	1
j. Structures of a nonrecreational nature that can be utilized for recreational activities	1

Recreational Spaces (80)

1. Land acquisition	25
2. Nomenclature land-use patterns	20
3. Location of land in relation to population density	20
4. Size of the land parcel	10
5. Topographic characteristics	5

Recreational Structures (60) 1 for each*:

1.	Municipal camp	3	50,000 pop. or less
2.	Band shell	1	80,000 pop. or less
3.	Shelter houses	2	3200 pop. or less
4.	Recreational piers	1	2500 pop. or less
5.	Stadium of 1500 seats or more	1	50,000 pop. or less
6.	Gymnasium	5	10,000 pop. or less
7.	Auditorium	3	13,000 pop. or less
8.	Recreational centers (neighborhood)	8	10,000 pop. or less
9.	Natatorium	1	3 percent of pop.
10.	Outdoor theater	1	78,000 pop. or less
11.	Club rooms	3	30,000 pop.or less
12.	Multipurpose rooms (should hold 40 persons)	3	3000 pop. or less
13.	Special activity rooms	1	8000 pop. or less
14.	Library	1	100,000 pop. or less
15.	Field houses	1	130,000 pop. or less
16.	Game room	5	8000 pop. or less
17.	Lounge	2	8000 pop. or less
18.	Bleachers	3	2500 pop. or less
19.	Pavilions	2	2300 pop. or less
20.	Maintenance and custodial operations	5	

Geographic and topographic factors will affect evaluation of the section.

Recreational Facilities (60)

1.	Playgrounds	3	1 acre per 150 pop. or less
2.	Play fields	3	1 acre per 150 pop. or less
3.	Parks	3	1 acre per 100 pop. or less
4.	Arboretum	1	1 per 180,000 pop. or less
5.	Zoo	1	1 per 2,500,000 pop. or less
6.	Bathing beach	1	1 per 3 percent pop. or less or 50,000 pop. or less where feasible
7.	Baseball diamond (lighted or unlighted)	2	1 per 8000 pop. or less.
8.	Softball diamond (lighted or unlighted)	2	1 per 2500 pop. or less
9.	Indoor-outdoor tennis courts (lighted or unlighted)	2	1 per 2000 pop. or less
10.	Basketball courts (indoor and outdoor)	2	1 per 10,000 pop. or less
11.	Football field (lighted or unlighted)	1	1 per 35,000 pop. or less
12.	Wading pools	1	1 per 1 percent pop. or less
13.	Volleyball and badminton courts (indoor and outdoor)	1	1 per 2000 pop. or less
14.	Handball courts (indoor and outdoor)	1	1 per 75,000 pop. or less
15.	Archery range (indoor and outdoor)	1	1 per 25,000 pop. or less
16.	Rifle range (indoor and outdoor)	1	1 per 100,000 pop. or less
17.	Locker rooms, showers, toilet facilities	2	1 per gymnasium
18.	Trailways	1	1 per 100,000 pop. or less

19. Kitchen facility	1	1 per every large recreational center (community center)
20. Bocce courts	½	1 per 250,000 pop. or less
21. Bowling greens	½	1 per 250,000 pop. or less
22. Soccer and field hockey field	½	1 per 150,000 pop. or less
23. Golf course	2	1 hole per 3000 pop. or less
24. Track field	1	1 per 150,000 pop. or less
25. Marina (where feasible)	1	1 per 150,000 pop. or less
26. Bicycle trails (where feasible)	1	1 per 10,000 pop. or less
27. Picnic area	2	1 per 2000 pop. or less
28. Botanical gardens	1	1 per 150,000 pop. or less
29. Nature trail (where feasible)	1	1 per 10,000 pop. or less
30. Indoor and outdoor skating rink (lighted or unlighted)	½	1 per 50,000 pop. or less
31. Apparatus, equipment, and supplies (as required)	5	
32. Design: indicates layout, functional use of space, safety features, supervisory features, availability and accessibility of facility, architectural features of layout, and functional use of space	5	
33. Construction: types of materials to be used, economical materials, materials that will blend with a surrounding design, all best suited for the purpose	5	
34. Maintenance and custodial operation: number of personnel necessary to maintain the facility, service inside and outside, and materials for this	5	

Public Relations (40)

1. Policy	10

   a. Community service attitude of staff personnel

   b. Definite community relations program in effect

   c. Periodic review of public relations

   d. Community relations committee

   e. One person responsible for public relations

   f. Coping with possible areas of friction

   g. Directing points of public conduct for goodwill

   h. Staff members taking active part in community affairs

2. Facilities	10

   a. Open house held recently

   b. Acceptable appearance of facility

   c. Established plan for taking care of visitors who just drop in

   d. Printed material to be handed to all people

   e. Encouragement of community members to visit the recreational agency and program

3. Mass media for communications	5

   a. Do local community people know where to go for information?

   b. Know where to get adequate information

c. Avoidance of trivial news releases

d. News releases made without discrimination

e. Adherence to deadlines

f. Means of communication to notify people concerning events of interest to them

4. Speakers bureau   5

   a. Procedure for handling requests for speaker

   b. Visual aid assistance when needed for speaker

   c. Available roster of staff members who can speak well on their specialization

   d. Manuscript cleared through administration channels

5. Technical assistance   5

   a. Agency acts as central coordinating agency for service.

   b. Agency furnishes technical assistance to other agencies or private individuals when requested.

   c. Specialists available to answer questions relative to their area.

   d. Facilities placed on priority basis for public and private uses.

6. Community awareness   5

   a. Conducting of periodic public opinion polls

   b. Citizen awareness of staff affiliation to the agency whenever they perform in the community

Patron Perception of Recreational Service (100)

1. Establishment of ongoing citizen monitoring program to determine effectiveness of the recreational service   25

2. Determination of knowledge of programmed offerings operated by the department   15

3. Determination of knowledge of recreational facilities available for use by citizens   10

4. Determination of knowledge of hours of activities scheduled by department   10

5. Determination of citizens' perception of personal safety at recreational areas or facilities   5

6. Determination of public relations program   10

7. Determination of attractiveness of facilities   15

   a. Heat, light, ventilation (when appropriate)

   b. Suitable interior decoration and appointments

   c. Suitable exterior plantings

   d. Maintenance and repair of facilities and areas

   e. Accessibility to potential users

8. Determination of perception of attitudes of employees insofar as helpfulness or consideration is concerned   10

Program (150)

1. Criteria for selection of activities   50

   a. Social acceptability

   b. Safety precautions necessary

   c. Skill required

   d. Participation required

   e. Self-expressiveness

2. Balanced program   60

   a. Art

   b. Crafts

   c. Dance

   d. Dramatics

   e. Education

   f. Hobbies

   g. Motor skills

   h. Music

   i. Nature-oriented activities

   j. Service activities

   k. Social activities

   l. Special events

3. Equalized opportunity   40

   a. Gender differences

   b. Age differences

   c. Economic levels

   d. Ethnic characteristics

   e. Religious affiliation

   f. Social status

   g. Active participation

   h. Passive participation

   i. Home bound

   j. Disabled

Summary

Assessment is an immediate appraisal of the value of a program to those who are engaged in it. It is the current status of how well given recreational activities meet the needs of the served constituency. Evaluation is postactivity examination designed to determine whether the program has satisfied preset standards of operation. The process finds how closely the operation has come to fulfilling whatever criteria were agreed upon.

Evaluation carried out continuously, with attention paid to all components of the program and its impact on the community's population, facilitates improvement. That is the only reason for activating this procedure. Comparison with other similar programs and with the predetermined conditions of ongoing activities enables accurate measures to be devised and taken whose outcome will produce a better recreational service.

Selected Further References

Bingham, R. D. C., and L. Felbinger. *Evaluation in Practice: A Methodological Approach.* Cottonwood, CA: Q. C. Press, 2002.

Riddick, C. C., and R. V. Russell. *Evaluative Research in Recreation, Park, and Sport Settings: Searching for Useful Information.* Champaign, IL: Sagamore Publishing, 1999.

Weinbach, R. W. *Evaluating Social Work Services and Programs.* Boston, MA: Allyn and Bacon, 2004.

Useful Sources for Enhancing the Recreational Service Program, by Category

Aquatics

Amateur Swimming Association
Harold Fun House
Derby Square
41 Granby St.
Loughborough, LE11 5AL, United Kingdom
http://www.britishswimming.org

American Boat and Yacht Council
3069 Solomons Island Road
Edgewater, MD 21037-1416
http://www.abycinc.org

American Casting Association
c/o Dale Lanser
1773 Lance End Lane
Fenton, MO 63026
http://www.americancastingassoc.org

American Sailing Association
P.O. Box 12079
Marina del Rey, CA 90295-3179
http://www.american-sailing.com

American Swimming Coaches Association
2101 North Andrews Ave., Suite 107
Fort Lauderdale, FL 33311
http://www.swimmingcoach.org

FishAmerica Foundation
225 Reinekers Lane, Suite 420
Alexandria, VA 22314
http://www.fishamerica.org

International Academy of Aquatic Art
c/o Nadine Pietrantoni
803 East Washington
Lombard, IL 60148
http://www.aquatic-art.org

National Swimming Pool Foundation
724 East Cheyenne Mountain Blvd.
Colorado Springs, CO 80916
http://www.nspf.com

U.S. Masters Swimming
P.O. Box 185
Londonderry, New Hampshire 03053-0185
http://www.usms.org

Art

Affiliated Woodcarvers
P.O. Box 104
Bettendorf, IA 52722
http://www.awcltd.org

African-American Visual Arts Association
3043 Milford Mill Road
Baltimore, MD 21244
http://www.aavaa.org

Allied Artists of America
15 Gramercy Park S.
New York, NY 10003
http://www.alliedartistsofamerica.org

American Art Pottery Association
c/o Patti Bourgeois
P.O. Box 834
Westport, ME 02790
http://www.amartpot.org

American Photographic Historical Society
28 Marksman Lane
Levittown, NY 11756-5110

American Society of Artists
P.O. Box 1326
Palatine, IL 60078
http://www.americansocietyofartists.com

American Watercolor Society
47 Fifth Ave.
New York, NY 10003
http://www.americanwatercolorsociety.com

Art Alliance for Contemporary Glass
P.O. Box 7022
Evanston, IL 60201
http://www.contempglass.org

Art Information Center
55 Mercer St., 3rd floor
New York, NY 10013

Art Through Touch
c/o Pocklington Resource Center
1c Yukon Road
London SW112 9PZ, United Kingdom
http://www.disabilityartsonline.org/art-through-touch

Arts International
251 Park Ave. S., 5th floor
New York, NY 10010-7302
http://www.artsinternational.org

Federation of Modern Painters and Sculptors
c/o Anneli Arms
113 Greene St.
New York, NY 10012
E-mail: aarms2001@yahoo.com

Folk Art Society of America
P.O. Box 17041
Richmond, VA 23226-7041
http://www.folkart.org

International Academy of Ceramics
Musee Ciriano
Ave. de la Paix, 10
CH-1202 Geneva, Switzerland
http://www.aic-iac.org

National Cartoonists Society
Membership Committee
P.O. Box 713
Suffield, CT 06078
http://www.reuben.org

National Society of Mural Painters
c/o American Fine Arts Society
215 W. 57th St.
New York, NY 10019
http://www.nationalsocietyofmuralpainters.com

Pastel Society of America
15 Gramercy Pk. S.
New York, NY 10003
http://www.pastelsocietyofamerica.org

Society for Calligraphy, Southern California
P.O. Box 6417
Los Angeles, CA 90064-0174
http://www.societyforcalligraphy.org

Crafts

Alliance for American Quilts
P.O. Box 6521
Louisville, KY 40206
http://www.quiltalliance.org

American Association of Woodturners
222 Landmark Center
75 W. 5th St.
St. Paul, MN 55102
http://www.woodturner.org

American Crafts Council
72 Spring St.
New York, NY 10012-4019
http://www.craftcouncil.org

Arts and Crafts Society
1194 Bandera Drive
Ann Arbor, MI 48103
http://www.arts-crafts.com

Embroiderers' Guild
Hampton Court Palace, Apt. 41
East Molesey KT8 9AU, United Kingdom
http://www.embroiderersguild.com

Guild of Glass Engravers
87 Nether St.
Finchley
London N12 7NP, United Kingdom
http://www.gge.org.uk

International Guild of Candle Artisans
1640 Garfield
Fremont, NE 68025
http://www.igca.net

International Internet Leathercrafter's Guild
3300 Hampton Ave.
Hopewell, VA 23860
http://www.iilg.org

National Council on Education for the Ceramic Arts
77 Erie Village Square, Suite 280
Erie, CO 80516-6996
http://www.nceca.net

North Star Needlework Guild
P.O. Box 80925
Fairbanks, AK 99708

Recycled Art Association
P.O. Box 1142
Eugene, OR 97405
http://www.recycarts.org

Dance

American Dance Festival
P.O. Box 90772
Durham, NC 27708-0772
http://www.americandancefestival.org

American Dance Guild
P.O. Box 2006
Lenox Hill Station
New York, NY 10021
http://www.americandanceguild.org

Art of Dance Community Association
30 Seminary Ave.
Chester, NJ 07930-2614
http://www.artofdance.org

Association for Dance Enrichment
120 E. Park Ave.
Fairmont, WV 26554-4018

County Dance and Song Society
132 Main St.
P.O. Box 338
Haydenville, ME 01039-0338
http://www.cdss.org

Cross-Cultural Dance Resources
578 South Agassiz St.
Flagstaff, AZ 86001-5711
http://www.ccdr.org

Dance Theater Workshop
219 W. 19th St.
New York, NY 10011
http://www.dtw.org

Dance/USA
1111 16th St. NW, Suite 300
Washington, DC 20036
http://www.danceusa.org

USDA Handicapable Dancers
904 South St. Marys
Sioux City, IA 51106
http://www.usda.org/handicap.htm

Drama

American Association of Community Theater
402 Brier Wood Cir.
Logo Vista, TX 78645
http://www.aact.org

American Mime Theatre
61 4th Ave.
New York, NY 10003-5204
http://www.americanmime.org

American Theater Arts for Youth
1429 Walnut St.
Philadelphia, PA 19102
http://www.atafy.org

Drama League
520 8th Ave., Suite 320
New York, NY 10018
http://www.dramaleague.org

National Theater of the Deaf
139 North Main St.
West Hartford, CT 06117
http://www.ntd.org

National Theater Workshop of the Handicapped
55 Greenwich St.
New York, NY 10013-1004
http://www.ntwh.org

Theatre Communications Group
520 8th Ave., 24th floor
New York, NY 10018-4156
http://www.tcg.org

Theatre for Young Audiences/USA
724 2nd Ave. S.
Nashville, TN 37210-2006
http://www.assitej-usa.org

Education

American Music Conference
5790 Armada Dr.
Carlsbad, CA 92008-4391
http://www.amc-music.org

American Park and Recreation Society
22377 Belmont Ridge Road
Ashburn, VA 20148-4150
http://www.nrpa.org/aprs

Crochet Guild of America
P.O. Box 3388
Zanesville, OH 43702-3388
http://www.crochet.org

Interlochen Center for the Arts
P.O. Box 199
Interlochen, MI 49643-0199
http://www.interlochen.org

National Association for Sport and Physical Education
1900 Association Dr.
Reston, VA 20191
http://www.aahperd.org/naspe/

Young Audiences Arts for Learning
115 E. 92nd St.
New York, NY 10128-1688
http://www.youngaudiences.com

Hobbies

Authentic Artifact Collectors Association
c/o Cliff Jackson
323 Hamme Mill Road
Warrenton, NC 27589
http://www.theaaca.com

International Association of Silver Art Collectors
P.O. Box 28415
Seattle, WA 98118
Email: iasacancy@comcast.net

Motor Skills

American Alliance for Health, Physical Education, Recreation and Dance
1900 Association Dr.
Reston, VA 20191-1598
http://www.aahperd.org

American Association for Leisure and Recreation
1900 Association Dr.
Reston, VA 20191-1595
http://www.aahperd.org/aalr

American Association of Riding Schools
375 Coldwater Road
Davison, MI 48423-8966
http://www.ucanride.com

American Bowling Congress
c/o Bowling Headquarters
5301 S. 76th St.
Greendale, WI 53129-1127
http://www.bowl.com

The Shuffleboard Federation
P.O. Box 549
South Lyon, MI 48178
http://www.shuffleboardfederation.com/shufhispar2.html

American Roquet and Croquet Association
P.O. Box 2304
Richmond, IN 47375-2304
Email: jacks@insightbf.com

Archery Shooters Association
P.O. Box 399
Kennesaw, GA 30156
http://www.asaarchery.com

National Amateur Dodge Ball Association
c/o Schaumburg Park District
235 E. Beach Dr.
Schaumburg, IL 60193
http://www.dodgeballusa.com

National Horseshoe Pitchers Association of America
c/o Dirk Hansen
3085 76th St.
Franksville, WI 53126
http://www.horseshoepitching.com

National Paddleball Association
7642 Kingston Dr.
Portage, MI 49002-4370
http://www.paddleball.org

National Sporting Clays Association
5931 Raft Road
San Antonio, TX 78253-9261
http://www.mynsca.com

USA Badminton
One Olympic Plaza
Colorado Springs, CO 80909
http://www.usabadminton.org

USA Gymnastics
201 S. Capitol St., Suite 300
Pan American Plaza
Indianapolis, IN 46225
http://www.usa-gymnastics.org

Music

Accordion Federation of North America
1101 W. Orangethorpe Ave.
Fullerton, CA 92833

America Sings!
6179 Grovedale Court, Suite 100
Alexandria, VA 22310
http://www.americasings.org

American Choral Directors Association
545 Couch Dr.
Oklahoma City, OK 73102
http://www.acdaonline.org

American Guild of English Handbell Ringers
1055 East Centreville Station Road
Centerville, OH 45459
http://www.agehr.org

American Guild of Music
P.O. Box 599
Warren, MI 48090-3048
http://www.americanguild.org

American Music Festival Association
P.O. Box 2987
Anaheim, CA 92814
Telephone: (714) 827-4562

American Musical Instrument Society
389 Main St., Suite 202
Malden, MA 02148
http://www.amis.org

American School Band Directors Association
227 North First St.
P.O. Box 696
Guttenberg, LA 52052-0696
http://www.asbda.com

Association of Concert Bands
6613 Cheryl Ann Dr.
Independence, OH 44131
http://www.acbands.org

Chamber Music America
305 7th Ave.
New York, NY 10001-6008
http://www.chamber-music.org

Conductors Guild
P.O. Box 18398
Richmond, VA 23226
http://www.conductorsguild.org

Drum Corps International
470 Irmen Dr.
Addison, IL 60101
http://www.dci.org

Guitar Foundation of America
c/o Gunnar Eisel
P.O. Box 1240
Claremont, CA 91711
http://www.guitarfoundation.org

Historical Harp Society
c/o Jean Humphrey
631 N. 3rd Ave.
St. Charles, IL 60174
http://historicalharps.org

League of American Orchestras
33 W. 60th St.
New York, NY 10023
http://www.americanorchestras.org

Music for All
39 W. Jackson Pl., Suite 150
Indianapolis, IN 46225
http://www.musicforall.org

Nature-Oriented Activities

Amateur Astronomers Association of New York
Gracie Station
P.O. Box 383
New York, NY 10028
http://www.aaa.org

American Camp Association
5000 State Rd. 67 North
Martinsville, IN 46151-7902
http://www.acacamps.org

American Geophysical Union
2000 Florida Ave., Northwest
Washington, DC 20009-1277
http://www.agu.org

American Indian Lore Association
460 Walhonding Ave.
Logan, OH 43138

American Museum of Natural History
Central Park West at W. 79th St.
New York, NY 10024-5192
http://www.amnh.org

Astronomical League
c/o Jackie Beucher
11305 King St.
Overland Park, KS 66210-3421
http://www.astroleague.org/

Federation of American Aquarium Societies
2508 Alton Dr.
Champaign, IL 61821
http://www.faas.info

Growth Through Aquatics
c/o Cathy Konrad, Senior Vice President
1073 Ruth Ann Dr.
Dallas, TX 75228-2015

National Speleological Society
2813 Cave Avenue
Huntsville, AL 35810-4431
http://www.caves.org

National Weather Association
1697 Capri Way
Charlottesville, VA 22911-3534
http://www.nwas.org

Wildlife Society
5410 Grosvenor Lane, Suite 200
Bethesda, MD 20814-2144
http://www.wildlife.org

Performing Arts

National Foundation for Advancement in the Arts
444 Brickell Ave., P-14
Miami, FL 33131
http://www.nfaa.org

Performing Arts Alliance
805 15th St. Northwest, Suite 500
Washington, DC 20036

Performing Arts Foundation
500 Riverside Dr.
New York, NY 10027

Service Activities

American Association of State Service Commissions
1400 I St. Northwest, Suite 560
Washington, DC 20005-6526
http://www.asc-online.org

Assistance League
P.O. Box 6637
Burbank, CA 91510-6637
http://www.assistanceleague.org

Center for Organizational and Community Development
University of Massachusetts
School of Education
470 Hills South
Amherst, MA 01003
Telephone: (413) 545-2933

Citizens Who Care
1260 Lake Blvd., Suite 208
Davis, CA 95616
http://www.dcn.davis.ca.us/GO/care

Holiday Project
104 Kingslend Road
Landing, NJ 05850
http://www.holiday-project.org

MATCH-UP Interfaith Volunteers
105 Chauncey St., Suite 801
Boston, MA 02111
http://www.matchelder.org

Social Activities

Alliance for Community Outreach
c/o W. K. McGregor
115 W. Main St.
Manchester, TN 37355-1542
Email: goodwork@cafes.net

Special Events

Institute of American Indian Arts
83 Avan Nu Po Road
Santa Fe, NM 87505
http://www.iaiancad.org

Index

Photo Credits

6-1 Courtesy of Prince William County Park Authority; **6-2** © Predrag Nova-kovic/Dreamstime.com; **6-3** © Stacy Barnett/ShutterStock, Inc.; **6-7** © Maslov Dmitry/ShutterStock, Inc.; **6-8** Courtesy of Sarasota County Government; **6-9** © 2009 Landscape Structures Inc.; **6-11, 6-12, 6-13, 6-14** Courtesy of Sarasota County Government; **6-16** © Shmeliova Natalia/ShutterStock, Inc.; **6-18, 6-19** Courtesy of Prince William County Park Authority; **6-20** Courtesy of Splash Down Waterpark, Manassas, Virginia; **8-1** © Brian Dunne/Dreamstime.com; **10-1** Courtesy of Ken Robinson; **11-1, 11-2** Courtesy of the University of Connecticut, The School of Fine Arts, Department of Dramatic Arts; **11-3** Courtesy of the University of Connecticut, The Jorgensen Center for Perform-ing Arts; **11-4, 11-6** Courtesy of the University of Connecticut, The School of Fine Arts, Department of Dramatic Arts; **13-1** © Joe Gough/Dreamstime.com; **13-8** Courtesy of Jay S. Shivers; **14-1** © Anke Van Wyk/Dreamstime.com; **14-2, 14-3** Courtesy of Prince William County Park Authority; **14-10** Courtesy of Jay S. Shivers; **14-11** Courtesy of Eric Tobin of Scuba Quest, Sarasota, Florida; **15-1** Courtesy of Sarasota County Government; **15-2** Courtesy of the University of Connecticut, The Jorgensen Center for Performing Arts; **17-1** Courtesy of Sarasota County Government; **17-2** © Photodisc; **17-3** © Bronwyn Photo/ShutterStock, Inc.; **17-4** Courtesy of Jay S. Shivers; **17-6** Cour-tesy of Sarasota County Government; **19-1, 19-2** © Monkey Business Images/Dreamstime.com

Unless otherwise indicated, all photographs and illustrations are under copyright of Jones and Bartlett Publishers, LLC.